Technologies for Constructing Intelligent Systems 1

Studies in Fuzziness and Soft Computing

Further volumes of this series can be found at our homepage.

Vol. 67. R.J. Howlett and L.C. Jain (Eds.)
Radial Basis Function Networks 2, 2001
ISBN 3-7908-1368-0

Vol. 68. A. Kandel, M. Last and H. Bunke (Eds.)
Data Mining and Computational Intelligence, 2001
ISBN 3-7908-1371-0

Vol. 69. A. Piegat
Fuzzy Modeling and Control, 2001
ISBN 3-7908-1385-0

Vol. 70. W. Pedrycz (Ed.)
Granular Computing, 2001
ISBN 3-7908-1387-7

Vol. 71. K. Leiviskä (Ed.)
Industrial Applications of Soft Computing, 2001
ISBN 3-7908-1388-5

Vol. 72. M. Mareš
Fuzzy Cooperative Games, 2001
ISBN 3-7908-1392-3

Vol. 73. Y. Yoshida (Ed.)
Dynamical Aspects in Fuzzy Decision, 2001
ISBN 3-7908-1397-4

Vol. 74. H.-N. Teodorescu, L.C. Jain and A. Kandel (Eds.)
Hardware Implementation of Intelligent Systems, 2001
ISBN 3-7908-1399-0

Vol. 75. V. Loia and S. Sessa (Eds.)
Soft Computing Agents, 2001
ISBN 3-7908-1404-0

Vol. 76. D. Ruan, J. Kacprzyk and M. Fedrizzi (Eds.)
Soft Computing for Risk Evaluation and Management, 2001
ISBN 3-7908-1406-7

Vol. 77. W. Liu
Propositional, Probabilistic and Evidential Reasoning, 2001
ISBN 3-7908-1414-8

Vol. 78. U. Seiffert and L.C. Jain (Eds.)
Self-Organizing Neural Networks, 2002
ISBN 3-7908-1417-2

Vol. 79. A. Osyczka
Evolutionary Algorithms for Single and Multicriteria Design Optimization, 2002
ISBN 3-7908-1418-0

Vol. 80. P. Wong, F. Aminzadeh and M. Nikravesh (Eds.)
Soft Computing for Reservoir Characterization and Modeling, 2002
ISBN 3-7908-1421-0

Vol. 81. V. Dimitrov and V. Korotkich (Eds.)
Fuzzy Logic, 2002
ISBN 3-7908-1425-3

Vol. 82. Ch. Carlsson and R. Fullér
Fuzzy Reasoning in Decision Making and Optimization, 2002
ISBN 3-7908-1428-8

Vol. 83. S. Barro and R. Marín (Eds.)
Fuzzy Logic in Medicine, 2002
ISBN 3-7908-1429-6

Vol. 84. L.C. Jain and J. Kacprzyk (Eds.)
New Learning Paradigms in Soft Computing, 2002
ISBN 3-7908-1436-9

Vol. 85. D. Rutkowska
Neuro-Fuzzy Architectures and Hybrid Learning, 2002
ISBN 3-7908-1438-5

Vol. 86. M.B. Gorzałczany
Computational Intelligence Systems and Applications, 2002
ISBN 3-7908-1439-3

Vol. 87. C. Bertoluzza, M.Á. Gil and D.A. Ralescu (Eds.)
Statistical Modeling, Analysis and Management of Fuzzy Data, 2002
ISBN 3-7908-1440-7

Vol. 88. R.P. Srivastava and T.J. Mock (Eds.)
Belief Functions in Business Decisions, 2002
ISBN 3-7908-1451-2

Bernadette Bouchon-Meunier
Julio Gutiérrez-Ríos
Luis Magdalena · Ronald R. Yager
Editors

Technologies for Constructing Intelligent Systems 1

Tasks

With 83 Figures
and 47 Tables

Springer-Verlag Berlin Heidelberg GmbH
A Springer-Verlag Company

Professor Bernadette Bouchon-Meunier
Université Paris VI
CNRS, LIP6
8 rue du Capitaine Scott
75015 Paris
France
Bernadette.Bouchon-Meunier@lip6.fr

Professor Julio Gutiérrez-Ríos
Universidad Politécnica de Madrid
Facultad de Informática
Campus de Montegancedo
28660 Boadilla del Monte, Madrid
Spain
jgr@fi.upm.es

Dr. Luis Magdalena
Universidad Politécnica de Madrid
Escuela Técnica Superior de Ingenieros
de Telecomunicación
Ciudad Universitaria s/n
28040 Madrid
Spain
llayos@mat.upm.es

Professor Ronald R. Yager
Iona College
Machine Intelligence Institute
New Rochelle, NY 10801
USA
yager@panix.com

ISSN 1434-9922

Cataloging-in-Publication Data applied for
Die Deutsche Bibliothek – CIP-Einheitsaufnahme
Technologies for constructing intelligent systems / Bernadette Bouchon-Meunier ... (ed.). – Heidelberg; New York: Physica-Verl.
1. Tasks: with 47 tables. – 2002
(Studies in fuzziness and soft computing; Vol. 89)

DOI 10.1007/978-3-7908-1797-3

a member of BertelsmannSpringer Science+Business Media GmbH

Originally published by Physica-Verlag Heidelberg in 2002
MyCopy version of the original edition 2002

Hardcover Design: Erich Kirchner, Heidelberg

SPIN 10858544 88/2202-5 4 3 2 1 0 – Printed on acid-free paper
www.springer.com/mycopy

Preface

At the beginning of this new century, Intelligent Systems represent a cutting edge of applied artificial intelligence. Most of the applications of Intelligent Systems are based upon an amalgamation of different techniques and methods. An Intelligent System resembles an ensemble rather than a soloist. Each attempt at constructing an intelligent system or improving the intelligence of a pre-existing system, has to deal with different aspects of information processing and uncertainty management. In the light of this situation the representation of uncertain information, the definition of suitable aggregation operators, the modelling of decisions and preferences, and the integration of learning capabilities become core technologies.

These technologies are the pieces of the ensemble, it is necessary to have them available when constructing intelligent systems. The focus of the International Conference on Information Processing and Management of Uncertainty in Knowledge Based Systems (IPMU) is on the development of intelligent systems and the allied technologies. The eighth IPMU conference, held in Madrid and organized by the Universidad Politécnica de Madrid in July 2000, brought together some of the worlds leading experts in these technologies. In these two companion volumes, Technologies for Constructing Intelligent Systems: Volume I Tasks and Volume II Tools, we have collected a selection of papers from this conference. The topics included in these volumes range from fundamental issues in uncertainty, information aggregation and preference modelling through technologies for effective decision making to applied research on pattern recognition for text classification or texture detection.

The first volume begins with a paper by Lotfi A. Zadeh presenting the new paradigm he proposes for the construction of intelligent systems, a Computational Theory of Perceptions. This new theory provides a machinery for computing and reasoning with perceptions described in a natural language. It provides an additional tool to help with decision making in problems where the available information is perceptual in nature. This of course, corresponds to many of the situations found in the real world.

Zadeh's paper makes clear a general concern underlying the content of these two volumes: the need for both theories and methodologies to help provide a computational solution to difficult problems in which the available knowledge and data may be imprecise, incomplete, linguistic and subjective. Various methodologies exist to manage such information in probabilistic, possibilistic, fuzzy, logical, evidential, and network-based frameworks. The purpose of these volumes is not to consider these methodologies separately, but rather to address key subjects in which they may be involved.

The first section of volume one is devoted to the issue of computing with words. This subject being an extension and generalization of the idea of using perceptions provides an important technique for enhancing the ability to have user friendly human–machine interactions and develop knowledge-based systems. Concepts such as linguistic modifiers, quantifiers and granulation of information are considered here. The following parts of this volume are concerned with subjects covering some of the important fields of intelligent systems. Decision making is the first domain covered. The notions of consensus, utility and preference are major items discussed in this part. Classification and clustering as well as example-based learning is the next domain considered. Another domain considered here, one which has great importance for the internet, concerns information retrieval and flexible queries in databases.

Volume two begins with a section devoted to fundamental issues of uncertainty. The concepts of independence and conditioning are discussed in different frameworks and this part is introduced in a paper by Richard Jeffrey proposing a "radical probabilism" in which probabilistic judgments are used instead of objective probabilities, and which also discusses the problem of probability updating.

Next issues related to aggregation, a necessary step in all aspects of intelligent systems construction, are discussed in great detail and several kinds of aggregation operators are presented.

The rest of this second volume deals with specific approaches underlying the development of intelligent systems. Fuzzy set theory is first addressed. Properties of basic tools in this field such as, fuzzy measures, fuzzy control, fuzzy relations and fuzzy temporal knowledge are discussed. Several of the papers in this volume are related to causal networks and neural networks. Finally, methods based on logics describe links between logic and the management of uncertain information.

In summary, these two companion volumes overview the various methods and domains involved in the construction of intelligent systems and provides a broad view of research in the field.

Bernadette Bouchon-Meunier
Julio Gutiérrez-Ríos
Luis Magdalena
Ronald R. Yager

Table of Contents

Computing with Words

A New Direction in AI Toward a Computational Theory of Perceptions*

Lotfi A. Zadeh

Abstract. Humans have a remarkable capability to perform a wide variety of physical and mental tasks without any measurements and any computations. Familiar examples are parking a car, driving in city traffic, playing golf, cooking a meal, and summarizing a story. In performing such tasks, humans use perceptions of time, direction, speed, shape, possibility, likelihood, truth, and other attributes of physical and mental objects. Reflecting the bounded ability of the human brain to resolve detail, perceptions are intrinsically imprecise. In more concrete terms, perceptions are f-granular, meaning that (1) the boundaries of perceived classes are unsharp and (2) the values of attributes are granulated, with a granule being a clump of values (points, objects) drawn together by indistinguishability, similarity, proximity, and function. For example, the granules of age might be labeled very young, young, middle aged, old, very old, and so on.

F-granularity of perceptions puts them well beyond the reach of traditional methods of analysis based on predicate logic or probability theory. The computational theory of perceptions (CTP), which is outlined in this article, adds to the armamentarium of AI a capability to compute and reason with perception-based information. The point of departure in CTP is the assumption that perceptions are described by propositions drawn from a natural language; for example, it is unlikely that there will be a significant increase in the price of oil in the near future.

In CTP, a proposition, p, is viewed as an answer to a question, and the meaning of p is represented as a generalized constraint. To compute with perceptions, their descriptors are translated into what is called the generalized constraint language (GCL). Then, goal-directed constraint propagation is utilized to answer a given query. A concept that plays a key role in CTP is that of precisiated natural language (PNL).

The computational theory of perceptions suggests a new direction in AI—a direction that might enhance the ability of AI to deal with real-world problems in which decision-relevant information is a mixture of measurements and perceptions. What is not widely recognized is that many important problems in AI fall into this category.

Since its inception in the early fifties, AI has scored a number of major successes, among them the defeat of Gary Kasparov by DEEP BLUE. How-

* This paper is a reproduction of:
Lotfi A. Zadeh, "A new Direction in AI: Toward a Computational Theory of Perceptions," from *AI Magazine* 22(1):73-84, Spring 2001.

ever, what we also see is that alongside the brilliant achievements lie areas in which progress has been slow and difficult to realize. In such areas, problems do not lend themselves to precise formulation, and the underlying modes of reasoning are approximate rather than exact. A case in point is the problem of summarization—a problem that is orders of magnitude more complex than the problem of machine translation. Although substantial progress has been realized (Mani and Maybury 1999), we are still far from being able to construct programs that are capable of summarizing a nonstereotypical story or providing a synopsis of a book.

Why is it that major successes have been achieved in some areas but not in others? A thesis that I should like to put on the table is that progress has been, and continues to be, slow in those areas where a methodology is needed in which the objects of computation are perceptions—perceptions of time, distance, form, direction, color, shape, truth, likelihood, intent, and other attributes of physical and mental objects.

Humans have a remarkable capability to perform a wide variety of physical and mental tasks without any measurements and any computations. Everyday examples of such tasks are parking a car, driving in city traffic, playing golf, cooking a meal, and summarizing a story. In performing such tasks, for example, driving in city traffic, humans base whatever decisions have to be made on information that, for the most part, is perception, rather than measurement, based. The computational theory of perceptions (CTP), which is outlined in this article, is inspired by the remarkable human capability to operate on, and reason with, perception-based information.

An essential difference between measurements and perceptions is that in general, measurements are crisp, whereas perceptions are fuzzy (figure 1). Furthermore, the finite ability of sensory organs to resolve detail necessitates a partitioning of objects (points) into granules, with a *granule* being a clump of objects (points) drawn together by indistinguishability, similarity, proximity, or function. Thus, perceptions, in general, are both fuzzy and granular or, for short, *f*-granular. For example, a perception of age can be described as very young, young, middle aged, old, and very old, with very young, young, and so on, constituting the granules of the variable *age* (figure 2). In this perspective, natural languages can be viewed as systems whose primary function is to describe perceptions.

Information granulation plays key roles in both human and machine intelligence. Modes of information granulation in which the granules are crisp, that is, *c*-granular (figure 3), play important roles in a wide variety of methods, approaches, and techniques. Among them are interval analysis, quantization, rough-set theory, diakoptics, divide and conquer, Dempster-Shafer theory, machine learning from examples, chunking, qualitative process theory, qualitative reasoning, decision trees, semantic networks, analog-to-digital conversion, constraint programming, Prolog, and cluster analysis.

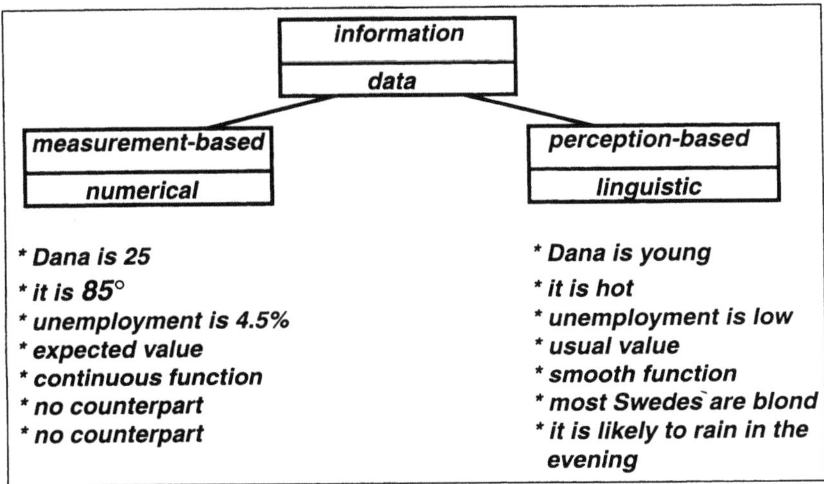

Fig. 1. Structure of Information.
Examples of measurement-based and perception-based information.

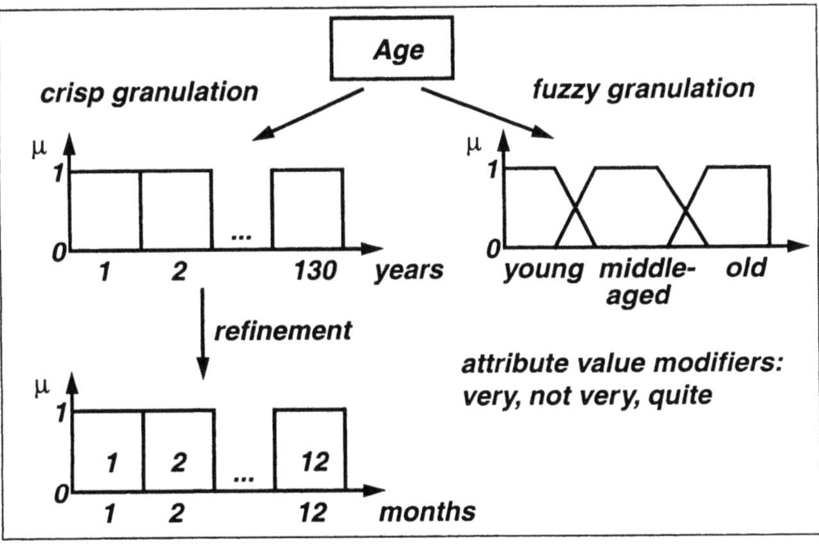

Fig. 2. *F*-Granulation and *C*-Granulation of Age.

Important though it is, crisp information granulation has a major blind spot. More specifically, it fails to reflect the fact that in much, perhaps most, of human reasoning and concept formation, the granules are fuzzy (f-granular) rather than crisp. In the case of a human body, for example, the granules are fuzzy in the sense that the boundaries of the head, neck, arms, legs, and so on, are not sharply defined. Furthermore, the granules are associated with fuzzy attributes, for example, length, color, and texture in

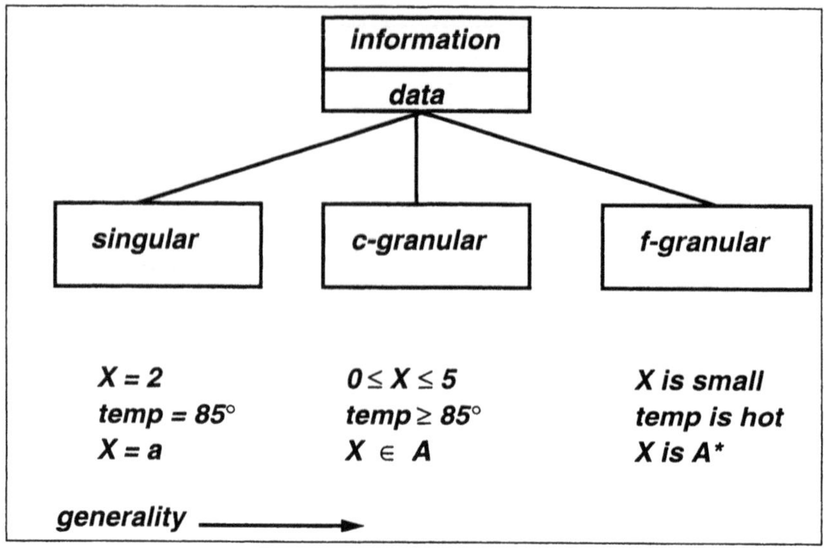

Fig. 3. Classification and Successive Generalization of Modes of Granulation: Singular, C-Granular, and F-Granular.

the case of hair. In turn, fuzzy attributes can have fuzzy values; for example, in the case of the fuzzy attribute *length (hair)*, the fuzzy values could be long, short, very long, and so on. The fuzziness of granules, their attributes, and their values is characteristic of the ways in which human concepts are formed, organized, and manipulated (Zadeh 1997; Dubois and Prade 1996).

There is an enormous literature on perceptions, spanning psychology, philosophy, linguistics, neuroscience, cognitive science, system theory, and other fields (Barsalou 1999; Vallee 1995). However, what is not in existence is a theory in which perceptions are objects of computation, as they are in CTP.

In the computational theory of perceptions, the point of departure is not, in general, a collection of perceptions; rather, it is a collection of descriptions of perceptions expressed in a natural language. Consider the following examples: (1) Dana is young, (2) Dana is much younger than her husband, (3) Michelle has long hair, (4) most Swedes are tall, (5) overeating causes obesity, (6) usually Robert returns from work at about 6 pm, and (7) it is very unlikely that there will be a significant increase in the price of oil in the near future. Thus, a basic assumption in CTP is that perceptions are represented as propositions in a natural language.

The principal aim of CTP is the development of a machinery for computing and reasoning with perceptions. A simple example of reasoning with perceptions is the following: Assume that we start with the antecedent perceptions that "most young men are healthy" and that "Robert is a young man," where *most* is a perceptual (fuzzy) quantifier that is defined by its membership function (figure 4). Then, it can be shown that the consequent

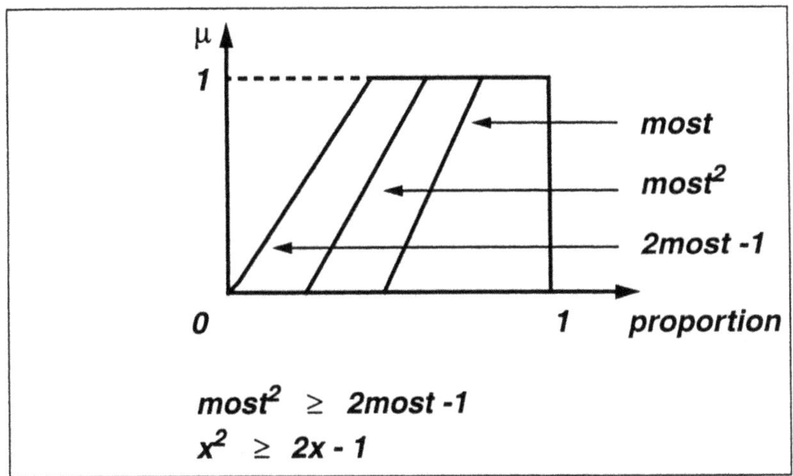

Fig. 4. Membership Functions of "Most" and Related Perceptual (Fuzzy) Quantifiers.

perception can be expressed as "it is likely that Robert is healthy," where *likely* is a fuzzy probability whose membership function coincides with that of *most*. Note that the result of computation in this case is in agreement with intuition.

Within AI, there are methodologies, prominent among which are qualitative reasoning and qualitative process theory (QPT) (Sun 1994; Raiman 1991; Davis 1990; de Kleer and Bobrow 1984; Forbus 1984; Kuipers 1984), that provide effective tools for dealing with interval-valued types of perception-based information. In relation to these methodologies, the computational theory of perceptions is complementary rather than competitive. More concretely, a basic difference between qualitative reasoning and CTP is that in qualitative reasoning, granulation is crisp, whereas in CTP, granulation is fuzzy. Because fuzzy granulation subsumes crisp granulation, CTP, in principle, has a higher level of generality than qualitative reasoning. However, in comparing the two theories, it is standard practice to exclude the less general theory from the more general theory, leaving a theory that complements the less general theory. Thus, in this sense, for example, linear system theory and nonlinear system theory are complementary. The same applies to the complementarity of qualitative reasoning and CTP. In more specific terms, the following examples illustrate the types of problems that fall within the scope of the computational theory of perceptions.

First is *perception-based function modeling.* Perception of a function can be described as a collection of linguistic if-then rules, with each rule describing a fuzzy granule. For example, in the case of the function, f, shown in figure 5, a description of a perception of f can be expressed as

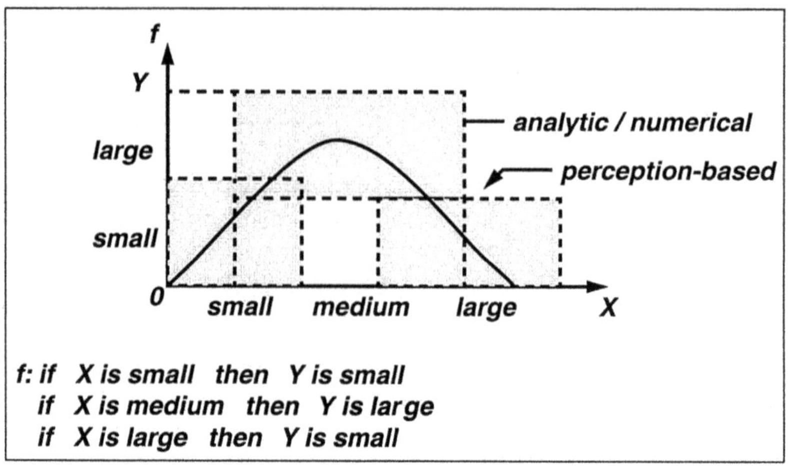

Fig. 5. Perception-Based Function Representation as a Collection of Linguistic If-Then Rules.
The granules in the (X, Y) space are Cartesian products of the granules in the X space and Y space.

If X is small, then Y is small.
If X is medium, then Y is large.
If X is large, then Y is small.

Given a perception-based description of a function, *f*, various standard questions can be raised; for example, what is the maximum value of *f*? Such questions are representative of perception-based computations in which the objects of computation are perception-based models of functions (Zadeh 1999).

Second is *perception-based system modeling.* A system, S, is assumed to be associated with temporal sequences of input $X_1, X_2, \ldots$; output $Y_1, Y_2, \ldots$; and states $S_1, S_2, \ldots$. S is defined by the state-transition function f

$$S_{t+1} = f(S_t, X_t)$$

and the output function g

$$Y_t = g(S_t, X_t).$$

In perception-based system modeling, the input, the output, and the states are assumed to be perceptions, as are the state-transition function, f, and the output function, g. Thus, a perception-based model of S would consist of a collection of linguistic if-then rules of the generic form "if X_t is A_t and S_t is B_t, then S_{t+1} is C_t, and Y_t is D_t, $t = 1, 2, \ldots$, where $A_t, B_t, C_t, D_t, t = 1, 2, \ldots$, are f-granular perceptions of the values of X_t, S_t, S_{t+1}, and Y_t (figure 6).

It is important to note that much of human decision making in everyday settings involves a knowledge of perception-based models of various systems,

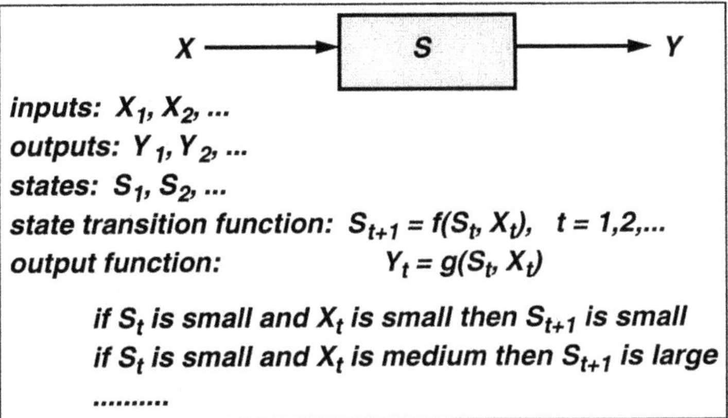

Fig. 6. Perception-Based System Modeling.
Transition and output functions are represented as collections of linguistic if-then rules.

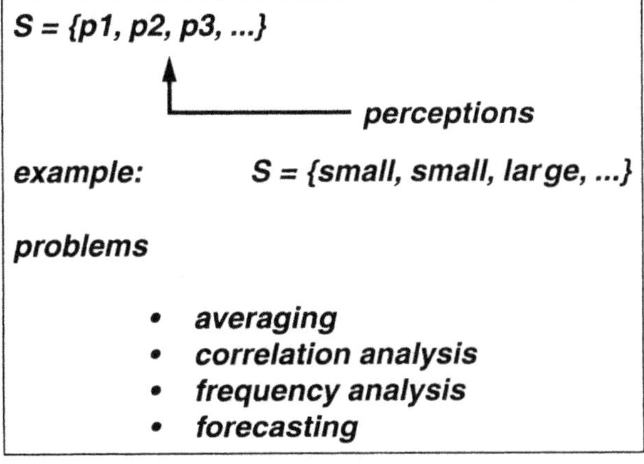

Fig. 7. Perception-Valued Time-Series Analysis.

for example, when we drive a car, balance a pole, and play golf. It is of interest to note that perception-based system modeling underlies what we normally view as commonsense and qualitative reasoning (Struss 1990; Mavrovouniotis and Stephanopoulos 1987; Forbus 1984; Kuipers 1984; Zadeh 1973; McCarthy and Hayes 1969).

Third is *perception-based time-series analysis*. In dealing with time series, the usual assumption is that their elements are numbers. In perception-based time-series analysis, the assumption is that the elements are perceptions, for example, small, medium, and large (figure 7). A question that can be raised is, What is the average value of a given time series? An important problem in perception-based time-series analysis is forecasting in the context of time series that are sequences of perceptions rather than measurements.

Fourth is the *solution of perception-based equations.* An example would be solving a system of equations with perception-based coefficients; for example,

$$\text{small} \cdot x + \text{large} \cdot y = \text{medium}$$
$$\text{medium} \cdot x + \text{small} \cdot y = \text{large}$$

Fifth is *computation with perception-based probabilities.* In probability theory, the usual assumption is that probabilities are numeric. In reality, most probabilities, and especially subjective probabilities, are perception based. For example, I might have the perception that most balls, in a box that contains balls of various sizes, are large. In this case, a perception of the probability that a ball drawn at random is large might be described as *most,* where *most* is interpreted as a fuzzy proportion (figure 2).

A less simple version of this example is the following: Assume that a box contains balls of various sizes and that my perceptions are (1) there are about 20 balls in the box; (2) most are large, and (3) a few are small. The question is, What is the probability that a ball drawn at random is neither large nor small?

As a further example of perception-based probabilistic reasoning, assume that I know that usually Robert returns from work at about 6 PM. The question is, What is the probability that Robert is home at 6:30 PM? Another question is, What is the earliest time that the probability that Robert is home is high?

As was stated at an earlier point, existing methods for dealing with perception-based information are effective when perceptions are interval valued or, more generally, *c*-granular. However, in most everyday settings, perception-based information is, as a rule, *f*-granular rather than *c*-granular. In this perspective, the importance of the computational theory of perceptions derives in large measure from the fact that it provides a capability to process perception-based information that is not constrained to be *c*-granular.

To be able to reason with perceptions, it is necessary to have a means of representing their meaning in a form that lends itself to computation. The expressive power of conventional predicate-logic-based meaning representation languages is insufficient for this purpose. This applies to very simple propositions such as "most balls are large" and "usually Robert returns from work at about 6 PM" and even more so to a proposition such as "it is very unlikely that there will be a significant increase in the price of oil in the near future."

In the computational theory of perceptions, meaning representation is based on the use of what is referred to as *constraint-centered semantics of natural languages* (CSNL). CSNL is a key part of CTP. The basic concepts underlying CSNL are outlined in the following section.

Constraint-Centered Semantics of Natural Languages

The point of departure in CSNL is a set of four basic assumptions.

First, a proposition, p, is an answer to a question, q. In general, q is implicit rather than explicit in p.

Second, the meaning of p is a generalized constraint on a variable. In general, both the variable and the constraint to which it is subjected are implicit in p. The canonical form of p, $CF(p)$, places in evidence the constrained variable and the constraining relation.

Third, a proposition, p, is viewed as a carrier of information. The canonical form of p defines the information that p carries.

Fourth, in CTP, reasoning is viewed as a form of computation. Computation with perceptions is based on propagation of generalized constraints from premises (antecedent propositions) to conclusions (consequent propositions).

In one form or another, manipulation of constraints plays a central role in a wide variety of methods and techniques, among which are mathematical programming, constraint programming, logic programming, and qualitative reasoning. However, in these methods and techniques, the usual assumption is that a constraint on a variable X is expressible as $X \in A$, where A is a crisp set, for example, $a \leq X \leq b$. In other words, conventional constraints are possibilistic in the sense that what they constrain are the possible values of variables.

The problem is that natural languages are much too rich to fit the Procrustean bed of conventional constraints. For, example, the sign in a hotel, "checkout time is 11 AM," constrains the checkout time. However, can it be represented as "checkout time = 11 AM" or as some other straightforward variation? Clearly, "checkout time is 11 AM" does not have a simple representation.

If our goal is to represent the meaning of a proposition drawn from a natural language as a constraint on a variable, then what is needed is a variety of constraints of different types—a variety that includes the standard constraint as a special case. This is what underlies the concept of a generalized constraint (Zadeh 1986) in CSNL.

A generalized constraint is represented as X isr R, where isr, pronounced "ezar," is a variable copula that defines the way in which R constrains X. More specifically, the role of R in relation to X is defined by the value of the discrete indexing variable r. The values of r and their interpretations are defined in figure 8.

As an illustration, when $r = e$, the constraint is an equality constraint and is abbreviated to $=$. When r takes the value d, the constraint is *disjunctive* (possibilistic), and *isd*, abbreviated to *is*, leads to the expression X is R, in which R is a fuzzy relation that constrains X by playing the role of the possibility distribution of X (Zadeh 1997; Lano 1991; Novak 1991).

As alluded to already, the key idea underlying CSNL is that the meaning of a proposition, p, can be represented as a generalized constraint on a variable.

e	: equal (abbreviated to =)
d	: disjunctive (possibilistic) (abbreviated to blank)
n	: veristic
p	: probabilistic
l	: probability value
u	: usuality
rs	: random set
rfs	: random fuzzy set
fg	: fuzzy graph
ps	: rough set (Pawlak set)
.	: ...

Fig. 8. Interpretations of Values of Indexing Variable, r.

Schematically, this is represented as

$$p \xrightarrow[\textit{explicitation}]{\textit{translation}} X \text{isr} R$$

with the understanding that the target language of translation is the language of generalized constraints, that is, GCL. Thus, translation is viewed as explicitation of the constrained variable, X; the defining indexing variable, r; and the constraining relation, R. In general, X, r, and R are implicit rather than explicit in p. Furthermore, X, r, and R depend on the question to which p is an answer. Thus, explicitation makes explicit what is implicit in p.

As a simple example consider the proposition

p : Mary is young.

In this case, there are two possible questions: (1) How old is Mary? and (2) Who is young? Typically, p would be an answer to question 1. Such a question is referred to as the *default* question, that is, the question that would normally be assumed unless explicitly stated to the contrary.

Assuming that the question is the first one, the meaning of p would be represented as

$$p \rightarrow \textit{Age(Mary)} \text{ is } \textit{young}$$

where *Age(Mary)* is the constrained variable; *young* is the constraining relation; and the constraint defines the possibility distribution of *Age(Mary)*. If the membership function of *young* is defined as shown in figure 2, then the same function defines the possibility distribution of *Age(Mary)*. More specifically, if the grade of membership of, say, 25 in *young* is 0.8, then the possibility that Mary is 25 given that Mary is young is 0.8.

If the question is the second one, the meaning of p would be represented as

$$p \rightarrow \textit{Person(young)} \text{ isv } \textit{Mary}$$

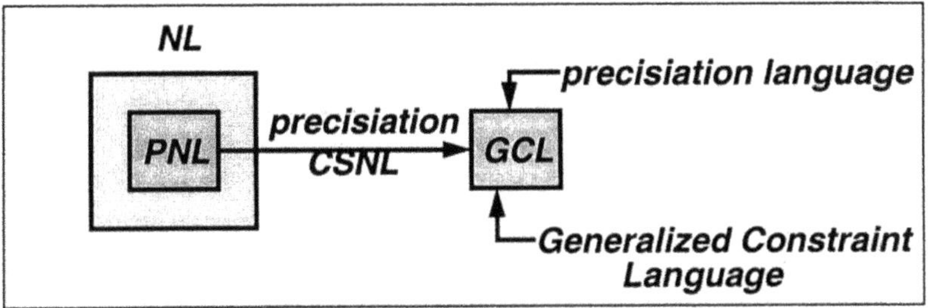

Fig. 9. PNL as a Precisiated Subset of a Natural Language.

in which the constrained variable is *Person(young)*, and *isv* is a veristic constraint. Thus, if Mary is 25, and the grade of membership of 25 in *young* is 0.8, then the verity (truth value) of the proposition "Mary is young" is 0.8.

As a further example, consider the proposition *p*: Carol lives in a small city near San Francisco. Assume that the question is, What is the location of residence of Carol? Representation of the meaning of *p* would proceed as follows:

Construct an explanatory database, *ED*, that consists of relations in terms of which the meaning of *p* is defined (Zadeh 1986). Assume that the relations in *ED* are

$$ED = \text{POPULATION[Name; Residence]} + \\ \text{SMALL[City; } \mu] + \\ \text{NEAR[City1; City2; } \mu]$$

In this case,

$$X = \text{Residence(Carol)} = {}_{\text{Residence}}\text{POPULATION[Name = Carol]}$$

and

$$R = \text{SMALL[City;}\mu] \cap {}_{\text{City1}}\text{NEAR[City2 = San Francisco]}$$

In *R*, the first constituent is the fuzzy set of small cities, the second constituent is the fuzzy set of cities that are near San Francisco, and $\cap$ denotes the intersection of these sets. A left subscript denotes projection on the domain of the displayed variable.

An important concept that emerges from a synthesis of the concepts of CSNL and GCL is *precisiated natural language* (PNL). In essence, PNL is a subset of a natural language that consists of propositions that are precisiable through translation into GCL (figure 9). In this perspective, GCL plays the role of a precisiation language, with the understanding that precisiation of meaning is not coextensive with representation of meaning. For example, in the proposition "usually Robert returns from work at about 6 PM," a request for precisiation might be expressed as "I understand what you mean but could you be more precise about the meaning of 'usually' and 'about 6 PM'."

The importance of the concept of PNL derives from the fact that by construction, GCL is maximally expressive because it incorporates all possible constraints and their combinations, modifications, and qualifications. It follows then that PNL is the largest subset of a natural language that admits precisiation. The high expressive power of PNL allows it to serve as a powerful definition language, opening the door to (1) definition of new concepts and (2) redefinition of existing concepts in a more general setting. Simple examples of definitions are the concept of a smooth function and the concept of the usual, rather than expected, value of a random variable. Examples of PNL-based redefinition are stability, Pareto optimality, and statistical independence.

A question arises about what can be said about concepts that do not admit precisiation within the framework of PNL. An example of such a concept is causality. Another example is randomness. Such concepts will be said to be amorphic.

Reasoning with Perceptions Based on Generalized Constraint Propagation

In the computational theory of perceptions, perceptions play the role of carriers of information. Thus, reasoning with perceptions involves a process of arriving at answers to specified questions given a collection of perceptions that constitute the initial data set (IDS). As a simple example, assume that the IDS consists of perceptions

p_1 : Most Swedes are tall.
p_2 : Most Swedes are blond.

The question is, What fraction of Swedes are both tall and blond?

The *generalized constraint propagation* (GCP) is a process that involves successive application of a collection of rules that govern combination, modification, qualification, and propagation of generalized constraints.

One of the basic rules governing GCP is the compositional rule. In its generalized generic form, it is expressed as

$$\frac{\begin{array}{l} X \text{ isr } R \\ (X,Y) \text{ iss } S \end{array}}{Y \text{ ist } T}$$

In particular, for probabilistic constraints, it reduces to the familiar Bayesian rule for combination of probabilities

$$\frac{\begin{array}{l} X \text{ isp } P \\ Y|X \text{ isp } Q \end{array}}{Y \text{ isp } P \bullet Q}$$

where $Y|X$ denotes Y conditioned on X, and $\bullet$ is the convolution of the probability distribution of X with the conditional probability distribution of Y given X.

Similarly, in the case of possibilistic constraints, the compositional rule reads

$$\frac{\begin{array}{l} X \text{ is } R \\ (X,Y) \text{ is } S \end{array}}{Y \text{ is } R \bullet S}$$

where $R \bullet S$ is the composition of the possibility distribution of X with the joint possibility distribution of X and Y. For example, from the perceptions

p_1: Mary is tall $\rightarrow$ *Height(Mary)* is *tall*
p_2: Chris is much taller than Mary $\rightarrow$
(Height(Chris), Height(Mary)) is *much.taller*

we can infer the perception "Chris is T," where $T = tall \bullet much.taller$. The $\bullet$ symbol is the operation of composition (Zadeh 1973). In this operation, conjunction and disjunction are usually assumed to be max and min, respectively. More generally, conjunction and disjunction can be, respectively, a t-norm and t-conorm (Pedrycz and Gomide 1998).

Computational rules governing GCP become more complex when the constituent constraints are heterogeneous. For example, if X is constrained probabilistically, and (X,Y) is constrained possibilistically, as in

$$\frac{\begin{array}{l} X \text{ isp } P \\ (X,Y) \text{ is } R \end{array}}{Y \text{ isrs } T}$$

then the constraint on Y is of random set type. Such constraints play a central role in the Dempster-Shafer theory of evidence (Shafer 1976).

The principal rule of inference in the computational theory of perceptions is the *generalized extension principle* (Zadeh 1999) (figure 10). For possibilistic constraints, it can be expressed as

$$\frac{f(X) \text{ is } R}{g(X) \text{ is } g(f^{-1}(R))}$$

In this constraint-propagation rule, $f(X)$ is R plays the role of an antecedent constraint that is an explicitation of a given perception or perceptions, X is the constrained variable, f is a given function, R is a relation that constrains $f(x)$, g is a given function, and $f^{-1}(R)$ is the preimage of R.

In effect, $f(X)$ is R is a generalized constraint that represents the information conveyed by antecedent perception(s), and $g(X)$ is $g(f^{-1}(R))$ defines the induced generalized constraint on a specified function of X. As an elementary example, assume that the initial data set consists of two perceptions:

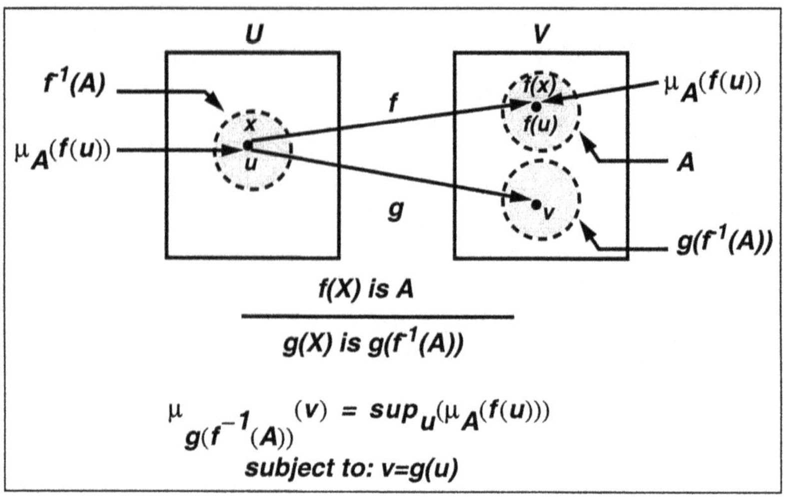

Fig. 10. Schematic of the Generalized Extension Principle. $f(X)$ is A is a given constraint on X, and $g(f^{-1}(A))$ is the induced constraint on $g(X)$. Computation of the induced constraint reduces to the solution of a variational problem.

p_1: Most Swedes are tall.
p_2: Most Swedes are blond.

Explicitations of p_1 and p_2 can be expressed as

$\sum$*Count(tall.Swedes/Swedes)* is *most*
$\sum$*Count(blond.Swedes/Swedes)* is *most*

where

$\sum$*Count(tall.Swedes/Swedes)*

and

$\sum$*Count(blond.Swedes/Swedes)*

represent, respectively, the proportions of tall Swedes and blond Swedes among Swedes. Application of the generalized extension principle leads to the following expression for the consequent constraint

$\sum$*Count(tall.and.blond.Swedes/Swedes)* is *2most - 1*

which retranslates into

(2most -1) Swedes are tall and blond

In this expression, the membership functions of *most* and *2most - 1* are related, as shown in figure 4. Details of the derivation are shown in the box.

Computation with propositions that contain perceptual quantifiers such as most, several, and few requires a definition of cardinality of a fuzzy set to make it possible to answer a question such as, What fraction of Swedes are tall?
In fuzzy logic, cardinality is defined in two ways: (1) crisp cardinality, which is simpler; and (2) fuzzy cardinality. In this article, I consider only crisp cardinality.
If A and B are fuzzy sets in $U = \{u_1, \ldots, u_N\}$ with respective grades of membership $\alpha_1, \ldots, \alpha_N$ and $\beta_1, \ldots, \beta_N$, then the sigma count of A is defined as

$$\sum Count(A) = \sum_i \alpha_i / u_i$$

and the relative sigma count of elements of A that are in B is defined as

$$\sum Count(A/B) = \frac{\sum_i \alpha_i \wedge \beta_i}{\sum_i \beta_i}$$

where $\wedge$ is min.
A basic identity involving sigma counts is the following:

$$\sum \text{Count}(A) + \sum \text{Count}(B) = \sum \text{Count}(A \cap B) + \sum \text{Count}(A \cup B)$$

which is analogous to the basic identity for probabilities:

$$P(A)+P(B) = P(A \cap B)+P(A \cup B)$$

From the identity, it follows that

$$\sum \text{Count}(A) + \sum \text{Count}(B) - \text{N} \leq \sum \text{Count}(A \cap B) \leq \sum \text{Count}(A) \wedge \sum \text{Count}(B)$$

Now, in the example under consideration, $A = tall.Swedes$, $B = blond.Swedes$, and

$$\frac{1}{N} \sum Count(tall.Swedes\ /\ Swedes) \text{ is most}$$
$$\frac{1}{N} \sum Count(blond.Swedes\ /\ Swedes) \text{ is most}$$

Substituting the given sigma counts into the inequalities, we obtain

$$2most - 1 \leq \frac{1}{N} \sum Count(tall.Swedes \cap blond.Swedes) \leq most$$

Assuming that most is monotonic (figure 2), we can conclude that

$$\frac{1}{N} \sum Count(tall.Swedes \cap blond.Swedes) \text{ is } 2most - 1$$

Note that in p_1, *tall* is quantifiable by height, but *blond* in p_2 is not. When an attribute is not quantifiable, the grade of membership is associated directly with an individual rather than through an attribute. In many applications, especially in the realm of control, elicitation of grades of membership is carried out through the use of automated learning techniques drawn from neurocomputing and evolutionary computing (Pedrycz and Gomide 1998).

In a general setting, application of the generalized extension principle transforms the problem of reasoning with perceptions into the problem of constrained maximization of the membership function of a variable that is constrained by a query. The examples considered earlier are simple instances of this process (Zadeh 1999).

What we see is that the machinery of the CTP bears little resemblance to the inference engine of predicate logic. At this juncture, CTP can be viewed as a direction—a direction that has a promise of enhancing the ability of AI to address problems in which the information that decisions are based on is perceptual in nature. This applies, in particular, to information about probabilities. More specifically, in most real-world settings, probabilities are not known precisely. What is known about them is, in the final analysis, based on perceptions rather than measurements.

Concluding Remarks

The CTP that is outlined in this article is not intended to replace traditional measurement-based methods. In effect, the theory is an additional tool that complements, rather than competes with, standard methods. The importance of CTP derives from the fact that much of human decision making and commonsense reasoning is, in reality, perception based. The principal features of CTP can be summarized as follows:

First, perceptions are assumed to be described by propositions drawn from a natural language. Second, perceptions are assumed to be f-granular. Third, the meaning of a perception is expressed as a generalized constraint of the form X isr R or as a combination of such constraints. Translation is viewed as explicitation of X, r, and R. Fourth, reasoning or computation with perceptions involves a goal-directed propagation of generalized constraints from premises to conclusions. The principal rule that governs GCP is the generalized extension principle. Application of the generalized extension principle reduces, in general, to the solution of a variational problem with constraints that represent the sought-after information.

Acknowledgment

This article is dedicated to Claude Shannon, John McCarthy, and Marvin Minsky. This research was supported in part by Office of Naval Research

(ONR) contract N00014-99-C-0298, National Aeronautics and Space Administration (NASA) contract NCC2-1006, NASA grant NAC2-117, ONR grant N00014-96-1-0056, ONR grant FDN0014991035, ARO grant DAAH 04-961-0341, and the BISC Program of the University of California at Berkeley.

Bibliography

Barsalou, L. W. 1999. Perceptual Symbol Systems. *Behavioral and Brain Sciences* 22:577-660.

Davis, E. 1990. *Representations of Commonsense Knowledge.* San Francisco, Calif.: Morgan Kaufmann.

Davis, E. 1987. Constraint Propagation with Interval Labels. *Artificial Intelligence* 32(3): 281-331.

de Kleer, J., and Bobrow, D. G. 1984. Qualitative Reasoning with Higher-Order Derivatives. In Proceedings of the Fourth National Conference on Artificial Intelligence. Menlo Park, Calif.: American Association for Artificial Intelligence.

Dubois, D., and Prade, H. 1996. Approximate and Commonsense Reasoning: From Theory to Practice. In *Proceedings of the Foundations of Intelligent Systems, Ninth International Symposium*, 19-33. Berlin: Springer-Verlag.

Dubois, D.; Fargier, H.; and Prade, H. 1994. Propagation and Satisfaction of Flexible Constraints. In *Fuzzy Sets, Neural Networks, and Soft Computing*, eds. R. R. Yager and L. A. Zadeh, 166-187. New York: Von Nostrand Reinhold.

Forbus, K. D. 1984. Qualitative Process Theory. *Artificial Intelligence* 24(1): 85-168.

Geng, J. Z. 1995. Fuzzy CMAC Neural Networks. *Journal of Intelligent and Fuzzy Systems* 3(1): 87-102.

Kaufmann A., and Gupta, M. M. 1985. *Introduction to Fuzzy Arithmetic: Theory and Applications.* New York: Von Nostrand.

Kuipers, B. J. 1984. *Qualitative Reasoning.* Cambridge, Mass.: MIT Press.

Lano, K. 1991. A Constraint-Based Fuzzy Inference System. In *Proceedings of EPIA 91, Fifth Portuguese Conference on Artificial Intelligence*, eds. P. Barahona, L. M. Pereira, and A. Porto, 45-59. Berlin: Springer-Verlag.

Lenat, D. B. 1995. cyc: A Large-Scale Investment in Knowledge Infrastructure. *Communications of the ACM* 38(11): 32-38.

McCarthy, J. 1990. *Formalizing Common Sense*, eds. V. Lifschitz and J. McCarthy. Norwood, N.J.: Ablex.

McCarthy, J., and Hayes, P. J. 1969. Some Philosophical Problems from the Standpoint of Artificial Intelligence. In *Machine Intelligence* 4, eds. B. Meltzer and D. Michie, 463-502. Edinburgh: Edinburgh University Press.

Mani, I., and Maybury, M. T., eds. 1999. *Advances in Automatic Text Summarization.* Cambridge, Mass.: MIT Press.

Mavrovouniotis, M. L., and Stephanopoulos, G. 1987. Reasoning with Orders of Magnitude and Approximate Relations. In Proceedings of the Sixth National Conference on Artificial Intelligence, 626-630. Menlo Park, Calif.: American Association for Artificial Intelligence.

Novak, V. 1991. Fuzzy Logic, Fuzzy Sets, and Natural Languages. *International Journal of General Systems* 20(1): 83-97.

Pedrycz, W., and Gomide, F. 1998. *Introduction to Fuzzy Sets.* Cambridge, Mass.: MIT Press.

Raiman, O. 1991. Order of Magnitude Reasoning. *Artificial Intelligence* 51(1): 11-38.

Sandewall, E. 1989. Combining Logic and Differential Equations for Describing Real-World Systems. In *Proceedings of the First International Conference on Principles of Knowledge Representation and Reasoning,* 412-420. San Francisco, Calif.: Morgan Kaufmann.

Shafer, G. 1976. A *Mathematical Theory of Evidence.* Princeton, N.J.: Princeton University Press.

Struss, P. 1990. Problems of Interval-Based Qualitative Reasoning. In *Qualitative Reasoning about Physical Systems,* eds. D. Weld and J. de Kleer, 288-305. San Francisco, Calif.: Morgan Kaufmann.

Sun, R. 1994. *Integrating Rules and Connectionism for Robust Commonsense Reasoning.* New York: Wiley.

Vallee, R. 1995. *Cognition et Systeme* (Cognition and Systems). Paris: l'Interdisciplinaire Systeme(s).

Zadeh, L. A. 1999. From Computing with Numbers to Computing with Words-From Manipulation of Measurements to Manipulation of Perceptions. *IEEE Transactions on Circuits and Systems* 45(1): 105-119.

Zadeh, L. A. 1997. Toward a Theory of Fuzzy Information Granulation and Its Centrality in Human Reasoning and Fuzzy Logic. *Fuzzy Sets and Systems* 90:111-127.

Zadeh, L. A. 1986. Outline of a Computational Approach to Meaning and Knowledge Representation Based on the Concept of a Generalized Assignment Statement. In *Proceedings of the International Seminar on Artificial Intelligence and Man-Machine Systems,* eds. M. Thoma and A. Wyner, 198-211. Heidelberg: Springer-Verlag.

Zadeh, L. A. 1973. Outline of a New Approach to the Analysis of Complex System and Decision Processes. *IEEE Transactions on Systems, Man, and Cybernetics* SMC-3(1): 28-44.

Combining Fuzzy and Case-Based Reasoning to Generate Human-like Music Performances

Josep Lluís Arcos and Ramon López de Mántaras

IIIA, Artificial Intelligence Research Institute
CSIC, Spanish Council for Scientific Research
Campus UAB, 08193 Bellaterra, Catalonia, Spain.
{arcos, mantaras}@iiia.csic.es, http://www.iiia.csic.es

Abstract. In this brief paper we describe several extensions and improvements of a previously reported system [2] capable of generating expressive music by imitating human performances. The system is based on Case-Based Reasoning (CBR) and Fuzzy techniques.

1 Introduction

One of the major difficulties in the automatic generation of music is to endow the resulting piece with the expressiveness that characterizes human performers. Following musical rules, no mater how sophisticated and complete they are, is not enough to achieve expression, and indeed computer music usually sounds monotonous and mechanical. The main problem is to grasp the performers personal touch, that is, the knowledge brought about when performing a score. A large part of this knowledge is implicit and very difficult to verbalize. For this reason, AI approaches based on declarative knowledge representations are very useful to model musical knowledge an indeed we represent such knowledge declaratively in our system, however they have serious limitations in grasping performance knowledge. An alternative approach, much closer to the observation imitation - experimentation process observed in human performers, is that of directly using the performance knowledge implicit in examples of human performers and let the system imitate these performances. To achieve this, we have developped the *SaxEx*, a case-based reasoning system capable of generating expressive performances of melodies based on examples of human performances. CBR is indeed an appropriate methodology to solve problems by means of examples of already solved similar problems.

In the next section we describe the system and in particular the fuzzy set-based extension of thereuse step. Then, we briefly mention some relevant related work and,finally, we give some conclusions.

2 System description

The problem-solving task of the system is to infer, via imitation, and using its case-based reasoning capability, a set of expressive transformations to be applied

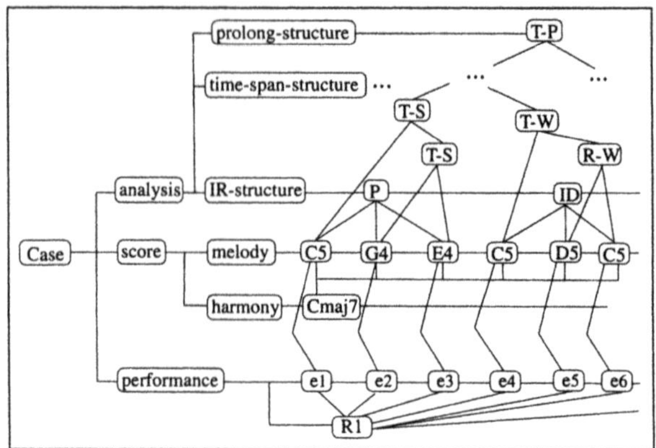

Fig. 1. Overall structure of the beginning of an 'All of me' case.

to every note of an inexpressive musical phrase given as input. To achieve this, it uses a case memory containing human performances and background musical knowledge, namely Narmours theory of musical perception [13] and Lerdahl & Jackendoffs GTTM [12]. The score, containing both melodic and harmonic information, is also given.

2.1 Modeling musical knowledge

Problems solved by *SaxEx*, and stored in its memory, are represented as complex structured cases embodying three different kinds of musical knowledge (see Figure 1): (1) concepts related to the score of the phrase such as notes and chords, (2) concepts related to background musical theories such as implication/realization (IR) structures and GTTM's time-span reduction nodes, and (3) concepts related to the performance of musical phrases.

A score is represented by a melody, embodying a sequence of notes, and a harmony, embodying a sequence of chords. Each note holds in turn a set of features such as its pitch (C5, G4, etc), its position with respect to the beginning of the phrase, its duration, a reference to its underlying harmony, and a reference to the next note of the phrase. Chords hold also a set of features such as name (Cmaj7, E7, etc), position, duration, and a reference to the next chord.

The musical analysis representation embodies structures of the phrase automatically inferred by *SaxEx* from the score using IR and GTTM background musical knowledge. The analysis structure of a melody is represented by a process-structure (embodying a sequence of IR basic structures), a time-span-reduction structure (embodying a tree describing metrical relations), and a prolongational-reduction structure (embodying a tree describing tensing and relaxing relations among notes). Moreover, a note holds the metrical-strength feature, inferred using GTTM theory, expressing the note's relative metrical importance into the phrase.

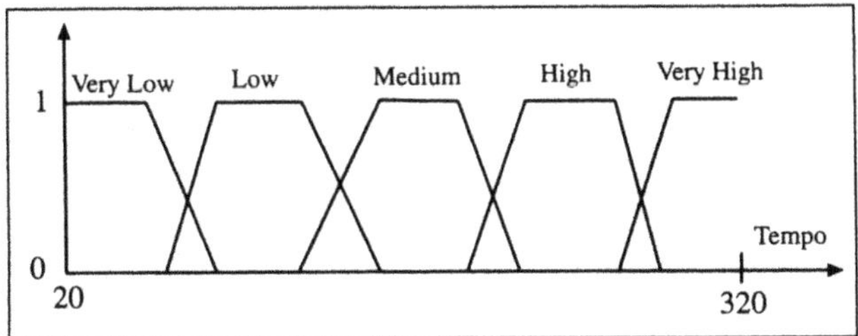

Fig. 2. Linguistic fuzzy values for rubato expressive parameter.

The information about the expressive performances contained in the examples of the case memory is represented by a sequence of *affective regions* and a sequence of *events*, one for each note, (extracted using the SMS sound analysis capabilities), as explained below.

Affective regions group (sub)-sequences of notes with common affective expressivity. Specifically, an affective region holds knowledge describing the following affective dimensions: *tender-aggressive*, *sad-joyful*, and *calm-restless*. These affective dimensions are described using five ordered qualitative values expressed by linguistic labels as follows: the middle label represents no predominance (for instance, neither tender nor aggressive), lower and upper labels represent, respectively predominance in one direction (for example, absolutely calm is described with the lowest label). For instance, a jazz ballad can start very tender and calm and continue very tender but more restless. Such different nuances are represented in *SaxEx* by means of different affective regions.

The expressive transformations to be decided and applied by the system affect the following expressive parameters: dynamics, rubato, vibrato, articulation, and attack. Except for the attack, the notes in the human performed musical phrases are qualified using the SMS (Spectral Modeling and Synthesis) system [14], by means of five different ordered values. For example, for dynamics the values are: very low, low, medium, high and very high and they are automatically computed relative to the average loudness of the inexpressive input phrase. The same idea is used for rubato, vibrato (very little vibrato to very high vibrato) and articulation (very legato to very staccato). In the previous system these values where mere syntactic labels but in the improved system, the meanings of these values are modeled by means of fuzzy sets such as those shown in figure 2 for Rubato. We will explain below the advantage of this extension. For the attack we have just two situations: reaching the pitch from a lower pitch or increasing the noise component of the sound.

2.2 The SaxEx CBR Task

The task of *SaxEx* is to infer a set of expressive transformations to be applied to every note of an inexpressive phrase given as input. To achieve this, *SaxEx* uses a CBR problem solver, a case memory of expressive performances, and background musical knowledge. Transformations concern the dynamics, rubato,

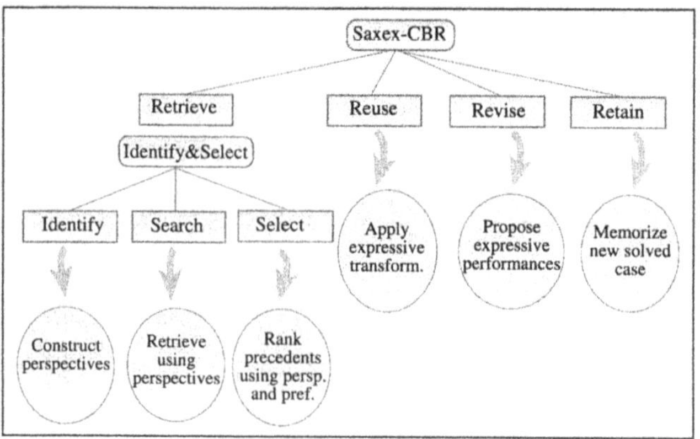

Fig. 3. Task decomposition of the *SaxEx* CBR method.

vibrato, articulation, and attack of each note in the inexpressive phrase. The cases stored in the episodic memory of *SaxEx* contain knowledge about the expressive transformations performed by a human player given specific labels for affective dimensions.

For each note in the phrase, the following subtask decomposition (Figure 3) is performed by the CBR problem solving method implemented in Noos:

- *Retrieve*: The goal of the retrieve task is to choose, from the memory of cases (pieces played expressively), the set of precedent notes—the cases—most similar for every note of the problem phrase. Specifically, the following subtask decomposition is applied to each note of the problem phrase:
  - *Identify*: its goal is to build retrieval perspectives (explained in the next subsection) using the affective values specified by the user and the musical background knowledge integrated in the system (retrieval perspectives are described in Subsection 2.3). These perspectives guide the retrieval process by focusing it on the most relevant aspects of the current problem, and will be used either in the *search* or in the *select* subtasks.
  - *Search*: its goal is to search cases in the case memory using Noos retrieval methods and some previously constructed perspective(s).
  - *Select*: its goal is to rank the retrieved cases using Noos preference methods. The collection of *SaxEx* default preference methods use criteria such as similarity in duration of notes, harmonic stability, or melodic directions.
- *Reuse*: its goal is to choose, from the set of most similar notes previously retrieved, a set of expressive transformations to be applied to the current note. The default strategy of *SaxEx* is the following: the first criterion used is to adapt the transformations of the most similar note. When several notes are considered equally similar, the transformations are computed using a fuzzy combination (see section 'The use of fuzzy techniques ...'). The user can, however, select alternative criteria, not involving this fuzzy combination such

as majority rule, minority rule, etc. When the retrieval task is not able to retrieve similar precedent cases for a given note, no expressive transformations are applied to that note and the situation is notified in the revision task. Nevertheless, using the current *SaxEx* case base, the retrieval perspectives allways retrieved at least one precedent in the experiments performed.
- *Revise*: its goal is to present to the user a set of alternative expressive performances for the problem phrase. Users can tune the expressive transformations applied to each note and can indicate which performances they prefer.
- *Retain*: the incorporation of the new solved problem to the memory of cases is performed automatically in *Noos* from the selection performed by the user in the *revise* task. These solved problems will be available for the reasoning process when solving future problems. Only positive feedback is given. That is, only those examples that the user judges as good expressive interpretations are actually retained.

In previous versions of *SaxEx* the CBR task was fixed. That is, the collection of retrieval perspectives, their combination, the collection of reuse criteria, and the storage of solved cases were pre-designed and the user didn't participate in the reasoning process. Moreover, the *retain* subtask was not present because it is mainly a subtask that requires an interaction with the user.

Now, in the current version of *SaxEx* we have improved the CBR method by incorporating the user in the reasoning process [1]. This new capability allows users to influence the solutions proposed by *SaxEx* in order to satisfy their interests or personal style. The user can interact with *SaxEx* in the four main CBR subtasks. This new functionality requires that the use and combination of the two basic mechanisms—perspectives and preferences— in the Retrieve and Reuse subtasks must be parameterizable and dynamically modifiable.

2.3 Retrieval perspectives

Retrieval perspectives are built by the *identify* subtask and can be used either by the *search* or the *select* subtask. Perspectives used by the *search* subtask will act as filters. Perspectives used by the *select* subtask will act only as a preference. Retrieval perspectives are built based on user requirements and background musical knowledge. Retrieval perspectives provide partial information about the relevance of a given musical aspect. After these perspectives are established, they have to be combined in a specific way according to the importance (preference) that they have.

Retrieval perspectives are of two different types: based on the affective intention that the user wants to obtain in the output expressive sound or based on musical knowledge.

1) *Affective labels* are used to determine the following declarative bias: we are interested in notes with affective labels similar to the affective labels required in the current problem by the user.

As an example, let us assume that we declare we are interested in forcing *SaxEx* to generate a calm and very tender performance of the problem phrase.

Based on this bias, *SaxEx* will build a perspective specifying as relevant to the current problem the notes from cases that belong first to "calm and very tender" affective regions (most preferred), or "calm and tender" affective regions, or "very calm and very tender" affective regions (both less preferred).

When this perspective is used in the *Search* subtask, *SaxEx* will search in the memory of cases for notes that satisfy this criterion. When this perspective is used in the *Select* subtask, *SaxEx* will rank the previously retrieved cases using this criterion.

2) *Musical knowledge* gives three sets of declarative retrieval biases: first, biases based on Narmour's implication/realization model; second, biases based on Lerdahl and Jackendoff's generative theory; and third, biases based on Jazz theory and general music knowledge.

Regarding Narmour's implication/realization model, *SaxEx* incorporates the following three perspectives:

- The "*role in IR structure*" criterion determines as relevant the role that a given note plays in an implication/realization structure. That is, the kind of IR structure it belongs to and its position (`first-note`, `inner-note`, or `last-note`). Examples of IR basic structures are the `P` process (a melodic pattern describing a sequence of at least three notes with similar intervals and the same ascending or descending registral direction) and the `ID` process (a sequence of at least three notes with the same intervals and different registral directions), among others. For instance, this retrieval perspective can specify biases such as "look for notes that are the `first-note` of a `P` process".
- The "*Melodic Direction*" criterion determines as relevant the kind of melodic direction in an implication/realization structure: `ascendant`, `descendant`, or `duplication`. This criterion is used for adding a preference among notes with the same IR role.
- The "*Durational Cumulation*" criterion determines as relevant the presence—in a IR structure—of a note in the last position with a duration significally higher than the others. This characteristic emphasizes the end of a IR structure. This criterion is used—as the previous—for adding a preference among notes with the same IR role and same melodic direction.

Regarding Lerdahl and Jackendoff's GTTM theory, *SaxEx* incorporates the following three perspectives:

- The "*Metrical Strength*" criterion determines as relevant the importance of a note with respect to the metrical structure of the piece. The metrical structure assigns a weight to each note according to the beat in which it is played. That is, the metrical weight of notes played in strong beats are higher than the metrical weight of notes played in weak beats. For instance, the metrical strength bias determines as similar the notes played at the beginning of subphrases since the metrical weight is the same.
- The "*role in the Time-Span Reduction Tree*" criterion determines as relevant the structural importance of a given note according to the role that the note plays in the analysis Time-Span Reduction Tree.

Fig. 4. Example of a Time-Span Tree for the beginning of the 'All of me' ballad.

Time-Span Reduction Trees are built bottom-up and hold two components: a segmentation into hierarchically organized rhythmic units and a binary tree that represents the relative structural importance of the notes within those units. There are two kinds of nodes in the tree: left-elaboration nodes and right-elaboration nodes.

Since the Time-Span Reduction Tree is a tree with high depth, we are only taking into account the two last levels. That is, given a note this perspective focuses on the kind of leaf the note belongs (left or right leaf) and on the kind of node the leaf belongs (left-elaboration or right-elaboration node).

For instance, in the 'All of me' ballad (see Figure 4) the first quarter note of the second bar (C) belongs to a left leaf in a right-elaboration node because the following two notes (D and C) elaborate the first note. In turn, these two notes belong to a left-elaboration (sub)node because second note (D) elaborates the third (C).

- The "*role in the Prolongational Reduction Tree*" criterion determines as relevant the structural importance of a given note according to the role that the note plays in the Prolongational Reduction Tree. Prolongational Reduction Trees are binary trees built top-down and represent the hierarchical patterns of tension and relaxation among groups of notes. There are two basic kinds of nodes in the tree (tensing nodes and relaxing nodes) with three modes of branch chaining: *strong prolongation* in which events repeat maintaining sonority (e.g., notes of the same chord); *weak prolongation* in which events repeat in an altered form (e.g., from I chord to I6 chord); and *jump* in which two completely different events are connected (e.g., from I chord to V chord).

  As in the previous perspective we are only taking into account the two last levels of the tree. That is, given a note this perspective focuses on the kind of leaf the note belongs (left or right leaf), on the kind of node the leaf belongs (tensing or relaxing node), and the kind of connection of the node (strong, weak, or jump).

Finally, regarding perspectives based on jazz theory and general music knowledge, *SaxEx* incorporates the following two:

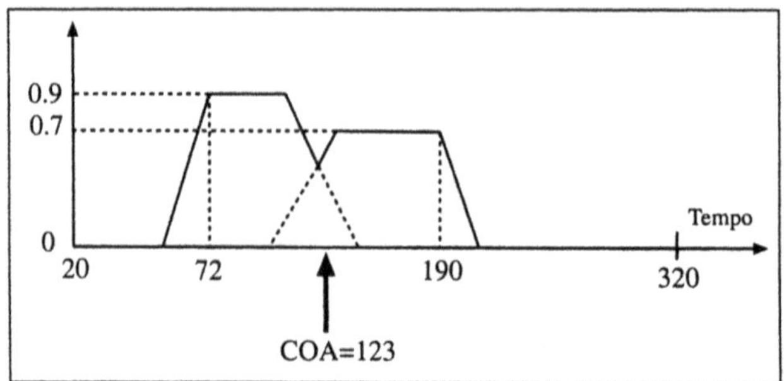

Fig. 5. Fuzzy combination and defuzzification of rubato value.

- The "*Harmonic Stability*" criterion determines as relevant the role of a given note according to the underlying harmony. Since *SaxEx* is focused on generating expressive music in the context of jazz ballads, the general harmonic theory has been specialized taking harmonic concepts from jazz theory. The Harmonic Stability criterion takes into account in the following two aspects: the position of the note within its underlying chord (e.g., first, third, seventh, ...); and the role of the note in the chord progression it belongs.
- The "*Note Duration*" criterion determines as relevant the duration of a note. That is, given a specific situation, the set of expressive transformations applied to a note will differ depending on whether the note has a long or a short duration.

2.4 The use of fuzzy techniques in the Reuse step

Having modeled the linguistic values of the expressive parameters by means of fuzzy sets, allows us to apply a fuzzy combination operator to these values of the retrieved notes in the reuse step. The following example describes this combination operation.

Let us assume that the system has retrieved two similar notes whose fuzzy values for the rubato are, respectively, 72 and 190, The system first computes the maximum degree of membership of each one of these two values with respect to the five linguistic values characterizing the *rubato* shown in figure 2. The maximum membership value of 72 corresponds to the fuzzy value *low* and is 0.90 (see figure 5) and that of 190 correponds to *medium* and is 0.70. Next, it computes a combined fuzzy membership function, based on these two values. This combination consists on the fuzzy disjunction of the fuzzy membership functions *low* and *medium* truncated, respectively, by the 0.90 and 0.70 membership degrees. That is:

$$Max(min(0.90, f_{low}), min(0.70, f_{medium}))$$

The result is shown in figure 5. Finally *defuzzifies* this result by computing the COA (Center of Area) of the combined function [11]. The defuzzification step gives the precise value for the tempo to be applied to the initially inexpressive note, in this example the obtained result is 123. An analogous process is applied to the other expressive parameters. The advantage of such fuzzy combination is that the resulting expression takes into account the contribution of all the retrieved similar notes whereas with criteria such as *minority rule*, *majority rule* etc. this is not the case. For example, if the system retrieves three notes from the expressive examples, and two of them had been played with low rubato and the third with medium rubato, the majority rule dictates that the inexpressive note should be played with *low rubato*. This conclusion is mapped into an a priori fixed value that is lower than the average rubato of the inexpressive input piece. It is worth noticing that each time the system concludes *low rubato* for several inexpressive notes, these note will be played with the same rubato even if the retrieved similar notes were different (*very low* would be mapped into a value much lower than the average rubato, *high* would be mapped into a value higher than the average and *very high* into a value much higher than the average and the same procedure applies to the other expressive parameters such as dynamics, vibrato and legato). With the fuzzy extension, the system is capable of increasing the variety of its performances because, after defuzzification, the final value for each expressive parameter is computed and this computation does not depend only on the linguistic value (low, etc.) of the retrieved similar notes but also on the membership degree of the actual numerical values that are used to truncate the membership functions as explained above, therefore the final value will not be the same unless, of course, the precedent retrieved notes is actually the same note.

The system is connected to the SMS (4) software for sound analysis and synthesis based on spectral modeling as pre and post processor. This allows to actually listen to the obtained results. These results clearly show that a computer system can play expressively. In our experiments, we have used Real Book jazz ballads.

3 Related work

Previous work on the analysis and synthesis of musical expression has addressed the study of at most two expressive parameters such as rubato and vibrato [4, 7, 9], rubato and dynamics [16, 3] or rubato and articulation [10]. Concerning instrument modeling, the work of Dannenberg and Derenyi [5] is an important step towards high-quality synthesis of wind instrument performances. Other work such as in [6, 8] has focalized on the study of how musicians expressive intentions influence performers. To the best of our knowledge, the only previous works using learning techniques to generate expressive performances are those of Widmer [16], who uses explanation-based techniques to learn rules for dynamics and rubato using a MIDI keyboard, and Bressin [3], who trains an artificial neural network to simulate a human pianist also using MIDI. In our work we deal with five expressive parameters in the context of a very expressive non-MIDI instrument (tenor sax). Furthermore, ours was the first attempt to use Case-based

Reasoning techniques. The use of CBR techniques was also done later by [15] but dealing only with rubato and dynamics for MIDI instruments.

4 Conclusions

We have briefly described a new improved version of our *SaxEx* system. The added interactivity improves the usability of the system and the use of fuzzy techniques in the reuse step increases the performance variety of the system. Some ideas for further work include further experimentation with a larger set of tunes as well as allowing the system to add ornamental notes and not to play some of the notes, that is moving a small step towards adding improvising capabilities to the system.

Acknowledgements

The research reported in this paper is partly supported by the ESPRIT LTR 25500-COMRIS *Co-Habited Mixed-Reality Information Spaces* project. We also acknowledge the support of ROLAND Electronics de España S.A. to our AI & Music project.

References

1. Josep Lluís Arcos and Ramon López de Mántaras. An interactive case-based reasoning approach for generating expressive music. *Journal of Applied Intelligence*, 2001. In press.
2. Josep Lluís Arcos, Ramon López de Mántaras, and Xavier Serra. Saxex : a case-based reasoning system for generating expressive musical performances. *Journal of New Music Research*, 27 (3):194–210, 1998.
3. R. Bresin. Artificial neural networks based models for automatic performance of musical scores. *Journal of New Music Research*, 27 (3):239–270, 1998.
4. Manfred Clynes. Microstructural musical linguistics: composers' pulses are liked most by the best musicians. *Cognition*, 55:269–310, 1995.
5. R.B. Dannenberg and I. Derenyi. Combining instrument and performance models for high-quality music synthesis. *Journal of New Music Research*, 27 (3):211–238, 1998.
6. Giovani De Poli, Antonio Rodà, and Alvise Vidolin. Note-by-note analysis of the influence of expressive intentions and musical structure in violin performance. *Journal of New Music Research*, 27 (3):293–321, 1998.
7. P. Desain and H. Honing. Computational models of beat induction: the rule-based approach. In *Proceedings of IJCAI'95 Workshop on AI and Music*, pages 1–10, 1995.
8. A. Friberg, R. Bresin, L. Fryden, and J. Sunberg. Musical punctuation on the microlevel: automatic identification and performance of small melodic units. *Journal of New Music Research*, 27 (3):271–292, 1998.
9. H. Honing. The vibrato problem, comparing two solutions. *Computer Music Journal*, 19 (3):32–49, 1995.
10. M.L. Johnson. An expert system for the articulation of Bach fugue melodies. In D.L. Baggi, editor, *Readings in Computer-Generated Music*, pages 41–51. IEEE Computes Society Press, 1992.

11. G. Klir and B. Yuan. *Fuzzy Sets and Fuzzy Logic*. Prentice Hall, 1995.
12. Fred Lerdahl and Ray Jackendoff. An overview of hierarchical structure in music. In Stephan M. Schwanaver and David A. Levitt, editors, *Machine Models of Music*, pages 289–312. The MIT Press, 1993. Reproduced from Music Perception.
13. Eugene Narmour. *The Analysis and cognition of basic melodic structures : the implication-realization model*. University of Chicago Press, 1990.
14. Xavier Serra, Jordi Bonada, Perfecto Herrera, and Ramon Loureiro. Integrating complementary spectral methods in the design of a musical synthesizer. In *Proceedings of the ICMC'97*, pages 152–159. San Francisco: International Computer Music Asociation., 1997.
15. T. Suzuki, T. Tokunaga, and H. Tanaka. A case-based approach to the generation of musical expression. In *Proceedings of IJCAI'99*, 1999.
16. Gerhard Widmer. Learning expressive performance: The structure-level approach. *Journal of New Music Research*, 25 (2):179–205, 1996.

A Fuzzy-Rough Approach to the Representation of Linguistic Hedges

Martine De Cock[1], Anna Maria Radzikowska[2], and Etienne E. Kerre[1]

[1] Dept. of Mathematics and Computer Science
Ghent University, Krijgslaan 281 (S9), B-9000 Gent, Belgium
E-mail: {Martine.DeCock, Etienne.Kerre}@rug.ac.be

[2] Faculty of Mathematics and Information Science
Warsaw University of Technology
Plac Politechniki 1, 00-661 Warsaw, Poland
E-mail: annrad@mini.pw.edu.pl

Abstract. We present a new representation for linguistic hedges using a framework of fuzzy rough sets. In traditional fuzzy–set theoretical representations, properties of objects such as *old* and *experienced*, are represented by a fuzzy set P, while linguistic hedges (i.e. expressions like very, more or less, rather) are modelled by means of some transformations applied to P. In contrast to these approaches, we propose a representation which allows us to express the meaning of a statement like "x is very P" also relative to mutual *resemblances* between objects in the domain of discourse. This allows for adequate context–dependent characteristics of objects. Technically, this is achieved by using fuzzy rough approximators with respect to fuzzy *resemblance relations* representing mutual resemblances between objects. We show that this framework allows for flexible representation of some linguistic terms.

1 Introduction

Linguistic hedges (also called *linguistic modifiers*) are special linguistic expressions such as very, more or less and rather by which other linguistic expressions are modified. During the last decades many fuzzy–set theoretical representations for linguistic modifiers are developed [6]. They are mostly only technical operators without an inheritant meaning. Denoting by $P(x)$ the degree to which an object x has a property P, the most popular representations for very and more or less, as proposed by Zadeh [14], dictate that very $P(x) = P(x)^2$ while more or less $P(x) = \sqrt{P(x)}$. Operations like $.^2$ and $\sqrt{.}$ result from studying membership functions of properties P and derived properties very P and more or less P (sometimes based on psycholinguistic research but mostly on own intuition) and should only be seen as technical operators that transform one degree into another, lacking any meaning of their own.

In natural language properties of objects are normally represented by adjectives; linguistic hedges applied to these adjectives, allow us to express a kind of emphasis imposed on these properties. For example, when we say "*Nico is a very good doctor*", we feel strongly about his qualifications. This conviction, in turn, may be viewed as an implicit reference to qualifications of other doctors – in other words, we have on mind other doctors who *resemble Nico* himself, which are found good also. The notion of *resemblance* cannot be viewed in a black-and-white scale. While saying that "*Nico* resembles *Bill*", we usually think about some degree to which they are similar to each other. Therefore, given a set $\mathfrak{X}$ of objects, the natural way for modelling mutual resemblance between these objects is a fuzzy relation R on $\mathfrak{X}$, where $R(x,y)$ represents the degree to which x resembles y.

Following an approach presented in [2], we propose a fuzzy–set theoretical representation of linguistic hedges, where the notion of *resemblance* is involved. In this paper we consider only the *inclusive interpretation*[1] of linguistic hedges. In this interpretation, all objects qualified as "very P" (P is the property of objects) are viewed as possessing P (e.g. all very tall people are referred to as tall as well). Properties of objects are represented by fuzzy sets (on the domain of all objects under consideration). In order to determine the degree to which x is qualified as very P (resp. more or less P), the set of all objects resembling x is taken into account. Informally: a flavour will be called more or less sweat if it resembles to another flavour also called sweat. Next, it will be called very sweat if all flavours to which it resembles are sweat. The mathematical representations of linguistic hedges resulting from this approach are closely related to the recently developed generalized concept of rough sets ([10],[11]). In this paper we will highlight this connection and show that the properties established for fuzzy rough sets have linguistic interpretations.

2 Preliminaries

Given a nonempty domain $\mathfrak{X}$, a *fuzzy set P in $\mathfrak{X}$* is characterized by its *membership function* $P : \mathfrak{X} \to [0,1]$, which assigns to every $x \in \mathfrak{X}$ the degree $P(x)$ to which x belongs to P. Throughout this paper, the family of all fuzzy sets in $\mathfrak{X}$ will be denoted by $\mathcal{F}(\mathfrak{X})$.

A *triangular norm* (t–norm) is an increasing, associative and commutative $[0,1]^2 \to [0,1]$ mapping that satisfies $\mathcal{T}(1,x)=x$, for all $x \in [0,1]$. Popular t–norms are the *min* operation $\mathcal{T}_M(x,y) = \min\{x,y\}$ and the Łukasiewicz t–norm $\mathcal{T}_L(x,y) = \max\{0, x+y-1\}$. For two fuzzy sets $A, B \in \mathcal{F}(\mathfrak{X})$ and a t–norm $\mathcal{T}$, the *$\mathcal{T}$-intersection* of A and B, in symbols $A \cap_{\mathcal{T}} B$, is the fuzzy set in $\mathfrak{X}$ defined by: $(A \cap_{\mathcal{T}} B)(x) = \mathcal{T}(A(x), B(x))$ for all $x \in \mathfrak{X}$.
An *implication* is a $[0,1]^2 \to [0,1]$ mapping with decreasing 1st and increasing 2nd partial mappings satisfying $\mathcal{I}(0,0) = \mathcal{I}(0,1) = \mathcal{I}(1,1) = 1$ and $\mathcal{I}(1,0) = 0$. We say that $\mathcal{I}$ is a *border* implication iff $\mathcal{I}(1,x) = x$ for all $x \in [0,1]$. Well–known implications are the Łukasiewicz implication $\mathcal{I}_L(x,y) = \min\{1, 1-x+y\}$

[1] Another commonly used interpretation of linguistic hedges is the *non–inclusive* interpretation: here some objects qualified as "very P" are not called P (e.g. a very good school grade is not thought of as just good). See also [6].

and the Kleene–Dienes implication $\mathcal{I}_{KD}(x,y) = \max\{1-x,y\}$. For a continuous t–norm $\mathcal{T}$, $\mathcal{I}$ is called a *residual implication based on* $\mathcal{T}$ (the residuum of $\mathcal{T}$) iff $\mathcal{I}(x,y) = \sup\{\alpha \in [0,1] : \mathcal{T}(x,\alpha) \leqslant y\}$ for all $(x,y) \in [0,1]^2$. For example, $\mathcal{I}_L$ is the residual implication based on $\mathcal{T}_L$.

Let $\mathfrak{X}$ be a nonempty universe. A *binary fuzzy relation on* $\mathfrak{X}$ is a function $R : \mathfrak{X} \times \mathfrak{X} \to [0,1]$. We say that R is:

- *reflexive* iff $R(x,x) = 1$ for all $x \in \mathfrak{X}$
- *symmetric* iff $R(x,y) = R(y,x)$ for all $(x,y) \in \mathfrak{X}^2$
- $\mathcal{T}$*-transitive* iff for all $(x,y,z) \in \mathfrak{X}^3$, $\mathcal{T}(R(x,y), R(y,z)) \leqslant R(x,z)$

If R is reflexive and symmetric then it is called a *tolerance* relation; for a t–norm $\mathcal{T}$, a $\mathcal{T}$–transitive tolerance relation is called a $\mathcal{T}$*-equivalence* relation. For $x \in \mathfrak{X}$, the R*-afterset of* x, written xR, is the fuzzy set on $\mathfrak{X}$ defined by: $(xR)(y) = R(x,y)$ for all $y \in \mathfrak{X}$.

3 Linguistic terms

In this paper we will study the mathematical representation of linguistic terms built up by the following scheme, where < *base term* > can be an arbitrary adjective:

Scheme 1

<*modifier*> := extremely | definitely | very | rather | more or less | roughly;
<*term*> := <*base term*> | <*modifier*> <*term*>.

Extremely, definitely and very are intensifying modifiers. They express a strengthened emphasis imposed on the term they are applied to. Conversely rather, more or less and roughly express a weakened emphasis.

The meaning of each term can be represented by a fuzzy set (in a universe $\mathfrak{X}$ of discourse). For simplicity, we will make no notational distinction between a fuzzy set P and the term P represented by that fuzzy set.

In this paper we will focus on the deduction of the membership function of a modified term from the membership function of that term. Our intuition dictates that in Scheme 1 extremely is the strongest intensifying modifier while very is the weakest one. If an object x is called "extremely P" then it can be called "definitely P" as well as "very P", but not conversely (e.g. only some *definitely good* painters may be called *extremely good*). Similarly, we feel that roughly has the most weakening force while rather has the least weakening effect. Formalizing these intuitive findings and following [8] we will assume that semantic entailment [7] holds: for $P \in \mathcal{F}(\mathfrak{X})$ and $x \in \mathfrak{X}$,

$$x \text{ is extremely } P \Rightarrow x \text{ is definitely } P \Rightarrow x \text{ is very } P \Rightarrow x \text{ is } P$$
$$\Rightarrow x \text{ is rather } P \Rightarrow x \text{ is more or less } P \Rightarrow x \text{ is roughly } P.$$

Representing linguistic terms by means of fuzzy sets, this corresponds to:

$$\text{extremely } P \subseteq \text{definitely } P \subseteq \text{very } P \subseteq P \tag{1}$$
$$P \subseteq \text{rather } P \subseteq \text{more or less } P \subseteq \text{roughly } P, \tag{2}$$

where for $A, B \in \mathcal{F}(\mathfrak{X})$, $A \subseteq B$ stands for: $A(x) \leqslant B(x)$ for all $x \in \mathfrak{X}$.
A linguistic modifier is represented in fuzzy set theory by a fuzzy modifier.

Definition 1 ([13]). A ***fuzzy modifier*** is a $\mathcal{F}(\mathfrak{X}) \to \mathcal{F}(\mathfrak{X})$ mapping. □

4 Fuzzy rough approximators

Fuzzy rough sets (see, for instance, [4], [5], [12], [10], [11]) were introduced as a fuzzy generalization of the concept of rough sets, originally proposed by Pawlak ([9]). The central notion is the ***fuzzy approximation space*** viewed as a pair $\text{FAS} = (\mathfrak{X}, R)$, where $\mathfrak{X}$ is a nonempty domain and R is a binary fuzzy relation on $\mathfrak{X}$.

While imposing additional assumptions on relations R, we actually obtain different classes of fuzzy rough approximation spaces. In particular, if the relation is required to be reflexive (resp. tolerance relation, $\mathcal{T}$–equivalence relation, for a t–norm $\mathcal{T}$), the corresponding class would be referred to as the class of *fuzzy R–approximation spaces* (resp. *fuzzy T–approximation spaces, fuzzy $E_{\mathcal{T}}$–approximation spaces*).

Definition 2. Given a fuzzy approximation space FAS, a border implication $\mathcal{I}$ and a t–norm $\mathcal{T}$, we define the $\mathcal{F}(\mathfrak{X}) \to \mathcal{F}(\mathfrak{X})$ mappings $\underline{\text{FAS}}_{\mathcal{I}}$ and $\overline{\text{FAS}}^{\mathcal{T}}$ such that for every $A \in \mathcal{F}(\mathfrak{X})$ and every $x \in \mathfrak{X}$,

$$\underline{\text{FAS}}_{\mathcal{I}}(A)(x) = \inf_{y \in \mathfrak{X}} \mathcal{I}(R(x,y), A(y)) \tag{3}$$
$$\overline{\text{FAS}}^{\mathcal{T}}(A)(x) = \sup_{y \in \mathfrak{X}} \mathcal{T}(R(x,y), A(y)). \tag{4}$$

$\underline{\text{FAS}}_{\mathcal{I}}$ (resp. $\overline{\text{FAS}}^{\mathcal{T}}$) is called an ***$\mathcal{I}$–lower*** (resp. ***$\mathcal{T}$–upper***) ***fuzzy rough approximator in*** FAS. □

Let us recall several basic properties of fuzzy rough approximators ([11]).

Proposition 1. *For every fuzzy approximation space* $\text{FAS} = (\mathfrak{X}, R)$*, every t–norm* $\mathcal{T}$*, every border implication* $\mathcal{I}$ *and every* $A, B \in \mathcal{F}(\mathfrak{X})$*:*

(P.1) $A \subseteq B$ *implies* $\overline{\text{FAS}}^{\mathcal{T}}(A) \subseteq \overline{\text{FAS}}^{\mathcal{T}}(B)$ *and* $\underline{\text{FAS}}_{\mathcal{I}}(A) \subseteq \underline{\text{FAS}}_{\mathcal{I}}(B)$.

(P.2) *If* $\mathcal{I}_1$ *and* $\mathcal{T}_1$ *are a border implication and a t–norm, respectively, such that* $\mathcal{I}_1 \leqslant \mathcal{I}$ *and* $\mathcal{T}_1 \leqslant \mathcal{T}$*, then*[2]

$$\overline{\text{FAS}}^{\mathcal{T}_1}(A) \subseteq \overline{\text{FAS}}^{\mathcal{T}}(A)$$
$$\underline{\text{FAS}}_{\mathcal{I}_1}(A) \subseteq \underline{\text{FAS}}_{\mathcal{I}}(A).$$

[2] For a mapping $\Phi, \Psi : [0,1]^2 \to [0,1]$, we write $\Phi \leqslant \Psi$ iff $\Phi(x,y) \leqslant \Psi(x,y)$ for all $(x,y) \in [0,1]^2$.

(P.3) *If* FAS *is a fuzzy R-approximation space then*

$$\underline{\text{FAS}}_{\mathcal{I}}(A) \subseteq A \subseteq \overline{\text{FAS}}^{\mathcal{T}}(A).$$

(P.4) *If* FAS *is a fuzzy T-approximation space and $\mathcal{I}$ is the residuum of $\mathcal{T}$ then*

$$\overline{\text{FAS}}^{\mathcal{T}}(\underline{\text{FAS}}_{\mathcal{I}}(A)) \subseteq A \subseteq \underline{\text{FAS}}_{\mathcal{I}}(\overline{\text{FAS}}^{\mathcal{T}}(A)).$$ ∎

Property **(P.3)** immediately implies:

Corollary 1. *For every border implication $\mathcal{I}$, every t-norm $\mathcal{T}$, every fuzzy R-approximation space* $\text{FAS} = (\mathfrak{X}, R)$ *and* $A \in \mathcal{F}(\mathfrak{X})$,

$$\begin{aligned} \overline{\text{FAS}}^{\mathcal{T}}(\overline{\text{FAS}}^{\mathcal{T}}(A)) &\supseteq \overline{\text{FAS}}^{\mathcal{T}}(A) \\ \underline{\text{FAS}}_{\mathcal{I}}(\underline{\text{FAS}}_{\mathcal{I}}(A)) &\subseteq \underline{\text{FAS}}_{\mathcal{I}}(A) \end{aligned}$$ ∎

However, in some restricted cases the above inclusions are equalities ([10]).

Proposition 2. *Let $\mathcal{T}$ be a continuous t-norm and let* $\text{FAS} = (\mathfrak{X}, R)$ *be a fuzzy* $E_{\mathcal{T}}$*-approximation space. For the residuum $\mathcal{I}$ of $\mathcal{T}$ and any* $A \in \mathcal{F}(\mathfrak{X})$,

$$\begin{aligned} \overline{\text{FAS}}^{\mathcal{T}}(\overline{\text{FAS}}^{\mathcal{T}}(A)) &= \overline{\text{FAS}}^{\mathcal{T}}(A) \\ \underline{\text{FAS}}_{\mathcal{I}}(\underline{\text{FAS}}_{\mathcal{I}}(A)) &= \underline{\text{FAS}}_{\mathcal{I}}(A). \end{aligned}$$ ∎

5 Modelling linguistic hedges by fuzzy rough approximators

$\underline{\text{FAS}}_{\mathcal{I}}$ and $\overline{\text{FAS}}^{\mathcal{T}}$ are $\mathcal{F}(\mathfrak{X}) - \mathcal{F}(\mathfrak{X})$ mappings and a fortiori fuzzy modifiers (see Definition 1). Hence we can use them to represent the linguistic modifiers extremely, definitely, very, rather, more or less and roughly. First, we have to choose a suitable class of fuzzy approximation spaces. For this purpose, we will need a fuzzy relation modelling *approximate equality*.

5.1 Modelling approximate equality

The intuitive meaning of the notion of *approximate equality* involves:

- *reflexivity*: the object x is approximately equal to itself to the degree 1;
- *symmetry*: x is approximately equal to y to the same degree as y is approximately equal to x.

However, in contrast to fuzzy equalities,[3] approximate equality should not be $\mathcal{T}$-transitive for some t-norm $\mathcal{T}$. The following example illustrates the underlying intuition.

[3] A *fuzzy equality on* $\mathfrak{X}$ is a $\mathcal{T}$-equivalence relation $E_{\mathcal{T}}$ ($\mathcal{T}$ is a t-norm) satisfying the following separation condition $E_{\mathcal{T}}(x,y) = 1 \Leftrightarrow x = y$ for all $(x,y) \in \mathfrak{X}^2$.

Example 1. In every-day life we usually don't feel the difference in temperature between 0° and 1°, neither between 1° and 2°, between 35° and 36° etc. For us 0° and 1° are certainly approximately equal, and so are 1° and 2°, and 35° and 36° etc. To formalize this, consider a universe $\mathfrak{X}$ of temperatures and, for a t–norm $\mathcal{T}$, let $E_{\mathcal{T}}$ be a $\mathcal{T}$–equivalence relation on $\mathfrak{X}$ used to represent "*approximately equal*". We would thus expect:

$$E(k, k+1) = 1 \text{ for every } k \in \mathbb{N}.$$

By induction it is easy to show that for every $k, n \in \mathbb{N}$, $E(k, k+n) = 1$, which means that all temperatures are approximately equal to the degree 1 – obviously, a completely contra–intuitive result. □

The above discussion leads us to defining pseudo–metric based resemblance relations (see [1]).

Definition 3. Let $\mathfrak{X}$ be a universe, $(\mathfrak{M}, d)$ be a pseudo–metric space and let $g : \mathfrak{X} \to \mathfrak{M}$. A binary fuzzy relation R on $\mathfrak{X}$ is called a ***(g,d)–resemblance relation on $\mathfrak{X}$*** iff for all $x, y, z, u \in \mathfrak{X}$,

(R.1) $E(x, x) = 1$
(R.2) $E(x, y) = E(y, x)$
(R.3) $d(g(x), g(y)) \leqslant d(g(z), g(u))$ implies $E(x, y) \geqslant E(z, u)$. □

If $\mathfrak{X}$ is already equipped with a pseudo–metric, then g can be the identical mapping $\mathbb{I}_{\mathfrak{X}}$ on $\mathfrak{X}$, i.e. $\mathbb{I}_{\mathfrak{X}}(x) = x$, for all x in $\mathfrak{X}$. Notice that for all $x \in \mathfrak{X}$ the R–afterset of x, denoted xR, is the fuzzy set of all objects resembling x.

5.2 Representational issues

Let R be a (g, d)–resemblance relation on $\mathfrak{X}$. Since R is reflexive and symmetric, $\text{FAS} = (\mathfrak{X}, R)$ is a fuzzy T–approximation space. For every border implication $\mathcal{I}$, every t–norm $\mathcal{T}$ and every $P \in \mathcal{F}(\mathfrak{X})$, $x \in \mathfrak{X}$:

$$\underline{\text{FAS}}_{\mathcal{I}}(P)(x) = \inf_{y \in \mathfrak{X}} \mathcal{I}(R(x,y), P(y)) = \inf_{y \in \mathfrak{X}} \mathcal{I}(xR(y), P(y)) \tag{5}$$

This expression is known as the degree to which xR, i.e. the fuzzy set of objects resembling x, is included in P. Furthermore:

$$\begin{aligned} \overline{\text{FAS}}^{\mathcal{T}}(P)(x) = \sup_{y \in \mathfrak{X}} \mathcal{T}(R(x,y), P(y)) &= \sup_{y \in \mathfrak{X}} \mathcal{T}(xR(y), P(y)) \\ &= \sup_{y \in \mathfrak{X}} (xR \cap_{\mathcal{T}} P)(y) \end{aligned} \tag{6}$$

which is known as the degree to which xR overlaps with P.
Let *IntModifier-1* and *IntModifier-2* be two linguistic intensifying modifiers such that the former one reflects a weaker emphasis than the latter one. Furthermore, let $\mathcal{I}$, $\mathcal{I}_1$ and $\mathcal{I}_2$ be border implications and $\mathcal{I}_2 \leqslant \mathcal{I}_1$. We propose the following two ways of modelling:

R1.i: $<$*IntModifier-1*$>$ $P = \underline{\text{FAS}}_{\mathcal{I}}(P)$
$<$*IntModifier-2*$>$ $P = \underline{\text{FAS}}_{\mathcal{I}}(\underline{\text{FAS}}_{\mathcal{I}}(P))$

R2.i: $<$*IntModifier-1*$>$ $P = \underline{\text{FAS}}_{\mathcal{I}_1}(P)$
$<$*IntModifier-2*$>$ $P = \underline{\text{FAS}}_{\mathcal{I}_2}(P)$.

A possible representation for the modifiers extremely, definitely and very is therefore given by:

$$\text{very } P = \underline{\text{FAS}}_{\mathcal{I}_1}(P) \tag{7}$$
$$\text{definitely } P = \underline{\text{FAS}}_{\mathcal{I}_2}(P) \tag{8}$$
$$\text{extremely } P = \underline{\text{FAS}}_{\mathcal{I}_2}(\underline{\text{FAS}}_{\mathcal{I}_2}(P)) \tag{9}$$

(P.2)–**(P.3)** in Proposition 1, together with Corollary 1 guarantee formula (1). Comparing with (5), (7) is read as: "x is very P" to the degree to which the set of objects resembling x is included in P. The expression (8) is similar, but the definition of inclusion is more severe because of the choice of $\mathcal{I}_2 \leqslant \mathcal{I}_1$. (9) reads as "$x$ is extremely P" to the degree to which the set of objects resembling x is included in definitely P.
Proceeding analogously, two weakening modifiers can be modelled. Namely, let $\mathcal{T}$, $\mathcal{T}_1$ and $\mathcal{T}_2$ be t–norms and let $\mathcal{T}_1 \leqslant \mathcal{T}_2$. For *WeakModifier-2* being more weakening then *WeakModifier-1* we propose the following two schemes :

R1.w: $<$ *WeakModifier-1*$>$ $P = \overline{\text{FAS}}^{\mathcal{T}}(P)$
$<$ *WeakModifier-2*$>$ $P = \overline{\text{FAS}}^{\mathcal{T}}(\overline{\text{FAS}}^{\mathcal{T}}(P))$

R2.w: $<$ *WeakModifier-1*$>$ $P = \overline{\text{FAS}}^{\mathcal{T}_1}(P)$
$<$ *WeakModifier-2*$>$ $P = \overline{\text{FAS}}^{\mathcal{T}_2}(P)$.

Specifically, rather, more or less and roughly can be represented as follows:

$$\text{rather } P = \overline{\text{FAS}}^{\mathcal{T}_1}(P) \tag{10}$$
$$\text{more or less } P = \overline{\text{FAS}}^{\mathcal{T}_2}(P) \tag{11}$$
$$\text{roughly } P = \overline{\text{FAS}}^{\mathcal{T}_2}(\overline{\text{FAS}}^{\mathcal{T}_2}(P)). \tag{12}$$

Again, Proposition 1 **(P.2)**–**(P.3)** and Corollary 1 guarantee formula (2). In view of (6), (10) can be read as: "x is rather P" to the degree to which the set of objects resembling x overlaps with P. (11) is similar but the definition of overlap is more soft because of the choice of $\mathcal{T}_1 \leqslant \mathcal{T}_2$. Finally, (12) reads as "x is roughly P" to the degree to which the set of objects resembling x overlaps with more or less P.

Example 2. Let $\mathfrak{X}$ be the universe of temperatures and let the $(\mathbb{I}_{\mathfrak{X}}, d_{|.|})$–resemblance relation R on $\mathfrak{X}$ be defined by: for all $(x,y) \in \mathfrak{X}^2$,

$$R(x,y) = min\left(max\left(2 - \frac{1}{2}|x-y|, 0\right), 1\right).$$

For the fuzzy set $P : \mathfrak{X} \to [0,1]$ representing the term *warm*

$$P(x) = \begin{cases} 0 & x \leqslant 15 \\ 2\left(\frac{x-15}{6}\right)^2 & 15 < x \leqslant 18 \\ 1-2\left(\frac{x-21}{6}\right)^2 & 18 < x \leqslant 21 \\ 1 & x > 21 \end{cases}$$

the membership functions for $\overline{\text{FAS}}^{\mathcal{T}_M}(\overline{\text{FAS}}^{\mathcal{T}_M}(P))$ (roughly *warm*), $\overline{\text{FAS}}^{\mathcal{T}_M}(P)$ (more or less *warm*), $\overline{\text{FAS}}^{\mathcal{T}_W}(P)$ (rather *warm*), P (*warm*), $\underline{\text{FAS}}_{\mathcal{I}_L}(P)$ (very *warm*), $\underline{\text{FAS}}_{\mathcal{I}_{KD}}(P)$ (definitely *warm*) and $\underline{\text{FAS}}_{\mathcal{I}_{KD}}(\underline{\text{FAS}}_{\mathcal{I}_{KD}}(P))$ (extremely *warm*) are depicted in Figure 1 from the left to the right. □

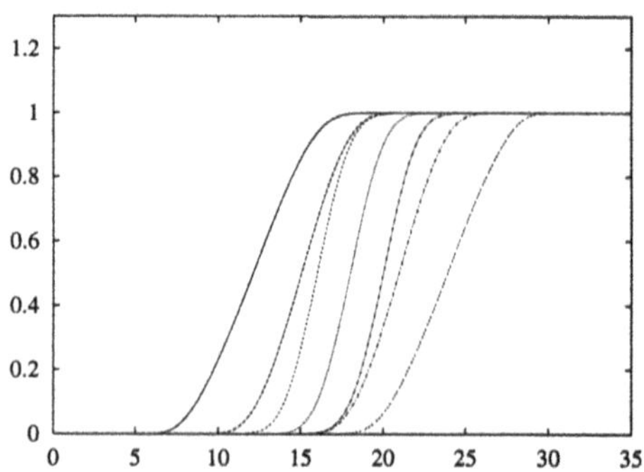

Fig. 1. Membership functions for the linguistic terms (from the left to the right) roughly *warm*, more or less *warm*, rather *warm*, *warm*, very *warm*, definitely *warm* and extremely *warm*.

Consider the following three statements:

"x is definitely more or less P" (13)
"x is rather very P" (14)
"x is P". (15)

In (13), a weakened emphasis is put on the fact represented by (15), yet stronger than in the statement "x is more or less P", so its expressive power is somewhere in between. Also, (14) is more expressive than (15), but less than "x is very P", so the expressivity of (14) is also intermediate, between these two expressions. In our framework (13) and (14) can be represented by $\underline{\text{FAS}}_{\mathcal{I}_2}(\overline{\text{FAS}}^{\mathcal{T}_2}(P))(x)$ and $\overline{\text{FAS}}^{\mathcal{T}_1}(\underline{\text{FAS}}_{\mathcal{I}_1}(P))(x)$, where $\mathcal{I}_1$ (resp. $\mathcal{I}_2$) is the residuum of a continuous t–norm $\mathcal{T}_1$ (resp. $\mathcal{T}_2$). By **(P.4)** in Proposition 1,

$$\overline{\text{FAS}}^{\mathcal{T}_1}(\underline{\text{FAS}}_{\mathcal{I}_1}(P)) \subseteq P \subseteq \underline{\text{FAS}}_{\mathcal{I}_2}(\overline{\text{FAS}}^{\mathcal{T}_2}(P)).$$

Clearly, this reflects our intuition.

The linguistic interpretations of other properties of fuzzy rough approximators are examined in [3].

6 Linguistic hedges in fuzzy modal logic

It is worth noting that intensifying modifiers are intuitively closely related to the notion of *certainty*, whereas weakening modifiers might be viewed in terms of *possibility*. Indeed, the expression "*x is certainly P*" is often interpreted as "y is P for all y's *accessible* from x". In our framework, "*x is very P*" means that all y's *resembling* x are P – threrefore, the notion of resemblance is viewed here in terms of accessibiliy. Furthermore, it is well–known that rough structures may be viewed as Kripke–style semantics for modal logics. The same holds in the fuzzy case: a fuzzy approximation space $\text{FAS} = (\mathfrak{X}, R)$ is in fact a fuzzy Kripke structure (R is the accessibility relation) and formulae are evaluated to fuzzy sets $A \in \mathcal{F}(\mathfrak{X})$. If a formula φ is evaluated to $A \in \mathcal{F}(\mathfrak{X})$ then $\Box\varphi$ (*necessary* φ) and $\Diamond\varphi$ ("*possibly* φ") are interpreted as $\underline{\text{FAS}}_{\mathcal{I}}(A)$ and $\overline{\text{FAS}}^{\mathcal{T}}(A)$, respectively. Therefore, linguistic terms with modifiers can be represented in the language of fuzzy modal logic.

Let us briefly present a propositional fuzzy modal logic (PFML) which language $\mathfrak{L}$ is determined by a denumerable set PV of propositional variables, logical connectives $\wedge$ and $\rightarrow$, and two *necessity* (resp. *possibility*) modal operators $\Box_1$ and $\Box_2$ (resp. $\Diamond_1$, $\Diamond_2$). The basis for the semantics of PFML are functions underlying the interpretations of the logical connectives and modal operators. In particular, $\wedge$ and $\rightarrow$ are often interpreted by a continuous t–norm $\mathcal{T}$ and its residuum $\mathcal{I}$, respectively. Furthermore, two continuous t–norms $\mathcal{T}_1$, $\mathcal{T}_2$ such that $\mathcal{T}_1 \leqslant \mathcal{T}_2$, and their residua $\mathcal{I}_1$ and $\mathcal{I}_2$ ($\mathcal{I}_2 \leqslant \mathcal{I}_1$) will be used for interpreting modal operators. A *fuzzy Kripke structure* is a pair $\mathcal{K} = (\mathfrak{X}, R)$, where $\mathfrak{X} \neq \emptyset$ is a set of objects and $R \in \mathcal{F}(\mathfrak{X} \times \mathfrak{X})$ is the *accessibility* relation. Given $\mathcal{K} = (\mathfrak{X}, R)$, an *interpretation* of $\mathfrak{L}$ based on $\mathcal{K}$ is a pair $\mathfrak{I} = (\mathcal{K}, v)$, where $v : PV \times \mathfrak{X} \rightarrow [0,1]$ is a valuation function. The function v is extended for all formulae as follows: **(i)** $v(\varphi \wedge \phi, x) = \mathcal{T}(v(\varphi, x), v(\phi, x))$ **(ii)** $v(\varphi \rightarrow \phi, x) = \mathcal{I}(v(\varphi, x), v(\phi, x))$ **(iii)** $v(\Box_k\varphi, x) = \inf_{y \in \mathfrak{X}} \mathcal{I}_k(R(x,y), v(\varphi, y))$, **(iv)** $v(\Diamond_k\varphi, x) = \sup_{y \in \mathfrak{X}} \mathcal{T}_k(R(x,y), v(\varphi, y))$ for $k = 1, 2$.
Comparing **(iii)**–**(iv)** with Definition 2 one can easily note the straightforward correspondence between fuzzy rough approximators and the interpretations of modal operators.

While modelling linguistic hedges we always work with tolerance relations. Hence, the proper logical system adequate for our purpose is some S4–like fuzzy modal logic. Here we have the following characteristic axioms: $\Box_k\varphi \rightarrow \varphi$, $\varphi \rightarrow \Diamond_k\varphi$, $\Diamond_k\Box_k\varphi \rightarrow \varphi$, $\varphi \rightarrow \Box_k\Diamond_k\varphi$, $k = 1, 2$, and $\Diamond_1\varphi \rightarrow \Diamond_2\varphi$, $\Box_2\varphi \rightarrow \Box_1\varphi$.

In view of the discussion in Section 5.2, we obtain the representation of some linguistic expressions in a PFML. Namely, every property P of objects is represented by a proposition p. By (7)–(9) and (10)–(12), linguistic terms of the form "very P", "definitely P" and "extremely P" are represented by formulae $\Box_1 p$, $\Box_2 p$ and $\Box_2\Box_2 p$, respectively, while expressions "rather P", "more or less P" and "roughly P" are represented by $\Diamond_1 p$, $\Diamond_2 p$ and $\Diamond_2\Diamond_2 p$, respectively. Finally, a compound term of the form "definitely more or less P" (resp. "rather very P") is represented by $\Box_2\Diamond_2 p$ (resp. $\Diamond_1\Box_1 p$).

7 Conclusions

We have proposed the fuzzy rough set theoretical representation of linguistic modifiers. By employing the concept of resemblance we can interprete linguisticterms like "x *is* very P" or "x *is* more or less P" relatively to similarity-based links between objects. It was also shown that these expressions can be naturally modelled in S4-like fuzzy modal logics. Several representational schemes have been proposed, which allow for flexibility in representation.

Acknowledgments

M. De Cock is supported by the Fund for Scientific Research Flanders (FWO). A. Radzikowska is partially supported by the KBN Grant No 8T11C01617.

References

1. De Cock M., Kerre E. E. (2000) On (un)suitable fuzzy relations to model approximate equality.Submitted.
2. De Cock M., Kerre E. E. (2000) A New Class of Fuzzy Modifiers. Proceedings of *ISMVL2000*, IEEE Computer Society, 121-126.
3. De Cock M., Radzikowska A. M., Kerre E. E. (2000) Modelling Linguistic Modifiers using Fuzzy–Rough Structures. Proceedings of *IPMU2000*, 1735-1742.
4. Dubois D., Prade H. (1990) Rough Fuzzy Sets and Fuzzy Rough Sets. *Int. J. of General Systems* **17**(2-3), 191-209.
5. Dubois D., Prade H. (1992) Putting fuzzy sets and rough sets together. *Intelligent Decision Support*, Roman Słowiński (ed.), Kluwer Academic, 203-232.
6. Kerre E. E., De Cock M. (1999) Linguistic Modifiers: an overview. *Fuzzy Logic and Soft Computing*, Guoqing Chen, Mingsheng Ying, Kai-Yaun Cai (eds), Kluwer Academic Publishers, 69-85.
7. Lakoff G. (1973) *Hedges : a Study in Meaning Criteria and the Logic of Fuzzy Concepts.* Journal of Philosophical Logic **2**, 458-508.
8. Novák V., Perfilieva I. (1999) *Evaluating Linguistic Expressions and Functional Fuzzy Theories in Fuzzy Logic.* Computing with Words in Information/Intelligent Systems 1: Foundations, L. A. Zadeh, J. Kacprzyk (eds.), Studies in Fuzziness and Soft Computing 33, Springer-Verlag, Heidelberg.
9. Pawlak Z. (1982) Rough sets. *Int. J. of Computer and Information Science* **11**(5), 341-356.
10. Radzikowska A. M., Kerre E. E. A Comparative Study of Fuzzy Rough Sets. To appear in*Fuzzy Sets and Systems.*
11. Radzikowska A. M., Kerre E. E. A General Calculus of Fuzzy Rough Sets. Submitted.
12. Thiele H. (1997) Fuzzy Rough Sets versus Rough Fuzzy Sets – an Interpretation and a Comparative Study using Concepts of Modal Logic. Proceedings of EUFIT-97, vol. I, 159-167
13. Thiele H. (1998) Interpreting linguistic hedges by concepts of functional analysis and mathematical logic. Proceedings of EUFIT-98, vol. I, 114-119
14. Zadeh L.A. (1972) A Fuzzy-Set-Theoretic Interpretation of Linguistic Hedges. Journal of Cybernetics **2,3**, 4-34

Dealing with Imprecise Inputs in a Fuzzy Rule-Based System using an Implication-based Rule Model*

Lluís Godo[1] and Sandra Sandri[2]

[1] Institut d'Investigació en Intel.ligència Artificial - CSIC,
Campus UAB s/n, 08193 Bellaterra, Spain
godo@iiia.csic.es

[2] LAC - Instituto Nacional de Pesquisas Espaciais
12201-970 S.J. Campos, Brazil
sandri@lac.inpe.br

Abstract. We discuss the means to efficiently propagate imprecise (but crisp) inputs in fuzzy control-like rule based systems in which fuzzy rules are chained in several levels. We consider a genuine implication-based model, in contrast to most of classical fuzzy control systems, using Rescher-Gaines implication to model the gradual relation between premises and conclusion of rules. The result of each inference is a crisp interval and we propose an efficient and sound method that provides with the tightest output intervals at one reasoning level, propagate them as input in the next level, and only pick a precise value at the very last level.

Keywords: fuzzy rules, inference, implication-based rule model.

1 Introduction

The most well-known fuzzy rule-based systems are certainly the so-called fuzzy-controllers [2]. Apart from being used in control applications, these systems usually share the characteristic of using only one level of reasoning, i.e., the set of rules infer values for a set of variables in the conclusions which are not propagated any further. One category of such controllers, sometimes called "classical", (e.g. Mamdani and Larsen controllers) have fuzzy sets both in the premise and the conclusion part of the rules. In this category of fuzzy controllers a precise single value is obtained for each output variable, after a process called defuzzification,.

In some more detail, the inference process in this fuzzy-control framework (but not only) is performed as follows. Let us suppose we have a set of m linguistic variables $\mathbf{x}_j$, each one associated to a set of fuzzy sets (terms) $\mathcal{A}_j = \{A_j^1, \ldots, A_j^r\}$, defined on domains Ω_j, and a linguistic variable[1] $\mathbf{y}$,

* This is a revised and expanded version of the paper '"Dealing with imprecise inputs in Fuzzy rule-based systems" appearing in the Proc. of IPMU'2000, Madrid (Spain), pp. 1055-1062.

[1] A single output variable is enough for the presentation of the framework, which however can be easily extended to systems with more than one output variable.

associated to a set of terms $\mathcal{B} = \{B^1, \ldots, B^s\}$, defined on a domain Ω'. Let us further suppose we have a set of n fuzzy rules R_i, of the kind

$$R_i : \text{If } \mathbf{x}_1 = A_{1,i} \text{ and } \ldots \text{ and } \mathbf{x}_m = A_{m,i} \text{ then } \mathbf{y} = B_i,$$

where each $A_{j,i}$ is taken out of $\mathcal{A}_j$ and each B_i is taken out of $\mathcal{B}$. Then the process follows the five steps below:

▷ **Step 1**: The *realization* of each input variable $\mathbf{x}_j$ is the *precise* value $x_j^* \in \Omega_j$ that it assumes at a given moment;

▷ **Step 2**: The *compatibility* of x_j^* with the j-th premise of the i-th rule is defined as:

$$\alpha_{j,i} = \mu_{A_{j,i}}(x_j^*),\ 1 \le j \le m,\ 1 \le i \le n;$$

▷ **Step 3**: The *global compatibility* of rule R_i with the realization of the input variables is determined using a t-norm[2] $\top$:

$$\alpha_i = \top(\alpha_{1,i},\ \ldots, \alpha_{m,i}),\ 1 \le i \le n;$$

▷ **Step 4**: The global compatibility value α_i obtained is put in relation with the fuzzy set B_i in rule R_i conclusion, originating B_i', through the implication operator I:

$$\mu_{B_i'}(y) = I(\alpha_i, \mu_{B_i}(y)),\ \ \forall y \in \Omega',\ 1 \le i \le n;$$

▷ **Step 5**: An operator ∇ performs the *aggregation* of the various contributions B_i', issued by the fired rules, into a single fuzzy set B':

$$\mu_{B'}(y) = \nabla(\mu_{B_1'}(y), \ldots, \mu_{B_n'}(y)), \forall y \in \Omega' .$$

The choice of operators I and ∇ depends on the model of fuzzy rule adopted, namely, either *conjunction-based* model or *implication-based* model. In conjunction-based models, generally used in the classical fuzzy controllers, the operator I is taken as a t-norm and then the ∇ operator is usually a t-conorm. For instance, Mamdani controllers use ∇ = max and I = min, whereas Larsen controllers use ∇ = max and $I = \times$ (the usual product operator). In an implication-based model of fuzzy rule, the operator I is a many-valued implication function and ∇ is a t-norm, usually ∇ = min. For instance, in the framework proposed in [3], ∇ = min and I is the "sharp" (or Rescher-Gaines) implication operator, given as

$$I(a, b) = \begin{cases} 1, & \text{if } a \le b \\ 0, & \text{otherwise} \end{cases}$$

[2] A t-norm operator $\top$ (respec. a t-conorm operator $\perp$) is a mapping from $[0,1]$ to $[0,1]$, which is commutative, associative, monotonic and with 1 (respec. 0) as neutral element.

After step 5, in either model, if needed, to obtain a single precise value for the output, the center of area of the resulting fuzzy set is generally used, or any other defuzzification method.

Fuzzy systems that need chaining between levels are usually implemented in more complex environments, possibily sometimes unnecessarily elaborated for some applications. Such is the case with systems using knowledge endowed with a simple structure but employing a large set of variables. In this case, it may be reasonable to create systems in a classical fuzzy-controller style, but allowing several levels of chaining (see e.g. [8]). The idea is to partition the initial set of input variables into smaller sets, and create rules for each of these subsets, that would infer values for intermediary variables. Finally, another set of rules would be created having the intermediary variables in the premise and the desired output variables in the conclusions. This partitioning, when feasible, induces a considerable decrease in the number of rules to be created. For instance, let us suppose we want to build a system with 9 input variables with n terms each. The partitioning of the variables in groups of 3 would demand the creation of 4 rules bases with n^3 rules each, which together totalize much less than the n^9 rules that would be necessary if the variables would not be partitioned.

To implement such a fuzzy system, we could straightforwardly defuzzify variable values at each level before propagating them further. This would however correspond to taking decisions too early in the process, possibly leading too far from optimal results. An alternative to that is to somehow propagate non-precise intermediary values to lower levels of reasoning. This can be done using an approach proposed in [3] for similarity-based reasoning whose core inference model turns out to be closely related to the use of *fuzzy gradual rules* [4,1] with Rescher-Gaines implication function. In that framework, given a precise (or imprecise but not fuzzy) input, the set of rules infer a crisp interval of values from which, if needed, the mid point may be chosen as a final precise output, provided that the interval is not empty. What we propose is to propagate the crisp interval obtained at one level as input to the next level, and pick a precise value only when the very last reasoning level has been reached. However there is a main problem in doing so with imprecise (even if crisp) inputs by just following the above 5-steps scheme: there is an important lack of precision of the whole inference process. Therefore, we basically have to deal with 2 problems: i) to be sure that the system is consistent for no matter which input values, i.e. the system must always provide a valid result (in our case, an non-empty interval) for each output variable at each reasoning level; and ii) to find a reasonably precise and efficient, and yet sound, manner of propagating imprecise results from one level to the other.

The first problem is related to the consistency of the system of fuzzy rules with potential inputs (also called *coherence*). The issue of consistency or coherence in fuzzy rule sets has been addressed in a number of papers in the literature, e.g. [10,6,5,9]. In particular, the problem of testing the coherence of systems of fuzzy gradual rules has been addressed by Dubois, Prade and Ughetto in [5]. The second problem is related to the propagation of imprecise/vague values in fuzzy rule-based systems. This problem has been addressed, for instance in [7], for the particular case of Mamdani fuzzy controllers, with rules having a single input variable in the premise.

In the present paper we address the second problem, in the context of an implication-based inference model when applied to an imprecise input to an already consistent set of fuzzy rules. Actually, in Section 2 we propose a general alternative inference model by splitting the input into a set of disjoint subsets, inferring separately from them, and finally aggregating the results. In Section 3 we describe and study in detail the method when the fuzzy model related to [3] is considered, which means imprecise but non fuzzy inputs and use of Rescher-Gaines implication, and the fuzzy rule base obeys the requirements presented in [5].

2 Dealing with non precise inputs: a new proposal

Let the rules in knowledge base K be given as

$$R_i : \text{If } \mathbf{x}_1 = A_{1,i} \text{ and } \ldots \text{ and } \mathbf{x}_m = A_{m,i} \text{ then } \mathbf{y} = B_i$$

with $1 \leq i \leq n$. We assume each rule[3] to be a *gradual* fuzzy if-then rule modelled by an implicational relation, which we represent[4] here as

$$R_i(\overline{x}, y) = I(\mu_{A_i}(\overline{x}), \mu_{B_i}(y)),$$

where $\overline{x} = (x_1, \ldots, x_n)$, with $x_j \in \Omega_j$, I is a residuated implication[5] and $\mu_{A_i}(\overline{x}) = \min(\mu_{A_{1,i}}(x_1), \ldots, \mu_{A_{m,i}}(x_m))$. Let X^* be a (possibly fuzzy) imprecise input for $\overline{x}$. Now, given X^*, it is known that a most specific output which can be inferred from X^* and K is obtained by applying the so-called *combination-projection* principle (see e.g. [1]) to X^* and the joint relation R_K induced by the whole rule set K as

$$(X^* \circ R_K)(y) = \sup_{\overline{x}} \min(\mu_{X^*}(\overline{x}), R_K(\overline{x}, y)),$$

which is nothing but the sup – min composition of the fuzzy relations induced by X^* and K. Here R_K is the intersection of the fuzzy relations induced by each rule, i.e.

$$R_K(\overline{x}, y) = \min_{i=1,n} R_i(\overline{x}, y).$$

[3] For the sake of an easier handling, we assume all the rules have the same variables in their premises. This is not restrictive at all since if the premise of a rule does not have a variable, say x, we can safely include the extra (and always satisfiable) condition $x = \Omega_x$ in that premise.

[4] Notice that we shall use the same symbols to denote ***linguistic variables*** and ***domain variables***, hoping that it will be clear from the context.

[5] That is, the residuum of a left-continuous t-norm $\top$ defined as $I(x, y) = \max\{z \in [0, 1] \mid \top(x, z) \leq y\}$.

Let us define $F_{opt}(X^*, K)$ as the output obtained in this way, that is,

$$F_{opt}(X^*, K) = X^* \circ R_K .$$

This inferential methodology provides us with the most specific outputs, but the fundamental problem, from an operational point of view, is the lack of modularity as soon as the input is not a precise value any longer, i.e. in general the output cannot be obtained as an aggregation of the corresponding outputs from each rule. Namely, the typical modular methodology, denoted by $F_{mod}(X^*, K)$, combines the input X^* with each rule and then aggregates them with intersection, yielding

$$\begin{aligned} F_{mod}(X^*, K)(y) &= \cap_{i=1,n} (X^* \circ R_i)(y) \\ &= \min_{i=1,n} \{\sup_{\overline{x}} \{\min(\mu_{X^*}(\overline{x}), R_i(\overline{x}, y))\}\} . \end{aligned}$$

Although both methodologies F_{opt} and F_{mod} are sound ways of performing inference in fuzzy rule bases, it can be checked that in general F_{mod} produces more imprecise outputs than F_{opt}. Namely, one can easily show that the (point-wise) inequality

$$F_{opt}(X^*, K) \leq F_{mod}(X^*, K) .$$

always holds, but not the converse one. In principle, one can only guarantee the equality $F_{mod}(X^*, K) = F_{opt}(X^*, K)$ whenever either K consists of just one rule R (in which case it is equal to $X^* \circ R$) or when X^* is in fact a precise observation, say $X^* = \{x_0\}$ (in which case it is equal to $\cap_i R_i(x_0, y)$). Moreover, the problems of lack of precision with F_{mod} are self-evident when the inputs are quite imprecise, even in the case of non-fuzzy rules; for instance, if $K = \{\text{If } \mathbf{x} = A_1 \text{ then } \mathbf{y} = B, \text{If } \mathbf{x} = A_2 \text{ then } \mathbf{y} = B\}$, then it is clear that $F_{opt}(A_1 \cup A_2, K) = B$ while $F_{mod}(A_1 \cup A_2, K) = \Omega_y$.

What we propose is an inference method which can be seen as a kind of trade-off between the accuracy of F_{opt} and the easiness of F_{mod}. Actually we shall see that we can improve the outputs for F_{mod} by suitably partitioning the input X^*.

Definition 1. Let $\{X_1^*, \ldots, X_r^*\}$ be a set of fuzzy sets such that $\cup_{k=1,r} X_k^* = X^*$. We define the inference method F_{part} as follows:

$$F_{part}(\{X_1^*, \ldots, X_r^*\}, K) = \cup_{k=1,r} [\cap_{i=1,n} (X_k^* \circ R_i)] .$$

for each rule base $K = \{R_i\}_{i=1,n}$, where $\cup$ and $\cap$ denote max-disjunction and min-disjunction of fuzzy sets respectively.

Then one can prove then the following inequalities:

$$\begin{aligned} F_{opt}(X^*, K) &= (\cup_k X_k^*) \circ (\cap_i R_i) = \cup_k [X_k^* \circ (\cap_i R_i)] \\ &\leq \cup_k [\cap_i (X_k^* \circ R_i)] = F_{part}(\{X_1^*, \ldots, X_r^*\}, K) \\ F_{mod}(X^*, K) &= \cap_i [(\cup_k X_k^*) \circ R_i] = \cap_i [\cup_k (X_k^* \circ R_i)] \\ &\geq \cup_k [\cap_i (X_k^* \circ R_i)] = F_{part}(\{X_1^*, \ldots, X_r^*\}, K) \end{aligned}$$

Thus, no matter how we decompose the input X^* into a set $\{X_1^*, \ldots, X_r^*\}$ we have

$$F_{opt}(X^*, K) \le F_{part}(\{X_1^*, \ldots, X_r^*\}, K) \le F_{mod}(X^*, K) .$$

In particular, these inequalities hold when the X_k^* are disjoint, i.e., when they form a partition of X^* stricto sensus. Actually, one can show that the finer is the partition of X^*, the better (more specific) will be the output $F_{part}(X^*, K)$, and conversely. Indeed, it is easy to show that:

- if we consider the roughest partition of X^*, i.e. the partition $\{X^*\}$ consisting of only one component, then $F_{part}(\{X^*\}, K) = F_{mod}(X^*, K)$;
- if we consider the finest partition $X^* = \cup_{\overline{x}_0 \in \Omega_x} \overline{x}_0^*$, where $\mu_{\overline{x}_0^*}(\overline{x}) = \mu_{X^*}(\overline{x}_0)$ if $\overline{x} = \overline{x}_0$, $\mu_{\overline{x}_0^*}(\overline{x}) = 0$ otherwise, i.e. when the support of each subset contains only one point, then F_{part} reaches the optimum output, that is, $F_{part}(\{\overline{x}_0^* \mid \overline{x}_0 \in \Omega_x\}, K) = F_{opt}(X^*, K)$.

Therefore, we propose to use F_{part} as an inference method in between the method F_{opt}, which produces optimal results (in the sense of most precise as possible) but with a difficult operational procedure, and the method F_{mod}, which is a modular and easy-to-implement procedure but producing more imprecise results. Moreover, F_{part} is a flexible methodology in the sense that, the finer is the input partition, a more precise output (closer to F_{opt}) will be got.

In the rest of the paper we show a suitable way to partition imprecise (but non fuzzy) inputs that allows an efficient and accurate use of F_{part} inference procedure for a particular choice of the implication function in the rule model. Namely, we choose the previously mentioned Rescher-Gaines implication. Actually this implication is the (point-wise) infimum of all residuated implications, although itself it is not the residuum of any left-continuous t-norm. The main advantage of using this implication, from an operational of view, is that the result of the inference from a crisp imprecise input X^* and a fuzzy rule $R =$ "If $\mathbf{x} = A$ then $\mathbf{y} = B$" is a again a crisp set, indeed, $X^* \circ R$ is the α-level cut of B, where $\alpha = \inf_{x \in X^*} \mu_A(x)$. Moreover, if the terms associated to the output variable are convex normalized fuzzy sets, then the resulting crisp set will also be convex (an interval). Therefore intervals can be safely propagated from one inference level to another.

3 A case study: F_{part} with imprecise input intervals and Rescher-Gaines implication

In this section we first present a basic framework, made simple to facilitate comprehension, which is used throughout the rest of the section. Then, in the second subsection, we show how the proposed method works with a single input variable and prove that we get optimal results in such a case. Finally, in the last subsection we show how the procedure can be extended to deal with multiple input variables.

3.1 Our working framework

Before presenting our working framework, we introduce some of the definitions we shall use in the remaining of this document.

- The *support* and the *core* of a fuzzy set D in Ω are respectively defined as $supp(D) = \{\omega \mid \mu_D(\omega) > 0\}$ and $core(D) = \{\omega \mid \mu_D(\omega) = 1\}$. The α-level cut of the fuzzy set D, is defined as $[D]_\alpha = \{\omega \mid \mu_D(\omega) \geq \alpha\}$.
- A fuzzy set D on the real numbers scale is said to be a *fuzzy number* if it is normalized (i.e., $\exists \omega \in \Omega, \mu_D(\omega) = 1$), unimodal, upper semi-continuous, and has a bounded support [9].
- We say that a set of terms $\{D_1, \ldots, D_n\}$ is in *consecutive order* when $supp(D_i) \cap supp(D_{i-1}) \neq \emptyset$, $supp(D_i) \cap supp(D_{i+1}) \neq \emptyset$, and $supp(D_i) \cap supp(D_j) = \emptyset, \forall j \notin \{i-1, i+1\}$. We define $mid(D_i, D_{i+1}) = \{w \mid \mu_{D_i}(w) = \mu_{D_{i+1}}(w)\}$ to be the intersection point of terms D_i and D_{i+1}.
- We denote the extremities of a (closed) interval I by $l(I)$ and $r(I)$ in such a way that $I = [l(I), r(I)]$.

In the present framework, we only consider the situations in which a system obeys the following restrictions:

- The terms associated with a linguistic variable are distinct fuzzy numbers in consecutive order.
- Let D and D' be consecutive terms associated with a linguistic *input variable* defined on Ω. Then, if $\omega \in supp(D) \cap supp(D')$, then $\mu_D(\omega) + \mu_{D'}(\omega) = 1$. This amounts to say that the terms of an input variable should form a Ruspini's fuzzy partition of the domain of the variable. For the *output* variable, it is enough (for ensuring coherence requirements) to require $\mu_D(\omega) + \mu_{D'}(\omega) \geq 1$.
- For any array x^*, representing the actual values for the input variables at a moment of time t, there exists at most 2 consecutive terms B and B' associated with the output variable y that are addressed by the rules fired with x^*.

Examples of two rule bases that obey the last restriction are given in Table 1. An example of terms obeying the first 3 restrictions is depicted in Figure 1. It is simple to verify that systems obeying the above restrictions are always consistent. Indeed, only two consecutive output terms B and B' are valid at each moment t. Therefore, the only problem we could possibly have would occur if the highest compatibility degrees assigned to these terms would both be higher than .5, which is clearly impossible, due to the restrictions on the terms and the use of t-norms in the premise.

These restrictions are more rigid than the ones presented in [5], but they make the basic ideas supporting our framework easier to present.

Let us suppose that at a given moment of time, the realization of an input variable is given as a crisp set X^*. We propose to partition this set

Table 1.

(a) Rule Base K_1

x_1/x_2	NM	NS	Z	PS	PM
NM	NM	-	NS	-	Z
NS	-	NS	-	Z	-
Z	NS	-	Z	-	PS
PS	-	Z	-	PS	-
PM	Z	-	PS	-	PM

(b) Rule Base K_2

x_1/x_2	NM	NS	Z	PS	PM
NM	NM	NS	NS	Z	Z
NS	NS	NS	Z	Z	Z
Z	NS	Z	Z	Z	PS
PS	Z	Z	Z	PS	PS
PM	Z	Z	PS	PS	PM

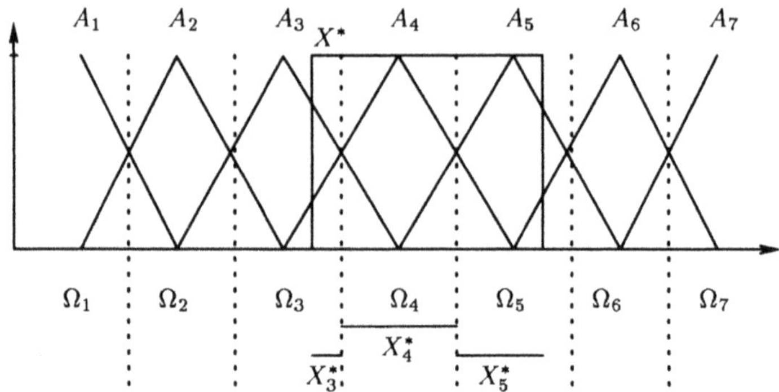

Fig. 1. Partitioning an imprecise input on a set of consecutive terms.

in a suitable way, say $X^* = X_1^* \cup \cdots \cup X_r^*$, such that, given a rule base K obeying the above mentioned requirements, it will allow us to: (i) get accurate outputs $F_{part}(\{X_1^*, \ldots, X_r^*\}, K)$ very close (if not equal) to $F_{opt}(X^*, K)$; (ii) propagate the imprecise input in a sound and efficient procedure. In the next section we detail the simple case of a single input variable, while the case of multiple input variables is dealt with in the final subsection.

3.2 Partitioning and treating imprecise inputs for a single input variable

First of all let us instantiate our working framework to the case of having a single input variable $\mathbf{x}$. The knowledge base $K = \{R_i \mid i = 1, n\}$ consists of a set of rules of the kind

$$R_i : \text{If } \mathbf{x} = A_i \text{ then } \mathbf{y} = B_i$$

where

(1) the A_i terms belong to a set of terms $\{D_1, \ldots, D_m\}$ which are in consecutive order and fulfill $\Sigma_{i=1,m}\mu_{D_i}(x) = 1$ for all $x \in \Omega_x$, thus the D_j's

form a fuzzy partition of the input domain Ω_x in the Ruspini's sense, and

(2) the B_i terms belong to a set of terms $\{E_1, \ldots, E_p\}$ which are in consecutive order and fulfill $\Sigma_{i=1,p}\mu_{E_i}(y) \geq 1$ for all $y \in \Omega_y$.

Then we partition the universe Ω_x into n adjacent intervals $\Omega_x^k = [mid(D_{k-1}, D_k), mid(D_k, D_{k+1})]$, $1 \leq k \leq n$, where by convention we take the extreme points of Ω_x for $mid(D_0, D_1)$ and $mid(D_n, D_{n+1})$ respectively.

According to this domain partition, an interval[6] X^*, corresponding to the realization of an input variable $\mathbf{x}$ is then partitioned into a set of n subsets X_k^*, given as $X_k^* = X^* \cap \Omega_x^k$ for $k = 1, n$. In Figure 1 we see the partitioning of an input interval into 7 subsets, of which only 3 are non-empty.

Next we show that using this kind of partitioning of the input interval in the inference model F_{part} allows us: (i) to get optimal outputs and (ii) to get these outputs by means of an efficient procedure.

Theorem 1. *Under the above hypothesis, it holds that* $F_{opt}(X^*, K) = F_{part}(\{X_1^*, \ldots X_n^*\}, K)$.

The detailed proof of this theorem can be found in the Appendix.

So far we have studied the accuracy of $F_{part}(\{X_1^*, \ldots X_n^*\}, K)$. Let us show now that we can compute $F_{part}(\{X_1^*, \ldots X_n^*\}, K)$ in a very efficient manner.

Notice that for each subset X_k^*, there are at most 3 rules that are relevant, R_{k-1}, R_k and R_{k+1}. Indeed, the results of all rules are aggregated using the intersection, and thus rules other than R_k, R_{k-1} and R_{k+1} can be disregarded since any value of X_k^* used as input in these rules will produce the totally imprecise result Ω_y as output.

Let us now focus in an interval X_k^* such that $X_k^* = \Omega_k$ (the case of X_4^* in Figure 1). In such a case X_k^* combined with the rules R_{k-1} and R_{k+1} will produce the whole domain Ω_y, and thus they will be disregarded as well. On the other hand, since $\mu_{A_k}(r(X_k^*)) = \mu_{A_k}(l(X_k^*)) = 1/2$, the result of the application of rule R_k with X_k^* will produce

$$Y_k^* = X_k^* \circ R_k = [B_k]_{1/2}$$

as result, i.e. the 1/2-level cut of B_k.

On the other hand, if $X_k^* \neq \Omega_k$, the only relevant rules will be R_{k-1}, R_k and R_{k+1}, and the outputs we get from them are the level-cuts $[B_{k-1}]_{\alpha_{k-1}}$, $[B_k]_{\alpha_k}$ and $[B_{k+1}]_{\alpha_{k+1}}$ respectively, where

$$\alpha_j = \min(\mu_{A_j}(l(X_k^*)), \mu_{A_j}(r(X_k^*)))$$

with $j = k-1, k, k+1$. Now, as outlined above, we have

$$Y_k^* = [B_{k-1}]_{\alpha_{k-1}} \cap [B_k]_{\alpha_k} \cap [B_{k+1}]_{\alpha_{k+1}} \,.$$

[6] We address here only simple intervals in order to make notation lighter, aiming at making the approach easier to understand, but union of intervals can be treated as well.

Actually, thanks to our working assumptions, one can easily check that Y_k^* is an interval $[l(Y_k^*), r(Y_k^*)]$, where [7]

$$l(Y_k^*) = \max(l([B_{k+1}]_{\alpha_{k+1}}), l([B_k]_{\alpha_k}), l([B_{k-1}]_{\alpha_{k-1}})) ,$$
$$r(Y_k^*) = \min(r([B_{k+1}]_{\alpha_{k+1}}), r([B_k]_{\alpha_k}), r([B_{k-1}]_{\alpha_{k-1}})) .$$

Finally, one can check that, when taking into account all intervals X_k^*, the final output we get is $F_{part}(\{X_1^*, \ldots X_n^*\}, K) = Y^*$ where

$$Y^* = \cup_{k=1,n} Y_k^* = [l(Y_1^*), r(Y_n^*)] .$$

Therefore, to calculate the final interval Y^* we have to examine few rules for a small amount of times, and only deal with the extremities of the intervals involved in the computations.

3.3 Treating imprecise inputs for a multiple input variable

We now suppose we have two input variables $\mathbf{x}$ and $\mathbf{z}$ and one output variable $\mathbf{y}$, but the framework we present here can be easily extended to any number of input variables.

Let $A_1, \ldots, A_n$ and $C_1, \ldots, C_m$ be the term sets for x and z respectively, and let us denote the rules as follows:

$$R_{rs} : \text{If } \mathbf{x} = A_r \text{ and } \mathbf{z} = C_s \text{ then } \mathbf{y} = B_{rs}$$

Let us suppose the input for both $\mathbf{x}$ and $\mathbf{z}$ are given as crisp intervals X^* and Z^* and assume these intervals are partitioned as $X^* = \cup_{k=1,n} X_k^*$ and $Z^* = \cup_{l=1,m} Z_l^*$, as in Section 3.2.

It is important to note that for each input for $\mathbf{x}$ and $\mathbf{z}$, inside a given pair of intervals X_k^* and Z_l^*, there are at most 9 rules that can fire: $\{R_{i,j}\}_{i=k-1,k+1;j=l-1,l+1}$. Due to the restriction of the framework presented at the beginning of this section, these rules address at most 2 terms associated with the output variable (this condition is taken for the sake of simplicity of the presentation, it is not a crucial point). Below we describe an efficient procedure to compute the output given the imprecise inputs X^* and Z^*.

Procedure *level − result*

▷ **Step 1:** For every k and l such that X_k^* and Z_l^* are non-empty do

$$Y_{kl}^* = calculate - output(X_k^*, Z_l^*);$$

▷ **Step 2:** Calculate the aggregated output concerning all the intervals X_k^* and Z_l^* as $Y^* = [l(Y^*), r(Y^*)]$, where

[7] Notice that, for each k, at most two of these α_j's will be strictly positive, which simplifies the expressions.

$$l(Y^*) = \min\{l(Y^*_{kl}) \mid k = 1, n; l = 1, m\}$$
$$r(Y^*) = \max\{r(Y^*_{kl}) \mid k = 1, n; l = 1, m\}.$$

Remember that n is the number of X^*_k's and m is the number of Z^*_l's in the partitions of X^* and Z^* respectively.

Procedure *calculate – output*(X^*_k, Z^*_l)

▷ **Step 1:** Let $X^*_k = [x^{*1}, x^{*2}], Z^*_l = [z^{*1}, z^{*2}]$. Calculate the compatibility degrees of the rules that are fired when the input is inside X^*_k and Z^*_l, for each of these intervals limit points, as

$$\alpha^{kl}_{rs} = \min(\min(\mu_{A_r}(x^{*1}), \mu_{A_r}(x^{*2})), \min(\mu_{C_s}(z^{*1}), \mu_{C_s}(z^{*2}))) ,$$

with $r \in \{k-1, k, k+1\}$ and $s \in \{l-1, l, l+1\}$.

▷ **Step 2:** Let B_1 and B_2 be the terms addressed by the set of rules that are fired when the input is inside X^*_k and Z^*_l. Calculate the highest compatibility degree associated to B_1 and B_2 in relation to the limits of intervals X^*_k and Z^*_l, as

$$\beta^{kl}_t = \max_{r,s}\{\alpha^{kl}_{rs} \mid B_{rs} = B_t\},$$

with $t \in \{1, 2\}$. If a rule R^{rs} does not exist, then its corresponding term in the expression of β^{kl}_t is simply disregarded.

▷ **Step 3:** Calculate the output for the set of rules, in relation to the limits of intervals X^*_k and Z^*_l, as

$$Y^*_{kl} = [B_1]_{\beta^{kl}_1} \cap [B_2]_{\beta^{kl}_2}.$$

We leave here as an open question to formally check that the union of the outputs Y^*_{kl} computed in Step 1 of the procedure *level-result* is actually an interval and that it coincides with the aggregated output Y^* computed in Step 2 of the same procedure.

4 Conclusion

In this paper we have proposed a sound methodology to efficiently propagate imprecise information in hierarchical fuzzy control-like rule-based systems under an implication-based model of fuzzy rules. With this methodology, instead of defuzzifying at each level, we propagate imprecise results from one level to the other and defuzzify, if needed, only at the final stage. Indeed, we have presented a mechanism, denoted F_{part}, to efficiently propagate, in a sound and accurate way, imprecise inputs in a framework that obeys restrictions appearing in the literature that ensure rule-base coherence. The efficiency is obtained by partitioning the input variable domains in a convenient manner. Namely, let us suppose we have p input variables, each associated to n terms.

The standard procedure with a precise input would yield a complexity of the order of n^p, for a complete rule-base. Using Ruspini's fuzzy partitions, the complexity can be reduced, by first searching the rule-base to find the region where the input is found. This yields a complexity of the order of $p \times \log n$ to locate the region plus 2^p to calculate and aggregate the output. In our approach, the procedure that partitions the (imprecise) input has a complexity of the order of $p \times n$. The complexity of procedure *calculate-output* is of the order of $c = 3^p$. Considering the number of non-empty intervals for each variable to be the same, say q, then the overall complexity of procedure *level-result* is $d = c \times q^p$. When we take only the intervals at the extremities for each variable we reduce the last complexity to $d = c \times 2^p$.

Future work includes both theoretical and practical issues. As for theoretical issues, it is our aim to generalize, if possible, the results obtained for the case of a single input variable to multiple input variable, namely Theorem 1, and for other implication-based rule models as well. On the other hand, regarding the problem of coherence, the use of fuzzy similarity relations can help in transforming an a priori not coherent fuzzy rule base into a coherent one. The idea is to *extrapolate* (or expand) rules of the type "If $\mathbf{x} = A$ then $\mathbf{y} = B$" into rules of the type "If $\mathbf{x} = approx(A)$ then $\mathbf{y} = approx(B)$" where $approx(A)$ and $approx(B)$ are just the images of A and B by a fuzzy similarity relation. By playing with the similarity relation one can eventually enforce coherence of the rule base.

As for practical issues, we envisage the application of the proposed methodology in a system monitoring the quality of multimedia devices emission in a multiple-users environment, e.g. videoconferences. Since this kind of system involves many variables, it is reasonable to deal with the parameters of sound, and image, in relation to both the system actual emission capacity and the user requirements, using separate sets of rules. Then, their results can be used as input to a set of rules that will set the new emission values for the individual users.

Acknowledgements. Sandra Sandri acknowledges support from the Brazilian research funding agencies CNPq (proc. 52.0176/96-0) and FAPESP (proc. 99/03989-4). Lluís Godo acknowledges support by the Spanish CICYT project SMASH (TIC96-1138-C04-01).

References

1. Bouchon-Meunier B., Dubois D., Godo L., Prade H. Fuzzy Sets and Possibility Theory in Approximate and Plausible Reasoning. In Bezdek et al. (eds.). *Fuzzy Sets in Approximate Reasoning and Information Systems*, 15–190, Kluwer,1999.
2. Driankov, D., Hellendoorn, H., Reinfrank, M. *An Introduction to Fuzzy Control.* Springer-Verlag, 1996.
3. Dubois D., Esteva F., Garcia P., Godo L., Prade H. A Logical approach to interpolation based on similarity relations. *Int. J. of Approximate Reasoning* 17 (1), 1–36, 1997.

4. Dubois D., Prade H. What are fuzzy rules and how to use them. *Fuzzy Sets and Systems* 84, 169–185, 1996.
5. Dubois D., Prade H., Ughetto L. Coherence of Fuzzy Knowledge Bases. In *Proc. Fuzz-IEEE'96*, New Orleans (USA), 1858–1864, 1996.
6. Gottwald S., Petri U. An algorithmic approach towards consistency checking for systems of fuzzy control rules. In *Proc. of EUFIT'95*, Aachen (Germany) 28–31, 1995.
7. Galichet S., Foulloy L. Fuzzy Control with non-Precise Inputs. In Bouchon-Meunier et al. (eds.). *Fuzzy Logic and Soft Computing*, 146–153, World Scientific Press, 1995.
8. Kóczy L.T., Hirota K. Approximate inference in hierarchical structured rule bases. In *Proc. of IFSA'93*, Seoul (Korea), 1262–1265, 1993.
9. Pedrycz W., Gomide F. *An introduction to Fuzzy sets: Analysis and Design*. MIT Press,1998.
10. Yager R.R., Larsen H.L. On discovering potential inconsistencies in validating uncertain knowledge bases by reflecting on the input. *IEEE Trans. on Systems, Man and Cibernetics* 21, 790–801, 1991.

Appendix: proof of Theorem 1

Let the universe Ω_x be partitioned into n adjacent intervals Ω_x^k, $1 \leq k \leq n$, as shown in Figure 1. According to this partition, the interval input X^*, for the variable **x** is then partitioned into a set of n subsets X_k^*, given as $X_k^* = X^* \cap \Omega_x^k$ for $k = 1, n$.

Theorem 1. *Under the above hypothesis, it holds that* $F_{opt}(X^*, K) = F_{part}(\{X_1^*, \ldots X_n^*\}, K)$.

Proof. Observe the following equalities:

$$F_{opt}(X^*, K) = (\cup_k X_k^*) \circ R_K = \cup_k (X_k^* \circ R_K) = \cup_k F_{opt}(X_k^*, K)$$
$$F_{part}(\{X_1^*, \ldots, X_n^*\}, K) = \cup_k [\cap_i \, (X_k^* \circ R_i)] = \cup_k F_{part}(\{X_k^*\}, K) \, .$$

Therefore, to prove the theorem it will suffice to prove that, for each k, $F_{opt}(X_k^*, K) = F_{part}(\{X_k^*\}, K)$, in other words,

$$X_k^* \circ (\cap_{i=1,n} R_i) = \cap_{i=1,n} (X_k^* \circ R_i) \, .$$

Actually, we can restrict our attention only to rules R_{k-1}, R_k and R_{k+1} by showing

(i) $X_k^* \circ (\cap_{i=1,n} R_i) = X_k^* \circ (\cap_{i \in \{l,k,r\}} R_i)$, and
(ii) $\cap_{i=1,n} (X_k^* \circ R_i) = \cap_{i \in \{l,k,r\}} (X_k^* \circ R_i)$,

where, for the sake of a simpler notation, we have taken $k-1 = l$ (left) and $k+1 = r$ (right). Let us prove (i). By definition,

$$\begin{aligned}
[X_k^* \circ (\cap_{i=1,n} R_i)](y) &= \sup_{x \in \Omega_k} \min(X_k^*(x), A_1(x) \Rightarrow B_1(y), \ldots, A_n(x) \Rightarrow B_n(y)) \\
&= \sup_{x \in X_k^*} \min(A_1(x) \Rightarrow B_1(y), \ldots, A_n(x) \Rightarrow B_n(y)) \, .
\end{aligned}$$

But, for all $x \in X_k^*$, we have $A_i(x) = 0$ for all i except for $i \in \{l, k, r\}$. Therefore, for all $i \notin \{l, k, r\}$, we have $A_i(x) \Rightarrow B_i(y) = 1$. Result (i) then follows the fact that

$$\min_{i=1,n} (A_i(x) \Rightarrow B_i(y)) = \min_{i \in \{l,k,r\}} (A_i(x) \Rightarrow B_i(y)) .$$

easily holds. Let us now prove (ii). Since $(X_k^* \circ R_i) = [B_i]_{\alpha_i}$, where $\alpha_i = \inf_{x \in X_k^*} \mu_{A_i}(x)$, we have actually to prove that

$$\cap_{i=1,n}[B_i]_{\alpha_i} = \cap_{i \in \{l,k,r\}}[B_i]_{\alpha_i} .$$

The result easily follows when we note that for all $i \notin \{l, k, r\}$ we have $[B_i]_{\alpha_i} = [B_i]_0 = \Omega_x$. We have now reduced our problem to show that

$$X_k^* \circ (R_l \cap R_k \cap R_r) = [B_l]_{\alpha_l} \cap [B_k]_{\alpha_k} \cap [B_r]_{\alpha_r} .$$

Actually, the real problem is to show the inclusion from left to right $\supseteq$, since the other inclusion always holds. Thus, for each $y \in \cap_{i \in \{l,k,r\}}[B_i]_{\alpha_i}$, we have to prove that $\sup_{x \in X_k^*} \min_{i \in \{l,r,k\}} (A_i(x) \Rightarrow B_i(y)) = 1$, and for this it is enough to show there exists $x_0 \in X_k^*$ for which $A_i(x_0) \leq B_i(y)$, $\forall i \in \{l, k, r\}$. Consider the following cases:

1. $\alpha_r > 0, \alpha_l = 0$.
   First of all, notice that, if $\alpha_r > 0$ then $X_k^* \subseteq supp(A_r)$, and consequentely, by the construction of the A_i's, $X_k^* \cap supp(A_l) = \emptyset$. Therefore, if $\alpha_r > 0$ then $\alpha_l = 0$. Moreover, the condition $A_l(x_0) \leq B_l(y)$ is trivially satisfied. Let us now examine the following cases:
   (a) $A_k(x) \leq B_k(y)$ for all $x \in X_k^*$.
   By continuity, we may take x_0 such that $A_r(x_0) = \alpha_r$. Then, $A_k(x_0) \leq B_k(y)$ and $A_r(x_0) = \alpha_r \leq B_r(y)$.
   (b) $A_k(x) > B_k(y)$ for some, but not all, $x \in X_k^*$.
   By continuity, there exists x_0 such that $A_k(x_0) = B_k(y)$. But $A_r(x_0) = 1 - A_k(x_0) = 1 - B_k(y)$, and since by hypothesis $B_k(y) + B_r(y) \geq 1$, we also have $A_r(x_0) = 1 - B_k(y) \leq B_r(y)$.
   The remaining case, $A_k(x) > B_k(y)$ for all $x \in X_k^*$, cannot actually happen. Indeed, we are assuming y such that $B_k(y) \geq \alpha_k$ and, on the other hand, $\alpha_k = \inf_{x \in X_k^*} A_k(x)$, and hence thus $A_k(x) \geq \alpha_k$ for all $x \in X_k^*$. But, since the functions A_k are continuous, for some $x' \in X_k^*$, $A_k(x') = \alpha_k$. So at least for these x''s, it is not the case that $A_k(x') > B_k(y)$.
2. $\alpha_l = \alpha_r = 0$.
   In this case, X_k^* contains the core of A_k and we can split the remaining part of X_k^* into two parts $X_k^* - \{core(A_k)\} = X_l \cup X_r$, where $X_l = X_k^* \cap su(A_l)$ and $X_r = X_k^* \cap su(A_r)$. We consider two subcases:
   (a) $A_k(x) \leq B_k(y)$ for all $x \in X_k^*$.
   It suffices to take $x_0 = core(A_k)$ since then $A_l(x_0) = A_r(x_0) = 0$.
   (b) $A_k(x) > B_k(y)$ for some $x \in X_k^*$.
   If $x = core(A_k)$ then $A_l(x) = A_r(x) = 0$. If $x \in X_r$ then we take the same x_0 as above in case 1(b). It follows then that $A_k(x_0) = B_k(y)$, $A_r(x_0) \leq B_r(y)$ and now $A_l(x_0) = 0 \leq B_l(y)$. Otherwise, if $x \in X_l$, the same proof applies exchanging r by l.

There are 2 remaining cases to be addressed. The case "$\alpha_l > 0, \alpha_r = 0$" is proved in a similar manner as in 1, and the case "$\alpha_l > 0, \alpha_r > 0$" cannot occur, by construction of the A_i's. This ends the proof. □

Constructing Rough Mereological Granules of Classifying Rules and Classifying Algorithms

Lech Polkowski[1,3], *Andrzej Skowron*[2]

Polish-Japanese Institute of Information Technology [1]
Koszykowa 86, 02008 Warsaw, Poland
Institute of Mathematics [2], Warsaw University
Banacha 2, 02-097 Warsaw, Poland
Department of Mathematics and Information Sciences [3], Warsaw University of Technology
Pl.Politechniki 1, 00661 Warsaw, Poland
emails:polkow@pjwstk.waw.pl, skowron@mimuw.edu.pl

Abstract

Rough Set Theory cf. [3] was conceived as an approach toward analysis of uncertainty as well as incompleteness. Its basic assumptions going back to logical and philosophical analysis by – among others – Leibniz, Frege and Russell – is that objects perceived by a given set of ***attributes*** should be regarded as ***indiscernible*** whenever the attributes have same values on them (***Leibnizian identity***). Sets of objects which may be represented as unions of classes of the indiscernibility relation are then complete (*exact, certain*) while all other sets may be described by means of approximations with complete sets. The framework of rough sets allows for construction of classifying as well as decision rules and algorithms cf. [9] as well as for many applications to real life problems (*op. cit.*).

Rough Mereology cf. [6], [7], [8], [11] is a paradigm based on the predicate of *being a part to a degree* and as such falls in the province of *mereological theories of reasoning* based on the notion of a *part* which go back to the tradition of the Polish School in particular to the work of S. Leśniewski cf. [2]. Rough Mereology is a paradigm allowing for a synthesis of main ideas of two potent paradigms for reasoning under uncertainty : Fuzzy Set Theory and Rough Set Theory. We present applications of Rough Mereology to the important theoretical idea put forth by Lotfi Zadeh [12], [13] i.e. Granularity of Knowledge. Granules of Knowledge are constructed in the framework of Rough Mereology via its *class operator* which allows for aggregation of objects close enough (or, *similar in a satisfactory degree*) with respect to the rough inclusion operator (which measures the degree of being a part for pairs of objects). This allows for constructing Logics for Reasoning in Multi–Agent environment. We present a basic outline of this approach. We propose a formal language for encoding reasoning schemes (the *Synthesis Grammar*) and here we carry the idea of Synthesis Grammar to a higher level of abstraction by constructing Granules of classifying rules as well as classifying algorithms. We finally discuss briefly the analogy between rough mereological and neural computations leading to the idea of hybrid rough–neural computation schemes.

Keywords

knowledge discovery, rough sets, rough mereology, information granulation, classification algorithms and rules

1 Introduction

We begin with basic notions of Rough Set Theory [3], [6], [7], [8], [9]. Knowledge is represented in rough set approach by means of an information system $\mathbf{A} = (U, A)$ where U is a (current) set of objects, A is a (current) set of (conditional) attributes and each attribute $a \in A$ is a mapping on the set U i.e. $a : U \to V_a$ where V_a is the set of values of a.

Objects with identical descriptions are not discernible: for each $u \in U$ and a set $B \subseteq A$ of attributes, we define the ***information set*** $Inf_B(u)$ of u over the set$B$ by

(INF) $Inf_B(u) = \{(a, a(u)) : a \in B\}$

and we express indiscernibility of objects with respect to B by the relation IND_B of *B–indiscernibility*:

(IND) $IND_B(u, w) \Longleftrightarrow Inf_B(u) = Inf_B(w)$.

The indiscernibility relation IND_B partitions the set U into classes $[u]_B$; these classes are regarded by us as *elementary granules* of knowledge and they in turn may be represented in predicate calculus of descriptors *(attribute=value)*: a descriptor $(a = v)$ is satisfied by u if $a(u) = v$ and given $[u]_B$ with $B = \{a_{i_1}, a_{i_2}, .., a_{i_k}\}$ and $a_{i_j}(u) = v_{i_j}$, we find that the formula $\wedge_j (a_{i_j} = v_{i_j})$ is satisfied by and only by elements of $[u]_B$. In what follows we refer to $[u]_B$ also as to the (B, v)*–template* where $v = < v_{i_j} >$.

Dependencies between templates say (B, v) and (C, w) are expressed by formulae of the form

$\wedge_j (a_{i_j} = v_{i_j}) \Longrightarrow \wedge_k (b_{i_k} = w_{i_k})$

where $B = \{a_{i_j}\}$, $C = \{b_{i_k}\}$; these dependencies in turn may be regarded as *classifying rules* allowing to define C–values of an object in terms of its B–values and they may be represented as *pairs* $([u]_B, [u']_C)$ of elementary granules with appropriate u, u'.

The power (quality) of a classifying rule $R : ([u]_B, [u']_C)$ is characterized by two parameters viz. (cf. [1] for a discussion)

$\alpha(R) = \frac{|[u]_B \cap [u']_C|}{|[u]_B|}$ *(classification accuracy)*;

$\kappa(R) = \frac{|[u]_B \cap [u']_C|}{|[u']_C|}$ *(coverage)*.

Both accuracy and coverage are based on the rough membership function [4]; in recent applications the need has been stressed for more relaxed approach based not only on indiscernibility but also on a variety of tolerance (similarity) relations [9]. The need arises thus for tools for expressing similarity in information systems and for algorithms based on these tools.

Here, we propose to introduce rough mereological approach to the granulation problem in which IND-classes are replaced with mereological classes of satisfactorily close objects and granules. We discuss in the following Ontology, Mereology and Rough Mereology in Information Systems.

2 Ontology in Information Systems

Our ontology is adapted from Ontology of S. Leśniewski [2]. We modify it in notational aspect. Ontology is a theory of the copula "is" and we render it here as the membership $\in$ to be read *is*. We adopt the Ontology Axiom of Leśniewski.

$$X \in Y \Longleftrightarrow \exists Z.Z \in X$$

$$\wedge \forall U, W.(U \in X \wedge W \in X \Longrightarrow U = W)$$

$$\wedge \forall T.(T \in X \Longrightarrow T \in Y).$$

These three conjuncts express respectively that: (i) X is a non–empty name; (ii) X is a singleton (i.e. an individual); (iii) any entity called X is also called Y.

This defines the meaning of the copula $\in$. In particular, $X \in X$ states that X is an individual.

2.1 Examples: Rough Set Ontology in Information Systems

As individuals, we consider elementary granules. For an elementary granule (template) (C, v) we denote by the symbol $[C, v]$ its *meaning*: $[C, v] = \{u \in U : \forall a \in C.a(u) = v_a\}$. We will write down the granule (C, v) as the pair $((C, v), [C, v])$. We introduce operations on elementary granules denoted by $\oplus, \odot, \ominus$

1. $((C, v), [(C, v)]) \oplus ((D, w), [(D, w)])$ is the granule whose meaning consists of those objects which are either in $[(C, v)]$ or in $[(D, w)]$;
2. $((C, v), [(C, v)]) \odot ((D, w), [(D, w)])$ is the granule whose meaning consists of those objects which fall both in $[(C, v)]$ and $[(D, w)]$;
3. $\ominus((D, w), [(D, w)])$ where is the granule whose meaning consists of those objects which fall in U but not in $[(D, w)]$.

We will often denote a granule $((C, v), [(C, v)])$ with the symbol g and then $[g]$ will denote the meaning of g. Then, a general granule g may be written down in a canonical form as $\oplus_{i=1}^{k}((C_i, v_i), [C_i, v_i])$ with $[g] = \bigcup_{i=1}^{k}[C_i, v_i]$ where each $((C_i, v_i), [C_i, v_i])$ is an elementary granule.

3 Mereology in Information Systems

Our Mereology is an adaptation of Mereology proposed by Leśniewski [2] which has offered a formal treatment of the predicate of being a part. We begin with the notion of a *part* functor (*pt*, for short). *pt* is introduced into Ontology by means of additional axioms. We formalize $pt(Y)$ as a set-forming functor of entities that are parts of Y. $pt(Y)$ is defined only for individual Y.

(ME1) $X \in pt(Y) \wedge Y \in pt(Z) \Longrightarrow Xpt(Z)$; (*symmetricity of pt*).

(ME2) $non(Xpt(X))$. (*non–reflexivity of pt*).

The concept of an improper part is reflected in the notion of an *element el* defined as follows: $X \in el(Y) \Longleftrightarrow X \in pt(Y) \vee X = Y$.

Basic feature of Mereology of Leśniewski is the presence of the class functor Kl making properties into single objects and defined as follows.

$$X \in Kl(Y) \Longleftrightarrow$$

$$\forall Z.(Z \in Y \Longrightarrow Z \in el(X))$$

$$\wedge \forall Z.(Z \in el(X) \Longrightarrow \exists U, W.$$

$$U \in Y \wedge W \in el(U) \wedge W \in el(Z)).$$

These respective conditions state that each individual in Y is an element of $Kl(Y)$ and the class $Kl(Y)$ consists of all individuals which have an element in common with an individual in Y.

One also requires

(ME3) $X \in Kl(Y) \wedge Z \in Kl(Y) \Longrightarrow Z = X$; ($Kl(Y)$ *is an individual*).

(ME4) $\exists Z.Z \in Y \Longleftrightarrow \exists Z.Z \in Kl(Y)$ (*the class existence*).

The class operator will be used by us as a granule–forming tool in the sequel.

4 Rough Mereology

Rough Mereology [6], [7], [11] has been proposed and studied as a tool for approximate reasoning. Its primitive notion is that of a *rough inclusion* i.e. a functor $\mu(r)$ of being a part in degree at least r for each $r \in [0, 1]$.

The following is a list of basic postulates about Rough Mereology. We introduce a graded family μ_r, where $r \in [0, 1]$ is a real number from the unit interval, of functors which would satisfy the following requirements ($\mu_r(X)$ is a new property derived from X via μ_r and we use relational notation $X \in \mu_r(Y)$ for the statement : X is a part of Y in degree at least r):

(RM1) $X \in \mu_1(Y) \Longleftrightarrow X \in el(Y)$; (*a part in degree 1 is an element*).

(RM2) $X \in \mu_1(Y) \Longrightarrow \forall Z.(Z \in \mu_r(X) \Longrightarrow Z \in \mu_r(Y))$; (*monotonicity*).

(RM3) $X = Y \wedge X \in \mu_r(Z) \Longrightarrow Y \in \mu_r(Z)$; (*identity is a μ–congruence*).

(RM4) $X \in \mu_r(Y) \wedge s \leq r \Longrightarrow X \in \mu_s(Y)$; (*degree at leat r*).

4.1 Rough Inclusions in Information Systems

The following procedure defines a rough inclusion in an information system (U, A).

Procedure 1

1. Consider a partition $P = \{A_1, A_2, ..., A_k\}$ of A.
2. Select a family of coefficients: $W = \{w_1, w_2, ..., w_k\}$ where $w_i \geq 0$, any i, and $\sum_{i=1}^{k} w_i = 1$.
3. Define $IND(A_i)(x, y) = \{a \in A_i : a(x) = a(y)\}$.
4. Let $r = \sum_{i=1}^{k} w_i \frac{card(IND(A_i)(x,y))}{card(A_i)}$.
5. Declare $x \in \mu_r(y)$.

μ_r thus defined is a pre–rough inclusion as it is defined on objects; we now propose a method for extending a measure defined for elements of two sets to a measure on these two sets.

Assume that we are given two individuals X, Y being classes of (finite) names: $X = Kl(X')$, $Y = Kl(Y')$ and that we have defined values of μ for pairs T, Z of individuals where $T \varepsilon X'$, $Z \varepsilon Y'$.

We extend μ to a measure μ^* on X, Y by letting:

$$Y \varepsilon \mu_r^*(X) \text{ for } r = min_{Z \in Y'}\{max_{T \in X'} max\{s : Z \varepsilon \mu_s(T)\}\}.$$

It may be proved straightforwardly that

Proposition 1. *The measure μ^* satisfies (RM1)–(RM4).*

Rough inclusions based on frequency count. In this case our strategy is based on counting frequencies by means of the rough membership function applied to specifically defined counted objects; particular strategies depend on the type of individual objects we consider. We point to few cases.

1. In case our individual objects g, g' are B–elementary granules, we may apply the strategy of counting the number of B–indiscernibility classes in respectively $[g] \cap [g']$ and $[g']$. Accordingly, for $[g] = \bigcup_{i=1}^{k} [(B, v_i)]$ and $[g'] = \bigcup_{j=1}^{m} [(B, w_j)]$, we let $g' \varepsilon \mu_r(g)$ where
$$r = \frac{\mid \{[(B, v_i)] : i \leq k\} \cap \{[(B, w_j)] : j \leq m\} \mid}{m};$$
2. In case our individual objects g, g' are elementary granules in A= (U, A), we may apply the strategy of counting rows: for two elementary granules g, g' with $[g] = \bigcup_{i=1}^{k} [(B_i, v_i)]$ and $[g'] = \bigcup_{j=1}^{m} [(C_j, w_j)]$, we let
$$g \varepsilon \mu_r(g')$$
where
$$r = \frac{\mid [g] \cap [g'] \mid}{\mid [g'] \mid}.$$

We also may apply the strategy of counting indiscernibility classes assuming

$$g \varepsilon \mu_r(g')$$

where

$$r = \frac{| \{[(B_i, v_i)] : i \leq k\} \cap \{[(C_j, w_j)] : j \leq m\} |}{m}.$$

3. We may apply a hybrid approach counting rows for indiscernibility classes and extending the received closeness measure to general individuals. First then, we define μ on atomic elementary granules $g = ((B, v), [(B, v)])$, $g' = ((C, w), [(C, w)])$: we begin with the set $IND(g, g') = \{a \in A : a \in B \cap C \wedge v(a) = w(a)\}$ and then we let $g' \varepsilon \mu_r(g)$ where $r = \frac{|IND(g,g')|}{|B|}$. Thus, the degree of partial containment of g' in g is determined by frequency count of identical elementary descriptors in templates (B, v) and (C, w).
Now, given individual entities being elementary granules g, g' with $[g] = \bigcup_{i=1}^{k} [(B_i, v_i)]$ and $[g'] = \bigcup_{j=1}^{m} [(C_j, w_j)]$, we let

$$g \varepsilon \mu_r^*(g')$$

where

$$r = min_{[(C_j, w_j)]}\{max_{[(B_i, v_i)]} max\{s : [(C_j, w_j)] \varepsilon \mu_s([(B_i, v_i)])\}\}.$$

Example 1. We give a simple example concerning the last method of calculating the measure μ. We begin with an example of an information system presented in Table 1.

	a_1	a_2	a_3
u_1	1	0	1
u_2	1	0	0
u_3	1	1	0
u_4	0	1	1
u_5	0	1	0
u_6	1	0	1
u_7	1	1	0

Table 1. *Binary1*: An example of an information table

Consider $B = \{a_1, a_2\}$, $C = \{a_2, a_3\}$, $v =< 1, 0 >$, $w =< 0, 1 >$. For $g = ((B, v), [B, v])$, $g' = ((C, w), [C, w])$, we have $IND(g, g') = \{a_2\}$ and accordingly, $g' \varepsilon \mu_{0.5}^*(g)$.

4.2 Rough Mereological Component of Granulation

The functors μ_r may enter our discussion of a granule:

1. Concerning the definitions of accuracy and coverage we may replace in them the rough membership function μ with a function μ_r possibly better suited to a given context.

2. The process of clustering may be described in terms of the class functor of mereology.

We will realize 1,2 in the sequel. Our setting will be the distributed environment of a multi–agent system.

5 Adaptive Calculi of Granules in Distributed Systems

We construct a mechanism for transferring granules of knowledge among agents by means of transfer functions induced by rough mereological connectives extracted from their respective information systems [7].

We now recall basic ingredients of our scheme of agents [6], [7], [11].

5.1 Distributed Systems of Agents

We refer to a model for approximate synthesis in a distributed system proposed in [6]– [8], [9].

Consider a distributed (multi-agent) system $M_A = \{Ag, Link, Inv\}$ where Ag is a set of agents, $Link$ is a finite list of words over Ag and Inv is a set of inventory objects. Each t in $Link$ is a word $ag_1 ag_2 ... ag_k ag$ meaning that ag is the parent node and $ag_1 ag_2 ... ag_k$ are children nodes in an elementary team t; both parties are related by means of the operation o_t which makes from a tuple $(x_1, ..., x_k)$ of objects, resp. at $ag_1, .., ag_k$ the object $o_t(x_1, .., x_k)$ at ag. Leaf agents $Leaf$ are those ag which are not any parent node. They operate on objects from Inv.

In addition, each agent ag is equipped with an information system $\mathbf{A(ag)} = (U(ag), A(ag)$ and a rough inclusion μ_{ag} on $U(ag)$ (cf. Procedure 1); a set $St(ag) \subseteq U(ag)$ of *standard individuals* is also defined for any ag.

Reasoning in M_A goes by way of standards and rough inclusions μ_{ag} at any ag. Instrumental in this reasoning process are rough connectives $f_{\sigma,t}$ where $\sigma = (st_1, ..., st_k, st)$ is a set of standards such that $o_t(st_1, .., st_k) = st$ (we call σ *admissible*). They propagate rough inclusion values from children nodes to the parent node according to the formula

$$\forall i. x_i \in \mu_{ag_i, r_i}(st_i) \Longrightarrow o_t(x_1, .., x_k) \in \mu_{ag, f(r_1, ..., r_k)}(st).$$

Approximate logic of synthesis We assume for simplicity that the distributed system M_A consists of $Ag = \{ag_1, ag_2, ag\}$ with $Link = ag_1 ag_2 ag$ and the operation o. This will not restrict the universality of our discussion but it will simplify the notation and make it easier to understand essential features of this approach.

We introduce a simplified logic $L(Ag)$ [7], [11] in which we can express global properties of the synthesis process.
Elementary formulae of $L(Ag)$ are $< st(a), \varepsilon(a) >$ where $st(a) \in St(a), \varepsilon(a) \in [0,1]$ for any $a \in Ag$. Formulae of $L(ag)$ form the smallest extension of the set of elementary formulae closed under propositional connectives $\vee$, $\wedge$, $\neg$ and under the modal operators $\Box$, $\Diamond$.
For $x \in U(a)$, we say that x satifies $< st(a), \varepsilon(a) >$, in symbols:

$$x \vdash < st(a), \varepsilon(a) >,$$

iff $x \in \mu(a)_{\varepsilon(a)}(st(a))$.

Notice that $st(a)$ may choose a formula (a choice is by no means unique) in descriptor language which it does satisfy and x has to be close enough to $st(a)$ in order to satisfy the chosen formula in degree $\varepsilon(a)$.

We extend satisfaction over formulae by recursion as usual.

By a *selection* over Ag we mean a function sel which assigns to each agent a an object $sel(a) \in U(a)$. For two selections sel, sel' we say that *sel induces sel'*, in symbols $sel \rightarrow_{Ag} sel'$ when $sel(a) = sel'(a)$ for $a = ag_1, ag_2$ and $sel'(ag) = o(ag)(sel'(ag_1), sel'(ag_2))$.

We extend the satisfiability predicate $\vdash$ to selections: for an elementary formula $< st(a), \varepsilon(a) >$, we let $sel \vdash < st(a), \varepsilon(a) >$ iff $sel(a) \vdash < st(a), \varepsilon(a) >$.

We now let $sel \vdash \Diamond < st(a), \varepsilon(a) >$ when there exists a selection sel' satisfying the conditions: $sel \rightarrow_{Ag} sel'; sel' \vdash < st(a), \varepsilon(a) >$.

In terms of $L(Ag)$ it is possible to express the problem of synthesis of an approximate solution to the problem posed to Ag.

In the process of top - down communication, a requirement Ψ received by the scheme from an external source (which may be called a *customer*) is decomposed into approximate specifications of the form $< st(a), \varepsilon(a) >$ for any agent a of the scheme. The decomposition process is initiated at the agent ag and propagated along the scheme. We now are able to formulate the synthesis problem.

Synthesis problem

Given $\alpha : < st(ag)), \varepsilon(ag) >$ *find a selection sel with the property sel* $\vdash \alpha$.

A solution to the synthesis problem with a given formula α is found by negotiations among the agents based on uncertainty rules and their successful result can be expressed by a top-down recursion as follows: it is sufficient that each agent ag_i choose a standard $st(ag_i) \in U(ag_i)$ and a coefficient $\varepsilon(ag_i) \in [0,1]$ such that

Criterion 5.1

1. $\sigma = (st(ag_1), st(ag_2), st(ag))$ is admissible i.e. $o(st(ag_1), st(ag_2)) = st(ag)$;
2. $f_\sigma(\varepsilon(ag_1), \varepsilon(ag_2)) \geq \varepsilon(ag)$.

We call an α - *scheme* an assignment of a formula $\alpha(a) : < st(a), \varepsilon(a) >$ to each $a \in Ag$ in such manner that 1, 2 in Crit. 5.1 are satisfied and $\alpha(ag))$ is α. We denote this scheme with the symbol $sch(\alpha)$.

We say that a selection *sel* is *compatible* with a scheme $sch(\alpha)$, in case $sel(a) \in \mu(a)_{\varepsilon(a)}(st(a))$ for $a = ag_1, ag_2$.

The goal of negotiations can be summarized now as follows.

Proposition 5.1

Given a formula $\alpha : < st(ag)), \varepsilon(ag)) >$, **if** a selection *sel* is compatible with a scheme $sch(\alpha)$ **then** $sel \vdash \Diamond\alpha$.

6 Calculi of Elementary Granules

We construct in a given system M_A of agents for each agent a, granules by means of a rough inclusion μ_a of the agent a.

For a standard $st(a)$ and $\varepsilon(a)$, we denote by the symbol $gr(st(a), \varepsilon(a))$ (*the granule of size* $\varepsilon(a)$ *about* $st(a)$) the class $Kl_{\varepsilon(a)}(st(a))$ where $Kl_{\varepsilon(a)}(st(a))$ is the class (i.e. the set) of those x for which $x \in \mu_{a,\varepsilon(a)}(st(a))$.

Example 1

Let us define the rough inclusion $\mu_{a,r}$ according to Procedure 1 with $w_1 = 1$ i.e. $x \in \mu(a)_r(y) \Longleftrightarrow r \geq \frac{|IND(x,y)|}{|A_a|}$.

For a given template (B, v), the elementary granule $gr(B, v)$ defined by (B, v) consists of all x with $a_i(x) = v_i$ for $a_i \in B$.

We regard now (B, v) as a standard say $st(a)_{B,v}$; for this standard, we define the rough inclusion $\mu_{a,st(a)_{B,v},r}$ according to Procedure 1 with $w_1 = 1$ i.e. $x \in \mu_{a,st(a)_{B,v},r}(y) \Longleftrightarrow r \geq \frac{|\{a \in A_a - B : a(x) = a(y)\}|}{|A_a|}$. Then, given ε, the granule $gr(st(a)_{B,v}, \varepsilon)$ consists of those x which agree with $st(a)_{B,v})$ on B and additionally agree with this standard on at least $\varepsilon \times 100$ percent of the remaining attributes.

Thus, granules $gr(st(a)_{B,v}, \varepsilon)$ provide a covering of the elementary granule $gr(B, v)$ by similarity classes of $\mu_{a,st(a)_{B,v}}$.

6.1 Synthesis in Terms of Granules

We say that $gr(st(a), \varepsilon(a))$ satisfies a formula $\alpha :< st(a), \varepsilon'(a) >$,

$$gr(st(a), \varepsilon(a)) \vdash \alpha$$

in case $\varepsilon(a) \geq \varepsilon'(a)$.

Given admissible $\sigma = \{st(ag), st(ag_1), st(ag_2)\}$ and $\varepsilon(ag), \varepsilon(ag_1), \varepsilon(ag_2)$ with $f_\sigma(\varepsilon(ag_1), \varepsilon(ag_2)) \geq \varepsilon(ag)$ (i.e. 1,2 in Crit. 5.1 are satisfied) we observe that: **if** $x \in gr(st(ag_1), \varepsilon(ag_1))$, $y \in gr(st(ag_2), \varepsilon(ag_2))$, **then** $o(x, y) \in gr(st(ag), \varepsilon(ag))$.

We may state the sufficiency of synthesis condition in terms of granules as follows.

Proposition 6.1

For the formula $\alpha :< st(a), \varepsilon(a) >$:

if $x \in gr(st(ag_1), \varepsilon(ag_1))$, $y \in gr(st(ag_2), \varepsilon(ag_2))$ with 1, 2 in Crit. 5.1 satisfied **then** $o(x, y) \vdash \alpha$.

It suffices thus that for a given granule $gr(st(ag), \varepsilon(ag)$, agents ag_1, ag_2 send to ag granules, respectively, $gr(st(ag_1), \varepsilon(ag_1))$ and $gr(st(ag_2), \varepsilon(ag_2))$.

7 Associated Synthesis Grammars

The above may be formulated in terms of a grammar Γ and a language $L(\Gamma)$ whose words code sufficient synthesis conditions [8]. With each agent $a \in Ag$, we associate a grammar $\Gamma(a) = (N(a), T(a), P(a))$. To this end, we assume that a finite set $\Xi(a) \subset [0,1]$ is selected for each a. We let $N(a) = \{(s_{st(a)}, t_{\varepsilon(a)}) : st(a) \in St(a), \varepsilon(a) \in \Xi(a)\}$ where $s_{st(a)}$ is a non–terminal symbol corresponding in a one - to - one way to the standard $st(a)$ and similarly $t_{\varepsilon(a)}$ corresponds to $\varepsilon(a)$.

The set of terminal symbols $T(ag)$ is defined for ag by letting
$T(ag) = \cup_{i=1,2}\{\{(s_{st(ag_i)}, t_{\varepsilon(ag_i)}) : \varepsilon(ag_i) \in \Xi(ag_i)\} : i = 1,2\}$.
The set $P(ag)$ contains productions of the form
$(s_{st(ag)}, t_{\varepsilon(ag)}) \longrightarrow (s_{st(ag_1)}, t_{\varepsilon(ag_1)})(s_{st(ag_2)}, t_{\varepsilon(ag_2)})$
where $st(ag_1), st(ag_2), st(ag)$, $\varepsilon(ag), \varepsilon(ag_1), \varepsilon(ag_2)$ satisfy 1, 2 in Crit. 5.1.

We define a grammar system $\Gamma = (T(ag), (\Gamma(a) : a = ag \vee a = Input), S)$ by introducing an additional agent *Input* with the non - terminal symbol S, terminal symbols of *Input* being non-terminal symbols of ag and productions of *Input* of the form:
$S \Longrightarrow (s_{st(ag))}, t_{\varepsilon((ag))})$

The meaning of S is that it codes an approximate specification (requirement) for an object; productions of *Input* code specifications for approximate solutions in the language of the agent ag. Subsequent rewritings produce terminal strings of the form
$(s_{st(ag_1)}, t_{\varepsilon(ag_1)})(s_{st(ag_2)}, t_{\varepsilon(ag_2)})$.
We have

Proposition 7.1

Suppose $(s_{st(ag_1)}, t_{\varepsilon(ag_1)})(s_{st(ag_2)}, t_{\varepsilon(ag_2)})$ is obtained from

$$S \longrightarrow (s_{st(ag))}, t_{\varepsilon(ag))})$$

by subsequent rewriting by means of productions in Γ. Then given any selection sel with $sel(ag_i) \in \mu(ag_i)_{\varepsilon(ag_i)}(st(ag_i))$ for $i = 1,2$ we have

$$sel \models \Diamond < st(ag), \varepsilon(ag) > .$$

Remarks

1. Synthesis grammars constructed above reflect processes in multi-agent systems which arise in a multi-agent system involved in cooperation, negotiation and conflict-resolving actions when attempting to provide a solution to a specification of a problem posed to its root.

2. Complexities of membership problems for languages generated by synthesis grammars may be taken ex definitione as complexities of the underlying synthesis processes.

8 Synthesis of Classifying Rules and Classifying Algorithms

As mentioned above classifying rules may be represented as pairs of granules. Thus, it is the first task to establish means for measuring the rough mereological distance between granules.

Consider granules g, g' in the universe U endowed with a rough inclusion μ. We propose the following *min-max* formula:

$$g \in \mu_r^*(g') \Longleftrightarrow min_x max\{r : x \in \mu_r(y) : y \in g'\} \geq r.$$

Then

Proposition 8.1

μ^g is a rough inclusion on granules as it satisfies (RM1)–(RM4).

Example 2

Consider templates (B, v) and (C, w) in an information system $\mathbf{A} = (U, A)$ with the rough inclusion μ defined in Procedure 1 with $w_1 = 1$.

It may be found straightforwardly that for $g = gr(B, v)$, $g' = gr(C, w)$, we have the worst–case estimate

$$g \in \mu_r^g(g') \Longleftrightarrow r \geq 1 - \frac{k - s}{n}$$

where $k = |C|$, s–the number of indices j with $j \in B \cap C$, $v_j = w_j$.

We have thus a trade–off: a short template (i.e. k small) means closeness of distinct granules and large size of the granule g'.

We extend this measure to pairs of granules i.e. clasifying rules by letting:

$$g \in \mu_r^g(g') \wedge g_1 \in \mu_s^g(g_1') \Longrightarrow$$
$$(g, g_1) \in \mu_{\top(r,s)}^{g*}(g', g_1')$$

where $\top$ is a *t-norm*.

Then μ^{g*} is a rough inclusion on classifying rules.

8.1 Rough Mereological Connectives on Classifying Rules

Given our system M_A, rough mereological connectives f may be extended to connectives propagating uncertainty about classifying rules. Although it would be possible to derive a general formula from our results above, we rather give an illuminating example.

Example 3: fusion of data

Consider M_A with ag_1, ag_2, ag where information systems of agents are $A_{ag_1} = (U, A_1)$, $A_{ag_2} = (U, A_2)$ and $A_{ag} = (U, A_1 \cup A_2)$ i.e. ag fuses tables of ag_1 and ag_2.

We find a formula for F, the rough mereological connective for granules generated by templates.

Consider thus templates (B_1, v_1), (C_1, w_1) at ag_1, (B_2, v_2), (C_2, w_2) at ag_2 and $(B = B_1 \cup B_2, v = v_1 \cup v_2)$ and $(C = C_1 \cup C_2, w = w_1 \cup w_2)$ at ag along with the corrresponding elementary granules for μ as in Example 2.

We have by Example 2 that :

1. $gr(B_1, v_1) \in \mu^g_{r_1}(gr(C_1, w_1))$ with $r_1 \leq 1 - \frac{k_1 - s_1}{n_1}$;
2. $gr(B_2, v_2) \in \mu^g_{r_2}(gr(c_2, w_2))$ with $r_2 \leq 1 - \frac{k_2 - s_2}{n_2}$;
3. $gr(B, v) \in \mu^*_r(gr(C, w))$ with $r \leq 1 - \frac{(k_1 - s_1) + (k_2 - s_2)}{n_1 + n_2}$.

From 1.–3. it follows that the connective F satisfies the formula

$$F(1 - \varepsilon_1, 1 - \varepsilon_2) \geq 1 - max(\varepsilon_1, \varepsilon_2) = min(1 - \varepsilon_1, 1 - \varepsilon_2).$$

An Application: a classifier query decomposition
In the setting of Example 3, we may select (C, w). Then the query

$$? < (.,.), (C, w), \delta >$$

means that we are searching for (B, v) with $gr(B, v) \in \mu^g_\delta(gr(C, w))$ i.e. for a classifier with a sufficient quality (measured by δ).

Then, the problem may be decomposed: it suffices that ag_1, ag_2 find granules $gr(B_1, v_1)$, $gr(B_2, v_2)$, respectively, satisfying:

- $gr(B_1, v_1) \in \mu^g_{1-\varepsilon_1}(gr(C_1, w_1))$;
- $gr(B_2, v_2) \in \mu^g_{1-\varepsilon_2}(gr(C_2, w_2))$

with $max(\varepsilon_1, \varepsilon_2) \leq 1 - \delta$.

The results presented here allow to

1. formulate counterparts of granule calculi for granules of classifiers;
2. define synthesis grammars in terms of classifiers;
3. extend these results to classification algorithms as these are finite collecctions of classifiers so one more application of our results would yield appropriate formulae in case of classification algorithms.

9 A Neural Model of Rough Mereological Computation

There is a parallelism between the proposed above calculi of granules in distributed systems and neural computing. Let us point to some analogies cf. [10].

1. Any elementary team of agents $t = ag$ may be regarded as a model of a neuron with inputs $ag_1, ag_2, ..., ag_k$, the output ag, and a parameterized family of activation functions represented as rough connectives $f_{\sigma,t}$ where $\sigma = (st_1, ..., st_k, st)$ is an admissible set of standards
2. Values of rough inclusions in the formula

$$\forall i. x_i \varepsilon \mu_{r_i, ag_i}(st_i) \Longrightarrow o_t(x_1, .., x_k) \varepsilon \mu_{f(r_1, ..., r_k), ag}(st)$$

are counterparts of weights in a traditional neural network. Let us observe that in our case the resulting network is a parameterized system of simple networks, indexed by synthesis schemes (α–schemes)

3. Learning in this new kind of a neural network is based also on back-propagation mechanisms in which the incoming signal (a specification Ψ) is assigned a proper α–scheme and a proper set of weights set in negotiation and cooperation processes among local teams and agents therein

These processes of learning would require new algorithms and one possible way out here is to base the process of learning on familiar techniques of neural networks by encoding all the constructs in a neural network whose activation functions are tractable (e.g. piece–wise differentiable) approximations to rough mereological connectives. As a result, we would obtain a closed–loop system providing feedback information from the distributed system to the neural network. The theory and practice of such systems is to come in future.

10 Conclusions

The reader of this work, after a scrutiny of the content, has undoubtedly noticed and made themselves familiar with the main ingredients of this approach: the formalism based on mereological ideas, the construction of reasoning schemes, the granule–forming mechanism, the analysis of correctness of problem solving procedure along with additional aspects i.e. the linguistic counterpart given in the guise of synthesis grammars and languages and rough–neuro–computing scheme.

In this way we propose to realize programs of *granulation of knowledge* and *computation with granules.* At the same time we propose a way toward *computing with words*: interfaces between natural language corpora and synthesis languages will allow for performing computing with words *sensu stricto.*

Acknowledgement

This work has been prepared under the Research Grant No 8T11C 024 17 from the State Committee for Scientific Research (KBN) of the Republic of Poland (Lech Polkowski) and under the Research Grant No 8T11C 025 19 from the State Committee for Scientific Research (KBN) of the Republic of Poland and a grant from the Wallenberg Foundation (Andrzej Skowron).

References

1. J. Bazan, Hung Son Nguyen, Sinh Hoa Nguyen, P. Synak, and J. Wróblewski, 2000, Rough set algorithms in Classification Problem, in; L. Polkowski, S. Tsumoto, and T. Y. Lin (eds.), *Rough Set Methods and Applications. New Developments in Knowledge Discovery in Information Systems*, Physica Verlag/ Springer Verlag, Heidelberg, pp. 49–88.
2. S. Leśniewski, 1927, O podstawach matematyki, *Przegląd Filozoficzny*, 30, pp.164-206; 31, pp. 261-291; 32, pp. 60-101; 33, 77-105; 34, 142-170; cf. also: S. Leśniewski, 1982, On the foundations of mathematics, Topoi 2, pp. 7–52.

3. Z. Pawlak, 1992, *Rough Sets: Theoretical Aspects of Reasoning about Data*, Kluwer, Dordrecht.
4. Z. Pawlak and A. Skowron, 1994, Rough membership functions, in: R.R. Yaeger, M. Fedrizzi, J. Kacprzyk (eds.), *Advances in the Dempster Shafer Theory of Evidence*, John Wiley and S., New York, pp. 251-271.
5. Z. Pawlak, 1999, Decision rules, Bayes' rule and rough sets, in: Ning Zhong, A. Skowron, S. Ohsuga (eds.), new Directions in Rough sets, Data Mining and Granular-Soft Computing, LNAI vol. 1711, Springer Verlag, Berlin, pp. 1–9.
6. L. Polkowski and A. Skowron, 1994, Rough mereology, in: *Lecture Notes in Artificial Intelligence*, vol. 869, Springer Verlag, Berlin, pp. 85-94.
7. L. Polkowski and A. Skowron, 1996, Rough mereology: a new paradigm for approximate reasoning, *International J. Approximate Reasoning*, 15(4), pp. 333-365.
8. L. Polkowski and A. Skowron, 1998, Grammar systems for distributed synthesis of approximate solutions extracted from experience, in: Gh. Paun and A. Salomaa (eds.), *Grammatical Models of Multi-Agent Systems*, Gordon and Breach Sci. Publ., Amsterdam, pp. 316-333.
9. L. Polkowski and A. Skowron (eds.), 1998, *Rough Sets in Knowledge Discovery*, vols. 18, 19 in the Series: *Studies in Fuzziness and Soft Computing*, J. Kacprzyk (ed.), Physica Verlag (Springer Verlag).
10. L. Polkowski and A. Skowron, 2001, Rough mereological calculi of granules: Rough Set approach to Computation, *Computational Intelligence*, in print.
11. A. Skowron and L. Polkowski, Rough mereological foundations for design, analysis, synthesis and control in distributed systems, *Information Sciences. An Intern. J.*, 104(1-2) (1998), pp. 129-156.
12. L.A. Zadeh, 1996, Fuzzy logic = computing with words, *IEEE Trans. on Fuzzy Systems*, 4, pp. 103-111.
13. L. A. Zadeh, 1997, Toward a theory of fuzzy information granulation and its certainty in human reasoning and fuzzy logic, *Fuzzy Sets and Systems*, 90, pp. 111-127.

Criticality in the Network with Imprecise Activity Times

Stefan Chanas[1] and Paweł Zieliński[2]

[1] Institute of Industrial Engineering and Management Technical University of Wrocław, Wybrzeże Wyspiańskiego 27, 50-370 Wrocław, Poland
chanas@ioz.pwr.wroc.pl
[2] Institute of Mathematics, Technical University of Opole, Luboszycka 3, 45-036 Opole, Poland
pziel@polo.po.opole.pl

Abstract. A review of the results obtained in the area of fuzzy network analysis is presented. The main approaches to the concept of criticality in a network with fuzzy activity times are described and classified. Against the background of this review some new results, obtained by the authors recently, are presented. The paper is an extended version of the work presented in IPMU'2000 (see [8]).

1 Introduction

In the paper we present some results, obtained by us recently, concerning the analysis of criticality (of paths and activities) in a network with interval and fuzzy activity durations. We give a natural, unconsidered in the literature so far, generalization of the criticality notion for the case of a network with interval and fuzzy activities duration times. We also consider the problem of determining a critical (in accordance with the introduced definition) path in a network with interval activities duration times and the problem of computing path degrees of criticality in a network with fuzzy activities duration times. All these results are presented in Sect. 3 and 4. Before that, however, we give (in Sect. 2) an extensive review of the main results obtained so far in the area of fuzzy network analysis. We describe and classify the main approaches to the concept of criticality in a network with fuzzy activity times.

2 Criticality in the network with fuzzy activity times – a review of some recent approaches

The criticality has been studied since the 80's. Several works have tried to cope with this problem. In this section we review and try to group together the existing approaches to defining the criticality notion in a network with fuzzy activity times. Before we pass on to the topic of the paper, let us recall the notions of the criticality of a path and an activity (an event) in a network with deterministic activities times.

A network $S = < V, A, t >$ being a project activity-on-arc model is given (the activities are represented by arcs of the network). V is the set of nodes (events) and $A \subset V \times V$ is the set of arcs (activities). The network S is a directed, connected, acyclic graph. The set $V = \{1, 2, \dots, n\}$ is labeled in such a way that $i < j$ for each activity $(i, j) \in A$. Let t be a nonnegative real function defined on the set of the activities, $t : A \rightarrow \mathbb{R}^+$, where $t(i, j) \stackrel{\text{def}}{=} t_{ij}$ is the duration time of activity $(i, j) \in A$.

The notions of the criticality of a path and an activity (an event) were born with the development of the Critical Path Method (CPM) (see [14]). The essence of the CPM method (from the numerical point of view) are two recurrence formulae which are used to determine the earliest and the latest moments of the occurrence of the events $i \in V$. The earliest moment, t_i^e, at which event $i \in V$ can occur, is determined according to the following recurrence formula (forward pass):

$$t_i^e = \begin{cases} 0 & \text{for } i = 1, \\ \max_{k \in P(i)} (t_k^e + t_{ki}) & \text{for } i > 1, \end{cases} \tag{1}$$

where $P(i) = \{k \in V \mid (k, i) \in A\}$ ($P(1) = \emptyset$). And the latest moment, t_i^l, at which event $i \in V$ can occur, may be found by means of the following formula (backward pass):

$$t_i^l = \begin{cases} t_n^e & \text{for } i = n, \\ \min_{k \in S(i)} (t_k^l - t_{ik}) & \text{for } i < n, \end{cases} \tag{2}$$

where $S(i) = \{k \in V \mid (i, k) \in A\}$ ($S(n) = \emptyset$).

The times obtained according to (1) and (2) are applied in the calculation of slack times (floats) $F_i = t_i^l - t_i^e$ of events $i \in V$, slack times (floats) $F_{ij} = t_j^l - t_i^e - t_{ij}$ of activities $(i, j) \in A$, the earliest start times $S_{ij}^e = t_i^e$ and the latest start times $S_{ij}^l = t_j^l - t_{ij}$ of activities $(i, j) \in A$. t_n^e is the minimum time required for the completion of the whole project. t_i^e is the length of the longest path from node 1 to i in S, assuming that the weights of the arcs are activities duration times. Let us denote by P the set of all the paths in S from node 1 to node n and by l_p the sum of duration times of the activities lying on path $p \in P$, i.e. $l_p = \sum_{(i,j) \in p} t_{ij}$. Of course, the following equation holds:

$$t_n^e = l_{p^*} = \max\{l_p \mid p \in P\}. \tag{3}$$

Now we give a series of equivalent definitions of the criticality of a path and an activity (an event) in S.

Definition 1. A path $p \in P$ is critical if and only if $t_n^e = l_p$ (according to (3) p is the longest path in S).

Definition 2. A path $p \in P$ is critical if and only if for each $(i, j) \in p$ the equation holds: $t_i^e + t_{ij} = t_j^e$.

Definition 3. An activity $(i,j) \in A$ (resp. an event $i \in V$) is critical if and only if $F_{ij} = 0$ $(F_i = 0)$.

Definition 4. An activity $(i,j) \in A$ (resp. an event $i \in V$) is critical if and only if $t_i^e + t_{ij} + t_j^{e'} = t_n^e$ $(t_i^e + t_i^{e'} = t_n^e)$, where $t_i^{e'}$ is the earliest moment of the occurrence of the event $i \in V$ while starting from the end of the network S, i.e.

$$t_i^{e'} = \begin{cases} 0 & \text{for } i = n, \\ \max_{k \in S(i)}(t_k^{e'} + t_{ik}) & \text{for } i < n. \end{cases} \tag{4}$$

Definition 5. A path $p \in P$ is critical if and only if all the activities belonging to p are critical.

Let us return to the fuzzy case now. A network $S =< V, A, \tilde{T} >$ is given. All the elements of this network are the same as in the deterministic case except for function $\tilde{T}$ which is now defined in the following way: $\tilde{T} : A \to F(\mathbb{R}^+)$, where $F(\mathbb{R}^+)$ is the set of nonnegative fuzzy numbers. We introduce the notation $\tilde{T}(i,j) \stackrel{\text{def}}{=} \tilde{T}_{ij}$, $(i,j) \in A$.

The use of fuzzy numbers in the network planning was proposed rather early (Chanas and Radosiński [5], Dubois and Prade [11], Prade [23], Chanas and Kamburowski [4]). The authors only studied the calculation of the fuzzy duration of the whole project (fuzzy earliest ending time), $\tilde{T}_n^e$. In all these papers the approach is similar. The formulae (1) and (2) used in the CPM for a network with deterministic activity times are used where the common operations $+$, $-$, max, min are replaced with the operations $\tilde{+}$, $\tilde{-}$, $\tilde{\max}$, $\tilde{\min}$ on fuzzy numbers. Since in the general case it is cumbersome to perform (1) by direct applying the definitions of $\tilde{+}$, $\tilde{-}$ and $\tilde{\max}$, Dubois and Prade [10] proposed to use for the representation of $\tilde{T}_{ij}$'s fuzzy numbers of a special form – of the $L-R$ type, i.e. $\tilde{T}_{ij} = (\underline{t}_{ij}, \bar{t}_{ij}, \alpha_{ij}, \beta_{ij})_{LR}$. The operations on fuzzy numbers of the $L-R$ type reduce themselves to the usual operations on the parameters. However, it should be stressed that from the mentioned operations only $\tilde{+}$, $\tilde{-}$ can be executed precisely. The $\tilde{\max}$, $\tilde{\min}$ have to be approximated.

In Chanas and Kamburowski [4] another way of performing the operations on fuzzy numbers has been presented. They considered only formula (1) and they proposed a decomposition of fuzzy activity times $\tilde{T}_{ij}$ into λ-cuts, i.e. $\tilde{T}_{ij}^{\lambda} = \{t_{ij} \in \mathbb{R}^+ \mid \mu_{\tilde{T}_{ij}}(t_{ij}) \geq \lambda\} = [\underline{t}_{ij}^{\lambda}, \bar{t}_{ij}^{\lambda}]$, $\lambda \in (0,1]$, and the use of formula (1) on each λ-cut with the operations on interval numbers.

Now we focus on the criticality in networks with fuzzy activity times. Two categories of approaches to defining the criticality in the fuzzy case are distinguished.

Category 1. The notion of criticality is introduced in a different way then in the deterministic case. As opposed to the deterministic case, the fuzzy criticality of a path, an activity and an event is defined as a fuzzy set in the set P, A and V, respectively. The fuzzy set $\tilde{P}$ in set P with the membership function $\mu_{\tilde{P}} : P \to [0,1]$ is called the fuzzy critical path in S. Similarly, the fuzzy set $\tilde{A}$ (resp. $\tilde{E}$) in set A (V) with the membership function $\mu_{\tilde{A}} : A \to [0,1]$ ($\mu_{\tilde{E}} : V \to [0,1]$) is called the fuzzy critical activity (event) in S. One may split this category into three subcategories.

(1.A) *Possibilistic approach using operations on fuzzy numbers.* Approaches of Kamburowski [13] (see also Chanas [2]), Mareš [17], Slyeptsov and Tyshchuk [25] can be classified in this subcategory.

In Kamburowski [13] (see also Chanas [2]) the degree of criticality of a path p is determined as

$$\mu_{\tilde{P}}(p) = \text{Poss}(\tilde{l}_p = \tilde{T}_n^e),\ p \in P, \tag{5}$$

and the degree of criticality of an activity (i,j) (resp. an event i) is determined as

$$\begin{aligned} \mu_{\tilde{A}}(i,j) &= \text{Poss}(\tilde{T}_i^e + \tilde{T}_{ij} + \tilde{T}_j^{e'} = \tilde{T}_n^e),\ (i,j) \in A, \\ (\mu_{\tilde{E}}(i) &= \text{Poss}(\tilde{T}_i^e + \tilde{T}_i^{e'} = \tilde{T}_n^e),\ i \in V), \end{aligned} \tag{6}$$

where $\tilde{l}_p = \tilde{\sum}_{(i,j)\in p}\tilde{T}_{ij}$, $\tilde{T}_i^e$ and $\tilde{T}_i^{e'}$ are the moments of the occurrence of event $i \in V$ computed by formulae (1) and (4) with $\tilde{+}$ and $\tilde{\max}$, respectively. The above definitions are a generalization of the criticality in the deterministic case to the fuzzy case (see Definitions 1 and 4).

Mareš's [17] approach is also a generalization of the criticality in the deterministic case to the fuzzy case (see Definition 1 and (3)). He proposed two equivalent definitions of the degree of criticality of a path p:

$$\mu_{\tilde{P}}(p) = \min\{\text{Poss}(\tilde{l}_p \geq \tilde{l}_s) \mid s \in P, s \neq p\}\ p \in P$$

or equivalently

$$\mu_{\tilde{P}}(p) = \sup_{x \leq 0}\{\min\{\mu_{\tilde{r}_{ps}}(x) \mid s \in P, s \neq p\}\}\ p \in P,$$

where $\tilde{r}_{ps}$ is the relative float, i.e. $\tilde{r}_{ps} = \tilde{l}_s \tilde{-} \tilde{l}_p$.

Slyeptsov and Tyshchuk [25] offer a generalized approach, which combines both existing ones. The degree of criticality of a path p is determined as

$$\mu_{\tilde{P}}(p) = \min\{\mu'_{\tilde{P}}(p), \mu''_{\tilde{P}}(p)\},\ p \in P,$$

and the degree of criticality of an activity (i,j) is determined as

$$\mu_{\tilde{A}}(i,j) \min\{\mu'_{\tilde{A}}(i,j), \mu''_{\tilde{A}}(i,j)\},\ (i,j) \in A,$$

where $\mu'_{\tilde{P}}(p) = \min\{\text{Poss}(\tilde{T}_i^e + \tilde{T}_{ij} = \tilde{T}_j^e) \mid (i,j), \in p\}$ and $\mu'_{\tilde{A}}(i,j) = \max\{\mu'_{\tilde{P}}(p) \mid (i,j) \in p\}$. The functions $\mu''_{\tilde{P}}(p)$ and $\mu''_{\tilde{A}}(i,j)$ are equal to the membership functions (5) and (6), respectively.

One may include to this subcategory the papers of Chang et al. [9] and McCahon [19]. In these papers the authors only take advantage of the proposed earlier methods and approaches to the criticality notions (see (5), (6)).
(1.B) *Possibilistic approach without using operations on fuzzy numbers.* The approaches proposed by Buckley [1], Chanas and Zieliński (see Sect. 4) can be classified in this subcategory. These approaches consist in a direct application of the extension principle of Zadeh to the notion of the criticality of a path (an activity, an event) treated as a function of the activities duration times in the network. They are a direct generalization of the criticality in the deterministic case to the fuzzy case.

Buckley [1] defined the degree of criticality of an activity (k, l) in the following way:

$$\mu_{\tilde{A}}(k,l) = \mathrm{Poss}(\tilde{F}_{kl} = 0) = \sup_{\substack{t_{ij} \in \mathbb{R}^+, (i,j) \in A \\ \text{and } F_{kl}=0 \text{ with} \\ \text{activities duration} \\ \text{times equal to } t_{ij}}} \min_{(i,j) \in A} \mu_{\tilde{T}_{ij}}(t_{ij}), \ (k,l) \in A.$$

However, one should point out that the possibility distribution of $\tilde{F}_{kl}$ is computationally difficult to determine. Taking advantage of the results obtained by Chanas and Zieliński [6], we may assert that this problem is NP-hard.

The approach proposed by Chanas and Zieliński is presented in Sect. 4.
(1.C) *Float approach.* Nasution's [21] approach can be classified in this subcategory. In the CPM method the times obtained according to (1) and (2) are applied in the calculation of floats, F_i, of events and F_{ij} of activities. These quantities are useful in the identification of the critical paths, activities and events in the network (see Definitions 3 and 5). In the fuzzy case a problem arises, when we apply backward pass (2) to compute the latest moments of the occurrence of event i, $\tilde{T}_i^l$, using operation $\tilde{-}$ and $\tilde{\min}$. These moments become more and more fuzzy as we get closer to the end of the calculation. Sometimes $\tilde{T}_i^l$ may be a fuzzy number with negative values. This anomaly is caused by the fact that fuzzy subtraction $\tilde{-}$ is not the inverse of fuzzy addition $\tilde{+}$. To overcome these problems Nasution [21] proposed to consider first the interactive fuzzy subtraction in backward pass, and then to observe that if the time was represented by fuzzy numbers then only the nonnegative part should be take into account. Based on these two assumptions he obtains the latest moment the occurrence of event i, $\tilde{T}_i^l$ and float $\tilde{F}_i$ for each $i \in V$. By means of such computed quantities he determines the degree of the criticality of events.
Category 2. In this category the notion of criticality is introduced in a different way then in Category 1. One does not talk about the degree of criticality. Namely, the criticality of a path (as well as an activity and an event) is treated, in the proposed approaches, as a two-value function. This function takes one of the two values *yes* or *no*, depending on whether the given path (activity, event) is critical or non-critical according to the introduced definitions of criticality. One may split this category into three subcategories.

(2.A) *Float approach.* Rommelfanger's [24] approach can be classified in this subcategory. In this approach he tried to cope with the problems pointed out in (1.C) by the elimination of $\tilde{-}$ from the backward pass. Namely, it is not formula (2) with $\tilde{-}$ and $\tilde{\min}$ that should be used for calculating $\tilde{T}_i^l$, $i \in V$, but the following equation:

$$\tilde{T}_i^l = \begin{cases} \tilde{T}_n^e & \text{for } i = n, \\ \min_{k \in S(i)} \{\tilde{T}_i^l \mid \tilde{T}_i^l \tilde{+} \tilde{T}_{ik} = \tilde{T}_k^l\} & \text{for } i < n. \end{cases}$$

Sometimes solving $\tilde{T}_i^l \tilde{+} \tilde{T}_{ik} = \tilde{T}_k^l$ may be impossible. So, in this case $\tilde{T}_i^l$, that fulfills inequality $\tilde{T}_i^l \tilde{+} \tilde{T}_{ik} \leq_\epsilon \tilde{T}_k^l$ is calculated, where $\leq_\epsilon$ is a preference relation defined in [24]. Similarly, the float of an activity $(i,j) \in A$ (resp. an event $i \in V$), $\tilde{F}_{ij}$ ($\tilde{F}_i$) is determined as a solution of equation $\tilde{T}_i^e \tilde{+} \tilde{T}_{ij} \tilde{+} \tilde{F}_{ij} = \tilde{T}_j^l$ ($\tilde{T}_i^e \tilde{+} \tilde{F}_i = \tilde{T}_i^l$). If it is impossible to find a solution of this equation, then the equation is replaced by the inequality with the preference relation $\leq_\epsilon$. The identification of a critical path, an activity (an event) is carried out as in the deterministic case, i.e. activity (resp. an event) is critical if and only if $\tilde{F}_{ij}$ ($\tilde{F}_i$) is the zero fuzzy number, and the critical path is composed of critical activities.

(2.B) *Approach using ranking functions.* Approaches proposed by Chanas [3], Yao and Lin [27], Loostma [15], Mačák [18] and Mon et al. [20] can be classified in this subcategory. These approaches use ranking function, i.e. a function $f : F(\mathbb{R}^+) \to \mathbb{R}^+$, which maps fuzzy activity times $\tilde{T}_{ij}$ into the real line $\mathbb{R}^+$. Applying such functions considerably simplifies the network analysis and allows to use the definitions of criticality from the deterministic case.

Chanas's [3] approach consists in replacing each fuzzy activity duration time $\tilde{T}_{ij}$ with a random variable of a probability distribution which in some sense coincide with this duration time. The random variable $X_{\tilde{T}_{ij}}$, $X_{\tilde{T}_{ij}} = \underline{t}_{ij}^T + S(\overline{t}_{ij}^T - \underline{t}_{ij}^T)$, may be associated with $\tilde{T}_{ij}$, where S and T are independent random variables uniformly distributed over $(0,1]$. The mean value and variance of $X_{\tilde{T}_{ij}}$ are expressed by the following formulae:

$$GE(\tilde{T}_{ij}) = \tfrac{1}{2} \int_0^1 (\underline{t}(\lambda) + \overline{t}(\lambda))\, \mathrm{d}\lambda, \tag{7}$$

$$GVar(\tilde{T}_{ij}) = \tfrac{1}{3} \int_0^1 (\underline{t}^2(\lambda) + \underline{t}(\lambda)\overline{t}(\lambda) + \overline{t}^2(\lambda))\, \mathrm{d}\lambda - [GE(\tilde{T}_{ij})]^2, \tag{8}$$

where $\underline{t}(\lambda) = \underline{t}_{ij}^\lambda = \inf\{t_{ij} \in \mathbb{R}^+ \mid \mu_{\tilde{T}_{ij}}(t_{ij}) \geq \lambda\}$, $\overline{t}(\lambda) = \overline{t}_{ij}^\lambda = \sup\{t_{ij} \in \mathbb{R}^+ \mid \mu_{\tilde{T}_{ij}}(t_{ij}) \geq \lambda\}$ are the ends of the interval constituting the λ-cut of $\tilde{T}_{ij}$. So the calculated quantities by (7) and (8) for each activity are used in the further project analysis in the same way as in the usual PERT method (see [16]). Note that (7) is Yager's [26] ranking function. It is possible to link other random values with $\tilde{T}_{ij}$, which would lead to other formulae for the expected value and variance.

The approach proposed by Yao and Lin [27] is partially similar to Chanas's [3] approach. They use Yager's [26] ranking function (see (7)) without any interpretation and reduce the fuzzy case to the deterministic one. Then a critical path, an activity and an event are determined in the same manner as in the CPM method.

In the approaches of Loostma [15] and Mačák [18] formulae (1) and (2) are applied with the operations $\tilde{+}$, $\tilde{-}$, $\tilde{\max}$, $\tilde{\min}$ on the triangular fuzzy numbers to compute the fuzzy moments of the occurrence of events. The operation $\tilde{\max}$ and $\tilde{\min}$ are approximated in order to preserve fuzzy number type. In the identification of a critical path by means of the calculated the fuzzy moments, only the modal values of the triangular fuzzy numbers are taken into account. Mačák [18] additionally determines critical paths for the boundary activities duration times (the lower and upper values of triangular fuzzy numbers).

In the approach of Mon et al. [20] the notions of a risk level $\lambda \in (0,1]$ and a degree of optimism α are introduced. The risk level λ and the degree of optimism $\alpha \in [0,1]$ are used in generating deterministic activity time $t_{ij}^{\lambda,\alpha}$, $(i,j) \in A$, i.e. $t_{ij}^{\lambda,\alpha} = \alpha \underline{t}_{ij}^{\lambda} + (1-\alpha)\overline{t}_{ij}^{\lambda}$, where $\underline{t}_{ij}^{\lambda}$, $\overline{t}_{ij}^{\lambda}$ are the ends of the interval constituting the λ-cut of $\tilde{T}_{ij}$. A larger λ indicates a lower risk. But a larger α indicates a higher optimism, vice versa. These values are given by the decision maker. In this way they reduce the problem to the deterministic case, and a critical path, an activity and an event are determined in the same manner as in the CPM method.

(2.C) *Another approach.* Gazdik's [12] approach can be classified in this subcategory. In this approach the identification of a critical path is equivalent to finding a path $p^* \in P$ such that $\tilde{l}_{p^*} = \tilde{\max}\{\tilde{l}_p \mid p \in P\}$. In other words, it is necessary to enumerate all the paths $p \in P$ in S.

3 Criticality in the network with interval activity times

A network $S = \langle V, A, T \rangle$ is given. All the elements of this network are the same as in the deterministic case except for function T, which maps the set of activities A into the set $I(\mathbb{R}^+)$ (the set of intervals with nonnegative ends), $T : A \to I(\mathbb{R}^+)$. We denote $T(i,j) \stackrel{\text{def}}{=} T_{ij} = [\underline{t}_{ij}, \overline{t}_{ij}]$, $(i,j) \in A$.

Definition 6. A path $p \in P$ is i-critical (interval critical) in S if and only if there exists a set of times t_{ij}, $t_{ij} \in [\underline{t}_{ij}, \overline{t}_{ij}]$, $(i,j) \in A$, such that p is a critical path in the usual sense, after replacing the interval times T_{ij} with the exact values t_{ij}, $T_{ij} := t_{ij}$.

Definition 7. An activity $(k,l) \in A$ (resp. an event $k \in V$) is i-critical (interval critical) in the network S if and only if there exists a set of times t_{ij}, $t_{ij} \in [\underline{t}_{ij}, \overline{t}_{ij}]$, $(i,j) \in A$, such that (k,l) (k) is a critical in the usual sense in the network S, after replacing the interval times T_{ij} with the exact values t_{ij}, $T_{ij} := t_{ij}$.

The key theorem for further considerations is Theorem 1 which determines a necessary and sufficient condition of i-criticality of a given path $p \in P$.

Theorem 1. *A path $p \in P$ is i-critical in S if and only if it is critical in the sense of definition 5 in the network S, after replacing the interval times $T_{ij} = [\underline{t}_{ij}, \overline{t}_{ij}]$, $(i, j) \in A$, with the exact values t_{ij} determined by means of the following formula*

$$t_{ij} = \begin{cases} \overline{t}_{ij} \text{ if } (i, j) \in p, \\ \underline{t}_{ij} \text{ if } (i, j) \notin p. \end{cases}$$

Proof. Obvious. The theorem is a direct consequence of Definition 6. □

It follows from Definition 6 and Theorem 1 that the problem of determining an arbitrary i-critical path and that of the estimation of the i-criticality of a fixed path $p \in P$ are easy problems and they can be solved in a time bounded by a polynomial in the size of the network.

In the first case it is enough to apply the CPM method (Sect. 2) to the network S with any fixed values t_{ij} of activity times chosen from the corresponding interval duration times, $t_{ij} \in [\underline{t}_{ij}, \overline{t}_{ij}]$. And in the second one it is sufficient to apply the CPM method to the network S, after replacing the interval times $[\underline{t}_{ij}, \overline{t}_{ij}]$ with the exact values t_{ij} determined as in Theorem 1. However, not all the problems concerning the i-criticality are so easy. Some of them have turned out to be hard ones. In paper [6] we have proved that the problem of estimating the i-criticality of a fixed activity (a fixed event) is NP-complete in the strong sense. We have also shown that the problem of determining K i-critical paths is NP-hard.

4 Criticality in the network with fuzzy activity times – a new approach

Let us define the fuzzy criticality of a path, an activity and an event.

Definition 8. The fuzzy set $\tilde{P}$ in set P with the membership function determined by formula:

$$\mu_{\tilde{P}}(p) = \text{Poss}(p \text{ is critical}) = \sup_{\substack{t_{ij} \in \mathbb{R}^+, (i,j) \in A \\ \text{and } p \text{ is critical with} \\ \text{activities duration} \\ \text{times equal to } t_{ij}}} \min_{(i,j) \in A} \mu_{\tilde{T}_{ij}}(t_{ij}), p \in P$$

is called the fuzzy critical path in S.

We say that a path p is critical to the degree $\mu_{\tilde{P}}(p)$. The value $\mu_{\tilde{P}}(p)$ stands for the path degree of criticality, the possibility of the criticality of path p. In other words, $\mu_{\tilde{P}}$ determines a possibility distribution of the criticality of the path in the set P which is generated by the possibility distributions of activities duration times $\mu_{\tilde{T}_{ij}}$, $(i,j) \in A$ (generated according to the extension principle of Zadeh).

Definition 9. The fuzzy set $\tilde{A}$ (resp. $\tilde{E}$) in set A (V) with the membership function determined by the formula:

$$\mu_{\tilde{A}}(k,l) = \text{Poss}((k,l) \text{ is critical}) = \sup_{\substack{t_{ij} \in \mathbb{R}^+, (i,j) \in A \\ \text{and } (k,l) \text{ is} \\ \text{critical with} \\ \text{activities duration} \\ \text{times equal to } t_{ij}}} \min_{(i,j) \in A} \mu_{\tilde{T}_{ij}}(t_{ij}), \ (k,l) \in A$$

$$(\mu_{\tilde{E}}(k) = \text{Poss}(k \text{ is critical}) = \sup_{\substack{t_{ij} \in \mathbb{R}^+, (i,j) \in A \\ \text{and } k \text{ is critical with} \\ \text{activities duration times} \\ \text{equal to } t_{ij}}} \min_{(i,j) \in A} \mu_{\tilde{T}_{ij}}(t_{ij}), \ k \in V)$$

is called the fuzzy critical activity (event) in S.

In [7], there have been shown relationships between the path degree of criticality and the degrees of the criticality of the activities and the events belonging to the path.

4.1 Determining the path degree of criticality

In this section, we present two effective methods of determining the path degree of criticality. Before we pass on to the essentials we introduce a notion of *feasibility* of a value $\lambda \in (0,1]$ under a path $p \in P$ and then we formulate the theorem which we substantially use in both methods.

Definition 10. The value $\lambda \in (0,1]$ is called feasible under the path $p \in P$ if and only if p is i-critical in the network S with interval activities duration times $T_{ij} = \tilde{T}_{ij}^{\lambda} = [\underline{t}_{ij}^{\lambda}, \overline{t}_{ij}^{\lambda}]$.

Theorem 2. *The following equality holds:* $\mu_{\tilde{P}}(p) = \sup\{\lambda \mid \lambda \text{ is a feasible value under the path } p \in P\}$.

Proof. Obvious. It follows directly from the theorem which asserts that every fuzzy set can be decomposed according to its λ-cuts (see [22]). □

An algorithm for computing the path degree of criticality Now we present an algorithm for computing the path degree of criticality. It is based on the idea of bisection of the unit interval of the possible values of λ and by means of the bisection the maximal feasible value λ under the path p is computed. In this algorithm at each iteration k we test if the value $\lambda_k \in (0,1]$ is feasible under the path p. The testing can be reduced to applying the CPM method to the network S, after replacing times $T_{ij} = \tilde{T}_{ij}^{\lambda_k} = [\underline{t}_{ij}^{\lambda_k}, \overline{t}_{ij}^{\lambda_k}]$, $(i,j) \in A$, with the exact values t_{ij} determined as in Theorem 1.

Algorithm 1

Step 1 *Assign* $k := 0$.
Step 2 *Test if* $\lambda = \epsilon$ *is a feasible value under the path* p. *If it is not then assign* $\lambda_{\max} := 0$ *and go to Step 6.*
Step 3 *Assign* $\lambda_k := 1$ *and test if* λ_k *is a feasible value under the path* p. *If it is then assign* $\lambda_{\max} := 1$ *and go to Step 6.*
Step 4 *Assign* $k := k + 1$,

$$\lambda_k := \begin{cases} \lambda_{k-1} + 1/2^k & \text{if } \lambda_{k-1} \text{ is a feasible value under the path } p, \\ \lambda_{k-1} - 1/2^k & \text{otherwise} \end{cases}$$

Test if λ_k *is a feasible value under the path* p. *If it is then assign* $\lambda_{\max} := \lambda_k$.
Step 5 *If* $k < K$ *then go to Step 4.*
Step 6 *Assign* $\mu_{\tilde{P}}(p) := \lambda_{\max}$, *stop.*

The length K of the generated sequence in Step 4 depends on the assumed accuracy of computation. If we want the absolute error of computation to be not greater than 10^{-N} then K has to fulfill the condition: $K \geq N/\log_{10} 2$. The value of ϵ used in Step 2 should be positive and not greater than the assumed absolute error of computation.

A linear programming approach Now we present another approach to the problem of determining the path degree of criticality showing that, under certain assumptions on the membership functions of fuzzy activities duration times $\tilde{T}_{ij}$, the problem can be reduced to that of determining the optimal solutions of a linear programming problem.

Let us return to the interval case considered in Sect. 3. Testing if path $p \in P$ is i-critical in network S with activity times equal to $T_{ij} = [\underline{t}_{ij}, \overline{t}_{ij}]$ can be reduced to the solution of the following system of linear equalities and inequalities:

$$\begin{aligned} & t_j - t_i - \overline{t}_{ij} = 0, && (i,j) \in p, \\ & t_j - t_i - \underline{t}_{ij} \geq 0, && (i,j) \notin p, \\ & t_1 = 0, && \\ & t_i \geq 0, && (i = 2, \dots, n), \end{aligned} \tag{9}$$

where variables t_i denote the moments of the occurrence of events $i \in V$ in S.

From Theorem 1 it follows that path p is i-critical if and only if the system (9) has a solution. Thus, asserting if $\lambda \in (0, 1]$ is feasible under the path p (in the fuzzy case) can be reduced to testing if the following system of equalities and inequalities has a solution:

$$\begin{aligned} & t_j - t_i - \overline{t}_{ij}^{\lambda} = 0, && (i,j) \in p, \\ & t_j - t_i - \underline{t}_{ij}^{\lambda} \geq 0, && (i,j) \notin p, \\ & t_1 = 0, && \\ & t_i \geq 0, && (i = 2, \dots, n), \end{aligned} \tag{10}$$

where $\underline{t}_{ij}^{\lambda}$ and $\overline{t}_{ij}^{\lambda}$ are the ends of the interval $\tilde{T}_{ij}^{\lambda} = [\underline{t}_{ij}^{\lambda}, \overline{t}_{ij}^{\lambda}]$. Hence, determination of the criticality degree of path $p \in P$, $\mu_{\tilde{P}}(p)$, can be reduced, according to Theorem 2, to the following mathematical programming problem:

$$\begin{array}{ll} \lambda \to \max & \\ t_j - t_i - \overline{t}_{ij}^{\lambda} = 0 & (i,j) \in p \\ t_j - t_i - \underline{t}_{ij}^{\lambda} \geq 0 & (i,j) \notin p \\ t_1 = 0 & \\ t_i \geq 0 & (i = 2, \dots, n), \end{array} \tag{11}$$

where $\lambda \in (0,1]$. If $\lambda_{\max}$ is the optimal objective value of (11) then $\mu_{\tilde{P}}(p) = \lambda_{\max}$. In the general case it may be difficult to find an optimal solution of problem (11).

Let us assume that fuzzy activities duration times $\tilde{T}_{ij}$, $(i,j) \in A$, are given by means of fuzzy numbers of the same $L - L$ type (see [10]), i.e. $\tilde{T}_{ij} = (\underline{t}_{ij}, \overline{t}_{ij}, \alpha_{ij}, \beta_{ij})_{L-L}$. In this case λ-cuts of a fuzzy number $\tilde{T}_{ij}$ have the form $\tilde{T}_{ij}^{\lambda} = [\underline{t}_{ij} - L^{-1}(\lambda)\alpha_{ij}, \overline{t}_{ij} + L^{-1}(\lambda)\beta_{ij}]$ and the problem (11) reduces itself to the following linear programming problem:

$$\begin{array}{ll} \Theta \to \min & \\ t_j - t_i - \overline{t}_{ij} - \beta_{ij}\Theta = 0 & (i,j) \in p \\ t_j - t_i - \underline{t}_{ij} + \alpha_{ij}\Theta \geq 0 & (i,j) \notin p \\ t_1 = 0 & \\ t_i \geq 0 & (i = 2, \dots, n), \end{array} \tag{12}$$

where $\Theta \in [\underline{\Theta}, \overline{\Theta})$, $\Theta = L^{-1}(\lambda)$, $\underline{\Theta} = L^{-1}(1)$, $\overline{\Theta} = L^{-1}(0)$. If $\Theta_{\min}$ is the optimal objective value of (12) then the path degree of criticality, $\mu_{\tilde{P}}(p)$, is equal to $L(\theta_{\min})$.

Examples Let us illustrate the utility of the methods of computing the path degrees of criticality with simple numerical examples.

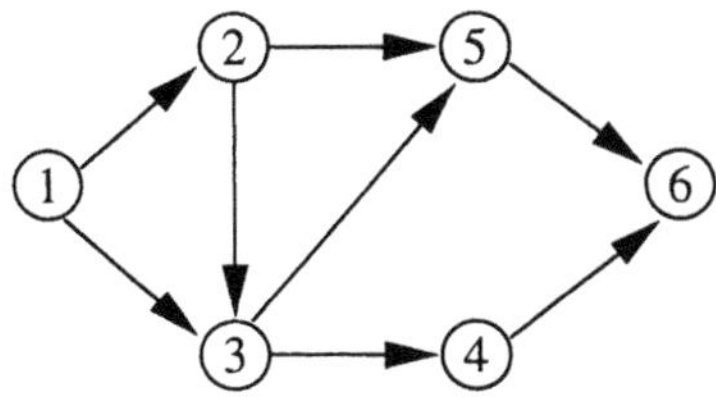

Fig. 1. The structure of the project in Examples 1, 2

Example 1. The network representing the project structure is given in Fig. 1. The activities duration times are fuzzy numbers of $L_{ij} - L_{ij}$ type. $\tilde{T}_{12} =$

$(3,4,2,2)_{L_{12}-L_{12}}$, $\tilde{T}_{13} = (6,6,2,4)_{L_{13}-L_{13}}$, $\tilde{T}_{23} = (3.5,4,2,0)_{L_{23}-L_{23}}$, $\tilde{T}_{25} = (4,5,0,2)_{L_{25}-L_{25}}$, $\tilde{T}_{35} = (7,7,2,2)_{L_{35}-L_{35}}$, $\tilde{T}_{34} = (3,3,2,4)_{L_{34}-L_{34}}$, $\tilde{T}_{46} = (5,5,2,2)_{L_{46}-L_{46}}$, $\tilde{T}_{56} = (6,6,0,0)_{L_{56}-L_{56}}$, $L_{12}(x) = L_{34}(x) = L_{35}(x) = \max(1-x^2,0)$, $L_{13}(x) = \max(0,1-x^4)$, $L_{23}(x) = L_{46}(x) = \max(0,1-x)$, $L_{25}(x) = \mathrm{e}^{-x^2}$ ($L_{25}^{-1}(y) = \sqrt{-\ln y}$, $y \in [0,1]$ we assume that $-\ln 0 = \infty$), $L_{56}(x) = \mathrm{e}^{-x}$.

By applying Algorithm 1, we have obtained the results which are listed in Table 1. The path degrees of criticality have been computed with accuracy 10^{-4}.

Table 1. The path degrees of criticality in Example 1

$p \in P$	$\mu_{\tilde{P}}(p)$
1-2-5-6	0.2867
1-2-3-5-6	1
1-2-3-4-6	0.5870
1-3-5-6	0.9998
1-3-4-6	0.5870

Example 2. The network representing the project structure of is given in Fig. 1. The activities duration times are fuzzy numbers of the same $L-L$ type, where $L(x) = \max(0, 1-x^2)$: $\tilde{T}_{12} = (3,4,2,2)_{L-L}$, $\tilde{T}_{13} = (6,6,2,4)_{L-L}$, $\tilde{T}_{23} = (3.5,4,2,0)_{L-L}$, $\tilde{T}_{25} = (4,5,0,2)_{L-L}$, $\tilde{T}_{35} = (7,7,2,2)_{L-L}$, $\tilde{T}_{34} = (3,3,2,4)_{L-L}$, $\tilde{T}_{46} = (5,5,2,2)_{L-L}$, $\tilde{T}_{56} = (6,6,0,0)_{L-L}$.

In this case we have determined the degree of criticality by solving for each paths $p \in P$ the linear programming problem (12). The results are listed in Table 2.

Table 2. The path degrees of criticality in Example 2

$p \in P$	$\mu_{\tilde{P}}(p)$	$\Theta_{\min}$
1-2-5-6	0.1597	0.9167
1-2-3-5-6	1	0
1-2-3-4-6	0.6093	0.625
1-3-5-6	0.9961	0.0625
1-3-4-6	0.6093	0.625

5 Summary

In the first part of the paper we have reviewed the results obtained in the area of fuzzy network analysis. We have described and classified the main approaches to the concept of criticality in a network with fuzzy activity times presented so far in the literature. Against the background of this review we have presented, in the second part of the paper, some new results concerning fuzzy network analysis. We have given a natural generalization of the notion of criticality to the case of a network with interval duration times of the activities, by introducing the notion of i-critical path, activity and event. We have shown that both the problem of determining an arbitrary i-critical path and that of the estimation of the i-criticality of a fixed path are easy problems. We have also presented another natural approach to the generalization of the criticality notion for the case of a network with fuzzy activities duration times. This generalization is done directly without using generalized arithmetic operations on fuzzy numbers. Due to a direct application of the extension principle of Zadeh to the classical criticality notion treated as a function of activity duration times this approach to the criticality concept is devoid of faults which are characteristic for the definitions of fuzzy criticality proposed in the literature till now. We have proposed two efficient methods of computing the path degree of criticality. There is no such method for calculating the criticality degree of an activity (an event). This problem is NP-hard since it includes, as a particular case, the problem of asserting the i-criticality of a fixed activity (a fixed event) in a network with interval activity times which is, as shown in [6], NP-complete in the strong sense.

Acknowledgments This work was supported by grant no. 7T11F02120 from the State Committee for Scientific Research (Komitet Badań Naukowych).

References

1. J. Buckley. Fuzzy PERT. In G. W. Evans, W. Karwowski, and M. R. Wilhelm, editors, *Applications of Fuzzy Set Methodologies in Industrial Engineering*, pages 103–114. Elsevier Science Publishers, Amsterdam-Oxford-New York-Tokyo, 1989.
2. S. Chanas. Fuzzy sets in few classical operational research problems. In M. M. Gupta and E. Sanchez, editors, *Approximate Reasoning in Decision Analysis*, pages 351–363. North-Holland Publishing Company, 1982.
3. S. Chanas. Fuzzy optimization in networks. In J. Kacprzyk and S. A. Orlovski, editors, *Optimization Models Using Fuzzy Sets and Possibility Theory*, pages 303–327. D. Reidel Publishing Company, Dordrecht Boston Lancaster Tokyo, 1987.
4. S. Chanas and J. Kamburowski. The use of fuzzy variables in PERT. *Fuzzy Set and Systems*, 5:11–19, 1981.
5. S. Chanas and E. Radosiński. A model of activity performance time in the light of fuzzy sets theory. *Problemy Organizacji*, 2:68–76, 1976. In Polish.
6. S. Chanas and P. Zieliński. The computational complexity of the criticality problems in a network with interval activity times. *European Journal of Operational Research*. To appear.

7. S. Chanas and P. Zieliński. Critical path analysis in the network with fuzzy activity times. *Fuzzy Sets and Systems.* To appear.
8. S. Chanas and P. Zieliński. Criticality in the Network with Imprecise Activity Times. In *Proceedings of 8-th International Conference IPMU*, pages 1233–1238, Madrid Spain, July 3-7 2000.
9. I. S. Chang, Y. Tsujimura, M. Gen, and T. Tozawa. An efficient approach for large scale project planning based on fuzzy Delphi method. *Fuzzy Sets and Systems*, 76:277–288, 1995.
10. D. Dubois and H. Prade. Operations on fuzzy numbers. *Int. J. Systems Sci.*, 30:613–626, 1978.
11. D. Dubois and H. Prade. Algorithmes de plus courts chemins pour traiter des donnees floues. *RAIRO-Recherche Opérationnelle/Operations Research*, 2(12):213–227, 1978.
12. I. Gazdik. Fuzzy network planning - FNET. *IEEE Transactions on Reliability*, R-32(3):304–313, 1983.
13. J. Kamburowski. Fuzzy activity duration times in critical path analyzes. In *Inter. Symp. on Project Management*, pages 194–199, New Delhi, November 30 - December 2 1983.
14. J. E. Kelley. Critical path planning and scheduling - Mathematical basis. *Operations Research*, 9:296–320, 1961.
15. F. A. Loostma. Stochastic and fuzzy PERT. *European Journal of Operational Research*, 43:174–183, 1989.
16. D. G. Malcolm, J. H. Roseboom, C. E Clark, and W. Fazar. Application of a technique for research and development project evaluation. *Operations Research*, 7:646–669, 1959.
17. M. Mareš. Some Remarks to Fuzzy Critical Path Method. *Ekonomicko-matematický obzor*, 27(4):367–370, 1991.
18. K. Mačák. On Fuzzy Critical Path Method. *Ekonomicko-matematický obzor*, 27(4):357–366, 1991.
19. C. S. McCahon. Using PERT as an Approximation of Fuzzy Project-Network Analysis. *IEEE Transactions on Engineering Management*, 40(2):146–153, 1993.
20. D. L. Mon, C. H. Cheng, and H. C. Lu. Application of fuzzy distributions on project management. *Fuzzy Sets and Systems*, 73:227–234, 1995.
21. S. H. Nasution. Fuzzy Critical Path Method. *IEEE Transactions on Systems, Man, and Cybernetics*, 24(1):48–57, 1994.
22. C. V. Negoită and D. A. Ralescu. *Applications of Fuzzy Sets to Systems Analysis.* Birkhäuser Verlag, Basel und Stuttgart, 1975.
23. H. Prade. Using fuzzy set theory in a scheduling problem: a case study. *Fuzzy Set and Systems*, 2:153–165, 1979.
24. H. J. Rommelfanger. Network analysis and information flow in fuzzy environment. *Fuzzy Sets and Systems*, 67:119–128, 1994.
25. A. I. Slyeptsov and T. A. Tyshchuk. Fuzzy critical path method for project network planning and control. *Cybernetics and System Analysis*, 3:158–170, 1999.
26. R. R. Yager. A procedure for ordering fuzzy subsets of the unit interval. *Information Sciences*, 24:143–161, 1981.
27. J. S. Yao and F. T. Lin. Fuzzy Critical Path Method Based on Signed Distance Ranking of Fuzzy Numbers. *IEEE Transactions on Systems, Man, and Cybernetics–Part A: Systems and Humans*, 30(1):76–82, 2000.

Object-Oriented Implementation of a Model for Fuzzy Temporal Reasoning

Slobodan Ribarić, Bojana Dalbelo-Bašić, Dražen Tomac*

Faculty of Electrical Engineering and Computing, University of Zagreb, Unska 3, 10000 Zagreb, Croatia,
E-mail: slobodan.ribaric@fer.hr, bojana.dalbelo@fer.hr
*Bell & Bandack SA, Route de la Conversion 271, 1093 La Conversion, Switzerland, E-mail: drazen@bellandbandack.com

Abstract. A program object-oriented implementation of a new formal model for fuzzy temporal knowledge representation and reasoning in temporally rich domains is described in the paper. The model is based on the modification of the Petri Nets, called the Petri Nets with Fuzzy Time Tokens (PNFTT). It is suitable for knowledge bases design in intelligent systems that deal with vague, human-like linguistic expressions.

1. Introduction

Intelligent systems used in temporally rich domains, i.e. domains that include concurrent actions that take time, simultaneous occurrence of many actions at once and domains with external events [1], require kind of knowledge that is time dependent. Human knowledge about time, which has to be implemented in intelligent systems, is usually pervaded with uncertainty and vagueness. Different formal models are proposed as a solution to the effective fuzzy temporal knowledge representation and reasoning: K. Khan and G. A. Gorry in their model, called time specialist [2], gave a clue of using vague terms for time specifications (e.g. "several days", "few weeks", "nearly a month"). Qian's model [3] and Fuzzy Temporal Constraint Satisfaction Network proposed by Barro *et al.* [4] are formal models which are based on Zadeh's fuzzy set theory [5], the possibility theory [6] and concepts of processing fuzzy temporal knowledge proposed by Dubois and Prade [7].

Our model for processing fuzzy temporal knowledge and reasoning is based on the originally defined Petri Nets with Fuzzy Time Tokens (PNFTT) [8]. Different approaches to time fuzzification in Petri Nets are given in papers [9] - [13]. Most of the above referenced models are primary intended for modelling dynamic discrete event system such as: analysing and monitoring manufacturing systems, performance evaluation, distributed real time systems specification and design, communications protocol verification, *etc*. Our Petri Net based model is designated for knowledge representation and reasoning about temporal relations which are expressed in natural language terms. It is also suitable for implementation in intelligent systems that deal with vague linguistic expressions and human like reasoning.

The paper is organized as follows. In Section 2, we give formal definition of the PNFTT and introduce Fuzzy Temporal Knowledge Representation Scheme. Then, in Section 3, the program object-oriented implementation of the Fuzzy Temporal Knowledge Representation Scheme is described. Section 4 provides the program description. An example of the use of proposed model for designing a knowledge base, as well as reasoning, is given in the Section 5.

2. Knowledge Representation Scheme Based on PNFTT

2. 1. Petri Net with Fuzzy Time Tokens

The Petri Net with Fuzzy Time Tokens (PNFTT) is 8-tuple PNFTT = (P, T, I, O, m, τ, λ, θ) where [8]:

P, T, I, O are components of ordinary Petri Nets [14], [15]. $P = \{p_1, p_2,\ldots,p_n\}$ is a finite set of places, $T = \{t_1,t_2,\ldots,t_m\}$ is a finite set of transitions, $P \cap T = \varnothing$. In general, $I : T \rightarrow P^{\infty}$ is an input function, a mapping from a set of transitions to bags of places. $O : T \rightarrow P^{\infty}$ is an output function, a mapping from a set of transitions to bags of places. For an ordinary Petri net there is a restriction: $\#(p_i, I(t_j)) \leq 1$ and $\#(p_i, O(t_j)) \leq 1$ for all $p_i \in P$ and $t_j \in T$, where # denotes the number of occurrences of p_i in $I(t_j)$, or p_i in $O(t_j)$, respectively.

m – marking function, $m : P \rightarrow [(\Im(TS) \cup \varnothing) \times (\Im(TS) \cup \varnothing)]$, where *TS* denotes a time scale. *TS* can be any linearly ordered set (e.g. R^+, Z^+). $\Im(TS)$ denotes a set of all normalized and convex possibility distributions [16] defined on *TS*. $m(p_i) = m_i$ is called a *fuzzy time token.* If $m(p_i) = \varnothing$ then place $p_i \in P$ is without a fuzzy time token. For all other places function m assigns to each place a ordered pair: $m(p_i) = m_i = (\pi_{b(i)}, \varnothing)$ or $(\varnothing, \pi_{e(i)})$ or $(\pi_{b(i)}, \pi_{e(i)})$, $i = 1,2,\ldots,n$. Possibility distributions π_b and π_e represent *beginning* and *end,* respectively, of some action, state or event [6], [7].

Function $\tau : P \rightarrow \Im(TS) \cup \varnothing$ defines the time of fuzzy time token detainment in the places. $\tau(p_i) = \tau_i$.

Function λ is a mapping from a set of transitions T to a set of fuzzy operations $\{\oplus\kappa, (-)\kappa, \underline{\min}, \underline{\max}, [\ ], \equiv, \ldots\}$, where κ is a fuzzy number [16] and $\oplus\kappa$, $(-)\kappa$, $\underline{\min}$, $\underline{\max}$, $[\ ]$ and $\equiv$ are fuzzy operations addition, subtraction, minimum, maximum, convex closure and identity of fuzzy numbers, respectively; $\lambda(t_j) = \lambda_j$. Operations are defined on the fuzzy time token and they modify the possibility distributions π_b, π_e or both.

Function $\theta : [\Im(TS) \times \varnothing)] \times \Im(TS) \rightarrow \Im(TS) \times \Im(TS)$ defines the effects of fuzzy time token detainment in a place. Token $m_i = (\pi_{b(i)}, \varnothing)$ is transformed by using function θ in $(\pi_{b(i)}, \pi_{e(i)})$, where $\pi_{e(i)} = \pi_{b(i)} \oplus \tau_i$.

Marking function m defines the state of the PNFTT, i.e. the distribution of fuzzy time tokens in places. The state of the PNFTT can be described by vector **m**, where i^{th} component of the vector is a fuzzy time token in place p_i. The initial state is denoted by $\mathbf{m}^{(0)}$.

Generally, fuzzy time tokens give to the PNFTT dynamic properties and they are used to define the execution of the PNFTT. Also, tokens have individuality and they carry information about the beginning of the interval (defined by the possibility distribution π_b), or the end of interval (π_e), or both (π_b, π_e). The pair (π_b, π_e) is the base for defining fuzzy time interval [7], [21].

The execution of the PNFTT is based on firing an enabled transition. In the PNFTT, a *transition is enabled* if each of its input places has a fuzzy time token *and* if time τ_i of token detainment in places p_i has elapsed, i.e. the transformation of the fuzzy time token from ($\pi_{b(i)}$, $\varnothing$) to ($\pi_{b(i)}$, $\pi_{e(i)}$), defined by function θ, is carried out. Such tokens are called "movable" fuzzy time tokens. By firing an enabled transition t_j, tokens are removed from its input places (elements in $I(t_j)$) and simultaneously new tokens are created and distributed to its output places (elements in $O(t_j)$).

The firing of an enabled transition in the PNFTT is performed *automatically* and *immediately* after the transition is enabled. However, the firing of enabled transition changes the information of the corresponding fuzzy time token according to the operation λ_j assigned to an enabled transition t_j. The execution of the PNFTT changes the initial state $\mathbf{m}^{(0)}$ to the next states $\mathbf{m}^{(1)},...,\mathbf{m}^{(k)}$.

New tokens in all output places with index z = 1, 2, ..., *l*, where *l* is the number of output places of the transition t_j, have a new possibility distribution defined by $\pi_b(z)=\lambda_j((\pi_b(1), \pi_e(1)), \ldots, (\pi_b(k), \pi_e(k)))$, where k is the number of input places of the transition t_j. In our model, the outcome of the fuzzy operation λ_j must have a form of convex and normalized possibility distribution [16] so that the process of firing a transition and thus performing the next fuzzy operation λ_j can proceed. If the outcome is not normalized i.e. height(π_b) < 1 then normalized possibility distribution π_b' is obtained $\pi_b'(t) = \pi_b(t)(1/\text{height}(\pi_b(t)))$, $\forall t \in TS$. The height π_b can be interpreted as certainty factor of the corresponding event or state [7].

The PNFTT can be represented by a bipartite directed graph. Graphically, places are represented by circles, transitions by bars and fuzzy time tokens by dots (•) in the places. Figure 1 illustrates the firing of an enabled transition.

In the proposed model, states known as conflict [14] and potential conflict in the classic Petri net theory are solved by multiplication of the fuzzy time token, so that the number of tokens in the places is equal to the number of directed arcs from that place to transitions.

2.2. Fuzzy Temporal Knowledge Representation Scheme

The Petri Net with Fuzzy Time Tokens is used as a main building block of the Fuzzy Temporal Knowledge Representation Scheme (FTKR). The scheme is defined as follows: FTKR = (PNFTT, FTLM, α, β, F), where PNFTT is a Petri Net with Fuzzy Time Tokens, FTLM is a Fuzzy Temporal Logical Module based on Allen's temporal logic [17] but extended on the fuzzy intervals [7].

Bijective function $\alpha : P \rightarrow C$, where C is set of states, actions or events. Surjective function $\beta : T \rightarrow \Sigma$, where Σ is a set of fuzzy temporal relations between states, actions or events. Both α and β give a semantic interpretation of the PNFTT.

F is a set of flags. A flag $f_i \in F$ represents the form of a query posed on the knowledge base designed by FTKR. Flags determine places from which fuzzy time tokens will be sent to the FTLM in order to evaluate fuzzy temporal relations *ftr*. Flags are represented by symbol |▸ in the graphical representation of the knowledge base. For example, a flag $f_i = (p_i, p_j, ftr)$ defines a query based on fuzzy time tokens in places p_i and p_j, and *ftr* specifies a fuzzy temporal relation (e.g. "much before"). The FTLM evaluates *ftr* relation and returns a value represented by a number from interval [0,1]. This number is a possibility measure which defines the degree of satisfaction of *ftr* relation between concepts assigned to places p_i and p_j.

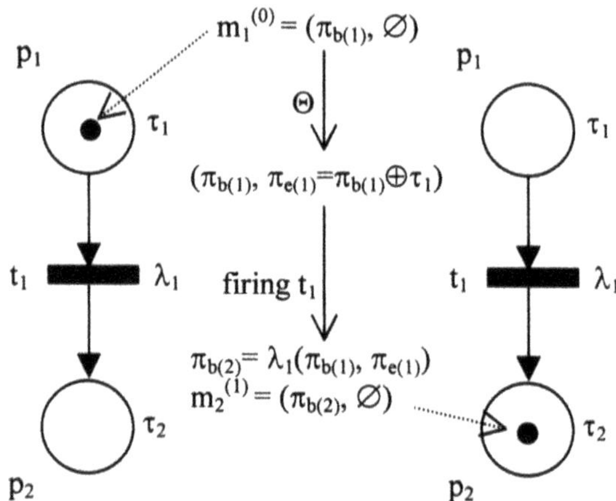

Figure 1. a) Before firing an enabled transition t_1
b) After firing an enabled transition t_1.

The reasoning process in the FTKR can be described as follows. The input is the initial marking of FTKR representation of the world. It determines current activities or states and initial fuzzy temporal relations among the activities or states. As soon as fuzzy time tokens became movable, the enabled transitions are automatically fired and tokens are moved through the net of the FTKR.

Depending on the path through the graph and fuzzy time duration of some activities (states), fuzzy time tokens carry information which is the result of the execution of the graph. This fuzzy time information is represented by possibility distributions. Owing to flags f_i, $i = 1, 2, 3,\dots$ the evaluation of the fuzzy temporal relations is enabled and performed by the FTLM during the execution process.

The above combination of the execution of the PNFTT and the evaluation of fuzzy temporal relations enables performing of different temporal reasoning tasks (e.g. determining the consistency of collections of intervals, finding a consistent scenario, deducing new relations).

For example, a new relation can be deduced by using flag $f_i = (p_i, p_j, ?)$ which specifies that fuzzy time tokens from places p_i and p_j (which correspond to concepts) have to be sent to the Fuzzy Temporal Logical Module (FTLM) for determining fuzzy temporal relations between the concepts (associated to p_i and p_j) and measures of their satisfaction.

3. Program Object-Oriented Implementation of Fuzzy Temporal Knowledge Representation Scheme

Object-oriented design includes the following elements [18]: abstraction into classes and objects, encapsulation, modularity, and inheritance with polymorphism. A Petri net structure is built from well-defined elements, with proper relationships, therefore, abstraction of these elements into classes is easy and straightforward. Behaviour and data of these elements, represented with methods and properties, are encapsulated in implementation of their classes. These classes represent building blocks for a class of Petri net, and can be bundled together in one module with only a Petri net class visible. Building a new type of Petri net involves adding or modifying some functions of underlying net, like adding a time component, or modifying a firing rule. Obviously, there exists hierarchy between nets, because new type is derived from old, inheriting most of its structure and behavior, and changing relevant parts. Although changes can be significant, public functions can be used in a unique way, regardless of net type, due to a polymorphism.

This program implementation uses C++ language to build an object-oriented model of a Petri net. There are four main classes implemented in a Petri net module: *token, place, transition* and *net.*

A *token class* is very important, because in a high-level Petri nets [22], such as the PNFTT, a token gives to the net dynamical properties and carries structured information. Because of it, a token class is only a wrapper class for a *token value* class, which can be a single integer, for a Petri net or fuzzy interval class in the PNFTT. Functions (e.g. comparison, assignment, index) with token data are encapsulated in its class, with unique names, so that other classes (place, transition and net) using them do not have to know anything about their implementation.

The basic property of a *place class* is a set of tokens, implemented with a parameterized set class with a token class as the parameter. Unique notation and description used in the knowledge scheme are other important properties of this class. Methods mostly include functions for token manipulation and setting properties.

Properties of a *transition class* include input and output sets of places, notation and description. In terms of methods, a transition class is a bit richer, because, besides manipulation of input and output sets and other properties, involves fundamental action of a Petri net – firing a transition. *Firing function* removes tokens from input places, and depending on the firing rule puts tokens into output places. It also checks additional parameters and optionally informs the user about the action performed.

Sets of places and tokens, implemented as fixed length arrays of place and transition classes, are main properties of a Petri net class. The static structure of a net is defined through input and output sets of transitions. For easier execution of a net a marking class is introduced. Its main property is a set of token sets associated with places. Methods include operators between markings: comparison, assignment and index. To ensure proper execution of a net without repeated markings, a net class includes a set of markings property. Additional properties include knowledge base parameters, boundaries, and output data. Methods provide the means for building the structure, executing a net and getting answers from a knowledge base. Input parameters for entry function define static structure and the knowledge base. A net can be executed continuously or step by step. In first case, a net is executed as long as there are enabled transitions and marking is not repeated, and in former case firing of a next transition is directed by the user. Additional functions check whether a marking is repeated or if there is a conflict, get the next enabled transition if there are any.

The above object-oriented model properly describes a general Petri net [14] and can be used in combination with the knowledge representation scheme based on Petri Net [19] to support "classic" inheritance and recognition procedures.

For the PNFTT, the structure of classes remains mostly intact. However, a new class has to be added for the PNFTT: a *fuzzy interval class*. A fuzzy interval class can be reached through a token value class due to polymorphism. The delay of a token, as additional property of a place class, is implemented as a fuzzy interval class. Similar happens to a transition class - a fuzzy interval class property is a parameter of the fuzzy operation associated with a transition. It is important that these operations are implemented in a fuzzy interval class, independent of a transition class.

A *net class* adds functions for temporal boundary, setting query parameters to the knowledge base implemented by the PNFTT, as well as getting answers from it.

Reasoning about temporal relations between fuzzy intervals is implemented in *fuzzy temporal logic module*. Functions defined in this module give linguistic as well as numeric values of relation between input fuzzy intervals according to modified Allen's interval logic [17].

4. Program Description

Based on above described Fuzzy Temporal Knowledge Scheme and underlying PNFTT, the program provides the means for describing situations from temporally rich domains and designing temporal knowledge base as well as temporal reasoning. The program gives the user an opportunity to describe a situation without the knowledge of Petri nets, only by entering concepts, temporal and other data associated with concepts, and then by entering relationships between these concepts thus generating corresponding knowledge base. Using entered information and the PNFTT primitives for modelling temporal linguistic expressions [8] the program generates the PNFTT and a knowledge base ready for reasoning. Besides, the program automatically generates a graphical representation of a knowledge base (in a form of a Petri net graph), which a user familiar with Petri nets can modify directly, or even graphically create a new net from scratch. Regardless of the way used to create a knowledge base, it is equally ready for queries about temporal relationships, or analysis of its behavior.

Table 1. Concept relationships and associated fuzzy operations

Relationship	**Fuzzy operation**
As soon as (Meets)	Identity; e.g. $\pi_{b(i+1)} \equiv \pi_{e(i)}$
κ units before-after	Addition; e.g. $\pi_{b(i+1)} = \pi_{e(i)} \oplus \kappa$
During	Creating of an interval [21]
Between possible beginnings and ends	Creating of an interval [7]
As soon as last begins	Maximum of beginnings; $\pi_{b(i+1)} = \underline{\max}(\pi_{b(i)}, \pi_{b(i-1)}, \ldots, \pi_{b(i-k)})$
As soon as first begins	Minimum of beginnings; $\pi_{b(i+1)} = \underline{\min}(\pi_{b(i)}, \pi_{b(i-1)}, \ldots, \pi_{b(i-k)})$
As soon as last finishes	Maximum of ends; $\pi_{b(i+1)} = \underline{\max}(\pi_{e(i)}, \pi_{e(i-1)}, \ldots, \pi_{e(i-k)})$
As soon as first begins	Minimum of ends; $\pi_{b(i+1)} = \underline{\min}(\pi_{e(i)}, \pi_{e(i-1)}, \ldots, \pi_{e(i-k)})$
At the same time	Intersection

The program is developed in a C++ environment for Windows 95/98 and Windows NT platforms. It has an open architecture and uses a highly user-friendly graphical interface. The main window of this program is shown in Figure 3. It consists of drop-down menus and a toolbar in the upper part for invoking functions. The left part shows all available data about a net and its main parts: places and transitions. The right panel is dedicated to the graphical presentation of temporal intervals associated with tokens before and after firing a transition. The lower part displays all available data about a transition being fired in textual format. The status bar, at the bottom of the window, displays some important data about the last fired transition: number and description of the transition and markings before and after firing.

A user can describe a situation in the following manner. First, the list of concepts is formed by entering the concepts through a simple window that is activated by pressing a corresponding button in a toolbar. By selecting the desired concept, a window is opened for entering data associated with the concept: description, temporal data in tokens and delay. Temporal data can be defined using temporal linguistic variables or it can be user-defined in the form of the trapezoidal fuzzy number. Predefined values of the temporal linguistic variables are *absolutely, exactly, almost exactly, approximately, about, around, before, after, between*. Possibility linguistic variable [20] is used for determining the possibility levels of situation, it includes values: *absolute, extreme, high, considerable, moderate, more-or-less, minor and no possibility*. The program automatically generates places, and tokens in the Petri net according to the initial marking.

The next step is entering relationships between these concepts. The program provides several predefined temporal relations, in terms of linguistic expressions, based on the PNFTT primitives [8] and fuzzy operations described in Table 1.

The user simply chooses a relationship, then one or more input concepts and one or more output concepts (depending on the operation) and adds it to the list of relationships. Behind this simple operation, the program generates transitions, assigns a fuzzy operation to them (according to the selected relationship), creates and fills input and output sets of places, and generates a Petri net graph. After all the relationships have been entered, the net is complete and ready for execution.

A user can execute a net in two ways. The first, more obvious, by making queries to a knowledge base. Queries available to the user are: temporal relationship, according to modified Allen's interval logic [17], between two concepts or between a concept and defined interval, time of desired concept with graphical and lexical representation of temporal information; and situation in a defined interval with threshold of possibility. First two queries give possibilities and relationships, in lexical format, between temporal intervals of concepts or defined ones, answering e.g. *"Can Concept 1 occur before 7 am?", or "What is the possibility that Concept 1 starts at the same time as Concept 2?"*. The third query describes temporal intervals of the concept of interest, giving an answer to the question "*When can Concept 1 happen*?". The last and the most complex query gives possibilities of all concepts in a defined interval, if they are higher than the defined possibility threshold. In this case the question can be "*What can happen after 8, with at least moderate possibility*?".

Another way of executing a net is step-by-step, in which the control is returned to the user after each transition is fired. This way, the user can see the behavior and execution of the PNFTT, explore a marking before and after firing transitions, see the graphical and linguistic presentation of the temporal information in tokens, and thus generate a space of events. Along with a part for changing and generating an PNFTT graph, this mechanism makes this program not only a temporal reasoning system for ordinary users, but a good educational tool for learning and exploring Petri nets and the knowledge representation scheme based on it.

Other program options include customization of lexical variables, setting temporal boundary for execution, definition of conversion parameters between a fuzzy and a crisp interval and file manipulation.

5. An Example

The following example will show the main elements of the program and explain basic usage: describing a situation and making queries about it, and give a proper set of results. The knowledge base is built on the following story:

Fred, John and Mark have a meeting as soon as all arrive to work. Fred leaves home about 7 o'clock. He goes by car and arrives to work about 20 minutes later. John comes to work a few minutes earlier than Fred. Mark leaves the house approximately at the same time as Fred. He takes a bus. It takes the bus about 20 minutes to the bus station nearest to Mark's work. It takes him few more minutes to get to work. As soon as Mark comes to work, he wakes his wife Jane by the phone, and goes to the meeting. Jane needs about 50 minutes to prepare and come to the mole by taxi. There she waits for Mark at most 20 minutes. Mark's meeting lasts almost exactly 90 minutes. As soon it ends, Mark is driving to meet Jane. It takes him approximately 10 minutes to the mole.

Table 2. Concepts and corresponding temporal data

Concept; $\alpha(p_i)$	**Place; p_i**	**Delay/Durations; τ_i**
Fred's leaving home	p_1	0
Fred's coming to work	p_2	0
Mark's in the bus	p_3	About 20 minutes (15, 20, 25)
Mark's arriving to work	p_4	0
John's arriving to work	p_5	0
Meeting	p_6	Almost exactly 90 minutes (87.5, 90, 92.5)
Mark calls his wife Jane	p_7	Few minutes (0, 5, 10)
Jane's preparing	p_8	About 50 minutes (40, 50, 60)
Jane waits	p_9	At most 20 minutes (0, 0, 20, 25)
Mark's driving to the mole	p_{10}	Approximately 10 minutes (7.5, 10, 12.5)

Here are some examples of the questions that can be put on the knowledge base: *What are the possible starting times of the meeting,?*

Will Mark and Jane meet at the mole?

What can happen at around 8.30 with at least moderate possibility?

The knowledge scheme is made by defining concepts, corresponding places, and their durations/delays (Table 2), which are easily entered in the program. Note, that in our program implementation the possibility distributions for fuzzy time concepts are in the form of trapeziodal or triangular fuzzy numbers [16].

The initial marking is defined as follows: the fuzzy time token m_1 = ((6.55, 7.00, 7.05), $\varnothing$) is placed in place p_1, where the triangular fuzzy number (6.55, 7.00, 7.05) describes the concept "about 7 o'clock".

Relationships between concepts and associated temporal data are given in Table 3. After entering data the program automatically generates the graph shown in Figure 2. Operations that correspond to the relations from Table 3 are given in the Table 1.

The answer to the first question above can be obtained in both manners:

- *Executing the net step-by-step* we can determine the possible starting time of the meeting. Figure 3 shows the result of firing transition t_6 that puts token in the place that represents the concept "meeting begins". The fuzzy interval of the output token (7.05, 7.30, 8.00) can be described as "Around 7.30" with absolute possibility.

- The same result we get with the *query about time* of the concept "meeting begins" that executes the net continuously.

Table 3. Relationships between concepts

t_i	$I(t_i)$	$O(t_i)$	Relation; $\beta(t_i)$	Data, fuzzy number κ
t_1	p_1	p_2	Later (after)	About 20 minutes (15, 20, 25)
t_2	p_1	p_3	Approximately at the same time (equals)	(-5, 0, 5)
t_3	p_3	p_4	Later (after)	Few minutes (0, 5, 10)
t_4	p_2	p_5	Earlier (before)	Few minutes (-10, -5, 0)
t_5	p_4	p_7	As soon as (meets)	
t_6	p_2, p_5, p_7	p_6	As soon as last	
t_7	p_7	p_8	As soon as (meets)	
t_8	p_8	p_9	As soon as (meets)	
t_9	p_6	p_{10}	As soon as (meets)	

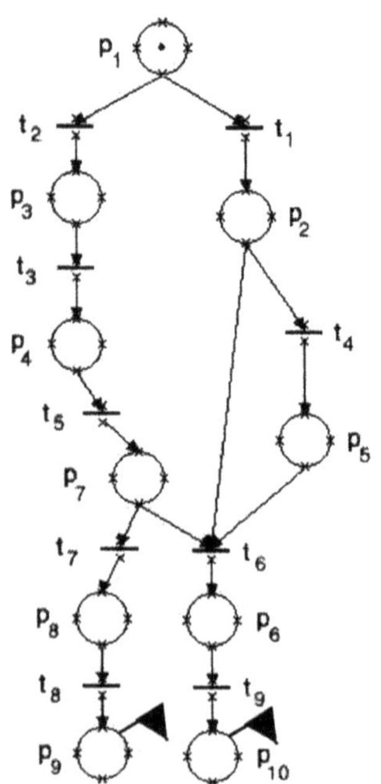

Figure 2. Automatically generated graphical representation of the knowledge base for the example.

Relationship between concepts "Jane waits" and "Mark's driving to the mole" gives the answer to the second question. From the Figure 4 it is clear that these two concepts intersect, and we conclude that there is moderate possibility that they will meet.

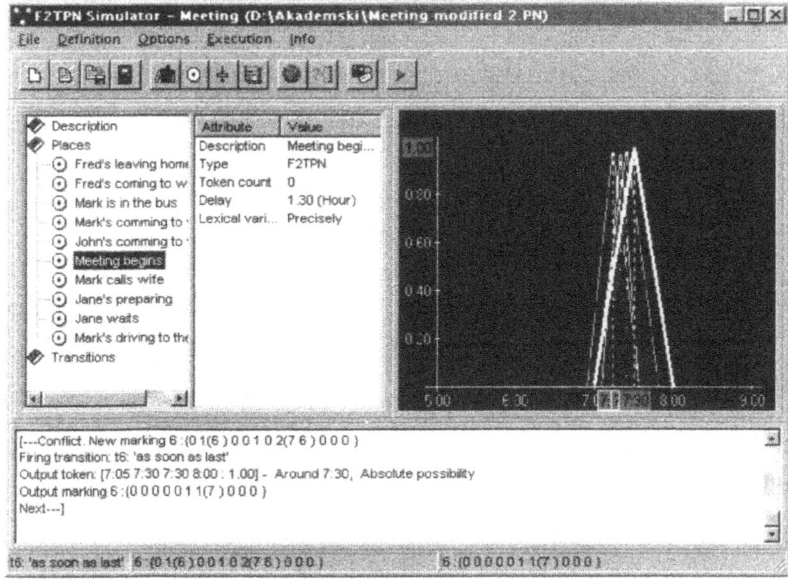

Figure 3. Main program window

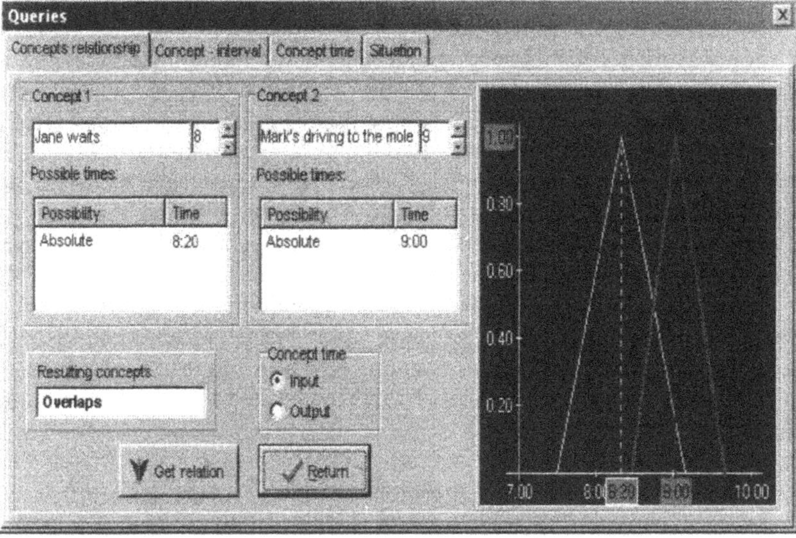

Figure 4. Query about relationship between concepts

To find an answer to the third question we make a *query about situation* at around 8.30 and set the minimal possibility to moderate. The result is given in Figure 5.

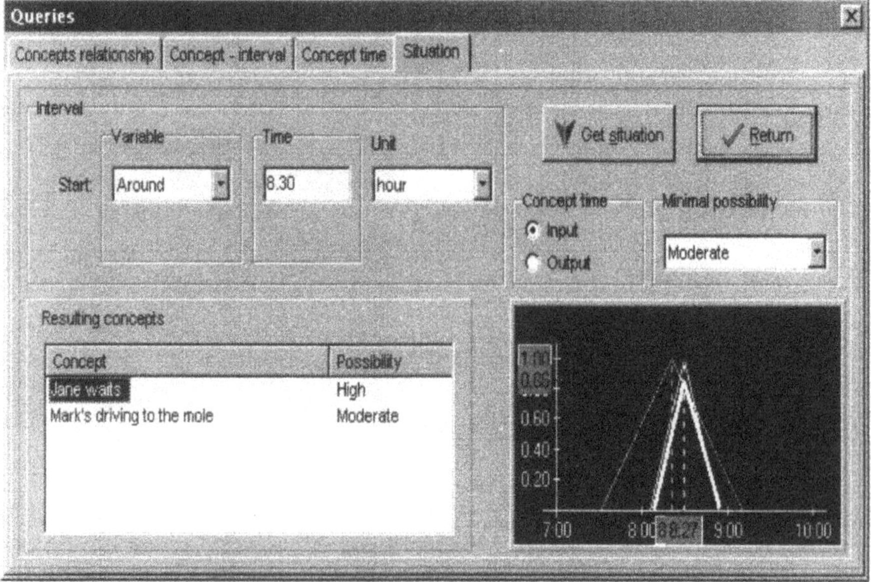

Figure 5. "Around 8.30"situation query

6. Conclusion

The proposed model for fuzzy temporal knowledge representation and reasoning based on the Petri Nets with Fuzzy Time Tokens is used to design knowledge bases with vague, fuzzy temporal, human-like linguistic expressions. The model effectively integrates temporal and fuzzy temporal information and metric, as well as fuzzy interval-based temporal logic. The major advantages of the model are: unified representation of different (fuzzy) temporal information, well defined methods for building temporal knowledge bases, analysing temporal relations among concepts, determining the consistency of the scenario and planning. The implementation of the model offers user-friendly interface, graphical representation of the knowledge base and fuzzy information, as well as straightforward view of the relations among concepts and results of queries.

References

[1] Pelavin, R., Allen, J. F., A Formal Logic of Plans in Temporally Rich Domains, *Proceed. of the IEEE,* Vol. 74, No. 10, pp. 1364-1382, 1986.

[2] Kahn, K., Gorry, G. A., Mechanizing Temporal Knowledge, *Artificial Intelligence,* Vol. 9, pp. 87-108, 1977.

[3] Qian, D., Representation and Use of Imprecise Temporal Knowledge in Dynamic Systems, *Fuzzy Sets and Systems,* Vol. 50, pp. 59-77, 1992.
[4] Barro, S. *et al.*, A Model and Language for the Fuzzy Representation and Handling of Time, *Fuzzy Sets and Systems,* Vol.61, No. 2, pp. 153-175, 1994.
[5] Zadeh, L. A., Fuzzy Sets, *Information and Control,* Vol. 8, No. 4, pp. 338-353, 1965.
[6] Zadeh, L. A., Fuzzy Sets as a Basis for Theory of Possibility, *Fuzzy Sets and Systems*, Vol. 1, pp. 3-28, 1978.
[7] Dubois, D., Prade, H., Processing Fuzzy Temporal Knowledge, *IEEE Trans. on Systems, Man and Cybernetics,* Vol. 19, No. 4, pp. 729-744, 1989.
[8] Ribarić, S., Dalbelo Bašić, B., Pavešić, N., A Model for Fuzzy Temporal Knowledge Representation and Reasoning, *Proceedings of the IEEE International Fuzzy System Conference - FUZZ-IEEE'99*, August 22-25, Seoul, Korea, Vol. 1, pp. 216-221, 1999.
[9] de Figueiredo Jorge, C.A., Perkusich, A., Faults and timing analysis in real-time distributed systems: A fuzzy time Petri-net-based approach, Fuzzy Sets and Systems (83) 2, pp. 143-168, 1996.
[10] Cardoso, J., Time Fuzzy Petri Nets, , in the book *Fuzziness in Petri Nets*, Eds. J.Cardoso, H. Camargo, Studies in Fuzziness and Soft Computing, Vol. 22, Springer-Verlag (Physica Verlag), Heidelberg, pp. 88-114, 1999.
[11] Künzle, L.A., Valette, R., Pradin-Chezalviel, B.,: Temporal Reasoning in Fuzzy Time Petri Nets, in the book *Fuzziness in Petri Nets*, Eds. J.Cardoso, H. Camargo, Studies in Fuzziness and Soft Computing, Vol. 22, Springer-Verlag (Physica Verlag), Heidelberg, pp. 146-173, 1999.
[12] Murata, T, Suzuki, T., Shatz, S., Fuzzy-Timing High-Level Petri Nets for Time-Critical Systems, in the book *Fuzziness in Petri Nets*, Eds. J.Cardoso, H. Camargo, Studies in Fuzziness and Soft Computing, Vol. 22, Springer-Verlag (Physica Verlag), Heidelberg, pp. 88-114, 1999.
[13] Bugarin, A., Carinena, P., Felix, P., Barro, S., Reasoning with Fuzzy Temporal Rules on Petri Nets, in the book *Fuzziness in Petri Nets*, Eds. J.Cardoso, H. Camargo, Studies in Fuzziness and Soft Computing, Vol. 22, Springer-Verlag (Physica Verlag), Heidelberg, pp. 174-201, 1999.
[14] Peterson, J.L., *Petri Net Theory and Modelling of Systems*, Prentice-Hall, 1981.
[15] Murata, T., Petri Nets Properties, Analysis and Applications, *Proceedings of the IEEE*, 1989, Vol. 77, pp. 541-580.
[16] Kaufmann, A. and M. M. Gupta, *Introduction to Fuzzy Arithmetic.* Van Nostrand Reinhold, N.Y., 1991.
[17] Allen, J. F., Maintaining Knowledge about Temporal Intervals, *Communications of the ACM,* Vol. 26, No. 11, pp. 832- 843, 1983.
[18] Booch, G, *Object-oriented analysis and design with applications*, Second edition, Addison Wesley, 1994.
[19] Ribarić, S, Knowledge Representation Scheme Based on Petri Net Theory, *Int. Journal of Pattern recognition and Artificial Intelligence,* 1988, Vol. 2, No. 4, pp. 691-700.

[20] Chen, S.M, Ke, J.S, Chang, J.F, Knowledge representation uzng fuzzy Petri Nets, *IEEE Transactions on knowledge and data engineering*, 1990, Vol. 2, No. 3, pp. 311-319.

[21] Dalbelo Bašić, B., Knowledge Representation Using Fuzzy and Fuzzy Time Petri Nets, Ph.D. thesis, Faculty of Electrical Engineering and Computing, University of Zagreb, 1997.

[22] Jensen, K., Rozenberg G.(Eds.), High-Level Petri Nets, Springer-Verlag, Berlin, 1991.

A Symbolic Approach to Syllogistic Reasoning

Mohamed Yasser Khayata, Daniel Pacholczyk

LERIA, U.F.R Sciences, 2, Boulevard Lavoisier
49045 ANGERS Cedex 01, FRANCE
{khayata, pacho}@info.univ-angers.fr

Abstract. In this paper we present a new approach to a symbolic treatment of quantified statements having the following form "Q A's are B's", knowing that A and B are labels denoting sets, and Q is a linguistic quantifier interpreted as a proportion evaluated in a qualitative way. Our model can be viewed as a symbolic generalization of statistical conditional probability notions as well as a symbolic generalization of the classical probabilistic operators. Our approach is founded on a symbolic finite M-valued logic in which the graduation scale of M symbolic quantifiers is translated in terms of truth degrees of a particular predicate. Then, we present symbolic syllogisms allowing us to deal with quantified statements.

1 Introduction

In this paper, we present a symbolic approach to linguistic quantification. In the natural language, one often uses statements qualifying statistical information like "Most students are single". More formally, they are represented under the form "Q A's are B's" where A and B are labels denoting sets, and Q is a linguistic quantifier. Zadeh [25] distinguishes between two types of quantifiers: *absolute* and *proportional.* An absolute quantifier evaluates the number of individuals of B in A. A proportional quantifier evaluates the proportion of individuals of B in A. The proportional quantifiers can be *precise* or *vague*. *A* precise quantifier translates an interval of proportions having precise bounds exemplified by "10%", "Between 10 and 20%", etc. A vague quantifier translates an interval of proportions having fuzzy bounds. Thus the vague proportional quantifiers express qualitatively and no quantitatively proportions. A proportional quantifier can be viewed as a kind of probabilities assigned to classes of individuals. Several approaches based on the theory of probabilities ([12], [18], [7], [4], [2], [5], [9]) deal with precise proportional quantifiers. Other probabilistic approaches ([13], [14], [6]) do not enable an adequate representation of proportional quantifiers, since these approaches are generally introduced to treat uncertainty. These authors interpret the probability degrees assigned to propositions as degrees of certainty in the truth of these propositions. They represent statistical assertions of type "Q A's are B's" as uncertain rules of the form: "if A then B" with a subjective degree of belief in the truth of the rule (A and B are interpreted as propositions). It has been pointed out by Bacchus [4] that a confusion in the representation is made between the probabilities interpreted as certainty degrees assigned to propositions about particular individuals and those interpreted as proportions assigned to classes of individuals. The probabilities of the first type are called subjective and the second statistical. The statistical probability that corresponds to the proportion is a particular case of probabilities where the distribution is uniform over the finite reference set. For example, the statistical probability attached to a subset A of the finite reference set Ω, Prop(A), is equal to the absolute proportion of individuals of A, i.e., Prop(A) = $|A|/|\Omega|$. Similarly, if A and B are two subsets of Ω, the relative proportion of individuals of B in A is expressed by the conditional statistical probability, Prop(B|A) with Prop(B|A)=Prop(A$\cap$B)/ Prop(A)=$|A\cap B|/||A|$. Some probabilistic approaches ([1], [18], [17], [4], [5]) are interested in a qualitative modeling of the proportional quantifier "Most" or "Almost-all" in the context of default reasoning. The approaches based on the fuzzy set theory ([25], [22,23], [7], [19]), deal with a vague proportional quantifier as a fuzzy number of the interval [0,1] which can be manipulated by using the fuzzy arithmetic. For example, the membership function of "Most" evaluates the degree to which a given proportion r is compatible with the quantifier "Most". The representation of quantified statements involving fuzzy sets is based on the concept of fuzzy subset cardinality. Recently, Dubois et al. [8] have proposed a semi-numerical approach to the vague quantifiers based upon the numerical results obtained in ([7], [2]) for precise quantifiers. It is concerned with a suitable ordered partition of the unit interval [0,1] in several subintervals, subinterval representing a vague quantifier. The subintervals obtained by applying the inference rules (on the precise quantifiers) to subintervals, representing the vague quantifiers, are approximately associated to subintervals of vague quantifiers.

In this paper, we propose a purely symbolic approach to represent vague proportional quantifiers with a statistical interpretation in terms of proportion evaluated in qualitative way[1]. More precisely, we define a semantic model of statistical probabilities (proportion) representation inspired by Bacchus's model [4]. The semantic model is built on the basis of the finite many-valued predicates symbolic logic proposed by Pacholczyk [15] for a symbolic treatment of vague information. We have introduced a new predicate in the language of this logic that takes into account the notion of proportions. There is a one to one correspondence between quantifiers and truth degrees in this logic. A graded scale symbolic quantifiers is associated to a graded scale of truth symbolic degrees of this predicate. In Section 2, we briefly present the many-valued symbolic logic. Section 3, describes our symbolic representation of statistical probability. The Axioms governing this representation are presented in Section 4. Section 5 deals with properties symbolically generalizing some classical properties. Inference rules called "syllogisms" manipulating the vague quantifiers are presented in Section 6. In Section 6.4, we present an example of syllogistic reasoning. Finally, in Section 7 we point out that our approach leads to similar syllogisms as the ones proposed by Bacchus [4].

[1] This model extends the work described in ([10], [11]).

2 M-valued predicates logic

Let $M \geq 2$ be an integer. Let $\mathcal{M}$ be the interval [1,M] totally ordered by the relation $\leq$, and **n** be the mapping defined by $n(\alpha)=M+1-\alpha$. $\{\mathcal{M},\vee,\wedge,n\}$ is a lattice of De MORGAN with: $\alpha \vee \beta = \max(\alpha,\beta)$ and $\alpha \wedge \beta = \min(\alpha,\beta)$. Let $\mathcal{L}_M = \{\tau_\alpha, \alpha \in \mathcal{M}\}$ be a set of **M** elements totally ordered by the relation $\leq$ such that: $\tau_\alpha \leq \tau_\beta \Leftrightarrow \alpha \leq \beta$. Thus $\{\mathcal{L}_M, \geq\}$ is a chain in which the least element is τ_1 and the greatest element is τ_M. We define in $\mathcal{L}_M$ two operators $\wedge$ and $\vee$ and a decreasing involution ~ as follows: $\tau_\alpha \vee \tau_\beta = \tau_{\max(\alpha,\beta)}$, $\tau_\alpha \wedge \tau_\beta = \tau_{\min(\alpha,\beta)}$ and $\sim\tau_\alpha = \tau_{n(\alpha)}$. We can interpret $\mathcal{L}_M$ as a set of linguistic truth degrees allowing dealing with vague predicates. For example, by choosing M = 7, we can introduce: $\mathcal{L}_7$ = {*not-at-all-true, very-little-true, little-true, moderately-true, very-true, almost-true, totally-true*}.[2]

In a statement having the following form "x is v_α *A*", the term v_α linguistically expresses the degree to which the object x satisfies the concept *A*. Each linguistic term v_α is associated to the truth degree τ_α*-true*. So we have: "Paul is *very* tall" is *true* $\Leftrightarrow$ "Paul is tall" is *very-true*. In the following, the lattice $\{\mathcal{L}_M,\vee,\wedge,\sim\}$ will be used as the support of the representation of M truth degrees. Let $\mathcal{L}$ be the many-valued predicates language and $\mathcal{F}$ the set of formulas of $\mathcal{L}$. We call an interpretation structure $\mathcal{A}$ of $\mathcal{L}$, the pair $<\mathcal{D}, \{\mathcal{R}_n \mid n \in N\}>$, where $\mathcal{D}$ designates the domain of $\mathcal{A}$ and $\mathcal{R}_n$ designates the multiset[3] associated with the predicate P_n of the language. We call a valuation of variables of $\mathcal{L}$, a sequence denoted v $=<v_0 \ldots v_{i-1}, v_i, v_{i+1}, \ldots>$. The valuation v(i/a) is defined by $v(i/a)=<v_0,\ldots,v_{i-1},a,v_{i+1},\ldots>$.

Definition 1 For a formula $P_n(z_{i_1},\ldots,z_{i_k})$ of $\mathcal{F}$, the relation of partial satisfaction "v *satisfies* $P_n(z_{i_1},\ldots,z_{i_k})$ to a degree τ_α *in-*$\mathcal{A}$" or "v τ_α*-satisfies* $P_n(z_{i_1},\ldots,z_{i_k})$ *in-*$\mathcal{A}$", denoted "$\mathcal{A} \models^v_\alpha P_n(z_{i_1},\ldots,z_{i_k})$", is defined as follows:
$\mathcal{A} \models^v_\alpha P_n(z_{i_1},\ldots,z_{i_k}) \Leftrightarrow <v_{i_1},\ldots,v_{i_k}> \in_\alpha \mathcal{R}_n$.
Definition 2 A formulas Φ is said to be τ_α*-true-in-*$\mathcal{A}$, if and only if there exists a valuation v such that v τ_α*-satisfies* Φ *in-*$\mathcal{A}$.

3 Symbolic representation of the statistical probabilities

The representation of statistical probabilities requires the reference to sets of individuals and also to assign probabilities to these sets [4]. To solve the first problem, we use the concept of *placeholder variables* in *lambda abstraction* used by [4], where one considers that a Boolean open formula can refer to the set of all instances of its free variables specified as placeholders, satisfying the formula. So given a many-valued predicate language $\mathcal{L}$, for an interpretation $\mathcal{A}^*$ with domain

[2] Note that "*not-at-all-true*" and "*totally-true*" correspond respectively with the truth classical values "*false*" and "*true*".

[3] The multiset theory [3] can be viewed as an axiomatic approach to the fuzzy set theory. In this theory, $x \in_\alpha A$, the membership degree α to which x belongs to *A*, corresponds with $\mu_A(x)=\alpha$ in the fuzzy set theory of Zadeh [24].

of discourse Ω and C the set of open well-formed formulas without bound variables ϕ of $\mathcal{F}$ such that, for any valuation v of Ω, ϕ is *totally satisfied in-*$\mathcal{A}^*$ or *not-at-all satisfied in-*$\mathcal{A}^*$: $C = \{\phi \in \mathcal{F} \mid \forall v, \mathcal{A}^* \models^v_M \phi \text{ or } \mathcal{A}^* \models^v_1 \phi\}$.

Since formulas of C contain only free variables, we can consider that free variables of formulas of C stand *implicitly* for placeholder variables. Thus in the multivalent interpretation $\mathcal{A}^*$, each formula of C will be able to make reference to the subset of individuals of Ω that satisfy this formula.

3.1 Representation of the absolute statistical probability

In order to define the symbolic statistical probabilities assigned to subsets referred by formulas of C, we add to the language $\mathcal{L}$, a new M-valued unary predicate denoted as **Prop** defined over formulas of C and which takes into account the notion of proportions of sets referred by formulas of C. We are going to extend the structure interpretation of the language $\mathcal{A}^*$ to $\mathcal{A}$ with domain $\Omega \cup C$, and we suppose that any valuation v comprises v_0 associated to the argument of **Prop**.

Definition 3 The predicate **Prop** is defined as follows:
- For any interpretation $\mathcal{A}$, $\forall\ \varphi \in C$, $\mathbf{Prop}(\varphi) \in \mathcal{F}$.
- Any interpretation $\mathcal{A}$ associates to predicate **Prop** a multiset of C, denoted as $\mathcal{RPS}$, so that for all valuation v, if ϕ is a some element of C, we have:

$$\mathcal{A} \models^{v(0/\phi)}_{\alpha} \text{Prop}(\varphi) \Leftrightarrow \langle\phi\rangle \in_{\alpha} \mathcal{RPS} \Leftrightarrow \text{Prop}(\phi) \text{ is } \tau_\alpha\text{-}\textit{true-in-}\mathcal{A}.$$

If no confusion is possible $\mathcal{A} \models_\alpha \text{Prop}(\phi)$ stands for $\mathcal{A} \models^{v(0/\phi)}_{\alpha} \text{Prop}(\varphi)$.

Definition 4 Let $\mathcal{Q}_M$ be the set of the proportional quantifiers: $\mathcal{Q}_M = \{Q_\alpha, \alpha \in [1,M]\}$. Then "$\mathcal{A} \models_\alpha \text{Prop}(\phi)$" will mean that "$Q_\alpha$ individuals of Ω *totally satisfy* ϕ in-$\mathcal{A}$", if and only if, the subset referred by ϕ belonging to the multiset $\mathcal{RPS}$ with a degree τ_α.

The basic idea of our definition is to translate the symbolic proportion Q_α of a subset of Ω, referred by ϕ, in terms of a symbolic degree of truth of the formula Prop(ϕ).Thus Q_α is considered as the symbolic degree of statistical probability of the set referred by ϕ in $\mathcal{A}$. Therefore, each symbolic truth degree τ_α-*true* of $\mathcal{L}_M$ of Prop(ϕ), is associated to a symbolic degree of statistical probability of the set referred by ϕ, i.e., to a linguistic quantifier Q_α of $\mathcal{Q}_M$.

Example 1 By choosing M = 7, we can introduce:
$\mathcal{Q}_7$ = {*None, Very-few (or Almost-none), Few, About-half, Most, Almost-all, All*}.

3.2 Representation of the conditional statistical probability

The idea proposed for the representation of "*Q A*'s are *B*'s" is to interpret it in terms of the symbolic relative (or conditional) proportion of individuals of *B* in *A*. We will generalize the classical definition of conditional statistical probability in a symbolic context by using the "symbolic probabilistic division" operator denoted

C or equivalently the "symbolic probabilistic multiplication" operator denoted **I**. These two operators have been defined in [16] (see also in [21]) for the symbolic representation of conditional uncertainty. The operator **I** is an application of $\mathcal{Q}_M^2$ into $\mathcal{Q}_M$, that verifies the classical properties of the probabilistic multiplication (commutativity, absorbent element: Q_1, neutral element: Q_M, monotony, associativity, idempotence: Q_2). The operator **C** is an application of $\mathcal{Q}_M^2$ into $\mathcal{P}(\mathcal{Q}_M)$. The definition of the operator **C** is deducted from **I** by a unique way as follows:

$$Q_\mu \in \mathrm{C}(Q_\alpha, Q_\lambda) \Leftrightarrow Q_\lambda = \mathrm{I}(Q_\alpha, Q_\mu).$$

Among the different tables of the operator **C**, which verify the axioms chosen in [16], in $\mathcal{L}_7$ we have chosen Table 1 presented in the Annex. The corresponding operator **I** is defined by Table 2.

Definition 5 Let formulas ϕ and ψ be formulas of C, we are going to introduce the symbolic conditional statistical probability, "Prop($\psi|\phi$)", expressing the symbolic degree of the relative proportion of individuals that satisfy the formula ψ among those satisfying ϕ. It will be defined by the symbolic division of the symbolic degree of Prop($\phi\wedge\psi$) by that of Prop(ϕ) as follows: $\{\mathcal{A}\models_\alpha$ Prop(ϕ), $\mathcal{A}\models_\lambda$ Prop($\phi\wedge\psi$)$\}$ $\Rightarrow$ $\mathcal{A}\models_\mu$ Prop($\psi|\phi$) with $Q_\mu \in \mathrm{C}(Q_\alpha, Q_\lambda)$. "$\mathcal{A}\models_\mu$ Prop($\psi|\phi$)" means that "Among the individuals of Ω which *totally satisfy* ϕ *in-*$\mathcal{A}$, Q_μ *totally satisfy* ψ *in-*$\mathcal{A}$".

In order to obtain an equivalent manipulation of sets and formulas of type "$\mathcal{A}\models_\mu$ Prop($\psi|\phi$)", we can use the usual notation of quantified statements. Suppose that ϕ and ψ refer respectively to subsets A and B of Ω in the interpretation $\mathcal{A}$. The equivalence between the two notations allows us to use "Q_μ A's are B's" instead of "$\mathcal{A}\models_\mu$ Prop($\psi|\phi$)". It can be established as follows: $\mathcal{A}\models_\mu$ Prop($\psi|\phi$) $\Leftrightarrow$ "Among the individuals of Ω which *totally satisfy* ϕ *in-*$\mathcal{A}$, Q_μ *totally satisfy* ψ *in-*$\mathcal{A}$" $\Leftrightarrow$ "Q_μ individuals of A are individuals of B" $\Leftrightarrow$ "Q_μ A's are B's". Then, knowing that $\top$ is a tautology, we obtain: $\mathcal{A}\models_\alpha$ Prop(ϕ) $\Leftrightarrow$ $\mathcal{A}\models_\alpha$ Prop($\phi|\top$). So, we can use "Q_α Ω's are A's" instead of "$\mathcal{A}\models_\alpha$ Prop(ϕ)". Thus the definition 5 can equivalently be written with notation of quantified statements as follows:

Definition 6 $\{Q_\alpha$ Ω's are A's, Q_λ Ω's are $(A\cap B)$'s$\}$ $\Rightarrow$ $\{Q_\mu$ A's are B's with $Q_\mu \in \mathrm{C}(Q_\alpha, Q_\lambda)\}$.

Remark 2 Definition 6 is a symbolic generalization of the classical definition: $\mathrm{Prop}(B|A) = \mathrm{Prop}(A \cap B) / \mathrm{Prop}(A) = |A \cap B| / |A|$.

Example 2. Let us suppose that: "Most residents of Paris are young" and "Half of residents of Paris are young single". By using $\mathcal{L}_7$, the two assertions are respectively written by "Q_5 Ω are *Young*" and "Q_4 Ω are *Young* $\cap$ *Single*". Definition 6 gives us: Q_μ *Young* are *Single* with $Q_\mu \in \mathrm{C}(Q_5, Q_4) = \{Q_5\}$. Then we obtain: "Most young people are single".

4 Axiomatic of the symbolic statistical probabilities

We can recall the axioms governing our representation of symbolic proportion. Let A and B be subsets of Ω, the axioms are defined as follows:

Axiom 1 $\{A \cap B \neq A$, Q_α Ω's are A's, Q_λ Ω's are $(A \cap B)$'s and $Q_\alpha \in$ [*Few*, *Almost-all*]$\}$ $\Rightarrow$ $\{$*Almost-all* A's are B's$\}$. (Axiom defining "Almost-all")

Qualitatively the subsets A and $A \cap B$ can have the same symbolic degree of proportions without being equal. This is the case, when $A \cap B$ is equal to the set A without one or some individuals. This can qualitatively translate by saying that "A and $A \cap B$ are *almost equal*" or "*Almost-all* A's are B's". This is not always the case, when the proportion of A is very weak (i.e., associated with Q_2 = *Very-few*).

Axiom 2 $\{Q_\alpha$ Ω's are A's, $Q_\alpha \in$ [*Very-Few*, *Almost-all*] and *Almost-all* A's are B's$\}$ $\Rightarrow$ $\{Q_\alpha$ Ω's are $(A \cap B)$'s$\}$ (Axiom defining "Almost-all")

When we have "*Almost-all* A's are B's", we know that $A \neq A \cap B$, but we can say that A and $A \cap B$ are almost equal and therefore A and $A \cap B$ have the same symbolic degree of proportions.

Remark 3 The chosen table of C is in agreement with Axiom 1 and Axiom 2, since respectively: for any $Q_\alpha \in$ [*Few*, *Almost-all*]$\}$, we have: Q_6 =*Almost-all*$\in C(Q_\alpha, Q_\alpha)$, and for any Q_α and $Q_\lambda \in$ [*Very-Few*, *Almost-all*] with $Q_\alpha \neq Q_\lambda$, we have: $Q_6 \notin C(Q_\alpha, Q_\lambda)$.

Axiom 3 $\{Q_\alpha$ Ω's are A's$\} \Leftrightarrow \{Q_{n(\alpha)}$ Ω's are $\overline{A}$'s with $n(\alpha)=M+1-\alpha\}$. (Axiom defining the *dual* quantifier)

Generally the dual quantifier of Q_α corresponds with $Q_{n(\alpha)}$ ("Few" is the dual quantifier of "Most")

Axiom 4 $\{Q_\alpha$ Ω's are A's, Q_α Ω's are B's, $A \cup B \neq \Omega$ and $A \cap B = \varnothing\}$ $\Rightarrow$ $\{Q_r$ Ω's are $(A \cup B)$'s with $Q_r \in S(Q_\alpha, Q_\beta)\}$.

(Axiom defining the symbolic proportion of disjoint set union)

Classically, when A and B are disjoint, the absolute proportion of their union is the sum of their absolute. We put that if the union A and B is different from Ω (otherwise, the symbolic proportion degree of their union is evidently Q_M) and that they are disjoint, then the symbolic proportion degree of their union belongs to the "symbolic sum" of their symbolic proportion degrees. The symbolic sum denoted **S** is introduced in a way that it gives an interval containing one or two values. The lower bound of this interval is greater than or equal to each symbolic value of two arguments of **S**. As the set $A \cup B$ is different from Ω, the maximal degree that can take the upper bound of the interval is Q_{M-1}. The use of an interval rather than a single degree is due to the degree Q_2. It is justified by the fact that the addition of one or some elements (i.e., very weak quantity) to a set can either preserve its symbolic degree of proportion or increase it at most one degree.

Definition 7 The symbolic sum **S** is a commutative application of $\mathcal{Q}_M^2$ into $\mathcal{P}(\mathcal{Q}_M)$. By supposing that $\alpha+\beta \leq M+1$, **S** is defined as follows:

$$S(Q_\alpha, Q_\beta) = \begin{cases} \{Q_\alpha\} \text{ if } \beta = 1 \\ [Q_{\alpha+\beta-2}, Q_{\alpha+\beta-1}] \text{ if } \alpha \neq 1, \beta \neq 1 \text{ et } \alpha+\beta \leq M \\ \{Q_{M-1}\} \text{ if } \alpha+\beta = M+1 \end{cases}$$

Remark 4 In agreement with Axiom 3, it is necessary to have $\alpha+\beta \leq M+1$. Indeed, $A \cap B = \emptyset$ implies that $B \subset \bar{A}$. Now (Axiom 3) gives $Q_{n(\alpha)}$ Ω's are $\bar{A}$'s. Intuitively, $\beta \leq n(\alpha)$ (for, $B \subset \bar{A}$) therefore, $\alpha+\beta \leq \alpha+n(\alpha)=M+1$.

Defining **Inf** and **Sup** as two applications of $\mathcal{Q}_M^2$ into $\mathcal{Q}_M$, we obtain respectively the lower bound and the upper bound of an interval of $\mathcal{Q}_M$ so we can write: $S(Q_\alpha,Q_\beta) = [\text{Inf}\circ S(Q_\alpha,Q_\beta), \text{Sup}\circ S(Q_\alpha,Q_\beta)]$ or more simply $[\text{Inf}S(Q_\alpha,Q_\beta), \text{Sup}S(Q_\alpha,Q_\beta)]$. We have proved that the applications **Inf∘S** and **Sup∘S** verify the properties of T-conorm.

Definition 8 For given **S**, we can define the "symbolic subtraction", denoted as **D,** as an application of $\mathcal{Q}_M^2$ into $\mathcal{P}(\mathcal{Q}_M)$ such that: if $Q_r \in S(Q_\alpha,Q_\beta)$, then $Q_\beta \in D(Q_r,Q_\alpha)$ and $Q_\alpha \in D(Q_r,Q_\beta)$. Then **D** can be deduced from **S** as follows:

$$D(Q_r, Q_\beta) = \begin{cases} \{Q_r\} \text{ if } \beta = 1 \\ \{Q_2\} \text{ if } r = \beta \in [2, M-1] \\ [Q_{r+1-\beta}, Q_{r+2-\beta}] \text{ if } 2 \leq \beta < r \leq M-1 \end{cases}$$

Table 3 and Table 4 presented in the Annex correspond to operator **S** and **D**.

5 Fundamental properties [4]

Let A and B be subsets of Ω. The following propositions can be viewed as symbolic generalizations of properties in classical statistical probabilities.

Proposition 1 If Q_α Ω's are A's and $A \subset B$, then Q_β Ω's are B's with $Q_\alpha \leq Q_\beta$.

Proposition 1 shows that the symbolic degree of proportion of a set is greater than or equal to its subsets. Classically, the proportion of a set is strictly greater than to one of its strict subsets. On the other hand, qualitatively, a set and one of its strict subsets can have the same symbolic degree of proportion (Cf. Axiom 1).

Proposition 2 If Q_α Ω's are A's, Q_λ Ω's are $(A \cap B)$'s, and $A \neq \Omega$, then $Q_{\alpha'}$ Ω's $(A \backslash B)$'s with $Q_{\alpha'} \in D(Q_\alpha,Q_\lambda)$.

It appears clearly that proposition 2 generalizes the classical property: $|A \backslash B|/|\Omega|=(|A|-|A \cap B|)/|\Omega|$.

[4] In this paper, all propositions are given without the corresponding proofs.

Proposition 3 Q_α Ω's are A's, Q_β Ω's are B's, Q_λ Ω's are $(A\cap B)$'s, and $A \cup B \neq \Omega$, then Q_r Ω's are $(A\cup B)$'s with $Q_r \in \mathrm{U}(Q_\alpha,Q_\beta,Q_\lambda)$ where $\mathrm{U}(Q_\alpha,Q_\beta,Q_\lambda) = [\mathrm{InfS}(Q_\alpha, \mathrm{InfD}(Q_\beta,Q_\lambda)), \mathrm{SupS}(Q_\alpha, \mathrm{SupD}(Q_\beta,Q_\lambda))]$ if $\alpha+\beta-\lambda \leq \mathrm{M}-1$, and $\mathrm{U}(Q_\alpha, Q_\beta, Q_\lambda) = \{Q_{\mathrm{M}-1}\}$ if $\alpha+\beta-\lambda = \mathrm{M}$.

Proposition 4 If Q_α Ω's are A's, Q_β Ω's are B's, Q_r Ω's are $(A \cup B)$'s, and $A \cup B \neq \Omega$, then Q_λ Ω's are $(A \cap B)$'s with $Q_\lambda = Q_2$ if $\alpha+\beta-r = 1$ and $Q_\lambda \in [\mathrm{InfD}(Q_\beta, \mathrm{SupD}(Q_r,Q_\alpha)), \mathrm{Inf}\{\mathrm{SupD}(Q_\beta, \mathrm{InfD}(Q_r,Q_\alpha)), Q_\alpha, Q_\beta\}]$ otherwise.

Proposition 3 and 4 generalize the classical property:

$$|A\cup B|/|\Omega|=(|A|+|B|-|A\cap B|)/|\Omega|.$$

6 Syllogistic reasoning

Reasoning with quantifiers is called by Zadeh [25] *syllogistic reasoning*, where a *syllogism* is an inference rule that consists in deducing a new quantified statement from quantified statements.

As an inference scheme, a *syllogism* may generally be expressed in the form:

$Q_{\mu1}$ A's are B's
$Q_{\mu2}$ C's are D's

Q_μ E's are F's, with $Q_\mu \in [Q_\alpha,Q_\beta] \subseteq$ [*None*, *All*],
where Q_α and Q_β are in accordance with $Q_{\mu1}$ or $Q_{\mu2}$, and E and F are sets resulting from application of operators set on A, B, C or D.

The quantifier "All" is represented by the implication using the quantifier $\forall$ in classical logic or by the inclusion in set theory. The classical implication and the inclusion propagate inferences by transitivity, contraposition, and disjunction or by conjunction. From statements quantified by "All", these inferences enable to generate new statements likely quantified by "All". Nevertheless, most of these inferences are not valid for other quantifiers, i.e., for $Q_\mu \in$ [*Very-few*, *Almost-all*]. The invalid inference has been considered as a case of *total ignorance*, i.e., $[Q_\alpha,Q_\beta]$ = [*None*, *All*].

6.1 Valid inferences

We consider that an inference is valid, if we deduce $Q_\mu \in [Q_\alpha,Q_\beta]$ with Q_α or Q_β are in accordance with $Q_{\mu1}$ or $Q_{\mu2}$. We present some valid inferences. Each of them is illustrated by an example.

Proposition 5 (Relative Duality)
$Q_{\mu 1}$ *A's are B's*

$Q_{\mu 2}$ *A's* are $(A \backslash B)$'s and $Q_{\mu 2}$ *A*'s are $\overline{B}$'s,
with $Q_{\mu 2} = Q_{n(\mu 1)}$ if $Q_{\mu 1} \neq Q_{n(\mu 1)}$
and $Q_{\mu 2} \in [Q_{n(\mu 1)}, Q_{n(\mu 1)+1}]$ otherwise.

Example 3
Almost all students are unmarried

Very few students are married

Proposition 6 (Mixed Transitivity)
$Q_{\mu 1}$ *A's are B's*
All B's are *C*'s

$Q_{\mu 2}$ *A*'s are *C*'s, with $Q_{\mu 1} \leq Q_{\mu 2}$.

Example 4
Most students are young
All young people are non retired

At least most students are non retired.

Proposition 7 (Intersection/Product Syllogism)
$Q_{\mu 1}$ *A's are B's*
$Q_{\mu 2}$ *(A∩B)'s are C's*

Q_{μ} *A*'s are $(B \cap C)$'s,
with $Q_{\mu} = \mathrm{I}(Q_{\mu 1}, Q_{\mu 2})$.

Example 5
Most students are young
Almost all young students are unmarried

Most students are young and unmarried.

6.2 Syllogisms with the quantifier "Almost-all"

We present three inferences only valid for the quantifier "Almost-all". They result from the axioms of quantifier "Almost-all" (Cf. Axioms 1-2). These inferences can be viewed as "counterparts" of inference rules of Adams [1] and Pearl [17][5] where in their approaches the quantifier "Almost-all" encoding a default is qualitatively interpreted as an infinitesimal proportion close to 1.

Proposition 8 (Contraction)
Almost-all *A*'s are *B*'s
Almost-all $(A \cap B)$'s are *C*'s

Almost-all *A*'s are *C*'s.

Example 6
Almost all students are young
Almost all young students are single

Almost all students are single

Proposition 9 (Cumulativity)
Almost-all *A*'s are *B*'s
Almost-al *A*'s are *C*'s.

Q_{μ} *(A∩B)'s are C's*,
with $Q_{\mu} \in$ [*Most*, *All*].

Example 7
Almost all students are young
Almost all students are single

At least most young students are single

[5] Pearl's approach is introduced for default reasoning, then his inferences are not exactly syllogisms, but they are rather non-monotonic inferences about particular individuals.

Proposition 10 (Union Left)
Almost-all A's are C's
Almost-al B's are C's

Q_μ $(A \cup B)$*'s are* C*'s*,
with $Q_\mu \in$ [*Most*, *Almost-all*].

Example 8
Almost all students are single
Almost all priests are single

Most or almost all students or priests are single.

6.3 Monotonic aspect of syllogistic reasoning

We can note that the syllogistic reasoning is monotonic ([20]) in the following sense: when a knowledge base contains: "$Q_{\mu 1}$ A's are B's" and "$Q_{\mu 2}$ C's are D's", when we deduce "Q_μ E's are F's" with $Q_\mu \in [Q_\alpha, Q_\beta]$, and if one adds in the base or one deduces by an other syllogism: "$Q_{\mu'}$ E's are F's" with $Q_{\mu'} \in [Q_{\alpha'}, Q_{\beta'}]$, then one must have $[Q_\alpha, Q_\beta] \cap [Q_{\alpha'}, Q_{\beta'}] \neq \varnothing$ and finally one will deduce: "Q_μ E's are F's" with $Q_\mu \in [Q_\alpha, Q_\beta] \cap [Q_{\alpha'}, Q_{\beta'}]$. In other words, the new knowledge can only tighten the interval $[Q_\alpha, Q_\beta]$, that maintains the coherence between the quantified statements. There is an inconsistency if $[Q_\alpha, Q_\beta] \cap [Q_{\alpha'}, Q_{\beta'}] = \varnothing$.

6.4 An example of syllogistic reasoning

Let us suppose that a knowledge base contains the quantified assertions:
S1 : *Almost all* students are young ; S2 : *Almost all* students are single
S3 : *Most* young students are single ; S4 : *All* young people are non retired
S5 : *Most* singles are young ; S6 : *Almost all* sportsmen students are young
S7 : *About half* of the sportsmen are students.

By using our *complete* model of syllogistic reasoning, we deduce the following quantified assertions "Q_β E's are F's" or "between Q_β and Q_γ E's are F's", denoted as Q_β(E, F) or [Q_β, Q_γ](E, F) .
[Very-few, Most] (Student *and* Young, Single *and* Sportsman)
[Most, Almost-all] (Student *and* Young, Single *or* Sportsman)
[Most, Almost-all] (Student *and* Young, Single)
[Most, Almost-all] (Student, Single *and* Young)
[Most, Almost-all] (Student *and* Single, Young)
[Most, All] (Student *and* Single, *Non* Retired)
[Very-few, All] (Student *and Non* Retired, Young *and* Single)
[Most, All] (Student *and Non* Retired, Young *or* Single)
[Most, All] (Student *and Non* Retired, Young)
[Most, Almost-all] (Student, *Non* Retired *and* Single)
[Most, All] (Student *and Non* Retired, Single)
[Most, Almost-all] (Student, Sportsman *and Non* Retired)
Almost-all (Student, Sportsman *or* Young)
Almost-all (Student, Sportsman *or* Single)
[Almost-all, All] (Student, Sportsman *or Non* Retired)
[Most, Almost-all] (Student, Sportsman)

[About-half, Almost-all] (Sportsman, Young *or* Student)
[About-half, Almost-all] (Sportsman, Young)
[About-half, All] (Sportsman *or* Young, *Non* Retired)
[About-half, All] (Sportsman, *Non* Retired *or* Student)
[About-half, All] (Sportsman, *Non* Retired)
Most (Student, Young *and* Sportsman)
About-half (Sportsman, Student *and* Young)
About-half (Sportsman, Student *and Non* Retired)
[Most, All] (Single *or* Young, *Non* Retired)
[Almost-all, All] (Student *or* Young, *Non* Retired)
Almost-all (Student, Single *or* Young)
[Almost-all, All] (Student, *Non* Retired *or* Single)
[Almost-all, All] (Student, *Non* Retired)
[Most, All] (Single, *Non* Retired)
[Almost-all, All] (Student *and* Sportsman, *Non* Retired)

7 Comparison with Bacchus's approach

About the quantifiers, Bacchus' framework [4] is defined upon statistical assertions using numerical values but it is only used for the symbolic values ''majority", denoted as "most" (which is interpreted as a proportion > 0.5) and ``minority". So, he only focuses on one linguistic quantifier (and its dual one) defining typicality. In our work, the aim is different since we do not want to represent the notion of majority but to capture the whole set of proportions. That's why we use several different quantifiers (seven in this paper) which describe a scale of quantifiers. If we focus on the syllogistic reasoning, we can verify that our approach leads to find similar syllogisms as the ones that can be found with Bacchus' proposal. If Q is associated with a numerical value (or a numerical interval [a, b]) then in Bacchus's approach, we obtain the following results.

- 1 - *Mixed Transitivity*

Q A's are B's
1 B's are C's (1 is equivalent to 100 \% or "All")
\---
[Q, 1] A's are C's (i. e. Q' A's are C's with $Q' \geq Q$).

Our approach gives the same result (Section 6.1, Proposition 6):

Q_α A's are B's
All B's are C's
\--------------------------------
Q_μ A's are C's with $Q_\mu \geq Q_\alpha$

- 2 - *Intersection/Product syllogism*

Q_1 A's are B's
Q_2 $(A \cap B)$'s are C's
\-------------------------------------
$Q_1 * Q_2$ A's are $(B \cap C)$'s (where * stands for the multiplication operator)

Our approach gives a similar result (Section 6.1, Proposition 7), since the operator I stands for an operator having in $\mathcal{L}_7$ the properties of the multiplication operator [16].

$Q_{\mu 1}$ A's are B's

$Q_{\mu 2}$ ($A \cap B$)'s are C's

Q_μ A's are ($B \cap C$)'s, with $Q_\mu = I(Q_{\mu 1}, Q_{\mu 2})$.

It is clear that they correspond to the same syllogisms since, for each syllogism, the resulting assertion is the same and the quantifier is obtained is the same way in the numerical and in the symbolic setting (that is using the same combination of the operators). Moreover, the operators C (division), I (product), S (addition), D (difference) are the symbolic counterparts of the four classical operators (see Annex and Sections 3-4). The operators defined for the symbolic setting respect properties of classical operators.

8 Conclusion

In this paper we have presented a symbolic approach to quantifiers used in the natural language to express a qualitative evaluation of proportions. This approach allows to reason qualitatively on quantified assertions, since we provide inference rules based upon statements involving linguistic quantifiers. In order to obtain belief symbolic degrees attached to propositions about *particular individuals*, and this, by using knowledge based upon quantified assertions and certain facts, it is necessary to propose a symbolic model based upon a *direct inference principle* and a choice the appropriate *reference class* ([12], [18], [4]). This point is actually on study.

References

1. E. Adams. *The logic conditionals*. D. Reidel, Dordercht, Netherlands, 1975.
2. S. Amarger, D. Dubois, H. Prade. Imprecise Quantifiers And Conditional Probabilities. *In ECSQARU'91*, R. Krause and *al* (eds.), 33-37, 1991.
3. H. Akdag, M. De Glas, D. Pacholczyk. A Qualitative Theory of Uncertainty. *Fundamenta Informatica*, 17(4): 333-362, 1992.
4. F. Bacchus. Representation and Reasoning with Probabilistic Knowledge. MIT Press, Cambridge, MA, 1990.
5. F. Bacchus, A. J. Grove, J. Y. Halpern, D. Koller. From statistical knowledge bases to degrees of belief. *Artificial intelligence*, 87 : 75-143, 1997.
6. P. Cheeseman. An inquiry into computer understanding. *Computational Intelligence*, 4(1): 58-66, 1988.
7. D. Dubois, H. Prade. On fuzzy syllogisms. *Computational Intelligence*, 4(2): 171-179, 1988.
8. D. Dubois, H. Prade, L. Godo, R. Mantaras. A symbolic approach to reasoning with linguistic quantifiers. *In UAI*, Stanford, 74-82, 1992.

9. M. Jaeger. *Default Reasoning about Probabilities*. Ph. D. Thesis, Univ. Of Saarbruchen, 1995.
10. M.Y. Khayata. D. Pacholczyk. A Symbolic Approach to Linguistic Quantifiers. Proc. of IPMU'2000, Madrid, Spain, Vol 3, p 1720-1727.
11. M.Y. Khayata, D. Pacholczyk. A Symbolic Approach to Linguistic Quantification. *In First FAST IEEE Student Conference*, 101-106, Lahore, 1998.
12. H.E. Kyburg. The reference class. *Philosophy of Science*, 50(3): 374-397, 1983.
13. N.J. Nilsson. Probabilistic logic. *Artificial Intelligence*, 28(1): 71-88, 1986.
14. G. Paass. Probabilistic logic. In *Non Standard Logic for Automated Reasoning*, P. Smet et *al.* (eds.), Academic Press, 213-251, 1988.
15. D. Pacholczyk. Contribution au Traitement Logico-symbolique de la Connaissance. Thèse d'Etat. Université de PARIS 6, 1992.
16. D. Pacholczyk. A Logico-symbolic Probability Theory for the Management of Uncertainty. *CC-AI*, 11(4): 417-484, 1994.
17. J. Pearl. Probabilistic Reasoning in Intelligent Systems: Networks of Plausible Inference. Revised second printing, Morgan Kaufmann, San Francisco, 1991.
18. J. L. Pollock. Nomic Probabilities and the Foundations of Induction. Oxford University Press, 1990.
19. A.L. Ralescu, *B*. Bouchon-Meunier, D.A. Ralescu. Combining Fuzzy Quantifiers. *Rapport interne de LAFORIA*, 1996.
20. L. Sombé. Reasoning under incomplete information in artificial intelligence, John Wiley, 1990.
21. Y. Xiang, M.P. Beddoes, D. Poole. Can Uncertainty Management be realized in a finite totally ordered Probability Algebra. *Uncertainty in Artificial Intelligence* 5: 41-57, 1990.
22. R.R. Yager. Reasoning with quantified statements. *Part I, Kybernetes*, 14, 233-240, 1985.
23. R.R. Yager. Reasoning with quantified statements. *Part II, Kybernetes*, 14,111-120, 1986.
24. L.A. Zadeh. Fuzzy sets. *Information and Control*, 8: 338-353, 1965.
25. L.A. Zadeh. Syllogistic reasoning in Fuzzy logic and its application to usuality and reasoning with dispositions. *IEEE Transactions on Systems, Man and Cybernetics*, 15(6): 754-763, 1985.

Annex. Tables of operators

Table 1: Operator C

C	Q_1	Q_2	Q_3	Q_4	Q_5	Q_6	Q_7
Q_1	$[Q_1,Q_7]$	$\varnothing$	$\varnothing$	$\varnothing$	$\varnothing$	$\varnothing$	$\varnothing$
Q_2	$\{Q_1\}$	$[Q_2,Q_7]$	$\varnothing$	$\varnothing$	$\varnothing$	$\varnothing$	$\varnothing$
Q_3	$\{Q_1\}$	$[Q_2,Q_5]$	$[Q_6,Q_7]$	$\varnothing$	$\varnothing$	$\varnothing$	$\varnothing$
Q_4	$\{Q_1\}$	$[Q_2,Q_4]$	$\{Q_5\}$	$[Q_6,Q_7]$	$\varnothing$	$\varnothing$	$\varnothing$
Q_5	$\{Q_1\}$	$[Q_2,Q_3]$	$\{Q_4\}$	$\{Q_5\}$	$[Q_6,Q_7]$	$\varnothing$	$\varnothing$
Q_6	$\{Q_1\}$	$\{Q_2\}$	$\{Q_3\}$	$\{Q_4\}$	$\{Q_5\}$	$[Q_6,Q_7]$	$\varnothing$
Q_7	$\{Q_1\}$	$\{Q_2\}$	$\{Q_3\}$	$\{Q_4\}$	$\{Q_5\}$	$\{Q_6\}$	$\{Q_7\}$

Table 2: Operator I

I	Q_1	Q_2	Q_3	Q_4	Q_5	Q_6	Q_7
Q_1	Q_1	Q_1	Q_1	Q_1	Q_1	Q_1	Q_1
Q_2	Q_1	Q_2	Q_2	Q_2	Q_2	Q_2	Q_2
Q_3	Q_1	Q_2	Q_2	Q_2	Q_2	Q_3	Q_3
Q_4	Q_1	Q_2	Q_2	Q_2	Q_3	Q_4	Q_4
Q_5	Q_1	Q_2	Q_2	Q_3	Q_4	Q_5	Q_5
Q_6	Q_1	Q_2	Q_3	Q_4	Q_5	Q_6	Q_6
Q_7	Q_1	Q_2	Q_3	Q_4	Q_5	Q_6	Q_7

Table 3: Operator S

S	Q_1	Q_2	Q_3	Q_4	Q_5	Q_6
Q_1	$\{Q_1\}$	$\{Q_2\}$	$\{Q_3\}$	$\{Q_4\}$	$\{Q_5\}$	$\{Q_6\}$
Q_2	$\{Q_2\}$	$[Q_2,Q_3]$	$[Q_3,Q_4]$	$[Q_4,Q_5]$	$[Q_5,Q_6]$	$\{Q_6\}$
Q_3	$\{Q_3\}$	$[Q_3,Q_4]$	$[Q_4,Q_5]$	$[Q_5,Q_6]$	$\{Q_6\}$	
Q_4	$\{Q_4\}$	$[Q_4,Q_5]$	$[Q_5,Q_6]$	$\{Q_6\}$		
Q_5	$\{Q_5\}$	$[Q_5,Q_6]$	$\{Q_6\}$			
Q_6	$\{Q_6\}$	$\{Q_6\}$				

Table 4: Operator D

D	Q_1	Q_2	Q_3	Q_4	Q_5	Q_6
Q_1	$\{Q_1\}$					
Q_2	$\{Q_2\}$	$\{Q_2\}$				
Q_3	$\{Q_3\}$	$[Q_2,Q_3]$	$\{Q_2\}$			
Q_4	$\{Q_4\}$	$[Q_3,Q_4]$	$[Q_2,Q_3]$	$\{Q_2\}$		
Q_5	$\{Q_5\}$	$[Q_4Q_5]$	$[Q_3,Q_4]$	$[Q_2,Q_3]$	$\{Q_2\}$	
Q_6	$\{Q_6\}$	$[Q_5,Q_6]$	$[Q_4,Q_5]$	$[Q_3,Q_4]$	$[Q_2,Q_3]$	$\{Q_2\}$

On Algebraic Foundations of Information Granulation*

Helmut Thiele

University of Dortmund,
Department of Computer Science I,
D-44221 Dortmund, Germany

Abstract. In his paper "Towards a theory of fuzzy information granulation and its centrality in human reasoning and fuzzy logic" L.A. ZADEH writes "There are three basic concepts that underline human cognition: granulation, organisation and causation. Informally, granulation involves decomposition of whole into parts; organisation involves integration of parts into whole; and causation involves association of causes with effects.

Granulation of an object A leads to a collection of granules of A, with a granule being a clump of points (objects) drawn together by indistinguishability, similarity, proximity or functionality."

Furthermore, he writes:

"Modes of information granulation (IG) in which the granules are crisp (c-granular) play important roles in a wide variety of methods, approaches and techniques. Crisp IG, however, does not reflect the fact that in almost all of human reasoning and concept formation the granules are fuzzy (f-granular)."

The contribution presented contains first steps to develop a systematic mathematical theory fitting ZADEH's approach. Because of lacking space we restrict our considerations to the generation of granulations by equivalence, tolerance, S_4, partial order, and linear order relations, however, in the crisp as well as in the fuzzy case.
Keywords: Crisp Granules, Fuzzy Granules, Crisp Granulations, Fuzzy Granulations, Binary Crisp Relations, Binary Fuzzy Relations.

1 Introduction

In his papers [42, 43] L.A. ZADEH has presented the concept of fuzzy information granulation and pointed out its pivotal role in fuzzy logic and human reasoning.

Following ZADEH, a granular is "a clump of points(objects) drawn together by indistinuishability, similarity, proximity or functionality"(see [43], page111). The papers [18–26, 28] can be interpreted as first steps to construct granulations using equivalence relations, tolerance relations, so-called a-b-c relations, and RUSPINI relations, that is in the crisp and in the fuzzy case. In the papers quoted above we have made more precise ZADEH's approach as follows.

Let U be a non-empty set interpreted as an object which is to be taken apart to pieces (parts, "granules"). We distinguished between the crisp and fuzzy case.

* This research was supported by the Deutsche Forschungsgemeinschaft as part of the Collaborative Research Center "Computational Intelligence"(531).

In the crisp case granules of U are defined as crisp subsets of U, while in the fuzzy case granules G are defined to be fuzzy sets on U, i.e. mappings $G : U \to \langle 0,1\rangle$ where $\langle 0,1\rangle$ denotes the unit interval of real numbers.

Again following ZADEH we defined "a granulation of U as a collection of (crisp or fuzzy) granules of U", i.e. a granulation $\mathfrak{G}$ on U is a subset of $\mathbb{P}U$ in the crisp case and a subset $\mathcal{F} \subseteq \mathbb{FP}U$ in the fuzzy case where $\mathbb{P}U$ denotes the classical power set and $\mathbb{FP}U$ denotes the fuzzy power set of U, i.e. the set of all mapping $G : U \to \langle 0,1\rangle$.

A characterisation of granulations using KRIPKE semantics is developed in [27] where a set of fuzzy sets is termed by "qualitative fuzzy set".

Note that in [26] we have "fuzzified" the concept of granulation, i.e. we suggested to consider not only subsets $\mathfrak{G} \subseteq \mathbb{P}U$ and $\mathcal{F} \subseteq \mathbb{FP}U$, but also "fuzzy granulations" on U, that means, mappings $\Gamma : \mathbb{P}U \to \langle 0,1\rangle$ and $\Phi : \mathbb{FP}U \to \langle 0,1\rangle$, hence, fuzzy sets on $\mathbb{P}U$ and $\mathbb{FP}U$.

The contribution presented is an updated version of [30] supplemented by concepts and results of [29].

Furthermore, we note that because of lacking space this paper contains only algebraic existence theorems (without proofs). An extended version with all proofs will be published soon. Moreover the "pure" existence theorems are to be supplemented by algorithms and numerical investigations.

With respect to the "philosophy" of our paper we have to mention that a procedure which generates a granulation from a given binary relation must satisfy the following fundamental "reconstructing property". Starting with the generated granulation the generating binary relations can be reconstructed. With other words, the procedure of generating a granulation can be carried out without lost of the "structural information" which the generating binary relation contains. Obviously, if this "reconstructing property" fails then the concerning generating procedure can be completely non-sense both for theory and applications, in general. To recognize that the "reconstructing property" is an important part of the investigations in this paper see, for instance, Corollary 1.

2 Binary Relations

In the following Sections 3-6 we shall only study the generation of granulations $\mathfrak{G} \subseteq \mathbb{P}U$ by crisp binary relations on U. For shortness we ommit the word "crisp" when speaking about crisp relations.

Let R be a binary relation on U, i.e. $R \subseteq U \times U$. We denote $[x,y] \in R$ also by xRy.

We assume that the reader is familiar with the concepts of equivalence relation, tolerance relation, and partial order relation on U.

For definiteness we recall

Definition 1. 1. R is said to be a preorder relation on $U =_{\text{def}}$
R is reflexive and transitive on U.

2. R is said to be a comparability relation on $U =_{\text{def}}$
   $\forall x \forall y(x, y \in U \rightarrow xRy \vee yRx)$.
3. R is said to be a linear order relation on $U =_{\text{def}}$
   R is a partial order and a comparability relation on U.

3 Generating Granulations by Equivalence Relations and by Tolerance Relations

For $R \subseteq U \times U$ we define

Definition 2. 1. $\mathrm{GRAN}(R) =_{\text{def}} \{xR | x \in U\}$ if R is an equivalence relation on U and $xR =_{\text{def}} \{y | y \in U \wedge xRy\}$.
2. $\mathrm{GRAN}'(R) =_{\text{def}} \{G | G \times G \subseteq R \wedge \neg\exists H(H \times H \subseteq R \wedge G \subset H)\}$ if R is a tolerance relation on U.

Furthermore, for $\mathfrak{G} \subseteq \mathbb{P}U$ we define

Definition 3. $\mathrm{REL}(\mathfrak{G}) =_{\text{def}} \{[x, y] | x, y \in U \wedge \exists G(G \in \mathfrak{G} \wedge x \in G \wedge y \in G)\}$.

For more information about equivalence relations see text books on algebra, for instance [7]. More information on tolerance relations one can find in [5,6,21,44,45].

4 Generating Granulations by Preorder Relations

The concepts and the results of the following chapters are partially new as far as we know.

In Section 4 we use the mapping GRAN. The mapping REL is unusable for generating binary relations in the Sections 4-6. Therefore we use the mapping REL$'$ defined as follows (see [29], definition 4.1)

Definition 4. $\mathrm{REL}'(\mathfrak{G}) =_{\text{def}} \{[x, y] | x, y \in U \wedge \forall G(G \in \mathfrak{G} \wedge x \in G \rightarrow y \in G)\}$.

Furthermore, we have to introduce the following new concepts if we want to characterize granulations of the form $\mathrm{GRAN}(R)$ where R is a preorder relation.

Definition 5. 1. $\mathfrak{G}$ is said to be reflexive-like $=_{\text{def}}$
   $\forall x(x \in U \rightarrow \bigcap\{G | G \in \mathfrak{G} \wedge x \in G\} \in \mathfrak{G})$.
2. $\mathfrak{G}$ is said to be transitive-like $=_{\text{def}}$
   $\forall G(G \in \mathfrak{G} \rightarrow \exists x(x \in U \wedge \bigcap\{H | H \in \mathfrak{G} \wedge x \in H\} = G))$.
3. $\mathfrak{G}$ is said to be preorder-like $=_{\text{def}}$
   $\mathfrak{G}$ is reflexive-like and transitive-like.

Lemma 1. $\forall R(R$ *is reflexive* $\rightarrow$

1. $\mathrm{GRAN}(R)$ *is reflexive-like* $\wedge$
2. $\mathrm{REL}'(\mathrm{GRAN}(R)) \subseteq R)$.

Lemma 2. $\forall R(R$ *is transitive* $\rightarrow$

1. $\mathrm{GRAN}(R)$ *is transitive-like* $\wedge$
2. $R \subseteq \mathrm{REL}'(\mathrm{GRAN}(R)))$.

Corollary 1. $\forall R(R$ *is a preorder relation on* $U \rightarrow \mathrm{REL}'(\mathrm{GRAN}(R)) = R)$.

Theorem 1. *The mapping* GRAN *is an injection from the set of all preorder relations on* U *into the set of all preorder-like granulation of* U.

Now, we shall show that GRAN is a mapping onto the set of all preorder-like granulations of U.

Lemma 3. *1.* $\forall \mathfrak{G}(\mathfrak{G} \subseteq \mathbb{P}U \rightarrow \mathrm{REL}'(\mathfrak{G})$ *is a preorder relation on* $U)$.
2. $\forall \mathfrak{G}(\mathfrak{G} \subseteq \mathbb{P}U \wedge \mathfrak{G}$ *is reflexive-like* $\rightarrow \mathrm{GRAN}(\mathrm{REL}'(\mathfrak{G})) \subseteq \mathfrak{G})$.
3. $\forall \mathfrak{G}(\mathfrak{G} \subseteq \mathbb{P}U \wedge \mathfrak{G}$ *is transitive-like* $\rightarrow \mathfrak{G} \subseteq \mathrm{GRAN}(\mathrm{REL}'(\mathfrak{G})))$.

Corollary 2. $\forall \mathfrak{G}(\mathfrak{G} \subseteq \mathbb{P}U \wedge \mathfrak{G}$ *is preorder-like* $\rightarrow \mathrm{GRAN}(\mathrm{REL}'(\mathfrak{G})) = \mathfrak{G})$.

Theorem 2. *1. The mapping* GRAN *is a bijection from the set of all preorder relations on* U *onto the set of all preorder-like granulations of* U.
2. *The mapping* REL' *is a bijection from the set of all preorder-like granulations of* U *onto the set of all preorder relations on* U.
3. REL' *is the inversion of* GRAN *and vice versa.*

5 Generating Granulations by Partial Order Relations

For an arbitrary granulation $\mathfrak{G} \subseteq \mathbb{P}U$ we define

Definition 6. 1. $\mathfrak{G}$ fulfills the separation property $=_{\mathrm{def}}$

$$\forall x \forall y(x, y \in U \wedge x \neq y \rightarrow \exists G(G \in \mathfrak{G} \wedge x \in G \wedge y \notin G) \vee \exists H(H \in \mathfrak{G} \wedge y \in H \wedge x \notin H)).$$

2. $\mathfrak{G}$ is said to be partial order-like $=_{\mathrm{def}}$
   $\mathfrak{G}$ is preorder-like and fulfills the separation property.

Lemma 4. $\forall R(R \subseteq U \times U \wedge R$ *is antisymmetric* $\wedge R$ *is reflexive on* $U \rightarrow \mathrm{GRAN}(R)$ *fulfills the separation property*$)$.

Lemma 5. $\forall \mathfrak{G}(\mathfrak{G} \subseteq \mathbb{P}U \wedge \mathfrak{G}$ *fulfills the separation property*$\rightarrow \mathrm{REL}'(\mathfrak{G})$ *is antisymmetric*$)$.

Using the results of Section 4 we obtain

Theorem 3. *1. The mapping* REL' *is a bijection from the set of all partial order-like granulations of* U *onto the set of all partial order relations on* U.
2. *The mapping* GRAN *is a bijection from the set of all partial order relations on* U *onto the set of all partial order like granulations of* U.
3. GRAN *is the inversion of* REL' *and vice versa.*

6 Generating Granulations by Linear Order Relations

For an arbitrary granulation $\mathfrak{G} \subseteq \mathbb{P}U$ we define

Definition 7. 1. $\mathfrak{G}$ is said to be comparability-like $=_{\mathrm{def}}$
$\forall x \forall y(x, y \in H \rightarrow$
$\forall G(G \in \mathfrak{G} \wedge x \in G \rightarrow y \in G) \vee \forall H(G \in \mathfrak{G} \wedge y \in G \rightarrow x \in H))$.
2. $\mathfrak{G}$ is said to be linear order-like $=_{\mathrm{def}}$
$\mathfrak{G}$ is partial order-like and comparability-like.

Lemma 6. $\forall R(R \subseteq U \times U \wedge R$ *is a comparability relation on* $U \wedge R$ *is transitive* $\rightarrow \mathrm{GRAN}(R)$ *is comparability-like*).

Lemma 7. $\forall R(R \subseteq \mathbb{P}U \wedge \mathfrak{G}$ *is comparability-like* $\rightarrow \mathrm{REL}'(\mathfrak{G})$ *is a comparability relation on* U).

Lemma 8. $\forall R(R \subseteq U \times U \wedge R$ *is a linear order-relation on* $U \rightarrow$

1. $\mathrm{GRAN}(R)$ *is linear-order like* $\wedge$
2. $\mathrm{REL}'(\mathrm{GRAN}(R)) = R$).

Lemma 9. $\forall \mathfrak{G}(\mathfrak{G} \subseteq \mathbb{P}U \wedge \mathfrak{G}$ *is a linear order-like* $\rightarrow$

1. REL' *is a linear-order relation on* $U \wedge$
2. $\mathrm{GRAN}(\mathrm{REL}'(\mathfrak{G})) = \mathfrak{G}$).

Theorem 4. *1. The mapping* GRAN *is a bijection from the set of all linear order relations on* U *onto the set of all linear order granulations of* U.
2. *The mapping* REL' *is a bijection from the set of all linear order-like granulations of* U *onto the set of all linear order-relations on* U.
3. REL' *is the inversion of* GRAN *and vice versa.*

7 Binary Fuzzy Relations

For definiteness we start with recalling some well-known concepts and facts drawn from the theory of binary fuzzy relations.

For all the following definitions and theorems we fix a function:

$$\pi : \langle 0,1 \rangle \times \langle 0,1 \rangle \rightarrow \langle 0,1 \rangle .$$

Assume $S : U \times U \rightarrow \langle 0,1 \rangle$.

Definition 8. 1. S is said to be fuzzy reflexive on $U =_{\mathrm{def}}$
$\forall x(x \in U \rightarrow S(x,x) = 1)$.
2. S is said to be π-implication based transitive on $U =_{\mathrm{def}}$
$\forall x \forall y \forall z(x, y, z \in U \rightarrow S(x,y) \leq \pi(S(y,z), S(x,z)))$.
3. S is said to be fuzzy symmetric on $U =_{\mathrm{def}}$
$\forall x \forall y(x, y \in U \rightarrow S(x,y) = S(y,x))$.

4. S is said to be fuzzy antisymmetric on $U =_{\text{def}}$
   $\forall x \forall y(x, y \in U \wedge S(x,y) = 1 \wedge S(y,x) = 1 \rightarrow x = y)$.
5. S is said to be a fuzzy comparability relation on $U =_{\text{def}}$
   $\forall x \forall y(x, y \in U \rightarrow S(x,y) = 1 \vee S(y,x) = 1)$.
6. S is said to be a π-implication based fuzzy equivalence relation on $U =_{\text{def}}$
   S satisfies the items 1, 2 and 3.
7. S is said to be a fuzzy tolerance relation on $U =_{\text{def}}$
   S satisfies the items 1 and 3.
8. S is said to be a π-implication based fuzzy preorder relation on $U =_{\text{def}}$
   S satisfies the items 1 and 2.
9. S is said to be a π-implication based fuzzy partial order relation on $U =_{\text{def}}$
   S satisfies the items 1, 2 and 4.
10. S is said to be a π-implication based fuzzy linear order relation on $U =_{\text{def}}$
   S satisfies the items 1, 2, 4 and 5.
11. $\lambda y\, S(x,y) =_{\text{def}} F_x$ where for fixed $x \in U$ the fuzzy set F_x is defined by $F_x(y) =_{\text{def}} S(x,y)$ for every $y \in U$.

8 Generating Fuzzy Granulations by Fuzzy Equivalence Relations

Assume $S : U \times U \rightarrow \langle 0,1 \rangle$ and $\mathcal{F} \subseteq \mathbb{FP}U$. Furthermore assume that τ_W denotes the weakest t-norm, i.e. τ_W satisfies for every $r, s \in \langle 0,1 \rangle$ the equations

$$\tau_W(r,1) = r,\quad \tau_W(1,s) = s,\quad \tau_W(r,s) = 0 \text{ if } r < 1 \text{ and } s < 1.$$

The papers [18, 32] contain the following concepts and results. Assume $x, y \in U$.

Definition 9. 1. $\mathrm{FGRAN}(S) =_{\text{def}} \{\lambda y\, S(x,y) | x \in U\}$.
2. $\mathrm{FREL}(\mathcal{F})(x,y) =_{\text{def}} \sup\{\tau_W(F(x), F(y)) | F \in \mathcal{F}\}$.

Definition 10. $\mathcal{F}$ is said to be π-implication based fuzzy partition of $U =_{\text{def}}$

1. $\forall F(F \in \mathcal{F} \rightarrow \exists x(x \in U \wedge F(x) = 1))$,
2. $\forall x(x \in U \rightarrow \exists F(F \in \mathcal{F} \wedge F(x) = 1))$, and
3. $\forall F \forall G \forall x \forall y(F, G \in \mathcal{F} \wedge x, y \in U \wedge F(x) = 1 \rightarrow G(x) \leq \pi(G(y), F(y)))$.

Lemma 10. *If*

1. $\forall s(s \in \langle 0,1 \rangle \rightarrow \pi(1,s) = s)$,
2. $\forall r \forall s(r, s \in \langle 0,1 \rangle \wedge \pi(r,s) = \pi(s,r) \rightarrow r = s)$, *and*
3. *S is a π-implication based fuzzy equivalence relation on U*

then

1. $\mathrm{FGRAN}(S)$ *is a π-implication based fuzzy partition of U, and*
2. $\mathrm{FREL}(\mathrm{FGRAN}(S)) = S$.

Lemma 11. *If*

1. $\forall s(s \in \langle 0,1\rangle \rightarrow \pi(1,s) = s)$,
2. $\forall r \forall s(r,s \in \langle 0,1\rangle \wedge \pi(r,s) = \pi(s,r) \rightarrow r = s)$, *and*
3. $\mathcal{F}$ *is a* π*-implication based fuzzy partition of* U

then

1. $\mathrm{FREL}(\mathcal{F})$ *is a* π*-implication based fuzzy equivalence relation on* U, *and*
2. $\mathrm{FGRAN}(\mathrm{FREL}(\mathcal{F})) = \mathcal{F}$.

Theorem 5. 1. *The mapping* FGRAN *is a a bijection from the set of all* π*-implication based fuzzy equivalence relations on* U *onto the set of all* π*-implication based fuzzy partitions of* U.
2. *The mapping* FREL *is a bijection from the set of all* π*-implication based fuzzy partitions of* U *onto the set of all* π*-implication based fuzzy equivalence relations on* U.
3. *The mapping* FREL *is the inversion of the mapping* FGRAN *and vice versa.*

9 Generating Fuzzy Granulations by Fuzzy Tolerance Relations

For fuzzy tolerance relations we can not use the mapping FGRAN in order to generate fuzzy granulations so that the given fuzzy tolerance relation S can be reconstructed using $\mathrm{FGRAN}(S)$.

Furthermore, we cannot use the mapping FREL in order to generate a fuzzy tolerance relation $\mathrm{FREL}(\mathcal{F})$ so that the given fuzzy granulation $\mathcal{F}$ can be reconstructed using $\mathrm{FREL}(\mathcal{F})$.

The following concepts and results are contained in the paper [19] (see also [23,24]) where we have solved the generation and reconstruction problem if we use fuzzy tolerance relations.

Let F and G be fuzzy sets on U and S, T binary fuzzy relations on U, i.e. $F, G : U \rightarrow \langle 0,1\rangle$ and $S, T : U \times U \rightarrow \langle 0,1\rangle$.

We use the following well-known definitions:

Definition 11. 1. $F \sqsubseteq G =_{\mathrm{def}} \forall x(x \in U \rightarrow F(x) \leq G(x))$.
2. $F \sqsubset G =_{\mathrm{def}} F \sqsubseteq G \wedge F \neq G$.
3. $S \sqsubseteq T =_{\mathrm{def}} \forall x \forall y(x,y \in U \rightarrow S(x,y) \leq T(x,y))$.
4. $(F \times G)(x,y) =_{\mathrm{def}} \min(F(x), G(y)) \quad (x,y \in U)$.

Now, we replace the mapping FGRAN and FREL by the mapping FGRAN$'$ and FREL$'$, respectively, defined as follows

Definition 12. 1. $\mathrm{FGRAN}'(S) =_{\mathrm{def}}$
$$\{F | F : U \rightarrow \langle 0,1\rangle \wedge F \times F \sqsubseteq S \wedge \neg\exists G(G : U \rightarrow \langle 0,1\rangle \wedge G \times G \sqsubseteq S \wedge F \sqsubset G)\}.$$
2. $\mathrm{FREL}'(\mathcal{F})(x,y) =_{\mathrm{def}}$
$$\sup\{\min(F(x), F(y)) | F \in \mathcal{F})\}.$$

Fuzzy sets F on U with $F \times F \sqsubseteq S$ are called fuzzy tolerance classes of S, hence $\mathrm{FGRAN}'(S)$ is the set of all maximal fuzzy tolerance classes of the binary fuzzy relation S.

Now, we want to characterize the set $\mathrm{FGRAN}'(S)$ if S is a fuzzy tolerance relation. Therefore we define

Definition 13. $\mathcal{F}$ is said to be a fuzzy tolerance covering of $U =_{\text{def}}$

1. $\mathcal{F}$ is a fuzzy covering of $U =_{\text{def}}$
   $\forall x(x \in U \rightarrow \sup\{F(x)|F \in \mathcal{F}\} = 1)$.
2. $\mathcal{F}$ is strongly fuzzy compact $=_{\text{def}}$
   $\forall F(F : U \rightarrow \langle 0,1\rangle \wedge$
   $\forall x \forall y(x, y \in U \rightarrow$
   $\min(F(x), F(y)) \leq \sup\{\min(G(x), G(y))|G \in \mathcal{F})\}) \longrightarrow$
   $\exists F^*(F^* \in \mathcal{F} \wedge F \sqsubseteq F^*))$.
3. $\mathcal{F}$ is a fuzzy anti-chain $=_{\text{def}}$
   $\forall F \forall G(F, G \in \mathcal{F} \wedge F \sqsubseteq G \rightarrow F = G)$.

Lemma 12. $\forall S(S$ *is a fuzzy tolerance relation on* $U \rightarrow$

1. $\mathrm{FGRAN}'(S)$ *is a fuzzy tolerance covering of* $U \wedge$
2. $\mathrm{FREL}'(\mathrm{FGRAN}'(S)) = S)$.

Lemma 13. $\forall \mathcal{F}(\mathcal{F}$ *is a fuzzy tolerance covering of* $U \rightarrow$

1. $\mathrm{FREL}'(\mathcal{F})$ *is a fuzzy tolerance relation on* $U \wedge$
2. $\mathrm{FGRAN}'(\mathrm{FREL}'(\mathcal{F})) = \mathcal{F})$.

Theorem 6. *1. The mapping* FGRAN' *is a bijection from the set of all fuzzy tolerance relations on* U *onto the set of all fuzzy tolerance coverings of* U.
2. *The mapping* FREL' *is a bijection from the set of all fuzzy tolerance coverings of* U *onto the set of all fuzzy tolerance relations on* U.
3. *The mapping* FREL' *is the inversion of the mapping* FGRAN' *and vice versa.*

10 Generating Fuzzy Granulations by Fuzzy Preorder Relations

The concepts and the results of the following chapters are new as far as we know.

For generating fuzzy granulations from binary fuzzy relations we return to the mapping FGRAN defined in Section 8, i.e. as

$$\mathrm{FGRAN}(S) =_{\text{def}} \{\lambda y S(x, y)|x \in U\}.$$

But, the mapping FREL (see Definition 9) and the mapping FREL' (see Definition 12) are unuseable for generating binary fuzzy relations in the following sections.

Therefore, we shall use the mapping FREL'' defined as follows.

Let π be the function $\pi : \langle 0,1\rangle \times \langle 0,1\rangle \rightarrow \langle 0,1\rangle$ fulfilling the axiom $\forall s(s \in \langle 0,1\rangle \rightarrow \pi(1, s) = s)$.

Definition 14. $\mathrm{FREL}''(\mathcal{F})(x,y) =_{\mathrm{def}} \inf\{\pi(F(x),F(y)) | F \in \mathcal{F}\} \quad (x,y \in U)$.

This definition is motivated by definition 4.1 in [29] where for a crisp granulation $\mathfrak{G} \subseteq \mathbb{P}U$ we have defined REL' by (see also Definition 4)

$$\mathrm{REL}'(\mathfrak{G}) =_{\mathrm{def}} \{[x,y] | x,y \in U \wedge \forall G(G \in \mathfrak{G} \wedge x \in G \rightarrow y \in G)\}.$$

Lemma 14. $\forall S(S : U \times U \rightarrow \langle 0,1\rangle \wedge S$ *is fuzzy reflexive on* $U \rightarrow$ $\mathrm{FREL}''(\mathrm{FGRAN}(S)) \subseteq S)$.

Lemma 15. $\forall S(S : U \times U \rightarrow \langle 0,1\rangle \wedge S$ *is* π*-implication based fuzzy transitive on* $U \rightarrow S \subseteq \mathrm{FREL}''(\mathrm{FGRAN}(S)))$.

Theorem 7. $\forall S(S : U \times U \rightarrow \langle 0,1\rangle \wedge S$ *is a* π*-implication based fuzzy preorder relation on* $U \rightarrow \mathrm{FREL}''(\mathrm{FGRAN}(S)) = S)$.

Corollary 3. 1. FGRAN *is an injection from the set of all* π*-implication based fuzzy preorder relations into the set of all fuzzy granulations of* U.
2. FREL'' *is the inversion of* FGRAN.

Now, we are going to characterize all fuzzy granulations of the form $\mathrm{FGRAN}(S)$ where S is a π-implication based fuzzy preorder relation.

Therefore we define where $\mathfrak{F} \subseteq \mathbb{FP}U$.

Definition 15. 1. $\mathfrak{F}$ is said to be fuzzy π-intersection closed $=_{\mathrm{def}}$
$\forall x(x \in U \rightarrow \lambda y \inf\{\pi(F(x),F(y)) | F \in \mathfrak{F}\} \in \mathfrak{F}) \quad (y \in U)$.
2. $\mathfrak{F}$ is said to be fuzzy π-complete $=_{\mathrm{def}}$
$\forall F(F \in \mathfrak{F} \rightarrow \exists x(x \in U \wedge F = \lambda y \inf\{\pi(G(x),G(y)) | G \in \mathfrak{F}\}))$.
3. $\mathfrak{F}$ is said to be a π-implication based fuzzy preorder granulation of $U =_{\mathrm{def}}$
$\mathfrak{F}$ satisfies the items 1 and 2 above.

Lemma 16. $\forall S(S : U \times U \rightarrow \langle 0,1\rangle \wedge S$ *is a* π*-implication based fuzzy preorder relation on* $U \rightarrow \mathrm{FGRAN}(S)$ *is a* π*-implication based fuzzy preorder granulation of* $U)$.

Corollary 4. FGRAN *is an injection from the set of all* π*-implication based fuzzy preorder relations on* U *into the set of all* π*-implication based fuzzy preorder granulations of* U.

Lemma 17. $\forall \mathfrak{F}(\mathfrak{F} \subseteq \mathbb{FP}U$ *is fuzzy* π*-intersection closed* $\rightarrow$ $\mathrm{FGRAN}(\mathrm{FREL}''(\mathfrak{F})) \subseteq \mathfrak{F})$.

Lemma 18. $\forall \mathfrak{F}(\mathfrak{F} \subseteq \mathbb{FP}U$ *is fuzzy* π*-complete* $\rightarrow \mathfrak{F} \subseteq \mathrm{FGRAN}(\mathrm{FREL}''(\mathfrak{F})))$.

Theorem 8. $\forall \mathfrak{F}(\mathfrak{F} \subseteq \mathbb{FP}U$ *is a* π*-implication based fuzzy preorder granulation of* $U \rightarrow \mathrm{FGRAN}(\mathrm{FREL}''(\mathfrak{F})) = \mathfrak{F}$.

Theorem 9. 1. FGRAN *is a bijection from the set of all* π*-implication based fuzzy preorder relations on* U *onto the set of all* π*-implication based fuzzy preorder granulations of* U.
2. FREL'' *is a bijection from the set of all* π*-implication based fuzzy preorder granulations of* U *onto the set of all* π*-implication based fuzzy preorder relations on* U.
3. *The mapping* FREL'' *is the inversion of the mapping* FGRAN *and vice versa.*

11 Generating Fuzzy Granulations by Fuzzy Partial Order Relations

For an arbitrary fuzzy granulation $\mathfrak{F} \subseteq \mathbb{FP}U$ we define

Definition 16. 1. $\mathfrak{F}$ satisfies the π-implication based fuzzy separation property $=_{\text{def}}$

$$\forall x \forall y (x, y \in U \wedge x \neq y \rightarrow \exists F(F \in \mathfrak{F} \wedge \pi(F(x), F(y) < 1) \vee \exists G(G \in \mathfrak{F} \wedge \pi(G(y), G(x) < 1)).$$

2. $\mathfrak{F}$ is said to be a π-implication based fuzzy partial order like granulation of U $=_{\text{def}}$
   $\mathfrak{F}$ is a π-implication based fuzzy preorder granulation of U and satisfies the π-implication based fuzzy separation property.

Lemma 19. $\forall S(S : U \times U \rightarrow \langle 0, 1\rangle \wedge S$ *is a fuzzy reflexive on* $U \wedge S$ *is fuzzy antisymmetric on* $U \rightarrow \mathrm{FGRAN}(S)$ *satisfies the* π*-implication based fuzzy separation property*).

Lemma 20. $\forall \mathfrak{F}(\mathfrak{F} \subseteq \mathbb{FP}U \wedge \mathfrak{F}$ *satisfies the* π*-implication based fuzzy separation property* $\rightarrow \mathrm{FREL}''(\mathfrak{F})$ *is fuzzy antisymmetric*).

Using the results of Section 10 we obtain

Theorem 10. *1.* FGRAN *is a bijection from the set of all* π*-implication based fuzzy partial order relations on* U *onto the set of all* π*-implication fuzzy partial order like granulations of* U*.*

2. *The mapping* FREL'' *is a bijection from the set of all* π*-implication based fuzzy partial order like granulations of* U *onto the set of all* π*-implication based fuzzy partial order relations on* U*.*
3. *The mapping* FREL'' *is the inversion of the mapping* FGRAN *and vice versa.*

12 Generating Fuzzy Granulations by Fuzzy Linear Order Relations

For arbitrary fuzzy granulations $\mathfrak{F} \subseteq \mathbb{FP}U$ we define

Definition 17. 1. $\mathfrak{F}$ satisfies the π-implication based fuzzy comparability property $=_{\text{def}}$

$$\forall x \forall y (x, y \in U \rightarrow \forall F(F \in \mathfrak{F} \rightarrow \pi(F(x), F(y) = 1) \vee \forall G(G \in \mathfrak{F} \rightarrow \pi(G(y), G(x) = 1)).$$

2. $\mathfrak{F}$ is said to be a π-implication based fuzzy linear order like granulation of U $=_{\text{def}}$
   $\mathfrak{F}$ is a π-implication based fuzzy partial order like granulation of U and satisfies the π-implication based fuzzy comparability property.

Lemma 21. *$\forall S(S : U \times U \to \langle 0,1\rangle \wedge S$ is a fuzzy comparability relation on $U \wedge S$ is fuzzy π-implication based fuzzy transitive on $U \to$ $\mathrm{FGRAN}(S)$ satisfies the π-implication based fuzzy comparability property).*

Lemma 22. *$\forall \mathfrak{F}(\mathfrak{F} \subseteq \mathbb{FP}U \wedge \mathfrak{F}$ satisfies the π-implication based fuzzy comparability property $\to$ $\mathrm{FREL}''(\mathfrak{F})$ is a fuzzy comparability relation on U).*

Lemma 23. *$\forall S(S : U \times U \to \langle 0,1\rangle \wedge S$ is a π-implication based fuzzy linear order relation on $U \to$*

1. *$\mathrm{FGRAN}(S)$ is a π-implication based fuzzy linear order granulation of $U \wedge$*
2. *$\mathrm{FREL}''(\mathrm{FGRAN}(S)) = S$).*

Lemma 24. *$\forall \mathfrak{F}(\mathfrak{F} \subseteq \mathbb{FP}U \wedge \mathfrak{F}$ is a π-implication based fuzzy linear order like granulation of $U \to$*

1. *$\mathrm{FREL}''(\mathfrak{F})$ is a π-implication based fuzzy linear order relation on $U \wedge$*
2. *$\mathrm{FGRAN}(\mathrm{FREL}''(\mathfrak{F})) = \mathfrak{F}$).*

Theorem 11.
1. *The mapping FGRAN is a bijection from the set of all π-implication based fuzzy linear order relations on U onto the set of all π-implication based fuzzy linear order like granulations of U.*
2. *The mapping FREL'' is a bijection from the set of all π-implication based fuzzy linear order like granulations of U onto the set of all π-implication based fuzzy linear order relations on U.*
3. *The mapping FREL'' is the inversion of the mapping FGRAN and vice versa.*

13 Conclusions and Final Remarks

1. We recall the well-known fact that the set of all equivalence relations on U as well as the set of all partitions of U form a lattice and, furthermore, that these lattices are isomorphic with respect to the mappings GRAN and REL, respectively.
   We have generalized this result to
   - the lattice of tolerance relations on U and the lattice of tolerance coverings of U [21],
   - the lattice of fuzzy equivalence relations on U and the lattice of fuzzy partitions of U [18,32],
   - the DE MORGAN algebra of all fuzzy tolerance relations on U and the DE MORGAN algebra of all fuzzy tolerance coverings of U [23].

   In a forthcoming paper we shall investigate the remaining cases discussed in this contribution.
2. By definition 8 we have introduced that

   "S is said to be π-implication based transitive on U".

   This concept is firstly introduced and used for characterizing (π-implication based) fuzzy equivalence relations and fuzzy partitions in [32]. Furthermore, for the same purpose in the paper mentioned we also used the well-known concept of fuzzy transitivity defined by

S is said to be κ-conjunction based transitive on $U =_{\text{def}}$
$$\forall x \forall y \forall z (x, y, z \in U \rightarrow \kappa(S(x,y), S(y,z)) \leq S(x,z))$$

where κ is a usual t-norm.
These approaches are not equivalent, in general. If we replace the π-implication based transitivity by the κ-conjunction based transitivity in Sections 7-12 of this contribution we get a series of new problems which will also be investigated in a forthcoming paper. Meanwhile we have recognized that for proving the concerning result in [32] we do not need all properties of a t-norm but only few of them.

3. Obviously, the concepts and results presented in Sections 4-6 have close interrelations to general topology. The same holds for fuzzy topology in Sections 10-12. So, for instance, the separation property (definition 6) means that $\mathfrak{G}$ fulfils the T_0-separation axiom, and that $\mathcal{F} \subseteq \mathbb{FP}U$ satisfies the π-implication based fuzzy separation property (definition 16) can be interpreted that $\mathcal{F}$ fulfils a special version of a fuzzy T_0-separation axiom. The interrelations mentioned above will be investigated in detail in a forthcoming paper.

Acknowledgements.
The author would like to thank Claus-Peter Alberts for his help in preparing the manuscript.

References

1. Bellmann R.E., Zadeh L.A. (1977) Local and fuzzy logics. In: Dunn J.M., Epstein G. (Eds.) Modern Uses of Multiple-Valued Logic – Invited Papers of 5th ISMVL Symposium 1975. Reidel, Dordrecht, 103–165
2. Bezdek J.C. (1981) Pattern Recognition with Fuzzy Objective Function Algorithms. Plenum Press, New York
3. Bezdek J.C., Pal S.K. (1992) Fuzzy Models for Pattern Recognition: Methods that Search for Patterns in Data. IEEE Press, New York
4. Bobrowski L., Bezdek J.C. (1991) C-means clustering with the l_1 and l_∞ norms. IEEE Trans. on Systems, Man and Cybernetics **21(3)**:545–554
5. Chajda I., Niederle J., Zelinka B. (1976) On existence conditions for compatible tolerances. Czechoslovak Mathematical Journal **26**:304–311
6. Chajda I., Zelinka B. (1977) Lattice of tolerances. Čassopis pro pěstováni matematiky **102**:10–24
7. Cohn P.M. (1981) Universal Algebra. Dordrecht, Boston, London
8. Dubois D., Prade H. (1994) Similarity-based approximate reasoning. In: Zurada J.M., Marks R.J., Robinson C.J. (1994) Computational Intelligence Imitating Life. IEEE Press, New York, 69–80
9. Duran B.S., Odell P.L. (1974) Cluster Analysis: A Survey. Springer, New York

10. Gottwald S. (1993) Fuzzy Sets and Fuzzy Logic. Foundations of Application – from a Mathematical Point of View. Artificial Intelligence, Vieweg
11. Hata Y., Mukaidono M. (1999) On some classes of fuzzy information granularity and their representations. 29th IEEE Symposium on Multi-Valued Logic(ISMVL'99), 28–287
12. Hirano S., Hata Y., Kamiura N. (1998) Medical image granulation by fuzzy inference. 17th Annual Meeting of the North American Fuzzy Information Processing Society NAFIPS, August, 1998. 188–192
13. Klawonn F. (1995) Similarity based reasoning. EUFIT '95 – Third European Congress on Intelligent Techniques and Soft Computing, Aachen, Germany, August 28-31, 1995. 34–38
14. Kruse R., Gebhardt J., Klawonn F. (1994) Foundations of Fuzzy Systems. Wiley, Chichester
15. Pedrycz W. (1998) Granular computing in fuzzy modeling and data mining. Talk held at the University of Dortmund, February 24
16. Ruspini E.H. (1969) A new approach to clustering. Information and Control **15(1)**:22–32
17. Ruspini E.H. (1970) Numerical methods for fuzzy clustering. Information Sciences **2(3)**:319–350
18. Schmechel N. (1996) On the isomorphic lattices of fuzzy equivalence relations and fuzzy partitions. Multiple Valued Logic – An International Journal **2(1)**:1–46
19. Thiele H. (1995) On the mutual definability of fuzzy tolerance relations and fuzzy tolerance coverings. The Twenty-Fifth International Symposium on Multiple-Valued Logic ISMVL'95, Bloomington, Indiana, May 23-25, 1995. 140–145
20. Thiele H. (1996) On similarity based fuzzy clusterings. In: Dubois D., Klement E.P., Prade H. (Eds.) Proceedings of Linz'96 – Fuzzy Sets, Logics, and Artificial Intelligence, Linz, Austria, February 20–24, 1996. 135–138
21. Thiele H. (1996) On isomorphisms between the lattice of tolerance relations and lattices of clusterings. Proceedings of the Twenty-Sixth International Symposium on Multiple-Valued Logic ISMVL'96, Santiago de Compostela, Spain, May 29-31, 1996. 198–202
22. Thiele H. (1996) A characterization of RUSPINI-partitions by similarity relations. International Conference on Information Processing and Management of Uncertainty in Knowledge-Based Systems IPMU '96, Granada, Spain, July 1-5, 1996. Volume I, 389–394
23. Thiele H. (1996) On isomorphisms between the DE MORGAN algebra of fuzzy tolerance relations and DE MORGAN algebras of fuzzy clusterings. Fifth IEEE International Conference on Fuzzy Systems FUZZ-IEEE'96, New Orleans, USA, September 8-11, 1996.
24. Thiele H. (1996) On mathematical foundations of fuzzy cluster analysis. Multiple Valued Logic – An International Journal **1(2)**:85–123
25. Thiele H. (1997) A characterization of arbitrary RUSPINI partitions by fuzzy similarity relations. Sixth IEEE International Conference on Fuzzy Systems FUZZ-IEEE'97, Barcelona, Spain, July 1-5, 1997. Volume I, 131–134
26. Thiele H. (1998) On Semantic Models for Investigating 'Computing with Words'. Keynote address. Second International Conference on Knowledge-Based Intelligent Electronic Systems, Adelaide, Australia, April 21-23, 1998. Extended Version: On Semantic Models for Investigating 'Computing with Words'. Technical Report CI-32/98, University of dortmund, Collaborative Research Center 531(Computational Intelligence)
27. Thiele H. (1999) On the concept of qualitative fuzzy set. The Twenty-Ninth International Symposium on Multiple-Valued Logic ISMVL'99, Freiburg, Germany, May 20-22, 1999. 282–287

28. Thiele H. (2000) On Fuzzy Clusterings with Variable Boundary Conditions. Fifth International Conference on Fuzzy Sets Theory and its Applications FSTA2000, Liptovsky Mikulas, The Slovak Republic, January 30-February 4, 2000. To appear in "Tatra Mountains Mathematical Publications".
29. Thiele H. (2000) On Algebraic Foundations of Information Granulation I (The Crisp Case). Fourth IEEE International Conference on Fuzzy Systems FUZZ'2000, Texas, USA, May 20–24, 2000.
30. Thiele H. (2000) On Algebraic Foundations of information Granulation II. The Fuzzy Case. 8th international Conference in Information Processing and Management of Uncertainty in Knowledge Based Systems IPMU2000, Madrid, Spain, July 3-7, 2000. Volume III, 1389-1396
31. Thiele H. (2000) On Algebraic Foundations of Information Granulation III. Investigating the Hata-Mukaidono Approach. 30th International Symposium on Multiple Valued Logic ISMVL 2000, Portland, Oregon, USA, May 23-25, 2000. 133–138
32. Thiele H., Schmechel N. (1995) On the mutual definability of fuzzy equivalence relations and fuzzy partitions. Fourth IEEE International Conference on Fuzzy Systems FUZZ-IEEE'95, Yokohama, Japan, March 20-24, 1995. Volume III, 1383–1390
33. Yager R.R., Ovchinnikov S., Tong R.M., Nguyen H.T. (1987) Fuzzy Sets and Applications – Selected Papers by L.A. ZADEH. John Wiley & Sons
34. Yuan B., Klir G.J., Swan-Stone J.F. (1995) Evolutionary fuzzy c-means clustering algorithm. Fourth IEEE International Conference on Fuzzy Systems FUZZ-IEEE'95, Yokohama, Japan, March 20-24, 1995. 2221–2226
35. Zadeh L.A. (1971) Similarity relations and fuzzy orderings. Information Sciences **3**:177–200
Reprinted in [33]
36. Zadeh L.A. (1973) Outline of a new approach to the analysis of complex systems and decision processes. IEEE Trans. on Systems, Man and Cybernetics **3(1)**:28–44
Reprinted in [33]
37. Zadeh L.A. (1975) The concept of a linguistic variable and its application to approximate reasoning – I. Information Sciences **8**:199–249
Reprinted in [33].
38. Zadeh L.A. (1975) Fuzzy logic and approximate reasoning. Synthese **30**:407–428
39. Zadeh L.A. (1979) Fuzzy sets and information granularity. In: Gupta M.M., Ragade R.K., Yager R.R., (Eds.) Advances in Fuzzy Set Theory and Applications. North-Holland, Amsterdam, New York, Oxford, 3–18
40. Zadeh L.A. (1996) Fuzzy logic = computing with words. IEEE Transactions On Fuzzy Systems **4(2)**:103–111
41. Zadeh L.A. (1996) Fuzzy logic and the calculi of fuzzy rules and fuzzy graphs: A precis. Multiple Valued Logic – An International Journal **1(1)**
42. Zadeh L.A. (1996) The Key Roles of Information Granulation and Fuzzy Logic in Human Reasoning, Concept Formulation and Computing with Words. Fifth IEEE International Conference on Fuzzy Systems FUZZ-IEEE'96, New Orleans, USA, September 8–11, 1996.
43. Zadeh L.A. (1997) Toward a theory of fuzzy information granulation and its centrality in human reasoning and fuzzy logic. Fuzzy Sets and Systems **90**:111–127
44. Zelinka B. (1970) Tolerance in algebraic structures. Czechoslovak Mathematical Journal **20**:281–292
45. Zelinka B. (1975) Tolerance in algebraic structures II. Czechoslovak Mathematical Journal **25**:157–178

Decision and Preferences

On the Issue of Consistency in Dynamical Consensual Aggregation

Mario Fedrizzi, Michele Fedrizzi, and R.A. Marques Pereira

Dipartimento di Informatica e Studi Aziendali, Università di Trento,
Via Inama 5, TN 38100 Trento, Italy

Abstract

In this paper we propose to use the consistency of preferences in order to endogenously assign different weights to decision makers in a consensual dynamics process. For this purpose, we first define a consistency index for preferences expressed by means of fuzzy preference relations. Then we introduce this index in an iterative law for updating the individual preferences. The updating law is formulated in the spirit of some previous papers on consensual dynamics (see for instance [5]) and, as a result, both the initially declared preferences and the present ones (in the ongoing process) act with a strength determined on the basis of their consistency.

Keywords: Group decision making, preference relations, transitivity, consistency, consensus reaching, opinion changing aversion, dynamical models.

1 Introduction

In group decision making under the equity or anonimity assumption it is assumed that the preferences of each decision maker have the same weight in the decision process. Nevertheless, different real-world situations need different assumptions. In some cases the weight of each decision maker necessarily results from his/her represented share in terms of voters, stocks, property, etc. In other cases, on the contrary, it is impossible to assign a priori different weights to the decision makers, but it can be quite reasonable to give more importance to preferences with 'good' properties and less importance to preferences with 'bad' properties. We think that consistency can be one of the good properties. We assume that the more consistent is a judgement, the more likely the decision maker is a good expert, has a deep insight into the problem and acts with attention and precision. Conversely, if judgements are far from consistency, it is likely that they were given with less competence and care. As consistency is an intrinsic property of preferences, the equity or anonimity assumption is preserved for what concern decision makers.

In the next section we present some basic notations and assumptions that we will use in the rest of the paper. In the third section some approaches to transitivity and consistency are considered and a consistency index is defined for preferences expressed by means of fuzzy preference relations. We then utilize this index in the context of consensual dynamics by introducing it in the iterative law that updates the individual preferences. The dynamics induced by this law acts iteratively on each decision maker by combining his present preference values with those of the other decision makers plus the preference values he initially declared [5]. In this way two fundamental and competing issues in group decision making are taken into account: the necessity of decreasing dissensus among decision makers and the individual opinion changing aversion. Finally, in the last section some numerical simulations are presented.

2 The problem formulation

Let $\{a_1, a_2, ..., a_n\}$ be a set of alternatives and let us denote the decision makers with the index $k = 1, ..., m$. We assume that preferences are expressed by means of fuzzy preference relations $r^k : A \times A \rightarrow [0,1]$. We use the shorter notation r^k_{ij} to indicate the preference degree $r^k(a_i, a_j)$ of decision maker k comparing a_i over a_j. It follows that $r^k_{ij} = 1$ when a_i is definitely preferred over a_j and $r^k_{ij} = 0$ in the opposite case. When the two alternatives a_i and a_j are indifferent, $r^k_{ij} = 0.5$. We also assume that the relation is reciprocal (in the additive sense) [19],

$$r^k_{ij} + r^k_{ji} = 1 \quad i, j = 1, ..., n. \tag{1}$$

¿From this condition it follows that $r^k_{ii} = 0.5 \ \forall i$. Moreover, the matrix $[r^k_{ij}]$, which can be identified with the fuzzy preference relation r^k, has only $n(n-1)/2$ degrees of freedom. Let us indicate with $s^k = [s^k_{ij}]$ the initial fuzzy preference relation of decision maker k. We assume that the decision makers are averse in changing their initial opinion but, on the other hand, they want to interact during the decision process in order to gradually reduce the disagreement inside the group [5]. In section 4 we propose an iterative law for updating r^k_{ij} which meets these assumptions.

3 Consistency of preferences

Consistency is a widely studied issue in decision theory [15] [1] [18] and some methods have been proposed for measuring how far from consistency are the expressed preferences of a decision maker [6] [21]. The problem has been studied mainly in the framework of pairwise comparison matrices $[a_{ij}]$ with judgement expressed on a ratio scale. Under this assumption, $a_{ij} = 3$, for example, means that a_i is three time preferred (better) than a_j. The well known Saaty's approach [17] [18] is of this type; the consistency condition for matrix $[a_{ij}]$ can be stated as

$$a_{ih} a_{hj} = a_{ij} \quad i, j, h = 1, ...n. \tag{2}$$

If (2) holds, the matrix $[a_{ij}]$ is also called supertransitive [15]. Let us assume that the judgements of the decision makers are expressed, as in our approach, by means of fuzzy preference relations $r = [r_{ij}]$, with $r_{ij} \in [0,1]$. In [3] a transformation of the Saaty's multiplicative approach into the additive one is proposed and some related properties are investigated. In fact, it can be shown that if the a_{ij}'s values are mapped into $[0,1]$ with a convenient function, the multiplicative type consistency condition (2) corresponds to the additive type condition

$$(r_{ih} - 0.5) + (r_{hj} - 0.5) = (r_{ij} - 0.5) \qquad i,j,h = 1,...,n. \tag{3}$$

In writing (3) we emphasize the role of the differences from indifference value 0.5. Condition (3) is also written as

$$r_{ih} + r_{hj} - 0.5 = r_{ij} \qquad i,j,h = 1,...,n. \tag{4}$$

and is referred to as additive transitivity [20] .

For the sake of simplicity, in practical situations it is often assumed that the judgements can be expressed only by means of a bounded set of numerical values. T. Saaty, for instance, suggests that a_{ij} can be chosen among the numbers 1, 2, ..., 9 and their reciprocal. It can be observed that the use of a bounded scale leads to a drawback for what concerns consistency. For fixed a_{ih} and a_{hj}, it can happen that no feasible value exists for a_{ij} in the given scale such that consistency condition (2) holds. The same may happen when the judgements are expressed by means of fuzzy preference relations: given $r_{ih}, r_{hj} \in [0,1]$, it is possible that no $r_{ij} \in [0,1]$ exists such that (4) holds. As an example, consider the extreme values $r_{ih} = r_{hj} = 0$ or $r_{ih} = r_{hj} = 1$. In Fishburn SSB theory [8] this drawback is not present, as he represents the degree of preference of a_i over a_j by means of a Skew-Symmetric Bilinear function $\phi(a_i, a_j)$ taking values in $\Re$. Under this assumption , the consistency condition can be stated as

$$\phi(a_i, a_h) + \phi(a_h, a_j) = \phi(a_i, a_j), \tag{5}$$

which corresponds to (3), taking into account that Fishburn represents indifference with $\phi(\cdot, \cdot) = 0$. If (5) holds $\forall ijk$, the function ϕ can be expressed in the additively separable form

$$\phi(a_i, a_j) = u(a_i) - u(a_j), \tag{6}$$

where clearly $u(a_i)$, or simply u_i, plays the role of a utility value. Analogous results can be stated if preferences satisfy consistency conditions (2) or (3) in the corresponding framework of preference formulation. More precisely: if (3) holds in the additive representation, it follows that r_{ij} can be expressed [19] as

$$r_{ij} - 0.5 = 0.5(u_i - u_j) \qquad i,j = 1,...,n, \tag{7}$$

where u_i are utility values assigned to the alternatives such that $| u_i - u_j| \leq 1$ $\forall ij$.

Analogously, if (2) holds, in the multiplicative representation, then each a_{ij} can be expressed as a ratio of positive numbers,

$$a_{ij} = \frac{w_i}{w_j} \qquad i, j = 1, ..., n, \tag{8}$$

where we write w_i instead of u_i to follow Saaty's notation.

Now we focus on (3), or (4), to derive our consistency measure. Let us consider decision maker k and let us fix two alternatives a_i and a_j. As consistency is a property which involves three alternatives, we take a third generic alternative a_h and we define the following index

$$\rho_{ij}^k = \sum_{h=1}^{n} (r_{ih}^k + r_{hj}^k - r_{ij}^k - 0.5)^2. \tag{9}$$

Taking into account (4), it follows that the value of ρ_{ij}^k is an *inconsistency* index of decision maker k judgements in comparing alternatives a_i and a_j with all the other alternatives a_h. Note that if $h = i$ or $h = j$ the corresponding term in the sum vanishes, as $a_{ii} = 0.5$. Finally we define the *consistency* index for decision maker k associated with the pair of alternatives (a_i, a_j) ,

$$w_{ij}^k = e^{-\tau \rho_{ij}^k}. \tag{10}$$

The exogenous parameter $\tau \geq 0$ controls the importance we want to assign to the consistency of preferences; if $\tau = 0$, all the weights are equal to 1 and the consistency plays no role in the process.

In analogy with (9), we need to define the inconsistency index σ_{ij}^k of decision maker k initial preferences:

$$\sigma_{ij}^k = \sum_{h=1}^{n} (s_{ih}^k + s_{hj}^k - s_{ij}^k - 0.5)^2, \tag{11}$$

and the corresponding consistency index for the initial preferences

$$\omega_{ij}^k = e^{-\tau \sigma_{ij}^k}. \tag{12}$$

4 Consensual dynamics and consistency

In this section we define an iterative process for updating the individual preferences r_{ij}^k on the basis of the objectives exposed in section 2: disagreement reduction and opinion changing aversion. The consistency indices w_{ij}^k and ω_{ij}^k introduced in the previous section play the role of weights in the preferences updating rule. Let us represent the process in the following way

$$r_{ij}^k \quad \longrightarrow \quad r_{ij}^k + \varepsilon \Delta r_{ij}^k \qquad i,j = 1,...,n. \tag{13}$$

That is, r_{ij}^k is iteratively updated by adding the correction term Δr_{ij}^k multiplied by the step ε ; we define the correction term as follows

$$\Delta r_{ij}^k \ = \ \omega_{ij}^k (s_{ij}^k - r_{ij}^k) \ + \frac{1}{m-1} \sum_{\substack{p=1 \\ p \neq k}}^{m} w_{ij}^p (r_{ij}^p - r_{ij}^k). \tag{14}$$

The term in the sum indexed with p represents the updating effect of the preferences of decision maker p on the preferences of decision maker k. The weight w_{ij}^p emphasizes the effect of the more consistent preferences and, conversely, it reduces the effect of the less consistent ones. The first term on the r.h.s. in (14) plays the role of a link with the initial preferences s_{ij}^k. The weight ω_{ij}^k acts as w_{ij}^p : the more consistent are the initial preferences of decision maker k, the stronger is the opposition to change them. At each step all the r_{ij}^k are simultaneously updated on the basis of (13). Then the w_{ij}^p are recalculated before the next step. From (13) and (14) we can write

$$r_{ij}^k + \varepsilon \Delta r_{ij}^k = \Big(1 - \frac{\varepsilon}{m-1} \sum_{\substack{p=1 \\ p \neq k}}^{m} (w_{ij}^p + \omega_{ij}^k)\Big) r_{ij}^k + \frac{\varepsilon}{m-1} \sum_{\substack{p=1 \\ p \neq k}}^{m} w_{ij}^p r_{ij}^p + \varepsilon \omega_{ij}^k s_{ij}^k. \tag{15}$$

It can be observed that the value of the updated preferences $r_{ij}^k + \varepsilon \Delta r_{ij}^k$ is written as a convex (for small values of ε) linear combination of the previous value r_{ij}^k , the initial value s_{ij}^k , and the preference values r_{ij}^p of the remaining decision makers.

In previous papers on consensual dynamics (see for instance [5]), the updating law for r_{ij}^k was obtained by minimizing a cost function W with the gradient descent scheme

$$r_{ij}^k \quad \longrightarrow \quad r_{ij}^k - \varepsilon \frac{\partial W}{\partial r_{ij}^k}. \tag{16}$$

Referring to [5], if the cost function $W = \sum_{i,j=1}^n W_{ij}$ does not include the so–called scaling function $f(x)$ (i.e. if $f(x) = x$), the terms W_{ij} concerning the comparison of a_i over a_j are

$$W_{ij} = (1/4) \sum_{k=1}^{m} \sum_{\substack{p=1 \\ p \neq k}}^{m} \frac{(r_{ij}^k - r_{ij}^p)^2}{m-1} + \ (1/2) \sum_{k=1}^{m} (r_{ij}^k - s_{ij}^k)^2. \tag{17}$$

It can be verified that the dynamical law (based on the gradient descent mechanism (16)) associated with (17) coincides with the particular case $\tau = 0$ of our dynamical law (15). Therefore the case in which consistency is not taken into account ($\tau = 0$) coincides with the so–called linear model.

With respect to the dynamical interaction among the preference values r_{ij}, which is already present in the standard model exposed in [5], notice that the presence of w_{ij}^p in (15) implies a more substantial and structured global interaction between the single preference values.

5 Numerical simulations

In this section we present some numerical simulations on the dynamics induced by (13). Let us consider the case of three decision makers and four alternatives. In order to emphasize the role of consistency, we choose decision maker $k = 1$ to be perfectly consistent, decision maker $k = 3$ to be very inconsistent and decision maker $k = 2$ to be somewhere between these two extremes. The initial preferences $s^k = [s_{ij}^k]$, $k = 1, 2, 3$ are the following:

$$s^1 = \begin{bmatrix} 0.5\ 0.8\ 0.7\ 0.9 \\ 0.2\ 0.5\ 0.4\ 0.6 \\ 0.3\ 0.6\ 0.5\ 0.7 \\ 0.1\ 0.4\ 0.3\ 0.5 \end{bmatrix} \quad s^2 = \begin{bmatrix} 0.5\ 0.4\ 0.3\ 0.1 \\ 0.6\ 0.5\ 0.6\ 0.2 \\ 0.7\ 0.4\ 0.5\ 0.1 \\ 0.9\ 0.8\ 0.9\ 0.5 \end{bmatrix} \quad s^3 = \begin{bmatrix} 0.5\ 0.2\ 0.7\ 0.9 \\ 0.8\ 0.5\ 0.3\ 0.3 \\ 0.3\ 0.7\ 0.5\ 0.1 \\ 0.1\ 0.7\ 0.9\ 0.5 \end{bmatrix}$$

It can be noted that each column in the matrix s^1 can be obtained from any other column of the matrix by adding a convenient fixed constant. It is easy to prove that this property holds for all matrices satisfying consistency condition (3).

In order to give a graphical representation of the consensual dynamics generated by (13), let us associate to each pairwise comparison matrix $[r_{ij}^k]$ a vector $u = (u_1, u_2, u_3, u_4)$ of utility values for the alternatives $\{a_1, a_2, a_3, a_4\}$. This can be done in different ways and several methods have been proposed in the literature. When the judgements are expressed on a ratio scale, Saaty [17] [18] proposes to compute the normalized eigenvector associated with the maximum eigenvalue of the pairwise comparison matrix $[a_{ij}]$. The most important alternative methods are the *least–squares* and *geometric means* methods [14]. As mentioned in section 3, the a_{ij} values can be mapped in a natural way into the interval $[0, 1]$ with a convenient logarithmic–type function [3], to obtain a fuzzy preference matrix $[r_{ij}]$. In this way, the geometric mean $(\prod_{j=1}^n a_{ij})^{1/n}$ of the ith–row elements of $[a_{ij}]$ is transformed into the arithmetic mean of the ith–row elements of $[r_{ij}]$. Thus, let us denote by u_i^k the utility value of alternative a_i obtained for decision maker k by computing the arithmetic mean of the elements of row i in matrix $[r_{ij}^k]$: $u_i^k = \frac{1}{n} \sum_{j=1}^n r_{ij}^k$.

As an example, Fig. 1 shows the updating process on the utility values u_1^1, u_1^2, u_1^3 of alternative a_1, for the three decision makers. Time is represented on the horizontal axis.

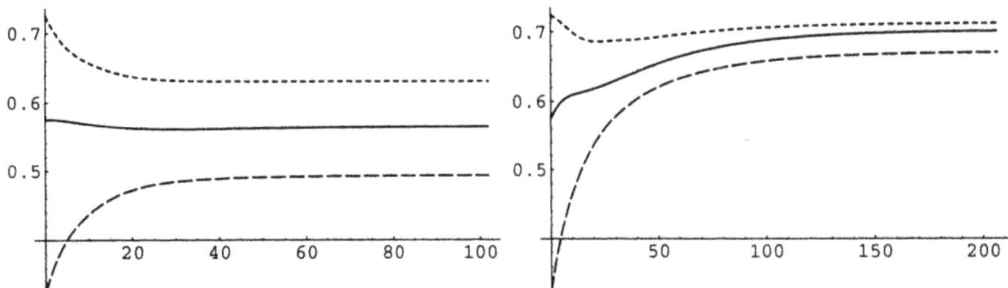

Fig. 1. Utility values of alternative a_1, for $\tau = 10$ (left) and $\tau = 50$ (right)

In Fig. 1 and in Fig. 2, the dotted, dashed, and continuous line is associated with decision maker 1, 2, and 3, respectively. The plot on the left is obtained with low inconsistency penalization, $\tau = 10$, while the plot on the right is obtained by giving more importance to consistency, $\tau = 50$. In the latter case, the dominant role of the consistent decision maker 1 is evident.

Fig. 2 shows how the consistency of the decision makers evolves during the process. To represent the complete information on the consistency of the kth decision maker's judgements, we need the entire matrix $[\rho_{ij}^k]$ (see (9)). However, a concise index of the kth decision maker's inconsistency can be obtained by summing the elements of $[\rho_{ij}^k]$:

$$\rho_k = \sum_{i=1}^{n} \sum_{j=1}^{n} \rho_{ij}^k$$

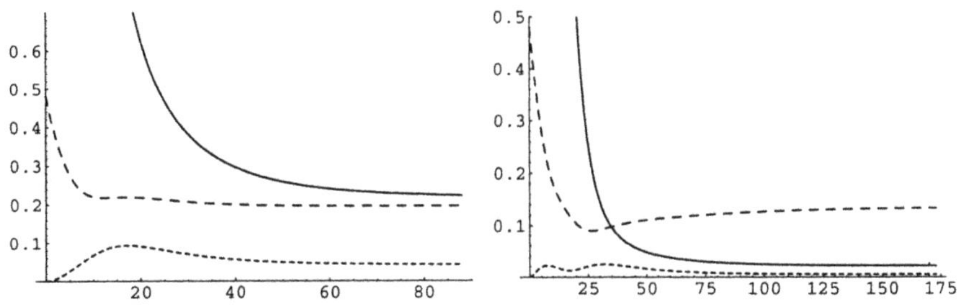

Fig. 2. inconsistency indices ρ_1, ρ_2, ρ_3 for $\tau = 3$ (left) and $\tau = 30$ (right)

The initial values, associated with s^1, s^2 and s^3 are: $\rho_1 = 0$, $\rho_2 = 0.48$, $\rho_3 = 10.92$. In Fig. 2 we represent how ρ_1, ρ_2, ρ_3 change for two different values of τ. It can be noted that (specially for $\tau = 30$) the initially less consistent decision maker 3 is heavily influenced by decision maker 1 even when his consistency improves, while decision maker 2 remains less influenced. This is due to the fact that the less consistent are the initial preferences, the weaker is their attraction power.

Finally, Fig. 3 illustrates how the degree of consensus changes during the process. As an index of the global dissensus between two decision makers, we consider the usual euclidean distance between the corresponding preference matrices, considered as elements of the vector space $\Re^{n\times n}$:

$$d_{12} = \sqrt{\sum_{i,j=1}^{n} (r_{ij}^1 - r_{ij}^2)^2}$$

and analogously for d_{13} and d_{23}. In Fig. 3, the dotted, dashed, and continuous line is associated with distance d_{12}, d_{13} and d_{23}, respectively. By comparing the two plots in Fig. 3, it can be observed that for sufficiently high penalization of the inconsistency, the dashed line converges to zero. This means that the preferences of the most inconsistent decision maker ($k = 3$) have been attracted by those of the most consistent one ($k = 1$).

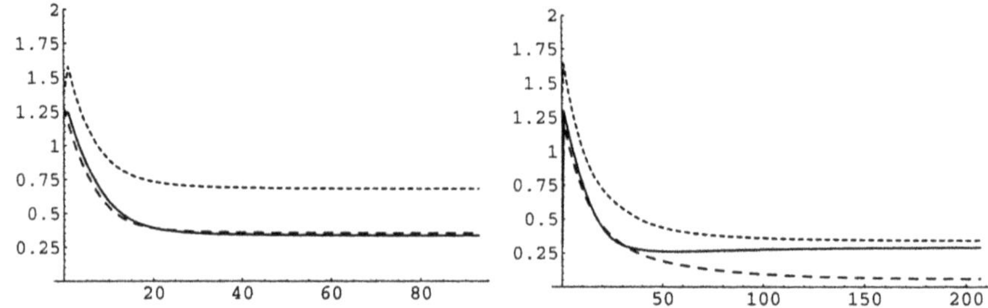

Fig. 3. Distances d_{12}, d_{13} and d_{23} for $\tau = 4$ (left) and $\tau = 50$ (right)

References

1. L. Basile, L. D'Apuzzo. Inconsistency in Analytic Hierarchy Process, in Proc. *21st Conference of the Associazione per la Matematica Applicata alle Scienze Economiche e Sociali* (Roma, Sept. 10–13, 1997), 61–66.
2. C. Carlsson, D. Ehrenberg, P. Eklund, M. Fedrizzi, P. Gustafsson, P. Lindholm, G. Merkuryeva, T. Riissanen, A. Ventre. Consensus in distributed soft environments, *European Journal of Operational Research*, 61 (1992) 165–185.
3. M. Fedrizzi. On a consensus measure in a group MCDM problem, in *Multiperson Decision Making Models using Fuzzy Sets and Possibility Theory* (Theory and Decision Library, series B: Mathematical and Statistical Methods, Vol. 18), J. Kacprzyk and M. Fedrizzi (eds.), Kluwer Academic Publishers, Dordrecht, The Netherlands, 1990.
4. M. Fedrizzi, M. Fedrizzi and R.A. Marques Pereira. Consensus, dynamics, and group decision making, in Proc. *20th Conference of the Associazione per la Matematica Applicata alle Scienze Economiche e Sociali* AMASES'96 (Urbino, Italy, September 1996), published by Università di Urbino, Italy (1996) 243–254.

5. M. Fedrizzi, M. Fedrizzi and R.A. Marques Pereira. Soft consensus and network dynamics in group decision making, *International Journal of Intelligent Systems* , 14, pages 63-77, 1999.
6. Fedrizzi Michele and R.A. Marques Pereira. Positive fuzzy matrices, dominant eigenvalues and an extension of Saaty's Analytical Hierarchy Process, in Proc. *VI International Fuzzy Systems Association World Congress*, São Paulo, Brasile, 21–28 luglio 1995, pages 245–247, 1995.
7. M. Fedrizzi, J. Kacprzyk and S. Zadrożny. An interactive multi-user decision support system for consensus reaching processes using fuzzy logic with linguistic quantifiers, *Decision Support Systems*, 4 (1988) 313–327.
8. P.C. Fishburn. SSB utility theory: an economic perspective, *Mathematical Social Sciences*, 8 (1984) 63–94.
9. J. Fodor, M. Roubens. *Fuzzy Preference Modelling and Multicriteria Decision Support.* (Theory and Decision Library, series D: System Theory, Knowledge Engineering and Problem Solving, Vol. 14), Kluwer Academic Publishers, Dordrecht, The Netherlands, 1994.
10. J. Kacprzyk and M. Fedrizzi. 'Soft' consensus measures for monitoring real consensus reaching processes under fuzzy preferences, *Control and Cybernetics*, 15 (1986) 309–323.
11. J. Kacprzyk and M. Fedrizzi. A 'soft' measure of consensus in the setting of partial (fuzzy) preferences, *European Journal of Operational Research*, 34 (1988) 316–325.
12. J. Kacprzyk and M. Fedrizzi. A human-consistent degree of consensus based on fuzzy logic with linguistic quantifiers, *Mathematical Social Sciences*, 18 (1989) 275–290.
13. J. Kacprzyk, M. Fedrizzi and H. Nurmi. Group decision making and consensus under fuzzy preferences and fuzzy majority, *Fuzzy Sets and Systems*, 49 (1992) 21–31.
14. J. Křovák. Ranking alternatives – Comparison of different methods based on binary comparison matrices, *European Journal of Operational Research*, 32 (1987) 86–95.
15. R. Narasimhan. A geometric averaging procedure for constructing supertransitive approximation to binary comparison matrices, *Fuzzy Sets and Systems*, 8, pages 53–61, 1982.
16. H. Nurmi. Approaches to collective decision making with fuzzy preference relations, *Fuzzy Sets and Systems*, 6 (1981) 249–259.
17. Saaty T. L. (1977), A scaling method for priorities in hierarchical structures, *J. Math. Psychology*, 15, 234–281.
18. Saaty T. L. (1980), *The Analytical Hierarchy Process.* McGraw-Hill, New York.
19. T. Tanino. Fuzzy preference relations in group decision making, in *Non-conventional preference relations in Decision Making* J. Kacprzyk and M. Roubens (eds.), Springer-Verlag, 1988.
20. T. Tanino. On group decision making under fuzzy preferences, in *Multiperson Decision Making Models using Fuzzy Sets and Possibility Theory* (Theory and Decision Library, series B: Mathematical and Statistical Methods, Vol. 18), J. Kacprzyk and M. Fedrizzi (eds.), Kluwer Academic Publishers, Dordrecht, The Netherlands, 1990.
21. X. Wang, E. E. Kerre and D. Ruan. Consistency of judgement matrix and fuzzy weights in fuzzy analytic hierarchy process, *International Journal of Uncertainty, Fuzziness and Knowledge-Based Systems*, 3 (1995) n. 1 35–46.

A Group Decision Support System Based on Linguistic Multicriteria Assessments

Janusz Kacprzyk and Sławomir Zadrożny

Systems Research Institute
Polish Academy of Sciences
ul. Newelska 6
01-447 Warsaw, Poland
E-mail: {kacprzyk,zadrozny}@ibspan.waw.pl

Abstract

A group decision support system is presented. The main concern is an effective support for the consensus reaching process. The point of departure are linguistic assessments of options with respect to multiple criteria. These are processed to obtain individual and group preference structures as well as an assessment of the consensus in the group. A pilot implementation of the system in the WWW environment is presented.

Keywords: consensus, fuzzy preferences, linguistic preferences, preference structures, fuzzy majority, multicriteria choice, Internet, WWW.

1. Introduction

The following group decision making setting is considered. We assume that there is a set of options characterised by a set of attributes/criteria, and a group of individuals (decision-makers, experts etc.). The individuals discuss the issues under consideration and present their opinions providing *assessments* of the fulfilment of a set of criteria by each option, as well as *importance weights* for the particular criteria. The former assessments are expressed using a set of linguistic terms expressing the compatibility of a particular option with the criteria. It may happen that a given individual is not able to assess the aforementioned compatibility or that, in his or her opinion, a given criterion is not applicable for the option considered. Hence, additional linguistic terms are provided for that. Then, the group decision support system automatically generates a preference structure corresponding to a given characterisation of all options in terms of the attributes/criteria considered. More precisely, it is an *additive preference structure*.

The next step is the assessment of (an extent of) consensus in the opinion of group members. It may be done on three levels: (1) linguistic evaluations in respect to the criteria, (2) a generated preference structure, or (3) implied individual choice sets. In this paper we concentrate on the second type of consensus evaluation, further developing our previous approach (see [4]). The other consensus evaluation schemes are only briefly discussed. Possible hints for a further group discussion, leading to a higher consensus degree, are also briefly mentioned.

We conclude the paper with the presentation of a preliminary implementation of the system. Recent advancements in ICT (Information and Communication Technology) have triggered a spectacular development of the Internet. One of the most popular services available is there the World Wide Web (WWW). The ease of access, use and maintenance of WWW based applications makes them a well-suited solution for group work tasks. These applications are equally attractive in case of spatially distributed groups as well as those connected by local area networks.

In particular, the WWW based applications may be useful for a decision making support. They provide an attractive and flexible user interface to the core of a decision support system as well as the access to a plethora of information available on the Internet. Thus, the decision-maker may have an immediate access to all data relevant to the problem. In case of group decision making, such systems may easily facilitate an open discussion between group members as well as support various processes within the group in a more structured way.

2. The data

Here we assume a classical group decision making setting. There is a *group of individuals* (decision makers, experts, etc.) and a *set of options* being potential solutions to the decision problem under consideration. Moreover, each option is evaluated in respect to a *set of criteria*. For the time being, we just assume that the set of criteria is given. Each individual assesses every option with respect to all criteria using linguistic labels such as *Very good*, *Good*, *Bad*, etc. A possible *inapplicability* of a criterion for a given option or the *inability* of an individual to rate an option with respect to a given criterion are represented by additional linguistic labels, *NA* and *UNK*, respectively.

Formally, let $X=\{x_1,...,x_M\}$ and $S=\{s_1,...,s_N\}$ denote the set of individuals and options, respectively. Let $C=\{c_1,...,c_K\}$ and $W^m=\{w_1^m,\dots,w_K^m\}$, $w_k\in[0,1]$, be sets of criteria characterising particular options and importance weights of these criteria, respectively. Notice that we assume the same set of criteria for all individuals and options but the importance weights are assigned to particular criteria independently by each individual. Additionally, we assume that $\max_k w_k^m = 1, \forall m$. Let

E_m: $S \times C \rightarrow LL \cup \{NA, UNK\}$

be a mapping representing the assessment of particular options as given by individual x_m, where LL={*Very good, Good, Fair, Bad, Very bad*}. We assume that there is a linear order $\succ$ defined on the set LL such that $\forall l_1, l_2 \in LL$ $l_1 \succ l_2$ means that label l_1 denotes a better performance of an option than label l_2. We assume that "*Very good* $\succ$ *Good* $\succ$ *Fair* $\succ$ *Bad* $\succ$ *Very bad*".

The interpretation of *NA* and *UNK* is as given in the previous paragraph. In what follows, we will refer to the elements of the set *LL* as *regular values*.

Example. Let the decision problem consist in the selection of proper candidates for the dean position at a university. The group of individuals is assessing the quality of particular candidates with respect to the following criteria: age, education, experience, self-presentation during an interview, language skills and the quality of scientific publications. We assume that, for an individual, some facts about a candidate may be unknown (e.g., their publications) or may be not applicable (e.g., an interview with some candidates was not conducted). As mentioned, each individual may assign different weights to particular criteria. Then, the part of source data of the *m*-th individual may look as follows:

S={Tom Adams, John Doe, Brian Kelly, John Smith, Alan Twain, Jim Welsh}

C={Age, Education, Experience, Interview, *Language skills, Publications*}

W^m={0.6, 1.0,1.0,0.5,0.8,0.7}

E_m(John Smith,Age) = Good, E_m(John Smith,Education)=Fair,

E_m(John Smith,Experience)=Fair, E_m(John Smith,Interview)=NA,

E_m(John Smith,Language skills)=Very good,

E_m(John Smith,Publications)=UNK

3. Preference structure

The source data mentioned above form the lowest level on which consensus may be sought. The perfect agreement among the individuals on such a low level may be unnecessary. Even if a basic evaluation of particular options, in terms of assigned linguistic labels, may be quite different, still implied preferences on pairs of options may be completely satisfactory. Thus in the next step the system automatically generates for each individual a *preference structure* corresponding in a specific sense to the input data he or she has given.

We adopt here the approach and notation proposed in [16], with some simplifications. A fuzzy preference structure is a triple of binary fuzzy relations (P,I,J) defined on the set $S{\times}S$. Originally, in [16], it is a sixtuple containing additionally the set of alternatives (options), S, as well as a t-norm and t-conorm used to express required properties of the relations. We will omit here these additional elements as the set of options is here always S, and we assume the Łukasiewicz t-norm and t-conorm (as advocated in [15,16]).

The binary fuzzy relations in the triple correspond to classical notions of strong preference, indifference and incomparability, respectively. Thus, usual properties are required for these relations, including the antisymmetry for P, and the symmetry for I and J. The completeness of the fuzzy preference structure is expressed, due to the use of the Łukasiewicz connectives, as $\mu_P(.,.) + \mu_{P^t}(.,.) + \mu_I(.,.) + \mu_J(.,.) = 1$, where P^t is the transpose of P, i.e., $P^t(s_i,s_j) = P(s_j,s_i)$. The completeness of the preference structure implies the pairwise disjointness, in the sense of the Łukasiewicz conjunction, of all relations P, P^t, I, J.

A fuzzy preference structure is automatically generated according to the following reasoning. Let us assume the following notation (we omit indices referring to the individual as all these computations are done separately for each individual):

$$UC : S \to 2^C \qquad UC(s_i) = \{k : E(s_i, c_k) = UNK\}$$

$$NC : S \to 2^C \qquad NC(s_i) = \{k : E(s_i, c_k) = NA\}$$

$$KC : S \to 2^C ; KC(s_i) = \{k : E(s_i, c_k) \notin \{UNK, NA\}\}$$

The above definitions distinguish some useful crisp subsets of indices of criteria, namely, those taking the value UNK (UC), the value NA (NC), and the values different from UNK and NA (KC).

Next, we define for each pair of options four other auxiliary entities:

$$ALLC : S \times S \to [1, K]; \quad ALLC(s_i, s_j) = \sum_{k \in AC} w_k;$$
$$AC = \{k : k \notin NC(s_i) \cap NC(s_j)\}$$

$$FFC : S \times S \to [1, K]; \quad FFC(s_i, s_j) = \sum_{k \in FF} w_k;$$
$$FF = \{k : k \in KC(s_i) \cap KC(s_j) \wedge E(s_i, c_k) \succ E(s_j, c_k)\}$$

$$FSC : S \times S \rightarrow [1, K]; \quad FSC(s_i, s_j) = \sum_{k \in FS} w_k$$

$$FS = \{k : k \in KC(s_i) \cap KC(s_j) \wedge E(s_i, c_k) \prec E(s_j, c_k)\}$$

$$FBC : S \times S \rightarrow [1, K]; \quad FBC(s_i, s_j) = \sum_{k \in FB} w_k$$

$$FB = \{k : k \in KC(s_i) \cap KC(s_j) \wedge E(s_i, c_k) = E(s_j, c_k)\}$$

In all the above formulas, the set of criteria is meant to be a fuzzy set with membership degrees equal to the importance weights (w_i) of the particular criteria. Thus, *ALLC* is equal to the cardinality (in the sense of ΣCounts) of the fuzzy set of criteria that do not simultaneously take value *NA* for both options. Intuitively, all the three remaining entities - *FFC*, *FSC* and *FBC* - count (in the same sense as *ALLC*) the criteria taking regular values for compared options and favouring the first options from the pair (*FFC*), the second (*FSC*), or not differentiating the options (*FBC*).

Then, the following formulas are used to compute the membership functions of the particular fuzzy preference relations constituting our fuzzy preference structure:

$$\mu_P(s_i, s_j) = FFC(s_i, s_j) / ALLC$$

$$\mu_{P'}(s_i, s_j) = FSC(s_i, s_j) / ALLC$$

$$\mu_I(s_i, s_j) = FBC(s_i, s_j) / ALLC$$

$$\mu_J(s_i, s_j) = \frac{\sum_{k \in UC(s_i) \cup UC(s_j) \cup NC(s_i) \cup NC(s_j) - NC(s_i) \cap NC(s_j)} w_k}{ALLC}$$

The following reasoning supports the adopted formulas. A degree of strong preference, *P*, of option s_i over option s_j should be proportional to the fraction of the number of criteria for which option s_i obtained a better score than s_j. Thus, a degree of strong preference is assumed to be equal to this fraction. The calculation of this fraction does not take into account the criteria that were classified by an individual as non-applicable for both options. If it were not arranged that way, such criteria - completely irrelevant for the comparison of that pair of options - would artificially diminish a degree of strong preference (the same applies to the indifference and incomparability relation). Exactly the same idea is applied for the calculation of a membership degree of a pair of options in the transposed strong preference relation. On the other hand, the degree of indifference of a pair of options is assumed to be the fraction of the number of criteria for which the score for both options is equal.

The calculation of a degree of incomparability is slightly more complicated as illustrated in Table 1. Table 1 shows which criteria are considered as supporting the incomparability of two options. Namely, if for the first option a criterion takes on a value listed in the first column and for the second option a value listed in the first row, and the "+" corresponds to that column and row, then such a combination of values is treated as contributing to the incomparability of options. On the other hand, pairs of values marked with "-" are excluded from the calculations of the incomparability degree. Thus, in fact only two combinations are excluded: (*NA*,*NA*) and a pair of regular values. The former is assumed as in the calculation of all other membership functions of fuzzy relations. The latter is obvious as two regular values may be evidently compared due to the "$\succ$" and identity relations assumed in our model.

Table 1

	UNK	*NA*	*LL*
UNK	+	+	+
NA	+	-	+
LL	+	+	-

This discussion clarifies the interpretation of non-regular values *UNK* and *NA*. The former should be used when an individual cannot assess an option with respect to given criteria due to lack of knowledge as to the appropriate regular value. Whenever *UNK* appears as the value of a criterion, it contributes to the incomparability of a pair of options, no matter what the value of the same criterion for the other option is. On the other hand, *NA* should be used if an individual finds a given criterion to be non-applicable for the option considered. If an individual finds the criterion non-applicable for both the options, then such a criterion is completely excluded from the calculation of membership degrees of preference relations.

It is obvious from the above definitions that $\mu_P(s_i,s_j) + \mu_P^t(s_i,s_j) + \mu_I(s_i,s_j) + \mu_J(s_i,s_j) = 1$. Thus, we obtain an *additive fuzzy preference structure*. It means that with each pair of options we have associated four numbers expressing the membership of this pair in particular fuzzy relations constituting our preference structure.

4. Consensus evaluation

Here we further develop the idea of a consensus reaching support system proposed in [7,4,3]. The main point was there to offer a new, flexible definition of a degree of consensus. From the perspective adopted there and here, the primary goal of a decision process support is to provide a framework for the selection of widely agreed, *consensual,* solutions to the decision problem. The classical concept of consensus meant as full and unanimous agreement, of all individuals involved as to all aspects of the decision problem, is hardly helpful in assisting a group of individuals in arriving at a satisfactory consensus. A flexible concept of consensus proposed earlier may be expressed as "the agreement of *most* of the individuals as to *most* of the decision problem aspects". Thus, basically, the idea was to replace the general quantifier "all", traditionally employed in the definition of consensus, by some flexible, linguistic quantifier as, e.g., "most".

In the previously proposed approach we have concentrated on the evaluation of consensus with respect to the fuzzy preference relation. In this paper, we would like to propose another way of calculating a consensus degree, now in the context of a preference structure. Another goal is to point out some other possible ways of exploiting different forms of preference related data for the evaluation of consensus.

In Sections 2 and 3 we have distinguished the following levels of preference related data:

- weights of the criteria, (1a)
- assessment of each option with respect to all criteria, (1b)
- a fuzzy preference structure (1c)

Usually, the ultimate goal of decision making is the selection of one or more options that may be treated as a best solution for the decision problem under consideration. This selection may take various forms - one option, subset of options, ranking of options etc. - depending on the nature of the decision process, requirements of an "ultimate" decision maker etc.

Anyway, we should add to the list mentioned above, another item, namely:

- a solution (1d)

A solution is meant as proposed by or generated for each individual separately. Usually, we expect as a result of a group decision making process another solution - this time supported by the group as a whole. As already stressed, here we are not dealing with such a solution directly. Anyway, reaching the agreement (consensus) in the group makes such a group solution more obvious and sound.

It is worth noticing that in our approach data belonging to levels (1a) and (1b) are directly provided by each individual, while (1c) and (1d) are automatically generated. In the previous section we have described the rules of transition from

(1a) and (1b) to (1c). For various ways of going from (1c) to (1d), see, e.g., [1, 8, 10, 11,12,13, 14].

Previously [7,4,3], we proposed some flexible scheme for consensus evaluation based on the level 3 data, i.e. fuzzy preference relations of all individuals. Here we extend the previous approach to a richer fuzzy preference structure and using some other aggregation technique, while preserving the basic idea of flexible consensus definition. After that, we briefly analyse other possibilities.

In [7,4,3] we started with a fuzzy preference relation R, interpreted as follows:

$$\mu_R(s_i,s_j)=\begin{cases}1 & s_i \text{ definitely preferred to } s_j\\ c\in(0.5,1) & s_i \text{ preferred to } s_j \text{ to some extent}\\ 0.5 & \text{indifference}\\ d\in(0,0.5) & s_j \text{ preferred to } s_i \text{ to some extent}\\ 0 & s_j \text{ definitely preferred to } s_i\end{cases}$$

The reciprocity of this relation was assumed, i.e., $\mu_R(s_i,s_j)=1-\mu_R(s_j,s_i)$, $\forall i \neq j$. Then, a flexible concept of consensus was introduced that may be expressed in natural language as:

"We will say that there is consensus among experts if *most* pairs of *important* experts *agree* as to *most* pairs of *important* options." (2)

This expression may be formalised using Zadeh's calculus of linguistically quantified propositions [18,19]. The *most* may be replaced by another quantifying expression and is modelled by a (fuzzy) *linguistic quantifier*. The notions of *importance* and *agreement* are modelled as fuzzy properties. Then, Zadeh's calculus provides a way to calculate the truth degree of (2). Here we adopt a richer preference structure that supports a more straightforward interpretation, and also makes possible a flexible consensus concept without additional definitions of an agreement degree among the experts.

Basically, we follow the previous approach, i.e. in the first step, for each pair of options we calculate a degree of agreement among *most* of the individuals. Then, we obtain the final consensus degree aggregating the partial consensus indicators computed in the first step, i.e. we calculate if these indicators are high for *most* of the pairs of options. The aggregation operator in both steps is a linguistic quantifier in the sense of Zadeh. Some other approaches to linguistic (fuzzy) quantification may be readily used, see, e.g., [9].

In the first step, there is an agreement among the individuals as to a pair of options if *most* of them support this pair of options due to the same fuzzy preference relation from our fuzzy preference structure. Thus, for a given pair of options we define four fuzzy properties of individuals, XP, XP^t, XI, XJ, basing on their support for particular preference relations. The membership functions of the fuzzy sets representing these fuzzy properties are as follows:

$$\mu_{XP}(x_m) = P(s_i,s_j)$$

$$\mu_{XP^t}(x_m) = P^t(s_i,s_j)$$

$$\mu_{XI}(x_m) = I(s_i,s_j)$$

$$\mu_{XJ}(x_m) = J(s_i,s_j)$$

Then the degree of consensus of *most* individuals as to the pair of options (s_i,s_j) may be expressed as:

$$\mathrm{con}(s_i,s_j) = \max\{\mathrm{Q_m}\, XP(x_m),\ \mathrm{Q_m}\, XP^t(x_m), \mathrm{Q_m}\, XI(x_m),\ \mathrm{Q_m}\, XJ(x_m)\} \quad (3)$$

where $\mathrm{Q_m}$ denotes a linguistic quantifier employed, e.g., *most,* and m iterates over the set of individuals.

The truth value of the expression, e.g, $\mathrm{Q_m}\ XP(x_m)$ is calculated according the original Zadeh's approach:

$$\mathrm{truth}(\mathrm{Q_m}\, XP(x_m)) = \Sigma\mathrm{Count}(XP) / M$$

In the second step we aggregate the results obtained above, for all pairs of options, thus producing the overall consensus degree:

$$\mathrm{CON} = \mathrm{Q}_{(i,j):i<j}\ \mathrm{con}(s_i,s_j)$$

Observe, that we have to take into account only those pairs of options (s_i,s_j) for which $i<j$ because the relations I and J are symmetric and P and P^t are the transposes of each other.

This concept of consensus is *constructive*. In the first step, we acknowledge consensus among the experts only if *most* of them support one of the preference relations. It may happen that their preferences are in perfect agreement but are more or less equally distributed among all four relations. Then, the computed consensus degree will be low. This may be somehow alleviated by replacing formula (3) by the following one:

$$\mathrm{con}(s_i,s_j) = \max\{\ \mathrm{Q_m}\, XP(x_m) \vee \mathrm{Q_m}\, XI(x_m), \mathrm{Q_m}\, XP^t(x_m) \vee \mathrm{Q_m}\, XI(x_m),\ \mathrm{Q_m}\, XJ(x_m)\ \} \quad (4)$$

Then the resulting consensus degree will be usually higher (especially in case of the Łukasiewicz disjunction) but still the concept does not completely loose its constructive character.

The question of incomparability requires a more careful consideration. Basically, we can employ the same approach, possibly with some modifications, for data on all remaining levels mentioned in (1a), (1b) and (1d). The resulting consensus degree concepts may be applicable in different contexts. For example, requiring a high consensus at the level of criteria weights, we focus on the very definition of the decision problem. If the weights chosen by particular individuals are essentially different (there is no consensus about them), then it may mean that the understanding of the decision problem among individuals is also rather distinct. Reaching consensus at this level may stimulate a discussion leading to a higher agreement on all other levels.

5. Implementation

The Internet, or more precisely the WWW environment, seems to be close to an ideal platform for the implementation of a group decision support system of the proposed type. The idea of browsing as a universal paradigm of human-computer interaction is very attractive and may prove to be also effective and efficient.

Basically, we have a simple client software (a WWW browser), focused on sending a document request to a WWW server selected by the user and displaying the document received applying some limited formatting commands. This fairly simple protocol turned out to be very efficient and attractive. Soon it started serving not only the purposes of a scientist but also a growing population of "ordinary" users. WWW has become a subject of commercial interest and activity what triggered a fast development of new applications and tools. Capabilities of a modern WWW-related software are much more sophisticated than it was a couple of years ago. Unfortunately, this happened, to some extent, at the expense of standardisation. Anyway, we decided to undertake our implementation using newest developments in this area, such as Dynamic HTML and XML. Before briefly presenting our pilot implementation, we will discuss how modern WWW-based software engineering meets the needs of decision support systems considered in this paper.

There is a vast literature related to the postulated features of (group) decision support systems. We can mention some of them after, e.g., Freyenfeld [5]:

1. an interactive way of data processing and presentation supporting individual (decision maker) involved,
2. user-friendliness,
3. a natural way of dialogue,
4. a filtering of information

The first two requirements are strictly of a software engineering nature. Here WWW provides a rich enough environment to accomplish those goals. The third feature may be connected with the idea of human consistency that is usually argued as a characteristic for fuzzy logic based approaches. Thus, in fact we are combining advanced software engineering solutions with sophisticated modelling and information processing methods. For example, the use of linguistic labels during the assessment of options should be much more comfortable for an "average" user.

There are also some requirements specific to group decision support systems. For example, the Internet may be a perfect communication media preserving the *anonymity* of individuals. It is well known from the literature that the participation in a decision making (or advising) process may imply a severe stress. Members of the group are afraid to express their real opinions in front of other people. They quite often quickly adopt positions of stronger personalities what, obviously, may have nothing to do with the merit of the decision problem. The Internet makes it possible to organise a session by "grouping" people being physically in very distant places and completely anonymous to each other. Huber [6] put stress on the use of software *in the session*. Again, a WWW based solution fits this requirement perfectly. A possible reason for breaking the session could be a need for more information on the topic. The use of an Internet based solution makes it possible to gather needed information from some millions of various sources of information available over the WWW as well as through a fast e-mail contact with other experts. All that may be done in the background without any discontinuation of the current session. In fact, on more and more occasions this is just the way we proceed now looking for some information!

DeSanctis and Gallupe [2] introduced three levels of group decision support systems, depending on their control of decision processes occurring in the group. The level 1 systems are to enhance these processes through a support of the exchange of information among the group members. The level 2 systems additionally provide some modelling tools and, finally, the level 3 systems should control the whole decision making session according to some flexible strategies. In fact, the Internet technology provides means for the implementation of features required by all three levels of the group decision-making systems. The integration of Web tools, e-mail agents, directory services or data transfer protocols makes this environment the richest information exchange forum. Moreover, it is easily accessible from virtually any desktop computer system. The system level 2 requirements may be also easily addressed as the WWW servers are no longer just file servers but full-fledged application servers.

The pilot implementation of the proposed system makes it possible to:

- set the weights of particular criteria,
- assess the quality of each option according to each criteria, and finally,
- compare opinions of the individuals including the consensus degree evaluation.

Most of the functionality is implemented on the client side using a WWW browser. We employed the Internet Explorer 5 supporting such recent advancements in Web technology as Dynamic HTML or XML. The server side of the application, based on the Internet Information Server, consists of a number of Active Server Pages files. Preferences and problem description data are represented in XML to provide for a high flexibility. The resulting user interface is illustrated in Exhibit 1.

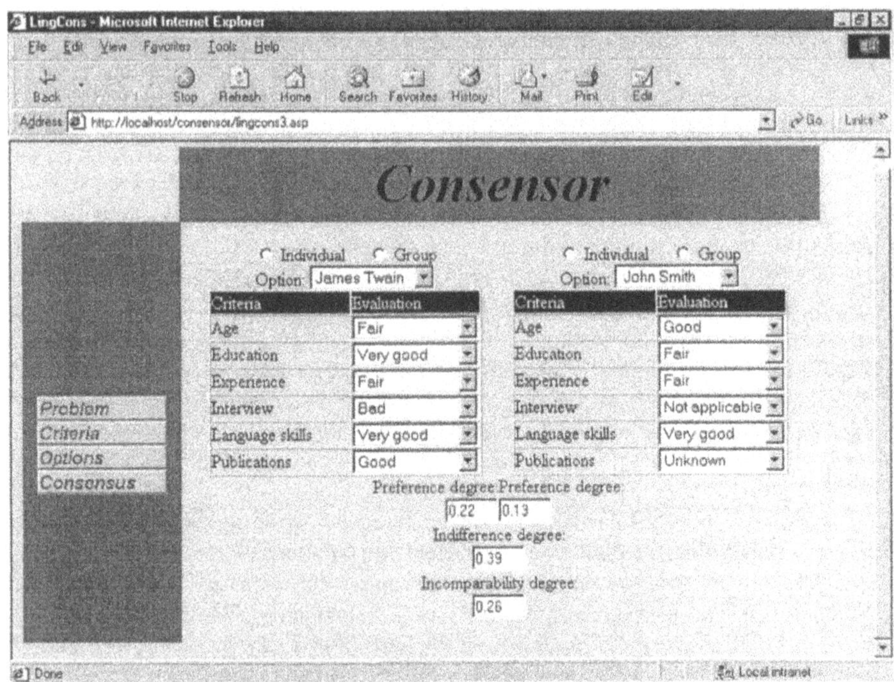

Exhibit 1. Assessment and comparison of options

6. Concluding remarks

We presented an idea of an Internet based group decision support system aimed mainly at supporting the consensus reaching process. We tried to couple a flexible software design with human consistent, sound theoretical foundations. The former was addressed by the use of modern tools and techniques available for system development in the WWW based environment. The latter relied on the application of recent preference modelling techniques elaborated in the framework of fuzzy sets and fuzzy logic.

There are many possible extensions and enhancements to the proposed system. From the software engineering perspective, it would be advantageous to develop a standard, XML based representation of preferences on all levels involved, i.e. linguistic labels, criteria importance weights, particular fuzzy relations constituting the preference structure, etc.

There are some extensions needed to support the completeness of the proposed group decision support system. These include, for example, a support for choosing a set of criteria to be used when assessing particular options. Another possible extension would be to offer more flexible a transition from a criteria based assessment of options to a fuzzy preference structure. Such a more flexible transition could, e.g., take into account compensatory interrelations among the criteria.

References

[1] Barrett CR, Pattanaik PK and M. Salles, "On choosing rationally when preferences are fuzzy", Fuzzy Sets and Systems 1990; 34: 197-212.

[2] DeSanctis G., Gallupe R.B., "A foundation for the study of group decision support systems", Management Sciences 33, 1987.

[3] Fedrizzi M., Kacprzyk J., Owsiński J.W. and S. Zadrożny, "Consensus reaching via a GDSS with fuzzy majority and clustering of preference profiles", Annals of Operations Research 1994; 51: 127-139.

[4] Fedrizzi M, Kacprzyk J and S. Zadrożny, "An interactive multi-user decision support system for consensus reaching processes using fuzzy logic with linguistic quantifiers", Decision Support Systems 1988; 4: 313-327.

[5] Freyenfeld W.A, Decision Support Systems, NCC Publications, Manchester, England, 1984.

[6] Huber G., Issues in the design of GDSS. Management Information Systems Quarterly 7, 1984, 195-204.

[7] Kacprzyk J and M. Fedrizzi, "A 'soft` measure of consensus in the setting of partial (fuzzy) preferences", European Journal of Operational Research 1988; 34: 316 - 325.

[8] Kitainik L., "Fuzzy Decision Procedures with Binary Relations: Towards a Unified Theory", Kluwer Academic Publishers, Boston/Dordrecht/London, 1993.

[9] Liu Y. And E.E. Kerre, "An overview of fuzzy quantifiers. (I). Interpretations", Fuzzy Sets and Systems 95, 1998, 1-21.

[10] Nurmi H., "Approaches to collective decision making with fuzzy preference relations". Fuzzy Sets and Systems 6, 1981, 249-259.

[11] Nurmi H. and J. Kacprzyk, "On fuzzy tournaments and their solution concepts in group decision making", EJOR 51, 1991, 223 - 232.

[12] Orlovsky S.A.: "Decision-making with a fuzzy preference relation", Fuzzy Sets and Systems 1, 1978, 155-167.

[13] Ovchinnikov S.V. and V.M. Ozernoy, "Identifying noninferior decision alternatives based on fuzzy binary relations", in: J. Kacprzyk and M. Roubens (Eds.): Non-Conventional Preference Relations in Decision Making. Springer Verlag, Berlin, 1988, 82-95.

[14] Świtalski Z., "Choice functions associated with fuzzy preference relations.", in: J. Kacprzyk and M. Roubens (Eds.): Non - conventional Preference Relations in Decision Making, Berlin: Springer-Verlag, 1988.

[15] Ovchinnikov S., "Modelling valued preference relations", in J. Kacprzyk and M. Fedrizzi (Eds.): Multiperson Decision Making Models Using Fuzzy Sets and Possibility Theory, Kluwer Academic Publishers, 1990, 64-70.

[16] Van de Walle B., B. De Baets and E. Kerre, "A plea for the use of Łukasiewicz triplets in fuzzy preference structures. Part 1: General argumentation", Fuzzy Sets and Systems 97, 1998, 349-359.

[17] Zadrożny S, "An approach to the consensus reaching support in fuzzy environment", in J. Kacprzyk, H. Nurmi and M. Fedrizzi (Eds.): Consensus under Fuzziness. Kluwer, Boston, 1996

[18] Zadeh LA., "A computational approach to fuzzy quantifiers in natural languages", Comp. and Maths. with Appls. 1983; 9: 149-184.

[19] Zadeh LA., "A computational theory of dispositions", International Journal of Intelligent Systems 1987; 2: 39-64.

Integral Representations and Decision Theory

Yasuo Narukawa[1], Toshiaki Murofushi[2], and Michio Sugeno[3]

[1] Toho Gakuen, 3-1-10, Naka, Kunitachi, Tokyo, 186-0004, Japan.
e-mail: narukawa@fz.dis.titech.ac.jp
[2] Comp. Intell. & Syst. Sci., Tokyo Inst. Tech. 4259 Nagatsuta, Midoriku, Yokohama, 226-8502, Japan.
e-mail: murofusi@fz.dis.titech.ac.jp
[3] Laboratory for Language-Based Intelligent Systems Brain Science Institute, RIKEN 2-1, Hirosawa, Wako, Saitama, 351-0198, Japan.
e-mail: msgn@brain.riken.go.jp

Abstract. A comonotonically additive and monotone functional (for short c.m.) on the class of continuous functions with compact support is represented by one Choquet integral if the universal set X is compact, while it is not represented by one Choquet integral but represented by the difference of two Choquet integral, if the universal set X is not compact but locally compact. This fact is expressed by the framework of decision making.
Keywords : Fuzzy measure, Non-additive measure, Choquet integral, Decision making, Utility theory.

1 Introduction

The Choquet integral with respect to a fuzzy measure proposed by Murofushi and Sugeno [8] is a basic tool for a subjective evaluation [22] and a decision analysis [4]. This integral is a functional on the class of measurable functions, which is comonotonically additive and monotone(for short c.m.).

Sugeno et al. [21] proved that a c.m. functional I can be represented by a Choquet integral with respect to a regular fuzzy measure when the domain of I is the class $C_0(X)^+$ of nonnegative continuous functions with compact support on a locally compact Hausdorff space. In [11], it is proved that a c.m. functional on the class $C_0(X)$ of continuous functions with compact support is a rank- and sign-dependent functional (for short a r. s. d. functional), that is, the difference of two Choquet integrals. The r. s. d. functional is used in utility theory [7] and cumulative prospect theory [23,24]. It is also proved in [11] that a r. s. d. functional is a c.m. functional if the universal set X is not compact. The conditions for which a c.m. functional can be represented by one Choquet integral is discussed in [12,16,13].

In this paper, we survey the results, and, as their application, we express these fact by the framework of decision-making, which has a finite or infinite state space.

In Section 2, basic properties of the fuzzy measure and the Choquet integral are shown. We show the representation of a c.m. functional by the Choquet integral with respect to regular fuzzy measures. One of the main theorem in this section is that a c.m. functional I on $C_0(X)$ is a r. s. d. functional which is the difference of two Choquet integral, if the universal set X is not compact, while it is represented by one Choquet integral if X is compact.

If the universal set X is not compact, a c.m. functional is not generally represented by one Choquet integral with respect to a regular fuzzy measure. In Section 3 and Section 4, we discuss this case.

In Section 3, the relations between a c.m. functional I and induced fuzzy measures μ_I^+ and μ_I^- are discussed. The boundedness of a c.m. functional I is discussed in Subsection 3.1. A necessary and sufficient condition for $\mu_I^+(X) < \infty$ is that I is bounded above, and that for $\mu_I^-(X) < \infty$ is that I is bounded below. We define the symmetry and ε-symmetry of a c.m. functional I in Subsection 3.2. The symmetry is a necessary and sufficient condition for I to be a Šipoš integral [19]. The ε-symmetry is a necessary and sufficient condition for $\mu_I^+(X) = \mu_I^-(X)$. In Subsection 3.3, we define the conjugate conditions for compact sets. The conditions are necessary and sufficient conditions for the representation of I by one Choquet integral.

In Section 4, the extension of the domain of a c.m. functional is discussed. The necessary and sufficient condition for the extension I^* of a c.m. functional I to be comonotonically additive is ε-symmetry. In Section 4.2, M-uniformly continuity is defined. The necessary and sufficient condition for monotonicity of the extension I^* of I is this continuity. The representation theorem of I^* is shown in the remainder of this section.

In Section 5, as an application of these theory, we interpret these fact by the framework of decision-making theory. Some examples show that the functionals in previous section is a utility functional which has been studied in various references [7,17,24].

2 Preliminaries

Throughout the paper we assume that X is a locally compact Hausdorff space, $\mathcal{B}$ is the class of Borel subsets, $\mathcal{O}$ is the class of open subsets and $\mathcal{C}$ is the class of compact subsets.

2.1 Fuzzy measure and Choquet integral

In this subsection, we define fuzzy measure, the Choquet integral and the rank- and sign-dependent functional, and show their basic properties.

Definition 2.11 [20] A *fuzzy measure* μ is an extended real valued set function,

$$\mu : \mathcal{B} \longrightarrow \overline{R^+}$$

with the following properties.

(i) $\mu(\emptyset) = 0$
(ii) $\mu(A) \leq \mu(B)$ whenever $A \subset B$, $A, B \in \mathcal{B}$

where $\overline{R^+} = [0, \infty]$ is the set of extended nonnegative real numbers.
When $\mu(X) < \infty$, we define *the conjugate* μ^c *of* μ by

$$\mu^c(A) = \mu(X) - \mu(A^c)$$

for $A \in \mathcal{B}$.

$C_0(X)$ denotes the class of continuous functions with compact support, $C_0(X)^+$ the class of nonnegative continuous functions with compact support and $C_0(X)_1^+$ denotes the class of nonnegative continuous functions with compact support which satisfies $0 \leq f \leq 1$.
supp(f) denotes the support of $f \in C_0(X)$, that is,

$$supp(f) = cl(\{x|f(x) \neq 0\}),$$

where $cl(A)$ means the closure of A.

Definition 2.12 [1,8] Let μ be a fuzzy measure on $(X, \mathcal{B})$.

(i) *The Choquet integral* of $f \in C_0(X)^+$ with respect to μ is defined by

$$(C)\int f d\mu = \int_0^\infty \mu_f(r)dr,$$

where $\mu_f(r) = \mu(\{x|f(x) \geq r\})$.
(ii) Suppose $\mu(X) < \infty$. The Choquet integral of $f \in C_0(X)$ with respect to μ is defined by

$$(C)\int f d\mu = (C)\int f^+ d\mu - (C)\int f^- d\mu^c,$$

where $f^+ = f \vee 0$ and $f^- = -(f \wedge 0)$. When the right hand side is $\infty - \infty$, the Choquet integral is not defined.

Definition 2.13 [3] Let $f, g \in C_0(X)$.
We say that f and g are *comonotonic* if

$$f(x) < f(x') \Rightarrow g(x) \leq g(x')$$

for $x, x' \in X$.
We denote $f \sim g$, when f and g are comonotonic.

Definition 2.14 Let I be a real valued functional on $C_0(X)$.
We say I is *comonotonically additive* if and only if

$$f \sim g \Rightarrow I(f+g) = I(f) + I(g)$$

for $f, g \in C_0(X)^+$, and I is *monotone* if and only if

$$f \leq g \Rightarrow I(f) \leq I(g)$$

for $f, g \in C_0(X)^+$.
If a functional I is comonotonically additive and monotone, we say that I is *a c.m. functional.*

Suppose that I is a c.m. functional, then we have $I(af) = aI(f)$ for $a \geq 0$ and $f \in C_0(X)^+$, that is, I is positive homogeneous.

2.2 Representation

Definition 2.21 Let I be a real valued functional on $C_0(X)$. I is said to be *a rank- and sign-dependent functional* (for short *a r.s.d. functional*) on $C_0(X)$, if there exist two fuzzy measures μ^+, μ^- such that for every $f \in C_0(X)$

$$I(f) = (C)\int f^+ d\mu^+ - (C)\int f^- d\mu^-$$

where $f^+ = f \vee 0$ and $f^- = -(f \wedge 0)$.

When $\mu^+ = \mu^-$, we say that the r.s.d. functional is the Šipoš functional [19]. If the r.s.d. functional is the Šipoš functional, we have $I(-f) = -I(f)$.
If $\mu^+(X) < \infty$ and $\mu^- = (\mu^+)^c$, we say that the r.s.d. functional is the Choquet functional.

Theorem 2.22 [10,11] *Let I be a c.m. functional on $C_0(X)$.*

(i) *A c.m. functional is a r.s.d functional, that is, there exist two fuzzy measure μ_I^+ and μ_I^- such that*

$$I(f) = (C)\int (f \vee 0) d\mu^+ - (C)\int -(f \wedge 0) d\mu^-.$$

for every $f \in C_0(X)$.
(ii) *If X is compact, then a c.m. functional can be represented by one Choquet integral.*
(iii) *If X is locally compact but not compact, then a r.s.d functional is a c.m. functional.*

Definition 2.23 Let I be a c.m. functional on $C_0(X)$. We say that μ_I^+ defined in Theorem 2.22 is *the regular fuzzy measure induced by the positive part of I* ,and μ_I^- *the regular fuzzy measure induced by the negative part of I.*

3 Conditions

Generally, a c.m. functional can not be represented by one Choquet integral if X is not compact. We consider the c.m. functional with some properties and its induced regular fuzzy measures.

3.1 Boundedness

In this subsection, we discuss the boundedness of a c.m. functional on $C_0(X)$.

Definition 3.11 Let I be a real valued functional on $C_0(X)$.

(i) I is said to be *bounded above* if there exists $M > 0$ such that

$$I(f) \leq M\|f\|$$

for all $f \in C_0(X)$.

(ii) I is said to be *bounded below* if there exists $M > 0$ such that

$$-M\|f\| \leq I(f)$$

for all $f \in C_0(X)$.

(iii) I is said to be *bounded* if I is bounded above and below.

Proposition 3.12 [10] *Let I be a c.m. functional on $C_0(X)$ and μ_I^+ and μ_I^- the regular fuzzy measure induced by I.*

(i) *I is bounded above if and only if $\mu^+(X) < \infty$.*
(ii) *I is bounded below if and only if $\mu^-(X) < \infty$.*

3.2 Symmetry

In this subsection, we define the symmetry and $\varepsilon-$ symmetry of a c.m. functional I and show some properties.

Definition 3.21 We say that a c.m. functional I is *symmetric* if $I(-f) = -I(f)$.

The next proposition presents a necessary and sufficient condition that a c.m. functional I is the Šipoš functional.

Proposition 3.22 [12] *Let I be a c.m. functional on $C_0(X)$. I is the* Šipoš *functional if and only if I is symmetric.*

Next we define ε-symmetry of a c.m. functional I.

Definition 3.23 Let I be a c.m. functional on $C_0(X)$. We say that I is *ε-symmetric* if for every $\varepsilon > 0$, there exists $f_\varepsilon \in C_0(X)^+$ such that

$$f \geq f_\varepsilon \Rightarrow |I(f) + I(-f)| < \varepsilon ||f||.$$

Obviously if a c.m. functional I is symmetric then I is ε-symmetric.

Theorem 3.24 [12] *Let I be a bounded c.m. functional on $C_0(X)$ and μ_I^+ and μ_I^- the regular fuzzy measures induced by I^+ and I^- respectively. The following conditions are equivalent to each other.*

(i) $\mu_I^+(X) = \mu_I^-(X)$
(ii) *I is ε-symmetric.*

If a c.m. functional I is a Choquet functional, then we have

$$\mu_I^+(X) = \mu_I^-(X).$$

Therefore a Choquet functional I is ε-symmetric.

3.3 Conjugate conditions for compact sets

In this subsection, we discuss the conditions for one Choquet integral representation. The proof of the main theorem is in [15]

Definition 3.31 Let I be a c.m. functional and $C \in \mathcal{C}$.

(i) We say that I satisfies the positive *conjugate condition for C* if there exists a positive real number M such that for any $\epsilon > 0$ there exist $f_1, f_2 \in C_0(X)_1$ satisfies the next condition.
   $1_C \leq g_1 \leq f_1$ and $f_2 \leq g2 \leq 1_{C^c}$ with $supp(f_2) \subset supp(g_2) \subset C^c$ imply

$$|I(-g_1) - I(g_2) + M| < \epsilon$$

   for $g_1, g_2 \in C_0(X)_1$.
(ii) We say that I satisfies *the negative conjugate condition for C* if there exists a positive real number M such that for any $\epsilon > 0$ there exist $f_1, f_2 \in C_0(X)_1$ satisfies the next condition.
   $1_C \leq g_1 \leq f_1$ and $f_2 \leq g_2 \leq 1_C^c$ with $supp(f_2) \subset supp(g_2) \subset C^c$ imply

$$|-I(g_1) + I(-g_2) + M| < \epsilon.$$

   for $g_1, g_2 \in C_0(X)_1$

We have the next theorem from the definition.

Theorem 3.32 *Let I be a c.m. functional and μ_I^+ and μ_I^- the regular fuzzy measure induced by I.*

(i) *I satisfies the positive conjugate condition for any $C \in \mathcal{C}$ if and only if*

$$\mu_I^-(C) = (\mu_I^+)^c(C).$$

for any $C \in \mathcal{C}$.

(ii) *I satisfies the negative conjugate condition for any $C \in \mathcal{C}$ if and only if*

$$\mu_I^+(C) = (\mu_I^-)^c(C).$$

for any $C \in \mathcal{C}$.

Corollary 3.33 *If a c.m. functional I satisfies the positive or negative conjugate condition for any $C \in \mathcal{C}$, then I is bounded.*

It follow from Theorem 3.32 that

$$\mu_I^-(\{x|f(x) \geq r\}) = (\mu_I^+)^c(\{x|f(x) \geq r\})$$

for all $f \in C_0(X)$ and $r \in R$. Therefore we have the next theorem.

Theorem 3.34 *Let I be a c.m. functional.*

(i) *If I satisfies the positive conjugate condition for all $C \in \mathcal{C}$, we have*

$$I(f) = (C)\int f d\mu_I^+$$

for all $f \in C_0(X)$.

(ii) *If I satisfies the negative conjugate condition for all $C \in \mathcal{C}$, we have*

$$I(f) = -(C)\int -f d\mu_I^-$$

for all $f \in C_0(X)$.

Theorem 3.35 *Let I be a c.m. functional on $C_0(X)$ which is bounded, and μ_I^+ and μ_I^- the regular fuzzy measure induced by I.*

(i) *If*

$$I(f) = (C)\int f d\mu^+$$

for all $f \in C_0(X)$, then I satisfies the positive conjugate condition for all $C \in \mathcal{C}$.

(ii) *If*

$$I(f) = -(C)\int -f d\mu^-$$

for all $f \in C_0(X)$, then I satisfies the negative conjugate condition for all $C \in \mathcal{C}$.

4 Extension and Representation

In this section, we discuss the case where X is not compact. We define the extension of I with constant of the domain of I and the extension of I. We show the Choquet integral representation of the extension with some condition. The proofs are shown in [16].

4.1 Extension with constant

We define the extension $(C_0(X)^+)^*$ of $C_0(X)^+$ by

$$(C_0(X)^+)^* = \{f + a | f \in C_0(X)^+, a \in R^+\},$$

$(C_0(X)^-)^*$ of $C_0(X)^-$ by

$$(C_0(X)^-)^* = \{f - a | f \in C_0(X)^-, a \in R^+\}$$

and $C_0(X)^*$ of $C_0(X)$ by

$$C_0(X)^* = (C_0(X)^+)^* + (C_0(X)^-)^*.$$

Definition 4.11 Let I be a c.m. functional on $C_0(X)$. We define the extension

$$(I^+)^*(f) : (C_0(X)^+)^* \longrightarrow \overline{R^+}$$

of $I^+ = I_{|C_0(X)^+}$ by

$$(I^+)^* = I(f_0) + a \sup\{I(f) | f \in C_0(X)_1^+\}$$

where $f = f_0 + a$, $f_0 \in C_0(X)^+$ and $a \geq 0$, and the extension

$$(I^-)^* : (C_0(X)^-)^* \longrightarrow -\overline{R^+}$$

of $I^- = I_{|C_0(X)^-}$ by

$$(I^-)^* = I(-f_0) - a \sup\{-I(-f) | f \in C_0(X)_1^+\}$$

where $f = f_0 + a$, $f_0 \in C_0(X)^+$ and $a \geq 0$.

It is obvious that $(I^+)^*$ and $(I^-)^*$ are well defined.

Definition 4.12 Let I be a c.m. functional on $C_0(X)$. We define the extension

$$I^* : (C_0(X))^* \longrightarrow \overline{R^+}$$

of I by

$$I^*(f) = (I^+)^*(f_0 \vee 0 + a \vee 0) + (I^-)^*(f_0 \wedge 0 + a \wedge 0)$$

where $f = f_0 + a$, $f_0 \in C_0(X)$ and $a \in R$.

Since

$$I^*(f) = (I^+)^*((f_0 \vee 0) + a) + (I^-)^*(f_0 \wedge 0)$$

if $a \geq 0$ and

$$I^*(f) = (I^+)^*(f_0 \vee 0) + (I^-)^*((f_0 \wedge 0) + a)$$

if $a < 0$, we have the next proposition.

Proposition 4.13 *Let I be a c.m. functional on $C_0(X)$, its extension I^* and μ^+ and μ^- the regular fuzzy measure induced by I. If $f = f_0 + a, f_0 \in C_0(X), a \in R$, then we have*

$$I^*(f) = I(f_0) + \begin{cases} a\ \mu^+(X) & \text{if } a \geq 0 \\ a\ \mu^-(X) & \text{if } a < 0. \end{cases}$$

The next theorem follows from Propsition 4.13

Theorem 4.14 *Let I be a c.m. functional on $C_0(X)$, I^* its extension and μ^+ and μ^- the regular fuzzy measure induced by I . I^* is comonotonically additive if and only if I is ε-symmetric.*

It seems that I^* is monotone. But it is not always true. See the example in [14]

Definition 4.15 *Let I be a bounded c.m. functional on $C_0(X)$. Suppose that*

$$M = (\sup\{I(f) | f \in C_0(X)_1^+\} \vee \sup\{-I(-f) | f \in C_0(X)_1^+\}).$$

We say that I is M-uniformly continuous if

$$f - g < \alpha \Rightarrow I(f) - I(g) < M\alpha$$

for all $f, g \in C_0(X)$ and $\alpha > 0$.

The next theorem is the necessary and sufficient condition for monotonicity of I^*.

Theorem 4.16 *Let I be a bounded c.m. functional on $C_0(X)$, which is ε-symmetric. The following conditions are equivalent to each other.*

(i) *The extension I^* of I is monotone.*
(ii) *I is M-uniformly continuous.*

If I is a Choquet functional then the extension I^* is monotone. Therefore a Choquet functional is M-uniformly continuous.

Theorem 4.17 *Let I be a bounded c.m. functional which is M-uniformly continuous and ε-symmetric, $C_0(X)^*$ be the extension of $C_0(X)$, and I^* be the extension of I. There exists an outer regular fuzzy measure μ^* on $\mathcal{B}$ such that*

$$I^*(f) = (C) \int f d\mu^*$$

for all $f \in C_0(X)^+$.

5 Decision theory

We apply the representation theorem in previous section to the decision theory under uncertainty. First, we begin with the definition in a decision theoretic framework.

Let S be a state space. X is a set of outcomes. We assume that $X = R$. $\mathcal{F}$ denotes the set of prospects, that is,

$$\mathcal{F} = \{f | f : S \longrightarrow X\}.$$

Let $\prec$ or $\preceq$ be a preference relation on $\mathcal{F}$. We say that a functional $I : \mathcal{F} \longrightarrow R$ represents a preference $\prec \quad (\preceq)$ if for all $f, g \in \mathcal{F}$, $f \prec g (f \preceq g)$ if and only if $I(f) < I(g)$(resp. $I(f) \leq I(g)$). If a functional in $\mathcal{F}$ represents a weak order $\prec$ ($\preceq$), we say that I is a utility functional. Let I be a utility functional. If there exists a probability measure P on $(S, \mathcal{B})$ such that

$$I(f) = \int f dP,$$

where $\mathcal{B} \subset 2^S$ is $\sigma-$algebra, we say that the preference is the expected utility (EU). If I is linear, the preference is EU.

We say that cumulative utility (CU) hold if there exists a fuzzy measure μ such that

$$I(f) = (C) \int f d\mu.$$

CU was introduced in Tversky and Kahneman[23]. CU is sometimes called Choquet expected utility. It is also identical to rank dependent utility as introduced by Quiggin[17].

Sign- dependent expected utility (SDEU) holds if there exist probability measures P^+, P^- such that

$$I(f) = \int f^+ dP^+ - \int f^- dP^-,$$

where $f^+ = f \vee 0, f^- = -(f \wedge 0)$.

Cumulative prospect theory (CPT) holds if there exist two fuzzy measures μ^+, μ^- such that

$$I(f) = \int f^+ d\mu^+ - \int f^- d\mu^-,$$

where $f^+ = f \vee 0, f^- = -(f \wedge 0)$. CPT was introduced by Tversky and Kahneman [23]. CPT combines CU and SDEU, which are generalization of expected utility (EU). The preference can be accommodated by rank- and sign- dependent utility, which suggests risk aversion for gains and risk seeking for losses or risk aversion for losses or risk seeking for gains.

CU, SDEU, CPT axiomatized by Wakker and Tversky [24].

Symmetric cumulative prospect theory (SCPT) holds if there exists a fuzzy measure μ such that

$$I(f) = \int f^+ d\mu^+ - \int f^- d\mu^-,$$

where $f^+ = f \vee 0, f^- = -(f \wedge 0)$. SCPT is investigated by Grabisch and Labreuche [5].

Example 1 (finite case)

Suppose that $S = \{1, \ldots, n\}$, that is, the state space is finite. Then S is a compact Hausdorff space with the discrete topology and the prospect $\mathcal{F}$ is the class of continuous functions with compact support. Therefore, from Theorem 2.6, if the utility I is comonotonic and monotone (c.m.), the preference is CU.

Example 2 (Ellsberg's paradox)

Let $S = \{R, B, W\}$, $f_R \in \mathcal{F}$ and

$$f_R(x) = \begin{cases} 1 & x = R \\ 0 & o.w. \end{cases}.$$

We denote $f_R = (1,0,0)$ $(f_R(R), f_R(B), f_R(W))$. We define $f_B, f_{RW}, f_{BW} \in \mathcal{F}$ by $f_B = (0,1,0)$, $f_{RW} = (1,0,1)$, $f_{BW} = (0,1,1)$. Suppose that $f_R \prec f_B$ and $f_{BW} \prec f_{RW}$. This preference is not EU. In fact, suppose that EU holds. Then there exists a linear functional I on $\mathcal{F}$ that represents the preference. We have

$$I(f_R) = I(f_{RW}) - I(f_W) > I(f_{BW}) - I(f_W) = I(f_B)$$

where $f_W = (0,0,1)$. This contradict $f_R \prec f_B$. Suppose that I is a c.m. functional. Since f_{RW} and $-f_W$ is not comonotonic, the inequality is not always true. Therefore it is possible that the preference is CU. In fact, we can define the regular fuzzy measure μ by $\mu(\{R\}) = 1/3$, $\mu(\{B\}) = \mu(\{W\}) = 2/9$, $\mu(\{R, W\}) = 5/9$ $\mu(\{B, W\}) = \mu(\{R, W\}) = 2/3$ and the utility functional I by

$$I(f) = (C) \int f d\mu.$$

Note that μ is non-additive and every fuzzy measure with a finite discrete topology is regular. The c.m. functional I represents the preference $\prec$. This CU-model is one of the solution of Ellseberg's paradox.

Example 3 (infinite case)

Let $S = \{1, 2, \cdots\}$ a countable state space. We consider 2^S with the discrete topology. Then a finite subset T of S is a compact set, that is,

$$\mathcal{C} = \{T | T \subset S, |T| < \infty\}.$$

$\mathcal{F}_0$ denotes the set of simple prospects, that is, the prospect f taking only a finite number of outcomes and $\{x|f(x) \neq 0\} \in \mathcal{C}$. We consider the preference on $\mathcal{F}_0$. It follows from the definition of $\mathcal{F}_0$ and $\mathcal{C}$ that $\mathcal{F}_0$ is a class of continuous functions with compact support. Suppose that I on $\mathcal{F}_0$ is a c.m. functional. Then I does not always represent CU, but represents CPT from Theorem 2.6 (i) and (ii). If a c.m. functional I satisfies the positive conjugate condition (Definition 3.8), the preference is CU from Theorem 3.10.

Example 4 *$\mathcal{F}_0^*$ denotes the extension with the constant of $\mathcal{F}_0$, that is,*

$$\mathcal{F}_0^* = \{f + a | f \in \mathcal{F}_0, a \in R\}.$$

Let $f(x) = 1$ for all $x \in S$. Then we have $f \in \mathcal{F}_0^*$ (extension, see Section 4) but $f \notin \mathcal{F}_0$. We can easily extend the preference $\prec$ ($\preceq$) on $\mathcal{F}_0$ to $\prec^*$ ($\preceq^*$) on $\mathcal{F}_0^*$ by

$$I^*(f_1) < I^*(f_2) \Longleftrightarrow f_1 \prec^* f_2.$$

The preference $\prec^*$ is not always CU even if $\prec$ is CU. If I satisfies the conditions of Theorem 4.7, then $\prec^*$ is CU.

Applying the theorems in Section 2 or Section 3, we have the next theorem.

Theorem 5.08 *Let S be a state space and X be a set of outcomes. We assume that $X = R$. $\mathcal{F}$ denotes the set of prospects.*

(i) *Suppose that S is a finite set.*
  (a) *The utility functional I on $\mathcal{F}$ represents CU if and only if I is c.m.*
  (b) *The utility functional I on $\mathcal{F}$ represents CPT if and only if the restriction $I_{\mathcal{F}^+}$ and $I_{\mathcal{F}^-}$ are c.m.*
  (c) *The utility functional I on $\mathcal{F}$ represents SCPT if and only if I is symmetric and the restriction $I_{\mathcal{F}^+}$ and $I_{\mathcal{F}^-}$ are c.m.*

(ii) *Suppose that S is a countable set.*
  (a) *The utility functional I on $\mathcal{F}$ represents CU if and only if I is c.m. and satisfies the conjugate condition.*
  (b) *The utility functional I on $\mathcal{F}$ represents CPT if and only if I is c.m.*
  (c) *The utility functional I on $\mathcal{F}$ represents SCPT if and only if I is c.m. and symmetric.*

We can obtain the table below. The table says that if the state space differ then we must take account of the difference of the conditions for CU, CPT or SCPT.

Table 1. State space and utility functional.

State space	finite (compact)	infinite (non compact)
EU	linear	linear
SDEU	$I_{\mathcal{F}^+}, I_{\mathcal{F}^-}$: linear	$I_{\mathcal{F}^+}, I_{\mathcal{F}^-}$: linear
CU	c.m.	conj. cond. & c.m.
CPT	$I_{\mathcal{F}^+}, I_{\mathcal{F}^-}$: c.m.	c.m.
SCPT	$I_{\mathcal{F}^+}, I_{\mathcal{F}^-}$: c.m. I: symmetric	c.m. & symmetric

References

1. G.Choquet . Theory of capacities. *Ann. Inst. Fourier, Grenoble.* 5 (1955) 131-295.
2. D. Denneberg, *Non additive measure and Integral,* Kluwer Academic Publishers, Dordrecht, 1994.
3. C. Dellacherie, Quelques commentaires sur les prolongements de capacités, *Séminaire de Probabilités 1969/1970, Strasbourg, Lecture Notes in Mathematics,* 191, Springer, 1971, 77- 81.
4. M. Grabisch, H.T. Nguyen and E. A. Walker, *Fundamentals of uncertainty calculi with applications to fuzzy inference,* Kluwer Academic Publishers, Dordrecht,1995.
5. M. Grabisch and C. Labreuche, The Šipoš integral for the aggregation of interactiong bipolar criteria. Proc. 8th Intern. Conf. Information Processing and Management of Uncertainty in Knowledge-based Systems (IPMU 2000) (2000) pp. 395-401.
6. G. Greco, Sulla rappresentazione di funzionali mediante integrali, *Rend. Sem. Mat. Univ. Padova,* 66 (1982) 21-42.
7. R. D. Luce and P. C. Fishburn, Rank- and sign-dependent linear utility models for finite first order gambles, *Journal of risk and uncertainty* 4 (1991) 29-59
8. T. Murofushi and M. Sugeno, An interpretation of fuzzy measures and the Choquet integral as an integral with respect to a fuzzy measure, *Fuzzy Sets and Systems,* 29 (1989) 201–227.
9. T. Murofushi and M. Sugeno, A Theory of Fuzzy Measures: Representations, the Choquet integral and null sets, *J. Math. Anal. Appl.* 159 (1991) 532–549.
10. Y. Narukawa, T. Murofushi, and M. Sugeno, The comonotonically additive functional on the class of continuous functions with compact support, *Proc. FUZZ-IEEE'97* (1997) 845-852.
11. Y. Narukawa, T. Murofushi, and M. Sugeno, Regular fuzzy measure and representation of comonotonically additive functionals, *Fuzzy Sets and Systems,* 112 (2) , (2000), 177-186.

12. Y. Narukawa, T. Murofushi, and M. Sugeno, Boundedness and Symmetry of Comonotonically Additive Functionals, *Fuzzy Sets and Systems* 118, no. 3 (2001) 539-545.
13. Y. Narukawa, T. Murofushi, and M. Sugeno, Conditions for Choquet Integral Representations, Proc. Eighth International Fuzzy System Association World Congress, (1999) 920-924.
14. Y. Narukawa, T. Murofushi, and M. Sugeno, Representation of Comonotonically Additive Functional by Choquet Integral, B. Bouchon-Meunier, R.R.Yager and L. A. Zadeh (eds), *Information, Uncertainty, Fusion,* 93-104 Kluwer Academic Publisher, Boston, 2000.
15. Yasuo Narukawa, Toshiaki Murofushi, Michio Sugeno, Conditions for Choquet Integral Representation, RIMS Kokyuroku 1100 (1999) 94-108.
16. Y. Narukawa, T. Murofushi, and M. Sugeno, Extension and Representation of Comonotonically Additive Functionals, to appear in Fuzzy Sets and Systems.
17. J. Quiggin, A Theory of Anticipated Utility, *Journal of Economic Behavior and Organization,* 3 (1982) 323-343.
18. D. Schmeidler, Integral representation without additivity, *Proceedings of the American Mathematical Society,* 97 (1986) 253–261.
19. J. Šipoš, Non linear integral, *Math. Slovaca,* 29 (3) (1979) 257-270.
20. M. Sugeno, *Theory of fuzzy integrals and its applications,* Doctoral Thesis, Tokyo Institute of Technology, (1974).
21. M. Sugeno, Y. Narukawa and T. Murofushi, Choquet integral and fuzzy measures on locally compact space, *Fuzzy sets and Systems,* 99 (2),(1998) 205–211.
22. K. Tanaka and M. Sugeno, A study on subjective evaluation of color printing image, *Int. J. of Approximate Reasoning,* 5 (1991) 213-222.
23. A. Tversky and D. Kahneman, Advances in prospect theory: cumulative representation of uncertainty, *Journal of Risk and Uncertainty,* 5 (1992) 297-323.
24. P.Wakker and A. Tversky, An axiomatization of cumulative prospect theory, *Journal of Risk and Uncertainty,* 7, (1993)147-176.

Can Qualitative Utility Criteria Obey the Sure Thing Principle ?

Hélène Fargier,
IRIT - Université Paul Sabatier - 31062 Toulouse Cedex (France)
e-mail: fargier@irit.fr
http://www.irit.fr/ACTIVITES/RPDMP/Helene.html

Régis Sabbadin,
INRA - Unité de Biométrie et Intelligence Artificielle
BP 27 - 31326 Castanet-Tolosan Cedex (France)
e-mail: sabbadin@toulouse.inra.fr
http://www.inra.fr/bia/T/sabbadin/WEB/accueilen.html

Abstract

Monotonic utilities are qualitative decision criteria that have been proposed for dealing with problems where preferences and uncertainty cannot be quantified. However, these criteria suffer from a double drawback: first, they may suffer from a lack of decisiveness power. Second, they do not fully satisfy the Sure-Thing Principle (STP), which is widely accepted as a fundamental property of decision criteria. We try to cope with these two problems, proposing refinements of these decision criteria that obey the Sure Thing Principle. These procedures are derived from the comparison of the monotonic utilities of acts, every state in which both acts give identical results being neglected.

1 Introduction

In the framework of decision under uncertainty, it has been pointed out that information about preference and uncertainty in decision problems cannot always be quantified in a simple way, but only qualitative evaluations can sometimes be attained. As a consequence, the topic of qualitative decision theory is a natural one to consider [1, 7, 3]. In [3] two qualitative criteria based on possibility theory, an optimistic and a pessimistic one, whose definitions only require a linearly ordered scale for utility and uncertainty are proposed. Later, a wider family of decision criteria called *monotonic utilities* and that embeds both possibilistic decision criteria, was proposed [4]. It is based, mathematically speaking, on a Sugeno integral.

Unfortunately, monotonic utilities in general and possibilistic utilities in particular, may suffer from a lack of decisiveness power. Especially, when two actions give an identical and extreme (either good or bad) consequence in some given, plausible state of the world, they may not be distinguished by possibilistic decision criteria, although they may give significantly different consequences in the other states of the world. In addition, the possibilistic utility criteria do not fully satisfy the Sure-Thing Principle (STP) of [8] which avoids this kind of lack of decisiveness power and is widely accepted as a fundamental property of decision criteria. The aim of this article is to provide some tools to cope with the undecisiveness of possibilistic decision criteria. In particular, it leads us to define a family of decision procedures that we call *discriminant monotonic decision procedures* that all satisfy the STP and may yield a gain in decisiveness power.

In Section 2, we first give some background on monotonic and possibilistic utilities, and point out the "drowning effect" that generates undecisiveness. More generally, this section shows that the only situations where possibilistic decision criteria obey the STP are degenerate. Then, in Section 3, two simple procedures derived from the possibilistic decision criteria, that obey the STP and allow to cope with the drowning effect are proposed. These two procedures are members of a general family that can be derived from the family of monotonic utilities, and of which we study the properties. In Section 4 we highlight an interesting subclass of decision procedures that embeds the two procedures derived from the possibilistic decision criteria and we study their decisiveness and transitivity properties.

2 Possibilistic decision-making

2.1 Possibilistic utility criteria

Let S be a set of potential states of the world and X be a set of possible consequences. $\mathcal{F} = X^S$ denotes the set of potential acts. In this paper, S and X are supposed to be finite.

Among the acts in $\mathcal{F} = X^S$ are the *constant acts*, that can be identified with consequences : the *constant act*, identified with $x \in X$ is such that $\forall s \in S, x(s) = x$. We will also often refer to the notion of *compound act* :

Definition 1 (Compound act) *$\forall A \subseteq S$, fAg is the act defined by: $fAg(s) = f(s)$ for all $s \in A$, and $fAg(s) = g(s)$ for all $s \in \overline{A}$.*

For any pair of consequences x and y in X, xAy will denote for short the act defined by: $xAy(s) = x$ for all $s \in A$, and $xAy(s) = y$ for all $s \in \overline{A}$. Such a compound act will be called a *binary act*.

Qualitative utility theory assumes that it is possible to evaluate uncertainty and preferences by means of a finite totally ordered scale $(L, \leq)$, with top and bottom elements of L denoted 1 and 0 respectively. The utility function over consequences is $\mu : X \to L$. Uncertainty is supposed to be captured by means of a set function $\sigma : 2^S \to L$ which is a monotonic measure (or a *capacity*), that is such that: $\sigma(\emptyset) = 0$, $\sigma(S) = 1$, $A \subseteq B \Rightarrow \sigma(A) \leq \sigma(B)$[1]. Then the utility of an act f can be defined as a Sugeno integral [9], a qualitative counterpart of expected sum, where the sum is replaced by a *sup* (a *max* in the finite case) and the product by a *inf* (a *min* in the finite case).

Definition 2 (Monotonic qualitative utility)
$U_\sigma(f) = \max_{s \in S} \min(\mu(f(s)), \sigma(F_s))$ *where* $F_s = \{s' \in S,\ \mu(f(s')) \geq \mu(f(s))\}$ *and* σ *is a monotonic measure.*

Notice that $U_\sigma(f) = \max_{x \in X} \min(\mu(x), \sigma(F_x)) = \max_{\lambda \in L} \min(\lambda, \sigma(F_\lambda))$ where $F_x = \{s \in S,\ \mu(f(s)) \geq \mu(x)\}$ and $F_\lambda = \{s \in S,\ \mu(f(s)) \geq \lambda\}$. This Sugeno integral defines a weak order $\succeq_\sigma$ representing the preferences of the Decision Maker over acts:

Definition 3 *Weak order on actions derived from the monotonic qualitative utility:*

$$f \succeq_\sigma g \Leftrightarrow U_\sigma(f) \geq U_\sigma(g).$$

Two qualitative possibilistic criteria for decision making that are special cases of Monotonic utility were proposed by [3]. These two criteria are respectively obtained when σ is forced into a possibility or a necessity measure:

Definition 4 (Possibilistic utilities)
- *Optimistic possibilistic utility:*

$$U_\Pi(f) = \max_{s \in S} \min(\pi(s), \mu(f(s))),$$

- *Pessimistic possibilistic utility:*

$$U_N(f) = \min_{s \in S} \max(n(\pi(s)), \mu(f(s))).$$

Where π *is a possibility distribution over* S *and* μ *a qualitative utility function over* X. n *is an order-reversing function of* L.

The second criteria can be seen as a refinement of the Wald criterion, which estimates the utility of an act by that of its worst possible consequence. Thus, U_N is "pessimistic" or "cautious", even if the pessimism is moderated by taking relative possibilities of states into account. $U_N(f)$ is high only if f gives good consequences in every "rather plausible" state. On the other side, U_Π is a mild version of the *max* criterion which is "optimistic", or "adventurous". Notice that two weak orders on actions, $\succeq_\Pi$ and $\succeq_N$ can be defined from U_Π and U_N, in the same way as $\succeq_\sigma$ is defined from U_σ.

[1] This kind of set-function is very general and represents the minimal requirement for the representation of partial belief. Especially the last condition is called *monotonicity*, and is verified by probability measures and most other well-known representations of partial belief (including belief and plausibility functions, necessity and possibility measures...).

2.2 The "drowning effect"

Both possibilistic criteria suffer from what is called a "drowning effect", illustrated in the following example.

Example 1 *Someone has to attend an important appointment at the other end of the city. The problem is to get there on time. The uncertainty lies in the uncertain event A:* "There is traffic jam". *Three routes are allowed : Routes f, g and h which consequences, depending on the traffic status, are listed below:*

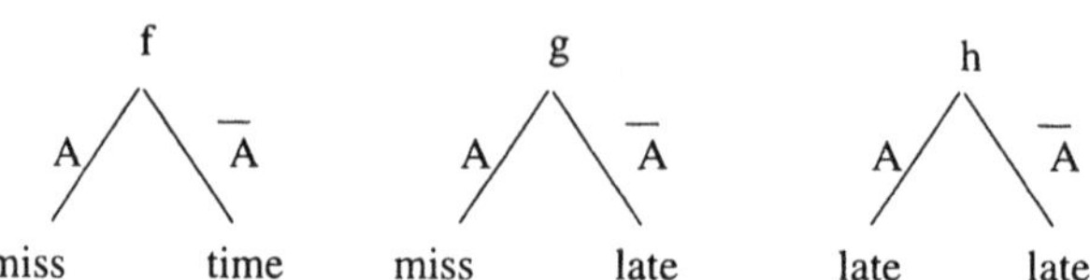

where $\Pi(A) = \Pi(\bar{A}) = 1$ *and* $0 = \mu(miss) < \mu(late) < \mu(time) = 1$. *One can check that* $f \succ_\Pi g \sim_\Pi h$ *and* $h \succ_N f \sim_N g$ *although* f *and* h *strictly dominate* g *in one situation.*

The drowning effect is not observed within expected utility theory since the following *Sure-Thing Principle* (STP) [8] insures that identical consequences do not influence the relative preference between two events.

STP: $\forall f, g, h, h', fAh \succeq gAh \Leftrightarrow fAh' \succeq gAh'$.

Our motivation will be, in the remainder of the paper, to see whether it is possible, in the possibilistic framework, to benefit from the STP, in order to escape the "drowning effect". In other terms the question we want to answer is: "can qualitative decision gain more decisiveness by using the STP ?"

2.3 Incompatibility with the sure thing principle

The critical point is that qualitative possibilistic criteria seem to be incompatible with the STP:

Proposition 1 *Let* $\succeq_\Pi$ *(resp.* $\succeq_N$*) be modeled by a qualitative possibilistic optimistic (resp. pessimistic) utility.* $\succeq_\Pi$ *(resp.* $\succeq_N$*) satisfies the STP iff* $\exists! s^* : \pi(s^*) = 1$ *and* $\forall s \neq s^*, \pi(s) = 0$.

Proof: (for $\succeq_\Pi$) The *if* part is trivial to show.
Only if part: Suppose that there exist s_1, s_2, $s_1 \neq s_2$, $\pi(s_1) \geq \pi(s_2) > 0$. Then, we have $1\{s_2\}0 \succ_\Pi 0$ and $1\{s_1, s_2\}0 \preceq_\Pi 1\{s_1\}0$, which is a violation of the STP. So, if $\succeq_\Pi$ satisfies the STP then there exists at most one s^* such that $\pi(s^*) > 0$. But, since π is normalized, such an s^* exists and $\pi(s^*) = 1$. □

In other terms, the possibilistic decision criteria do not obey the STP, except in a very particular case: when the actual state of the world is known, i.e. when there is no uncertainty at all! This result can be compared to the one (concerning preferential independance) obtained by Marichal [6] in the context of multi-criteria decision making.

3 The discri-monotonic decision procedures

3.1 Discriminant possibilistic utility criteria

In order to escape from the drowning effect, it is tempting to modify $\succeq_\Pi$ and $\succeq_N$ in such a way that they obey the STP. A simple way to restore the STP is to limit the comparison of two acts to the states in which they give different consequences. This leads to defining the *Discri-opt* order $\succeq_{\Pi\Delta}$ and *Discri-pes* order $\succeq_{N\Delta}$:

Definition 5 (Discri-opt and Discri-pes order)
- $f \succeq_{\Pi\Delta} g \Leftrightarrow \max_{s\in\Delta(f,g)} \min(\pi(s), \mu(f(s))) \geq \max_{s\in\Delta(f,g)} \min(\pi(s), \mu(g(s)))$
- $f \succeq_{N\Delta} g \Leftrightarrow \min_{s\in\Delta(f,g)} \max(n(\pi(s)), \mu(f(s))) \geq \min_{s\in\Delta(f,g)} \max(n(\pi(s)), \mu(g(s)))$,
where $\Delta(f,g) = \{s \in S, f(s) \neq g(s)\}$. *Furthermore,* $\Delta(f,g) = \emptyset \Rightarrow f \sim_{\Pi\Delta} g; f \sim_{N\Delta} g$.

One can notice that the drowning effect disappears in Example 1 when $\succeq_{\Pi\Delta}$ or $\succeq_{N\Delta}$ are used instead of $\succeq_\Pi$ or $\succeq_N$: $f \succ_{\Pi\Delta} h \succ_{\Pi\Delta} g$ and $h \succ_{N\Delta} f \succ_{N\Delta} g$. More generally, it can be proved that $\succeq_{\Pi\Delta}$ refines $\succeq_\Pi$ and $\succeq_{N\Delta}$ refines $\succeq_N$:

Proposition 2 $f \succ_\Pi g \Rightarrow f \succ_{\Pi\Delta} g$ *and* $f \succ_N g \Rightarrow f \succ_{N\Delta} g$.

Proof: (for $\succ_{\Pi\Delta}$) $f \succ_\Pi g \Rightarrow \exists s^* \in S, \min(\pi(s^*), \mu(f(s^*))) > \min(\pi(s), \mu(g(s))), \forall s \in S$. So, $\min(\pi(s^*), \mu(f(s^*))) > \min(\pi(s), \mu(g(s))), \forall s \in \Delta(f,g)$ since $\Delta(f,g) \subseteq S$. But $s^* \in \Delta(f,g)$, since, if it is not the case, we cannot have $\min(\pi(s^*), \mu(f(s^*))) > \min(\pi(s^*), \mu(g(s^*)))$. Finally, we have :
$\exists s^* \in \Delta(f,g), \min(\pi(s^*), \mu(f(s^*))) > \min(\pi(s), \mu(g(s))), \forall s \in \Delta(f,g)$, that is: $f \succ_{\Pi\Delta} g$. □

Since $\Delta(fAh, gAh) \subseteq A$, it is also easy to prove that both $\succeq_{\Pi\Delta}$ and $\succeq_{N\Delta}$ satisfy the STP:

Proposition 3 $\succeq_{\Pi\Delta}$ *and* $\succeq_{N\Delta}$ *satisfy the STP.*

Finally, notice that the indifference part of the preference relation based on $\succeq_{\Pi\Delta}$ and $\succeq_{N\Delta}$ is not necessarily transitive. This is easy to accept, if we consider that the indifference relation between acts encompasses not only the notion of equivalence between acts, but also models incomparability, which is obviously not transitive. Anyway, it holds that the corresponding strict preference relations ($\succ_{\Pi\Delta}$ and $\succ_{N\Delta}$) fortunately remain transitive.

3.2 A general family of decision procedures derived from monotonic utilities

Actually, $\succeq_{N\Delta}$ and $\succeq_{\Pi\Delta}$ are particular cases of a more general family of decision procedures that can be derived in a simple way from the family of monotonic utilities. In order to get this new family, we change the decision procedure based on the comparison of the monotonic utilities of two acts, by forcing the two acts to take a fixed value on those states where they give identical consequences. The obtained orderings on acts are indexed by this given value:

Definition 6 (Discri-monotonic decision)
Let α be a given consequence. $\succeq_{\sigma\Delta\alpha}$ is defined by:

$$f \succeq_{\sigma\Delta\alpha} g \Leftrightarrow U_\sigma(f\Delta\alpha) \geq U_\sigma(g\Delta\alpha)$$

where $\Delta = \Delta(f,g) = \{s \in S, f(s) \neq g(s)\}$ and $f\Delta\alpha(s) = f(s)$ if $s \in \Delta$ and $f\Delta\alpha(s) = \alpha$ otherwise.

We can notice that $\succeq_{\Pi\Delta} \equiv \succeq_{\Pi\Delta 0}$ and $\succeq_{N\Delta} \equiv \succeq_{N\Delta 1}$. It is also interesting to notice that $U_\sigma(f\Delta\alpha)$ may be rewritten as a function of $U_\sigma(f\Delta 0)$ and $U_\sigma(f\Delta 1)$.

Proposition 4 *$\forall f, \alpha$ and $\forall \Delta \subseteq S$,*
$U_\sigma(f\Delta\alpha) = \max\{\min(\mu(\alpha), U_\sigma(f\Delta 1)), U_\sigma(f\Delta 0)\}$.

Proof: $U_\sigma(f\Delta\alpha) = \max_{\lambda \in L} \min(\lambda, \sigma([f\Delta\alpha]_\lambda))$ where $[f\Delta\alpha]_\lambda = \{s \in S, \mu(f\Delta\alpha(s)) \geq \lambda\}$, that is $[f\Delta\alpha]_\lambda = F_\lambda \cap \Delta$ if $\mu(\alpha) < \lambda$ and $[f\Delta\alpha]_\lambda = F_\lambda \cup \Delta$ if $\mu(\alpha) \geq \lambda$. So, $U_\sigma(f\Delta\alpha) = \max\{\max_{\lambda \leq \mu(\alpha)} \min(\lambda, \sigma(F_\lambda \cup \Delta)), \max_{\lambda > \mu(\alpha)} \min(\lambda, \sigma(F_\lambda \cap \Delta))\}$. But, $\forall \lambda \leq \mu(\alpha), \min(\lambda, \sigma(F_\lambda \cup \Delta)) \geq \min(\lambda, \sigma(F_\lambda \cap \Delta))$, since $F_\lambda \cap \Delta \subseteq F_\lambda \cup \Delta$. So, $U_\sigma(f\Delta\alpha) = \max\{\max_{\lambda \leq \mu(\alpha)} \min(\lambda, \sigma(F_\lambda \cup \Delta)), U_\sigma(f\Delta 0)\}$. We also have $\max_{\lambda \leq \mu(\alpha)} \min(\lambda, \sigma(F_\lambda \cup \Delta)) = U_\sigma(f\Delta 1)$ if $U_\sigma(f\Delta 1) \leq \mu(\alpha)$ and $\mu(\alpha)$ if not. Finally, $U_\sigma(f\Delta\alpha) = \max\{\min(\mu(\alpha), U_\sigma(f\Delta 1)), U_\sigma(f\Delta 0)\}$□

The following corollary can be deduced from the expression of $U_\sigma(f\Delta\alpha)$:

Corollary 1 *$\forall \alpha, \alpha_1, \alpha_2 \in X$, s.t. $\mu(\alpha_1) \leq \mu(\alpha) \leq \mu(\alpha_2)$,*
$[(f \succeq_{\sigma\Delta\alpha_1} g$ and $f \succeq_{\sigma\Delta\alpha_2} g) \Rightarrow f \succeq_{\sigma\Delta\alpha} g]$.

3.3 Properties of the discri-monotonic decision procedures

First of all, notice that every $\succeq_{\sigma\Delta\alpha}$ relations obviously satisfy the STP:

Proposition 5 *$\forall \sigma, \alpha, \succeq_{\sigma\Delta\alpha}$ satisfies the STP.*

Proof: Just notice that for all A, f, g, h, h', $fAh \succeq_{\sigma\Delta\alpha} gAh \Leftrightarrow fA\alpha \succeq_{\sigma\Delta\alpha} gA\alpha \Leftrightarrow fAh' \succeq_{\sigma\Delta\alpha} gAh'$ □

Since discri-monotonic decision procedures obey the STP, it is possible to derive an uncertainty relation over events (i.e. subsets of the state space), by restricting $\succeq_{\sigma\Delta\alpha}$ to "binary acts" :

Definition 7 (Uncertainty relations) *$\forall A, B \subseteq S$,*
$A \trianglerighteq_{\sigma\Delta\alpha} B \Leftrightarrow \forall x, y, s.t.\ \mu(x) > \mu(y), xAy \succeq_{\sigma\Delta\alpha} xBy$.

Since the STP holds, it is easy to check that $\trianglerighteq_{\sigma\Delta\alpha}$ is well-defined, that is, can be rewritten as: $\forall A, B \subseteq S$, $A \trianglerighteq_{\sigma\Delta\alpha} B \Leftrightarrow \exists x, y, s.t.\ \mu(x) > \mu(y), xAy \succeq_{\sigma\Delta\alpha} xBy$. $\trianglerighteq_{\sigma\Delta\alpha}$ can be understood as a "projection" of $\succeq_{\sigma\Delta\alpha}$ on 2^S. Notice that $\trianglerighteq_{\sigma\Delta\alpha}$ is different from $\trianglerighteq_\sigma$, the preorder on events induced by the original uncertainty relation based on σ. Especially, $\trianglerighteq_{\sigma\Delta\alpha}$ is generally not a preorder (see [2, 5] for similar types of settings).

The equivalence of $\trianglerighteq_{N\Delta 1}$ and $\trianglerighteq_{\Pi\Delta 0}$ is a particular case of the following general property :

Proposition 6 $\trianglerighteq_{\sigma^T\Delta\alpha} \equiv \trianglerighteq_{\sigma\Delta n(\alpha)}$ *where* $\sigma^T(A) = n(\sigma(\bar{A}))$ *and* $n(\alpha) = \alpha'$ *such that* $\mu(\alpha') = n(\mu(\alpha))$.

Proof: $A \trianglerighteq_{\sigma\Delta n(\alpha)} B$
$\Leftrightarrow \max\{\min(n(\mu(\alpha)), \sigma(A \cap \bar{B})), \sigma(A \cup \bar{B})\} \geq \max\{\min(n(\mu(\alpha)), \sigma(\bar{A} \cap B)), \sigma(\bar{A} \cup B)\}$
$\Leftrightarrow n(\max\{\min(n(\mu(\alpha)), \sigma(\bar{A} \cap B)), \sigma(\bar{A} \cup B)\}) \geq n(\max\{\min(n(\mu(\alpha)), \sigma(A \cap \bar{B})), \sigma(A \cup \bar{B})\})$.
But, $n(\max\{\min(n(\mu(\alpha)), \sigma(\bar{A} \cap B)), \sigma(\bar{A} \cup B)\}) = \min\{\max(\mu(\alpha), n(\sigma(\bar{A} \cap B))), n(\sigma(\bar{A} \cup B))\} = \max\{\min(\mu(\alpha), n(\sigma(\bar{A} \cup B)), \min(n(\sigma(\bar{A} \cap B)), n(\sigma(\bar{A} \cup B))\}$
$= \max\{\min(\mu(\alpha), n(\sigma(\bar{A} \cup B)), n(\sigma(\bar{A} \cap B))\}$ (since $\bar{A} \cap B \subseteq \bar{A} \cup B$ and σ is monotonic)
$= \max\{\min(\mu(\alpha), \sigma^T(A \cap \bar{B})), \sigma^T(A \cup \bar{B})\}$.
In the same way, $n(\max\{\min(n(\mu(\alpha)), \sigma(A \cap \bar{B})), \sigma(A \cup \bar{B})\}) = \max\{\min(\mu(\alpha), \sigma^T(\bar{A} \cap B)), \sigma^T(\bar{A} \cup B)\}$, so that $A \trianglerighteq_{\sigma\Delta n(\alpha)} B \Leftrightarrow A \trianglerighteq_{\sigma^T\Delta\alpha} B$. □

Let us go back to $\succeq_{\sigma\Delta\alpha}$. First, recall that in general the indifference part of the preference relation based on discri-monotonic decision procedures is not transitive, which is acceptable as already mentionned. Anyway, it can be shown that even the strict preference between acts ($\succ_{\sigma\Delta\alpha}$) can fail to satisfy the requirement of transitivity, which is not acceptable.

Proposition 7 $\succ_{\sigma\Delta 0}$ *and* $\succ_{\sigma\Delta 1}$ *are not transitive nor acyclic in general, i.e. :* $\exists f, g, h, \sigma$ *such that :*
- $f \succ_{\sigma\Delta 0} g$, $g \succ_{\sigma\Delta 0} h$ *and* $h \succ_{\sigma\Delta 0} f$,
- $f \succ_{\sigma\Delta 1} g$, $g \succ_{\sigma\Delta 1} h$ *and* $h \succ_{\sigma\Delta 1} f$.

Proof: (for $\succ_{\sigma\Delta 0}$) Just take σ a capacity such that for some $A, B, C \subseteq S$, ($A \cap \bar{B} \neq \emptyset$, $B \cap \bar{C} \neq \emptyset$ and $C \cap \bar{A} \neq \emptyset$):
$\sigma(W) = 1$ if $A \cap \bar{B} \subseteq W$ or $B \cap \bar{C} \subseteq W$ or $C \cap \bar{A} \subseteq W$ and $\sigma(W) = 0$ otherwise. Now $f = 1A0, g = 1B0$ and $h = 1C0$ are such that $f \succ_{\sigma\Delta 0} g$, $g \succ_{\sigma\Delta 0} h$ and $h \succ_{\sigma\Delta 0} f$. □

Now, it is also worth noticing that although $\succeq_{\sigma\Delta\alpha}$ satisfies the STP, it does not necessarily refine $\succeq_\sigma$.

Proposition 8 $\exists f, g, \sigma / g \succ_\sigma f$, $f \succ_{\sigma\Delta 0} g$, $f \succ_{\sigma\Delta 1} g$.

Proof: (for $\succ_{\sigma\Delta 0}$) Let $S = \{s_1, s_2, s_3\}, A = \{s_1, s_3\}$ and $B = \{s_2, s_3\}$, $\sigma(\emptyset) = \sigma(\{s_2\}) = 0$, $\sigma(\{s_1\}) = \sigma(\{s_3\}) = \sigma(\{s_1, s_2\}) = \sigma(A) = a$ and $\sigma(B) = \sigma(S) = 1$ with $0 < a < 1$: σ is a capacity. Let now $f = 1A0$ and $g = 1B0$, obviously, $f \succ_{\sigma\Delta 0} g$ and $g \succ_\sigma f$. □

Notice that even the restriction $\trianglerighteq_{\sigma\Delta\alpha}$ of $\succeq_{\sigma\Delta\alpha}$ on events does not possess the acyclicity and refinement properties:

Proposition 9 $\triangleright_{\sigma\Delta\alpha}$ *is not necessarily acyclic and* $\trianglerighteq_{\sigma\Delta\alpha}$ *does not necessarily refine* $\trianglerighteq_\sigma$.

Proof: (for $\triangleright_{\sigma\Delta 0}$) Just notice that in the proofs of Prop. 7 and 8, f, g and h are binary acts, and thus represent events. □

4 The Discri-possibilistic decision procedures

We have described a general family of qualitative decision criteria denoted $\succeq_{\sigma\Delta\alpha}$ that generalize $\succeq_{\Pi\Delta}$ and $\succeq_{N\Delta}$ and that obey the Sure-thing principle. Unfortunately, unlike $\succeq_{\Pi\Delta}$ and $\succeq_{N\Delta}$, $\succeq_{\sigma\Delta\alpha}$ can fail to satisfy two important requirements : first, the transitivity (and even the acyclicity) of its strict part cannot always be ensured. Second, $\succeq_{\sigma\Delta\alpha}$ can be less decisive that the original monotonic utility-based decision procedure it is derived from. In this Section, we focus on the subclass of Discri-possibilistic decision procedures ($\sigma = \Pi$ or N). We search for conditions on α under which they refine the possibilistic decision procedures, and are acyclic or transitive. We study $\succeq_{\Pi\Delta\alpha}$ only, but similar properties can be derived for $\succeq_{N\Delta\alpha}$.

4.1 When does $\succeq_{\Pi\Delta\alpha}$ refine $\succeq_{\Pi}$?

First of all, as a particular case of σ, notice that

Lemma 1 $U_\Pi(f\Delta\alpha) = \max\{\min(\alpha, \Pi(\bar{\Delta})), U_\Pi(f\Delta 0)\}$.

Proof: $U_\Pi(f\Delta\alpha) = \max\{\min(\mu(\alpha), U_\Pi(f\Delta 1)), U_\Pi(f\Delta 0)\}$.
But, $U_\Pi(f\Delta 0) = \max_{s\in\Delta} \min(\pi(s), \mu(f(s)))$
and $U_\Pi(f\Delta 1) = \max\{\max_{s\in\Delta} \min(\pi(s), \mu(f(s))), \max_{s\in\bar{\Delta}} \pi(s)\}$
$= \max\{U_\Pi(f\Delta 0), \Pi(\bar{\Delta})\}$, so that: $U_\Pi(f\Delta\alpha) = \max\{\min(\alpha, \Pi(\bar{\Delta})), U_\Pi(f\Delta 0)\}$. □

Then, we can show that:

Proposition 10 $\forall \alpha, \alpha'$ *s.t.* $\mu(\alpha) \leq \mu(\alpha'), f \succ_{\Pi\Delta\alpha'} g \Rightarrow f \succ_{\Pi\Delta\alpha} g$.

Proof:
$f \succ_{\Pi\Delta\alpha'} g \Leftrightarrow \max\{\min(\mu(\alpha'), \Pi(\bar{\Delta})), U_\Pi(f\Delta 0)\} > \max\{\min(\mu(\alpha'), \Pi(\bar{\Delta})), U_\Pi(g\Delta 0)\}$
$\Leftrightarrow U_\Pi(f\Delta 0) > \max\{\min(\mu(\alpha'), \Pi(\bar{\Delta})), U_\Pi(g\Delta 0)\}$
$\Rightarrow U_\Pi(f\Delta 0) > \max\{\min(\mu(\alpha), \Pi(\bar{\Delta})), U_\Pi(g\Delta 0)\}$, since $\mu(\alpha) \leq \mu(\alpha')$.
So, $\max\{\min(\mu(\alpha), \Pi(\bar{\Delta})), U_\Pi(f\Delta 0)\} > \max\{\min(\mu(\alpha), \Pi(\bar{\Delta})), U_\Pi(g\Delta 0)\}$,
that is $f \succ_{\Pi\Delta\alpha'} g$. □

Corollary 2 $\succeq_{\Pi\Delta 0}$ *refines* $\succeq_\Pi$ *which refines* $\succeq_{\Pi\Delta 1}$.

So, it appears that $\succeq_{\sigma\Delta\alpha}$ can actually be less specific that $\succeq_\sigma$. In other terms, one can say that the family we have proposed offers different ways to ensure the STP : refining $\succeq_\sigma$ (as $\succeq_{\Pi\Delta 0}$ does for $\succeq_\Pi$) or drowning it more (as $\succeq_{\Pi\Delta 1}$ does for $\succeq_\Pi$). At this point, two questions maybe raised about the choice of an α, according to the problem of refinement:

- First, does it exist an α, such that whatever the knowledge modeled by π, $\succeq_{\Pi\Delta\alpha}$ refines $\succeq_\Pi$?

The answer is "yes" since $\alpha = 0$ provides such a value (Corollary 2). More generally, we formulate the conjecture that $\alpha = 0$ is the *only* such value:

Conjecture 1 $\succeq_{\Pi\Delta\alpha}$ refines $\succeq_\Pi$ for all π iff $\alpha = 0$.

- Second : an uncertainty model π and a preference model μ being given, can we give an easy-to-apply procedure for computing the subset $X' \subseteq X$ of values, such that $\forall\alpha \in X', \succeq_{\Pi\Delta\alpha}$ refines $\succeq_\Pi$ and $\forall\alpha \notin X'$, $\succeq_\Pi$ refines $\succeq_{\Pi\Delta\alpha}$? From proposition 10 and corollary 2, we can deduce the existence of an α^* such that, $\forall\alpha$ s.t. $\mu(\alpha) \leq \mu(\alpha^*)$, $\succeq_{\Pi\Delta\alpha}$ refines $\succeq_\Pi$ and $\forall\alpha$ s.t. $\mu(\alpha) > \mu(\alpha^*)$, $\succeq_\Pi$ refines $\succeq_{\Pi\Delta\alpha}$. Still, we have not found yet a procedure for computing directly α^* from π and μ: this is a topic for further research.

4.2 When is $\succ_{\Pi\Delta\alpha}$ transitive?

In this section, we show that $\succ_{\Pi\Delta\alpha}$ is acyclic in general, and under some restrictive condition on α, $\succ_{\Pi\Delta\alpha}$ is even transitive.

Proposition 11 (Acyclicity of $\succ_{\Pi\Delta\alpha}$)
$f \succ_{\Pi\Delta\alpha} g$ and $g \succ_{\Pi\Delta\alpha} h$ implies $f \succeq_{\Pi\Delta\alpha} h$.

Proof: Let
$A = \{s \in S, f(s) \neq g(s), g(s) \neq h(s)$ and $f(s) = h(s)\}$, $B = \{s \in S, f(s) \neq g(s), g(s) \neq h(s)$ and $f(s) \neq h(s)\}$, $C = \{s \in S, f(s) \neq g(s), g(s) = h(s)$ and $f(s) \neq h(s)\}$, $D = \{s \in S, f(s) = g(s), g(s) \neq h(s)$ and $f(s) = h(s)\}$ and $E = \{s \in S, f(s) = g(s) = h(s)\}$. Hence, $\Delta(f,g) = A \cup B \cup C, \Delta(g,h) = A \cup B \cup D$ and $\Delta(f,h) = B \cup C \cup D$.

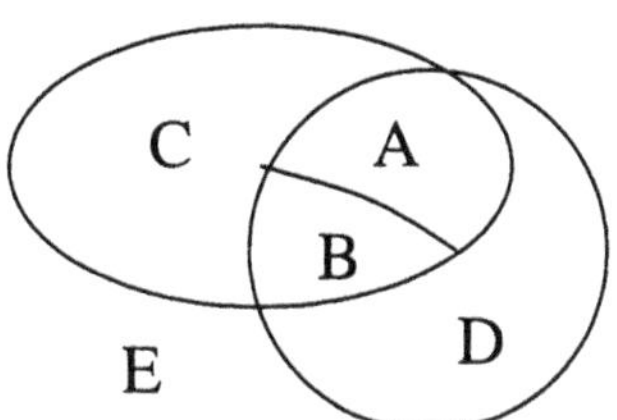

We note also $\mathcal{F}_W = \max_{s\in W} \min\{\mu(f(s)), \pi(s)\}$; $\mathcal{G}_W = \max_{s\in W} \min\{\mu(g(s)), \pi(s)\}$ and $\mathcal{H}_W = \max_{s\in W} \min\{\mu(h(s)), \pi(s)\}$ (Remark: $\mathcal{X}_{W\cup Y} = \max\{\mathcal{X}_W, \mathcal{X}_Y\}$, $\forall\mathcal{X} \in \{\mathcal{F}, \mathcal{G}, \mathcal{H}\}$. $f \succ_{\Pi\Delta\alpha} g \Leftrightarrow \max\{\min(\mu(\alpha), \Pi(D\cup E)), \mathcal{F}_{A\cup B\cup C}\} > \max\{\min(\mu(\alpha), \Pi(D\cup E)), \mathcal{G}_{A\cup B\cup C}\}$. This implies $\mathcal{F}_{A\cup B\cup C} > \mathcal{G}_{A\cup B\cup C}$. In the same way, $g \succ_{\Pi\Delta\alpha} h \Rightarrow \mathcal{G}_{A\cup B\cup D} > \mathcal{H}_{A\cup B\cup D}$. $\mathcal{F}_{A\cup B\cup C} > \mathcal{G}_{A\cup B\cup C} \Leftrightarrow \max\{\mathcal{F}_A, \mathcal{F}_{B\cup C}\} > \max\{\mathcal{G}_{A\cup B}, \mathcal{G}_C\}$ and $\mathcal{G}_{A\cup B\cup D} > \mathcal{H}_{A\cup B\cup D} \Leftrightarrow \max\{\mathcal{G}_{A\cup B}, \mathcal{G}_D\} > \max\{\mathcal{H}_A, \mathcal{H}_{B\cup D}\}$. Notice that $\mathcal{G}_D = \mathcal{F}_D$ since $D \cap \Delta(f,g) = \emptyset$, $\mathcal{G}_C = \mathcal{H}_C$ since $C \cap \Delta(g,h) = \emptyset$ and $\mathcal{H}_A = \mathcal{F}_A$ since $A \cap \Delta(f,h) = \emptyset$. So, from $f \succ_{\Pi\Delta\alpha} g$ and $g \succ_{\Pi\Delta\alpha} h$ we get $\max\{\mathcal{F}_A, \mathcal{F}_{B\cup C}\} > \max\{\mathcal{G}_{A\cup B}, \mathcal{H}_C\}$ and $\max\{\mathcal{G}_{A\cup B}, \mathcal{F}_D\} > \max\{\mathcal{F}_A, \mathcal{H}_{B\cup D}\}$. Then, combining the two inequalities by a max: $\max\{\max\{\mathcal{F}_A, \mathcal{G}_{A\cup B}\}, \mathcal{F}_{B\cup C\cup D}\} > \max\{\max\{\mathcal{F}_A, \mathcal{G}_{A\cup B}\}, \mathcal{H}_{B\cup C\cup D}\}$. Thus, $\mathcal{F}_{B\cup C\cup D} > \mathcal{H}_{B\cup C\cup D}$. From $\mathcal{F}_{B\cup C\cup D} > \mathcal{H}_{B\cup C\cup D}$
we get $\max\{\min(\alpha, \Pi(A\cup E)), \mathcal{F}_{B\cup C\cup D}\} \geq \max\{\min(\alpha, \Pi(A\cup E)), \mathcal{H}_{B\cup C\cup D}\}$, that is $f \succeq_{\Pi\Delta\alpha} h$. □

Now, the question is: is there an α that guarantees that $\succ_{\Pi\Delta\alpha}$ is transitive?

Proposition 12 *$\succ_{\Pi\Delta 0}$ is transitive.*

Proof: Let f, g and h be three acts such that $f \succ_{\Pi\Delta 0} g$ and $g \succ_{\Pi\Delta 0} h$. We are to prove that $f \succ_{\Pi\Delta 0} h$. Let us use the same notations as in the preceding proof. It holds that $f \succ_{\Pi\Delta 0} g \Leftrightarrow \mathcal{F}_{A \cup B \cup C} > \mathcal{G}_{A \cup B \cup C}$ and $g \succ_{\Pi\Delta 0} h \Leftrightarrow \mathcal{G}_{A \cup B \cup D} > \mathcal{H}_{A \cup B \cup D}$. As in the preceding proof, from $\mathcal{F}_{A \cup B \cup C} > \mathcal{G}_{A \cup B \cup C}$ and $\mathcal{G}_{A \cup B \cup D} > \mathcal{H}_{A \cup B \cup D}$ we get $\mathcal{F}_{B \cup C \cup D} > \mathcal{H}_{B \cup C \cup D}$. That is $f \succ_{\Pi\Delta 0} h$. □

Thus, we have proven that $\succ_{\Pi\Delta 0}$ is transitive. Unfortunately, $\succ_{\Pi\Delta\alpha}$ is not transitive in general, as soon as there exists $\alpha \in X'$ such that $\mu(\alpha) > \mu(\alpha') > 0$.

Proposition 13 (Non-transitivity) *As soon as* $|S| \geq 2$ *and* $|X| \geq 3$, $\forall \alpha$ *such that* $(\exists \alpha', \mu(\alpha) > \mu(\alpha') > 0)$, $\exists, \pi, \mu$ *such that* $\succ_{\Pi\Delta\alpha}$ *is not transitive.*

Proof: Let $S = \{s_1, s_2\}$, $X = \{x_0, x_1, x_2\}$, $\pi(s_1) = \pi(s_2) = 1$, $\mu(\alpha) \geq \mu(x_2) > \mu(x_1) > \mu(x_0)$ and $f(s_1) = h(s_1) = h(s_2) = x_0$, $g(s_1) = g(s_2) = x_1$ and $f(s_2) = x_2$. $f \succ_{\Pi\Delta 0} g$ since $\Delta(f,g) = S$ and $U_\Pi(f) = \mu(x_2) > U_\Pi(g) = \mu(x_1)$. $g \succ_{\Pi\Delta 0} h$ since $\Delta(g,h) = S$ and $U_\Pi(g) = \mu(x_1) > U_\Pi(h) = \mu(x_0)$. But, $\Delta = \Delta(f,h) = \{s_2\}$ and $U_\Pi(f\Delta\alpha) = \max\{\mu(f(s_2)), \alpha\} = \mu(\alpha)$ and $U_\Pi(h\Delta\alpha) = \max\{\mu(h(s_2)), \alpha\} = \mu(\alpha)$, so $f \sim_{\Pi\Delta 0} h$ that is $\succ_{\Pi\Delta\alpha}$ is not transitive. □

So, the only possible values of α that ensure transitivity independently of the particular possibility distribution seem to be those corresponding to the two lowest levels of L. Actually, we conjecture that only the lowest level ensures this property, that is: *When* $|S| \geq 2$ *and* $|X| \geq 3$, $\succ_{\Pi\Delta\alpha}$ *is transitive for every* π *if and only if* $\mu(\alpha) = 0$.

4.3 Conclusions about the choice of α in $\succeq_{\Pi\Delta\alpha}$ and $\succeq_{N\Delta\alpha}$

We have shown that choosing $\alpha = 0$ is a good choice with respect to both the requirement of refinement ($\succeq_{\Pi\Delta 0}$ refines the $\succeq_{\Pi\Delta\alpha}$ for all α) and the requirement of the transitivity of $\succ_{\Pi\Delta\alpha}$. We conjecture that $\alpha = 0$ is actually the only value that guarantees the satisfaction of these requirements, independtly of π. Every proposition in the two previous subsections has its exact counterpart concerning $\succeq_{N\Delta\alpha}$. In particular, one can show that $\alpha = 1$ is the best choice in this case, insofar as $\succ_{N\Delta 1}$ is both transitive and the most refined among the family of $\succ_{N\Delta\alpha}$ orderings.

5 Concluding remarks

In order to cope with the drowning effect that pertains to possibilistic decision criteria, we have investigated the introduction of the Sure-Thing Principle in such a qualitative setting. At a first glance, it seems that the STP is incompatible with possibilistic decision criteria. But, as soon as one accept to forget the transitivity of the indifference relation (attitude that is natural since the indifference relation between acts can come from their incomparability, which is obviously not transitive), it is possible to meet this important requirement of decision under uncertainty. Our new decision procedure is based on the comparison of the monotonic utilities of two acts, by forcing the two acts to take a fixed value of reference α on those states where they give identical consequences.

Moreover, the only good choice for α seems to be the worst consequence when considering the optimistic qualitative utility (respectively, the best one, when considering the pessimistic qualitative utility). We thus get new and appealing decision procedures that are both compatible with the STP and with a qualitative, possibilistic, approach of decision under uncertainty.

This work naturally extends to the search of a Savage-like axiomatization of the discri-possibilistic decision procedures. We already know that these procedures obey the Sure Thing Principle and are no more representable by a weak order (although the strict preference relation is transitive). A careful study of their behavior in front of the axioms of expected utility and possibilistic utility should help in finding this axiomatization. The second direction for further research would then consist in determining those uncertainty models for which acyclicity is guaranteed and in identifying which conditions on the capacity function used to model uncertainty can ensure the choice of a suitable level of reference. Good candidates are qualitative beliefs and plausibilities [10], for which suitable α seems still to be 1 and 0, respectively.

References

[1] R. Brafman and M. Tennenholtz. On the axiomatization of qualitative decision criteria. In *AAAI'97*, pages 76–81, Providence, R. I., Aug. 4-8 1997. AAAI Press / MIT Press.

[2] D. Dubois, H. Fargier, and H. Prade. Possibilistic likelihood relations. In *IPMU'98*, pages 1196–1203, Paris, La Sorbonne, 1998. EDK.

[3] D. Dubois and H. Prade. Possibility theory as a basis for qualitative decision theory. In *IJCAI'95*, pages 1925–1930, Montreal, Canada, Aug. 20-25 1995. Morgan Kaufman.

[4] D. Dubois, H. Prade, and R. Sabbadin. Qualitative decision theory with Sugeno integrals. In *UAI'98*, pages 121–128, Madison, WI, July 24-26 1998. Morgan Kaufmann.

[5] H. Fargier and P. Perny. Qualitative models for decision under uncertainty without the commensurability assumption. In *UAI'99*, pages 188–195, Stockholm, Sweden, July 30-Aug. 1 1999. Morgan Kaufmann.

[6] J. L. Marichal. On Sugeno integrals as an aggregation function. Technical Report 9710, GEMME, Faculté d'Economie, de Gestion et de Sciences Sociales, Liège, Belgium, May 1997.

[7] J. Pearl. From conditionnal oughts to qualitative decision theory. In *UAI'93*, pages 12–20, San Mateo, CA, 1993. Morgan Kaufmann.

[8] L. J. Savage. *The Foundations of Statistics*. J. Wiley and Sons, New York, 1954.

[9] M. Sugeno. Fuzzy measures and fuzzy integrals - A survey. In *Fuzzy Automata and Decision Processes*, pages 89–102. M. M. Gupta, G. N. Saridis et B. R. Gaines éditeurs, North-Holland, Amsterdam, 1977.

[10] S. K. M. Wong, Y. Y. Yao, and P. Lingras. Comparative beliefs and their measurements. *Int. Journal of General Systems*, 22:69–89, 1993.

Pseudo-additive Measures and the Independence of Events

Didier Dubois[1], Endre Pap[2], and Henri Prade[1]

[1] I.R.I.T., Université Paul Sabatier, 118 route Narbonne, 31062 Toulouse Cedex 4, France, e-mail: dubois@irit.fr, e-mail:prade@irit.fr
[2] Institute of Mathematics, University of Novi Sad, 21000 Novi Sad, Yugoslavia, e-mail: pap@unsim.ns.ac.yu , pape@eunet.yu

Abstract. This paper is devoted to the investigation of independence (separability) of events with respect to a pseudo-additive measure that combine probabilistic and possibilistic behaviours via a threshold. It is based on a restricted family of t-conorm/ t-norm pairs which are very special ordinal sums. Any practically useful theory of pseudo-additive measures must use such special pairs of operations in order to conjointly extend the additivity property, and the notion of probabilistic independence.
Keywords: triangular conorm, decomposable measure, conditional distributivity, independence.

1 Introduction

Natural independence structures exist for probability measures, and maybe less well-known, for possibility measures (e.g. De Campos and Huete [3], [4], Vejnarová [18]). The aim of this paper is to address the following question: what can be a counterpart to probabilistic independence for pseudo-additive measures([9,15]). Namely what type of operation is mathematically consistent for obtaining the uncertainty of a conjunction of prescribed events, here called separable, as a function of the individual uncertainty of such events? This question is addressed, from a mathematical point of view, by taking advantage of a result of Klement et al. obtained in [13] on the relaxed distributivity of a triangular norm over a triangular conorm (called conditional distributivity). This distributivity property must be satisfied between the t-conorm characterizing the pseudo-additive measure, and the triangular norm expressing separability. This result has a drastic consequence on the choice of suitable pseudo-additive measures. Almost nothing else remains possible beyond possibility and probability measures, when preserving a natural notion of independence? Only a form of hybridization is possible such that the measure is possibilistic under a certain threshold, and probabilistic above.

The role of the operation expressing independence is to let the probability of a sequence of events conditioned by other events in composite lotteries be evaluated. Probability distributions on finite sets can then be represented by probability trees, a natural, and historically very old, representation, as pointed out by Shafer [17]. This paper thus addresses a key question in the theory of pseudo-additive measures, since the possibility of specifying separable events is a basic epistemological and practical issue in any uncertainty theory.

Section 2 is a refresher on triangular norms and pseudo-additive measures and recalls the mathematical result concerning the conditional distributivity on t-norm theory. Section 3 defines separable events and states two properties which separability must obey. It lays bare the families of pseudo-additive measures where this notion makes sense due to conditional distributivity. It is a necessary condition for the decomposability of S-measures into binary trees. Only a simple hybridization of possibility and probability measures remain meaningful from this point of view.

2 Mathematical background

For triangular conorms and norms see [13].

Definition 1. A triangular conorm (t-conorm for short) is a binary operation on the unit interval $[0,1]$, i.e., a function $S : [0,1]^2 \to [0,1]$ such that for all $x, y, z \in [0,1]$ the following four axioms are satisfied:

(S1) *Commutativity* $S(x,y) = S(y,x)$,
(S2) *Associativity* $S(x, S(y,z)) = S(S(x,y),z)$,
(S3) *Monotonicity*
$S(x,y) \leq S(x,z)$ whenever $y \leq z$,
(S4) *Boundary Condition* $S(x,0) = x$.

If S is a t-conorm, then its dual t-norm $T : [0,1]^2 \to [0,1]$ is given by

$$T(x,y) = 1 - S(1-x, 1-y).$$

Basic t-norms and co-norms are:
Minimum T_M and maximum S_M given by

$$T_M(x,y) = \min(x,y), \quad S_M(x,y) = \max(x,y),$$

Product T_P and probabilistic sum S_P given by

$$T_P(x,y) = x \cdot y, \quad S_P(x,y) = x + y - x \cdot y,$$

Lukasiewicz t-norm T_L and Lukasiewicz t-conorm S_L given by

$$T_L(x,y) = \max(x+y-1, 0),$$

$$S_L(x,y) = \min(x+y, 1).$$

A general way of constructing new t-norms (t-conorms) from given t-norms (t-conorms) is by means of ordinal sums after the following theorem, see [13]:

Theorem 1. *Let $(T_k)_{k\in K}$ be a family of t-norms and let $\{]\alpha_k, \beta_k[\}_{k\in K}$ be a family of pairwise disjoint open subintervals of the unit interval $[0,1]$ (i.e., K is an at most countable index set). Consider the linear transformations $(\varphi_k : [\alpha_k, \beta_k] \to [0,1])_{k\in K}$ given by*

$$\varphi_k(u) = \frac{u - \alpha_k}{\beta_k - \alpha_k}.$$

Then the function $T : [0,1]^2 \to [0,1]$ defined by

$$T(x,y) = \begin{cases} \varphi_k^{-1}(T_k(\varphi_k(x), \varphi_k(y))) \\ \qquad\qquad \text{if } (x,y) \in]\alpha_k, \beta_k[^2, \\ \min(x,y) \quad \text{otherwise,} \end{cases}$$

is a triangular norm, which is called ordinal sum of summands $T_k, k \in K$. We shall write

$$T = (< \alpha_k, \beta_k, T_k >)_{k\in K}.$$

In a quite analogous way, a triangular conorm S can be defined as an ordinal sum of a family $(S_k)_{k\in K}$ of t-conorms, putting max instead of min in the ordinal sum representation and we shall write $S = (< \alpha_k, \beta_k, S_k >)_{k\in K}$.

The following representations hold, see [13]:

Theorem 2. *A function $S : [0,1]^2 \to [0,1]$ is a continuous Archimedean triangular conorm,i.e., for all $x \in]0,1[$ we have $S(x,x) > x$, if and only if there exists a continuous, strictly increasing function $s : [0,1] \to [0,+\infty]$ with $s(0) = 0$ such that for all $x, y \in [0,1]$*

$$S(x,y) = s^{-1}(\min(s(x) + s(y), s(1))).$$

The analogous theorem holds for continuous Archimedean triangular norms:

Theorem 3. *A function $T : [0,1]^2 \to [0,1]$ is a continuous Archimedean triangular norm,i.e., for all $x \in]0,1[$ we have $T(x,x) < x$, if and only if there exists a continuous, strictly decreasing function $t : [0,1] \to [0,+\infty]$ with $t(1) = 0$ such that for all $x, y \in [0,1]$*

$$T(x,y) = t^{-1}(\min(t(x) + t(y), t(0))).$$

The functions s and t from Theorems 2 and 3 are then called additive generators of S and T, respectively. They are uniquely determined by S and T, respectively, up to a positive multiplicative constant.

We have the following representation for arbitrary continuous t-conorm and t-norm, see [13].

Theorem 4. *A function $S : [0,1]^2 \to [0,1]$ (resp. a function $T : [0,1]^2 \to [0,1]$) is a continuous t-conorm (resp. t-norm) if and only if S (T) is an ordinal sum whose summands are continuous Archimedean t-conorms (t-norms).*

The t-conorm S (t-norm T) is called strict if it is continuous and strictly monotone on the open square $]0,1[^2$. The continuous t-conorm S (t-norm T) is called nilpotent if each $a \in]0,1[$ is a nilpotent element of S (of T), i.e., for every $a \in]0,1[$ there exists $n \in \mathbb{N}$ such that $a_S^{(n)} = 1$ (respectively $a_T^{(n)} = 0$), where $a_S^{(n)}$ is the n-th power of a given by $S(a, \dots, a)$ (respectively $T(a, \dots, a)$) repeating a n-times. The class of continuous Archimedean t-conorms (t-norms) consists of two disjoint classes: strict and nilpotent.

The following important characterization of a strict t-norm and a nilpotent t-conorm will enable us to simplify the approach in this paper, see [13].

Theorem 5. *A function $T : [0,1]^2 \to [0,1]$ is isomorphic to T_P, i.e., there is a strictly increasing bijection $\varphi : [0,1] \to [0,1]$ such that for all $x, y \in [0,1]$ we have $T(x,y) = \varphi^{-1}(T_P(\varphi(x), \varphi(y))$ if and only if it is a strict t-norm.*

Theorem 6. *A function $S : [0,1]^2 \to [0,1]$ is isomorphic to S_L, i.e., there is a strictly increasing bijection $\varphi : [0,1] \to [0,1]$ such that for all $x, y \in [0,1]$ we have $S(x,y) = \varphi^{-1}(S_L(\varphi(x), \varphi(y))$ if and only if it is a nilpotent t-conorm.*

It is well-known (see [13]) that a t-norm T is distributive over a t-conorm on the whole square $[0,1]^2$ if and only if $S = S_M$. We shall relax this condition to require distributivity only on a smaller region, see [13].

Definition 2. A t-norm T is conditionally distributive over a t-conorm S if for all $x, y, z \in [0,1]$ such that $S(y,z) < 1$, it holds:

$$(CD) \quad T(x, S(y,z)) = S(T(x,y), T(x,z)).$$

The continuity of T and S implies that distributivity can be extended for a wider domain.

Proposition 1. *Let a continuous t-norm T be conditionally distributive over a continuous t-conorm S. Let $x, y, z \in [0,1]$ and y and z are such that $S(y,z) = 1$ and for every $b < y$ we have $S(b,z) < 1$ or for every $c < z$ we have $S(y,c) < 1$, then the distributivity $T(x, S(y,z)) = S(T(x,y), T(x,z))$ holds.*

We shall need the following theorem from [13] which gives the complete characterization of the family of continuous pairs (S, T) which satisfy the condition (CD). The proof is recalled due to the centrality of the result for the paper.

Theorem 7. *A continuous t-norm T is conditionally distributive over a continuous t-conorm S if and only if there exists a value $a \in [0,1]$, a strict t-norm T^* and a nilpotent t-conorm S^* such that the additive generator s^* of S^* satisfying $s^*(1) = 1$ is also a multiplicative generator of T^* such that*

$$T = (< 0, a, T_1 >, < a, 1, T^* >)$$

where T_1 is an arbitrary continuous t-norm and

$$S = (< a, 1, S^* >).$$

Proof. Suppose that a continuous t-norm T is conditionally distributive over a continuous t-conorm S. If $b \in [0,1[$ is an idempotent element of S, then, for each $x \in [0,1]$, $T(x,b)$ is an idempotent element of S. Therefore by the continuity of T each element in $[0,b]$ is an idempotent element of S. Hence, from Theorem 4 it follows that either $S = S_{\mathbf{M}}$ (in which case we have proved the theorem for $a = 0$) or $S = (\langle a, 1, S^*\rangle)$, where S^* is a continuous Archimedean t-conorm and $a \in [0,1[$.

If $S = (\langle a, 1, S^*\rangle)$ for some continuous Archimedean t-conorm S^* and some $a \in [0,1[$, then a is an idempotent element also of T. This follows from the fact that for all $x \in]a,1[$ with $S(x,x) < 1$ we have $T(a, S(x,x)) = S(T(a,x), T(a,x)) = T(a,x)$, i.e., $T(a,x) = T(a, x_S^{(2)})$, and consequently, for all $x \in]a,1[$ we have $T(a,x) = T(a, x_S^{(\frac{1}{2})})$ (see Remark 3.5 in [13]), implying $a = T(a,1) = T(a, x_S^{(\frac{1}{2})})$ for each $x \in]a,1[$. Therefore, T can be written as an ordinal sum (see Theorem 4), one of its summands being $\langle a, 1, T^*\rangle$, where T^* is some continuous t-norm. Since T is conditionally distributive over S, T^* must be conditionally distributive over the Archimedean t-conorm S^*.

We will show that T^* is also Archimedean. Namely, the existence of a non-trivial idempotent element c of T^* would imply the existence of $x \in [0,1]$ with $x < c < S^*(x,x) < 1$, leading to the contradiction

$$c = T^*(c, S^*(x,x)) = S^*(T^*(c,x), T^*(c,x)) = S^*(x,x).$$

Moreover, T^* cannot be nilpotent: if $0 < d = \sup\{x \in [0,1] \mid T(x,x) = 0\}$ then there exists $y \in [0,1]$ with $y < d < S^*(y,y) < 1$, leading to the contradiction

$$0 < T^*(d, S^*(y,y)) = S^*(T^*(d,y), T^*(d,y)) = 0.$$

Let θ be an arbitrary but fixed multiplicative generator of the strict t-norm T^* and s an additive generator of the continuous Archimedean t-conorm S^*. Remark that we have $S(y,z) = s^{-1}(s(x) + s(y))$ for all $(y,z) \in [0,1]^2$ with $S(y,z) < 1$. We define the continuous, strictly increasing function $f : [0, s(1)] \to [0,1]$ by $f = \theta \circ s^{-1}$ and note that $f(s(1)) = 1$. Taking $u = s(x)$, $v = s(y)$ and $w = s(z)$, the conditional distributivity of T^* over S^* can be rewritten as

$$f(u) \cdot f(v + w) = f(f^{-1}(f(u) \cdot f(v)) + f^{-1}(f(u) \cdot f(w))) \qquad (1)$$

for all $u, v, w \in [0, s(1)]$ and $v + w < s(1)$. For a fixed $u \in]0, s(1)]$,we define the continuous, strictly increasing function $g_u : [0, s(1)] \to [0, s(1)]$ by $g_u(x) = f^{-1}(f(u) \cdot f(x))$ and observe that $g_u(0) = 0$ and $g_u(s(1)) = u$. Then (1) transforms into the Cauchy equation

$$g_u(v + w) = g_u(v) + g_u(w)$$

for all $v, w \in [0, s(1)]$ and $v + w \leq s(1)$, where the case $v + w = s(1)$ follows from the continuity of g_u. If $s(1) = \infty$ then this equation has no solution, so

S^* must be a nilpotent t-conorm. From [1, Section 2.1,Theorem 3] it follows that $g_u(x) = \frac{u}{s(1)}x$, i.e.,

$$f\left(\tfrac{u}{s(1)}x\right) = f(u) \cdot f(x)$$

for all $x, u \in [0, s(1)]$ (the case $u = 0$ follows from $f(0) = 0$). The only solutions of this modified Cauchy equation are given by $f(x) = \left(\frac{x}{s(1)}\right)^c$, where $c \in]0, \infty[$. Since $s(1)$ can be chosen arbitrarily in $]0, \infty[$ we may take $s(1) = 1$, leading to $f(x) = x^c$ and, consequently, we have $\theta = s^c$, i.e., s is a multiplicative generator of T^*.

Conversely, assume that a continuous t-norm T and a continuous t-conorm S have the forms from theorem, then obviously T is conditionally distributive over S. □

We denote by $(< S_M, S^* >, < T_1, T^* >)_a$ the pair of continuous t-conorm S and t-norm T from Theorem 7. We restrict ourselves to the situation $(< S_M, S_L >, < T_1, T_P >)_a$, since this is the most important case and all other cases can be obtained by isomorphisms (see Theorems 5, 6).

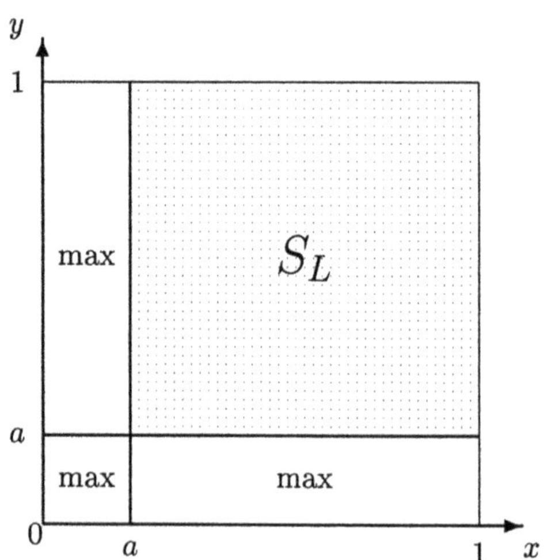

Fig. 1. Case of $0 < a < 1$, t-conorm

The extreme case $a = 0$ gives us the pair S_L and T_P. The other extreme case $a = 1$ gives us the pair S_M and T_1.

Let $0 < a < 1$. Then the pair

$$(< S_M, S_L >, < T_1, T_P >)_a$$

is given on Figures 1, 2. Let X be a fixed non-empty finite set.

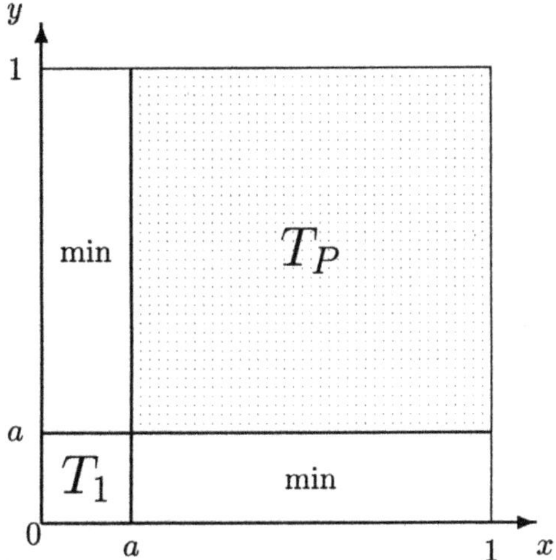

Fig. 2. Case of $0 < a < 1$, t-norm

Definition 3. Let S be a t-conorm and let $\mathcal{A}$ be a σ-algebra of subsets of X. A mapping $m : \mathcal{A} \to [0, 1]$ is called a pseudo-additive measure, shortly S-measure [15], if $m(\emptyset) = 0, m(X) = 1$ and if for all $A, B \in \mathcal{A}$ with $A \cap B = \emptyset$ we have $m(A \cup B) = S(m(A), m(B))$.

Compare with (σ-) S-decomposable measures [15]. Each S-measure $m : \mathcal{P}(X) \to [0, 1]$ is uniquely determined by the values $m(\{x\})$ with $x \in X$. Each measure $m : \mathcal{A} \to [0, \infty]$ with Range$(m) \subseteq [0, 1]$ is an S_L-measure. A set function $m : \mathcal{P}(X) \to [0, 1]$ is an S_M-measure if and only if for all $A, B \in \mathcal{A}$ we have $m(A \cup B) = S_M(m(A), m(B))$. Completely maxitive measures are called possibility measures, denoted by Π and the corresponding distribution by f, see [11,13,15,19]. Namely for an arbitrary function $f : X \to [0, 1]$, the set function $\Pi : \mathcal{P}(X) \to [0, 1]$ defined by $\Pi(A) = \sup\{f(x) \mid x \in A\}$ is an S_M-measure. We remark that only for X finite the notions of S_M-measure and possibility measures coincide.

3 From Independence to Event Separability in Pseudo-additive Measures

A basic notion in probability theory is independence. The main issue in probabilistic independence is the existence of special events $A_1, \ldots, A_n$ such that

$$P(A_1 \cap \ldots \cap A_n) = \prod_{i=1}^{n} P(A_i).$$

Such events are called independent events. In order to preserve the computational advantages of independence, any operation $*$ for which it could be established that

$$P(A_1 \cap \ldots \cap A_n) = *_{i=1}^{n} P(A_i),$$

would do. However the Boolean structure of sets of events and the additivity of the probability measure, impose considerable constraint on the choice of operation $*$. Especially for any pair of events A and B, the following properties are requested if a single operation $*$ is used for all events:

$$P(A \cap B) = P(A) * P(B), P(\overline{A} \cap B) = P(\overline{A}) * P(B)$$

$$P(A \cap \overline{B}) = P(A) * P(\overline{B}), P(\overline{A} \cap \overline{B}) = P(\overline{A}) * P(\overline{B}),$$

These conditions express that independence is *stable under complementation.* The only possible choice for $*$ is the product. See [6] for the case when $*$ may depend on A and B (that is $*_{AB} \neq *_{\overline{A}B}$).

Moreover we wish to keep the property stating that if A and B are mutually exclusive events, each one being independent from a third event C, then the disjunction $A \cup B$ is also independent from C. We shall say that the disjoint union of sets preserves independence (*disjoint union stability*).

Here we shall study the possible operations $*$ that remain complementation-stable and disjoint union stable when changing P for a pseudo-additive measure based on a t-conorm S. A first remark is that it is natural to require that $*$ be a continuous triangular norm. For instance, if $A = X$ is a sure event, then A and X are independent, and it follows that

$$m(A \cap X) = m(A) * m(X) = m(A) * 1 = m(A).$$

Commutativity and associativity of $*$ reflect the corresponding properties for conjunctions. It is also very natural that $*$ be non-decreasing in each place and continuous. When the universe is finite, the range of m is a finite subset of the unit interval, and the above natural properties of $*$ cannot be enforced on the whole unit interval([12,16]). However, these properties remain worth considering as defining the most convenient setting for generalizing independence.

So, we try to find which continuous triangular norms can be used for extending the notion of independence to pseudo-additive measures in the sense of a prescribed triangular conorm. Since the term independence has a precise meaning in probability theory, we shall speak of separability in the framework of S-measures. In particular

Definition 4. Two events A and B are said to be $*$-separable if $m(A \cap B) = m(A) * m(B)$ for a continuous triangular norm $*$.

Moreover, we shall assume than the S-measure is properly normalized (that is, no truncating effect occurs when computing $S(X)$ by summing the terms $S(\{x\}), x \in X$ in the sense of the t-conorm). Namely, the weights of the singletons in the finite referential X must be such that for any disjoint events A and B, if $S(A) > 0$ then $S(A \cup B) > S(B)$, while $S(X) = 1$.

In order to be meaningful, it is natural to require that separability be preserved via complementation and disjoint union of sets. Complementation stability is achieved if the same separability operation is used for any pair of events. Disjoint union stability reads:
$S(m(A), m(B)) * m(C) = S(m(A) * m(C), m(B) * m(C))$
whenever $A \cap B$ is empty. This is conditional distributivity when the pseudo-additive measure is normalized so as to avoid thresholding effects (otherwise the condition of disjoint union stability requires the full conditional distributivity). Under these natural constraints, the only reasonable pseudo-additive measures admitting of an independence-like concept, are based on conditionally distributive pairs (S, T) of conorms and t-conorms, namely:

- probability measures (and $*$ = product);
- possibility measures (and $*$ is any t-norm);
- suitably normalized hybrid set-functions m such that there is $a \in]0, 1[$ which gives for A and B disjoint

$$m(A \cup B) = \begin{cases} m(A) + m(B) - a & \text{if } m(A) > a, m(B) > a, \\ \max(m(A), m(B)) & \text{otherwise,} \end{cases}$$

and for separability:

$$m(A \cap B) = \begin{cases} a + \frac{(m(A)-a)(m(B)-a)}{1-a} & \text{if } m(A) > a, m(B) > a, \\ a \cdot T_1(\frac{m(A)}{a}, \frac{m(B)}{a}) & \text{if } m(A) \leq a, m(B) \leq a, \\ \min(m(A), m(B)) & \text{otherwise,} \end{cases}$$

The separability condition also leads to a natural definition of conditional pseudo-additive measure $m(A \mid B)$ such that ([5]):

$$m(A \cap B) = m(A \mid B) * m(B)$$

when $m(B) > 0$. It is natural, when $*$ is not invertible, to define $m(A \mid B)$ as the greatest solution to this equation, in agreement with possibility theory, that is ([10]):

$$m(A \mid B) = m(B) \rightarrow m(A \cap B)$$

where $\rightarrow$ is obtained from $*$ by residuation. The definition of conditioning is not well behaved for any choice of the t-norm T_1. Namely choosing a nilpotent t-norm, a conditional possibility measure is no longer a possibility measure. Indeed we then find for $S = S_{\mathbf{M}}$ and $T_1 = T_{\mathbf{L}}$ (the parameter $a = 1$) the equality

$$\Pi(A \mid B) = -\Pi(B) + \Pi(A \cap B) + 1$$

Let A be an impossible event, such that, $\Pi(A) = 0$, and B a not fully possible event, such that $0 < \Pi(B) < 1$. This definition leads to $\Pi(A \mid B) = 1 - \Pi(B) > 0$. This is quite unnatural, and all the more so if $A = \emptyset$ (see [10]. Note that when moving to an infinite setting, the use of T_M for constructing conditional possibility measures becomes debatable as well because the conditioning may not preserve σ-maxitivity (De Baets et al. [2]).

The preceding consideration enforces the choice of the t-norm T_1 to be restricted to an ordinal sum of strict t-norms.

4 Hybrid possibilistic/probabilistic event trees

Any probability distribution on a finite set X can be represented as a sequence of binary lotteries forming a probability event tree. An event tree can be built from a sequence of events $(A_1, A_2, \ldots, A_k)$ such that $A_1 = X$. Any node of depth level i of the tree correspond to a sequence of events $(A_2^\varepsilon, \ldots, A_i^\varepsilon)$, $\varepsilon \in \{0,1\}$, where $A_j^\varepsilon = A_j$ if $\varepsilon = 1$ and the complement of A_j if $\varepsilon = 0$. Each path from the root to a leaf node corresponds to a particular element of X which has been obtained via the sequence of events. Each subtree consisting of a non-leaf node A_i and its two sons A_{i+1} and $\overline{A}_{i+1}$ forms a conditional binary lottery such that $P(A_{i+1} \mid B) = \alpha$, and $B = A_2^\varepsilon \cap \ldots \cap A_i^\varepsilon$. For simplicity, consider P, a probability on X such that $p_i = P(x_i), x_i \in X$. Assume $X = \{x_1, x_2, x_3\}$ then p can be described by the elementary tree on fig. 3.

A binary tree is obtained as follows: First partition X into $\{x_1\}$ and $\{x_2, x_3\}$

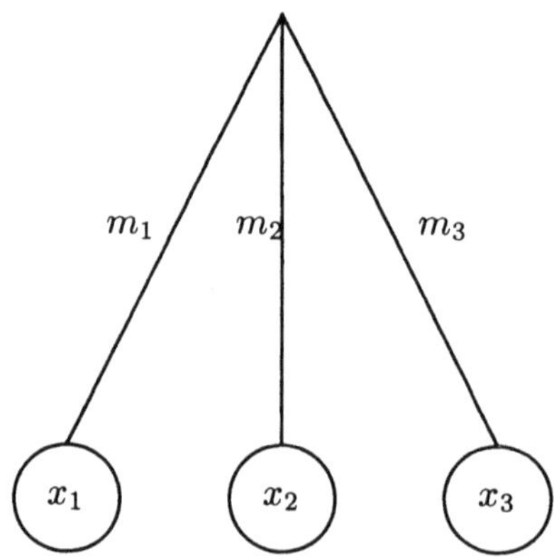

Fig. 3. S-measure tree

with probabilities p_1 and $p_2 + p_3$, respectively, then partition $X \setminus \{x_1\}$ into $\{x_2\}$ and $\{x_3\}$ with probabilities $p_2/(p_2 + p_3)$ and $p_3/(p_2 + p_3)$, respectively. The two trees are equivalent, provided that the probability of x_i is calculated by performing the product of weights on the path from the root of the tree until the leaf x.

Consider now m is a S-measure on $X = \{x_1, x_2, x_3\}$ and $m_i = m(\{x_i\})$. Suppose we want to decompose the ternary tree on Figure 3 into the event tree on Figure 4 so that they are equivalent. Then the following equations are obtained by stating the conditions: $S(m(\{x_2\} \mid \{x_2, x_3\}), m(\{x_3\} \mid \{x_2, x_3\}) = 1$, $m(\{x_3\}) = m(\{x_3\} \mid \{x_2, x_3\}) * m(\{x_2, x_3\})$ and $m(\{x_3\}) = m(\{x_2\} \mid \{x_2, x_3\}) * m(\{x_2, x_3\})$:

$$S(v_1, v_2) = 1, \quad T(\mu, v_1) = m_2, \quad T(\mu, v_2) = m_3,$$

where T is the triangular norm that expresses separability for S-measures. The first condition expresses normalization (with no truncating effect for t-conorm S allowed). If these equations have unique solutions, then by iterating this construction, any distribution of a S-measure can be decomposed into a sequence of binary lotteries, or more generally, a probability tree. This property is basic in probability theory since probability trees have been originally used as a primitive notion for developing the notion of probability, as recalled by Shafer [17]. Turning an S-measure into a sequence of binary trees leads to the necessity of

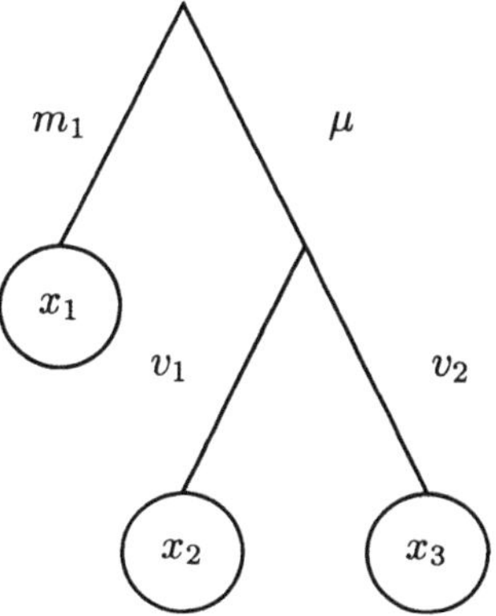

Fig. 4. The corresponding binary tree

solving the following system of equations

$$\alpha_1 = T(\mu, v_1),\ \alpha_2 = T(\mu, v_2),\ S(v_1, v_2) = 1 \tag{2}$$

for given α_1 and α_2. Applying Corollary 2 from [7] we know that there generally exists a unique solution (μ, v_1, v_2) (except for purely possibilistic cases with equipossibility, where a unique natural solution emerges anyway using a principle od least commitment). Assuming that $T_1 = \min$ we have solved (2) completely in [8] and exhibited the analytical forms of (μ, v_1, v_2). .

5 Conclusions

This paper has shown that using pseudo-additive measures to represent uncertainty, thus requiring a well-behaved independence structure, considerably reduces the range of meaningful set-functions. Only possibility and probability theories resist to the introduction of natural conditions on independence and conditioning, and what is new, hybrid set-fuctions based on ordinal sums. Moreover nilpotent t-norms, in particular Lukasiewicz's, cannot capture possibilistic independence in a reasonable way. More details and applications to utility theory can be found in [8].

The pair of t-conorm S and t-norm T which satisfies (CD) and the corresponding S-measure also give a basis for an integration theory, so called (S,T)-integral, see [13,14].

Among future works, Cox's well-known theorem [5,16], which justifies the use of probability for treating uncertainty, should be reconsidered in the light of the above results. Indeed, some relaxed axioms have been proposed, enabling non-additive functions to be admissible solutions, see [10,12].

References

1. Aczél, J., Lectures on Functional Equations and their Applications. Academic Press, New York, 1966.
2. De Baets B., Tsiporkova E., and Mesiar R., Conditioning in possibility with strict order norms, Fuzzy Sets and Systems, 106(1999), 221-229.
3. de Campos, L.M., Huete, J.F., Independence concepts in possibility theory: Part 1. Fuzzy Sets and Systems 103 (1999), 127-152.
4. de Campos, L.M., Huete, J.F., Independence concepts in possibility theory: Part 2. Fuzzy Sets and Systems 103 (1999), 487-505.
5. Cox, R., Probability, frequency, and reasonable expectation. American Journal of Physics **14** (1) (1946) , 1-13
6. Dubois, D., Generalized probabilistic independence and its implications for utility. Operations Res. Letters **5** (1986), 255-260
7. Dubois D., Fodor,J.C., Prade, H., Roubens,M., Aggregation of decomposable measures with applications to utility theory, Theory and Decision **41** (1996), 59-95
8. Dubois D., Pap, E., Prade, H., Hybrid probabilistic-possibilistic mixtures and utility functions, (Eds. J. Fodor, B.de Baets, P. Perny) Preferences and Decisions under Incomplete Knowledge , Springer-Verlag, 2000, 51-73.
9. Dubois D., Prade, H., A class of fuzzy measures based on triangular norms, Internat. J. Gen. System **8** (1982), 43–61

10. Dubois D., Prade,H., The logical view of conditioning and its application to possibility and evidence theories. Internat. J. of Approximate Reasoning **4** (1) (1990), 23-46
11. Dubois, D., Prade, H., Possibility theory: qualitative and quantitative aspects. The Handbook of Defeasible Reasoning and Uncertainty Management Systems Vol I (Ed. Ph. Smets), Kluwer, Dordrecht, pages 169-226, 1998.
12. Halpern, J.Y., A counterexample to theorems of Cox and Fine. Journal of Artif. Int. Research **10** (1999), 67-85.
13. Klement,E.P., Mesiar,R., Pap, E., Triangular Norms. Kluwer Academic Publishers, Dordrecht, 2000.
14. Klement,E.P., Mesiar, R., Pap, E., (S, U)-integral. Proc. EUSFLAT - 99, Palma de Mallorca, pages 371-374, 1999.
15. Pap, E., Null-Additive Set Functions, Kluwer Academic Publishers, Dordrecht and Ister Science, Bratislava, 1995.
16. Paris, J.B., The Uncertain Reasoner's Companion, A Mathematical Perspective. Cambridge, U.K.: Cambridge University Press, 1994.
17. Shafer, G., The Art of Causal Conjecture. The MIT Press, Cambridge, Massachusetts, 1996.
18. Vejnarová, J., Conditional independence relations in possibility theory. Int. J. Uncertainty, Fuzziness and Knowledge-Based Systems 8 (2000), 253-269.
19. Zadeh, L., Fuzzy sets as a basis for a theory of possibility. Fuzzy Sets and Systems **1** (1978), 3-28.

On Discrete Preference Structures *

Bernard De Baets[1] and János Fodor[2]

[1] Department of Applied Mathematics, Biometrics and Process Control
Faculty of Agricultural and Applied Biological Sciences, Ghent University
Coupure links 653, B-9000 Gent, Belgium
Bernard.DeBaets@rug.ac.be

[2] Department of Biomathematics and Informatics
Faculty of Veterinary Science, Szent István University
István u. 2, H-1078 Budapest, Hungary
jfodor@univet.hu

Abstract. In this paper, we introduce and study discrete preference structures. Such structures are expressed on finite chains and arise in the context of ordinal or linguistic preference modelling. Two classes of discrete preference structures are identified and characterized.

1 Introduction

Preference structures are mathematical tools for formally expressing a decision maker's strict preferences, indifferences and incomparabilities among a set of alternatives. As preference structures are based on classical set theory and are therefore restricted to classical relations, they do not allow to express degrees of strict preference, indifference or incomparability. This is seen as an important drawback to the practical use of these structures, leading researchers already at an early stage to the theory of fuzzy sets.

The axiomatic definition and construction of fuzzy preference structures is a well-established area of research when the evaluation scale is a compact real interval (typically $[0,1]$) [1]. However, in practical situations experts are often asked to use only a finite number of (very often linguistic) values for expressing degrees of preference between alternatives. For example, such a typical scale is given by *None, Very Low, Low, Medium, High, Very High, Perfect*, or in short form:

$$\mathcal{L} := \{\mathrm{N}, \mathrm{VL}, \mathrm{L}, \mathrm{M}, \mathrm{H}, \mathrm{VH}, \mathrm{P}\} ,$$

where the letters refer to the previous linguistic terms, and are listed in an increasing order:

$$\mathrm{N} \prec \mathrm{VL} \prec \mathrm{L} \prec \mathrm{M} \prec \mathrm{H} \prec \mathrm{VH} \prec \mathrm{P} .$$

* This work has been supported in part by OTKA T025163, by FKFP 0051/2000, and by the Bilateral Scientific and Technological Cooperation Flanders–Hungary BIL00/51 (B-08/2000).

Then, one might be curious if in such a discrete case we can "copy" the axiomatic approach to fuzzy preference modelling, with all of its notions, constructions, characterizations and other results. The main aim of the present paper is to clarify some of these issues about discrete preference structures.

2 Smooth De Morgan triplets on finite chains

Assume that $\mathcal{L} := \{x_0, x_1, \ldots, x_n, x_{n+1}\}$ is a totally ordered finite set of $n+2$ elements that are indexed increasingly: $x_0 \prec x_1 \prec \ldots \prec x_n \prec x_{n+1}$, according to a relation $\prec$ (that is asymmetric and negatively transitive on $\mathcal{L}$). For $x \in \mathcal{L}$, let $\mathrm{ind}(x)$ be the index of x according to this increasing ordering. Clearly, thus defined ind is a function from $\mathcal{L}$ to $\mathbb{N}$ such that $\mathrm{ind}(x)$ is the number of elements y such that $y \prec x$.

In the sequel, we use the notations $\mathbf{0} := x_0$ and $\mathbf{1} := x_{n+1}$. For any $x_i, x_j \in \mathcal{L}$ such that $x_i \preceq x_j$, let us define

$$\langle x_i, x_j \rangle := \{x_k \in \mathcal{L} \mid x_i \preceq x_k \preceq x_j\} \ ,$$

which can be considered as the discrete "closed interval" of points in $\mathcal{L}$ between x_i and x_j (note that $x \preceq y$ if and only if either $x \prec y$, or $x = y$).

The appropriate definition of logical operations on $\mathcal{L}$ plays a crucial role. Luckily, this knowledge is at our disposal.

2.1 Strong negations

First we consider *strong negations* on $\mathcal{L}$. That is, decreasing functions $\mathcal{N} : \mathcal{L} \to \mathcal{L}$ with $\mathcal{N}(\mathbf{0}) = \mathbf{1}$ that are *involutive*: $\mathcal{N}(\mathcal{N}(x)) = x$ for all $x \in \mathcal{L}$.

Theorem 1. [8] *The unique strong negation $\mathcal{N}$ on $\mathcal{L} := \{x_0, \ldots, x_{n+1}\}$ is given by*

$$\mathcal{N}(x_i) = x_{n-i+1} \ ,$$

for all $x_i \in \mathcal{L}$.

Clearly, this strong negation on $\mathcal{L}$ corresponds to the standard negation $x \mapsto 1 - x$ on the unit interval. Notice however that $\mathcal{N}$ does not have a fixed point (i.e. an $x \in \mathcal{L}$ such that $\mathcal{N}(x) = x$) when n is even.

2.2 Smooth t-norms and t-conorms

Mayor and Torrens [8] have determined all associative, commutative, increasing binary operations $\mathcal{T} : \mathcal{L} \times \mathcal{L} \to \mathcal{L}$ that satisfy $\mathcal{T}(\mathbf{1}, \mathbf{1}) = \mathbf{1}$, and for all $x, y \in \mathcal{L}$

$$x \preceq y \iff (\exists \in \mathcal{L})(x = \mathcal{T}(y, z)) \ . \tag{1}$$

Such a binary operation $\mathcal{T}$ is called a *smooth t-norm on $\mathcal{L}$*. Indeed, it can be seen that $\mathcal{T}$ satisfies all the four axioms of t-norms, and condition (1) is just equivalent with the continuity of $\mathcal{T}$ when it is considered on $[0,1]$. For more details on the smoothness property of binary operations, we refer to [6,3,4].

A smooth t-norm on $\mathcal{L}$ is *Archimedean* if $\mathcal{T}(x,x) \prec x$ for all $x \in \langle x_1, x_n \rangle$ [8].

Theorem 2. [8] *The only Archimedean smooth t-norm on* $\mathcal{L} := \{x_0, \dots, x_{n+1}\}$ *is given by:*

$$\mathcal{T}(x_i, x_j) = \begin{cases} x_{i+j-(n+1)} & , \textit{if } i+j > n+1 \\ \mathbf{0} & , \textit{elsewhere} \end{cases} , \tag{2}$$

for all $x_i, x_j \in \mathcal{L}$.

One recognizes that the above t-norm corresponds to the Łukasiewicz t-norm on $[0,1]$; hence, it is denoted by $\mathcal{T}_L$ in the sequel. As a consequence, one essential difference between the finite case and the usual unit interval is that there exists only one Archimedean smooth t-norm on a given finite $\mathcal{L}$, and it depends basically on the cardinality (i.e., the number of elements) of $\mathcal{L}$. No counterpart of any strict t-norm (like the product on $[0,1]$) exists on $\mathcal{L}$.

If, in the remaining case, $\mathcal{T}$ is a non-Archimedean smooth t-norm then it has idempotent(s) other than $\mathbf{0}$ and $\mathbf{1}$: $\exists\ x_i \in \langle x_1, x_n \rangle$ such that $\mathcal{T}(x_i, x_i) = x_i$. Then $\mathcal{T}(x_k, x_\ell) = x_{\min\{k,\ell\}}$ if there exists an idempotent x_i between x_k and x_ℓ. In any other case, there are two consecutive idempotents x_i, x_j such that $x_i \preceq x_k, x_\ell \preceq x_j$, and

$$\mathcal{T}(x_k, x_\ell) = \begin{cases} x_i & , \text{if } \ell + k \le i + j \\ x_{\ell+k-i} & , \text{elsewhere} \end{cases} .$$

Denote by $\mathcal{T}_M$ the smooth t-norm on $\mathcal{L}$ which corresponds to the minimum; it is the only t-norm that has all elements as idempotents. Moreover, there are exactly 2^n different smooth t-norms on $\mathcal{L}$ (where $|\mathcal{L}| = n+2$) [8].

We say that a t-norm $\mathcal{T}$ on $\mathcal{L}$ has *zero divisors* if and only if there exist $x, y \in \langle x_1, x_n \rangle$ such that $\mathcal{T}(x,y) = \mathbf{0}$. In the opposite case, $\mathcal{T}$ is called *positive*.

Smooth t-conorms can be obtained by duality w.r.t. the unique strong negation $\mathcal{N}$. Obviously, the only Archimedean smooth t-conorm can be obtained from Eq. (2) as follows:

$$\mathcal{S}_L(x_i, x_j) = \begin{cases} x_{i+j} & , \text{if } i+j < n+1 \\ \mathbf{1} & , \text{elsewhere} \end{cases} , \tag{3}$$

for all $x_i, x_j \in \mathcal{L}$.

In what follows, we consider only smooth De Morgan triplets $(\mathcal{T}, \mathcal{S}, \mathcal{N})$ on $\mathcal{L}$. That is, $\mathcal{T}$ is a smooth t-norm on $\mathcal{L}$, $\mathcal{N}$ is the unique strong negation on $\mathcal{L}$ and $\mathcal{S}(x,y) := \mathcal{N}(\mathcal{T}(\mathcal{N}(x),\mathcal{N}(y)))$ is the dual of $\mathcal{T}$. Obviously, such a De Morgan triplet depends *only* on the choice of the smooth t-norm $\mathcal{T}$. The triplet $L = (\mathcal{T}_L, \mathcal{S}_L, \mathcal{N})$ is called *the* Łukasiewicz triplet.

3 Definition of discrete preference structures

Let us start by recalling the classical definition of a preference structure.

Definition 1. A *preference structure* on a set of alternatives A is a triplet (P, I, J) of binary relations in A that satisfy:

(P1) P and J are irreflexive, I is reflexive;

(P2) P is asymmetrical, I and J are symmetrical;

(P3) $P \cap I = \emptyset$, $P \cap J = \emptyset$ and $I \cap J = \emptyset$;

(P4) $P \cup P^t \cup I \cup J = A^2$.

Meaningful fuzzy counterparts of this classical definition need a rather careful study of the essential underlying components. There are at least two of them.

First, the completeness condition (P4) can be formulated in a number of equivalent ways. Then, which one should we choose in the fuzzy definition?

Second, there are many possible De Morgan triplets for modelling the logical operations. Which one of them is appropriate in the fuzzified definition?

By meaningful extension we mean a notion of preference structures allowing at least one of the four values $P(a,b)$, $P(b,a)$, $I(a,b)$, $J(a,b)$ lying anywhere in the evaluation scale $\mathcal{L}$ for any pair of alternatives $(a,b) \in A^2$, $a \neq b$. In the sequel, by a fuzzy relation we mean an $\mathcal{L}$-fuzzy relation, i.e. an $\mathcal{L}$-valued relation.

The completeness condition (P4) can be written as follows, where the formulations are pairwise equivalent:

(C1) $\operatorname{co}(P \cup I) = P^t \cup J$;

(C2) $\operatorname{co}(P \cup P^t) = I \cup J$;

(C3) $\operatorname{co}(P \cup I \cup J) = P^t$;

(C4) $\operatorname{co}(P \cup P^t \cup J) = I$;

(C5) $\operatorname{co}(P \cup P^t \cup I) = J$;

(C6) $P \cup P^t \cup I \cup J = A^2$.

Let $(\mathcal{T}, \mathcal{S}, \mathcal{N})$ be a smooth De Morgan triplet defined on $\mathcal{L} := \{x_0, \dots, x_{n+1}\}$, A be a set of alternatives and (P, I, J) be a triplet of binary fuzzy relations in A. Then the above conditions are of the following form, and are no longer pairwise equivalent in general:

(FC1) $\mathrm{co}_{\mathcal{N}}(P \cup_{\mathcal{S}} I) = P^t \cup_{\mathcal{S}} J$;

(FC2) $\mathrm{co}_{\mathcal{N}}(P \cup_{\mathcal{S}} P^t) = I \cup_{\mathcal{S}} J$;

(FC3) $\mathrm{co}_{\mathcal{N}}(P \cup_{\mathcal{S}} I \cup_{\mathcal{S}} J) = P^t$;

(FC4) $\mathrm{co}_{\mathcal{N}}(P \cup_{\mathcal{S}} P^t \cup_{\mathcal{S}} J) = I$;

(FC5) $\mathrm{co}_{\mathcal{N}}(P \cup_{\mathcal{S}} P^t \cup_{\mathcal{S}} I) = J$;

(FC6) $P \cup_{\mathcal{S}} P^t \cup_{\mathcal{S}} I \cup_{\mathcal{S}} J = A^2$.

Definition 2. Consider a smooth de Morgan triplet $M = (\mathcal{T}, \mathcal{S}, \mathcal{N})$ and $i \in \{1, \dots, 6\}$. An *M-discrete preference structure* on A w.r.t. completeness condition (FCi) – shortly, an M-DPS on A w.r.t. (FCi) – is a triplet (P, I, J) of binary fuzzy relations in A that satisfy:

(M1) P and J are irreflexive, I is reflexive;

(M2) P is $\mathcal{T}$-asymmetrical, I and J are symmetrical;

(M3) $P \cap_{\mathcal{T}} I = \emptyset$, $P \cap_{\mathcal{T}} J = \emptyset$ and $I \cap_{\mathcal{T}} J = \emptyset$;

(M4) completeness condition (FCi).

Theorem 3. *Consider a smooth de Morgan triplet $M = (\mathcal{T}, \mathcal{S}, \mathcal{N})$ with a positive t-norm $\mathcal{T}$, and let $i \in \{1, \dots, 6\}$. Then any M-DPS on A w.r.t. (FCi) is a classical (i.e.* **0**-**1**-*valued) preference structure.*

Therefore, $\mathcal{T}$ must have zero divisors. That is, there exists $x_{\mathcal{T}} \in \langle x_1, x_{n+1} \rangle$ such that $\mathcal{T}$ is the Łukasiewicz t-norm on the square $\langle x_0, x_{\mathcal{T}} \rangle \times \langle x_0, x_{\mathcal{T}} \rangle$. We consider first the non-Archimedean case (i.e. $x_{\mathcal{T}} \prec x_{n+1}$). Then none of the fuzzy relations in the corresponding discrete preference structure (P, I, J) can take values between $x_{\mathcal{T}}$ and x_n (inclusive).

Theorem 4. *Consider a smooth de Morgan triplet $M = (\mathcal{T}, \mathcal{S}, \mathcal{N})$ with a non-Archimedean t-norm $\mathcal{T}$ having zero divisors, and let $i \in \{1, \dots, 6\}$. Then there exists a value $x_{\mathcal{T}} \in \langle x_1, x_n \rangle$ such that for any M-DPS on A w.r.t. (FCi) it holds that:*

(i) $P(a, b) \prec \mathbf{1}$ *implies* $P(a, b) \prec x_{\mathcal{T}}$,

(ii) $I(a, b) \prec \mathbf{1}$ *implies* $I(a, b) \prec x_{\mathcal{T}}$,

(iii) $J(a, b) \prec \mathbf{1}$ *implies* $J(a, b) \prec x_{\mathcal{T}}$,

for all $a, b \in A$.

Corollary 1. *Meaningful discrete preference structures must have the Łukasiewicz triplet as corresponding smooth De Morgan triplet.*

Next, we show that if $\mathcal{T}$ is the Łukasiewicz t-norm then there exists only one type of discrete preference structures (i.e. under the remaining conditions in Definition 2, any two of the completeness conditions are equivalent).

Theorem 5. *Let L be the Łukasiewicz triplet and (P, I, J) be a triplet of binary fuzzy relations in A that satisfy conditions (M1)–M(3) in Definition 2. Then (P, I, J) satisfies also completeness condition (FCi) for some $i \in \{1, 2, \ldots, 6\}$ if and only if (P, I, J) satisfies (FCj) for all $j \in \{1, 2, \ldots, 6\}$.*

As a consequence, we can formulate a sound and unambiguous notion of a discrete preference structure in the following way.

Definition 3. A triplet (P, I, J) of binary fuzzy relations in A is called a *discrete preference structure (DPS)* on A if it satisfies:

(D1) P and J are irreflexive, I is reflexive;

(D2) P is $\mathcal{T}_L$-asymmetrical, I and J are symmetrical;

(D3) $P \cap_{\mathcal{T}_L} I = \emptyset$, $P \cap_{\mathcal{T}_L} J = \emptyset$ and $I \cap_{\mathcal{T}_L} J = \emptyset$;

(D4) $P \cup_{\mathcal{S}_L} P^t \cup_{\mathcal{S}_L} I \cup_{\mathcal{S}_L} J = A^2$.

There is still an open question related to this definition: does there exist any meaningful discrete preference structure? The positive answer is a corollary of the following proposition, which mentions a minimal definition that is equivalent to Definition 3.

Proposition 1. *A triplet (P, I, J) of binary fuzzy relations in A is a discrete preference structure on A if and only if*

(i) *I is reflexive;*

(ii) *I is symmetric;*

(iii) *for any $(a, b) \in A^2$ we have*

$$n + 1 = \mathrm{ind}(P(a, b)) + \mathrm{ind}(P(b, a)) + \mathrm{ind}(I(a, b)) + \mathrm{ind}(J(a, b)) \ .$$

4 Axiomatic construction of discrete preference structures

As it is well known, from any given reflexive binary relation R in A one can construct a classical preference structure (P, I, J) on A as follows:

(i) $P := R \cap \mathrm{co}R^t$,

(ii) $I := R \cap R^t$,

(iii) $J := \mathrm{co}R \cap \mathrm{co}R^t$.

In addition, we always have $R = P \cup I$ and $\mathrm{co}R^t = P \cup J$, whence R is the large preference relation attached to (P, I, J).

Consider a reflexive binary fuzzy relation R in A and a smooth de Morgan triplet $(\mathcal{T}, \mathcal{S}, \mathcal{N})$ on $\mathcal{L}$. The following general axioms guiding the construction of P, I and J are required:

(IA) Independence of Irrelevant Alternatives:

- *For any two alternatives $a, b \in A$, the values $P(a,b)$, $I(a,b)$ and $J(a,b)$ depend only on the values $R(a,b)$ and $R(b,a)$.*

According to (IA), there exist three functions p, i, j from $\mathcal{L} \times \mathcal{L}$ to $\mathcal{L}$ such that

$$P(a,b) := p(R(a,b), R(b,a)),$$

$$I(a,b) := i(R(a,b), R(b,a)),$$

$$J(a,b) := j(R(a,b), R(b,a)).$$

(PA) Positive Association Principle:

- *The functions $p(x, \mathcal{N}(y))$, $i(x,y)$, $j(\mathcal{N}(x), \mathcal{N}(y))$ ($x, y \in \mathcal{L}$) are non-decreasing w.r.t. both arguments.*

(S) Symmetry:

- *i and j are symmetric functions.*

(LP) Preserving Large Preference:

- $P \cup_{\mathcal{S}} I = R$, $P \cup_{\mathcal{S}} J = \mathrm{co}_{\mathcal{N}} R^t$.

The key axiom is (LP), which can be written in the following form of a system of two functional equations:

$$\mathcal{S}(p(x,y), i(x,y)) = x, \tag{4}$$

$$\mathcal{S}(p(x,y), j(x,y)) = \mathcal{N}(y), \tag{5}$$

for all $x, y \in \mathcal{L}$, with $x := R(a,b)$, $y := R(b,a)$, $a, b \in A$. In the following theorem we summarize some results about Eqs. (4) and (5).

Theorem 6. *Consider a reflexive binary fuzzy relation R in A. Suppose $\langle p, i, j, \mathcal{T}, \mathcal{S}, \mathcal{N} \rangle$ satisfies axioms (IA), (PA), (S) and (LP). Then:*

(i) *$(\mathcal{T}, \mathcal{S}, \mathcal{N})$ must be the Łukasiewicz triplet.*

(ii) *The following inequalities are valid for all $x, y \in \mathcal{L}$:*

$$\mathcal{T}(x,y) \preceq p(x, \mathcal{N}(y)) \preceq \min(x,y),$$

$$\mathcal{T}(x,y) \preceq i(x,y) \preceq \min(x,y),$$

$$\mathcal{T}(x,y) \preceq j(\mathcal{N}(x), \mathcal{N}(y)) \preceq \min(x,y).$$

(iii) *The resulting triplet (P, I, J) is a discrete preference structure on A such that $R = P \cup_{\mathcal{S}} I$.*

(iv) *If R is strongly complete, i.e.*

$$\max(R(a,b), R(b,a)) = \mathbf{1}$$

for all $a, b \in A$, then the following unique forms are obtained:

$$P(a,b) = \mathcal{N}(R(b,a)),$$
$$I(a,b) = \min(R(a,b), R(b,a)),$$
$$J(a,b) = \mathbf{0},$$

for all $a, b \in A$.

This theorem leads us to defining the large preference relation R of a general discrete preference structure (P, I, J) as follows: $R := P \cup_{\mathcal{S}_L} I$.

There is an extremely important and nice theorem on the solutions of Eqs. (4) and (5) on the unit square when $p(x,y) := \mathcal{T}_1(x, \mathcal{N}(y))$ and $i(x,y) := \mathcal{T}_2(x,y)$ with some t-norms $\mathcal{T}_1$ and $\mathcal{T}_2$, see Theorem 3.3 in [5]. It states that then $\mathcal{T}_1$ and $\mathcal{T}_2$ belong to the Frank family of t-norms with parameters reciprocal to each other. Moreover, in that case $j(x,y) := \mathcal{T}_2(\mathcal{N}(x), \mathcal{N}(y))$.

The question is natural: what remains true for discrete preference structures? Since there are no strict t-norms on finite chains, only the two extreme cases might be expected to be valid.

Applying the function ind, Eq. (4) can be formulated as follows:

$$\mathrm{ind}(\mathcal{T}_1(x, \mathcal{N}(y))) + \mathrm{ind}(\mathcal{T}_2(x,y)) = \mathrm{ind}(x) \ , \tag{6}$$

for all $x, y \in \mathcal{L}$.

Lemma 1. *Both t-norms $\mathcal{T}_1$ and $\mathcal{T}_2$ must satisfy the following functional equation*

$$\mathrm{ind}(\mathcal{S}_i(u,v)) + \mathrm{ind}(\mathcal{T}_i(u,v)) = \mathrm{ind}(u) + \mathrm{ind}(v) \ , \tag{7}$$

for all $u, v \in \mathcal{L}$, where $\mathcal{S}_i$ is the dual of $\mathcal{T}_i$ ($i = 1, 2$).

Eq. (7) is exactly that one which was formulated in [7] analogously to the original Frank equation, not necessarily for dual t-norms and t-conorms.

The following observation is vital in our framework.

Proposition 2. [7] *All t-norms and t-conorms satisfying Eq. (7) are smooth.*

Now we can state the expected proposition as follows.

Theorem 7. *There are exactly two pairs of solutions to Eq. (6):*

(i) $\mathcal{T}_1 = \mathcal{T}_M$ *and* $\mathcal{T}_2 = \mathcal{T}_L$ *,*

(ii) $\mathcal{T}_1 = \mathcal{T}_L$ *and* $\mathcal{T}_2 = \mathcal{T}_M$ *.*

Combining the results in this section then leads to the following two t-norm-based constructions of discrete preference structures.

Theorem 8. *Consider a reflexive binary fuzzy relation R in A, then the following two discrete preference structures on A can be constructed:*

1. *The structure (P_0, I_0, J_0) defined by*
   (i) $P_0(a,b) := \mathcal{T}_L(R(a,b), \mathcal{N}(R(b,a)))$,
   (ii) $I_0(a,b) := \min(R(a,b), R(b,a)))$,
   (iii) $J_0(a,b) := \min(\mathcal{N}(R(a,b)), \mathcal{N}(R(b,a)))$,

   for all $a, b \in A$.
2. *The structure $(P_\infty, I_\infty, J_\infty)$ defined by*
   (i) $P_\infty(a,b) := \min(R(a,b), \mathcal{N}(R(b,a)))$,
   (ii) $I_\infty(a,b) := \mathcal{T}_L(R(a,b), R(b,a))$,
   (iii) $J_\infty(a,b) := \mathcal{T}_L(\mathcal{N}(R(a,b)), \mathcal{N}(R(b,a)))$,

   for all $a, b \in A$.

The indices 0 and ∞ are inspired by the notations for the corresponding classes of fuzzy preference structures on the unit interval [10].

5 Characterization of discrete preference structures

One final question needs to be addressed, namely that of the reconstructability of a discrete preference structure. Is it possible to reconstruct a discrete preference structure (P, I, J) from its large preference relation $R := P \cup_{\mathcal{S}_L} I$? Only when this question can be answered positively, do we have a sound concept of a discrete preference structure. It turns out that the above two t-norm-based constructions lead to two characterizable classes of discrete preference structures. To that end, we first introduce some definitions.

Definition 4. A discrete preference structure (P, I, J) on A is called:

(i) a 0-DPS on A if and only if $P \cap_{\mathcal{T}_M} P^t = \emptyset$, i.e. if and only if

$$\min(P(a,b), P(b,a)) = \mathbf{0} \ ,$$

for all $a, b \in A$;

(ii) an ∞-DPS on A if and only if $I \cap_{\mathcal{T}_M} J = \emptyset$, i.e. if and only if

$$\min(I(a,b), J(a,b)) = \mathbf{0} \ ,$$

for all $a, b \in A$.

One easily verifies that the structure (P_0, I_0, J_0) defined above is a 0-DPS and that the structure $(P_\infty, I_\infty, J_\infty)$ is an ∞-DPS.

The following conclusive theorem expresses that reconstructability holds for the two classes considered.

Theorem 9. *Consider a discrete preference structure (P, I, J) on A with large preference relation R.*

1. *(P, I, J) is a 0-DPS if and only if*

$$\text{(i)}\quad P(a,b) = \mathcal{T}_L(R(a,b), \mathcal{N}(R(b,a)))\,,$$
$$\text{(ii)}\quad I(a,b) = \min(R(a,b), R(b,a))\,,$$
$$\text{(iii)}\quad J(a,b) = \min(\mathcal{N}(R(a,b)), \mathcal{N}(R(b,a)))\,,$$

for all $a, b \in A$.

2. *(P, I, J) is an ∞-DPS if and only if*

$$\text{(i)}\quad P(a,b) = \min(R(a,b), \mathcal{N}(R(b,a)))\,,$$
$$\text{(ii)}\quad I(a,b) = \mathcal{T}_L(R(a,b), R(b,a))\,,$$
$$\text{(iii)}\quad J(a,b) = \mathcal{T}_L(\mathcal{N}(R(a,b)), \mathcal{N}(R(b,a)))\,,$$

for all $a, b \in A$.

6 Conclusion

So far, three approaches to preference modelling have been gradually built up: classical preference structures [9] and discrete preference structures in the present paper, corresponding to discrete evaluation scales; and fuzzy preference structures [5,10,1], corresponding to continuous evaluation scales. It is shown in [2] that the associated degrees of freedom gradually increase.

References

1. B. De Baets and J. Fodor, *Twenty years of fuzzy preference structures (1978–1997)*, Riv. Mat. Sci. Econom. Social. **20** (1997), 45–66.
2. B. De Baets and J. Fodor, *Preference scales: from discrete to continuous*, Proc. of the 3rd Int. Workshop on Preferences and Decisions (Trento, Italy, 2000), pp. 21–25.
3. J. Fodor, *Smooth associative operations on finite chains*, Proc. 1999 EUSFLAT-ESTYLF Joint Conference (Palma de Mallorca, Spain), 1999, pp. 359–362.
4. J. Fodor, *Smooth associative operations on finite ordinal scales*, IEEE Trans. on Fuzzy Systems **8** (2000), 791–795.
5. J. Fodor and M. Roubens, *Fuzzy Preference Modelling and Multicriteria Decision Support*, Kluwer Academic Publishers, 1994.

6. L. Godo and C. Sierra, *A new approach to connective generation in the framework of expert systems using fuzzy logic*, in: Proc. 18th Int. Symposium on Multiple-Valued Logic (Palma de Mallorca, Spain), Computer Society Press, Washington D.C., 1988, pp. 157–162.
7. L. Godo and V. Torra, *On aggregation operators for ordinal qualitative information*, IEEE Trans. Fuzzy Systems **8** (2000), 143–154.
8. G. Mayor and J. Torrens, *On a class of operators for expert systems*, Int. J. of Intelligent Systems **8** (1993), 771–778.
9. M. Roubens and Ph. Vincke, *Preference Modelling*, Springer-Verlag, 1985.
10. B. Van de Walle, B. De Baets and E. Kerre, *Characterizable fuzzy preference structures*, Annals of Operations Research, Special Issue "Preference modelling" (D. Bouyssou and Ph. Vincke, eds.), **80** (1998), 105–136.

Families of Valued Sets as Media

Alexander Dukhovny and Sergei Ovchinnikov[1]
Mathematics Department
San Francisco State University
San Francisco, CA 94132
dukhovny@math.sfsu.edu, sergei@sfsu.edu

Abstract
It is shown that the family of all valued sets on a finite universe with values in a finite linear order is a medium. Stochastic properties of these media are investigated.

Key words: Media theory, Wellgradedness, Markov chains

1 Introduction

The concept of a medium was introduced by J.-Cl. Falmagne in [5] as a special case of a general 'token system'. The initial motivation for his work came from some situations in social and behavioral sciences. In particular, in the framework of preference evolution [4, 6], the individuals may be asked to provide their initial preference relations (called *states*) over a given set of alternatives. As time evolves, the individuals are bombarded with a discrete stream of (unobservable) 'particles' of information (called *tokens*) which may alter the individual states. The effect of these tokens is formalized by transformations of the individual states. The states can be probed by interviewing the individuals at some arbitrary chosen times $t_1, \dots, t_n$. General axioms are given that cast the theory as a Markov process having as a state space the set of individual preferences.

A comprehensive coverage of media theory and preference evolution as well as a large scale application are found in [4]–[9] and [12]. Here, we just present the basic concepts of the media theory [5].

Definition 1.1. Let $\mathcal{V}$ be a finite set of states. A token (of information) is a function $\tau : S \mapsto S\tau$ mapping $\mathcal{V}$ into itself. We shall use the abbreviations $S\tau = \tau(S)$, and $S\tau_1 \dots \tau_n = \tau_n[\dots[\tau_1(S)]]$ for the function composition. We denote by τ_0 the identity function on $\mathcal{V}$ and suppose that τ_0 is not a token. Let $\mathcal{T}$ be a set of tokens on $\mathcal{V}$. The pair $(\mathcal{V}, \mathcal{T})$ is called a *token system.*

A token τ' is a *reverse* of a token τ if for all distinct $S, V \in \mathcal{V}$

$$S\tau = V \quad \Leftrightarrow \quad V\tau' = S.$$

[1]Ovchinnikov's work is supported by NSF grant No SES–9986269 to J.–Cl. Falmagne at UC Irvine.

A finite composition $\mathbf{m} = \tau_1 \dots \tau_n$ of not necessarily distinct tokens $\tau_1, \dots, \tau_n$ in $\mathcal{V}$ such that $S\mathbf{m} = V$ is called a *message producing V from S*. We write $l(\mathbf{m}) = n$ to denote the *length* of $\mathbf{m}$. The *content* of a message $\mathbf{m} = \tau_1 \dots \tau_n$ is the set $\mathcal{C}(\mathbf{m}) = \{\tau_1, \dots, \tau_n\}$ of its tokens. (We adopt the standard set theoretical convention that $\{\dots, y, x, x, z, \dots\} = \{\dots, y, x, z, \dots\}$.) A message $\mathbf{m}$ is *effective* (resp. *ineffective*) for a state S if $S\mathbf{m} \neq S$ (resp. $S\mathbf{m}{=}S$). A message $\mathbf{m} = \tau_1 \dots \tau_n$ is *stepwise effective* for S if

$$S\tau_1 \dots \tau_k \neq S\tau_0 \dots \tau_{k-1}, \qquad 1 \leq k \leq n.$$

A message is called *consistent* if it does not contain both a token and its reverse, and *inconsistent* otherwise. A message which is both consistent and stepwise effective for some state S is said to be *straight* for S. A message $\mathbf{m} = \tau_1 \dots \tau_n$ is *vacuous* if the set of indices $\{1, \dots, n\}$ can be partitioned into pairs $\{i, j\}$, such that one of τ_i, τ_j is a reverse of the other. Two messages $\mathbf{m}$ and $\mathbf{n}$ are *jointly consistent* if $\mathbf{mn}$ (or, equivalently, $\mathbf{nm}$) is consistent.

The next definition introduces the main concept of media theory.

Definition 1.2. A token system is called a *medium* if the following axioms are satisfied.

[**M1**] Every token τ has a unique reverse, which we denote by $\tilde{\tau}$.

[**M2**] For any two distinct states S, V, there is a consistent message transforming S into V.

[**M3**] A message which is stepwise effective for some state is ineffective for that state if and only if it is vacuous.

[**M4**] Two straight messages producing the same state are jointly consistent.

In this paper, we present preliminary results that are aimed to developing a stochastic media theory of valued preference relations. The paper is organized as follows.

In Section 2, we construct a token system based on valued sets with a finite domain and prove that this token system is a medium. It is shown in Section 3 how general principles of stochastic media theory can be applied to this particular medium.

2 The set of all valued sets as a medium

In what follows the symbols $\vee$ and $\wedge$ stand for supremum and infimum, respectively.

Definition 2.1. *Let L be an ordered set and X be a set. An L*–valued set *A with domain X is a function $A : X \to L$.*

If $L = \mathbf{2} = \{0, 1\}$, we have the usual sets, and in the case $L = [0, 1]$ we have fuzzy sets. In this paper, we assume that $L = \boldsymbol{n} = \{0, 1, \ldots, n-1\}$ is a linearly ordered set consisting of n elements ($n > 2$).

The set of all L–valued sets with a given domain X forms a finite distributive lattice L^X. Operations of union and intersection are defined in terms of lattice operations as follows.

$$(S \cup T)(x) = S(x) \vee T(x), \quad (S \cap T)(x) = S(x) \wedge T(x),$$

for $x \in X$.

For a given $S \in L^X$ we define a subset $\hat{S}$ of $X \times L$ by

$$\hat{S} = \{(x, i) \in X \times L : S(x) \geq i\}.$$

It is easy to verify that the correspondence $\theta : L^X \to \mathbf{2}^{X \times L}$ defined by $S \mapsto \hat{S}$ is a *lattice monomorphism* [2, Ch. II, § 3]. In other words, this correspondence is one–to–one, isotonic, and preserves unions and intersections.

The concept of well–graded family of sets plays an important role in media theory. This concept was introduced in [5, 3] and (independently and under a different name) in [10, 11]. As usual, we define the distance between two finite subsets as the cardinality of the symmetric difference of these sets, $d(S, T) = |S \Delta T|$.

Definition 2.2. *A family of subsets of a given finite set is said to be* well–graded *if for any two distinct subsets Y and Z there is a sequence of subsets $Y_0 = Y, Y_1, \ldots, Y_m = Z$ such that*

(i) $d(Y_i, Y_{i+1}) = 1$ for $i = 0, 1, \ldots, m-1$, and

(ii) $d(Y, Z) = m$.

Theorem 2.1 ([7]). *Any well-graded family $\mathcal{F}$ of subsets of a set is representable as a medium $(\mathcal{F}, \mathcal{T})$, where $\mathcal{T}$ contains, for all $x \in \cup\mathcal{F} \setminus \cap\mathcal{F}$ the transformations $\tau_x, \tilde{\tau}_x$ of $\mathcal{F}$ into $\mathcal{F}$ defined by*

$$\tau_x : Y \mapsto Y\tau_x = \begin{cases} Y \cup \{x\}, & \text{if } x \notin Y \text{ and } Y \cup \{x\} \in \mathcal{F}, \\ Y, & \text{otherwise.} \end{cases} \tag{1}$$

$$\tilde{\tau}_x : Y \mapsto Y\tilde{\tau}_x = \begin{cases} Y \setminus \{x\}, & \text{if } x \in Y \text{ and } Y \setminus \{x\} \in \mathcal{F}, \\ Y, & \text{otherwise.} \end{cases} \tag{2}$$

In some precise sense, any medium is isomorphic to a medium of well–graded sets [9].

Theorem 2.2. *The image $\theta(L^X)$ of L^X in $\mathbf{2}^{X \times L}$ is a well-graded family of subsets of $X \times L$.*

Proof. Let $\hat{S} = \theta(S)$, $\hat{T} = \theta(T)$ be two distinct elements in $\mathbf{2}^{X \times L}$ and let $m = d(\hat{S}, \hat{T})$. By symmetry, we may assume that there is a point $a \in X$ such that $S(a) < T(a)$. We define a valued set V by

$$V(x) = \begin{cases} S(x), & \text{if } x \neq a, \\ S(a) + 1, & \text{if } x = a. \end{cases}$$

Clearly, $d(\hat{S}, \hat{V}) = 1$ and $S \cap T \subset V \subseteq S \cup T$. The latter implies

$$\hat{S} \cap \hat{T} \subset \hat{V} \subseteq \hat{S} \cup \hat{T}.$$

Thus we have (see [1, Chapter 1, Section 3])

$$d(\hat{S}, \hat{T}) = d(\hat{S}, \hat{V}) + d(\hat{V}, \hat{T}) = 1 + d(\hat{V}, \hat{T}),$$

i.e., $d(\hat{V}, \hat{T}) = m - 1$. A simple induction completes the proof.

□

Following Theorem 2.1, we consider the medium $(\theta(L^X), \mathcal{T})$ with tokens in the form $\tau_{(a,i)}$ and $\tilde{\tau}_{(a,i)}$, where $a \in X$ and $i \in L \backslash \{0\}$. Since L^X and $\theta(L^X)$ are isomorphic, we may consider a medium $(L^X, \mathcal{T})$ with the set of tokens $\mathcal{T}$ defined by (1) and (2). More precisely, we have the following theorem.

Theorem 2.3. *Let $\mathcal{T}$ be a set of tokens defined on L^X by*

$$(S\tau_{(a,i)})(x) = \begin{cases} S(a) + 1, & \textit{if } x = a,\ i = S(a) + 1, \\ S(x), & \textit{otherwise}. \end{cases}$$

$$(S\tilde{\tau}_{(a,i)})(x) = \begin{cases} S(a) - 1, & \textit{if } x = a,\ i = S(a), \\ S(x), & \textit{otherwise}. \end{cases}$$

Then $(L^X, \mathcal{T})$ is a medium.

Note, that in the case $L = \mathbf{2}$, the set of states $\mathbf{2}^X$ is the set of all subsets of X (a logic cube of dimension $|X|$). The medium $(\mathbf{2}^X, \mathcal{T})$ is called a complete oriented medium in [9] and plays an important role in general media theory.

3 Evolution of states

In the definition of a *probabilistic token medium* ([5, Definition 5.1]), it is supposed that there is a proper probability distribution $\{\theta_\tau\}$ on the set $\mathcal{T}$ of tokens. A Markov chain model is constructed by assuming that stochastic stream of tokens is delivered by the environment. It is proved in [5, Theorem 5.2] that under certain assumptions this Markov chain has a stationary distribution in which the probability of every state S is equal, up to a normalizing constant, to $\prod_{\tau \in \hat{S}} \theta_\tau$, where $\hat{S}$ is the *content family* of the state S (see [5] for details).

In this section, we consider a process in which the states of the medium $(L^X, \mathcal{T})$ interact with tokens that arrive at instances $\{t_k,\ k=0,1,\dots\}$ in such a way that in the sequence $\{\tau_k\}$, the nature of the token τ_{k+1} is controlled in a random fashion by the transition over the interval $[t_k, t_{k+1}]$ of a Markov control parameter sequence $\{\nu_k\}$.

In what follows we assume that

$$X = \{x_1, \dots, x_m\} \text{ and } L = \{0, 1, \dots, n-1\}.$$

We also assume that $\{\nu_k\}$ is an irreducible and aperiodic Markov chain with the transition probabilities

$$\Pi_{rs} = P(\nu_{k+1} = s \,|\, \nu_k = r),\ k = 0, 1, \dots.$$

Definition 3.1. *Token arrival process is said to be* Markov controlled *if*

$$P(\tau_{k+1} = \tau_{(x,i)} \,|\, \nu_{k+1} = s) = \alpha_{s,i} > 0,$$
$$P(\tau_{k+1} = \tilde{\tau}_{(x,i)} \,|\, \nu_{k+1} = s) = \beta_{s,i} > 0,$$
$$\sum_{i=1}^{n-1} \alpha_{s,i} + \sum_{i=1}^{n-1} \beta_{s,i} = 1,\ \forall s = 1, \dots, m.$$

We denote the current state of the medium $(L^X, \mathcal{T})$ at a moment t_k by an L-valued set A_k, and represent it by the string of numbers

$$\vec{Q}_k = (Q_{k,1}, \dots, Q_{k,m}),$$

where $Q_{k,r} = A_k(x_r)$ is the current *value* of the element x_r. By Definition 3.1, Markov control implies that the value of ν_{k+1} specifies the element that may change over the interval $[t_k, t_{k+1}]$.

Theorem 3.1. *The sequence $\{\nu_k, \vec{Q}_k\}$ is an aperiodic and irreducible Markov chain.*

Proof. By Definition 3.1 and the definition of token actions in Theorem 2.3, the transition probabilities of the sequence can be expressed as follows:

$$P(\nu_{k+1} = s,\ \vec{Q}_k = \vec{j} \,|\, \nu_k = r,\ \vec{Q}_k = \vec{i}) \ = \ \Pi_{rs} c^s_{i_s j_s} \prod_{u \neq r} \delta^{j_u}_{i_u}, \tag{3}$$

where $\vec{i} = (i_1, \dots, i_m)$, $\vec{j} = (j_1, \dots, j_m)$, δ^j_i is the Kroneker symbol, and

$$c^s_{ij} = \begin{cases} \alpha_{s,j} & i = 0, \dots, n-2,\ j = i+1; \\ \beta_{s,i} & i = 1, \dots, n-1,\ j = i-1; \\ 1 - \alpha_{s,i+1} - \beta_{s,i} & i = j = 1, \dots, n-2; \\ 1 - \alpha_{s,1} & i = j = 0; \\ 1 - \beta s, n-1 & i = j = n-1; \\ 0, & \text{otherwise.} \end{cases} \tag{4}$$

Now, the Markov property follows from (3). Under the assumptions made on Π_{rs}, $\alpha_{s,i}$ and $\beta_{s,i}$, the chain $\{\nu_k, \vec{Q}_k\}$ can make a transition with a positive probability (not necessarily in one step) between any two of possible states. this makes the chain irreducible. Finally, aperiodicity follows from the fact that, by (3) and (4), $P(\nu_{k+1} = 1, \vec{Q}_{k+1} = \vec{0} \mid \nu_k = 1, \vec{Q}_k = \vec{0}) > 0$.

□

The number of possible states of the chain $\{\nu_k, \vec{Q}_k\}$ is n^{m+1}. Since the chain is irreducible and aperiodic, it means that it has a stationary probability distribution. Denote by $(\nu, \vec{Q}) = (\nu, Q^1, \ldots, Q^m)$ a random vector whose probability distribution is the stationary distribution of the chain $\{\nu_k, \vec{Q}_k\}$. To find the distribution of $\vec{Q}$, we need the following special property of $\{\nu_k, \vec{Q}_k\}$.

Definition 3.2. (cf. [9, Definition 6.1]) *Let $\{\nu_k,\ k = 0, 1, \ldots\}$ be an irreducible and aperiodic Markov chain with values in $\{1, 2, \ldots, n\}$ and transition probability matrix*

$$\Pi = (\Pi_{rs}),\ \Pi_{rs} = P(\nu_{k+1} = s \mid \nu_k = r).$$

A sequence of random vectors $\vec{Q}_k = (Q_k^1, \ldots, Q_k^n)$, $k = 0, 1, \ldots$ whose components Q_k^r take vales $0, 1, \ldots$ is said to have disjoint Markov–controlled one–dimensional transitions *if*

$$P(\nu_{k+1} = s, \vec{Q}_{k+1} = \vec{j} \mid \nu_k = r, \vec{Q}_k = \vec{i}) = \Pi_{rs} a^s_{i_s j_s} \prod_{u \neq r} \delta^{j_u}_{i_u},$$

$$\sum_{j=0}^{\infty} a^s_{ij} = 1,\ s = 1, \ldots, n,\ i = 0, 1, \ldots.$$

Now, based on [9, Theorem 6.1], we obtain the stationary probability distribution of $\vec{Q}$.

Theorem 3.2. *The stationary joint distribution of the sequence $\{\vec{Q}_k\}$ is given by*

$$P(\vec{Q} = \vec{i}) = \prod_{s=1}^{m} p^s_{i_s}, \tag{5}$$

where

$$p^s_i = p^s_0 \prod_{j=0}^{i} \rho_{s,j}, \tag{6}$$

$$p^s_0 = \left[\sum_{i=0}^{n-1} \prod_{j=0}^{i} \rho_{s,j} \right]^{-1}, \tag{7}$$

$$\rho_{s,j} = \frac{\alpha_{s,j}}{\beta_{s,j}}\ (j = 1, \ldots, n-1),\ \rho_{s,0} = 1\ (s = 1, \ldots, M). \tag{8}$$

Proof. By Definition 3.1 and the definition of token actions in Theorem 2.3, in every transition of the chain $\{\nu_k, \vec{Q}_k\}$ only one component of $\vec{Q}_k$ may undergo a transition (the probabilities of which are presented in (4)). Therefore, the sequence $\{\vec{Q}_k\}$ has disjoint Markov–controlled one–dimensional transitions with

$$a_{ij}^s = \begin{cases} c_{ij}^s, & i, j = 0, 1, \ldots, n-1, \\ 0, & \text{otherwise}. \end{cases} \tag{9}$$

By (9) and (4), Markov chains $\{\hat{Q}_k^r\}$ with transition matrices

$$A^r = (a_{ij}^r,\ i = 0, 1, \ldots, n-1),\ r = 1, \ldots, n$$

are irreducible and aperiodic. Therefore, along with the chain $\{\nu_k, \vec{Q}_k\}$, they too have stationary distributions which will be denoted by $\vec{P}^r = (p_0^r, \ldots, p_{n-1}^r)$. These distributions are unique solutions of the system of equations

$$\vec{P}^r = \vec{P}^r A^r,\ \sum_{j=0}^{n-1} p_j^r = 1. \tag{10}$$

Now, (5) follows from Theorem 6.1 in [9], while (6), (7), and (8) follow from (10) on the strength of (4).

□

It follows from (5) that the stationary joint probabilities of $\vec{Q}$ are products of the stationary marginal probabilities of individual element values (described by formulas (6)–(8)) – a sort of independence of element values in the limit. An apparent reason for this phenomenon is the assumption of *disjoint token action*, that is, that tokens are assumed to be applied to only one element of X at a time.

Another remarkable consequence of Theorem 3.2 is that the parameters $\alpha_{s,i}$ and $\beta_{s,i}$ are involved only by their ratios $\rho_{s,i}$. In particular, when for a given s the ratios are constant, formulas (6)–(8) yield the following result.

Corollary 3.1. *If, for some s, $\rho_{s,i} = \rho_s$, $i = 1, \ldots, n-1$, then the steady–state value distribution for the element x_s is either finite geometric*

$$P(Q^s = i) = (\rho_s)^i(\rho_s - 1)\left[(\rho_s)^n - 1\right]^{-1},\ \textit{if}\ \rho_s \neq 1,$$

or discrete uniform

$$P(Q^s = i) = \frac{1}{n},\ \textit{if}\ \rho_s = 1.$$

References

[1] M. Barbut and B. Monjardet, Ordre et Classification (Collection Hachete Université, 1970).

[2] G. Birkhoff, *Lattice Theory* (AMS Colloquium Publications, 3rd ed., vol. XXV, AMS, Providence, R.I., 1967).

[3] J.-P. Doignon and J.-Cl. Falmagne, "Well–graded families of relations", *Discrete Math.* **173** (1997) 35–44.

[4] J.-Cl. Falmagne, "A stochastic theory for the emergence and the evolution of preference structure", *Math. Social Sci.* **31** (1996) 63–84.

[5] J.-Cl. Falmagne, "Stochastic Token Theory", *J. Math. Psych.* **41(2)** (1997) 129–143.

[6] J.-Cl. Falmagne and J.-P. Doignon, "Stochastic evolution of rationality", *Theory and Decision* **43** (1997) 107–138.

[7] J.-Cl. Falmagne and S. Ovchinnikov, "Media theory", *Discrete Appl. Math.* (to appear)

[8] J.-C. Falmagne, M. Regenwetter and B. Grofman, "A stochastic model for the evolution of preferences", in *Choice, Decision, and Measurement: Essays in Honor of R. Duncan Luce*, ed. A.A.J. Marley (Lawrence Erlbaum Associates, NJ, 1997) pp. 111–129.

[9] S. Ovchinnikov and A. Dukhovny, "Advances in media theory", *Int. J. of Uncertainty, Fuzziness and Knowledge–Based Systems* **8**(1) (2000) 45–71.

[10] V. B. Kuz'min and S. V. Ovchinnikov, "Geometry of preference spaces I", *Automat. Remote Control* **36** (1975) 2059–2063.

[11] S. V. Ovchinnikov, "Convexity in subsets of lattices", *Stochastica* **IV** (1980) 129–140.

[12] M. Regenwetter, J.-Cl. Falmagne, and B. Grofman, "A stochastic model of preference change and its applications to 1992 Presidential Election Panel Data", *Psychological Review*, **106** (1999) 362–384.

A General Framework for Ordering Fuzzy Sets

Ulrich Bodenhofer

Software Competence Center Hagenberg, A-4232 Hagenberg, Austria

Abstract. Orderings and rankings of fuzzy sets have turned out to play a fundamental role in various disciplines. Throughout the previous 25 years, a lot a different approaches to this issue have been introduced, ranging from rather simple ones to quite exotic ones. The aim of this paper is to present a new framework for comparing fuzzy sets with respect to a general class of fuzzy orderings. This approach includes several known techniques based on generalizing the crisp linear ordering of real numbers by means of the extension principle, however, in its general form, it is applicable to any fuzzy subsets of any kind of universe for which a fuzzy ordering is known – no matter whether linear or partial.

1 Introduction

There is no doubt that orderings and rankings are essential in any field related to decision making. Admitting vagueness or impreciseness naturally results in the need for specifying vague preferences in crisp domains, but also in the demand for a framework in which it is even possible to decide between fuzzy alternatives. It is, therefore, not surprising that orderings and rankings of fuzzy sets have become main objects of study in fuzzy decision analysis and related disciplines.

Albeit only scarcely recognized, orderings of fuzzy sets are also important in areas related to fuzzy systems and fuzzy control, where the ordering of a numerical domain is most often used when defining fuzzy sets – there might only be a minority of fuzzy systems or controllers in which expressions like "small", "medium", or "large" do not occur. This ordering, however, is even more crucial as soon as automatic tuning procedures are concerned, which are supposed to give *interpretable*, i.e. understandable, results [1,5]. Similar questions arise in *linguistic approximation* [7,19] which may be considered as a kind of inverse procedure – finding a linguistic label for a given fuzzy set. A third application scenario is *rule interpolation* [15,16] which is concerned with obtaining conclusions for observations which are not covered by any antecedent in a fuzzy rule base. Orderings of fuzzy sets are able to provide criteria for determining between which rules the interpolation should take place [15].

Since the 1970s, a host of different methods for ordering or ranking fuzzy sets has been published (see [6,20–22] for detailed reviews). In order to find profound motivations for adding yet another approach, let us review some common characteristics of these methods:

1. As long as linguistic expressions are represented by fuzzy subsets of numerical domains, there is a certain context-dependent notion of indistinguishability. It could be desirable to take this indistinguishability into account, since not only the ranking of alternatives itself, but also the information that the difference between two alternatives is, more or less, negligible could be of interest. All existing methods, however, do not offer the opportunity to integrate indistinguishability which often leads to undesired, counter-intuitive preciseness.
2. All methods are defined for so-called *fuzzy quantities* – fuzzy subsets of the real numbers. Not only from the theoretical, but also from the practical point of view, it could be interesting to consider arbitrary ordered domains, without any restriction in terms of the underlying domain or linearity of the ordering.
3. The applicability of many ordering methods is restricted to fuzzy quantities having special properties, such as convexity, normality, or continuity (often called *fuzzy numbers*). The motivation for such restrictions is to guarantee some desirable properties, for example, antisymmetry.

The purpose of this paper is to introduce and investigate an ordering method for arbitrary fuzzy subsets of an arbitrary (fuzzy) ordered domain where indistinguishability is taken into account, too. For proof details and theoretical basics, the reader is referred to [3].

2 Preliminaries

In this paper, uppercase letters will be used synonymously for denoting fuzzy sets and their corresponding membership functions. The reader is assumed to be familiar with the basics of triangular norms and their corresponding residual implications [8,10,14]. Throughout the whole text, the symbol T is supposed to denote a left-continuous t-norm.

Since, according to the above discussions, the ordering method should be able to cope with vagueness and indistinguishability, all studies in this paper will be based on the similarity-based definition of fuzzy orderings (for extensive studies, see [3,4,11]). We only recall the very basic definitions.

Definition 1. A binary fuzzy relation E on a domain X is called *fuzzy equivalence relation* with respect to T, for brevity *T-equivalence*, if and only if the following three axioms are fulfilled for all $x, y, z \in X$:

(i)	Reflexivity:	$E(x, x) = 1$
(ii)	Symmetry:	$E(x, y) = E(y, x)$
(iii)	T-transitivity:	$T\big(E(x, y), E(y, z)\big) \leq E(x, z)$

Definition 2. Let $L : X^2 \to [0,1]$ be a T-transitive fuzzy relation. L is called *fuzzy ordering* with respect to T and a T-equivalence E, for brevity *T-E-ordering*, if and only if it additionally fulfills the following two axioms for all $x, y \in X$:

(i) E-Reflexivity: $E(x,y) \leq L(x,y)$
(ii) T-E-antisymmetry: $T\big(L(x,y), L(y,x)\big) \leq E(x,y)$

A subclass, which will be of special importance in the following, are so-called direct fuzzifications.

Definition 3. A T-E-ordering L is called a *direct fuzzification* of a crisp ordering $\preceq$ if and only if it admits the following resolution:

$$L(x,y) = \begin{cases} 1 & \text{if } x \preceq y \\ E(x,y) & \text{otherwise} \end{cases}$$

It is worth to mention that there is a one-to-one correspondence between direct fuzzifications of crisp linear orderings and fuzzy orderings L which additionally fulfill *strong completeness* [3,4]

$$\max\big(L(x,y), L(y,x)\big) = 1 .$$

The modifiers 'at least' and 'at most' with respect to a fuzzy ordering L will be essential for all further investigations. They can be defined by means of hulls/closures.

Definition 4. Suppose that X is supplied with some T-E-ordering L. Then, for a fuzzy subset A of X, the fuzzy sets 'at least A' and 'at most A' (with respect to L), abbreviated $\mathrm{ATL}(A)$ and $\mathrm{ATM}(A)$, respectively, can be defined as follows:

$$\mathrm{ATL}(A)(x) = \sup\{T(A(y), L(y,x)) \mid y \in X\}$$
$$\mathrm{ATM}(A)(x) = \sup\{T(A(y), L(x,y)) \mid y \in X\}$$

If L coincides with a crisp ordering $\preceq$, we will use the symbols $\mathrm{LTR}(A)$ and $\mathrm{RTL}(A)$ instead (standing for left-to-right and right-to-left continuation, respectively), where one can easily show the following identities:

$$\mathrm{LTR}(A)(x) = \sup\{A(y) \mid y \preceq x\}$$
$$\mathrm{RTL}(A)(x) = \sup\{A(y) \mid x \preceq y\}$$

In words, $\mathrm{LTR}(A)$ is the smallest superset of a fuzzy set A the membership function of which is non-decreasing with respect to $\preceq$. Correspondingly, for any fuzzy set A, $\mathrm{RTL}(A)$ is the smallest superset whose membership function is non-increasing. In direct analogy, $\mathrm{ATL}(A)$ can be regarded as the smallest superset of A the membership function of which is non-decreasing with respect to the fuzzy ordering L; analogously for $\mathrm{ATM}(A)$ (for a detailed and mathematically exact argumentation, see [3]).

Theorem 1. *Provided that a T-E-ordering L is a direct fuzzification of a crisp ordering $\preceq$, the following holds for all fuzzy sets A*

$$\begin{aligned} \mathrm{ATL}(A) &= \mathrm{LTR}(\mathrm{EXT}(A)) = \mathrm{EXT}(\mathrm{LTR}(A)) \, , \\ \mathrm{ATM}(A) &= \mathrm{RTL}(\mathrm{EXT}(A)) = \mathrm{EXT}(\mathrm{RTL}(A)) \, , \end{aligned}$$

where $\mathrm{EXT}(A)$ *is the so-called extensional hull of A with respect to E* [13,17], *which is defined as*

$$\mathrm{EXT}(A)(x) = \sup\{T(A(y), E(y, x)) \mid y \in X\} \, .$$

Example 1. Figure 1 shows an simple example demonstrating the actual meaning of the operators ATL and ATM as well as the correspondences of Theorem 1. We consider the following two fuzzy relations on the real numbers:

$$E(x, y) = \max(1 - |x - y|, 0)$$

$$L(x, y) = \begin{cases} 1 & \text{if } x \leq y \\ \max(1 - x + y, 0) & \text{otherwise} \end{cases}$$

One easily verifies that E is a $T_{\mathbf{L}}$-equivalence and that L is a $T_{\mathbf{L}}$-E-ordering, which directly fuzzifies the natural ordering of real numbers, where $T_{\mathbf{L}}$ stands for the Łukasiewicz t-norm

$$T_{\mathbf{L}}(x, y) = \max(x + y - 1, 0).$$

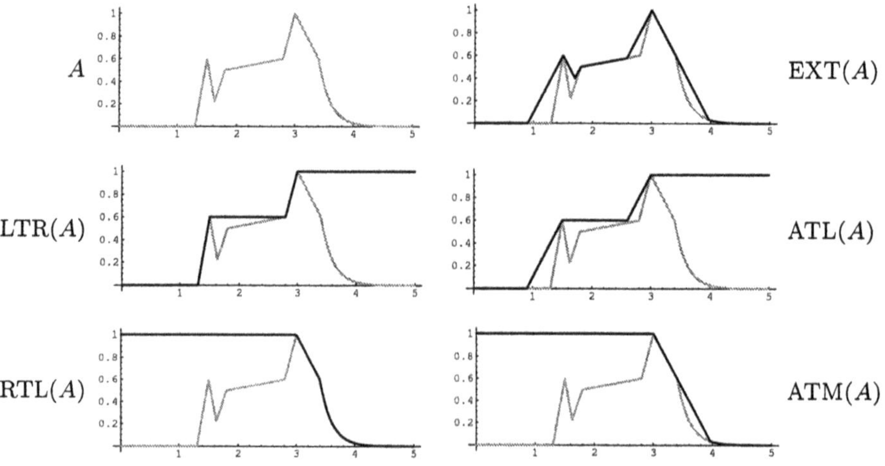

Fig. 1. A fuzzy quantity A and the results which are obtained when applying various ordering-based operators.

3 The Basic Approach

In order to have a clear motivation, let us start from a well-known ordering procedure for real intervals (with respect to the usual ordering of real numbers):

$$[a,b] \leq_I [c,d] \iff a \leq c \wedge b \leq d \tag{1}$$

It is easy to check that $\leq_I$ is a partial ordering. The inequality $a \leq c$ means that there are no elements of the set $[c,d]$ which are below the entire interval $[a,b]$. The inequality $b \leq d$, analogously, means that there are no elements of $[a,b]$ which lie completely above $[c,d]$. This criterion can be generalized to arbitrary crisp subsets of an ordered set $(X, \preceq)$ as follows:

$$M \preceq_I N \iff (\forall x \in N \; \exists y \in M: \; y \preceq x) \wedge (\forall x \in M \; \exists y \in N: \; x \preceq y)$$

The following lemma provides an equivalent formulation by means of hulls which will be the basis of all our further generalizations.

Lemma 1. *Let a domain X be equipped with an ordering $\preceq$. With the above notations, the following holds for all crisp subsets $M, N \subseteq X$:*

$$\begin{aligned} \mathrm{LTR}(M) \supseteq \mathrm{LTR}(N) &\Leftrightarrow \forall x \in N \; \exists y \in M: \; y \preceq x \\ \mathrm{RTL}(M) \subseteq \mathrm{RTL}(N) &\Leftrightarrow \forall x \in M \; \exists y \in N: \; x \preceq y \end{aligned}$$

As an immediate consequence, we obtain that the assertion $M \preceq_I N$ is always equivalent to

$$\mathrm{LTR}(M) \supseteq \mathrm{LTR}(N) \wedge \mathrm{RTL}(M) \subseteq \mathrm{RTL}(N) \, .$$

Since the operators LTR and RTL are not restricted to crisp sets, we can write down an extension of $\preceq_I$ to fuzzy subsets immediately:

$$A \preceq_I B \iff (\mathrm{LTR}(A) \supseteq \mathrm{LTR}(B) \; \wedge \; \mathrm{RTL}(A) \subseteq \mathrm{RTL}(B))$$

This means that we are able to order fuzzy sets with respect to a crisp ordering $\preceq$. The generalization to an arbitrary fuzzy ordering is now straightforward.

Definition 5. Let L be a fuzzy ordering on X. Then the relation $\preceq$ on $\mathcal{F}(X)$ is defined in the following way:

$$A \preceq_L B \iff (\mathrm{ATL}(A) \supseteq \mathrm{ATL}(B) \; \wedge \; \mathrm{ATM}(A) \subseteq \mathrm{ATM}(B))$$

Reconsidering Example 1 and Fig. 1, it may be clear that, in a more general setting, the properties $\mathrm{ATL}(A) \supseteq \mathrm{ATL}(B)$ and $\mathrm{LTR}(A) \supseteq \mathrm{LTR}(B)$ correspond to the property that the "left flank" of A is to the left of the "left flank" of B. Analogously, $\mathrm{ATM}(A) \subseteq \mathrm{ATM}(B)$ and $\mathrm{RTL}(A) \subseteq \mathrm{RTL}(B)$ relate to the fact that the "right flank" of A is to the left of the "right flank" of B. This demonstrates the appropriateness of the approach if we compare these two correspondences with the simple interval order (1).

Example 2. Figure 2 shows two simple convex fuzzy quantities A_1 and B_1 for which naturally $A_1 \preceq_I B_1$ (implying $A_1 \preceq_L B_1$ for any L directly fuzzifying the natural ordering of real numbers) holds.

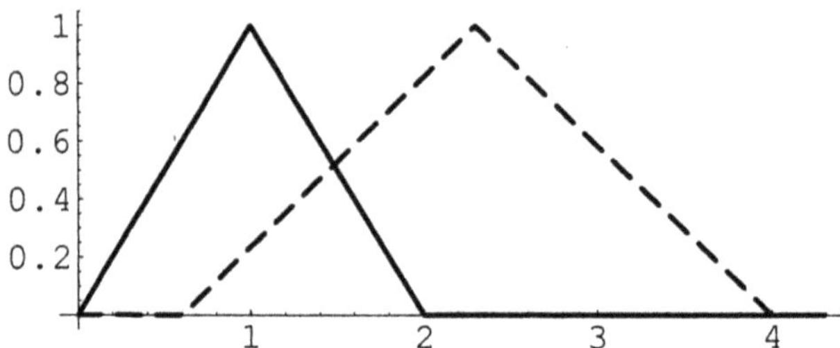

Fig. 2. Two simple convex fuzzy quantities A_1 (solid line) and B_1 (dashed line) for which $A_1 \preceq_I B_1$ holds.

Correspondingly, Fig. 3 shows two non-convex fuzzy quantities A_2 and B_2. In this example, approaches assuming the convexity of the fuzzy sets are not applicable, although it may be obvious from intuition that A_2 is, in some sense, smaller than B_2. In the proposed framework, $A_2 \preceq_I B_2$ actually holds (again implying $A_2 \preceq_L B_2$ for any L directly fuzzifying the natural ordering of real numbers).

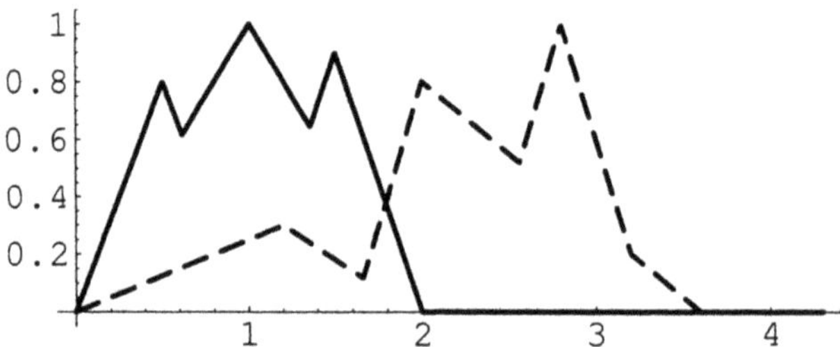

Fig. 3. Two non-convex fuzzy quantities A_2 (solid line) and B_2 (dashed line) for which $A_2 \preceq_I B_2$ holds.

Remark 1. Note that two fuzzy sets A and B are a priori incomparable if their heights do not coincide, i.e. if

$$\sup\{A(x) \mid x \in X\} \neq \sup\{B(x) \mid x \in X\} .$$

For simplicity, therefore, let us assume that the fuzzy sets we deal with are normalized, where we call a fuzzy set A *normalized* if and only if its height is 1, i.e. $\sup\{A(x) \mid x \in X\} = 1$.

4 Analysis

In order to study the properties of relations of type $\preceq_L$, let us assume that L is an arbitrary but fixed fuzzy ordering with respect to some t-norm T and a fuzzy equivalence relation E.

First of all, it is trivial to see that the relation $\preceq_L$ is reflexive and transitive, since it is nothing else than the intersection of two inclusion relations, which are, of course, reflexive and transitive. The next result characterizes antisymmetry, or better, non-antisymmetry in a unique way.

Theorem 2. *The following holds for all fuzzy subsets $A, B \in \mathcal{F}(X)$*

$$\big(A \preceq_L B \wedge A \succeq_L B\big) \;\Leftrightarrow\; \mathrm{ECX}(A) = \mathrm{ECX}(B)\;,$$

where the operator ECX *is defined as the minimum intersection of* ATL *and* ATM*:*

$$\mathrm{ECX}(A) = \mathrm{ATL}(A) \cap \mathrm{ATM}(A)$$

Theorem 2, however, only provides a valuable insight if we know more about the inside of the operator ECX. If we go back to crisp orderings for a moment, we will see that the above property corresponds to the equality of the convex hulls. In contrast to vector space-based definitions of convexity [18,23], we will use a general ordering-based definition of convexity, where it is easy to check that, for the real number and their natural ordering, the two definitions are equivalent.

Definition 6. Assume we are given a crisp ordering $\preceq$. Then a fuzzy set A is called *convex* (with respect to $\preceq$) if and only if the following property holds for all $x, y, z \in X$:

$$x \preceq y \preceq z \;\Rightarrow B(y) \geq \min\big(B(x), B(z)\big)$$

Proposition 1. *Given a crisp ordering $\preceq$ on X, the smallest convex superset of a given fuzzy set A – the so-called* convex hull *of A – is uniquely given as*

$$\mathrm{CVX}(A) = \mathrm{LTR}(A) \cap \mathrm{RTL}(A)\;.$$

Almost needless to mention, if L is a crisp ordering, the two operators CVX and ECX coincide.

Hence, we obtain that, for some crisp ordering $\preceq$, the relation $\preceq_I$ is unable to distinguish between two fuzzy sets A and B if and only their convex hulls coincide.

In the case that we are dealing with an ordering relation L which is not crisp, this argumentation becomes more subtle. It is intuitively clear that $\mathrm{ECX}(A)$ is always something like a generalized convex hull, but this should be made more precise. If L is a direct fuzzification, a clear answer can be given.

Theorem 3. *Let L be a T-E-ordering which is a direct fuzzification of some crisp ordering $\preceq$. Then the following equalities hold for all $A \in \mathcal{F}(X)$:*

$$\mathrm{ECX}(A) = \mathrm{CVX}(\mathrm{EXT}(A)) = \mathrm{EXT}(\mathrm{CVX}(A))$$

In words, for direct fuzzifications, the operator ECX can be interpreted as a kind of "extensional convex hull".

In any case, we see that neither $\preceq_I$ nor $\preceq_L$ is guaranteed to be antisymmetric. However, we have found equivalence relations uniquely describing non-antisymmetry. Of course, we can obtain orderings by factorization with respect to the symmetric kernels of $\preceq_I$ and $\preceq_L$, respectively. From the above consideration, we know that the symmetric kernels can be represented as

$$A \cong_I B \iff \mathrm{CVX}(A) = \mathrm{CVX}(B)$$
$$A \cong_L B \iff \mathrm{ECX}(A) = \mathrm{ECX}(B)$$

and we obtain the following result.

Theorem 4. *The relation $\preceq_I$ is an ordering on $\mathcal{F}(X)_{/\cong_I}$ which is isomorphic to the set of convex fuzzy subsets:*

$$\mathcal{F}_I(X) = \{A \in \mathcal{F}(X) \mid A = \mathrm{CVX}(A)\}$$

Analogously, the relation $\preceq_L$ is an ordering on $\mathcal{F}(X)_{/\cong_L}$ which is isomorphic to the set of extensional convex fuzzy subsets:

$$\mathcal{F}_L(X) = \{A \in \mathcal{F}(X) \mid A = \mathrm{ECX}(A)\}$$

The above results have a different quality if we compare them with the existing approaches which restricted to some special classes of fuzzy subsets in advance (e.g. [12,16]) just to preserve properties, such as antisymmetry. The new method is not restricted to (extensional) convex fuzzy sets. It can distinguish between any two arbitrary fuzzy subsets as long as their (extensional) convex hulls do not coincide. Since non-antisymmetry is characterized by an equivalence relation, it is possible to define orderings of the equivalence classes in order to obtain an even broader class of fuzzy subsets for which antisymmetry is satisfied [3].

5 Fuzzification

If we consider the two convex fuzzy quantities in Fig. 4, it is easy to see that, if we construct $\preceq_I$ by means of the natural ordering of real numbers, these two triangular fuzzy quantities are incomparable. The question is whether it is natural at all to compare vague phenomena crisply or if, as the example in Fig. 4 suggests, this directly leads to artificial preciseness.

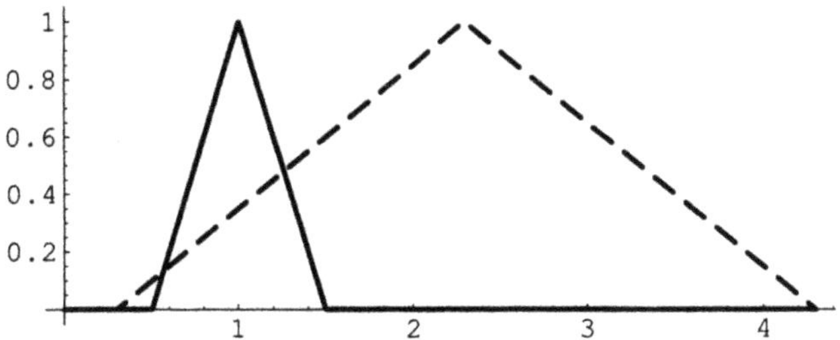

Fig. 4. Two convex fuzzy quantities A_3 (solid line) and B_3 (dashed line) which are incomparable.

In this section, we want to overcome this problem by allowing intermediate degrees to which a fuzzy set is smaller or equal than another. For this purpose, let us reconsider the definition of $A \preceq_L B$:

$$\mathrm{ATL}(A) \supseteq \mathrm{ATL}(B) \wedge \mathrm{ATM}(A) \subseteq \mathrm{ATM}(B)$$

If we want to make this crisp expression fuzzy, we have to specify (1) a fuzzy concept of subsethood and (2) a conjunction operation.

Definition 7. For a left-continuous t-norm T, the *residual implication* (residuum) is defined as

$$\vec{T}(x,y) = \sup\{z \in [0,1] \mid T(x,z) \leq y\} ,$$

while the corresponding *biimplication* (equivalence) is defined as

$$\overleftrightarrow{T}(x,y) = \min\left(\vec{T}(x,y), \vec{T}(y,x)\right) .$$

In the framework of many-valued predicate logics based on residuated lattices [9,10], it is natural to define the degree of inclusion of a fuzzy set A in another fuzzy set B as [2,3,8]

$$\mathrm{INCL}_T(A,B) = \inf_{x\in X} \vec{T}\big(A(x), B(x)\big) ,$$

where the infimum can be considered as a generalization of the universal quantifier.

Theorem 5. *The relation* INCL_T *is a fuzzy ordering on* $\mathcal{F}(X)$ *with respect to* T *and the* T*-equivalence*

$$\mathrm{SIM}_T(A,B) = \inf_{x\in X} \overleftrightarrow{T}\big(A(x), B(x)\big) .$$

If we replace the Boolean conjunction $\wedge$ by the minimum t-norm and the usual inclusion $\subseteq$ by INCL_T, we obtain the following generalization of $\preceq_L$:

$$\mathcal{L}_L(A,B) = \min\Big(\mathrm{INCL}_T(\mathrm{ATL}(B), \mathrm{ATL}(A)), \mathrm{INCL}_T(\mathrm{ATM}(A), \mathrm{ATM}(B))\Big)$$

which is, in fact, a fuzzy ordering of fuzzy sets – perfectly fitting to the results of Theorems 2 and 4:

Theorem 6. *The fuzzy relation $\mathcal{L}_L$ is fuzzy ordering on $\mathcal{F}(X)$ with respect to T and the fuzzy equivalence relation*

$$\mathcal{E}_L(A, B) = \mathrm{SIM}_T\big(\mathrm{ECX}(A), \mathrm{ECX}(B)\big) .$$

So far, it remains an open question in which way the crisp ordering $\lesssim_L$ and the fuzzy ordering $\mathcal{L}_L$ are related to each other. The next result gives an exhaustive answer:

Theorem 7. *The following characterization of the kernel of $\mathcal{L}_L$ holds:*

$$\forall A, B \in \mathcal{F}(X) : \ \big(\mathcal{L}_L(A, B) = 1 \Longleftrightarrow A \preceq_L B\big)$$

The relationship between $\mathcal{E}_L$ and $\cong_L$ is given analogously:

$$\forall A, B \in \mathcal{F}(X) : \ \big(\mathcal{E}_L(A, B) = 1 \Longleftrightarrow A \cong_L B\big)$$

In particular, this entails that $\preceq_L$ is a subrelation of $\mathcal{L}_L$ which implies that the comparability of two fuzzy sets with respect to $\mathcal{L}_L$ cannot be worse than comparability with respect to $\preceq_L$. The following example will show that the problem of artificial strictness when comparing fuzzy sets with $\preceq_L$ is perfectly solved if they are compared with the relation $\mathcal{L}_L$.

Example 3. If we choose L to be the crisp linear ordering of real numbers, i.e. $L = \chi_{\leq}$, and $T = T_{\mathbf{L}}$, Theorem 7 implies the following if we apply $\mathcal{L}_L$ to the fuzzy quantities from Example 2:

$$\begin{aligned} \mathcal{L}_L(A_1, B_1) &= 1 \\ \mathcal{L}_L(A_2, B_2) &= 1 \end{aligned}$$

Moreover, it is easy to verify the following equalities:

$$\begin{aligned} \mathcal{L}_L(B_1, A_1) &= 0 \\ \mathcal{L}_L(B_2, A_2) &= 0 \end{aligned}$$

Now let us reconsider the two fuzzy quantities A_3 and B_3 shown in Fig. 4. Using the same L and T as above, we obtain

$$\begin{aligned} \mathcal{L}_L(A_3, B_3) &= 0.9 \\ \mathcal{L}_L(B_3, A_3) &= 0 \end{aligned}$$

which seems quite a reasonable result.

Figure 5 shows two fuzzy quantities A_4 and B_4 which would be incomparable with respect to $\preceq_I$, too. Using the fuzzification we obtain

$$\begin{aligned} \mathcal{L}_L(A_4, B_4) &= \frac{5}{8} = 0.625 , \\ \mathcal{L}_L(B_4, A_4) &= \frac{5}{12} = 0.41\dot{6} . \end{aligned}$$

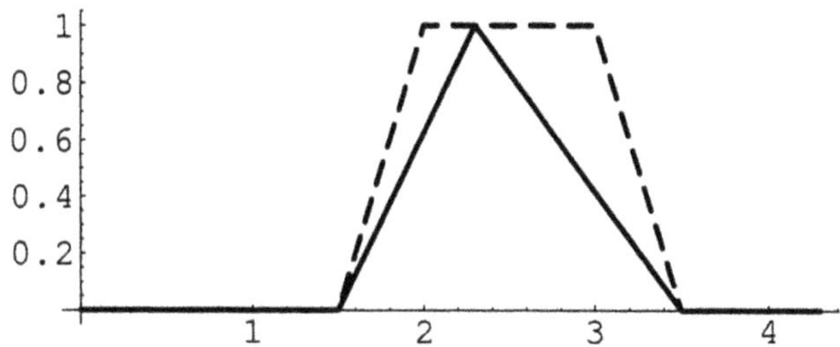

Fig. 5. Two convex fuzzy quantities A_4 (solid line) and B_4 (dashed line).

6 Concluding Remarks

In this paper, a general method for ordering fuzzy sets with respect to fuzzy orderings was introduced. We have seen that the restriction to certain subclasses of fuzzy sets is not necessary in this approach.

Since it is often not desirable or natural to compare fuzzy sets crisply, a straightforward fuzzification of the ordering approach has been carried out – leading to fuzzy orderings of fuzzy sets.

The reader should be aware, as noted in Remark 1, that different heights of two fuzzy sets immediately imply incomparability with respect to $\precsim_L$. If the fuzzy variant $\mathcal{L}_L$ is taken, this problem is slightly solved, but still in a way which is far from being satisfactory. For a detailed discussion and a possible solution, the reader is referred to [3].

Acknowledgements

This work has partly been done in the framework of the Kplus Competence Center Program which is funded by the Austrian Government, the Province of Upper Austria and the Chamber of Commerce of Upper Austria, and partly at the Fuzzy Logic Laboratorium Linz-Hagenberg which is part of to the Department of Algebra, Stochastics, and Knowledge-Based Mathematical Systems of the Johannes Kepler University, Linz, Austria.

References

1. R. Babuška. Construction of fuzzy systems—interplay between precision and transparency. In *Proc. ESIT 2000*, pages 445–452, Aachen, 2000.
2. W. Bandler and L. Kohout. Fuzzy power sets and fuzzy implication operators. *Fuzzy Sets and Systems*, 4:183–190, 1980.
3. U. Bodenhofer. *A Similarity-Based Generalization of Fuzzy Orderings*, volume C 26 of *Schriftenreihe der Johannes-Kepler-Universität Linz.* Universitätsverlag Rudolf Trauner, 1999.

4. U. Bodenhofer. A similarity-based generalization of fuzzy orderings preserving the classical axioms. *Internat. J. Uncertain. Fuzziness Knowledge-Based Systems*, 8(5):593–610, 2000.
5. U. Bodenhofer and P. Bauer. Towards an axiomatic treatment of "interpretability". In *Proc. IIZUKA2000*, pages 334–339, Iizuka, October 2000.
6. G. Bortolan and R. Degani. A review of some methods for ranking fuzzy subsets. *Fuzzy Sets and Systems*, 15:1–19, 1985.
7. F. Eshrag and E. H. Mamdani. A general approach to linguistic approximation. *Int. J. Man-Mach. Stud.*, 11:501–519, 1979.
8. S. Gottwald. *Fuzzy Sets and Fuzzy Logic*. Vieweg, Braunschweig, 1993.
9. S. Gottwald. *A Treatise on Many-Valued Logics*. Studies in Logic and Computation. Research Studies Press, Baldock, 2001.
10. P. Hájek. *Metamathematics of Fuzzy Logic*, volume 4 of *Trends in Logic*. Kluwer Academic Publishers, Dordrecht, 1998.
11. U. Höhle and N. Blanchard. Partial ordering in L-underdeterminate sets. *Inform. Sci.*, 35:133–144, 1985.
12. E. E. Kerre, M. Mareš, and R. Mesiar. On the orderings of generated fuzzy quantities. In *Proc. IPMU'98*, volume 1, pages 250–253, 1998.
13. F. Klawonn and R. Kruse. Equality relations as a basis for fuzzy control. *Fuzzy Sets and Systems*, 54(2):147–156, 1993.
14. E. P. Klement, R. Mesiar, and E. Pap. *Triangular Norms*, volume 8 of *Trends in Logic*. Kluwer Academic Publishers, Dordrecht, 2000.
15. L. T. Kóczy and K. Hirota. Ordering, distance and closeness of fuzzy sets. *Fuzzy Sets and Systems*, 59(3):281–293, 1993.
16. L. T. Kóczy and K. Hirota. Size reduction by interpolation in fuzzy rule bases. *IEEE Trans. Syst. Man Cybern.*, 27(1):14–25, 1997.
17. R. Kruse, J. Gebhardt, and F. Klawonn. *Foundations of Fuzzy Systems*. John Wiley & Sons, New York, 1994.
18. R. Lowen. Convex fuzzy sets. *Fuzzy Sets and Systems*, 3:291–310, 1980.
19. V. Novák. *Fuzzy Sets and Their Applications*. Adam-Hilger, Bristol, 1989.
20. X. Wang and E. E. Kerre. On the classification and the dependencies of the ordering methods. In D. Ruan, editor, *Fuzzy Logic Foundations and Industrial Applications*, International Series in Intelligent Technologies, pages 73–90. Kluwer Academic Publishers, Boston, 1996.
21. X. Wang and E. E. Kerre. Reasonable properties for the ordering of fuzzy quantities (I). *Fuzzy Sets and Systems*, 118:375–385, 2001.
22. X. Wang and E. E. Kerre. Reasonable properties for the ordering of fuzzy quantities (II). *Fuzzy Sets and Systems*, 118:387–405, 2001.
23. L. A. Zadeh. Fuzzy sets. *Inf. Control*, 8:338–353, 1965.

Learning, Classification and Clustering

Pattern Extraction Method for Text Classification

Hung Son Nguyen[1] **and Hui Wang**[2]

[1] Institute of Mathematics, Warsaw University, Banacha 2, Warsaw 02095, Poland
E-mail: son@mimuw.edu.pl
[2] School of Information and Software Engineering University of Ulster at Jordanstown N Ireland, BT37 0QB. Email: h.wang@ulst.ac.uk

Abstract. The quality of classification can be increased by using some feature extraction algorithm, i.e. the algorithm that finds new and more relevant features, before application of learning procedure. In this paper, we investigate a novel feature extraction method for textual data. Usually, texts (documents) are represented as collections of words or keywords. We present a method for finding new numerical attributes that improve the quality of classification. New features are based on a set of words (text pattern) and are defined as number of words occurring in both text pattern and the considered document. Our approach is based on Rough set methods and Lattice Machine theory. The experimental results show that the presented methods improve the classification quality on almost all textual data.

1 Introduction

Pattern extraction is one of most important tasks in Data Mining [3]. In previous papers we investigated some problems of pattern extraction from data and relevant feature selection by using Rough Set approach [4,7,8]. We considered the *generalized patterns* being conjunctions of descriptors of form $(attribute \in value\_set)$ (instead of ordinary descriptors of form $(attribute = value)$). We also presented an approach based on *Lattice Machine* [12] for text classification. In some sense, Lattice Machine technique joins data by using some "sum" operations (defined by users) to produce some generalized patterns. In this paper we propose the general scheme for classification systems, in which both feature extraction and feature selection processes are performed automatically from data. This scheme combines the pattern extraction methods as a feature extraction process and Rough Set methods as a feature selection process. We illustrate our proposition by example of text classification problem. Experiment results – performed by simplest application of our approach – show advantages of our proposition.

2 Preliminaries

An *information system* [9] is a pair $\mathbb{A} = (U, A)$, where U is a non-empty, finite set called the *universe* and A is a non-empty finite set of *attributes (or features)*, i.e. $a : U \to V_a$ for $a \in A$, where V_a is called *the value set of a*. Elements of U are called *objects or records*. Two objects $x, y \in U$ are said to be discernible by attributes from A if there exists an attribute $a \in A$ such that $a(x) \neq a(y)$. Any information system of the form $\mathbb{A} = (U, A \cup \{dec\})$ is called *decision table* where $dec \notin A$ is called *decision attribute* (or decision for short). Without loss of generality we assume that $V_{dec} = \{1, \ldots, d\}$. Then the set $DEC_k = \{x \in U : dec(x) = k\}$ will be called the kth *decision class of* $\mathbb{A}$ for $1 \leq k \leq d$.

2.1 Templates as Patterns in Data

Let $\mathbb{A} = (U, A)$ be an information table. By *descriptors* (or simple descriptors) we mean terms of the form $(a = v)$, where $a \in A$ is an attribute and $v \in V_a$ is a value in the domain of a (see [7]). One can define *generalized descriptors* by expressions of form $(a \in S_a)$, where $S_a \subseteq V_a$ is a set of values. By a *template* we mean the conjunction of descriptors:

$$\mathbf{T} = D_1 \wedge D_2 \wedge \ldots \wedge D_m$$

where $D_1, \ldots D_m$ are either simple or generalized descriptors. We denote by $length(\mathbf{T})$ the number of descriptors being in $\mathbf{T}$.

For the given template with length m:

$$\mathbf{T} = (a_{i_1} \in S_1) \wedge \ldots \wedge (a_{i_m} = S_m)$$

the object $u \in U$ is said to satisfy the template $\mathbf{T}$ if and only if $\forall_j a_{i_j}(u) \in S_j$. We denote the set of objects satisfying the template $\mathbf{T}$ by $\mathbf{Supp}(\mathbf{T})$. In this way the template $\mathbf{T}$ describes the set of objects $\mathbf{Supp}(\mathbf{T})$ having the common property: "*values of attributes* $a_{i_1}, \ldots, a_{i_m}$ belong to $S_1, \ldots, S_m$, respectively". The template $\mathbf{T}$ is *consistent with a given decision table* $\mathbb{A} = (U, A \cup \{d\})$ (or simply: consistent) if all objects from $\mathbf{Supp}(\mathbf{T})$ belong to one decision class.

The main purpose of pattern extraction methods is to find the minimal set of consistent templates $\mathbf{P} = \{\mathbf{T}_1, \ldots, \mathbf{T}_m\}$ that $\bigcup_{i=1}^{m} \mathbf{Supp}(\mathbf{T}_i) = U$. In this way, one can obtain more compact representation for the given decision table.

One can find in [7,6] many methods extracting templates from data. In this paper we present a method based on Lattice Machine [12].

2.2 Lattice Machine

Let us consider a given information table $\mathbb{A} = (U, A)$, where $A = \{a_1, \ldots, a_k\}$. Every object $u \in U$ is associated with a simple template of length k:

$$T_u = (a_1 = a_1(u)) \wedge \ldots \wedge (a_k = a_k(u))$$

In Lattice Machine [12], every simple template T_u is called *tuple*, and templates are called *hyper_tuples*. The original decision table is called *relation*,

ID	Attribute		Class
	A_1	A_2	
t_0	a	1	0
t_1	a	2	1
t_2	a	3	1
t_3	b	1	0
t_4	b	2	1
t_5	b	3	1
t_6	c	2	0
t_7	c	3	0

$\Longrightarrow$

ID	Attribute		Class
	A_1	A_2	
t'_0	$\{a, b\}$	$\{1\}$	0
t'_1	$\{a, b\}$	$\{2, 3\}$	1
t'_2	$\{c\}$	$\{2, 3\}$	0

Table 1. A simple (database) relation and a hyper relation obtained from the relation in Table 1 by the Lattice Machine.

and its compact version using templates is called *hyper_relation*. Examples of a relation and hyper relation are shown in Tables 1 and 1, respectively.

One can define a ordering relation $\leq$ over templates as follows:

$$\mathbf{T}_1 \leq \mathbf{T}_2 \Leftrightarrow_{def} \left| \begin{array}{l} \text{for any descriptor } D = (a \in S) \text{ from } \mathbf{T}_2 \text{ there exists} \\ \text{a descriptor } D' = (a \in S') \text{ from } \mathbf{T}_1 \text{ such that } S' \subseteq S \end{array} \right.$$

It has been shown [12] that an elegant structure is implied among generalized templates – the collection of all hyper tuples in a given domain is a semilattice under the following ordering relation $\leq$. We call this *domain lattice*. The templates T_u for $u \in U$ are minimal elements in the *domain lattice*.

In a domain lattice, a labelling of objects by decision attribute induces a labelling of the minimal elements of lattice. For example, the following decision table corresponds to the labelled lattice in Figure 1.

E: {Large, Red, Triangle} $\rightarrow \oplus$
G: {Large, Blue, Circle} $\rightarrow \oplus$
J: {Small, Blue, Triangle} $\rightarrow \ominus$
L: {Small, Green, Rectangular} $\rightarrow \ominus$

Given a labelled lattice, a straightforward representation of the labelling is by sets – each set consisting of all data units with the same label, and a simple classification is by enumeration – if a new data unit is the same as one element in the set representation, then it is classified by the label of this element; otherwise, it is marked as unknown. This is in fact the idea of rote learning. Clearly there is no generalisation in this kind of learning. The nearest neighbour method goes one step further. In its basic form, the representation is also by sets, but the classification is based on some distance measure. There is generalisation in this kind of learning, but distance measures can be troublesome in cases where discrete attributes are involved.

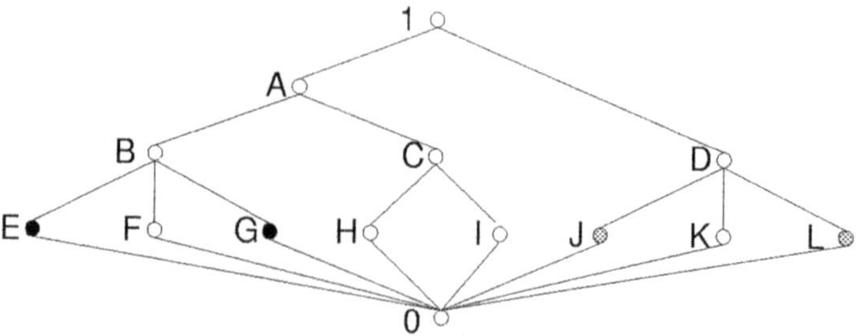

Fig. 1. *A labelled lattice.*

The Lattice Machine takes a different approach to this problem. It represents the labelling by a subset of the elements in the lattice – usually much less than the number of labelled elements. These elements have the property that all elements below them have the same label or are unlabelled, and we called them *equilabelled.* The classification is governed by the following simple rule:

family given an equilabelled element, any elements below it will have the same label as the equilabelled element (if any).

The hyper relation in Table 1 is in fact the set of equilabelled elements found by the Lattice Machine from the decision table in Table 1.

The core of the Lattice Machine is the following algorithm [12]. Let $\mathbb{A} = (U, A \cup \{dec\})$ be a decision table and let $DEC_k = \{x \in U : dec(x) = k\}$ the kth *decision class of* $\mathbb{A}$ induced by *dec* for $1 \leq k \leq d$. For any decision class DEC_k, the algorithm finds a set H_k of equilabelled maximal elements (in the sense that the sum of any pair of them is not equilabelled any more). This algorithm is based on the lattice operation *sum* (+) for finding the unique least upper bound of a set of elements.

Let $\mathcal{E}$ be the set of all (possible) equilabelled elements in a labelled lattice.

$C_1 \quad :=_{df} DEC_k$.

$C_{n+1} :=_{df}$ The set of maximal elements of $[\downarrow (C_n + DEC_i)] \cap \mathcal{E}$.

Note that, for a lattice L and $e \in L$, $\downarrow e = \{y \in L : y \leq e\}$. It has been shown [12] that there is some n such that $C_n = C_{n+1}$, and therefore $C_n = C_r$ for all $r \geq n$. It has also been proved that $C_n = H_k$. This H_k is called *interior* of class DEC_k.

One of the advantage of Lattice Machine is possibility of its implementation on parallel computers where the lattice sum operations (in Step 2) can be done in short time.

3 Feature extraction and selection algorithms for textual data

In this section we describe some pattern extraction methods for textual data. On the simplest text classification model, one can assume that every textual object (document) is represented by a set of words. The training data set consists of labelled documents. The task is to label new documents by using training data.

One of the most important notions of Rough set theory is: "*indiscernibility relation*". We say that two objects x and y from the domain are indiscernible by the set of attributes $A = \{a_1, ..., a_k\}$ if $\forall_{a \in A} a(x) = a(y)$. In this situation we say that objects x and y are in the relation IND_A and denote by $x \; IND_A \; y$. It is easy to see that the defined above IND_A is equivalent relation, hence it produces a partition of the set of objects into "*equivalent classes*".

In the feature selection process we would like to generate such a set of attributes A that the partition of objects defined by IND_A is consistent with the partition of objects into (decision) classes. In other words, the partition defined by IND_A must be more detail than the partition defined by the decision attribute d. The ***discernibility quality*** of the set of attributes A can be measured by the number of pairs of different class objects discerned by A i.e.

$$Disc(A) = |\{x, y \in U : d(x) \neq d(y) \wedge \neg(x \; IND_A \; y)\}|$$

The (inside) conflict of the set of objects is defined by

$$conflict(S) = card\left(\{x, y \in S : d(x) \neq d(y)\}\right)$$

Hence, the discernibility quality of A can be computed by

$$Disc(A) = conflict(U) - \sum_i conflict(DEC_i)$$

where $C_i(A)$ are equivalent classes of IND_A.

In the feature selection method based on Rough Set Theory, the set of attributes is initiated by the empty set and in the consecutive steps it is increased by adding the new feature that best improves the discernibility quality of the whole set of attributes. This process is continued until the quality improvement of the next attribute is too small (e.g. when it is equal to 0).

This simple scheme has been adopted to solve many problems in data mining e.g.: attribute reduction, discretization of real value attributes, decision tree construction. The general scheme for solving decision problems based on Rough Set Theory can be presented in Figure 2.

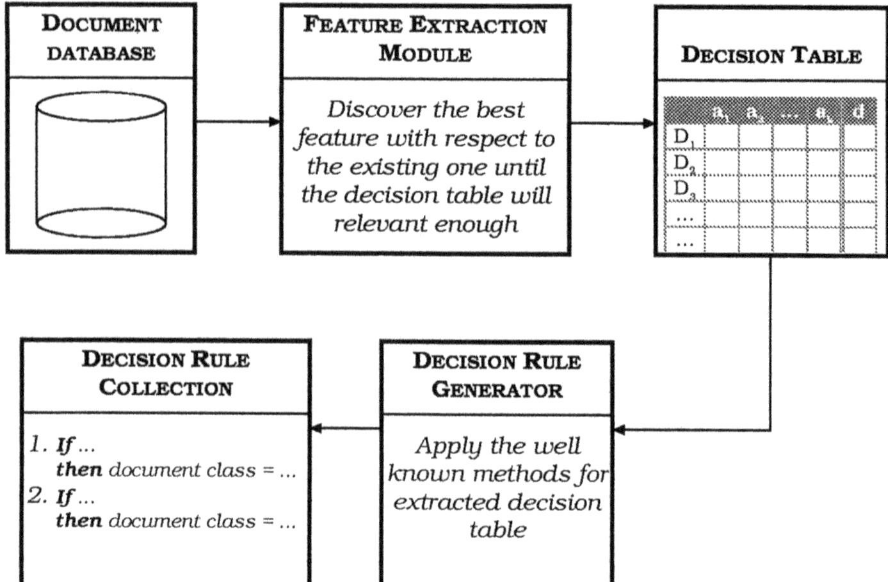

Fig. 2. The general scheme for solving decision problems based on Rough Sets theory

In the next section we describe several methods of searching for *pattern texts* that allow to discern the particular set of documents from another. We define the feature $f_{\mathbf{T}}$ associated to the given pattern text $\mathbf{T}$ as follows:

$$f_{\mathbf{T}}(D) = card(\mathbf{T} \cup D)$$

4 Pattern Text extraction Methods

One consider two possible tasks in the successive step of the feature extraction process for document classification (i.e. some set of attributes has been found). The *global problem* can be formulated as follows:

> *Given the set of attributes A find a new feature which best improve the quality of A.*

The *local problem* can be formulated as follows:

Given the set of attributes A:
- *find the set $\mathbf{S}$ of indiscernible objects by A with maximal value of $conflict(\mathbf{S})$.*
- *find a new feature which discern $\mathbf{S}$ best.*

Let $\mathbf{S}_1$ and $\mathbf{S}_2$ be given two sets of documents. We say that the pattern text $\mathbf{T}$ and the integer k discerns $\mathbf{S}_1$ from $\mathbf{S}_2$ if one of the next conditions satisfies:

$$\forall_{D \in \mathbf{S}_1} f_{\mathbf{T}}(D) > k \tag{1}$$

$$\forall_{D \in \mathbf{S}_2} f_{\mathbf{T}}(D) \leq k \tag{2}$$

Any such pair $(\mathbf{T}, k)$ will be called "*the discriminator for* $\mathbf{S}_1$ *and* $\mathbf{S}_2$" and denoted by $a_{\mathbf{T},k}$. The *discernibility power* of the discriminator $f_{\mathbf{T},k}$ over $\mathbf{S}_1$ and $\mathbf{S}_2$ is defined by:

$Disc_{\mathbf{T},k}(\mathbf{S}_1; \mathbf{S}_2) = |\{D \in \mathbf{S}_1 : f_{\mathbf{T}}(D) > k\}| \times |\{D \in \mathbf{S}_2 : f_{\mathbf{T}}(D) \leq k\}|$

The problem is to find the smallest pattern text $\mathbf{T}$ and the corresponding integer k such that for given two sets of documents $\mathbf{S}_1$ and $\mathbf{S}_2$ the value $Disc_{\mathbf{T},k}(\mathbf{S}_1; \mathbf{S}_2)$ is maximal.

Our methods are based on the Lattice Machine and Boolean reasoning approach. We will describe some basic technique of searching for pattern text in the simplest situations. These techniques will be used to describe the pattern text extraction method.

4.1 Boolean reasoning based method

Let us consider the simplest situation when we would like to discern the only one text document D from the set of documents $\mathbf{S} = \{D_1, ..., D_n\}$. One consider the *Minimal Hitting Set* problem of the family of sets. This problem is NP-complete, but one can apply the greedy heuristics to determine the semi-minimal hitting set of words T for $D - D_1, ..., D - D_n$. as a pattern text. Then the pair $(T, |T|)$ is a good classifier. For any word $w \in D$, we denote by $n_{\mathbf{S}}(w)$ the number of documents $D_i \in \mathbf{S}$ containing the word w. The simplest version of greedy heuristic can be described as follows:

ALGORITHM Basic algorithm
Input: the document D and the set of documents
 $\mathbf{S} = \{D_1, ..., D_n\}$ to be distinguished from D.
Output: The minimal hitting set of words $T \subset D$ for
 $D \backslash D_1, ..., D \backslash D_n$.

1. $T := \emptyset$;
2. while $\mathbf{S} \neq \emptyset$ **do**
 Search for the word $w \in D$ that
 $n_{\mathbf{S}}(w)$ is minimal;
 Reduce $\mathbf{S}$ to the set of documents
 containing w i.e.
 $\mathbf{S} := \{D : w \in D\}$
endwhile

We assume that $\mathbf{S}_1 = \{D_1, D_2, ..., D_n\}$ and $\mathbf{S}_2 = \{D_{n+1}, ..., D_{n+m}\}$. Using Basic Algorithm, one can find the semi-optimal pattern texts $T_1, ...T_n$ for $D_1, D_2, ..., D_n$, respectively, with regards to $\mathbf{S}_2$. Then we set $T := T_1 \cup ... \cup T_n$. The parameter k can be determined by applying MD algorithm for discretization problem (see [4]).

4.2 Lattice Machine based method

Lattice Machine is a general framework for supervised learning. The basic elements can be re–configured to suit different learning problem. In this section we are going to show how to re-configure the Lattice Machine for the task of text classification.

Representation Lattice Machine was originally proposed to work on structured data. Text documents, however, are unstructured data. A common representation of text document is by boolean feature vector. For example, one could construct a feature for each word appearing in the corpus – a set of documents. A corpus with m documents and n words would thus be represented as a $m \times n$ matrix. This representation in fact turns unstructured datasets into structured. However, this representation is inefficient in its usage of space, since even a moderate sized corpus usually contains many different words. Lattice Machine has a natural solution to this problem.

The ordering relation In the context of text classification, if the documents are relatively large hence different documents have large number of common elements, it would be more efficient to use $\supseteq$ rather than $\subseteq$ to define the ordering relation. This amounts to classifying a document using a subset of the words in the document either in a fixed order or in any order. If the documents are relatively small, however, it would be more effective to use $\subseteq$ instead. This amounts to classifying a document according to whether it is a subset of an already classified document. In what follows, our presentation is mainly for $\supseteq$. Where a result doesn't apply to $\subseteq$, we will clearly spell it out, and an alternative solution will be provided accordingly.

Since we choose to represent a document by a set of words, the ordering relation between documents, denoted by $doc_1 \leq doc_2$, can be specified by:

$$set\_of\_words(doc_1) \supseteq set\_of\_words(doc_2),$$

where $set\_of\_words(doc_i)$ is the set of words in doc_i.

The sum operation Now that documents are represented by sets (word list) and the ordering relation is (inverse) set inclusion, the sum operation (denoted by $+$) is simply set intersection.

ID	SET OF WORDS	CLASS
[1]	97 doc code r area 02 18 n america by state lewen	commun
[2]	97 j code text area 02 18 n america 2 memo by state megibow	commun
[3]	97 doc at t answer machin code 10 15 command for 1343 dave diehl	commun
[4]	97 doc at t answer machin control code 10 15 1545 r frisbi	commun
[5]	97 doc 11 at t answer machin 1339 control code text michael choi	commun
[6]	97 at code text r 02 18 2 hard drive rev sutherland	comput
[7]	97 code text r 02 18 2 xt hard drive rev sutherland	comput
[8]	97 code text 02 18 ibm irq and pc diagnost w taucher	comput
[9]	97 doc j at command 04 09 modem karam	comput
[10]	97 doc j code 02 18 7 error system mac 20k simpson	comput

Table 2. A sample of the MEMO data.

4.3 Example of Lattice Machine Approach

Now we use a sample of the MEMO data shown in Table 2 to illustrate our solution to the text classification problem. This dataset was used in [2]. It was 11 classes, but we use only samples from two classes. Each line corresponds to one document, and it is a list of words in the document (stemmed with the Porter Stemmer algorithm [10,14]). Since the documents have been processed, they may not be readable to humans any more. So are the interiors to be found later.

[1+1]: 97 doc code r area 02 18 n america by state lewen
[1+2]: 97 code area 02 18 n america by state
[1+3]: 97 doc code
[1+4]: 97 doc code r
[1+5]: 97 doc code
[2+2]: 97 j code text area 02 18 n america 2 memo by state megibow
[2+3]: 97 code
[2+4]: 97 code
[2+5]: 97 code text
[3+3]: 97 doc at t answer machin code 10 15 command for 1343 dave diehl
[3+4]: 97 doc at t answer machin code 10 15
[3+5]: 97 doc at t answer machin code
[4+4]: 97 doc at t answer machin control code 10 15 1545 r frisbi
[4+5]: 97 doc at t answer machin control code
[5+5]: 97 doc 11 at t answer machin 1339 control code text michael choi

Table 3. The sum of all pairs of tuples from class "commun" in Table 2

For the "commun" class, we sum all pairs of documents using $\supseteq$ and we get the hyper tuples in Table 3. The set of maximal equilabelled hyper tuples

[6+6]:	97 at code text r 02 18 2 hard drive rev sutherland
[6+7]:	97 code text r 02 18 2 hard drive rev sutherland
[6+8]:	97 code text 02 18
[6+9]:	97 at
[6+10]:	97 code 02 18
[7+7]:	97 code text r 02 18 2 xt hard drive rev sutherland
[7+8]:	97 code text 02 18
[7+9]:	97
[7+10]:	97 code 02 18
[8+8]:	97 code text 02 18 ibm irq and pc diagnost w taucher
[8+9]:	97
[8+10]:	97 code 02 18
[9+9]:	97 doc j at command 04 09 modem karam
[9+10]:	97 doc j
[10+10]:	97 doc j code 02 18 7 error system mac 20k simpson

Table 4. The sum of all pairs of tuples from class "comput" in Table 2

[1+2]:	97 code area 02 18 n america by state	commun
[1+4]:	97 doc code r	commun
[3+5]:	97 doc at t answer machin code	commun
[6+7]:	97 code text r 02 18 2 hard drive rev sutherland	comput
[8+8]:	97 code text 02 18 ibm irq and pc diagnost w taucher	comput
[9+10]:	97 doc j	comput

Table 5. Maximal equilabelled hyper tuples for class "commun" and "comput"

is shown in Table 5. The same operation is applied to this table, and it is clear that the result is the same as this table. Therefore this is the interior for the "commun" class. The same is done for the "comput" class, and the interior for this class is shown in Table 4.

5 Experimental results

To evaluate our approach as a tool for text classification, we applied it to nine benchmark problems which were used in [2]. Table 6 lists the problems and gives a summary description of each domain, the number of classes and number of terms found in each problem, and the number of training and testing examples used in the experiment. On smaller problems 10-fold cross-validation was used, and on larger problems a single hold out set of the specified size was used.

We applied the pattern text extraction method presented in Section 4 for these data tables. As a result, we obtained a decision table, where the founded patterns are attributes and documents are objects (see Table 2).

Datasets	#Train	#Test	#Classes	#Terms	Text-valued field	Label
memos	334	10cv	11	1014	document title	category
cdroms	798	10cv	6	1133	CD-Rom game name	category
birdcom	914	10cv	22	674	common name of bird	phylogenic order
birdsci	914	10cv	22	1738	common scientific name of bird	phylogenic order
hcoarse	1875	600	126	2098	company name	industry (coarse grain)
hfine	1875	600	228	2098	company name	industry (fine grain)
books	3501	1800	63	7019	book title	subject heading
species	3119	1600	6	7231	animal name	phylum
netvet	3596	2000	14	5460	URL title	category

Table 6. Description of benchmark problems.

Afterward, we applied a Rough Set based decision tree construction method for classification (see [4,5]).

Dataset	default	RIPPER	C4.5	LM/Text	Combined
memos	19.8	50.9	57.5	59.8	59.6
cdroms	26.4	38.3	39.2	40.0	40.5
birdcom	42.8	88.8	79.6	90.4	88.9
birdsci	42.8	91.0	83.3	92.3	92.4
hcoarse	11.3	28.0	30.2	20.2	46.1
hfine	4.4	16.5	17.2	13.8	15.7
books	5.7	42.3	52.2	45.3	60.2
species	51.8	90.6	89.4	89.4	89.6
netvet	22.4	67.1	68.8	67.8	68.9
Average	31.6	57.1	57.5	57.7	58.6

Table 7. Experimental results of the Lattice Machine, along with those of C4.5 and RIPPER cited from [2].

The experimental results are listed in Table 7. As a comparison we cite from [2] experimental results on the same set of problems using two state-of-the-art learning algorithms – C4.5 [11], RIPPER [1], Lattice Machine [13] and the proposed method called *Combined method.*

Acknowledgement

This paper has been partially supported by Polish State Committee of Research (KBN) grant No 8T11C02519, grant of the Wallenberg Foundation and

British Council/KBN grant "Uncertainty Management in Information Systems: Foundations and Applications of Non-Invasive Methods (1999-2001)".

References

1. W. W. Cohen. Fast effective rule induction. In *Machine Learning: Proceedings of the Twelfth International Conference*. Morgan Kaufmann, 1995.
2. William W. Cohen and Haym Hirsh. Joins that generalize: Text classification using whirl. In *Proc. KDD-98, New York*, 1998. `http://www.research.att.com/~wcohen/`.
3. V.M. Fayad, G.Piatetsky Shapiro, P. Smyth, R. Uthurusamy (eds): *Advanced in Knowledge Discovery and Data Mining*, AAAI/MIT Press 1996.
4. Nguyen H.Son, Skowron A., 1997. Boolean reasoning for feature extraction problems. In: Z.W. Raś and A.Skowron (Eds.): Proceedings of Tenth International Symposium on Foundation of Intelligent Systems, ISMIS'97, Oct. 1997, NC, USA, *Foundation of Intelligent Systems* **LNAI 1325**, Springer Verlag, pp. 117-126.
5. H.S. Nguyen and S.H. Nguyen. Pattern extraction from data, *Fundamenta Informaticae* **34** (1998) 129–144.
6. Nguyen H. Son, Nguyen S. Hoa (1999). Rough Sets and Association rule Generation. *Fundamenta Informaticae* **40**, pp. 383-405.
7. Nguyen S. Hoa, A. Skowron, P. Synak, 1998. Discovery of data pattern with applications to decomposition and classification problems. In L. Polkowski, A. Skowron (eds.): *Rough Sets in Knowledge Discovery* **2**. Physica-Verlag, Heidelberg, pp. 55–97.
8. Nguyen S.Hoa, 1999. Discovery of Generalized Patterns. In Z.W. Raś and A.Skowron (Eds.): Proceedings of 11th International Symposium on Foundation of Intelligent Systems, ISMIS'99, *Foundation of Intelligent Systems* **LNAI 1609**, pp. 574–582.
9. Pawlak Z., 1991. Rough Sets. Theoretical Aspects of Reasoning about Data, Kluwer Academic Publishers, Dordrecht.
10. M. Porter. An algorithm for suffix stripping. *Program*, 14(3):130–137, 1980.
11. Ross Quinlan. *C4.5: Programs for Machine Learning.* Morgan Kaufmann, San Mateo, 1993.
12. Hui Wang, Ivo Düntsch, and David Bell. Data reduction based on hyper relations. In *Proceedings of KDD98, New York*, pages 349–353, 1998.
13. Hui Wang, Son Nguyen. Text classification using Lattice Machine. In *Proceedings of ISMIS'99*, Springer–Verlag, Warsaw, pages 349–353, 1999.
14. Jinxi Xu and W.B. Croft. Corpus-based stemming using co-occurrence of word variants. *ACM TOIS*, 16(1):61–81, Jan. 1998.

A Comparison of Rough Set Strategies for Pre-Term Birth Data

Jerzy W. Grzymala-Busse [1], Linda K. Goodwin [2], Witold J. Grzymala-Busse [3], and Xinqun Zheng [1]

[1] Department of Electrical Engineering and Computer Science, University of Kansas, Lawrence, KS 66045, USA, E-mail: Jerzy@eecs.ukans.edu, Zheng@eecs.ukans.edu

[2] Department of Information Services and the School of Nursing, Duke University, Durham, NC 27710, USA, E-mail: goodw010@mc.duke.edu

[3] RS Systems, Inc., Lawrence, KS 66047, USA, E-mail: Witek@argus.rs-systems.com

Abstract. In many applications data are inconsistent: for two distinct cases attribute values are the same but the decisions are different. For example, two patients are characterized identically by all tests, demographic variables, etc., however, one delivers a baby prematurely and the other delivers at full term.

Our main objective was to increase sensitivity, i.e., a conditional probability of true positives. In order to achieve this objective we changed a strength multiplier for rules describing preterm cases. In our experiments we induced rules from preterm birth data using LERS (Learning from Examples using Rough Sets). The problem was to make the best use of certain and possible rule sets induced by LERS from inconsistent data. To solve this problem we used eight different strategies: using only certain rules, only possible rules, first certain then possible rules, and both rule sets; combined with two different ways to use rules in complete and partial matching.

1 Introduction

Prediction of preterm birth is an important but difficult medical problem. The problem is important because it affects a lot of cases—for example, in 1995, 11% of all babies born in USA were premature. Among preterm births, about 10% need intensive medical care, a very expensive procedure [3]. Prediction of preterm birth is difficult, since current methods of preterm birth diagnosis have limited prediction power [13].

In medical diagnosis, the objective is not to achieve a small error rate, computed as the ratio of all erroneously diagnosed cases to the total number of cases. In our domain, the error rate would be the ratio of all misdiagnosed preterm and fullterm cases to the total number of all cases. Fullterm cases do not require special attention. Only predicting preterm cases is important. Diagnosticians are interested mostly in correctly diagnosing preterm cases. The accuracy of preterm birth, i.e., the ratio of correctly recognized preterm cases (true-positives) to the number of all preterm cases is a *sensitivity*. The ratio of correctly recognized fullterm cases (true-negatives) to the number of all fullterm cases, is a *specificity*, a secondary parameter characterizing diagnosis.

A large database, describing preterm births, was collected at the Duke University Medical Center. After initial preprocessing, the database contained 19,970 cases characterized by 1,229 attributes. The database was divided into two parts: training with 14,977 cases and testing with 4,993 cases. The training data set was used as the input data set for a rule induction system LERS (Learning from Examples based on Rough Set theory). The testing data set was used to compute sensitivity and specificity of the rule set induced by LERS.

Both training and testing data sets were unbalanced: each data set contained more fullterm cases than preterm cases. As a result, there was more rules describing fullterm cases, and additionally, these rules were stronger, meaning that more training cases were correctly recognized by fullterm case rules. Thus, specificity was higher, at the cost of sensitivity that was lower.

The main objective of our research was to increase sensitivity, keeping specificity within a reasonable range. To accomplish this objective, two methods were used. The first method was to change a parameter, called a *rule strength*, associated with every rule induced by LERS. The second method was to change the strategy of using the two rule sets, induced by LERS from inconsistent data sets.

A preliminary version of this paper was presented at the Eighth International Conference on Information Processing and Management of Uncertainty in Knowledge Based Systems, Madrid, Spain, July 3–7, 2000 [8].

2 Data mining by LERS

Frequently, prenatal data sets are conflicting (inconsistent). Two women, characterized by the same values of all attributes, have different outcome: preterm birth in one case, fullterm in the other. The best tool to deal with inconsistency is rough set theory [15, 16]. Rough set theory is the foundation for a data mining system LERS, used in our experiments. For inconsistent data, LERS computes lower and upper approximations for each class.

Rules induced from the lower approximation of the class *certainly* describe the class, so they are called *certain*. On the other hand, rules induced from the upper approximation of the class describe only *possibly* (or *plausibly*) cases, so they are called *possible* [5]. In our experiments the LERS algorithm LEM2 [5, 6] was used to induce rule sets. An example of another data mining system based on rough sets is presented in [17].

For classification of unseen cases system LERS uses a modified "bucket brigade algorithm" [2, 12]. The decision to which class a case belongs is made on the basis of two parameters: strength and support. They are defined as follows: *Strength* is the total number of cases correctly classified by the rule during training. The second parameter, *support*, is defined as the sum of scores of all matching rules from the class. The class C for which the support, i.e., the value of the following expression

$$\sum_{\text{matching rules } R \text{ describing } C} \text{Strength}(R)$$

is the greatest is the winner and the case is classified as being a member of C. The above scheme reminds non-democratic voting in which voters vote with their strengths. Note that in our experiments we did not used the possibility of awarding rules proportionally to the number of conditions (attribute-value pairs), because this option usually decrease accuracy [11].

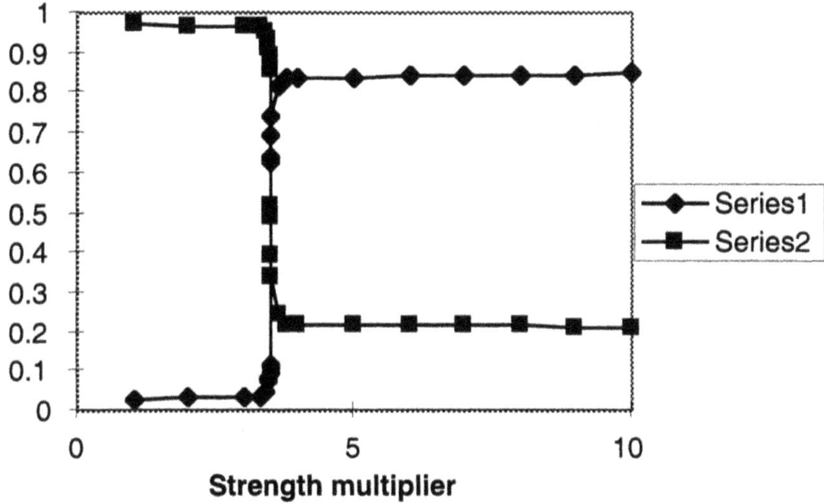

Figure 1. Sensitivity (series 1) and specificity(series 2) versus rule strength multiplier in a typical data set describing preterm birth.

If a case is not completely matched by any rule, some classification systems use *partial matching*. During partial matching, system AQ15 uses the probabilistic sum of all measures of fit for rules [14]. Another approach to partial matching is presented in [17]. Holland *et al.* [12] do not consider partial matching as a viable alternative to complete matching and rely on a default hierarchy instead. In LERS partial matching does not rely on the input of the user. If complete matching is impossible, all partially matching rules are identified. These are rules with at least one attribute-value pair matching the corresponding attribute-value pair of a case.

For any partially matching rule R, the additional factor, called *Matching factor*

(R), is computed. In partial matching, the class C for which the value of the following expression

$$\sum_{\text{partially matching rules } R \text{ describing } C} \text{Matching\_factor}(R) * \text{Strength}(R)$$

is the greatest is the winner and the case is classified as being a member of C. In our experiments, two matching options were : complete matching first, followed by using partial matching if necessary and using both complete matching and partial matching at the same time. Hence, in partial matching, Matching_factor was always used.

In our experiments, we used four combinations for using rule sets: using only certain rules, using only possible rules, using certain rules first, then possible rules if necessary, and using both certain and possible rules. Since we used four options for choosing rule sets and two options for matching, eight different strategies were tested in our experiments:

1. Using only certain rules and complete matching, then partial matching if necessary,

2. Using only possible rules and complete matching, then partial matching if necessary,

3. Using certain rules first, then using possible rules if necessary and complete matching, then partial matching if necessary,

4. Using both certain rules and possible rules and using complete matching, then partial matching if necessary,

5. Using certain rules first, then using possible rules if necessary and both complete matching and partial matching,

6. Using only certain rules and both complete matching and partial matching,

7. Using only possible rules and both complete matching and partial matching,

8. Using both certain rules and possible rules and both complete matching and partial matching,

3 Unbalanced data sets

For simplicity we will assume that data sets have only two classes (concepts). Frequently medical data sets are unbalanced: one class is represented by the majority of cases while the other class is a minority. Unfortunately, in medical data the smaller class—as a rule—is more important. We will call this class *basic*. In Duke's perinatal training data, only 20.7% of the cases represent the basic class, preterm birth. During rule induction, the average of all rule strengths for the bigger class is also greater than the average of all rule strengths for the more important but smaller basic class. During classification of unseen cases, rules matching a case and voting for the basic class are overvoted by rules voting for the bigger, complementary class. The total accuracy, measured as a ratio of the total number of well classified cases to the total number of cases, is good, because almost every case from the majority class is well classified. On the other hand, many cases from the basic class may not be classified correctly. Thus the sensitivity is poor and the resulting classification system will be rejected by diagnosticians.

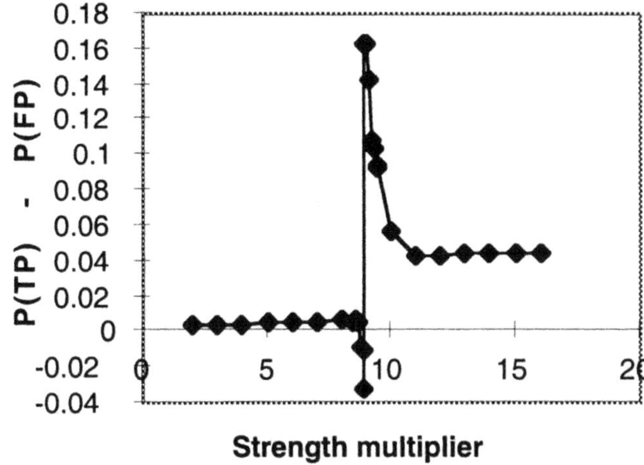

Figure 2. P(TP) – P(FP) versus rule strength multiplier for Duke-1 data set using certain rules and complete matching first, then partial matching.

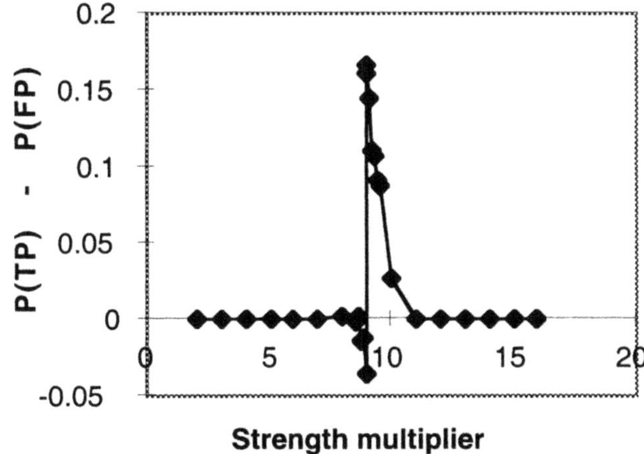

Figure 3. P(TP) – P(FP) versus rule strength multiplier for Duke-1 data set using certain rules and both, complete matching and partial matching at the same time.

Therefore it is necessary to increase sensitivity. The simplest idea is to add cases to the basic class in the data set, e.g., by adding duplicates of the available cases. The total number of training cases will increase and that will increase the total running time of the rule induction system. However, adding duplicates will not change the knowledge hidden in the original data set, but it may create a balanced data set so that the average rule set strength for both classes will be approximately equal. The same effect may be accomplished by increasing the average rule strength for the basic class. In our experiments we multiplied the rule strength for every rule describing the basic class by the same real number called *strength multiplier*.

Results of our experiments, in which we measured the accuracy for both classes (the accuracy for the basic class, i.e., sensitivity, and the accuracy of the complementary class, i.e., specificity) with changing strength multiplier are presented in the next section.

4 Description of data sets and experiments

Data sets used for our experiments come from the Duke University Medical Center. First, a large data set, with 1,229 attributes and 19,970 cases was partitioned into two parts: training (with 14,977 cases) and testing (with 4,993 cases). We selected three mutually disjoint subsets of the set of all 1,229 attributes, the first set containing 52 attributes, the second with 54 attributes and the third subset contained eight attributes; the new data names were Duke-1, Duke-2, and Duke-3, respectively. The Duke-1 data set contains laboratory test results. The Duke-2 test represents the most essential remaining attributes that, according to experts, should be used in diagnosis of preterm birth. Duke-3 represents demographic information about pregnant women. All three data sets were unbalanced because only 3,103 cases were preterm, all remaining 11,874 cases were fullterm. Similarly, in the testing data set, there were only 1,023 preterm cases while the number of fullterm cases was 3,970. All three data sets, Duke-1, Duke-2, and Duke-3, had many missing attribute values, see Table 1.

Table 1. Input data—missing attribute values

Number of missing attribute values in data sets		
	training	testing
Duke-1	505,329	167,371
Duke-2	291,796	96,997
Duke-3	4,742	1,579

First, missing attribute values were replaced by actual values [4, 7]. Duke-1 and Duke-2 data sets were processed by the most common value algorithm of the OOMIS system, while Duke-3 was preprocessed by a concept closest fit algorithm of OOMIS.

To reduce the error rate during classification we used a very special discretization method. First, in the training data set, for any numerical attribute, values were sorted. Every value *v* was replaced by the interval [*v*, *w*), where *w* was the next bigger value than *v* in the sorted list. Our approach to discretization was the most cautious since, in the training data set, we put only one attribute value in each interval. For testing data sets, values were replaced by the corresponding intervals taken from the training data set. It could happen that a few values come into the same interval.

Table 2. Input data—conflicting and unique cases

Number of conflicting and unique cases in the data sets				
	training		testing	
	conflicting	unique	conflicting	unique
Duke-1	10,028	4,994	2,748	2,242
Duke-2	8,687	6,295	2,297	2,533
Duke-3	9,070	5,229	1,863	2,958

All of our training and testing data sets, after replacing missing attribute values by actual attribute values and by applying our cautious discretization, were inconsistent. The input data sets are described in Table 2.

Table 3. Rule sets

			certain	possible
Duke-1	Number of rules	Preterm	572	618
		Fullterm	876	775
	Average strength of rule set	Preterm	1.50	8.97
		Fullterm	8.47	44.73
Duke-2	Number of rules	Preterm	884	1,022
		Fullterm	2068	1,642
	Average strength of rule set	Preterm	1.19	4.60
		Fullterm	3.28	11.37
Duke-3	Number of rules	Preterm	455	847
		Fullterm	993	659
	Average strength of rule set	Preterm	2.44	5.49
		Fullterm	6.91	38.56

Some statistics about rule sets are presented in Table 3. As a result of unbalanced data sets, the average rule strength for rules describing fullterm births is much greater than the corresponding rule strength for preterm births. Consequently, the error rate in the original rule sets is not a good indicator of rule set quality, as follows from [9, 10].

Table 4. Results of experiments

Complete matching first, then partial matching

Certain rules

	Duke-1	Duke-2	Duke-3
Initial total error rate	21.85	22.19	22.41
Critical total error rate	44.94	49.33	48.45
Maximum of P(TP) – P(FP)	0.1633	0.1336	0.13969
Minimum of P(TP) – P(FP)	–0.0327	–0.0321	0.0065
Critical number of true-positives	649	684	677
Critical number of true-negatives	2100	1846	1897
Critical rule strength multiplier	9	7.15	7.96.5

Since the basic concept is the class of preterm cases, the set of all correctly predicted preterm cases are called true-positives, incorrectly predicted preterm cases (i.e., predicted as fullterm) are called false-negatives, correctly predicted fullterm cases are called true-negatives, and incorrectly predicted fullterm cases are called false-positives.

Sensitivity is the conditional probability of true-positives given actual preterm birth, i.e., the ratio of the number of true-positives to the sum of the number of true-positives and false-negatives. It will be denoted by P(TP), following notation from [18]. Specificity is the conditional probability of true-negatives given fullterm birth, i.e., the ratio of the number of true-negatives to the sum of the number of true-negatives and false-positives. It will be denoted by P(TN). Similarly, the conditional probability of false-negatives, given actual preterm birth, and equal to 1 – P(TP), will be denoted by P(FN) and the conditional probability of false-positives, given actual fullterm birth, and equal to 1 – P(TN), will be denoted by P(FP). Obviously,

$$\text{Sensitivity} + \text{Specificity} = P(TP) - P(FP) + 1,$$

so all conclusions drawn from the observations of the sum of sensitivity and specificity can be drawn from observations of P(TP) – P(FP). Another study of the sum of sensitivity and specificity was presented in [1].

For completeness, a typical chart (Fig. 1) shows how sensitivity and specificity change as a function of the rule strength multiplier.

Table 5. Results of experiments

Complete matching first, then partial matching

	Possible rules		
	Duke-1	Duke-2	Duke-3
Initial total error rate	22.01	22.07	23.47
Critical total error rate	54.18	44.18	31.68
Maximum of P(TP) – P(FP)	0.1242	0.1599	0.1349
Minimum of P(TP) – P(FP)	–0.0704	–0.0084	0.0091
Critical number of true-positives	755	631	380
Critical number of true-negatives	1533	2156	3031
Critical rule strength multiplier	8.04	2.04	6.5

Following [9, 10], we computed the maximum of the difference between the conditional probabilities for true-positives given actual preterm births and false-positives given actual fullterm births as a function of the rule strength multiplier for the preterm rule set. Representative charts are presented in Fig. 2–3.

Again, following the idea from [9, 10], in our experiments we were increasing the strength multiplier and observed P(TP) – P(FP). For each rule set, there exists some value of the rule strength multiplier, called *critical*, for which the values of P(TP) – P(FP) jumps from the minimal value to the maximal value. The respective values of true positives, true negatives, etc., and the total error rate, are also called *critical*. The results are summarized in Tables 4–11. The total error rate is defined as the ratio of the number of true-positives and true-negatives to the total number of testing cases. The total error rate, corresponding to the rule strength multiplier that is equal to one, is called *initial*.

The corresponding values of P(TP) – P(FP) are presented also in Tables 4–11. The critical total error rate from Tables 4–11 is computed as the total error rate for the maximum of P(TP) – P(FP).

Table 6. Results of experiments

	Complete matching first, then partial matching		
	Certain rules first, then possible rules		
	Duke-1	Duke-2	Duke-3
Initial total error rate	22.37	22.33	23.53
Critical total error rate	45.04	48.67	31.0
Maximum of P(TP) – P(FP)	0.1607	0.1383	0.1348
Minimum of P(TP) – P(FP)	–0.0353	–0.0277	0.0141
Critical number of true-positives	647	679	368
Critical number of true-negatives	2097	1884	3077
Critical rule strength multiplier	8.99	7.15	7.1

Table 7. Results of experiments

	Complete matching first, then partial matching		
	Union of certain and possible rules		
	Duke-1	Duke-2	Duke-3
Initial total error rate	22.21	22.13	23.45
Critical total error rate	52.35	41.96	33.01
Maximum of P(TP) – P(FP)	0.121	0.1668	0.1299
Minimum of P(TP) – P(FP)	–0.0746	–0.0051	0.0125
Critical number of true-positives	719	602	396
Critical number of true-negatives	1660	2296	2949
Critical rule strength multiplier	8.14	2.26	8

Table 8. Results of experiments

Both, complete and partial matching at the same time

Certain rules

	Duke-1	Duke-2	Duke-3
Initial total error rate	20.49	20.49	20.49
Critical total error rate	44.44	52.53	50.65
Maximum of P(TP) – P(FP)	0.1653	0.1376	0.1112
Minimum of P(TP) – P(FP)	–0.035	–0.0286	0.0
Critical number of true-positives	643	745	676
Critical number of true-negatives	2131	1625	1788
Critical rule strength multiplier	9	7.15	7.1

Table 9. Results of experiments

Both, complete and partial matching at the same time

Possible rules

	Duke-1	Duke-2	Duke-3
Initial total error rate	20.49	20.49	20.49
Critical total error rate	64.69	45.86	48.49
Maximum of P(TP) – P(FP)	0.0717	0.1482	0.1282
Minimum of P(TP) – P(FP)	–0.1228	–0.0132	0.0
Critical number of true-positives	865	644	662
Critical number of true-negatives	898	2059	1910
Critical rule strength multiplier	8.03	2.04	5.5

Table 10. Results of experiments

	Both, complete and partial matching at the same time		
	Certain rules first, then possible rules		
	Duke-1	Duke-2	Duke-3
Initial total error rate	20.49	20.49	20.49
Critical total error rate	44.36	52.53	50.65
Maximum of P(TP) – P(FP)	0.1653	0.1376	0.1112
Minimum of P(TP) – P(FP)	–0.035	–0.0286	0.0
Critical number of true-positives	638	745	676
Critical number of true-negatives	2140	1625	1788
Critical rule strength multiplier	9	7.15	7.19

Table 11. Results of experiments

	Both, complete and partial matching at the same time		
	Union of certain and possible rules		
	Duke-1	Duke-2	Duke-3
Initial total error rate	20.49	20.49	20.49
Critical total error rate	64.25	42.02	52.33
Maximum of P(TP) – P(FP)	0.0737	0.1639	0.1256
Minimum of P(TP) – P(FP)	–0.1219	–0.0028	0.0
Critical number of true-positives	860	599	725
Critical number of true-negatives	925	2296	1655
Critical rule strength multiplier	8.14	2.26	5.9

5 Conclusions

The main objective of our work was to increase the sum of sensitivity and specificity. As was shown in [1], this was a compromise, in which sensitivity was considerably increased, while specificity decreased but not too much. This objective was accomplished by increasing rule strengths for all rules describing preterm birth cases. At the same time, eight different strategies for using certain and possible rules, induced by LERS, were used. The only conclusion is that using complete matching first, then partial matching is a better strategy than using both, complete and partial matching at the same time. We may conclude this not only on the basis of the critical number of true positives but also on the basis of the AUC (the area under the ROC curve).

On the other hand, using the following four strategies: only certain rules, only possible rules, certain rules and then possible rules and using both certain rules and possible rules at the same time does not show any obvious advantage. Similar results were reported in [11]. It seems that there is no one single best strategy among these four strategies used for classifying preterm cases.

References

[1] Bairagi, R. and Suchindran C. M. (1989) An estimator of the cutoff point maximizing sum of sensitivity and specificity. *Sankhya*, Series B, *Indian Journal of Statistics* **51**, 263–269.

[2] Booker, L. B., Goldberg, D. E., and Holland, J. F. (1990) Classifier systems and genetic algorithms. In *Machine Learning. Paradigms and Methods.* Carbonell, J. G. (ed.), The MIT Press, 235–282.

[3] Feldman, W. E. and Wood, B. (1997) The economic impact of high-risk pregnancies. *Journal of Health Care Finance* **24**, 64–71.

[4] Grzymala-Busse, J. W. (1991) On the unknown attribute values in learning from examples. *Proc. of the ISMIS*-91, *6th International Symposium on Methodologies for Intelligent Systems*, Charlotte, North Carolina, October 16–19. *Lecture Notes in Artificial Intelligence*, vol. 542, Springer-Verlag, 368–377.

[5] Grzymala-Busse, J. W. (1992) LERS—A system for learning from examples based on rough sets. In *Intelligent Decision Support. Handbook of Applications and Advances of the Rough Sets Theory*. Slowinski, R. (ed.), Kluwer Academic Publishers, 3–18.

[6] Grzymala-Busse, J. W. (1998) LERS—A knowledge discovery system. In *Rough Sets in Knowledge Discovery* 2, *Applications, Case Studies and Software Systems*, ed. by L. Polkowski and A. Skowron, Physica-Verlag, 562–565.

[7] Grzymala-Busse, J.W. and Goodwin, L.K. (1997) Predicting preterm birth risk using machine learning from data with missing values. *Bull. of Internat.*

Rough Set Society **1**, 17–21.

[8] Grzymala-Busse, J. W., Goodwin, L. K., Grzymala-Busse, W. J. and Zheng, X. (2000). Comparing different rough set strategies in using rules induced from pre-term birth data. Proc. of the IPMU-2000 Information Processing and Management of Uncertainty in Knowledge-Based Systems, Madrid, Spain, July 3–7, pp. 388–394.

[9] Grzymala-Busse, J. W., Goodwin, L. K., and Zhang, X. (1999) Increasing sensitivity of preterm birth by changing rule strengths. Proc. of the 8th Workshop on Intelligent Information Systems (IIS'99), Ustronie, Poland, June 14–18, pp. 127–136.

[10] Grzymala-Busse, J. W., Grzymala-Busse, W. J., Goodwin K. L. (1999) A closest fit approach to missing attribute values in preterm birth data. *Proc. of the Seventh Int. Workshop on Rough Sets, Fuzzy Sets, Data Mining and Granular-Soft Computing* (RSFDGrC'99), Ube, Yamaguchi, Japan, November 8–10, 1999. *Lecture Notes in Artificial Intelligence*, No. 1711, Springer Verlag, 405–413.

[11] Grzymala-Busse, J. W. and Zou X. (1998) Classification strategies using certain and possible rules. *Proc. of the First International Conference on Rough Sets and Current Trends in Computing*, Warsaw, Poland, June 22–26, 1998. *Lecture Notes in Artificial Intelligence*, No. 1424, Springer Verlag, 37–44.

[12] Holland, J. H., Holyoak K. J., and Nisbett, R. E. (1986) *Induction. Processes of Inference, Learning, and Discovery.* The MIT Press.

[13] McLean, M., Walters, W. A. and Smith, R. (1993) Prediction and early diagnosis of preterm labor: a critical review. *Obstetrical & Gynecological Survey* **48**, 209–225.

[14] Michalski, R. S., Mozetic, I., Hong, J. and Lavrac, N. (1986) The AQ15 inductive learning system: An overview and experiments. Department of Computer Science, University of Illinois, Rep. UIUCDCD-R-86-1260.

[15] Pawlak, Z. (1982) Rough sets. *International Journal Computer and Information Sciences* **11**, 341–356.

[16] Pawlak, Z. (1991) *Rough Sets. Theoretical Aspects of Reasoning about Data.* Kluwer Academic Publishers.

[17] Stefanowski, J. (1998) On rough set based approaches to induction of decision rules. In Polkowski L., Skowron A. (eds.) *Rough Sets in Data Mining and Knowledge Discovery*, Physica-Verlag, 500–529.

[18] Swets, J. A. and Pickett, R. M. (1982) *Evaluation of Diagnostic Systems. Methods from Signal Detection Theory.* Academic Press.

Toward the Intelligent Control of Hierarchical Clustering

Ronald R. Yager
Machine Intelligence Institute
Iona College
New Rochelle, NY 10801
yager@panix.com

ABSTRACT: The importance of the inter-cluster distance measure in the determination of the clusters in hierarchical clustering is pointed out. We note a fundamental distinction between the nearest neighbor cluster distance measure, Min, and the furthest neighbor measure, Max. The first favors the merging of large clusters while the later favors the merging of smaller clusters. We introduce a family of inter-cluster distance measures which can be parameterized along a scale characterizing their preference for merging larger or smaller clusters. We then consider the use of this distinction between distance measures as a way of controlling the hierarchical clustering process. Combining this with the ability of fuzzy systems modeling to formalize linguistic specifications we see the emergence of a tool that can aid in the inclusion of intelligence in the clustering process.

1. Introduction

As a step toward providing intelligent methods for performing clustering, we are interested in looking at different methods of controlling the process of merging clusters in hierarchical clustering techniques.

In **H**ierarchical **A**g**G**lomerative (HAG) clustering [1, 2] clusters are built up by combining existing clusters based upon their proximity. The following algorithm summarizes the basic steps in the HAG clustering approach:

1. Select an initial set of clusters
2. Find the nearest pair of clusters and merge them
3. Repeat Step 2 until the stopping rule is satisfied

In each of these steps there exists a degree freedom that can affect the results of the clustering process. In the first step, the procedure for selecting the initial clusters is unspecified. In the second step the method of measuring the "nearness" of clusters is unspecified. In the third step the stopping rule is unspecified. Let us look at each of these steps and begin to describe some possible methods for implementing the available freedom.

The most common method of initialization is to assign each data point to a distinct cluster. However *seeding* is another way of initializing the clustering process. In this process we collect some of the data into clusters and let the remaining data form singleton clusters. Using this approach we are providing some guidance as to how the clusters will be formed.

In the second step it is the selection of the method used to evaluate the proximity of clusters that provides us with freedom. This selection has two components, first, we decide upon a method for measuring the proximity between two individual elements in the data space. Once having this measure we must then select a method for determining the proximity of clusters. It is the process of measuring the proximity of clusters that shall mainly interest us in this work.

In the third step the stopping rule is not specified. We can make some preliminary comments on how to do this. The stopping rule has to depend upon information available in the clustering process. One piece of information we can use is the number of clusters. Indicating that when we have N^* clusters we stop is often used. Another piece of information that can be used is information about the number of elements in the clusters, the cluster cardinalities. For example, we can decide to stop if the cardinality of the biggest cluster is equal or greater than some specified value. Another method that is often used to determine the stopping rule is to stop the clustering process when the two nearest clusters are beyond a certain specified value. Combinations of these individual stopping criteria can be used

*if the number of clusters is greater than N_1 **and** the minimal cluster distance is greater than D_1 then stop.*

2. Measuring Proximity

Central to HAG clustering is the measurement of the proximity of two clusters. Underlying this is the measurement of the proximity between individual observations. The measurement of proximity between data points is strongly domain dependent. In order to more directly focus on our concern, the measurement of proximity of clusters, we shall assume the availability of a measure of proximity between individual elements. Letting $X = \{x_1, x_2, \ldots, x_n\}$ be our data set we denote the proximity of two observations x_i and x_j as $Prox(x_i, x_j)$. This measure can be of two types, "a distance type" or "a similarity type". By distance type measure, $Dist(x_i, x_j)$, we mean a proximity measure such that the smaller its value the nearer the objects. By a similarity type, $Sim(x_i, x_j)$, we mean a proximity measure such that the larger its value the nearer the objects. One property required of proximity measures, whether of the distance or similarity type is that they are symmetric, $Prox(x_i, x_j) = Prox(x_i, x_j)$. Another property required of proximity measures is that the proximity of an element with itself should have a value indicating that they are the closest elements. This condition manifests itself differently for the distance type measure and similarity type measure. For the distance type measure this means $Dist(x_j, x_j) = 0$. For the similarity measures $Prox(x_i, x_j)$ should be the largest possible value. If similarity is measured on the unit interval this means $Sim(x_j, x_j) = 1$. Another property often associated with these kinds of measure is the triangular inequality and the related idea of transitivity.

We shall most often view things from the perspective of a distance type measure. With this perspective in mind we shall assume that we have available an $n \times n$ matrix S such that s_{ij} is the distance between object x_i and object x_j, $s_{ij} = Dist(x_i, x_j)$. It is assumed that $s_{jj} = 0$ and $s_{ij} = s_{ji}$. Extending this notation if A and B are two clusters we shall let Dist(A, B) indicate the distance between these two clusters. We sometimes shall refer to this as the inter-cluster distance.

The basic step in the HAG clustering can now be formally described. Assume at some point in the clustering process we have q clusters, C_k for k = 1 to q. If $Dist[C_i*, C_j*] = Min_{ij}[Dist(C_i, C_j)]$ we select the clusters C_i* and C_j* to merge together. We shall call C_i* and C_j* the winning clusters.

We now focus on measuring the distance between two clusters. Let A and B be two clusters. In particular A and B are two disjoint subsets of X, $A \cap B = \varnothing$. We shall denote $A = \{y_1,..., y_{n_a}\}$ and $B = \{z_1,..., z_{n_b}\}$, here n_a and n_b are respectively the cardinality of A and B. Since we have assumed the availability of the matrix S we have the distance between any element in A and any any element in B, $Dist(y_i, z_j)$. In the following we let d_{ij} indicate the distance between y_i and z_j. We consider the question of obtaining Dist(A, B) from the d_{ij}.

Two methods which have been often used for calculating the distance between two clusters are the nearest and furthest neighbor rules. The nearest neighbor rule defines the inter-cluster distance as the distance between the elements in each of the two clusters that are nearest,

$$Dist[A, B] = Min_{y_i \in A \text{ and } z_j \in B}[d_{ij}].$$

The furthest neighbor rule defines the inter-cluster distance as the distance between the elements in each of the two clusters that are furthest,

$$Dist[A, B] = Max_{y_i \in A \text{ and } z_j \in B}[d_{ij}].$$

We shall for simplicity denote these as Min[A, B] and Max[A, B] respectively.

Whichever of these methods we are using we are looking for the two clusters that are closest. In this respect some useful general observations can be made about these two approaches. Using the Min method we see that if A and A' are two clusters such that $A \subset A'$ then for any B

$$Min[A, B] \geq Min[A', B]$$

Hence when using the Min inter-cluster distance measure the **more** elements in a cluster the more likely it is to be "nearer" to a neighboring cluster. This implies that this nearest neighbor clustering type approach tends to favor the formation of **big** clusters, at any point in the cluster merging process there is a propensity for the two largest clusters to unite. In this method there is an inclination for a few big clusters to form while the remaining elements will be in isolated small clusters.

Under the Max method if A and A' are two clusters such that $A \subset A'$ then for any other cluster B

$$Max[A, B] \leq Max[A', B]$$

The implications here is that the fewer the elements in the cluster the more likely it is to be "near" to a neighboring cluster. Here there is a tendency to form clusters of uniform size.

The two methods, the nearest and furthest neighbor method, can be seen as providing two extreme approaches to cluster aggregation. Another method, also commonly used is to calculate the distance between two clusters by taking the average of distances between the elements in the two clusters. Here

$$\text{Dist}[A, B] = \frac{1}{n_a}\frac{1}{n_b} \sum_{i \in A} \sum_{j \in B} d_{ij}$$

When using this method the number of elements in a cluster has no effect on the determination of Dist[A, B].

3. Inter-Cluster Distance Measures

To enable the development of computationally intelligent methods for performing hierarchical clustering we are interested in methods for controlling the process of merging clusters. Since the cluster merging process is greatly effected by the technique used to measure the distance between clusters an understanding and particularly the association of a semantics with different methods of measuring the distance between clusters will help enable us to implement HAG clustering guided by intelligent human-like imperatives.

We now look at the general issue of defining inter-cluster distance measures, Dist[A, B]. We begin by considering the properties required of such a function. The first property that we require is that the distance function be symmetric, Dist[A, B] = Dist[B, A]. A second requirement is that the proximity of two singleton clusters should be the proximity of the two individual elements. Thus if $A = \{y_1\}$ and $B = \{z_1\}$ then $\text{Dist}[A, B] = \text{Dist}(y_1, z_1) = d_{11}$. A third property is a kind of monotonicity. Assume $A = \{y_i, y_2, \quad , y_{n_a}\}$ and $\tilde{A} = \{\tilde{y}_1, \tilde{y}_2, \quad , \tilde{y}_{n_a}\}$ are two clusters containing all the same elements except the first. If $B = \{z_1, ..., z_{n_b}\}$ is another cluster such that $\tilde{y}_1$ is at least as closer to all the elements in B as y_1, $\text{Dist}[y_1, z_i] \geq \text{Dist}(\tilde{y}_1, z_i]$ for all i, then $\text{Dist}[A, B] \geq \text{Dist}[\tilde{A}, B]$, B is at least as close to $\tilde{A}$ as it is to A. We also require that the distance between the two clusters should be no smaller than the two closest elements, that is $\text{Dist}(A, B) \geq \text{Min}_{\substack{i \in A \\ j \in B}}[d_{ij}]$ and the distance between A and B should be no greater than the distance between the two furthest elements, $\text{Dist}(A, B) \leq \text{Max}_{\substack{i \in A \\ j \in B}}[d_{ij}]$.

The three examples of inter-cluster distance measure previously introduced, Max, Min and Average, satisfy these conditions. Actually the three methods can be seen as special examples of a more general class of methods available for defining the distances between clusters based on mean operators.

Definition: A mapping $M: R^n \to R$ is called a mean operator if it satisfies the following three properties

1. M is *symmetric*: the ordering of the arguments of M is irrelevant
2. M is *idempotent*: if $a_k = a$ for k then $M(a_1, a_2, ..., a_n) = a$
3. M is *monotonic*:

$$\text{if } a_k \geq b_k \text{ for all k then } M(a_1, a_2, \ldots\ldots, a_n) \geq M(b_1, b_2, \ldots\ldots, b_n)$$

We note that these three conditions imply a boundedness,

$$Min_k[a_k] \leq M_k[a_k] \leq Max_k[a_k].$$

Consider the use of these operators as inter-cluster distance measures. Let $A = \{y_1, y_2, \quad y_{na}\}$ and $B = \{z_1, z_2, \quad z_{n_b}\}$ be two clusters. Let $d_{ij} = Dist[y_i, z_j]$ and $D = <d_{ij}>$ indicates the collection of all the distances between the elements in A and B, the cardinality of D, $|D| = n_a \times n_b$. If M is a mean aggregation operator we say that Dist[A, B] is a mean type inter-cluster measure if Dist(A, B) = $M(< d_{ij}>)$. We note that for this type of measure the distance between clusters is dependent upon the distances between the elements in each of the clusters. The three properties associated with the mean operator reflect into appropriate properties for the cluster distance measure. Property one, symmetry, says that we make no distinction between any element pair distances, each d_{ij} is treated the same. Idempotency says that if all the pair distances have the same value this is the inter-cluster distance. The third condition implies a positive association between pair distances and cluster distance, an increase in pair distances can't decrease the cluster distances. Since the exact denotation of the elements formulating the d_{ij} plays no role in the calculation of $M(<d_{ij}>)$ at times we shall find it more convenient to use a single subscript to indicate the components in the aggregation, d_k.

There exists one issue that requires discussion with respect to the use of mean type inter–cluster distance measures, it is the issue of consistency [3]. At any level of iteration, when using the cluster distance function, we must aggregate over many different number of arguments. When measuring the distance between clusters C_1 and C_2 we may have to aggregate $n_1 \times n_2$ distances while when measuring the distance between C_3 and C_4 we may have to aggregate $n_3 \times n_4$ distances. Thus when defining an inter cluster distance in terms of a mean operator we must provide a version to work for each different number of arguments, essentially we are defining a group of measures, $M_1, M_2, M_3, \ldots., M_n$ in which M_q is the operation used for combining q arguments. The ability to provide these aggregation operators, which are defined over the different argument cardinalities, in an consistent manner is important in providing meaningful comparisons of inter-cluster distances..

A useful property for the construction of aggregation operators over different argument cardinalities is associativity [4]. Associativity enables one to define an aggregation operators in terms of a binary operation and then uniquely extend it to the aggregation of any number of arguments. Specifically if R is an associative operator, R(a, b, c) = R(a, R(b,c)) = R(R(a, b), c). Associativity provides a unified way of defining aggregations over different argument cardinalities. The operations of addition and multiplication are associative.

Unfortunately, except in the special cases of Max and Min, operators that are idempotent are not associative. [4] Thus in the general case of mean operators we don't have associativity and we must look elsewhere to provide consistency between the distance measure at different cardinalities.

4. Generalized Mean Based Cluster Distance Measures

One whole class of consistently extendable mean operators are the generalized mean operators [5]. The generalized mean is defined as

$$G_\alpha(d_1, \quad , d_n) = \left(\frac{1}{n} \sum_{k=1}^{n} d_k{}^\alpha\right)^{\frac{1}{\alpha}}$$

where $\alpha \in [-\infty, \infty]$ is a parameter which determines a specific member of this family. Some special members of this family are Min operator ($\alpha = -\infty$), Harmonic mean ($\alpha = -1$), Geometric mean ($\alpha = 0$), Arithmetic mean ($\alpha = 1$), Euclidian Mean ($\alpha = 2$) and Max Operator ($\alpha = \infty$). Thus using this class of operators we have a whole family of ways for defining the inter-cluster distance by choosing a value α.

For the generalized means there exists a monotonicity with respect to the α value, for $\alpha_1 \geq \alpha_2$, $G_{\alpha_1}(d_1, \ldots\ldots, d_n) \geq G_{\alpha_2}(d_1, \ldots\ldots, d_n)$. Another property that is associated with the generalized mean is the centering property [6], this property says is that if we add some element to the aggregation then the aggregation should either remain the same or move in the direction of this element. Implicit in this is the property called <u>self identity</u>, if $e = G_\alpha(d_1, \ldots\ldots, d_n)$ then $G_\alpha(d_1, \ldots\ldots, d_n, e) = e$. What is clear is that choice α affects the determination of the distance between clusters. The implication of this is that the selection of α will have an effect on the process of merging clusters. The effect of α is essentially on determining which clusters will be the winning clusters.

When $\alpha = -\infty$, $G_\alpha(d_1, \ldots\ldots, d_n) = \mathrm{Min}_i[d_i]$, as we already noted when using the Min measure the more arguments being aggregated the smaller the aggregation. The implication here is that a cluster with a large number of members will have a propensity to be a cluster that is nearest another cluster. With the Min large clusters will tend to be the winning clusters.

When $\alpha = \infty$, $G_\alpha(d_1, \ldots., d_n) = \mathrm{Max}_i[d_i]$. In this case the more arguments being aggregated the larger the aggregation, the less arguments the smaller the aggregation. The implication here is that clusters with smaller number of members will have a propensity to be "nearer" other clusters. Thus small clusters will tend to be winning clusters when using the Max. For the case when $\alpha = 1$, $G_\alpha(d_1, \ldots\ldots, d_n) = \frac{1}{n} \sum_{k=1}^{n} d_k$. In this case the cluster size doesn't effect aggregation.

In the preceding we have observed a useful relationship between α and the merging process, as α increases there exists a propensity for smaller clusters to be winning clusters while as α decreases larger clusters become more favorable to be winning clusters. Thus the selection of α is going to significantly effect the process of growing clusters in this HAG method. The general effect here is that, the smaller α, the more likely it is a cluster containing many members will be the winning cluster, while for larger α the tendency is for smaller size clusters to be the winning cluster. Thus as α goes from $-\infty$ to ∞, the process of cluster merging is one going from a propensity of big clusters being a winning cluster to small clusters being the winning cluster.

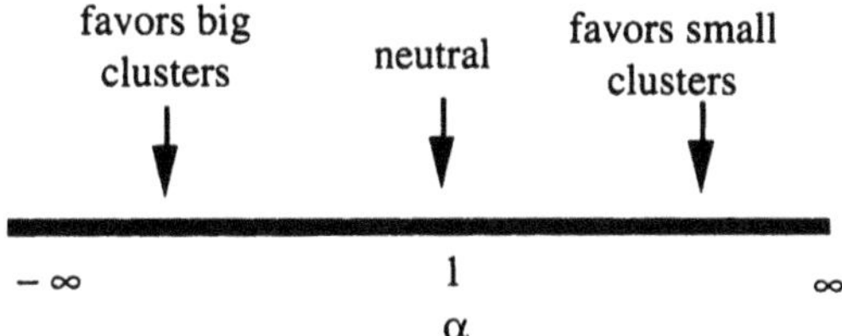

Figure #1 Cluster size preference

5. Functionally Generated Cluster Distance Measures

There exists another class of consistent mean operators, related to the OWA operators [7], that can be used to obtain inter–cluster distance measures. In this class each operator is characterized by a mapping $f:[0, 1] \rightarrow [0, 1]$ such that:: $f(0) = 0$, $f(1) = 1$ and $f(x) \geq f(y)$ if $x > y$. We call these **B**asic **U**nit-interval **M**onotonic (BUM) functions.

Using these functions we can define the mean operator over different cardinalities of aggregates in a consistent manner. Using a BUM function f we obtain an OWA aggregation function

$$F_f(d_1, \ldots\ldots, d_n) = W^T B$$

where B is an n dimensional vector in which b_j is the jth largest of d_i and W is also an n vector in which $w_j = f(\frac{j}{n}) - f(\frac{j-1}{n})$.

This operator is clearly parameterized by the choice of f. Different choices of f lead to different properties of the resulting inter-cluster distance measure. Let us look at the properties associated with different selections of f. First we shall introduce a useful perspective in which to view the different functions. We shall say $f_1 \geq f_2$ if for each x, $f_1(x) \geq f_2(x)$.

Consider first the BUM function f^* defined by $f^*(0) = 0$ and $f^*(x) = 1$ for all $x \neq 0$. It can be shown that for any BUM function f it is the case that $f^* \geq f$, f^* is the maximal BUM function. Using this BUM function we get $w_1 = 1$ and $w_j = 0$ and hence $F_{f^*}(d_1, \ldots, d_n) = Max_j[d_j]$. Thus f^* gives Max as the inter cluster distance measure.

On the other hand, if we define f_* as $f_*(1) = 1$ and $f_*(x) = 0$ for $x \neq 1$ then for all f, $f_* \leq f$. Using this BUM function we get $w_n = 1$ and $w_j = 0$ for all $j \neq n$. In this case $F_{f_*}(d_1, \ldots, d_n) = Min_j[d_j]$. Thus f_* gives Min as the inter cluster distance measure.

For the case when $f(x) = x$ we get that $w_j = \frac{1}{n}$. In this case

$f_f(d_1, ..., d_n) = \frac{1}{n}\Sigma_j d_j$,

it is the average The three standard cluster distance measures are also in this class.

The following theorem provides an important relationship with respect to this type of operators.

Theorem: If f and $\hat{f}$ are two BUM functions such that $f \geq \hat{f}$ then for all arguments

$$F_f(d_1, ..., d_n) \geq F_{\hat{f}}(d_1, ..., d_n).$$

Depending upon the function f we get different types of aggregation; different forms for the inter cluster distance measure. We have already indicated three members of this class, let us look at some other ones. Consider the function f where $f(x) = 0$ for $x < 0.5$ and $f(x) = 1$ for $x \geq 0.5$. In this case when n is even we get $w_{n/2} = 1$ and $w_j = 0$ for $j \neq \frac{n}{2}$. While if n is odd we get $w_{\frac{n+1}{2}} = 1$ and $w_j = 0$ for all others. Using this the inter-cluster distance measure is the median of the distances between the individual elements in the two clusters.

Another example of a BUM function, one which can be seen as a generalization of the median, is $f(x) = 0$ for $x < \alpha$ and $f(x) = 1$ for $x \geq \alpha$. In this case $w_j = 1$ for the index j where $n\alpha + 1 \geq j \geq n\alpha$. In this case we taking as our aggregated value the argument such that α portion of the arguments are below this value. In the case of the median we are taking the argument value such that half the argument values are below it. Actually this can as generating a family of cluster distance measures, parameterized by α, where when $\alpha = 0$ we get the Min, when $\alpha = 0.5$ we get the Median and when $\alpha = 1$ we get the Max.

Another BUM function is the function f where $f(0) = 0$. $f(x) = \alpha$ for $0 < x < 1$ and $f(1) = 1$. In this case $w_1 = \alpha$, $w_n = 1 - \alpha$ and $w_j = 0$ for all other j. The resulting aggregation operator is $F_f(d_1, ..., d_n) = \alpha \, Max_j[d_j] + (1 - \alpha)Min_j[d_j]$. It is a weighted average of the maximal and minimal distances.

Different selections of BUM function lead to different manifestations of inter-cluster distance measure. This in turn will lead to different final clustering of the data. With this in mind it becomes imperative to try to understand the effect of the selection of f on the process of cluster formation.

The Min inter-cluster distance measure leads to a situation in which there exists a propensity for big clusters to be winning clusters. The Max inter-cluster distance measure leads to a situation in which smaller clusters have more of a propensity to be winning clusters. The average measure of inter-cluster distance is one in which the number of elements in a cluster doesn't effect its propensity to be a winning cluster. We also note that for a median type inter-cluster distance measure, as in the case of the average, the number of elements in a cluster doesn't affect its propensity to be a winning cluster.

As we have also previously indicated the function f_*, which is the smallest BUM function, induces the Min distance measure. The function f^*, which is the largest BUM function, is the one that induces the Max distance measure and the average lies midway between these. Thus we see that there exists an ordering over the class of BUM functions with respect to their propensity to favor small or large clusters in the cluster merging process, if $f_1 > f_2$ then f_1 has more of a propensity then f_2 to favor smaller clusters as winning clusters.

As an aid in characterizing these BUM generated inter-cluster distance measures we introduce a measure of *Propensity* associated with a BUM function,

$$Propensity(f) = 1 - 2\ Area(f).$$

where $Area(f) = \int_0^1 f(x)dx$. Consider the function f_*, which induces the Min aggregation and favors large clusters. For this function $Area(f_*) = 0$ and hence $Propensity(f_*) = 1$. For the function f^*, which induces the Max inter-cluster distance measure and favors small clusters we have $Area(f^*) = 1$ and hence $Propensity(f^*) = -1$. Since these provide the bounding functions, $Propensity(f) \in [-1, 1]$, where the bigger the value the more the propensity to favor larger clusters in the merging process. Consider now $f(x) = x$, which generates the simple average and is neutral with respect the size of the clusters formed. The Area under this function is $\frac{1}{2}$, and hence $Propensity(f) = 0$, reflecting its neutrality. Consider the parameterized family of BUM functions where $f(0) = 0$, $f(x) = \alpha$, $0 < x < 1$ and $f(x) = 1$. For this family the we have $Area(f) = \alpha$, hence $Propensity(f) = 1 - 2\alpha$. We note that for the median, which is a member of this class with $\alpha = 0.5$ we get $Propensity(f) = 1 - 2\alpha = 0$.

Consider the family $f(x) = x^r$ where $r \in [0, \infty]$. It can be shown that $Area(x^r) = \frac{1}{r+1}$ and hence $Propensity(x^r) = 1 - 2\frac{1}{r+1}$.. We see as r moves from zero, Max aggregation, to infinity, Min Aggregation, our measure $Propensity(x^r)$ moves from -1 to 1 and in the case where r = 1, the average, it assumes as desired the value zero

In figure # 2 we show the BUM functions that generate the average and median type aggregation operators. It is easily shown that both these functions have the same area, the same *propensity*. However, there exists a fundamental distinction between these two aggregation operators. In the case of the average, the aggregation uses all the arguments while in the case of the median only one value is being used to determine the aggregated value. We see that the median is more brittle in that it depends on only one value while the average can be seen as providing a smoother or softer aggregation. In order to try to capture this type of distinction between operators and provide some additional characterization for the associated aggregation methods let us look further at the situation. A feature that seems to characterize the distinction between the median and average aggregation is a dissymmetry between the weights used in the aggregation process. In the case of the average all the weights are the same while for the median all the allotted weight is assigned to one component.

In [7] Yager suggested a tool for measuring this distinction which he called the entropy. In particular if the weights of the aggregation are w_j then he suggested using $\sum_{j=1}^{n} w_j \ln(w_j)$ to classify aggregations along this dimensions. While the entropy measure suggested by Yager works well it is defined in terms of the weights and not directly in terms of the underlying BUM function. Since the weights are related to the

BUM function by $w_j = f(\frac{j}{n}) - f(\frac{j-1}{n})$ we can calculate this entropy measure for any function f at any cardinality n. However our more global goal is to try to understand this characteristic directly in terms of the BUM function.

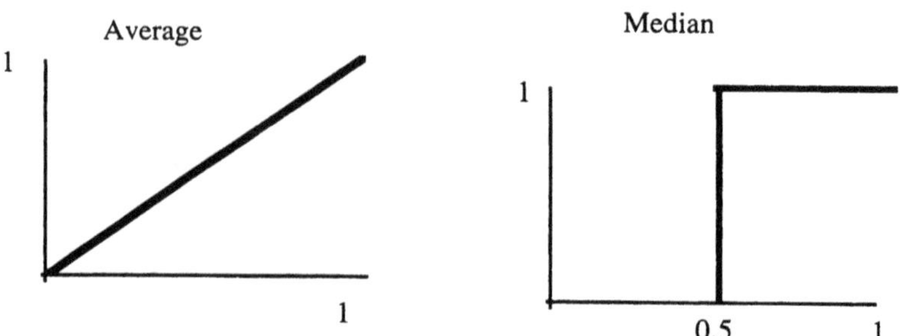

Figure #2. Average and Median generating functions

In figure # 2 we show the BUM functions that generate the average and median. What appears to be at the heart of the distinction between the average and median aggregations is related to the <u>derivative</u> of the underlying functions. At a first level the function representing the median has a discontinuity while the average has no discontinuity. More generally we see that the larger the derivative the more weight will be assigned to one element.

One preliminary approach we can suggest to capture this idea is based upon use of the maximum of the derivative. Thus for continuous functions if we use Max $\frac{\partial f(x)}{\partial x}$ we get some indication in the sense that the larger this maximum derivative the more weight we push to one element. For discontinuous functions the height of the largest discontinuity is some indication of this property.

There exists a unified way we can look at this class of aggregation type functions which helps accent the role of the derivative and may aid in the development of the characterization we seek. Let f be a BUM function, and let $\frac{df(x)}{dx}$ indicate its derivative Using this we can express

$$F_f(d_1, ..., d_n) = \int_0^1 G(x)\, df(x) = \int_0^1 G(x) \frac{df(x)}{dx} dx$$

where G(x) is a function, G: I → R, defined on the unit interval by

$$G(x) = b_j \qquad \text{for } \frac{j-1}{n} < x \le \frac{j}{n}$$

where b_j is the jth largest of the d_i and j = 1 to n. G is monotonically non-increasing, $G(x_1) \ge G(x_2)$ if $x_2 \ge x_1$

We note that this can be used even when f is discontinuous. If f is discontinuous at x = a with discontinuity Δ, we define $f'(a) = \Delta\delta(x - \alpha)$ where δ is the Dirac delta function. The dirac delta function has the property that

$$\int_{a^-}^{a^+} G(x)\, \delta(x - a)\, dx = G(a).$$

6. Dynamically Controlling the Clustering Process

As we have indicated in the preceding there exists a relationship between the choice of cluster distance measure and the propensity of the clustering algorithm for favoring large or small clusters as the winning clusters. This situation allows one to consider the possibility of controlling the clustering process by approximate selection of the inter-cluster distance measure. While a predetermined choice of one inter–cluster distance clearly offers some control over the clustering process a more interesting possibility is to dynamically change the inter-cluster distance measure as we move through the clustering process. This will of course offer us a fine control over the clustering process. In order to accomplish this we can make use of fuzzy systems modeling [6] to dynamically build our inter-cluster distance function based on information available at the time the measurement of distance between clusters is being performed.

In the following we shall describe one example of the use of fuzzy systems modeling to construct an inter-cluster distance measure. In this example we shall determine a distinct inter–cluster distance measure for each pair of clusters. Let A and B be two arbitrary clusters, we shall denote Dist(A, B), as the distance between these two clusters, this is the function we are trying to obtain. Let V_1 and V_2 indicate the cardinalities of A and B respectively. Let V indicate the cardinality of A plus B, it is the number of elements that would be in a cluster formed by merging these two clusters. We let d_j for $j = 1$ to $V_1\ V_2$, be the collection of inter element distances, that is $d_j = \text{dist}(x_i, x_k)$ for some $x_i \in A$ and $x_k \in B$. Let *E* and *F* be linguistic concepts corresponding to possible values for V, the number of elements in the union of A and B. For example, these could be concepts like *at least q*, *about five*, *many* or *few*. These concepts can be expressed as fuzzy subsets of the set $\mathbf{n} = \{0, 1, \quad , n\}$, where n is the total number of elements to be clustered. Using concepts of this type we can consider a specification of our inter-cluster distance measure in the form

if V is *E* then $\text{Dist(A,B)} = \text{Min}_j[d_j]$

if V is *F* then $\text{Dist(A,B)} = \text{Max}_j[d_j]$

Here we are saying if the cluster resulting from merging A and B will have *E* elements then use the Min inter-cluster distance measure and if the resulting cluster will have *F* elements then use the Max inter-cluster distance measure. If the value of V is q then using the inference mechanism of fuzzy systems modeling [6] we get as our inter cluster distance measure

$$\text{Dist(A, B)} = \frac{E(q)\ \text{Min}_j[d_j] + F(q)\ \text{Max}_j[d_j]}{E(q) + F(q)},$$

where E and F are the fuzzy subsets representing the concepts *E* and *F*. Here we see that the measure we use is a function of the number of elements in $A \cup B$, V, it depends upon the clusters whose distance is being measured.

If we let U = V/n, the proportion of the total elements , we can express *E* and *F* as proportional type linguistic terms and represent E and F as fuzzy subsets of the unit interval. That is, we can use terms such as *about half, most* and *at least a quarter.* It is often the case that using these proportional quantifiers is easier.

Consider now a situation in which we want a clustering of the objects that results in four clusters of "about equal size" and uses, whenever possible, a nearest neighbor distance measure. We can accomplish this using our control mechanism. Let E be a fuzzy subset of the unit interval corresponding to *about a quarter at most* . In this case, if A and B are any clusters and U is the proportion of the number of objects to be in the cluster that is the union of A and B, $U = \frac{\text{Card}(A \cup B)}{n}$, then the cluster measure is defined as

$$\text{If } U \textit{ is } E \text{ then } \text{Dist}(A, B) = \text{Min}_j[d_j]$$

$$\text{If } U \textit{ is } \bar{E} \text{ then } \text{Dist}(A, B) = \text{Max}_j[d_j]$$

If V = q then using the fuzzy systems modeling we get

$$\text{Dist}(A, B) = E(q)\,\text{Min}_j[d_j] + (1 - E(q))\,\text{Max}_j[d_j]$$

In this model p indicates a size of clusters, defined in terms of a proportion of the elements to be clustered, which we don't want to exceed and p - 0.25 can be viewed as our slack in the concept "about equal."

We can consider a case in which we have m primary or basic cluster distance measures, $D_1, D_2, \ldots\ldots, D_m$. Let our effective inter-cluster distance measure be made of some combination of these as expressed by the specifications

$$\text{If } U \textit{ is } E_j \text{ then } \text{Dist}(A, B) = D_j(A, B) \qquad j = 1 \text{ to } m.$$

In this case for U = q we get $$\text{Dist}(A, B) = \frac{\sum_{j=1}^{m} E_j(q)\, D_j(A, B)}{\sum_{j=1}^{m} E_j(q)}$$

An interesting related formulation could be based upon use of the generalized mean. We recall that the generalized mean is characterized by the parameter $\alpha \in [-\infty, \infty]$, however for all intents and purposes we can restrict $\alpha \in [-20, 20]$. We can consider a description of our distance function in terms of the α value. Thus we can have for j = 1 to m

$$\text{If } U \textit{ is } E_j \text{ then } \alpha = \alpha_j$$

If in the case of measuring the distance between the clusters A and B value of U = q we obtain α as

$$\alpha^* = \frac{\sum_{j=1}^{m} E_j(q)\, \alpha_j}{\sum_{j=1}^{m} E_j(q)}$$

Using this we can get our particular inter cluster distance measure Dist(A, B), which would be a generalized mean with parameter α^*. It should be emphasized that the distance measures obtained are specific to a pair of clusters, that is each pair of clusters would have a different α^*.

In the preceding we have essentially considered controlling the inter-cluster distance measure solely based upon the number of elements that would be contained in the resulting merged cluster. Using this allows us to implement different agenda's for cluster formation based upon our observation that different distance measures tend to favor different cardinalities as being the winning cluster. We can introduce an even further degree of control by using more information. Consider the clusters $A = \{x_1, x_2\}$ and $B = \{z_1, z_2, z_3\}$ the merging of these clusters will lead to a cluster C with five elements. If the cardinality of the merged cluster is a size we want to encourage then we can use a Min type aggregation, as this will lead to a smaller cluster distance and increase the chances that A and B are the closest clusters. Hence we may have a rule that says

If V is "about five" then use Dist = Min.

Consider now the two clusters $A' = \{x_1\}$ and $B' = \{z_1, z_2, z_3, z_4\}$, the merging of these two clusters will also result in a cluster of size five. Hence it will also fire the rule above. However, there exists a distinction between these two situations, in the first case we have six, 3 * 2, inter-element distances while in the second case we have only four. As we have indicated the Min has a propensity to favor aggregations with many elements. This leads us to consider the possibility of additionally using the number of arguments as a control variable. Thus with V_1 and V_2 respectively being the number of elements in each the clusters whose inter cluster distance is being calculated and $V = V_1 + V_2$ we can let $W = V_1 \bullet V_2$, the number element distance pairs. In this case we can consider rules of the form

If V is E_j **and** W is F_j then $\text{Dist}(A, B) = D_j(A, B)$

when D_j is some standard distance measure. Here then we are controlling the structure of the effective inter-cluster distance measure as a function of both V and U. In this case with V = q and W = r we get

$$\text{Dist}(A, B) = \frac{\sum_{j=1}^{m} E_j(q)\, F_j(r) D_j(A, B)}{\sum_{j=1}^{m} E_j(q)\, F_j(r)}$$

Another parameter that could be used to control the cluster merging process is the number of clusters existing at the current stage of the process which is usually closely related to the inverse of the index of the iteration step as each iteration reduces the number of clusters by one. This allows the possibility for globally setting a distance measure for each stage of the iteration with a rule of the type

if its early in the iteration process then use ....

This iteration stage parameter can also be used in combination with other characteristics to control the process based upon some property over all the clusters over all the clusters at the current stage. For example, if it is early in the iteration process and we have a large cluster we may want to use a Max distance measure so as to give other clusters a chance to form. This can be expressed as a the specification

if the iteration stage is *early* and there exists a *large* cluster then D = Max

We note that if at a particular iteration stage we have m clusters each with cardinality n_j and L is the fuzzy subset corresponding to *large* then the degree to which we have a large cluster is $Max_j[L(n_j)]$. We further note that the concept of large cluster can be dependent upon the iteration step.

7. Conclusion

The the basic process of hierarchical agglomerative clustering was described. The significance of the role cluster distance measure in the determination of resulting clusters was pointed out. We noted a fundamental distinction between the nearest neighbor cluster distance measure, Min, and the furthest neighbor measure, Max. The first favors the merging of large clusters while the later favors the merging of smaller clusters. We discussed a family of inter-cluster distance measures, the generalized mean, which was shown to be parameterized along a scale characterizing their preference for merging larger or smaller clusters. We then showed how this distinction between distance measures can be used as a way of controlling the hierarchical clustering process. Combining this with fuzzy systems modeling we saw the emergence of a tool to add human like control to the clustering process.

8. References

[1]. Sokal, R. R. and Sneath, P. H. A., Principles of Numerical Taxonomy, W. H. Freeman: San Francisco, 1963.

[2]. Duda, R. O., Hart, P. E. and Stork, D. G., Pattern Classification, Wiley Interscience: New York, 2001.

[3]. Yager, R. R., "On mean type aggregation," IEEE Transactions on Systems, Man and Cybernetics 26, 209-221, 1996.

[4]. Dubois, D. and Prade, H., "A review of fuzzy sets aggregation connectives," Information Sciences 36, 85 - 121, 1985.

[5]. Dyckhoff, H. and Pedrycz, W., "Generalized means as model of compensative connectives," Fuzzy Sets and Systems 14, 143-154, 1984.

[6]. Yager, R. R. and Filev, D. P., Essentials of Fuzzy Modeling and Control, John Wiley: New York, 1994.

[7]. Yager, R. R., "On ordered weighted averaging aggregation operators in multi-criteria decision making," IEEE Transactions on Systems, Man and Cybernetics 18, 183-190, 1988.

Combining Both a Fuzzy Inductive Learning and a Fuzzy Repertory Grid Method

J.L. Castro, J.J. Castro-Schez*, J.M. Zurita

Dpto. Ciencias de la Computación e I.A.
E.T.S.I. Informática. Universidad de Granada
Avenida de Andalucía, 38, 18071 Granada
castro@decsai.ugr.es zurita@decsai.ugr.es

*Dpto. Informática
Escuela Universitaria de Informática.
Universidad de Castilla-La Mancha
Ronda de Calatrava, 5, 13071 Ciudad Real
jjcastro@inf-cr.uclm.es

Abstract

In this paper we describe a new approach to the problem of management of the inconsistency in expert systems which can be used for acquiring knowledge. The method proposed is used for planning interviews with the domain expert. The validation method searches for inconsistent areas in the knowledge base and asks the expert questions with the aim of resolving the conflict present in these areas. The questions asked will depend on the area in which the inconsistency arises.

1 Introduction

The knowledge acquisition step in the design of knowledge-based systems is one of the more difficult activities faced by knowledge engineers. The expert's inaccessibility, the different terminology employed by both the knowledge engineer and the expert, the expert's difficulty in transmitting his knowledge, incorrect translations carried out by the knowledge engineer from the knowledge acquired into operational forms and the performance of incomplete immediate analysis on the knowledge acquired for continuing to interview the expert, all of the latter complicate the acquisition stage.

We have developed a technique (*Castro*[3]) that reduces the *different terminology problem*. This technique is useful in decision and classification problems. We acquire the concepts, attributes and their domains and possible or used values that are employed by the expert, and a set of very general rules that model the way the expert reasons, by means of a fuzzy repertory grid.

There is an important requirement when knowledge is acquired from the expert and that is that both the knowledge engineer and the expert understand the chosen representation. Moreover, this representation must allow the expert to express himself as he usually does. The expert must never be forced to express his knowledge according to a representation that is not natural for him. In this sense, we have proposed a representation that allows the inclusion and management of various types of knowledge. The taxonomy of the knowledge used by the expert when he expresses his experience may be seen in Figure 2.

We have suggested the trapezoidal fuzzy membership function (see Figure 1) for representing any value shown in Figure 2.

$$\Pi(u;a,b,c,d)=\begin{cases}0 & u<a,\\ (u-a)/(b-a) & a\le u<b,\\ 1 & b\le u\le c,\\ (d-u)/(d-c) & c<u\le d,\\ 0 & u>d.\end{cases}$$

Figure 1. Trapezoidal fuzzy membership function.

With the technique based on the fuzzy repertory grid we obtain three sets, which are V, DDV and R_g. With V being $\{v_1,v_2,v_3,...\}$ the set of variables employed by the expert for deciding or classifying, DDV being $\{DDV_1,DDV_2,DDV_3,...\}$ the set of fuzzy sets describing each variable belonging to V and with R_g being $\{R_1,R_2,R_3,...,R_m\}$ the set of rules that identify the evident knowledge from the expert.

Each $DDV_i \in DDV$ is defined as the set $DDV_i=\{(a_1,b_1,c_1,d_1),(a_2,b_2,c_2,d_2),...\}$ and it contains all possible values that can take the v_i variable.

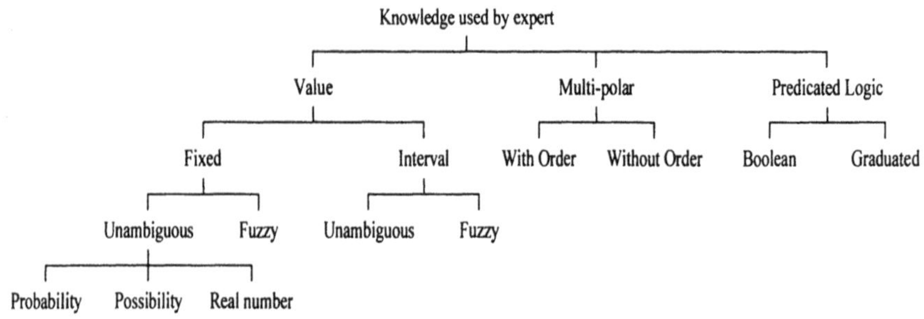

Figure 2. Expert's knowledge taxonomy.

In *Castro*[4] we developed a machine learning technique that resolves the *expert's inaccessibility problem* and reduces the *expert's difficulty for transmitting his knowledge problem.* Organisations are always ready to provide the knowledge engineer with a set of the expert's past actions, which shows the way the expert reasons.

Moreover, there are cases in which the expert is not able to totally explain his way of performing, i.e., the processes or heuristic which leads to solving the problem because the expert will provide a set of examples. The knowledge engineer analyses this set and attains general conclusions from specific examples. We propose a machine learning technique for doing this work.

The suggested algorithm of inductive machine learning suggested basically is made up by two stages. In the first stage, a set of very particular rules is constructed from a set of examples. After this, in the second stage those particular rules are generalised yielding a set of general rules. This algorithm divides the domains of the input variables into fuzzy regions, here we propose not making such a division and making use of the set DDV obtained by means of the fuzzy repertory grid-based technique. The generalisation rule process consists of adding to each variable of the rule v_i those values from DDV_i that yet have must not been considered for v_i in the rule when it will be possible.

This suggested technique, as with any other machine learning technique, acquires some knowledge but not enough knowledge for building knowledge-based systems. From now on, the knowledge engineer must analyse the rules obtained by the machine learning technique and fuzzy repertory grid-based technique for planning future interviews with the domain expert designed to obtain a complete knowledge base.

In this paper, we propose a validation technique as a method for combining both fuzzy inductive learning and a fuzzy repertory grid method. The suggested technique will be a very efficient mechanism for performing an immediate analysis on the acquired knowledge with the aim of asking the expert more interesting questions for acquiring a complete knowledge base.

2 Validation

There is a fundamental problem during the process of building knowledge-based systems, and that is the problem of finding and resolving potential inconsistencies. The search for inconsistencies is a time-consuming process that often cannot be applied to real-life applications. Many surveys on the detection of inconsistent inputs and inconsistency handling have been described in the literature. The state-of-the-art for this problem is represented by:

1. Approaches that search inconsistency by means of comparisons of two rules. For instance, the CHECK system [8] checks for contradictory conclusions by comparing rules two-by-two.

2. Approaches that search for inconsistency not only between two rules but an arbitrary number of rules. To do so, they compute and explore the deductive closure of a rule base.

   2.1. COVADIS [9] computes the deductive closure by forward chaining and checks whether this set violates one or more integrity constraints. The cost of using such a strategy increases exponentially with the number of rules. This approach does not solve the problem of validating knowledge-based systems with uncertainty.

   2.2. *Larsen-Nonfjall* approach [6] for knowledge bases with uncertainty, it is modelled by the possibility necessity measure and is very similar to the COVADIS system. This approach requires less computation since it searches for γ**-inconsistency* in the knowledge base with γ^* being the effective lower bound for the belief of $\perp$ in the knowledge base. Thus, it yields a controlled way to reason with a consistent part of knowledge base. Moreover, it is suitable for handling the more general knowledge base from represented by Horn clause bases.

   2.3. *Yager-Larsen* approach [11] for knowledge bases with uncertainty for a number of different basic uncertainty calculus. They propose that the existence of potential conflicts in a database may be obtained by making a kind of backward inference in the knowledge base (the authors called this act *reflecting on the input*). The suggested methodology uses various uncertainty representations (Possibilistic logic, Probabilistic environment, and Fuzzy logic). Moreover, they present a general model for uncertainty qualification.

3. Approaches that search for inconsistency in an arbitrary number of rules. They do so by computing and exploring the deductive closure of each element in an incompatibility base.

   Castro-Trillas approach [1] reducing the validation problem to the capture of the deductive closure of the incompatibilities introduced by the expert, each possible incompatibility will be an element in an *incompatibility base*. This incompatibility base will be provided for the domain expert by means of a set of facts, which cannot be simultaneously true.

   Other non-logical conflicts are presented in *Castro-Trillas-Zurita* approach [2] where the detection of potential conflicts is reduced to the capture of the deductive closure of the conflicts base. Input will be problematic if and only if it is in the deductive closure of the conflicts base.

The validation approach suggested in this paper also searches for inconsistencies in an arbitrary number of rules and it is employed in decision or classification problems. Our knowledge base is constituted by rules that do not have deductible facts in its antecedent part. The principal role in the suggested approach corresponds to the conflicting areas, which are general inputs in which inconsistency is produced. The validation system searches in inconsistent areas for the rules that operate on those areas and the facts that can be deduced in those areas. The expert must resolve the problem that there is in this area bearing in mind the conflict in its totality, in a co-ordinated manner. This is the main difference with the approaches developed until now, which consider the base of facts as the mechanism that allows us to find the inconsistency present in the knowledge base and handle particular inconsistencies in the knowledge base. Moreover, the suggested method carries out a validation on a knowledge base that merges various kinds of knowledge (see Figure 2) though all kinds will be dealt with as if they were fuzzy. Another advantage of the proposed method is its condition of *incremental*, that is we assure that once a rule has been validated this will never be validated again in its present level. Since each inconsistency found is resolved in an independent resolution module.

3 A validation method useful in the knowledge acquisition stage

We intend to acquire a set of rules that model the way the expert performs in a decision or classification problem. For doing it, we have the collaboration of the expert and a set of examples that shows the way in which he acted in similar situations in the past. In the following section, we show the starting point for our validation method, since this is very important for understanding the way in which our validation method performs.

3.1 Working environment

Let us suppose a very simple example, we want to decide or distinguish a set of three different classes $\{O_1,O_2,O_3\}$. We intend to acquire the knowledge that the expert uses for deciding between or classifying these different outputs and to represent them by means of a set of rules. Let us suppose that we can distinguish or decide among the three classes mentioned above making use of only two variables. Let us look at the structure of rules with which the validation system works and the problems that can appear between the rules obtained from this *two-dimensional* space.

We have obtained the variables v_1 and v_2 and their sets DDV_1 and DDV_2, which are made up by: $DDV_1=\{E_1,E_2,E_3\}$ y $DDV_2=\{E_1',E_2',E_3'\}$ where each E_i and E_i' is a fuzzy set defined by means of a four value membership function, (i.e. $E_i=(a,b,c,d)$).

We recall that $V=\{v_1,v_2\}$ and $DDV=\{DDV_1,DDV_2\}$ are obtained making use of a fuzzy repertory grid-based technique. We have also obtained the R_1' rule by means of the fuzzy repertory grid-based technique. The rule R_1' is the following:
R_1': If v_2 is E_3' then O_3

Let us suppose that the expert or organisation to which he belongs gives us the set of examples shown in Figure 3. If we run the fuzzy inductive learning algorithm over this set of examples we obtain the following set of general rules:

R_1: If v_1 is $\{E_1,E_2\}$ and v_2 is $\{E_1'\}$ then O_1.
R_2: If v_1 is $\{E_2,E_3\}$ and v_2 is $\{E_1'\}$ then O_2.
R_3: If v_1 is $\{E_1,E_2\}$ and v_2 is $\{E_2',E_3'\}$ then O_3.
R_4: If v_1 is $\{E_2,E_3\}$ and v_2 is $\{E_2'\}$ then O_1.

	E_1'	E_2'	E_3'
E_1	O_1	O_3	
E_2			O_3
E_3	O_2	O_1	

Figure 3. Set of examples.

As we can verify, the rules obtained have a tendency to absorb inputs in which there is no response about its belonging to one class or another.

In Figure 4 we show in an illustrated manner all the rules acquired after applying the fuzzy inductive learning algorithm and the fuzzy repertory grid-based technique.

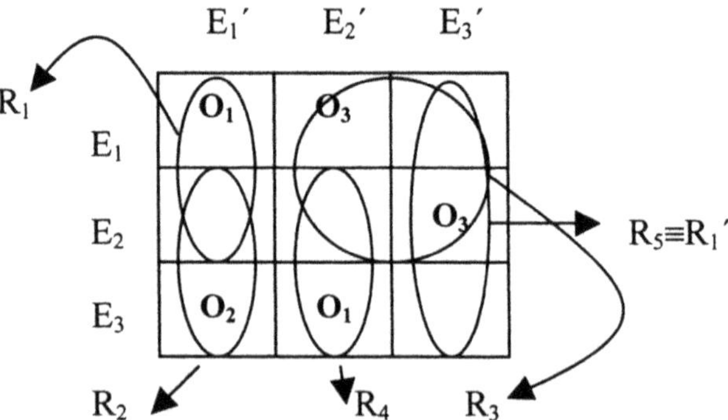

Figure 4. Rules acquired using both methods.

As we can verify by studying the set of rules obtained R_g or in a more illustrated manner by means of Figure 4, we have two conflicting areas (E_2,E_1') and (E_2,E_2'), that is to say, two inconsistencies. We are not able to decide when the input of the system is $v_1=E_2$ and $v_2=E_1'$or E_2'.

If these problems occur in a *two*-dimensional space they will also occur in an *n*-dimensional space. Moreover, the greater the number of variables and values employed by the domain expert that is the dimension space, the larger the conflicting areas and the greater their number. In a four-dimensional space (*Iris Plants Database*[5]) we can find conflicting areas such as the following:

({HN,MN,SN,Z,SP,MP,HP},{HN,MN,SN,Z,SP,MP,HP},{HN,MN,SN,Z,MP},{SP})

Where the definition domain sets DDV_1, DDV_2, DDV_3 and DDV_4 are made up by:

DDV_1={HN,MN,SN,Z,SP,MP,HP}={(4.3,4.3,4.75,5.2),(4.75,5.2,5.2,5.65),(5.2,5.65,5.65,6.1),(5.65,6.1,6.1,6.55),(6.1,6.55,6.55,7),(6.55,7,7,7.45),(7,7.45,7.9,7.9)}

DDV_2={HN,MN,SN,Z,SP,MP,HP}={(2,2,2.3,2.6),(2.3,2.6,2.6,2.9),(2.6,2.9,2.9,3.2),(2.9,3.2,3.2,3.5),(3.2,3.5,3.5,3.8),(3.5,3.8,3.8,4.1),(3.8,4.1,4.4,4.4)}

DDV_3={HN,MN,SN,Z,SP,MP,HP}={(1,1,1.74,2.47),(1.74,2.47,2.47,3.21),(2.47,3.21,3.21,3.95),(3.21,3.95,3.95,4.68),(3.95,4.68,4.68,5.42),(4.68,5.42,5.42,6.16),(5.42,6.16,6.9,6.9)}

DDV_4={HN,MN,SN,Z,SP,MP,HP}={(0.1,0.1,0.4,0.7),(0.4,0.7,0.7,1),(0.7,1,1,1.3),(1,1.3,1.3,1.6),(1.3,1.6,1.6,1.9),(1.6,1.9,1.9,2.2),(1.9,2.2,2.5,2.5)}

And the rules obtained after applying the inductive learning are:

R_0: IF v_4 is {HN,MN} THEN Y is Iris Setosa
R_1: IF v_4 is {SN,Z} THEN Y is Iris Versicolor
R_2: IF v_3 is NOT HP and v_4 is {SN,Z,SP} THEN Y is Iris Versicolor
R_3: IF v_4 is {MP,HP} THEN Y is Iris Virginica
R_4: IF v_3 is NOT SP and v_4 is {SP,MP,HP} THEN Y is Iris Virginica

The validation method is the module used for detecting these conflicting areas and gives them to a module generator of questions. This module will ask the domain expert questions with the aim of resolving the inconsistency detected and will help to develop a multi-level rule-based system. The question asked will depend on the area in which the inconsistency arises, the information available in the fuzzy repertory grid and the examples provided by the organisation or domain expert. Let us see in the following section, how the validation method performs.

3.2 Suggested validation method

Let us make some definitions before studying the way for performing the validation method in the search of conflicting areas.

Definition 1. Each rule $R_i \in R_g$ will have the following form:

$$R_i:\ ZD_{1i}\ ZD_{2i} \ldots ZD_{|V|i} \rightarrow O_x$$

where ZD_{ij} is the definition area of variable v_i in the rule R_j, it verifies that $ZD_{ij} \subseteq DDV_i$

Definition 2. The OR(x) function will have as its output the consequent part of the rule R_x.

Definition 3. The intersection between two rules R_i and R_j will be noted as $I(R_i,R_j)$, and is defined as:

$$I(R_i,R_j) = ZD_{1i} \cap ZD_{1j}, ZD_{2i} \cap ZD_{2j}, \ldots, ZD_{|V|i} \cap ZD_{|V|j}$$

$I(R_i,R_j) \neq 0$ if and only if $ZD_{1i} \cap ZD_{1j} \neq 0 \wedge ZD_{2i} \cap ZD_{2j} \neq 0 \wedge \ldots \wedge ZD_{|V|i} \cap ZD_{|V|j} \neq 0$.

Definition 4. The inconsistency between two rules R_i y R_j will be noted as $IC(R_i,R_j)$ and is defined as:

$$IC(R_i,R_j)= \begin{cases} 1 \text{ if } I(R_i,R_j)\neq 0 \text{ and } OR(i)\neq OR(j). \\ 0 \text{ in some other case.} \end{cases}$$

Definition 5. The set of rules that have intersection non null with the rule R_i in the conflicting area ZC will be noted as $CRIR_i(ZC)$ and is defined as:

$$CRIR_i(ZC)=\{R_j \in R_g \,/\, I(R_j,R_i) \text{ in } ZC\} \cup R_i$$

Definition 6. The set of conflicting areas found by means of the rule R_i will be noted as CR_i and is defined as:

$$CR_i=\{(ZC,CRIR_i)_j\} \text{ for } j=0\ldots NZCR_i$$

with $NZCR_i$ being the number of conflicting areas found in the knowledge base using R_i as the mechanism of revelation.

Now let us see how the proposed validation method performs:

- To use in each step a rule $R_i \in R_g$ as the mechanism of revelation or searching of conflicting areas and the set of rules that act over these areas, check whether these areas are inconsistent areas (Algorithm 1).
- To show area by area to the expert and ask for the resolution of such an inconsistency. The system will recommend some solutions to him for resolving the inconsistent area (Algorithm 4), which can be:
  - Mark this inconsistent area as a non possible real input.
  - Mark this inconsistent area as input that requires a specific research.
  - Mark this inconsistent area as input that requires more information to be able to resolve the inconsistent area.
  - Restrict the area in the rules in which this inconsistent input appears.

Any suggested solution does not introduce new inconsistencies in the current level of validation. The last two solutions involve the creation of new modules over which we shall have to acquire more knowledge and consequently apply the validation method. Therefore, we can guarantee that the rule employed as a mechanism of revelation is free from inconsistencies. That is because it will not be employed any more in the process for the detection of conflicting areas.

Let us see our algorithm for searching the conflicting areas. See Algorithm 1.

Algorithm 1

Input: A rule $R_x \in R_g$ that will be used as a mechanism of revelation of conflicting areas and a set of rules $R_g=\{R_1,R_2,R_3,...,R_q\}$ over which these areas will be searched.

Output: A set of inconsistent areas and the set of rules that are affected by these inconsistencies.

Step 1. For each rule $R_i \in R_g$ i=x...q

Step 1.1. If $I(R_x,R_i) \neq 0$ then $ZC=I(R_x,R_i)$

Step 1.1.1. If $(ZC,\{\}) \subseteq CR_x$

then *Add*(R_j,(ZC,$CRIR_x$))

Step 1.1.2. If $(ZC,\{\}) \not\subset CR_x$ and $ZC \notin CZCR$

then $CR_x=CR_x \cup (ZC,\{R_j\})$

Step 2. Apply the Detection of Conflicting Areas Algorithm (Algorithm 2) to CR_x.

Step 3. Provide the questions generator algorithm (Algorithm 4) with CR_x.

Step 4. End.

The $\subseteq$ and *Add*() operations are defined as:

Definition 7. We assert that $(ZC,\{\}) \subseteq CR_i$ when it is verified that there is a $(A,CRIR_i) \in CR_i$ such as $ZC \subseteq A$.

Definition 8. The *Add*(R_j,(ZC,$CRIR_i$)) operations is defined as: $CRIR_i=R_j \cup CRIR_i$

Let us see how Detection of Conflicting Areas algorithm performs. See Algorithm 2.

Algorithm 2

Input: A set of conflicting areas found by means of the rule R_x, CR_x.

Output: A set of inconsistent areas found in CR_x.

Step 1. For each $(Z,CRIR_x) \in CR_x$

Step 1.1. Apply Confirmation Conflicting areas Algorithm (Algorithm 3)

Step 1.2. If there are none, then do: $CR_x - (Z,CRIR_x)$

Step 2. End.

Let us see how the Confirmation Conflicting areas algorithm performs. See Algorithm 3.

Algorithm 3

Input: A conflicting area Z and a set of rules CRZ with intersections other than null in that area.

Output: A decision on whether that conflicting area is an inconsistent area.

Step 1. For each $R_i \in CRZ$

Step 1.1. For each $R_j \in CRZ$ with $i \neq j$

Step 1.2. If $OR(i) \neq OR(j)$ then Z is an inconsistent area, go to step 2.

Step 2. Return decision.
Step 3. End.

In the following section, we show how the questions generator algorithm performs. We have studied it apart from the validation method (even though it is part of it) with the aim of showing its utility in the knowledge acquisition process in a multi-level rule-based expert system.

3.3 Using the suggested validation method for acquiring knowledge

As mentioned above, when we find a conflicting area, several situations can occur. It is possible that the conflicting area will be an input non-possible of the system over which we want to acquire knowledge. In this case, the output that is produced by the system does not matter to us, since it will never occur. As a result of that, we allow the inconsistency in that area. However, it is necessary to mark this area as a resolved conflicting area for avoiding that this area will be presented again to the expert.

Definition 9. The set of resolved conflicting areas will be noted as CZCR and is defined as:

$$CZCR=\{ZC \;/\; ZC \text{ have been resolved by the expert}\}$$

At the beginning of the validation process, the set CZCR will be the empty set.

Another situation that may occur is that the conflicting area will be so complex that a special research will be required over that input. The expert has never been faced with a similar problem and he is not able to decide or classify. In this case, we mark this area as a resolved conflicting area to avoid this area from being presented again to the expert and we add a control rule for indicating that in that case special research is required.

Definition 10. The set of control rules will be noted as RCL and is defined as: $RCL=\{R_{cl1},\ldots,R_{cln}\}$

The control rules are rules that will be used for surfing the multilevel rule-based system and as a mechanism for preventing certain rules from being fired when conflicting inputs occur.

It may also arise that the expert will require new variables for resolving a conflicting area, that is to say, it means increasing the space dimension. If these new variables are only required for resolving a particular area, we create a new module in which we take into account the new variables and add to it only those rules that work over that area. We propose that the new variables could be acquired by means of a fuzzy repertory grid-based technique. Fuzzy inductive learning may also be applied for learning rules when the domain expert is able to provide a set of examples belonging to the inconsistent area that contains the newly acquired variables. In this case, we mark this area as a resolved conflicting area and we add a control rule for indicating that this case is resolved in a resolution module of the inconsistency.

Finally, we mention those cases in which the expert partially agrees with the rules but he requires restricting some values of the variables that form the inconsistent area for his total approval.

Definition 11. A restriction of a (a,b,c,d) value implies converting that value into (a′,b′,c′,d′). The new value verifies: $b \leq b', c' \leq c$, $a \leq a'$ y $d' \leq d$.

The restrictions will be carried out over a new module that will be fired when the inconsistent area is produced as system input. This area is marked as a resolved conflicting area and we add a control rule for indicating that this case is resolved in a resolution module of the inconsistency.

Let us see how the algorithm performs for generating questions for the expert and guiding the process for building a multi-level rule-based expert system. See Algorithm 4.

Algorithm 4

Input: An inconsistent area ZC and a set of rules $CRIR_i$ that have intersection non-null with that conflicting area.
Output: A solution to that inconsistent area.

Step 1. Check whether there are examples in the set of examples provided by the domain expert belonging to that area.
Step 1.1. If there are no examples that verify the aforementioned condition
Step 1.1.1. Generate the following question: *Is ZC a non-possible input to the system?* If the answer is YES then incorporate ZC to CZCR. Go to Step 4.
Step 1.1.2. Generate the following question: *Do ZC require a specific treatment?* If the answer is YES then create the following control rule: R_{cl}: IF Input=ZC THEN *carry out specific research into ZC*, and add it to the set of control rules RCL, $RCL=RCL \cup R_{cl}$. Go to Step 4.

Step 2. For each $R_j \in CRIR_i$ do:
Step 2.1. If there are no examples that verify that they fire the rule with the greater *degree of convenience* (*Castro*[4]) than some other rule.
Step 2.1.1. Generate the following question: *There is no example that fires the rule R_j in ZC, Do we remove this input from the rule?* If the answer is YES then create the following control rule: R_{cl}: IF Input = ZC THEN *do not take into account R_j*, and add it to the set of control rules RCL, $RCL=RCL \cup R_{cl}$ and extract R_j from $CRIR_i$. Go to Step 4.

Step 3. Apply the Confirmation Conflicting areas algorithm to ($ZC,CRIR_i$) for checking whether there is inconsistency in ZC.
Step 3.1. If there is inconsistency in ZC
Step 3.1.1. Generate the following question: *Is ZC a special input to the system in which more information is required?* If the answer is YES then create

the following control rule: R_{cl}: IF Input = ZC THEN *to go to inconsistency resolution module for ZC (MRC{ZC})*, and add it to the set of control rules RCL, RCL=RCL$\cup$$R_{cl}$, and ZC to CZCR. Start the knowledge acquisition process in the new module. Go to Step 4.

Step 3.1.2.Generate the following question: *The rule is correct but it is necessary to restrict the values of inconsistent area?* If the answer is YES then create the following control rule: R_{cl}: IF Input = ZC THEN *to go to inconsistency resolution module for ZC (MRC{ZC})*, and add it to the set of control rules RCL, RCL=RCL$\cup$$R_{cl}$, and ZC to CZCR. Restrict the values of DDV for the rules and variables, that cause the inconsistency in the new module. After this validating this new module. Go to Step 4.

Step 3.1.3.Generate the following question: *Do ZC require a specific treatment?* If the answer is YES then create the following control rule: R_{cl}: IF Input = ZC THEN *carry out specific research in ZC,* and add it to the set of control rules RCL, RCL=RCL$\cup$$R_{cl}$. Go to Step 4.

Step 4.End.

The degree of convenience of one rule is calculated as the lowest value of the functions that are associated with each input variable in the rule (*Castro*[4]).

In the end, we shall obtain a system without inconsistencies. The structure of the resulting system will be modular, that is, it will have a structure similar to that shown in Figure 5. With the suggested validation method and its questions generator module, we acquire a system that works on various abstraction levels passing from one level to another, by means of more information or restricting the variables values of the inconsistent rules, only when it is strictly necessary.

This system classifies or decides as follows: It first checks whether that input belongs to the set of resolved conflicting areas (CZCR). If it belongs to this set and it is an input that requires a special research indicating this to the domain expert and stopping the classification or decision process. If it is a possible input firing the control rule associated with this input and employing the rules belonging to the resolution conflict area module to which the control rule has led. If it does not belong to CZCR then the system fires the rules in the knowledge base.

4 Conclusions

In this paper, we have suggested a validation method that validates a knowledge base. We propose that the tests over KB will be performed incrementally, that is to say that the test will be carried out over those parts that have been modified. We acted in accordance with the *Meseguer-Verdaguer*'s ideas set out in IN-DEPTH II [7]. They proposed carrying out the verification on five levels. Moreover, they propose verifying only those KB parts that are affected by one modification. We extend their level idea and we think about working with sub-levels from their level

0 (*facts*) idea. When we found a conflicting in the level 0 that requires more information or restricting its values, we create a new module which constitutes a new level of the Multi-Level Rule-based expert system. We propose starting the process of knowledge acquisition over this new module and validating it. Our validation method analyses the knowledge base object taking into account the way in that they will be used during expert systems execution. Because of this, the suggested validation method performs over general conflicting areas, in contrast to other validation methods proposed in the validation knowledge base literature, which performs over particular conflicting areas.

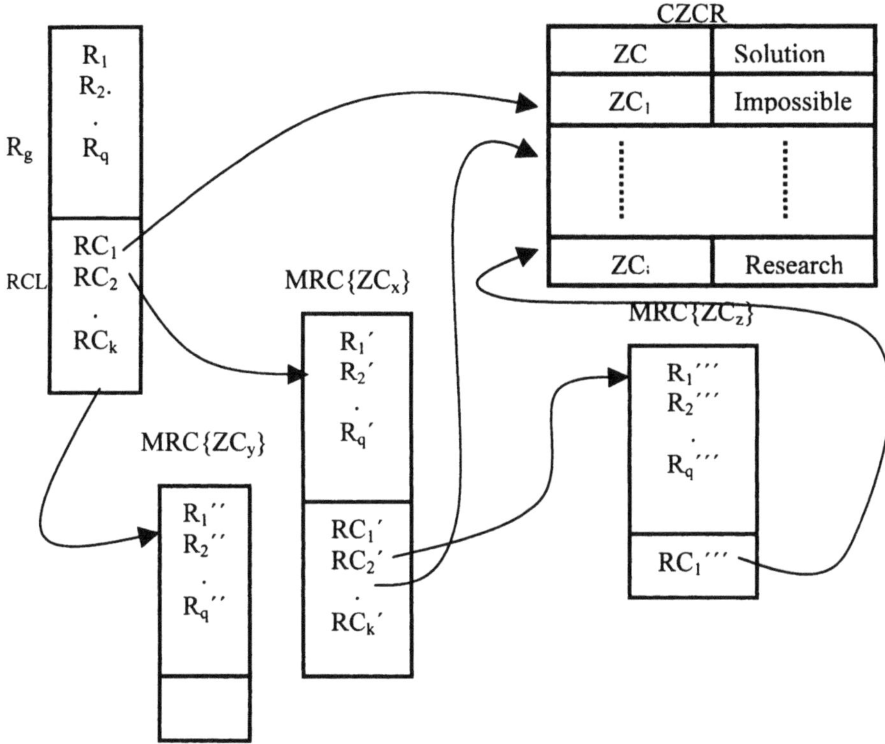

Figure 5. Structure of the suggested rule-based expert system.

We have employed the suggested validation method as a mechanism for acquiring knowledge. It is used for designing interviews with the domain expert who extends, updates and improves a knowledge base by answering the questions formulated by a questions generator module. The idea of generating a newer knowledge base from an older one is not original (*Tecuci*[10]). *Tecuci* develops a learning system shell, NeoDISCIPLE, that is defined as an expert system building tool that incorporates both the capabilities of an expert system shell and those of a knowledge acquisition tool. This tool built expert systems in three phases. In the first phase the expert defines a preliminary knowledge base. In the second phase, the system extends, updates and improves the knowledge base through learning from new input information provided by the human expert. In the last phase, the knowledge base is reorganised for improving efficiency in problem-solving.

We define the source knowledge base by means of a fuzzy repertory grid-based technique and a fuzzy inductive learning algorithm. This knowledge base contains rules that employed more kinds of knowledge but that will be represented as if they were fuzzy (by means of a membership function). By means of the proposed validation method, we improve the source KB and obtain a multi-level rule-based expert system that resolves classification or decision problems.

References

[1] Castro, J.L, and Trillas, E. The management of the inconsistency in expert systems. *Fuzzy Sets and Systems*, 58:51-57, 1993.

[2] Castro, J.L, Trillas, E. and Zurita, J.M. Searching potential conflicts in medical expert systems. *Fuzzy Sets and AI*, Vol 3(1):79-94, 1994.

[3] Castro, J.L., Castro-Schez, J.J., and Zurita, J.M. Fuzzy Repertory Table, a method for acquiring knowledge about input variables to machine learning algorithms (in review).

[4] Castro, J.L. Castro-Schez, J.J., and Zurita, J.M. Learning Maximal Structure Rules in Fuzzy Logic for Knowledge Acquisition in Expert Systems. *Fuzzy Sets and Systems,* 101:331-342, 1999.

[5] Fisher, R.A. The use of multiple measurements in taxonomic problems. *Annual Engenics,*7-II:179-188.

[6] Larsen, H.L., and Nonfjall, H. Modelling in the design of a KBS verification system. *International Journal of Intelligence System,* 1991.

[7] Meseguer, P. and Verdaguer, A. Verification of Multi-Level Rule-Based Expert Systems: Theory and Practice. *International Journal of Expert Systems.* Vol. 6 (2):163-192, 1993.

[8] Nguyen, T.A., Perkins, W.A., Laffey, T.J., and Pecora, D. Knowledge base verification. *AI Magazine* 8(2):69-79, 1987.

[9] Rousset, M. On the consistency of knowledge bases: The COVADIS system. In Proc. of ECAI-88, Munich, Germany, 79-84, 1988.

[10] Tecuci, G. Automating Knowledge Acquisition as Extending, Updating and Improving a Knowledge Base. *IEEE Transactions on Systems, Man and Cybernetics,* 22(6):1444-1460, 1992.

[11] Yager, R.R., and Larsen, H.L. On discovering potential inconsistencies in validating uncertain knowledge bases by reflection on the input. Tech. Report #MII-100, 1990 or In Proc. Verification, Validation, and Testing of KBS Workshop of the AAAI-91 Conference.

An Approach to Computational Microtexture Perceptual Detection with Management of Uncertainty

E.Montseny Dept. Eng. Sistemes Automàtica i Informàtica Industrial, Universitat Politècnica de Catalunya. Pau Gargallo5, 08028. Barcelona, Spain. E-mail: montseny@esaii.upc.es
P. Sobrevilla Dept. Matemàtica Aplicada II, Universitat Politècnica de Catalunya. Pau Gargallo5, 08028. Barcelona, Spain. E-mail: pilars@ma2.upc.es

Abstract. The aim of this work is determining a minimum set of perceptual features allowing microtexture description, in the textured aerial images domain, and adequate computational methods for the evaluation of those features. Moreover, fuzzy techniques are introduced in the features evaluation process to be faithful to the principle of least commitment, and to make easier the management of uncertainty inherent to perceptual features of microtextures.

Choosing aerial images for the fulfillment of the work is based on the broad range of microtextures contained in this kind of images, their uncertainty, variability and inherent complexity.

Obtaining a *"minimum"* set of perceptual features has been possible considering how experts usually describe microtextures of aerial images, what features are important in visual texture perception, and how they are used. On the other hand, texture measures that correlate well with human perception have been picked to evaluate previously selected features.

To illustrate the effectiveness of incorporating fuzzy techniques within our approach, the resulting computational method is applied to detect some textures of aerial images.
Keywords: Attentive Microtexture Perception, Perceptual Features, Feature Extraction, Principal Component Analysis, Fuzzy Rules.

1. Introduction

Texture is an important visual cue, and has been studied by several researches in psychophisics as well as computer vision (Haralick [4], Julesz and Bergen[7], and Rao [24]). It is related to qualitative properties of surfaces, but due to its complexity and wide diversity, there exists neither a unique definition of texture nor an accepted computational representation of it.

Several authors have attempted qualitatively to define texture. One of the widely accepted definitions was given by Pickett [21]. He states that a texture is an optical pattern that contains a large number of elements (spatial variations in intensity or wavelength), each visible to some degree, and, on the whole, densely and evenly arrayed over the field of view.

It is known that the human visual system is essential in understanding the basic functionality of machine vision and the principal properties that can be measured by image processing and analysis. Therefore, to apply image-processing techniques, it is essential to understand that there are basic differences in the purpose and functionality of human and machine vision.

From a human point of view, texture perception can be *preattentive* or *attentive*. *Preattentive perception* takes place when two textures in an image can be easily sorted out by human vision, what is possible when two textures are constituted by components clearly identifiable by their shape or size. On the contrary, *attentive perception* happens when a detailed observation is required for discriminating between two different textures in an image, as it is usually the case of microtextures.

Preattentive texture analysis is based on the *texton theory*, developed by Julesz [7]. This theory considers textures as formed by local components called *textons*, characterized by their contrast, orientation, length and width. Unfortunately, there are textures that can't be preattentively discriminated but require higher level features, such as coarseness or directionality. So, attentive perception is necessary, for example, in biomedical image analysis, manufactured products inspection or aerial image segmentation.

The study of perceptual features used by humans for attentive analysis of textures started in the seventies (Haralick [3], Nevatia [15], Tamura et al. [27] and Weszka [33]), when the first texture features and some ad-hoc computational measures for their evaluation were introduced. Even though more related work has been carried out in the eighties and nineties (Nevatia [16], Rao and Lohse [22] and [23], and Rao [24]), the study of the relevance of perceptual features, and the way in which these features can be evaluated are currently open problems.

Following aforementioned classifications, research in textures description and analysis can be grouped in three lines: 1) Analysis of high level perceptual features based on qualitative properties of texture, such as coarseness, granularity, linearity, etc. 2) Study of shapes and spatial organization oriented to extract basic primitives and their relationships. Often, those primitives extraction is difficult to achieve and it is not applicable to microtextures. 3) Study of receptive channels of human visual system, based on photometry and spatial characteristics used in preattentive perception.

First line has been widely used and it is suitable for all kinds of textures, particularly microtextures. Moreover the kind of analysis it performs conforms well to the human mind analysis and objects description, which is a goal of our approach. Therefore, present work may be considered as included within this line.

As a visual process, considerable uncertainty is introduced at different stages of the microtexture feature analysis. Some of the sources of this uncertainty include presence of noise in the images, dispersion of the light, digitalization process, imprecision in computations, vagueness in texture features definitions, ambiguities in natural textures and their interpretations, and ill-posed questions.

Fuzzy set theory and fuzzy logic provide powerful and flexible framework to represent vague and ill-defined concepts, and they represent and numerically manipulate linguistic rules in a natural way. Moreover, since some works in eighties (Pal et al.[17], and Pao [19]) introduced the presence of a non-random vagueness component in the variables taking part in computer vision systems, many researchers, as Gupta and Knopf [2], have used fuzzy techniques to improve vagueness treatment.

In this sense our approach, after fixing a set of relevant high level perceptual features and computational methods to evaluate them, make use of fuzzy techniques to take into account images uncertainty.

In section 2 taking into account the aforementioned works on analysis of microtexture perceptual features a *"minimum"* set of microtexture features is proposed. Based on the selection of the more suitable method to evaluate each original feature, section 3 contains a computational method to evaluate the new set of features which considers uncertainty factors. Experimental results of microtextures feature evaluation and fuzzy segmentation are given in Section 4. Some conclusions are given in section 5.

2. Determination of the Minimum Microtexture Feature Set

The quality of the features is critical for a good classification. At first glance, we might think that as many features as possible would be the best solution. Generally, this is not the case because some features can be strongly correlated. Moreover, it is important to find the right features, i.e., to study the relationship between the features of the objects and those in the image very carefully.

Tamura et al. [27], and Rao and Lohse [23] have tried to determine the relevant features used in texture perception. Some of them include repetition, directionality, complexity, coarseness, contrast and granularity.

Some research (Brady and Xie [1], Haralick et al.[3], Lumia et al.[13], Nevatia et al.[15] and [16], Sobrevilla et al.[26], and Weszka et al.[33]) has been focused on the sight of groups of features with texture segmentation and classification aims. The majority of studies consider groups having from 5 to 12 features. Since many of these groups have common components, the most voted constitute our starting perceptual feature set. These are *granularity*, *linearity*, *homogeneity*, *coarseness*, *continuity*, *abruptness*, and *contrast*.

Taking into account the aim of present work, every initial feature must be defined in such a way that intuitive and imprecise concepts can be translated, as clear as possible, to a computational implementation. According to this principle, our proposed definitions are the following:

- *Granularity*: Denotes the presence of either a large number of isolated pixels or many small groups of pixels, forming spots in a region, with similar intensity, different from the background intensity.
- *Linearity*: Points out the presence of neighboring pixels forming lineal structures in a region with similar intensity, but different from background.

- *Homogeneity*: Denotes presence of smooth intensity changes in any direction in a region.
- *Coarseness*: Is given when groups of pixels with variable size presenting sudden changes of intensity in any direction appear at a region.
- *Continuity*: Denotes presence of neighboring pixels with similar intensity, different from background intensity, forming continuous lineal structures in a region.
- *Abruptness*: Points out presence either of sudden transitions or strong changes in the direction of lineal structures.
- *Contrast*: Denotes the presence of a wide range of gray levels in a region, being a meaningful representation of every gray level of the range.

Issues related to texture point to the fundamental problem of identifying relevant texture features. So, with the aim of getting fairly generic features, which can be expected to work in a wide set of domains, reduction of the initial features set might satisfy following conditions:

1^{est} It must contain a number of features as small as possible to reduce the complexity of automatic segmentation algorithms based on them.

2nd As many features as necessary to segment any pair of microtextures must be included.

3rd Chosen features must allow the identification of microtextures in a particular context, such as aerial images.

As our target is not only determining a minimum set of perceptual features allowing microtexture aerial images description, but also an efficient and as accurate as possible computational method for their evaluation, a representative set of perceptual textures must be selected

Our selection process has been carried out starting from the prototype elements (surfaces) considered by Haralick [4], some of which have been later on used by other researchers at their works (Brady and Xie[1], Lumia et al.[13], and Weszka et al.[33]). Moreover, to be faithful to the aims of present work, next requirements have been considered in the selection process: (a) The number of selected surfaces must be as small as possible (redundant elements could distort subsequent studies). (b) Each surface has to represent as many types of elements as possible, attending to their features. (c) A new surface is selected if its type of texture is different from the one of already considered elements.

This process have led us to consider *forests, scrub, road, orchard, sown field* and *urban area* as prototype surfaces.

At this point it is important to consider the implication of initial perceptual features within the selected prototype set. Following this general outline, the level of human perception for the seven selected features, is studied for each one of the six surfaces or texture prototypes. We selected fifty subjects who were asked to rate the seven perceptual features, for each texture on a four-interval scale. These intervals were [i-0.5, i+0.5) for $0 \leq i \leq 3$, and most voted intervals for each feature/texture (represented by its mean points, as depicted at Table 1) were selected after this rating process.

Table 1: Feature values obtained by human perception

	Forest	Scrub	Road	Orchard	Sown Field	Urban Area
Granularity	3	2	0	2	0	1
Linearity	0	0	3	2	0	3
Homogeneity	1	1	2	1	2	1
Coarseness	3	2	1	2	1	2
Continuity	0	0	3	2	0	2
Abruptness	0	0	1	1	0	3
Contrast	1	1	1	2	1	3

At first glance Table 1 points out that there aren't textures with the same feature estimated values, which is favorable to the discrimination purpose of this microtexture feature set. However, a more attentive observation suggests certain correlation between some features.

Considering previous conditions, textures showing similar values in one feature should differ in another, that is to say, features should be non-correlated. The correlation of the features can be studied by means of some statistical method. One of them is Principal Components Analysis (PCA), a descriptive variable-directed technique, which main benefit lies in allowing us to reduce the dimensionality of the problem so as to simplify subsequent analyses.

Applying this method we'll transform the original set of features to a new subset of non correlated ones (principal components), and thus reduce the computational costs of segmentation and classification algorithms. These new features will be lineal combinations of the originals, and derived in decreasing order of importance so that, for example, the first principal component accounts as much as possible of the information in the original data.

To get round the scaling problem, a normalized PCA has been performed. It means that principal components are gotten from the correlation matrix of the initial 7 features, and the components turn out to be the eigenvectors of this matrix. As this matrix shows a strong correlation between some couples of features, the fitting of the PCA to get a lower number of features can be guaranteed.

After calculating the eigenvalues and principal components of the correlation matrix, we look at the first components accounting for the 95% of total information, but making possible to explain the differences among microtextures. These objectives have been attained retaining the first three components.

From Table 2 can be observed that correlation among the components and the original features is very high, and which out of the 7 initial features have more influence in the interpretation of each selected independent component, which is in the line of the work developed by Rao [23].

Table 2: Eigenvectors and Component correlation for the first 3 components

	Component C_1		***Component C_2***		***Component C_3***	
	Eigenv.	***Correl.***	***Eigenv.***	***Correl.***	***Eigenv.***	***Correl.***
Granularity	-0.376	-0.707	0.395	0.66	*0.348*	0.25
Linearity	*0.490*	0.92	0.172	0.287	*0.348*	0.25
Homogeneity	0.195	0.366	*-0.542*	-0.905	0.028	0.02
Coarseness	-0.318	-0.597	*0.454*	0.758	0.195	0.14
Continuity	*0.468*	0.88	0.087	0.145	*0.613*	0.44
Abruptness	*0.415*	0.779	0.341	0.57	-0.301	-0.216
Contrast	0.298	0.56	*0.437*	0.73	*-0.502*	-0.36
Inertia		**50.449**		**39.844**		**7.355**
Percentage of supported information					**97.648**	

From Table 2 can be observed that correlation among the components and the original features is very high, and which out of the 7 initial features have more influence in the interpretation of each selected independent component, which is in the line of the work developed by Rao [23].

3. Computational Evaluation of the Aerial-Image-Based Microtexture Set

After obtaining the components, our approach proceeds to get a suitable computational method to evaluate them. It has been carried out considering some of the most significant computational methods used during the last years, for microtexture analysis and segmentation. Within the framework of Reed [25], Van Gool [30], and Wechsler [32], these methods can be classified into the next four groups:

- *Linear Filtering Operators.* Based on local texture energy measures formulated by Laws [10]. Other measures of this type were proposed by Unser [29].
- *Statistical Methods.* Are based on spatial gray level dependence analysis. This yields a co-occurrence matrix of dimension equal to the number of gray levels in the image, considering every distance and orientation. Many measures have been extracted from these matrixes (Haralick [4], Lohmann [10], and Van Gool et al.[30]).
- *Transform Domain Methods.* They are based on local energy measures obtained from frequency domain, which is represented by means of the discrete Fourier transform (He and Wang [5], Tomita and Tsuji [28], and Van Gool et al.[30]), Gabor functions [21], and wavelet transforms (Lu et al.[12], Pichler et al.[20]).
- *Methods based on Texture Models.* These methods assume some kind of dependence between a pixel and its neighborhood. This dependence can be linear, or based on joint probability, as in the Markov fields [9]. Moreover, fractal functions have been proposed as textural models, and fractal dimension is used as a measure for texture segmentation (Reed et al.[25]).

3.1. Selection of Computacional Methods

Our approach for getting a computational method to evaluate the independent components is based on selecting the fitting method to evaluate each perceptual feature. To do it, for each perceptual feature, we compute the distances between the values obtained by human perception (Table 1), and those obtained applying the computational methods (Table 3). So, the lower distance values the more precisely the method captures the perceptual concept denoted by the feature.

Table 3: Distances between perceptual features and the most relevant computational measures. The range of the distances is [0, 45]. Lower distances are in bold-faced type

COMPUTATIONAL METHODS	PERCEPTUAL FEATURES						
	Granul.	*Linear.*	*Homog.*	*Coarse.*	*Contin.*	*Abrupt.*	*Contrast*
Laws (E5E5)	12,86	3,69	5,31	10,11	3,01	***1,46***	2,10
Laws (E5L5)	14,39	***3,15***	4,40	10,81	***2,32***	2,00	2,48
Laws (R5R5)	***6,48***	6,93	4,43	***3,59***	6,18	4,58	***1,55***
Statistic(Variance)	15,27	***2,61***	4,84	10,29	2,66	1,92	1,68
Statistic(Homogeneity)	10,10	21,49	***2,30***	8,46	17,01	16,31	9,58
Statistic(Contrast)	11,74	4,20	5,49	9,18	3,66	***1,36***	1,68
Fourier (r1)	13,61	4,06	4,92	11,38	2,75	1,85	3,07
Fourier (r2)	12,82	3,26	4,48	9,53	***2,45***	2,06	2,22
Fourier(r2-r3)	11,66	4,03	3,97	8,97	2,75	2,56	2,50
Wavelet(Haar 2)	9,73	4,24	5,20	5,68	4,16	3,45	***1,50***
Gabor	13,25	9,12	***2,39***	11,08	6,56	5,35	4,25
Fractal	***6,50***	20,13	4,02	***1,79***	17,84	15,64	6,35

To understand better these values, next we explain the steps for the particular case of the *feature "granularity"* and the *Linear Filtering Operator "Laws R5R5"*.

1. This method is separately evaluated for each different texture, obtaining one probability density function (PDF) per prototype texture. To leave out problems due to noise, the 10% of extreme values are eliminated in all PDF's (Figure 1-a).

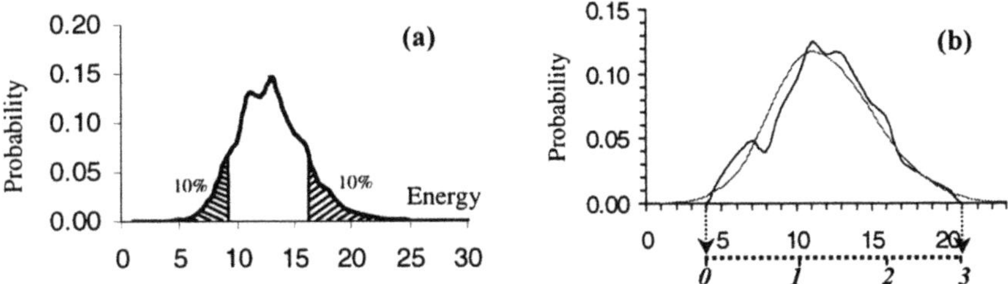

Figure 1: (a) LawsR5R5 Probability Density Function. Approximated. (b) *LawsR5R5* Probability Density Function and its projection over the continuous interval [0,3]

2. The resultant PDF's (PDF´) are brought together obtaining a new PDF, and its interval of energy values is projected onto the interval [0,3] (Figure 1-b).

3. Considering the new axis of abscissas, the mean of the PDF´ is calculated for each texture. So, the mean for the texture *"forest"* is 1,49. Third line of Table 3 shows the results after applying this process to the textures. Next, the square of the differences between the level of response given by the computational method, and the level of *granularity* of human perception (Table 1), is calculated for every texture (Table 4).

Table 4: Means for *"LawsR5R5"* PDF's, and values of the distances between the perceptual feature Granularity and the computational measure Laws R5R5.

	Forest	*Scrub*	*Road*	*Sown Field*	*Urban Area*
Granularity	3	2	0	0	1
Laws (R5R5)	***1,49***	1,12	1,41	0,40	2,13
Square of differences	2,28	0,77	1,99	0,16	1,28
	Total Difference		**6,48**		

The total difference value represents the fitting of the computational method *"Laws R5R5"* to evaluate the perceptual feature *"granularity"*. This process is repeated for each computational method and each feature, obtaining the results of Table 3. Methods giving the lower distance value (marked in bold-faced type) are chosen to evaluate the features.

3.2. Evaluating the Independent Components Using Fuzzy Techniques

To carry out the evaluation of the independent components, taking into account features and textures uncertainty, and being faithful to the principle of least commitment, fuzzy techniques are introduced.

As our aim is to get an image segmentation algorithm, based on pixel classification, our approach considers that a pixel can present four activation levels for each component, so-called: *Very Low*, *Low*, *Medium* and *High*. Next, in order to fuzzify the information supplied by the components, a fuzzy set is associated to each activation level per component (Table 5).

Table 5: Fuzzy sets associated to each activation level per component

	Very Low	Low	Medium	High
C_1	$FS_{1,1}$	$FS_{1,2}$	$FS_{1,3}$	$FS_{1,4}$
C_2	$FS_{2,1}$	$FS_{2,2}$	$FS_{2,3}$	$FS_{2,4}$
C_3	$FS_{3,1}$	$FS_{3,2}$	$FS_{3,3}$	$FS_{3,4}$

With the aim to obtain these fuzzy sets, it is necessary to get the activation perceptual levels of the components within the prototype textures, which is performed projecting, over each component, the minimum and maximum of the intervals wherein the human perception values of the features. Table 6 shows, for each component, two lines corresponding to the values of the minimum and maximum activation levels per feature.

Table 6: Activation perceptual levels for the components in the perceptual prototype textures

		Forest	*Scrub*	*Road*	*Orchard*	*Sown Field*	*Urban Area*
C_1	*min*	***-2.175***	-1.48	3.073	1.148	-0.216	3.142
	max	-1.003	-0.31	4.245	2.32	0.956	***4.314***
C_2	*min*	1.77	0.921	0.253	2.217	***-0.865***	3.113
	max	3.114	2.265	1.597	3.561	0.479	***4.457***
C_3	*min*	0.7905	0.248	1.967	1.3665	***-0.6155***	0.2625
	max	1.5195	0.977	***2.696***	2.0955	0.1135	0.9915

Given a component, the minimum and maximum values determine the theoretic interval of variability of the component, say $I_{Ci} = [min(C_i\, min), max(C_i\, max)]$, which is divided into four subintervals $I_{Ci,1}$, $I_{Ci,2}$, $I_{Ci,3}$, $I_{Ci,4}$, having the same length and related to the aforementioned activation levels like this:

$I_{Ci,1} \leftrightarrow VeryLow$ $\quad I_{Ci,2} \leftrightarrow Low$ $\quad I_{Ci,3} \leftrightarrow Medium$ $\quad I_{Ci,4} \leftrightarrow High$

Considering these intervals, the four fuzzy sets associated to each component are given by trapezoidal membership functions, as depicted at Figure 2.

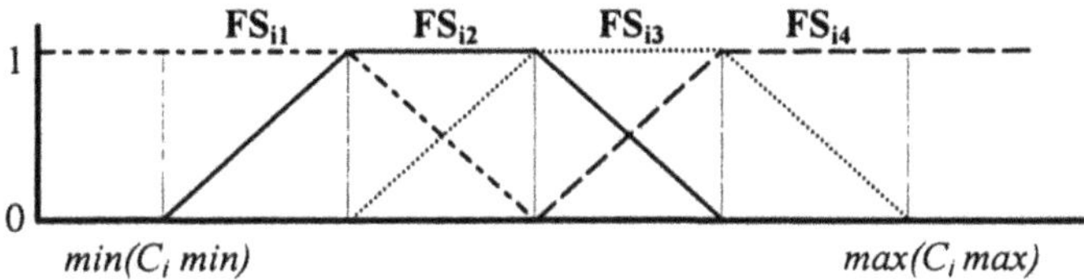

Figure 2: Trapezoidal fuzzy sets for the Component C_i.

- Obtaining the Fuzzy Sets associated to the textures

To define the textures' fuzzy sets it is necessary to know their activation levels per component, which has been performed evaluating the training textures in the previous framework. Obtaining the results depicted at Table 7.

Table 7: Activation levels of the components per texture.

	Forest	*Scrub*	*Road*	*Orchard*	*Sown Field*	*Urban Area*
C_1	Very Low	Low	High	Medium	Low	High
C_2	Low / Med.	Medium	Low / Med.	Low	Low	Medium
C_3	Low / Med.	V.Low / Low	High / Med.	Low / Med.	V.Low / Low	V.Low / Low

The fuzzy set of a texture per component is determined considering jointly the results of Tables 7 and 5. Finally, the membership degree of a pixel to a given texture is determined aggregating by the OWA operator W=(0, 0.3, 0.7) the membership degrees of the pixel to the three fuzzy sets.

When a texture has two levels of activation per component we use the maximum (as shown at [1] for the texture Forest).

[1] $\mu_{Forest}(i,j) = h_W(\mathrm{FS}_{1,1}(i,j), max(\mathrm{FS}_{2,2}(i,j), \mathrm{FS}_{2,3}(i,j)), max(\mathrm{FS}_{3,2}(i,j), \mathrm{FS}_{3,3}(i,j)))$

4. Experimental Results

According to the design of the algorithm, we are going to present some results of the adjusting of the selected computational methods to evaluate the considered perceptual features, as well as the behavior (adjustment) of the fuzzy sets.

Even though many images have been used to test the efficiency of the algorithm, due to space shortage here only the results of the tests performed over not many textured aerial images, owning some perceptual features at different levels, are presented. Figure 3 depicts the images used for these tests.

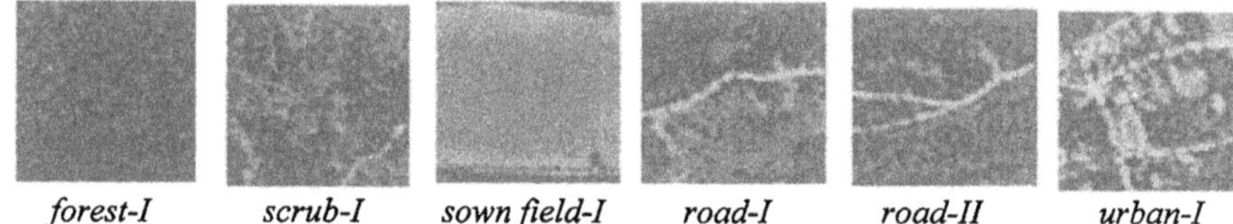

Figure 3: Textured aerial images used for the tests.

- Fitting of the selected computational methods evaluating the perceptual features

Figure 4 depicts the results when *Granularity* is evaluated when three computational methods, having the best, intermediate and worst adjusting levels, are used to evaluate the feature. Figure 4-(a) shows that applying Laws R5R5 to images having decreasing granularity level, the evaluated result retains this decreasing degree. Nevertheless, this property isn't fulfilled when Markov (Figure 4-(b)) or Statistic-Variance (Figure 4-(c)) are applied.

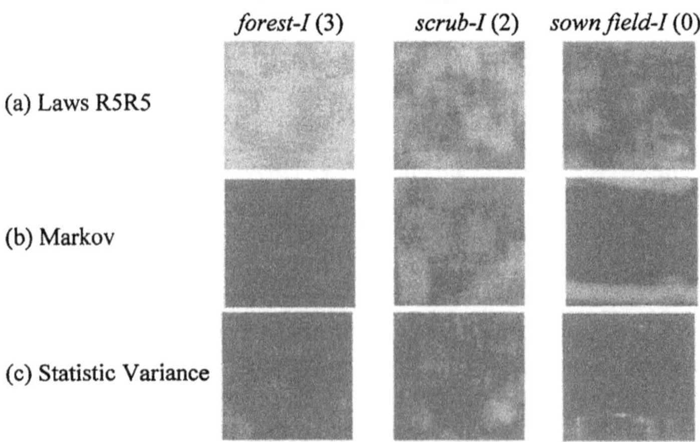

Figure 4: Results of Granularity tests

For *Abruptness*, when the operator Statistic-Contrast is applied over images with decreasing texture level (Figure 5-(a)), the result retains this decreasing degree after evaluating the feature. Nevertheless, applying the operator Statistic-Homogeneity (Figure 5-(b)) over the images an increasing degree is observed. Moreover, when the Laws R5R5 operator is applied (Figure 5-(c)), the maximum degree is obtained for the image with the smallest abruptness degree.

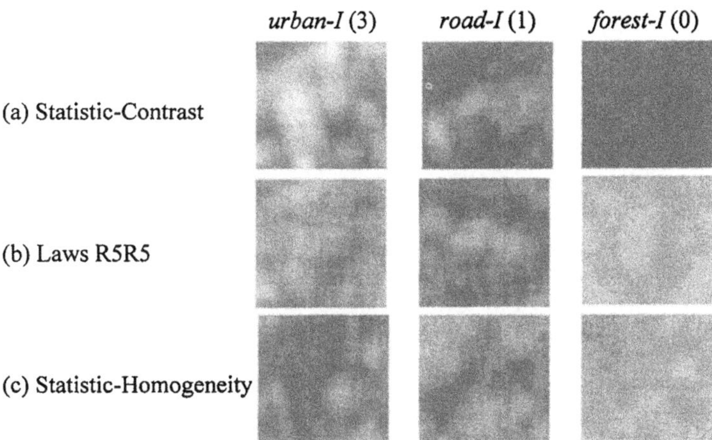

Figure 5: Computational results of Abruptness tests

- Fuzzy Sets Evaluation

The results corresponding to the behavior of the fuzzy sets have been very powerful, allowing the detection of all kind of textures we are working with. Here, due to space shortage, we present the results for two test images, *Scrub-I* and *Road_II*.

Within Figures 6 and 7, image (a) correspond to the original image. Images (b) to (g) represent the fuzzy sets: Forest, Orchard, Road, Scrub, Sown-field, and Urban respectively, obtained for the original image. At these images the greatest membership degree to the corresponding fuzzy set the brightest representation within the corresponding fuzzy image. Moreover, white pixels of images (h) at both Figures, represent the pixels having the highest membership degree to the fuzzy set Scrub and road respectively.

Having a look at images (h) of both Figures, can be observed that most pixels have been correctly classified, because of their membership degrees are the highest for the correct Fuzzy Set (Scrub for Figure 6, and Road for Figure 7). Furthermore, must be noticed that pixels not well classified are uniformly distributed. Needless to say that false alarms are due to the pixel classification algorithm we are working with.

Previous considerations are proving to be very advantageous for the implementation of this approach within a fuzzy segmentation algorithm wherein the authors are actually working.

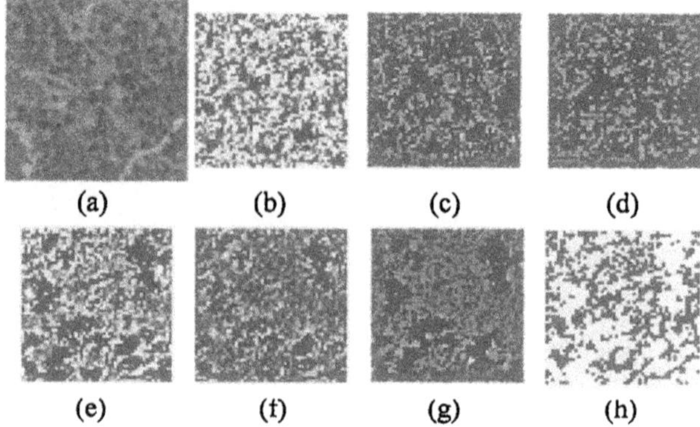

Figure 6: (a) Original Image Scrub I; (b) to (g) Forest, Orchard, Road, Scrub, Sown-field, and Urban Fuzzy Sets obtained for Original Image; (h) brightest pixels have the highest membership degree to the Fuzzy Set Scrub.

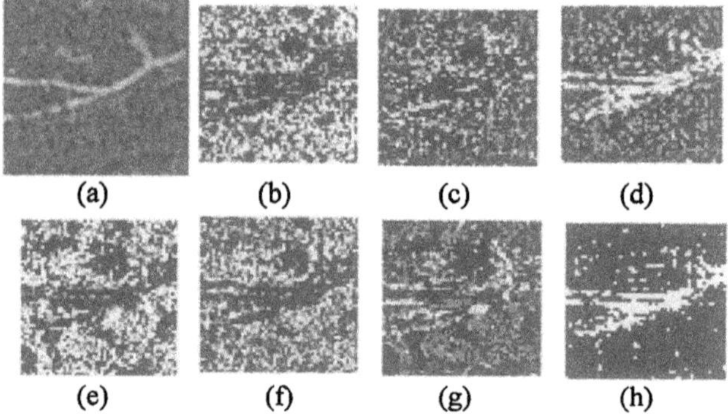

Figure 7: (a) Original Image Road II; (b) to (g) Forest, Orchard, Road, Scrub, Sown-field, and Urban Fuzzy Sets obtained for Original Image; (h) brightest pixels have the highest membership degree to the Fuzzy Set Road.

5. Conclusions

The study performed in this paper introduces a computational method to evaluate perceptual features. Moreover, an approach to reduce the number of necessary features to identify the several textures is presented, and a computational method to evaluate them is proposed.

On the other hand, the use of fuzzy techniques allows to introduce a robust method to describe the textures appearing within the aerial images, which takes into account the vagueness connected with this kind of images.

The system allows to get very good results detecting textures, when these present small or medium general difference in gray level with respect the training texture gray level. Nevertheless, some problems appear if the texture to be detected presents big differences in gray level with respect the training texture gray level. Actually we are analyzing this problem in order to solve it.

Acknowledgements

We are thankful to D. Puig for his helpful work.
This work was partially supported by the spanish CICYT Project TIC1999-1230-C02-01.

References

[1] Brady, M., Xie, Z.Y., "Feature Selection for Texture Segmentation", *IEEE PAMI*, pp. 29-44, 1996.

[2] Gupta,M.M. and Knopf,G.K., "Fuzzy Logic and Uncertainty in Image Processing", Proc. SPIE, Vol. 1902, pp. 210-223, 1993.

[3] Haralick,R.M., Shanmugam,K. and Distein,I., "Textural Features for Image Classification", IEEE Trans. SMC, 3, pp. 610-621, 1973.

[4] Haralick,R.M., "Statistical and Structural Approaches to Texture", Proc. IEEE, Vol 67, pp. 786-804, 1979.

[5] He,D.H. and Wang,L., "Texture Features Based on Texture Spectrum", Pattern Recognition, Vol.24, No. 5, pp. 391-399, 1991.

[6] Iisaka, J., Sakurai-Amano, T., "Terrain Feature Recognition for Sar Imagery employing Spatial Attributes of Targets", Proc. ISPRS 3th Symposium Spatial Information from Digital Photogrametry and Computer Vision, Munich, Germany, pp. 399-408, Sept.1994.

[7] Julesz,B. and Bergen,J.R., "Textons, the Fundamental Elements in Preattentive Vision and Perception of Textures", Bell Syst. Tech. Journal, Vol. 62, No. 6, pp. 1619-1645, 1983.

[8] Krishnamachari,S. and Chellappa,R., "Multiresolution Gauss-Markov Random Field Models for Texture Segmentation", IEEE Trans. on Image Processing, Vol. 6, No. 2, pp. 251-260, 1997.

[9] Laws,K.I., "Textured Image Segmentation", Technical Report USCIPI-940, Univ. of Southern California, Los Angeles, 1980.

[10] Lohmann,G., "Co-Ocurrence-based Analysis and Synthesis of Textures", Proc. 12th IAPR Inter. Conf. Pattern Recognition, Vol. 1, pp. 449-453, Jerusalem, 1994.

[11] Lotti,J.L., Giraudon,G., "Adaptive Window Algorithm for Aerial Image Stereo", Proc. 3th ISPRS, pp. 517-524, Munich, 1994.

[12] Lu,C.S., Chung,P.C. and Chen,C.F., "Unsupervised Texture Segmentation via Wavelet Transform", Pattern Recognition, Vol. 30, No. 5, pp. 729-742, 1997.

[13] Lumia,R., Haralick,RM., Zuniga,O.A. and Shapiro,L.G., "Texture Analysis of Aerial Photographs", Pattern Recognition, Vol. 16, No. 1, pp. 39-46, 1983.

[14] Montseny,E., Sobrevilla,P., "Application of Fuzzy Techniques to the Design of Algorithms in Computer Vision", Mathware & Soft Computing, Vol. V, No. 2-31, pp. 223-230, 1998.

[15] Nevatia,R., Price,K. and Vilnrotter,S., "Describing Natural Scenes", Proc. IJCAI-79, pp. 642-644, Tokyo, 1979.
[16] Nevatia,R. and Babu,K.R., "Linear Feature Extraction and Description", Computer Graphics and Image Processing, Vol. 13, pp. 257-269, 1980.
[17] Pal,K. et al., "Image Description and Primitive Extraction Using Fuzzy Sets", IEEE Trans. SMC, 13, 1983.
[18] Palubinskas,G., "A Comparison of Texture-based and Fuzzy Classification Approaches for Regenerating Tropical Forest Mapping Using Landsat TM", Proc. 3th ISPRS, pp. 640-647, Munich, 1994.
[19] Pao,Y.H., "Vague Features and Vague Decision Rules: the Fuzzy-Set Approach", Adaptative Pattern Recognition and Neural Networks, Ed. Adison Wesley, 1989.
[20] Pichler,O., Teuner,A. and Hosticka,B.J., "A Comparison of Texture Extraction Using Adaptive Gabor Filtering, Pyramidal and Tree Structured Wavelet Transforms", Pattern Recognition, Vol. 29, No. 5, pp. 733-742, 1996.
[21] Pickett,R.M., "Visual Analysis of Texture in the Detection and Recognition of Objects", Picture Processing and Psychopictorics, Ed. Academic Press, pp. 298-308, 1970.
[22] Rao,A.R. and Lohse,G.L., "Identifying High Level Features of Texture Perception", CVGIP: Graphical Models and Image Processing, Vol. 55, No. 3, pp. 218-233, 1993.
[23] Rao,A.R. and Lohse,G.L., "Towards a Texture Naming System: Identifying Relevant Dimensions of Texture", Vision Research, Vol. 36, No. 12, pp. 1649-1669, 1996.
[24] Rao,A.R., "A Taxonomy for Texture description and Identification", Ed. Springer, New York, 1990.
[25] Reed,T.R. and Hans du Buf,J.M., "A Review of Recent Texture Segmentation and Feature Extraction Techniques", CVGIP: Image Understanding, Vol. 57, No. 3, pp. 359-372, 1993.
[26] Sobrevilla,P., Puig,D., Montseny,E., "Segmentation of Textured Aerial Images Using OWA Operators", Proc. 6th IPMU, pp. 1513-1518, Granada, 1996.
[27] Tamura,H., Mori,S. and Yamawaki,T., "Textural Features Corresponding to Visual Perception", IEEE Trans. SMC, 8, pp. 460-473, 1978.
[28] Tomita,F. and Tsuji,S., Computer Analysis of Visual Textures, Kluwer Academic Publishers, 1990.
[29] Unser,M., "Local Linear Transforms for Texture Measurements", Signal Processing, Vol. 12, pp. 61-79, 1986.
[30] Van Gool,L., Dewaele,P. and Oosterlinck,A., "Survey: Texture Analysis Anno 1983", Computer Vision Graphics and Image Processing, No. 29, pp. 336-357, 1985.
[31] Vanrell,M. and Vitrià,J., "A Four-Dimensional Texture Representation Space", VII National Symposium on Pattern Recognition and Image Analysis, Vol. 1, pp. 245-250, Barcelona, 1997.
[32] Wechsler,H., "Texture Analysis, a Survey", Signal Processing, Vol. 2, pp. 271-282, 1980.
[33] Weszka,J.C., Dyler,C.R. and Rosenfeld,A., "A Comparative Study of Texture Measures for Terrain Classification", IEEE Trans. SMC, 6, pp. 269-285, 1976.

Bagging Improves Uncertainty Representation in Evidential Pattern Classification

Jérémie François[1,2], Yves Grandvalet[1], Thierry Denœux[1], and Jean-Michel Roger[2]

[1] Université de Technologie de Compiègne, Heudiasyc, UMR CNRS 6599, F-60205 Compiègne, France
[2] Cemagref, GIQUAL Research Unit, 361 rue Jean-François Breton, F-34033 Montpellier, France

Abstract. Uncertainty representation is a major issue in pattern recognition when the outputs of a classifier do not lead directly to a final decision, but are used in combination with other systems, or as input to an interactive decision process. In such contexts, it may be advantageous to resort to rich and flexible formalisms for representing and manipulating uncertain information, such as the Dempster-Shafer theory of Evidence. In this paper, it is shown that the quality and reliability of the outputs from an evidence-theoretic classifier may be improved using an adaptation from a resample-and-combine approach introduced by Breiman and known as "bagging". This approach is explained and studied experimentally using simulated data. In particular, results show that bagging improves classification accuracy and limits the influence of outliers and ambiguous training patterns.

Keywords: Supervised Pattern Recognition, K-Nearest Neighbor Rule, Decision Fusion, Dempster-Shafer Theory, Evidence Theory, Bootstrap, Bagging.

1 Introduction

In the last thirty years, the issue of uncertainty representation and management in supervised pattern recognition has received considerable attention. New theoretical frameworks have been proposed as alternatives to Bayesian Probability theory to describe, manipulate, and reason with partial knowledge and unreliable information. In particular, the so-called Dempster-Shafer (D-S) theory of Evidence, first proposed by Shafer [10] and further elaborated by many authors has been shown to constitute a rich and flexible framework, in which the concepts of a probability and possibility measures are recovered as special cases of the more general concept of *belief function*. This theory has been successfully applied in many areas such as diagnosis [12], sensor fusion [1] and pattern classification [9,3].

When applying D-S theory to classification tasks, the construction of belief functions from observation data is a crucial step. Typically, a training set of patterns with known classification is given, and one wishes to quantify one's beliefs concerning the category of a new pattern submitted to the system. The evidential K-NN rule, previously introduced by one of the authors [3,15], is such a method for inferring a belief function by pooling the evidence from the nearest neighbors in the training set. In this paper, it is proposed to improve this method using a new variant of a technique, known as "bagging", proposed by Breiman [2] in a conventional statistical context to improve the stability of classification rules. This method is shown experimentally to provide a more "realistic" description of the uncertainty pertaining to the classification task, leading to improved classification performances.

The paper is organized as follows. Section 2 introduces the main concepts of Evidence Theory and their use in pattern recognition. Section 3 depicts the adaption of the bagging approach to evidential classifiers, followed by the presentation and discussion of experimental results obtained in an artificial learning task (Sections 4-6). Finally, Section 7 concludes the paper and presents directions for further research.

2 Background

2.1 Theory of Belief Functions

Only the main concepts of the Dempster-Shafer theory of belief functions that we use in this paper will be recalled here. The reader is referred to Shafer's book [10] for a detailed exposition of the mathematical background, and to more recent papers such as, e.g., Refs. [14,13] for up-to-date presentations of the latest developments in both the theoretical aspects and practical applications of belief functions. Although our approach is not tied to a particular interpretation of belief functions, we shall adopt the non-probabilistic view of Smets' Transferable Belief Model (TBM), which constitutes a particularly coherent and justified approach [14,13].

In short, the main assumptions underlying the TBM are that (1) degrees of belief are quantified by numbers between 0 and 1; (2) there exists a two-level structure composed of a *credal level* where beliefs are entertained, and a *pignistic level* where decisions are made; (3) beliefs at the credal level are quantified by belief functions, while decisions at the pignistic level are based on probability functions; (4) when a decision has to be made, beliefs are transformed into probabilities using the so-called pignistic transformation.

The Credal Level Let $\Omega = \{\omega_1, \ldots, \omega_M\}$ be a finite possibility space containing *all* the possible answers to a certain question (the truth lies necessarily somewhere in Ω). In the type of applications envisaged here, Ω is the set of possible classes for an object with unknown class membership. It is assumed that any item of evidence can be represented by a belief structure, or basic belief assignment, defined as a function m from 2^Ω (the power set of Ω) to the [0,1] interval, verifying:

$$\sum_{A \subseteq \Omega} m(A) = 1. \tag{1}$$

and $m(\emptyset) = 0$. The value of $m(A)$ can be interpreted as the "mass" of belief that is given to A and that cannot be given to any other subset without further information; if $m(A) > 0$, A is called a focal element. For example, $m(\Omega) = 1$ represents total ignorance (m is then called the vacuous belief structure), $m(\{\omega_1\}) = 0.5$ stands for a moderated belief in hypothesis 1, and $m(\{\omega_1, \omega_2\}) = 1$ means complete certainty that either hypothesis 1 or hypothesis 2 is true (with no evidence in favor of any of one them individually).

A new reliable piece of information can be incorporated by use of the Dempster's rule of combination [11], if and only if the two sources of belief (denoted m_1 and m_2) are independent and non-totally contradictory. The combination results in a new belief structure $m = m_1 \oplus m_2$ on Ω that represents the new state of knowledge.

The pignistic level Given a belief structure, different criteria can be used to choose one hypothesis. We will use here the pignistic risk minimization as defined and justified by Smets [14] on an axiomatic basis.

Let Pbet be the so-called pignistic probability distribution, defined by uniformly distributing the mass of belief given to each subset of Ω among its elements:

$$\mathtt{Pbet}(\omega) = \sum_{\{A \subseteq \Omega | \omega \in A\}} \frac{m(A)}{|A|} \qquad \forall \omega \in \Omega, \tag{2}$$

where $|A|$ is the number of elements in A.

In the TBM, the pignistic probability function is used for decision making according to the Bayes decision theory. Let $\mathcal{A}$ denote a set of actions, and $\lambda(\alpha|\omega)$ the loss incurred if action $\alpha \in \mathcal{A}$ is selected, $\omega \in \Omega$ being the true state of nature. Then, the expected cost (or risk) of choosing action α, relative to the pignistic distribution, is:

$$\mathtt{Rbet}(\alpha) = \sum_{\omega \in \Omega} \lambda(\alpha|\omega)\ \mathtt{Pbet}(\omega) \tag{3}$$

$$= \sum_{A \subseteq \Omega} \frac{m(A)}{|A|} \sum_{\omega \in A} \lambda(\alpha|\omega). \tag{4}$$

The Bayes decision theory then recommends the action α with the lowest expected cost $\mathtt{Rbet}(\alpha)$.

2.2 Application to Pattern Classification

Recently, Denœux proposed an evidence-theoretic distance-based classifier [3] which takes fully advantage of the evidence theory, by staying free of any intermediate probabilistic representation. The outline of this approach is summarized below.

Let x be the sample to be classified, and let $\mathcal{L} = \{(x_i, y_i)\}_{i=1}^N$ be the learning set of known patterns, where $y_i \in \Omega$ is the class of pattern x_i.

First, the K-nearest neighbors of x in $\{x_i\}_{i=1}^N$ are selected according to the Euclidean distance. Each neighbor x_k is then considered as an item of evidence about the class of x. If $y_k = \omega_q$, this evidence induces a belief structure m_k with focal elements $\{\omega_q\}$ and Ω [3,5]:

$$m_k(A) = \begin{cases} \alpha \exp(-\gamma_q \|x_k - x\|^2) & \text{if } A = \{\omega_q\} \\ 1 - \alpha \exp(-\gamma_q \|x_k - x\|^2) & \text{if } A = \Omega \\ 0 & \text{otherwise} \end{cases} \quad (5)$$

where $\|x_k - x\|$ is the Euclidean distance between x_k and x. Parameter $\alpha \in [0, 1]$ sets the minimum belief mass given to Ω, thus limits the certainty expressed by training patterns. Parameters $\gamma_q \in \mathbb{R}^+$ adjust the influence of the patterns of class q according to their distance to x. These coefficients can be determined from the data using a learning scheme proposed in Ref. [15].

Then, as they are independent from each other, the K belief structures m_k are combined into a single structure m by means of Dempster's rule. This structure summarizes the available information about the class of x, provided by its neighborhood in the training set.

Finally, m is used to compute pignistic probabilities $\texttt{Pbet}(\omega_k|x)$, from which class assignment can be performed, using the approach described in Section 2.1 [4]. We define $\mathcal{A} = \{\alpha_0, \alpha_1, \ldots, \alpha_M\}$ the set of actions, where α_i for $i = 1, \ldots, M$ is the decision to classify x in class ω_i, and α_0 denotes rejection. The loss is assumed to be 1 in case of a wrong classification and 0 for correct classification. The rejection loss is assumed to be constant, and equal to some value $\lambda_0 \in [0, 1]$. We thus have:

$$\lambda(\alpha_i|\omega_j) = 1 - \delta_{ij} \quad \forall i, j \in \{1, \ldots, M\} \quad (6)$$

$$\lambda(\alpha_0|\omega_j) = \lambda_0 \quad \forall j \in \{1, \ldots, M\}, \quad (7)$$

where δ_{ij} is the Kronecker symbol ($\delta_{ij} = 1$ if $i = j$, and 0 otherwise).

With these costs, the risks are defined, for each action, as follows :

$$\texttt{Rbet}(\alpha_i) = 1 - \texttt{Pbet}(\omega_i), \quad i = 1, \ldots, M \quad (8)$$

$$\texttt{Rbet}(\alpha_0) = \lambda_0 \quad (9)$$

Each pattern is thus assigned to the class with highest pignistic probability, provided that this probability is greater than $1 - \lambda_0$. Otherwise, it is rejected. Consequently, parameter λ_0 allows to control the rejection rate of the classifier.

3 Sampling, Learning and Uncertainty

Problem The basic belief assignment defined by Eq. 5 handles the uncertainty that stems from the possibly novel characteristics of the query sample.

However, additional causes of uncertainty exist. First, the known instances x_k are usually not "prototypical" patterns, such as measurements obtained from some careful experimental design. They are records of past solved cases, which are supposed to be representative of future unsolved cases. In probabilistic terms, they may be considered as randomly sampled from the distribution of future cases. This random sampling is responsible for some uncertainty in the global belief assignment which cannot be taken into account by the basic belief assignment which is conditioned on a given realization of the training set. Additionally, when the parameters of the basic belief assignment are tuned by minimizing some performance criterion on the training set, the learned parameters are also random variables, whose variability is responsible for another part of uncertainty.

This is why we propose here the use of bagging, introduced in the probabilistic framework by Breiman [2] to limit the effects of sampling on a learned decision rule.

Bagging Decision Rules Bagging is a procedure for improving a classification using a resample-and-combine technique. Breiman argues that its main effect is to decrease the variance of the estimator, and advocates its use for unstable classification methods, i.e. methods which are sensitive to perturbations of the training set.

From the original decision rule, the bagged estimator is produced by aggregating using a majority vote on several replicates of the rule, trained on bootstrap resamples of the learning set. A bootstrap sample [7] is created by drawing with replacement N examples from the learning set $\mathcal{L} = \{(x_i, y_i)\}_{i=1}^N$. It has thus the same size as the original sample but may contain replicates of some given examples, while other ones are not represented. The drawing with replacement in $\mathcal{L}$ simulates the original sampling from the distribution that generated $\mathcal{L}$. Empirical evaluations showed that the method almost systematically compares favorably with the original predictor [2,6].

Bagging in the TBM In pattern classification, bagging is usually applied to the decisions. In this paper, however, we propose to use it upstream, at the credal level.

The main goal is to better take into account the uncertainty attached to the finite training set, in order to allow steadier decisions and, consequently, to improve the result of further combinations when new sources are available.

Practically, as in decision rule bagging, B bootstrap learning sets $\mathcal{L}_b$ ($b = 1, \ldots, B$) are obtained by drawing with replacement N examples from the original learning set $\mathcal{L}$. Here, the bootstrap is balanced, which means that each sample (x_i, y_i) is globally drawn B times over the B resamples. Then, for a given unknown sample x, each training set $\mathcal{L}_b$ produces a belief structure m_b through a given K-NN classifier. These are finally aggregated into the average structure $m_{\mathbf{B}}$, defined as:

$$\forall A \subseteq \Omega, \quad m_{\mathbf{B}}(A) = \frac{1}{B} \sum_{b=1,B} m_b(A). \tag{10}$$

In contrast to the usual bagging by majority vote on the B decision rules, aggregation thus takes place at the credal level, using the average operator. While it is clear that aggregation should operate on beliefs, other operators could be used, such as weighted averaging, or the selection of the median or some other particular element among the B structures[1]. Averaging was chosen as a good simple candidate as it is idempotent, commutative and linear: first, getting B times the same structure should lead to this same structure after aggregation (idempotency), second, the resulting structure should be independent from the aggregation order (commutativity), and third, the linear relationship between credal and probabilistic levels, introduced by Smets [14] in the decision process, also supports linear aggregation (linearity).

Remark: In our method, each bootstrap resample of the training set generates a belief structure for each x. These B structures are first aggregated by averaging, and the decision is then based on this average belief structure. The faithful transposition of the original proposition of Breiman would have been to perform a majority vote between the decisions provided by the B classifiers. Experimental results (not shown here) show that this strategy is a poor choice in the TBM framework. This suggests that the evidential K-NN procedure already provides stable decision rules, a finding in agreement with Breiman's results concerning the standard K-NN [2].

4 Experimental Settings

So as to investigate the benefits of bagging, we will focus on an artificial learning task. For easy problems, with well-separated classes and large training sets, many different algorithms yield similar results. A learning task of interest should therefore involve overlapping class distributions and a small learning set. Additionally, it should contain outliers as frequently encountered in real data sets. Finally, a bidimensional problem allows clear representation and interpretation of the results.

We thus consider three bidimensional Gaussian distributions with common covariance matrix $\Sigma = 2.25I$ and mean vectors $(0,0)$, $(3,0)$ and $(0,5)$. Each training set $\mathcal{L}$ is constructed by drawing 15 points from each distribution. Additionally, to simulate the contamination of the training set by outliers, 6 points with randomly selected class labels are drawn from a uniform distribution on $[-5,9] \times [-3,8]$. To exhibit general trends, 15 training

[1] The Dempster's rule of combination cannot be used because the belief sources are not independent.

sets were generated from the same distribution. Fig. 1 shows an example of such a generated set.

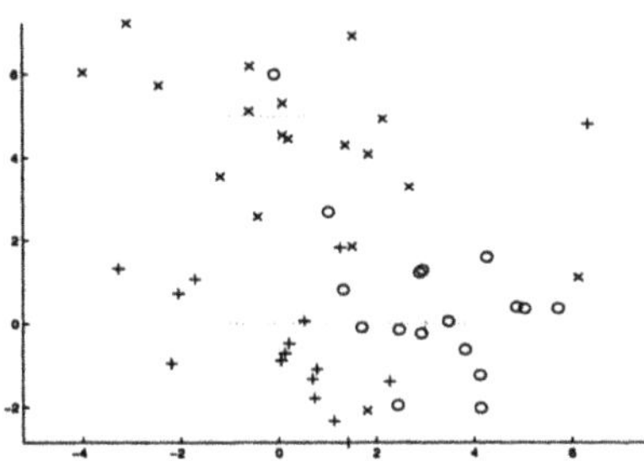

Fig. 1. Example of a generated learning set. The intersections of dotted lines indicate the class means.

Evaluation For each training set, the decision rule is evaluated on a single independent test set $\mathcal{T}$ generated from the same distribution as $\mathcal{L}$ with $N_\mathcal{T} = 2000 \times 3 + 800$ items. The mean classification cost $\mathbf{C}$ is estimated by the average of the classification costs on the $N_\mathcal{T}$ test points of $\mathcal{T}$:

$$\mathbf{C} = \frac{1}{N_\mathcal{T}} \sum_{(x,y)\in\mathcal{T}} \lambda(D(x)|y) \tag{11}$$

where $D(x) \in \mathcal{A} = \{\alpha_0, \ldots, \alpha_M\}$ denotes the decision made by the classifier for pattern x. The costs are defined according to Eqs. 6 and 7.

The classification error rate $\mathbf{E}$ is estimated by the proportion of bad predictions (rejection is not an error) and the rejection rate $\mathbf{R}$ is defined as the proportion of rejected items. We thus have the relation $\mathbf{C} = \mathbf{E} + \lambda_0 \mathbf{R}$.

Finally, we will also make use of the mean quadratic difference between the pignistic probabilities $\mathtt{Pbet}(\omega_i)$ and the class posterior probabilities $p(\omega_i|x)$:

$$\mathbf{Q} = \int \sum_i (\mathtt{Pbet}(\omega_i|x) - p(\omega_i|x))^2 p(x) dx, \tag{12}$$

The mean classification cost and the error rate are also computed for the Bayes classifier, whose optimal solution provides a baseline to compare results with and without bagging. Its performances also characterize the intrinsic difficulty of the task. For instance, the minimal rejection rates to achieve classification error rates of 10% and 5% are here respectively 23% (for $\lambda_0 = 0.34$) and 42% (for $\lambda_0 = 0.19$).

Results are reported according to two decision strategies. In the first one, the rejection cost λ_0 is fixed and may correspond, e.g., to the cost of the information needed to resolve the ambiguity. The performance is then measured by the mean classification cost $\mathbf{C}$. In the second one, a given classification error rate is required. Practically, the tuning parameter is still λ_0, but the interesting quantity is now the minimum rejection rate required to meet the criterion.

Implementation The method proposed by Denœux bears some resemblance with the Parzen method when the neighborhood is extended to the whole training set ($K = N$), because the influence of a neighboring vector decreases with its distance to the query point. Setting $K = 8$ achieves a near-asymptotic behavior while limiting the computational expense.

The influence of training patterns depends on parameters α and γ (see Eq. 5). As the influence of α on the classification is low [3], and in order to reduce the complexity of the analysis, it was set to the "standard" 0.95 value. Regarding γ, we will proceed here in two steps. First, all γ_q are fixed (Section 5); they are set to the same value (0.5) since the three classes have the same shape and the same number of items. Then, different learning strategies are tested in Section 6.

Finally, the average structure $m_{\mathbf{B}}$ estimates the expected structure over training sets. The expectation over training samples is ideally estimated by the expectation over bootstrap samples. Hence, the number B of bootstrap samples should tend towards infinity. In fact, the effect of bagging is quite visible for values as low as $B = 10$. We used $B = 50$, as the small improvement achieved by higher values is not worth the computation cost. Note that Breiman recommends values around 25.

5 Results without Learning

In this section, the results with and without bagging will be compared from two viewpoints: first, the quality of the decisions (measured by the mean classification cost or by the rejection rate needed to achieve a given error rate), and then the closeness of the pignistic probabilities to the class posterior probabilities.

5.1 Decision Level

The first plot of figure 2 shows mean classification costs vs. rejection costs for the 15 experiments. The horizontal segments in boxplots represent the lower quartile, median, and upper quartile results. Minimal and maximal values are indicated by the whiskers, and the plotted curve itself is the average over experiments. Bagging clearly improves classification for low classification costs $\lambda_0 < 0.3$, *i.e.* higher rejection rates. Its cost is half-way between the original algorithm and the Bayes classifier. However, this benefit vanishes for high values of λ_0 (low rejection rates). The improvement due to bagging is thus linked to its higher capacity to reject truly ambiguous patterns. but the pignistic probabilities values may be significantly modified so that rejection is more common.

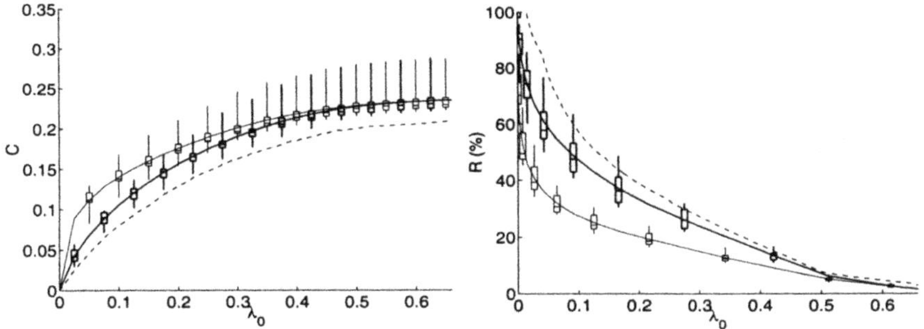

Fig. 2. Mean classification cost (left) and rejection rate (right) as a function of rejection cost for classic (thin line) and bagged (bold line) methods. The dotted line corresponds to the Bayes classifier

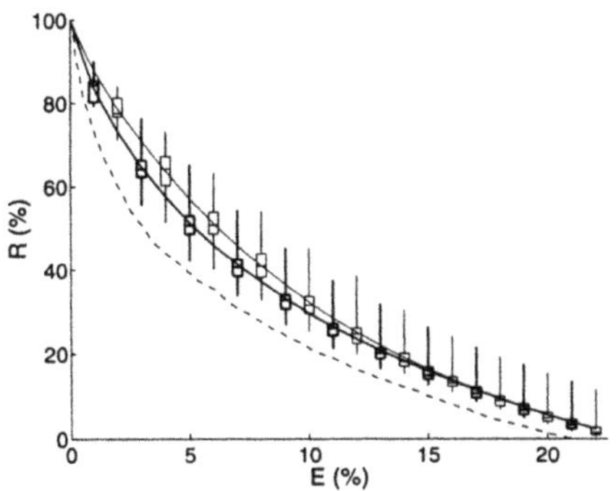

Fig. 3. Rejection rate **R** as a function of classification error rate **E** for original (thin line) and bagged (bold line) methods. The dotted line corresponds to the Bayes classifier

The second plot of Fig. 2 shows that the rejection rate of the bagged rule is much higher than that of the original rule. This means that bagging increases the uncertainty attached to the classification, that is, the uncertainty about conclusions. Rejection rate with bagging is also much closer to the Bayes classifier rate (for low λ_0 values), but however still lower. Bagging thus weakens the tendency of the original algorithm to over-estimate the confidence in classification.

These observations are confirmed when looking at the fixed error rate strategy in Fig. 3, where classification is visibly improved for the most stringent error rates requirements. Table 1 displays the mean rejection rates obtained with and without bagging for several error rates. The improvements are higher than what the boxplot in Fig. 3 suggests, because the boxplots show the global variability in performance for different training sets. The individual comparisons for each training set are summarized in Table 1. In this table, the second column (S-0-F) reports the number of trials for which the bagged version performed significantly better or significantly worse (first and third figure, respectively) than the non-bagged version at the 5 % significance level, according to the exact McNemar test for matched samples (see, for instance, [8]). The middle figure is the remaining number of cases, for which differences between the two methods were not significant. These results show that bagging never performs worse than the original classifier for error rates below 15%, and that it significantly improves the mean results for all error rates below 20%.

Table 1. Mean Rejection rates **R** (in %) for some given target error rates **E** (in %). Column S–0–F reports the number of significant success and failures (at the 5% level) of bagging for each training set. The p-values reporting the smallest level for which mean rejection rates differ significantly are all below 0.02%

E	S–0–F	Original	Bagged
2.5	12–3–0	74.2	68.9
5.0	15–0–0	57.0	51.5
10.0	15–0–0	32.3	29.6
15.0	7–8–0	16.4	15.9
20.0	6–6–3	5.8	5.6

For a classification task with a small number of classes, taking into account the uncertainty due to the finite size of the training sample hardly modifies the rank of the highest pignistic probability. Its value is however duly lowered, which is interpreted as a more uncertain outcome. Bagging is thus beneficial when the values attached to belief assignments are of interest. Besides rejection, all applications where a measure of uncertainty should be attached to the decision are concerned.

5.2 Pignistic Level

While it may be possible to display the effect of bagging at the credal level, there is no satisfactory criterion for measuring the relevance of a belief structure. We thus resort to the study of pignistic probabilities which give more information on beliefs than the decisions themselves. Results of the previous sections provided hints suggesting that, with bagging, the pignistic probabilities **Pbet** should be closer to the posterior probabilities p. Indeed, the mean quadratic errors $\mathbf{Q}$ on posterior class probabilities (Eq. 12) are about 40% lower on the whole space when bagging is applied to the K-NN rule.

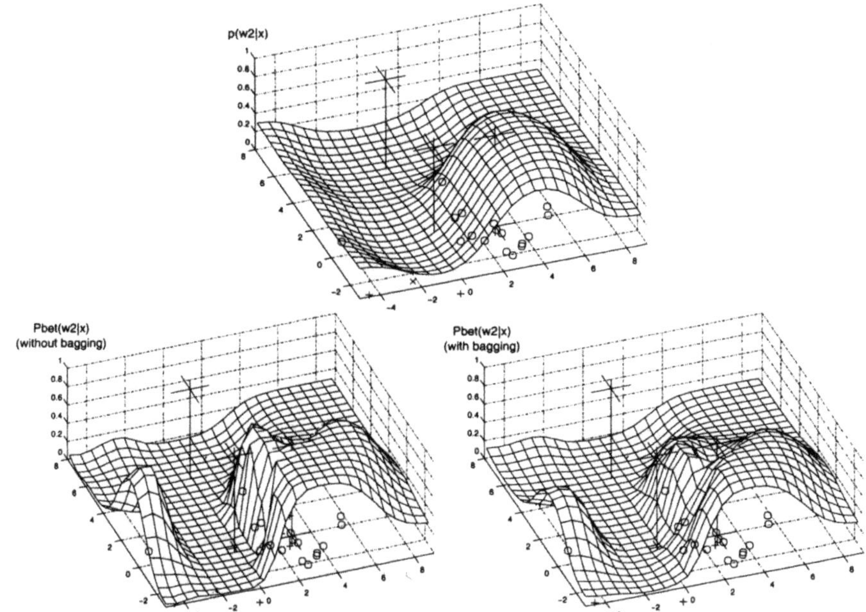

Fig. 4. Posterior probability $p(\omega_2|x)$ (top) and pignistic probability $\mathtt{Pbet}(\omega_2|x)$ without bagging (bottom left) and with bagging (bottom right). Vertical lines locate the centers of the three class distributions

We can easily illustrate situations where bagging is the most beneficial by plotting the probability surfaces, An example is given in Fig. 4, which shows that the main improvements occur at class boundaries and for outliers (one is situated in the lower-left corner of the graph). Bagging thus yields a better representation of uncertainties, stemming either from ambiguity (where classes overlap) or from lack of information (in regions of low density of training patterns).

The correction of these two types of uncertainties does not have the same impact on the estimation of posterior class probabilities, and on the mean classification rate (decision level). This is illustrated in Fig. 5, which gives the quadratic error contours weighted by the mixture density $p(x)$. For example, as the outlier is situated in a region of low density, the weakening of its influence by the bagging procedure results in a negligible contribution to the mean error rate improvement. However, this effect could be much more

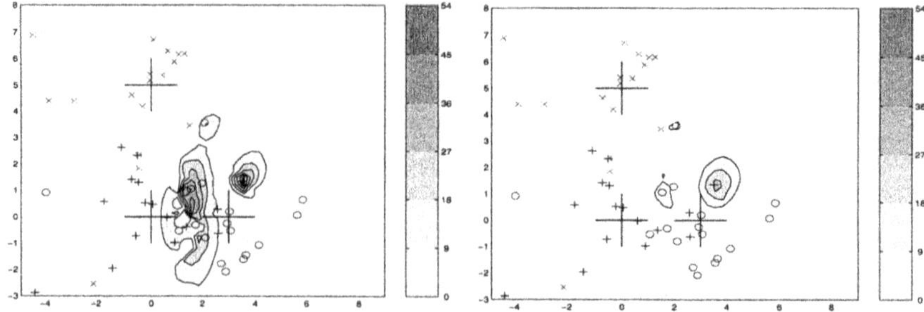

Fig. 5. Contours of the quadratic error on $p(\omega_2|x)$, weighted by the mixture density $p(x)$ ($\times 10^{-4}$). left: without bagging; right: with bagging.

noticeable with other misclassification costs : in a medical diagnosis application, for example, an outlier in the "healthy" class can cause an absence of illness detection.

6 Remarks about Learning

In the previous sections, the parameters α and γ of the basic belief assignment were set at arbitrary values. The effect of bagging regarding uncertainty due to the finite sample size was thus isolated. This section depicts the effect of bagging regarding the uncertainty pertaining to the learning of parameters. Here, α is kept at 0.95 as it was shown to have only marginal influence on the classification results [3,15].

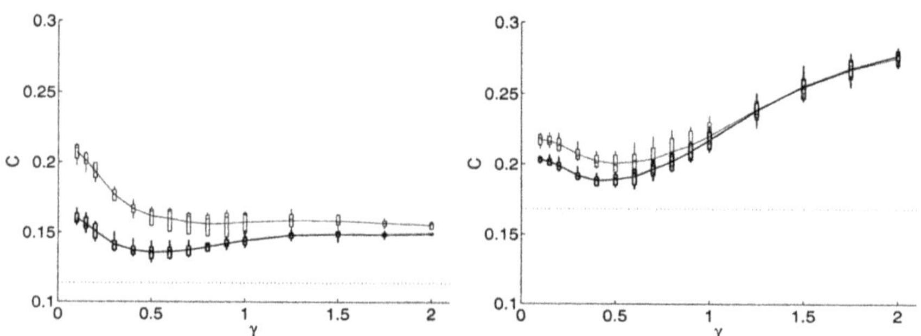

Fig. 6. Mean classification cost **C** as a function of γ for $\lambda_0 = 0.15$ (top) and $\lambda_0 = 0.3$ (bottom). The dotted line represents the Bayes classification cost, thin lines and bold lines represent respectively classic and bagged K-NN classifications

As explained in Section 2.2, the influence regions of training patterns are controlled by γ (Eq. 5). Fig. 6 shows the mean classification cost as a function of γ for the original classifier and its bagged version.

The bagged K-NN mean classification cost according to γ is always lower than that of the original algorithm for any given rejection cost. Thus, the results presented in the previous sections are representative of what would be obtained for any value of γ. The comparison of the two plots in Fig. 6 also shows that the differences between the two methods are larger for small rejection costs, regardless of γ.

Bagging is more effective in improving the original method for small values of γ, i.e., when all neighbors have the same influence, regardless of their distance to the query sample. In this case, the resulting belief is too confident, and bagging neatly corrects it.

In comparing the two graphs, it may be noted that, for the bagged algorithm, the optimal γ value is identical for both rejection costs, while it depends on λ_0 for the standard algorithm. Indeed, these two values should ideally not interact, as beliefs should not be affected by the consequences of actions. These consequences should only be taken into account in the decision process.

Finally, the lower variability of $\mathbf{C}$ provides a steadier optimal γ value and a lower sensitivity to errors in γ, in terms of misclassification cost.

7 Conclusion

Standard classifiers are sensitive to ambiguous training items such as mislabeled patterns or outliers. Regarding this point, the evidential K-NN rule improves upon the original probabilistic rule, as the certainty expressed by training patterns can be limited to weaken the influence of ambiguous items. In this paper, we show that bagging the belief structure construction process further improves this robustness.

Classification error is shown to be significantly reduced for high to intermediate rejection rates, and is always observed to be lower than that of the non-bagged K-NN rule. Pignistic probabilities are much closer to posterior probabilities, which in turns supports the idea that bagging defines more relevant belief structures.

Beyond the evidential K-NN, this paper illustrates the necessity to build generic tools for inferring beliefs. It is probably the first attempt to take into account the uncertainty due to the presence/absence of an information source upon which beliefs are constructed. In the classical pattern recognition paradigm, where information sources are points assumed to be sampled from some fixed distribution, resample and combine techniques provide a fully automatic means to correct undue certainty in inferred beliefs.

Work in progress shows that the gain is more important for classifiers that make a more intensive use of data (with more learning parameters).

More sophisticated inference methods such as decision trees or fuzzy K-means should thus also be improved. Investigations could be done on other operators to combine the belief structures in the bagging procedure in order to further improve the quality of belief representation at the credal level.

References

1. A. Appriou. Uncertain data aggregation in classification and tracking processes. In B. Bouchon-Meunier, editor, *Aggregation and Fusion of imperfect information*, pages 231–260. Physica-Verlag, Heidelberg, 1998.
2. L. Breiman. Bagging predictors. *Machine Learning*, 24:123–140, 1996.
3. T. Denœux. A k-nearest neighbor classification rule based on Dempster-Shafer theory. *IEEE Trans. on Systems, Man and Cybernetics*, 25(05):804–813, 1995.
4. T. Denœux. Analysis of evidence-theoretic decision rules for pattern classification. *Pattern Recognition*, 30(7):1095–1107, 1997.
5. T. Denœux. Application du modèle des croyances transférables en reconnaissance de formes. *Traitement du Signal*, 14(5):443–451, 1998.
6. T.G. Dietterich. An experimental comparison of three methods for constructing ensembles of decision trees: Bagging, boosting and randomization. *Machine Learning*, 40(2):1–19, 2000.
7. B. Efron and R. Tibshirani. *An introduction to the bootstrap*, volume 57 of *Monographs on Statistics and Applied Probability*. Chapman and Hall, New York, 1993.
8. B. D. Ripley. *Pattern Recognition and Neural networks*. Cambridge University Press, Cambridge, 1996.
9. G. Rogova. Combining the results of several neural network classifiers. *Neural Networks*, 7(5):777–781, 1994.
10. G. Shafer. *A mathematical theory of evidence*. Princeton University Press, Princeton, N.J., 1976.
11. P. Smets. The combination of evidence in the Transferable Belief Model. *IEEE Transactions on Pattern Analysis and Machine Intelligence*, 12(5):447–458, 1990.
12. P. Smets. The application of the Transferable Belief Model to diagnosis problems. *International Journal of Intelligent Systems*, 13:127–158, 1998.
13. P. Smets. The Transferable Belief Model for quantified belief representation. In D. M. Gabbay and P. Smets, editors, *Handbook of Defeasible reasoning and uncertainty management systems*, volume 1, pages 267–301. Kluwer Academic Publishers, Dordrecht, 1998.
14. P. Smets and R. Kennes. The Transferable Belief Model. *Artificial Intelligence*, 66:191–243, 1994.
15. L. M. Zouhal and T. Denœux. An evidence-theoretic k-NN rule with parameter optimization. *IEEE Trans. on Systems, Man and Cybernetics C*, 28(2):263–271, 1998.

Non-Euclidean Genetic FCM Clustering Algorithm

Sergio López García[1], Luis Magdalena[2], Juan R. Velasco[2]

[1] Lince Telecomunicaciones S.A. C/ Ortega y Gasset, 100. 28006 Madrid. E-mail: slopez@uni2.es
[2] ETSI Telecomunicación, UPM. Ciudad Universitaria s/n. 28080 Madrid. E-mail: llayos@mat.upm.es / juanra@dit.upm.es

Abstract. The standard FCM clustering algorithm is a powerful mathematical tool widely used in many practical problems. Nevertheless, it is dependent on initial conditions and either the number of clusters and the distance definition must be predefined. In [15,11] the authors presented the Genetic FCM clustering, that improves the first and second drawbacks, but not the third one. This article shows how the definition of the distance can be included in the genetic structure. Several results applied to the Iris data set are also shown.

1 Introduction

The Fuzzy C-Means [3] clustering algorithm is a mathematical tool that detects similarities in a collection of data. It is widely used in different fields, such as pattern recognition, data analysis and image processing.
However, FCM has several drawbacks, such as the predefinition of the distance (Euclidean by default). In [15,11] the authors have presented a genetic fuzzy c-means (GFCM) clustering algorithm. The key point is the use of Genetic Algorithms [5], a known optimisation method. GFCM algorithm overcomes several drawbacks of FCM, but not the distance definition. In this paper will be presented an improved GFCM that also treats about the distance definition problem.

2 Standard FCM Clustering Algorithm

Consider a set of n objects $X = \{x_1, x_2,...,x_n\}$ where $x_i \in R^S$. Each x_i is an object that is described by s real-valued measurements of their features. A fuzzy c-partition of X is a class of c fuzzy sets $V_1, V_2, ..., V_C$, where c is an integer in the range [2,n]. Then, a fuzzy c-partition space for X is the set:

$$M_{fcn} = \left\{ \begin{array}{l} U \in R^{cxn} \middle| u_{ik} \in [0,1], \forall i,k; \\ \sum_{i=1}^{c} u_{ik} = 1, \forall k; 0 < \sum_{k=1}^{n} u_{ik} < n, \forall i \end{array} \right\} \quad (Eq.\ 1)$$

The aim of the algorithm is to find the best partition matrix U in M_{fcn}. This objective is reached when the following function is minimised:

$$J_M(U,V)=\sum_{k=1}^{n}\sum_{i=1}^{c}u_{ik}^{m}\cdot d_{ik}^{2}(v_i,x_k), \qquad (Eq.\ 2)$$
$$U\in M_{fcn,}\ 1<m<\infty$$

In this function, v_i are the prototypes (or cluster centroids) of each class, m is a weighting exponent and d is the Euclidean distance. The cluster centroids are obtained with the following expression:

$$v_i=\frac{\sum_{k=1}^{n}u_{ik}^{m}\cdot x_k}{\sum_{k=1}^{n}u_{ik}^{m}} \qquad (Eq.\ 3)$$

The steps of FCM algorithm are the following:
(a) Select an initial partition $U^{(0)}$.
(b) Compute the cluster centroids v_i.
(c) Update the fuzzy membership

$$u_{ik}=\frac{\left(\frac{1}{d_{ik}^{2}(v_i,x_k)}\right)^{1/(m-1)}}{\sum_{j=1}^{c}\left(\frac{1}{d_{jk}^{2}(v_j,x_k)}\right)^{1/(m-1)}} \qquad (Eq.\ 4)$$

(d) Repeat steps (b) and (c) until the value of J_M is no longer decreasing.

3 Genetic Algorithms

Genetic Algorithms [5] are a known optimisation method that can be used in a great variety of problems. GA systems need four main elements:

- Population: the group of individuals to optimise. Applied to function optimisation, individuals are values of R^n.
- Environment: the place where individuals live. In function optimisation, the environment is the function itself.
- Goal: to reach the maximum of a 'fitness function'. This 'fitness function' measures the adaptation of the individual to the environment
- Reproduction mechanisms: algorithms that create new individuals from existing ones. They are usually selection, crossover, mutation and insertion.

The general structure of a GA is:
(a) Generate an initial population
(b) Evaluate this population
(c) Obtain a new population from the previous one:
    1) Select a number of parents from population

2) Take a number of pairs of individuals and mix their genetic code
3) Mutate a number of individuals
4) Insert new children into the old population, replacing the non-adapted individuals

(d) Evaluate the new population
(e) If the termination condition is met, stop
(f) Go to step 3

4 Genetic FCM Clustering Algorithm

The GFCM Clustering Algorithm [15,11] is designed to overcome the drawbacks of the FCM Algorithm. This work is divided into three main parts.

4.1 Initial partition of the space

The first problem detected on the FCM algorithm is its sensitivity to the initial partition of the features space. Due to this fact, certain initial partitions can lead to incorrect results.

In [15], the use of genetic algorithms was proposed to overcome this problem. Although algorithm structures are different, GFCM and FCM share the same functionals. The next figure shows the scheme of the aforementioned algorithm, such as it was proposed in [15].

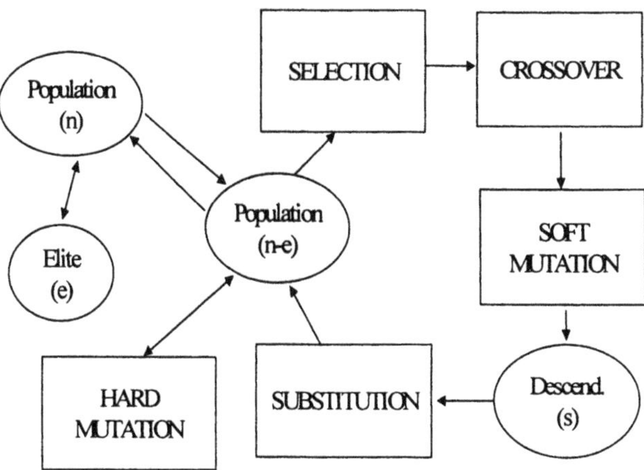

Fig. 1. GFCM Algorithm Scheme

Similar schemes can be found in references [6], [9] and [13]. However, in [11] the authors extend the scope of the algorithm showing how it can be used for the automatic generation of fuzzy partitions. It implies that, automatically, all the points of the features space are classified.

4.2 Problem of finding the number of clusters

One of the main disadvantages of the FCM algorithm is that the number of clusters (*c*) has to be fixed in advance, before the application of the algorithm. Although in some clustering problems the number of clusters is known beforehand, there are many other cases in which some method to find this value is needed. This situation happens because the FCM objective function, *J(U,V)* cannot be compared directly for different values of parameter *c*. Several references with different solutions to this problem can be found in the bibliography. Briefly, they are:

(a) Validation indexes

Originally, this kind of functionals was proposed to make a validation of the partitions created by the FCM algorithm. In this way, validation can be understood as a way to know the quality of the partition found by a clustering algorithm. Obviously, it is a subjective idea, but the validation indexes are independent on the number of clusters, what can be useful for the global problem. Some known indexes are:

- Xie-Beni [17,14]:

$$J(U,V) \Big/ c \cdot min(d(v_i,v_j)) \quad (Eq.\ 5)$$

- Fukuyama-Sugeno [14]:

$$J(U,V) - \sum_{k=1}^{n}\sum_{i=1}^{c} u_{ik}^2 \cdot d_{ik}^2(v_i,\bar{x}) \quad (Eq.\ 6)$$

- Gath-Geva [4]: It measures the 'hypervolume', based on the fuzzy covariance matrix of the clusters. In the same paper it is presented another index that measures the partition density, what is based in the hypervolume too.
- Mountain potential method [18,2]: this family of methods consists on the calculation of a *potential function* such as:

$$\sum_{k=1}^{n} e^{-\alpha \cdot d(x_k,N_i)} \quad (Eq.\ 7)$$

  where *n* is the number of points, x_k is every point of the space and *N* is a node (the point of the space where the potential is calculated).

(b) Uniform data functional methods

Windham showed in [16] a method that solves this problem in a different way. In this case, a function (or its coefficients) is looked for to equalize the value of *J(U,V)* for the different values of *c*. These coefficients can be obtained by means of making the FCM clustering to a uniform data distribution. In this kind of

distributions there is no substructure in the data. In this way, the value of the functionals should be the same for different values of the c parameter.
In references [15,10,11], the authors have proposed a solution based on the model of the uniform data functional, but structured inside a GFCM scheme. It has its source in the idea of the *species* of the natural genetic. A species is made of all the solutions of a certain clustering problem that have the same number of clusters. To implement this, a new concept is introduced: *the selection between species*, where an uniform data functional is included. Therefore, the stronger species has a higher number of individuals than the weaker species. It is shown in the following figure:

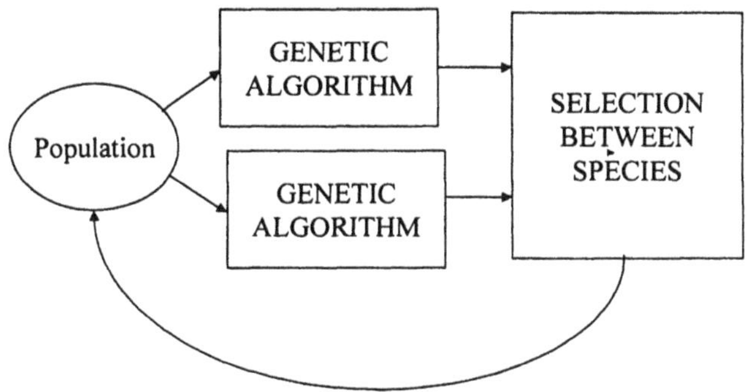

Fig. 2. Species scheme

In [12] a study of a validity functional, which will be applied in this work, is presented.

(c) Problem of the clusters shape

The problem of the shape of clusters is the last matter to deal with. As it was previously mentioned, standard FCM algorithm distance is Euclidean. In this way, the clusters detected by FCM are hyperspherical, having as many dimensions as the features space has. If the natural shape of clusters for the problem is hyperspherical Euclidean distance is suitable (sometimes, normalization in an appropriate way leads to this kind of solutions). Nevertheless, in several problems hyperspherical clusters are not fitted at all.

5 Non-Euclidean GFCM Algorithm

In a first approximation, it is easy to change Euclidean distance definition by another non-spherical one. In reference [19] are collected several distance functions. Perhaps the most interesting one is the Mahalanobis distance, defined by

$$d(a,b)=(a-b)^T \cdot A \cdot (a-b) \quad (Eq.\ 8)$$

where A is a positive definite matrix.

The difficulties appear when it is intended the coefficients calculation for A matrix. For Mahalanobis distance, matrix A has the shape:

$$A = \begin{pmatrix} a_{11} & a_{12} & \cdots & a_{1n} \\ a_{21} & \cdots & \cdots & a_{2n} \\ \cdots & \cdots & \cdots & \cdots \\ a_{n1} & a_{n2} & \cdots & a_{nn} \end{pmatrix}$$

where n is the number of space dimensions.

Each a_{ij} must be known for calculating J(U,V). Sometimes the coefficients are known in advance, but it is not usual. In a general case, the clustering algorithm must find the coefficients by itself. A less ambitious option is only to find coefficients for the main diagonal. This option leads to a ellipsoidal definition of clusters, being the values of a_{ii} the axis values of the unit circle. In this way, matrix A has the following shape:

$$A = \begin{pmatrix} a_{11} & 0 & \cdots & 0 \\ 0 & a_{22} & \cdots & 0 \\ \cdots & \cdots & \cdots & \cdots \\ 0 & 0 & \cdots & a_{nn} \end{pmatrix}$$

Obviously, if A = I (identity matrix), the distance definition is Euclidean. Using this matrix, the distance function has the form:

$$d(a,b) = \sum_{i=1}^{s} w_i \cdot (a_i - b_i)^2 \quad (Eq.\ 9)$$

where $w_i = a_{ii}$ of the matrix A.

In the references there are several methods for detecting hyperellipsoidal clusters, by means of calculating w_i.

- In [19] it is used an evolutionary algorithm that modifies w_i adding a gaussian noise function.
- On the other hand, [7] is a FCM-like algorithm finding the coefficients w_i by means of a Lagrange function. It is based in the classical Gustafson-Kessel clustering algorithm.
- Lastly, it can be mentioned the Gath-Geva [4] method based on the maximum likelihood estimation.

Here it is presented a non-Euclidean GFCM clustering algorithm. The values of w_i will be calculated in the genetic structure of the GFCM algorithm. In this way, the diagonal matrix of distances is one of the features of the individuals and it will evolve according to the known reproduction mechanisms of GA. Therefore, there will be one diagonal matrix per individual.

There is only one constraint in this structure: the determinant of the diagonal matrix must be constant (equal to one) for every individual. In this way, the fitness function of GFCM is consistent indeed. In addition, this non-euclidean GFCM

algorithm allows a linear normalization of the features space, if it were required. It would be done in the beginning of the algorithm.
The next section will present some results of the non-euclidean GFCM clustering algorithm for the Iris data set.

6 Results

6.1 Non-Euclidean GFCM Results

One of the most known data sets used for algorithm testing is the Iris data. The data set contains three kinds of flowers:

- Iris versicolor
- Iris virginica
- Iris setosa

The number of points for each set are 50. The features considered are:

- Sepal length
- Sepal width
- Petal length
- Petal width

It has been tested the overall algorithm using different values of parameter m. It is known that the algorithm converges for any $m \in (1, \infty)$, but the partitions become fuzzier as m increases (see [8]). Therefore, a good selection of this parameter will improve the results.
The figures 3, 4 and 5 will show the equalized J(U,V) functional. The reference case chosen was a 4-dimension sphere where r=1. In addition to this, features data was normalized to [0,1].

(a) m=1.5

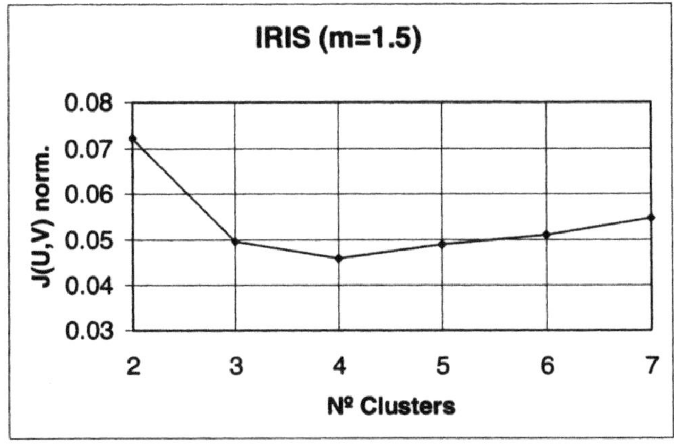

Fig. 3. Results for m=1.5

(b) m=2

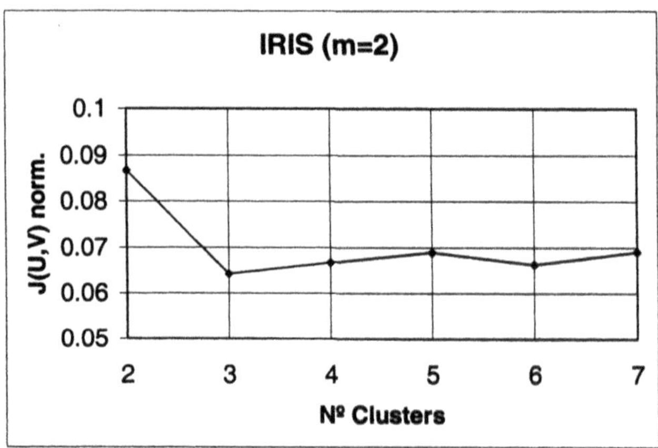

Fig. 4. Results for m=2

(c) m=3

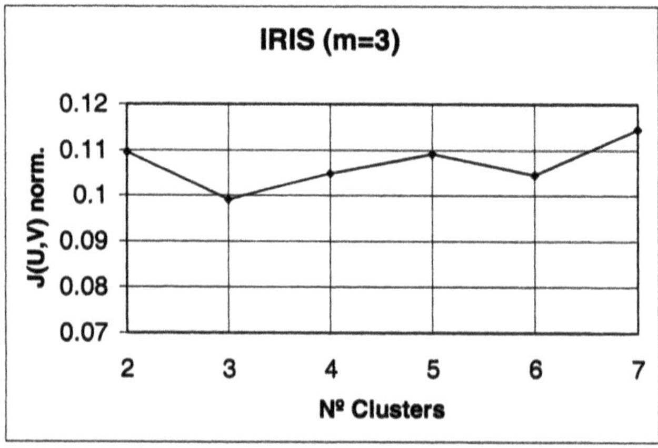

Fig. 5. Results for m=3

Due to the definition of data, the algorithm will work well if there would be a minimum in c=3. Using this hypothesis, it can be seen that the equalization function works better when m increases. It could be a deviation due to the reference case, but maybe it is caused because the best value of m is between 2 and 3 indeed.

The figure 6 shows the results for m=2 when the features data is not normalized. Compared with Figure 4, the results are poorer (and the number of misclassifications is higher too). As the reference case is normalized, this result is expected.

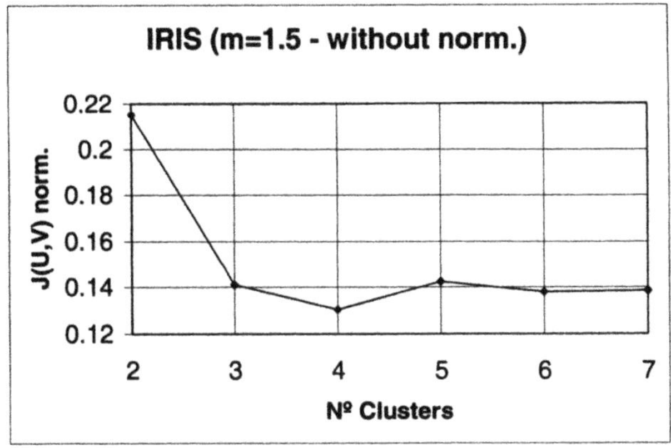

Fig. 6. Results for m=2 without normalization

Lastly, the table 1 shows the best and the average percentage of success point classifications for different values of m when the feature data is normalized. The success percentage is very high; for example, for m=2 there are only 7 misclassifications.

M	BEST	AVERAGE
1.5	96%	93.3%
2	95.3%	93.1%
3	94.7%	92.4%

Tab. 1. Percentage of missclassifications

6.2 Comparison between Validation Indexes

Until now, the results presented show that the non-euclidean GFCM algorithm works well in the Iris clustering problem. Now, it is time to test the method of calculating the number of clusters, by means of a comparison with the other functionals referenced in this paper.

We have run the algorithm using normalized data calculating four indexes: Xie-Beni [17], Fukuyama-Sugeno [14], Gath-Geva [4] (hypervolume) and the one proposed for the authors [6, 11], which will be called 'UDF' (which stands for 'uniform data functional'). As the results seem to be dependant on the values of m, three cases (m=1.5; m=2 and m=3) will be shown in the tables 2, 3 and 4.

It is pointed out in the columns of each table the best value of the indexes. Xie-Beni and Fukuyama-Sugeno ones do not seem to be appropriate for this problem, although both can be good indexes for the original validation problem. The hypervolume calculus proposed by Gath and Geva works fine in m=3, but it does not work well in m=2 and m=1.5. Finally, UDF is right in m=2 and m=3 but fails for m=1.5. However, UDF shows a good property: it avoids the edge values (c=2 and c=7), what are the main weakness of the rest of the indexes.

c	Xie-Beni	Fukuy.-Sugeno	Gath-Geva	UDF
2	**0.07769**	-1.3476	**0.00017**	0.07297
3	0.14549	-24.213	0.01106	0.05297
4	0.14577	-15.929	0.00503	**0.04893**
5	0.30035	-44.566	0.00130	0.05019
6	1.78471	-17.888	0.01425	0.05529
7	0.68502	**-50.816**	0.00081	0.05103

Tab. 2. Comparison of indexes for m=1.5

c	Xie-Beni	Fukuy.-Sugeno	Gath-Geva	UDF
2	**0.06887**	6.81018	**0.00896**	0.08738
3	0.11275	3.07927	0.01803	**0.06926**
4	1.72126	-10.144	0.02565	0.07636
5	0.30267	-14.869	0.01728	0.07028
6	0.52882	-7.3359	0.01274	0.07845
7	0.99286	**-24.987**	0.01273	0.08353

Tab. 3. Comparison of indexes for m=2

c	Xie-Beni	Fukuy.-Sugeno	Gath-Geva	UDF
2	**0.04622**	5.18875	0.00945	0.10829
3	0.17753	1.00477	**0.00441**	**0.10135**
4	0.8787	0.82912	0.00896	0.10832
5	0.25019	-1.1859	0.01219	0.10487
6	0.16833	-0.9889	0.02238	0.10491
7	0.61825	**-2.1221**	0.01319	0.11898

Tab. 4. Comparison of indexes for m=3

7 Conclusions

In this work it is presented the non-euclidean GFCM clustering algorithm. This algorithm is more complex than FCM, but overcomes the weaknesses of it. It is also shown a successful test on Iris data. In addition to this, the way of calculating the number of clusters has been tested, compared with other methods, with a satisfactory outcome. About the future works, there are three different ways for improving the algorithm:

- First of all, in this paper it has not been tested the mountain method as a way of calculating the number of clusters. There are two difficulties with this method: it cannot match well with the species scheme and it has several parameters which are difficult to find out. However, we think that it is a very interesting idea and we will test it in future works
- Secondly, it has been used a diagonal matrix A in the distance definition. However, finding the coefficients for the whole matrix can improve the results.
- Finally, it has not been mentioned the algorithm performance. In a AMD K6-II 350 MHz (Linux OS) the algorithm lasts about 7 hours, with the parameters: 100 individuals, 100 iterations and 6 species. An optimization of this performance will be tried in following works.

References

[1] Bezdek, J.C.; Pal, S.K. 'Fuzzy Models for Pattern Recognition'. Chap. 1.3. in *Pattern Recognition: Models and Approaches.* IEEE Press, 1992.

[2] Chiu, S.L. 'A cluster estimation method with extension to fuzzy model identification' in *Proc. FUZZ-IEEE'94*, pp. 1240- 1245. 1994.

[3] Dunn, J. 'A fuzzy relative of the isodata process and its use in detecting compact well separated clusters' in *J. Cybernetics*, 3(3):32-57. 1973.

[4] Gath, I.; Geva, A.B. 'Unsupervised optimal fuzzy clusterings' in *IEEE Trans. Pattern Analysis and Machine Intelligence*, 11(7):773-781. 1989.

[5] Goldberg, D. *Genetic Algorithms in search, optimization and machine learning*. Addison-Wesley, 1989.

[6] Hall, L.; Bezdek, J.C. ;Boggavarpu, S.; Bensaid S. 'Genetic Fuzzy Clustering' in *Proc. NAFIPS'94*. pp. 411-415. 1994.

[7] Keller, A.; Klawonn, F. 'Fuzzy Clustering with Weighting of Data Variables' in *EUSFLAT-ESTYLF Joint Conference 1999* pp. 497-500. 1999.

[8] Klir, G.J.; Yuan, B. *Fuzzy sets and fuzzy logic theory and applications*. Prentice-Hall, 1995.

[9] Liu, J.; Xie, W. 'A genetics-based approach to fuzzy clustering' in *Proc. FUZZ-IEEE'95*. pp 2233-2237. 1995.

[10] López, S.; Velasco, J.R; Magdalena, L. 'Generación de Particiones Borrosas mediante técnicas de Agrupamiento mejoradas con Algoritmos Genéticos' in *Revista Iberoamericana de Inteligencia Artificial*, N° 5 V/98, pg. 74-79. 1998.

[11] López, S.; Magdalena, L.; Velasco, J.R. 'Genetic Fuzzy C-Means Algorithm for the Automatic Generation of Fuzzy Partitions' in *Proc. IPMU'98*. pp. 705-711 Paris. 1998.

[12] López, S.; Magdalena, L.; Velasco, J.R. 'Cluster validity for FCM clustering algorithm using uniform data' in *EUSFLAT-ESTYLF Joint Conference 1999*, pp. 501-504. 1999.

[13] Nascimento, S.; Moura-Pires, F. 'A genetic fuzzy c-means algorithm' in *Proc IPMU'96*. pp 745-750. 1996.
[14] Pal, N.R.; Bezdek, J. 'On cluster validity for the fuzzy c-means model' in *IEEE Trans. Fuzzy Systems*, 3(3):370-379. 1995.
[15] Velasco, J.R.; López S.; Magdalena, L. 'Genetic Fuzzy Clustering for the definition of the fuzzy sets' in *Proc. FUZZ-IEEE'97.*, pp. 1665-1670. 1997.
[16] Windham, M.P. 'Cluster validity for the Fuzzy c-Means Clustering Algorithm' in *IEEE Trans. on Pattern Analysis and Machine Intelligence*, 4(4):357-363. July, 1982.
[17] Xie, X.; Beni, G. 'A validity measure for fuzzy clustering' in *IEEE Trans. Pattern Analysis and Machine Intelligence,* 13(8):841-847. 1991.
[18] Yager, R.R.; Filev, D.P. 'Aproximate clustering via the Mountain Method' in *IEEE Trans. on Systems, Man and Cybernetics*, 24 (8):1279-1284. August, 1994.
[19] Yuan B.; Klir G.J.; Swan-Stone F.J. 'Evolutionary Fuzzy C-Means clustering algorithm' in *Proc. FUZZ-IEEE'95*, pp. 2221-2226. 1995.
[20] Zadeh, L.A. 'Fuzzy Sets' *in Information and Control*, vol 8. pp. 338-352. 1965.

Different Approaches to Induce Cooperation in Fuzzy Linguistic Models Under the COR Methodology*

Jorge Casillas, Oscar Cordón, and Francisco Herrera

Dept. Computer Science and Artificial Intelligence,
Computer Engineering School, University of Granada,
E-18071 Granada, Spain

Abstract. Nowadays, Linguistic Modeling is considered to be one of the most important areas of application for Fuzzy Logic. It is accomplished by linguistic Fuzzy Rule-Based Systems, whose most interesting feature is the interpolative reasoning developed. This characteristic plays a key role in their high performance and is a consequence of the cooperation among the involved fuzzy rules.

A new approach that makes good use of this aspect inducing cooperation among rules is introduced in this chapter: the Cooperative Rules methodology. One of its interesting advantages is its flexibility allowing it to be used with different combinatorial search techniques. Thus, four specific metaheuristics are considered: simulated annealing, tabu search, genetic algorithms and ant colony optimization. Their good performance is shown when solving a real-world problem.

1 Introduction

At present, system modeling is one of the main applications of fuzzy rule-based systems (FRBSs) [2,17]. It may be considered as an approach to model a system making use of a descriptive language based on fuzzy logic with fuzzy predicates [19]. In this framework, one of the most interesting areas is *Linguistic Modeling*, where the interpretability of the obtained model is the main requirement. This task is developed by means of linguistic FRBSs, which use fuzzy rules composed of linguistic variables [22] that take values in a term set with a real-world meaning. Thus, the linguistic model consists of a set of linguistic descriptions regarding the behavior of the system being modeled [19].

Several tasks have to be performed in order to design an FRBS (linguistic model) for a concrete application. One of the most important and difficult ones is to derive an appropriate knowledge base (KB) about the problem being solved. The KB stores the available knowledge in the form of fuzzy linguistic IF-THEN rules. It consists of the rule base (RB), constituted by the collection of rules in their symbolic forms, and the data base (DB), which contains the linguistic term sets and the membership functions defining their meanings.

* This research is supported by CICYT, project PB98-1319

In this sense, numerous methods have been proposed to automatically generate fuzzy rules from numerical data. Usually, they consider complex rule generation mechanisms based on neural networks [9,15] or genetic algorithms (GAs) [5,11,18], among others.

Opposite to them, this chapter is devoted to present the Cooperative Rules (COR) learning methodology (initially proposed in [3,4]), whose good performance is related to the consideration of cooperation among rules. The methodology simplifies the rule generation process and is capable of being used with any combinatorial search technique. Thus, four different neighborhood-based and global search metaheuristics will be selected to be applied in COR:

- simulated annealing (SA) algorithms,
- tabu search (TS) algorithms,
- GAs, and
- ant colony optimization (ACO) algorithms.

The paper is organized as follows. Section 2 introduces the methodology proposed to improve the accuracy of linguistic models by means of more cooperative rules. Section 3 shows how to learn cooperative rules with the four said metaheuristics. Section 4 analyzes the behavior of our proposals and other methods when solving a real-world problem. Finally, Sect. 5 outlines some concluding remarks.

2 The Cooperative Rules Methodology

A family of efficient and simple methods to derive fuzzy rules guided by covering criteria of the data in the example set, called *ad hoc data-driven methods*, has been proposed in the literature in the last few years [3]. Their high performance, in addition to their quickness and easy understanding, make them very suitable for learning tasks.

However, ad hoc data-driven methods usually look for the fuzzy rules with the best individual performance (e.g. [21]) and therefore the global interaction among the rules of the RB is not considered. This sometimes causes KBs with bad cooperation among the rules to be obtained, thus not being as accurate as desired. This is due to the interpolative reasoning developed by FRBSs, which is one of the most interesting features of these kinds of systems and plays a key role in their high performance, being a consequence of the cooperative action among the linguistic rules. Moreover, the fact of locally processing these rules makes these learning methods be more sensitive to noise.

With the aim of addressing these drawbacks keeping the interesting advantages of ad hoc data-driven methods, a new methodology to improve the accuracy obtaining better cooperation among the rules is proposed in [3,4]: the COR methodology. Instead of selecting the consequent with the highest performance in each subspace like ad hoc data-driven methods usually do, the COR methodology considers the possibility of using another consequent, different from the best one, when it allows the FRBS to be more accurate thanks to having a KB with better cooperation.

In this way, its operation mode consists of two stages:

1. Obtain a set of candidate consequents for each rule.
2. Perform a *combinatorial search* among these sets looking for the combination of consequents with the best global accuracy.

A wider description of the COR-based rule generation process is shown in Fig. 1, whilst an example of the operation mode for a simple problem with two input variables and three labels in the output fuzzy partition is graphically illustrated in Fig. 2.

Since the search space – Fig. 2d in the example – tackled in step 2 of the algorithm is usually large, it is necessary to use approximate search techniques. Any combinatorial search approach may be used for such a purpose. In this contribution, four different well-known techniques are proposed: SA algorithms, TS algorithms, GAs, and ACO algorithms. The following section introduces the particular aspects for applying the considered techniques to the COR methodology.

3 Different Approaches to Learn Fuzzy Linguistic Rules Inducing Cooperation Among Them

3.1 Learning with Simulated Annealing

Introduction

SA [20] is a neighborhood-based search technique based on the analogy with the physical annealing process of solids. The SA-based algorithm begins with an initial solution and generates a neighbor of this solution by means of a suitable mechanism. If the latter is better than the former, the current solution is replaced by the generated neighbor; otherwise, this replacement is accomplished with a specific probability that will be decreased during the algorithm progress. This process is iterated a large number of times.

Simulated Annealing Algorithms Applied to the COR Methodology

The proposed COR-based learning method with an SA algorithm is characterized as follows:

- *Representation* — An integer-valued vector (c) of size N_S is employed. Each cell of the vector represents the index of the consequent used to build the rule in the corresponding subspace:

$$\forall s \in \{1, \ldots, N_S\},\ c[s] = k_s\ s.t.\ B_{k_s} \in \mathbf{B}^s\ .$$

Inputs:

- An input-output data set – $E = \{e_1, \ldots, e_l, \ldots, e_N\}$, with $e_l = (x_1^l, \ldots, x_n^l, y^l)$, $l \in \{1, \ldots, N\}$, N being the data set size, and n being the number of input variables – representing the behavior of the problem being solved.
- A fuzzy partition of the variable spaces. In our case, uniformly distributed fuzzy sets are regarded:

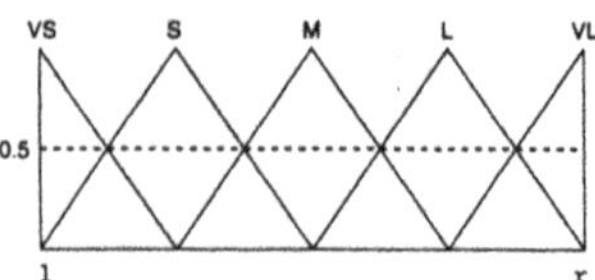

Let $\mathcal{A}_i$ be the set of linguistic terms of the i-th input variable – with $i \in \{1, \ldots, n\}$ –, and $\mathcal{B}$ be the set of linguistic terms of the output variable, with $|\mathcal{A}_i|$ ($|\mathcal{B}|$) being the number of linguistic terms of the i-th input (output) variable.

Algorithm:

1. *Generate candidate rules in each subspace* — For each n-dimensional fuzzy input subspace containing at least an example, $S_s = (A_1^s, \ldots, A_i^s, \ldots, A_n^s)$ such that $E_s' = \{e_l \in E \mid \mu_{A_1^s}(x_1^l) \cdot \ldots \cdot \mu_{A_n^s}(x_n^l) \neq 0\} \neq \emptyset$ – with $A_i^s \in \mathcal{A}_i$ being a label, $\mu_{A_i^s}(\cdot)$ being its membership function, $s \in \{1, \ldots, N_S\}$, and $N_S \leq \prod_{i=1}^n |\mathcal{A}_i|$ being the number of subspaces with examples –, do:
   (a) Let $\mathbf{B}^s = \{B_k \in \mathcal{B},\ k \in \{1, \ldots, |\mathcal{B}|\}\ \textit{such that}\ \exists e_{l^s} \in E_s'\ \textit{with}\ \mu_{B_k}(y^{l^s}) \neq 0\}$ be the set of linguistic labels in the output variable term set which contain examples belonging to E_s', and let $|\mathbf{B}^s|$ be the number of candidate consequets in the subspace S_s.
   (b) For each linguistic label $B_{k^s}^s \in \mathbf{B}^s$ compute the covering value, CV, of the linguistic rule associated with the S_s subspace built using this term as a value in the consequent, $R_{k^s}^s$ = IF X_1 is A_1^s and ... and X_n is A_n^s THEN Y is $B_{k^s}^s$, over each example $e_{l^s} \in E_s'$ as follows:

$$CV(R_{k^s}^s, e_{l^s}) = Min(\mu_{A_1^s}(x_1^{l^s}), \ldots, \mu_{A_n^s}(x_n^{l^s}), \mu_{B_{k^s}^s}(y^{l^s})).$$

2. *Select the most cooperative rule in each subspace* — This stage is performed by running a combinatorial search algorithm to look for the combination $\{B_{k^1}^1, \ldots, B_{k^s}^s, \ldots, B_{k^{N_S}}^{N_S}\}$ with the best accuracy.
   To evaluate the quality of each solution, an index measuring the cooperation degree of the encoded rule set is considered. In our case, the algorithm uses a global error function called *mean square error* (MSE), which is defined as

$$\mathsf{MSE} = \frac{1}{2 \cdot N} \sum_{l=1}^{N} (F(x_1^l, \ldots, x_n^l) - y^l)^2,$$

   with $F(x_1^l, \ldots, x_n^l)$ being the output obtained from the FRBS when the example e_l is used, and y^l being the known desired output. The closer to zero the measure, the greater the global performance and, thus, the better the rule cooperation.

Fig. 1. Learning generic scheme followed by the COR methodology

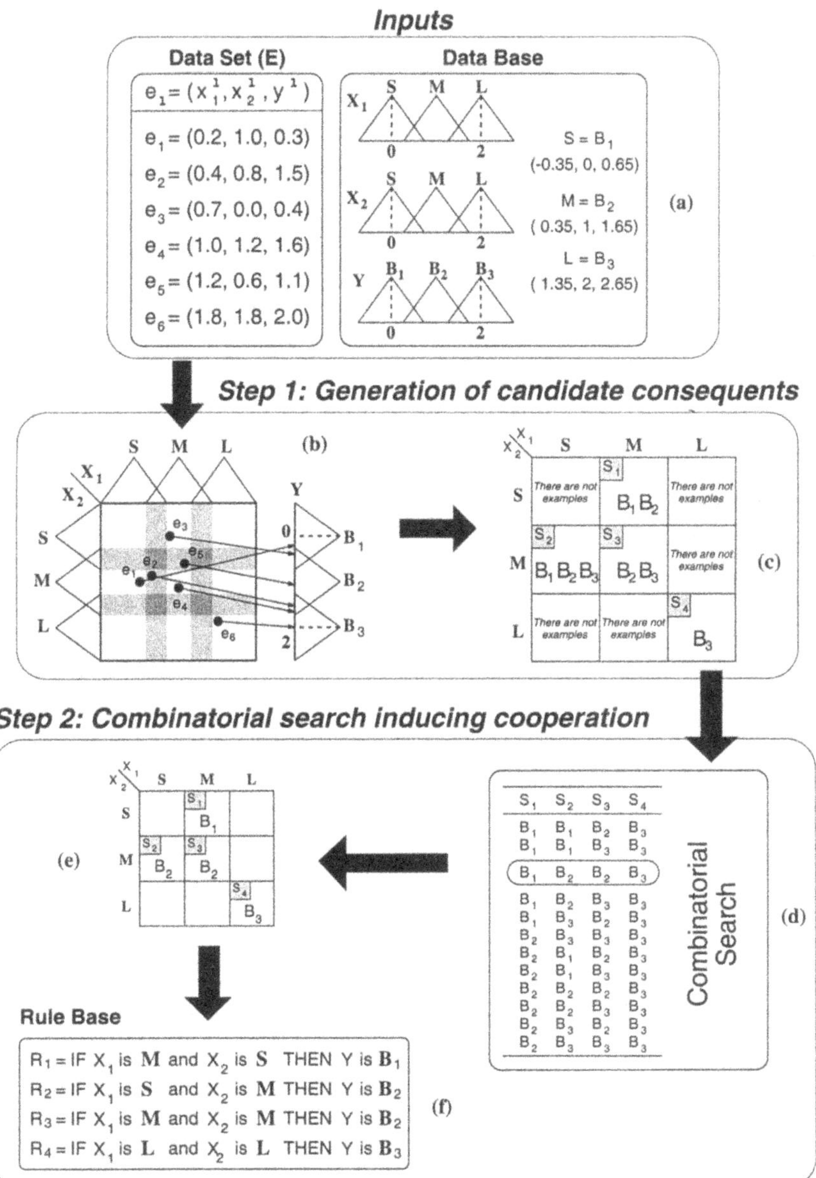

Fig. 2. COR-based learning process for a simple problem with two input variables ($n = 2$) and three labels in the output fuzzy partition ($|\mathcal{B}| = 3$): (a) data set (E) and DB previously defined; (b) the six examples are located in four ($N_S = 4$) different subspaces that determine the antecedent combinations and candidate consequents of the rules; (c) set of possible consequents for each subspace; (d) combinatorial search accomplished within a space composed of twelve different combinations of consequents; (e) rule decision table for the third combination; (f) RB generated from the third combination

- *Objective function* — The said MSE function (Fig. 1) is used.
- *Cooling scheme* — The cooling scheme used is the exponential one proposed by Kirkpatrick [13] ($T_{t+1} = T_t \cdot C$).
- *Trials per temperature* — The equilibrium at a specific temperature is achieved when a maximum number of neighbors has been generated.
- *Initial solution* — The initial solution is obtained by generating a possible combination at random.
- *Neighbor generation* — The operator considered to obtain a neighbor randomly selects a specific $s \in \{1, \ldots, N_S\}$ where $|\mathbf{B^s}| \geq 2$, and changes at random k^s by $k^{s\prime}$ such that $B^s_{k^{s\prime}} \in \mathbf{B^s}$ and $k^{s\prime} \neq k^s$.
- *Stopping criterion* — The algorithm stops when no neighbor is accepted for a specific temperature.

3.2 Learning with Tabu Search Algorithms

Introduction

TS [10] is an adaptive procedure for solving combinatorial optimization problems, which guides a hill-descendent heuristic to continue exploration without becoming confounded by a lack of improving moves, and without falling back into a local optimum from which it previously emerged.

At each iteration, an admissible move is applied to the current solution, transforming it into its neighbor with the smallest cost. Solutions that increase the cost function are permitted, the reverse move is prohibited for some iterations in order to avoid cycling. The restrictions are based on a short term memory function that determines how long a tabu restriction will be enforced or, alternatively, which moves are admissible at each iteration.

Tabu Search Algorithms Applied to the COR Methodology

The proposed COR-based learning method with a TS algorithm has the following components:

- *Representation* — The same proposed for the SA approach (Sect. 3.1).
- *Objective function* — The said MSE function (Fig. 1) is used.
- *Tabu criterion* — The tabu list (or history record) contains the moves applied to obtain the most recently accepted solutions. The movement considered is the pair subspace–consequent, i.e., $(s, k^{s\prime})$.
- *Aspiration criterion* — Moves that yield solutions better than the best one obtained in the search are allowed even if they are tabu active.
- *Initial solution* — It is obtained as in the SA approach (Sect. 3.1).
- *Neighbor generation* —The same proposed in the SA approach (Sect. 3.1).
- *Intensification restart* — The current solution is replaced by the best one obtained till now when a specific *intensification convergence criterion* is meet. The tabu list size is also changed by randomly reducing or increasing it by 50%. The convergence criterion involves making a restart when the *best* and *current costs* differ during a specific number of iterations.

- *Diversification restart* — A *long term memory* is used to keep an account of the use frequency of each successful move. To do that, the array LTM is initialized to zero and whenever a move is accepted (say $(s, k^{s'})$), its corresponding counter is increased by one, i.e., $LTM[s][k^{s'}] \leftarrow LTM[s][k^{s'}]+1$. Subsequently, when a specific *diversification convergence criterion* is meet, a new solution is generated by selecting a consequent in each subspace according to a probability inversely proportional to the corresponding LTM value:

$$c[s] = k^s \quad with\ a\ probability\ of \quad \frac{\dfrac{1}{LTM[s,k^s]+1}}{\sum\limits_{B^s_{q^s} \in \mathbf{B}^s} \dfrac{1}{LTM[s,q^s]+1}} \ .$$

The convergence criterion is meet when the *best cost* has not been improved during a specific number of iterations.

3.3 Learning with Genetic Algorithms

Introduction

GAs are general-purpose global search algorithms that use principles inspired by natural population genetics to evolve solutions to problems. The basic principles of the GAs were first laid down rigorously by Holland [12] and are well described in many texts as [14].

The basic idea is to maintain a population of knowledge structures that evolves over time through a process of competition and controlled variation. Each structure in the population represents a candidate solution to the specific problem and has an associated *fitness* to determine which structures are used to form new ones in the process of competition. The new individuals are created using genetic operators such as crossover and mutation. Figure 3 shows the structure of a simple GA.

Genetic Algorithms Applied to the COR Methodology

The proposed COR-based learning method with a GA is characterized as follows:

- *Coding scheme* — The same proposed for the SA approach (Sect. 3.1).
- *Fitness function* — The objective will be to minimize the said MSE function (Fig. 1).
- *Genetic approach* — An elitist generational GA with the Baker's stochastic universal sampling procedure [1].

```
Procedure Genetic Algorithm
begin
    t = 0;
    initialize P(t);
    evaluate P(t);
    while (not termination-condition) do
        t = t + 1;
        select P(t) from P(t - 1);
        cross P(t) with an specific probability;
        mutate P(t) with an specific probability;
        evaluate P(t);
    end-while
end
```

Fig. 3. Basic structure of a GA

- *Initial pool* — The population is initially generated with the first individual as follows

$$\forall s \in \{1, \ldots, N_S\},$$

$$c_1[s] = arg \max_{B_{k_s} \in \mathbf{B}^s} \left\{ \max_{e_{l^s} \in E'_s} \{CV(R^s_{k^s}, e_{l^s})\} \cdot \frac{\sum_{e_{l^s} \in E'_s} CV(R^s_{k^s}, e_{l^s})}{|E'_s|} \right\},$$

  and the remaining chromosomes generated at random:

$$\forall p \in \{2, \ldots, pool\_size\},\ \forall s \in \{1, \ldots, N_S\},\ c_p[s] = \ some\ k_s\ s.t.\ B_{k_s} \in \mathbf{B}^s \ .$$

- *Crossover* — The standard two-point crossover is used.
- *Mutation* — The same that the said SA neighbor generation mechanism (Sect. 3.1).

3.4 Learning with Ant Colony Optimization Algorithms

Introduction

ACO algorithms [7] constitute a new family of global search bio-inspired algorithms that has recently appeared. Since the first proposal, the Ant System algorithm [8] – applied to the Traveling Salesman Problem –, numerous models has been developed to solve a wide set of optimization problems (refer to [7] for a review of models and applications).

ACO algorithms draw inspiration from the social behavior of ants to provide food to the colony. In the food search process, consisting of the food find and the return to the nest, the ants deposit a substance called *pheromone*. The ants have the ability of sniffing the pheromone and pheromone trails guide the colony during the search. When an ant is located at a branch, it decides to take the path according to the probability defined by the pheromone existing in each trail. In this way, the depositions of pheromone terminate in constructing a path between the nest and the food that can be followed by new ants. The progressive action of the colony members involves the length of the path is progressively reduced. The shortest paths are finally the more frequently visited ones and, therefore, the pheromone concentration is higher on them. On the contrary, the longest paths are less visited and the associated pheromone trails are evaporated.

The basic operation mode of ACO algorithms is as follows [8]: at each iteration, a population of a specific number of ants progressively construct different tracks on the graph (i.e., solutions to the problem) according to a *probabilistic transition rule* that depends on the available information (heuristic and pheromone trails). After that, the pheromone trails are updated. This is done by first decreasing them by some constant factor (corresponding to the evaporation of the pheromone) and then reinforcing the solution attributes of the constructed solutions considering their quality. This task is developed by the *global pheromone trail update rule.*

Ant Colony Optimization Algorithms Applied to the COR Methodology

The proposed COR-based learning method with an ACO algorithm has the following main aspects:

- *Problem representation* — To use ACO algorithms in the COR methodology, it is convenient to see it as a combinatorial optimization problem with the capability of being represented on a graph. In this way, we can face the problem interpreting the COR methodology as the way of assigning consequents ($B_j \in \mathcal{B}$) – i.e., labels of the output fuzzy partition – to n-dimensional fuzzy input subspaces containing examples (S_s) with respect to an optimality criterion (MSE).
  Thus, the graph is constructed taking the steps described in Fig. 4. Following these steps, the graph corresponding to the example presented in Fig. 2 would be the one shown in Fig. 5.
- *Heuristic information* — The heuristic information on the potential preference of selecting a specific consequent, B_j, in each antecedent combination (subspace) is determined as follows:

$$\eta_{sj} = \max_{e_{l^s} \in E'_s} \{CV(R^s_j, e_{l^s})\} \cdot \frac{\sum\limits_{e_{l^s} \in E'_s} CV(R^s_j, e_{l^s})}{|E'_s|},$$

  with $R^s_j =$ IF X_1 is A^s_1 and ... and X_n is A^s_n THEN Y is B_j.

1. *Set a node for each subspace* — Use a node for each n-dimensional fuzzy input subspaces containing examples (S_s), thus having a total of N_S subspace nodes.
2. *Link the subspaces to consequents* — The subspace S_s will be linked to the consequent B_j, with $j \in \{1, \ldots, |\mathcal{B}|\}$, if and only if it meets the following condition:
$$\exists e_l \in E \text{ such that } \mu_{A_1^s}(x_1^l) \cdot \ldots \cdot \mu_{A_n^s}(x_n^l) \cdot \mu_{B_j}(y^l) \neq 0 .$$
That is, if there is at least one example located in the fuzzy input subspace that is covered by such a consequent.

Fig. 4. Graph construction process

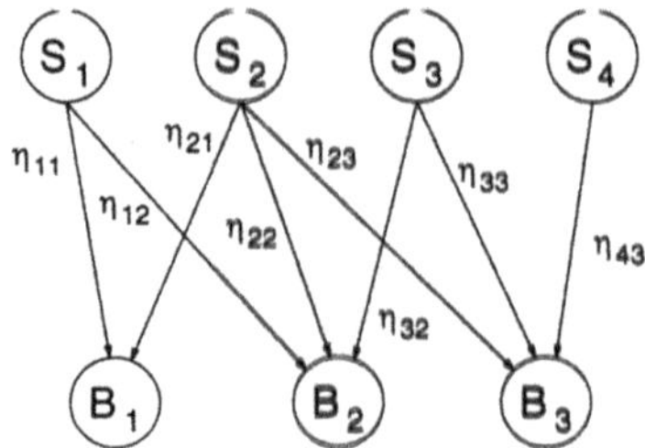

Fig. 5. ACO graph corresponding to the example of Fig. 2

- *Pheromone initialization* — The initial pheromone value of each assignment is obtained as follows:

$$\tau_0 = \frac{\sum_{s=1}^{N_S} \max_{j=1}^{|\mathcal{B}|} \eta_{sj}}{N_S} .$$

  In this way, the initial pheromone will be the mean value of the path constructed taking the best consequent in each rule according to the heuristic information (greedy assignment).
- *Fitness function* — The said MSE function (Fig. 1).
- *ACO approach* — The well-known Ant System [8] algorithm is considered.

4 Experimental Study Solving the Rice Taste Evaluation Problem

This experimental study will be devoted to analyze the behavior of the proposed COR-based methods. With this aim, we have chosen the problem of rice taste evaluation [16]. We will analyze the accuracy of the linguistic models generated from the processes introduced in the previous section compared to two well-known ad hoc data-driven methods, the ones proposed by Wang and Mendel (WM) [21] and Nozaki, Ishibuchi, and Tanaka (NIT) [16].

With respect to the FRBS reasoning method used, we have selected the *minimum t-norm* playing the role of the implication and conjunctive operators, and the *center of gravity weighted by the matching* strategy acting as the defuzzification operator [6].

4.1 Problem Description

Subjective qualification of food taste is a very important but difficult problem. In the case of the rice taste qualification, it is usually put into effect using a subjective evaluation called the *sensory test*. In this test, a group of experts, usually composed of 24 persons, evaluate the rice according to a set of characteristics associated with it. These factors are *flavor*, *appearance*, *taste*, *stickiness*, and *toughness* [16].

Because of the large quantity of relevant variables, the problem of rice taste analysis becomes very complex, thus requiring the design of a model representing the existing non-linear relationships. Moreover, the problem-solving goal is not only to obtain an accurate model, but to obtain a user-interpretable model as well, capable of putting some light on the reasoning process performed by the expert for evaluating a kind of rice in a specific way. Due to all these reasons, in this section we deal with obtaining a linguistic model to solve the said problem.

To do that, we use the data set presented in [16]. This set is composed of 105 data arrays collecting subjective evaluations of the six variables in question (the five mentioned and the overall evaluation of the kind of rice), made up by experts on the number of kinds of rice grown in Japan (e.g., Sasanishiki, Akita-Komachi, etc.). The six variables are normalized, thus taking values in the real interval [0, 1].

With the aim of not biasing the learning, we have randomly obtained ten different partitions of the mentioned set, composed by 75 pieces of data in the training set and 30 in the test one, to generate 10 different linguistic models in each experiment. Two labels will be considered to partition each linguistic variable domain.

4.2 Experiments and Analysis Results

The following values have been considered for the parameters of each COR-based method:

- *COR-SA*: cooling factor (C), 0.9; trials per temperature, 32; and initial temperature, 70.
- *COR-TS*: number of iterations, 150; initial tabu list size, 32; intensification convergence criterion, 10 iterations; and diversification convergence criterion, 7 iterations;

- *COR-GA*: number of generations, 500; population size, 61; crossover probability, 0.6; and mutation probability, 0.2.
- *COR-AS*: number of ants, 32; pheromone evaporation (ρ), 0.6; pheromone trail weight (α), 1; and heuristic information weight (β), 2.

The results obtained by the six methods analyzed are collected in Table 1, where #R stands for the number of rules, MSE_{tra} and MSE_{tst} respectively for the error obtained over the training and test data sets, EBS for the number of evaluations needed to obtain the best solution, and $\bar{x}$ and σ respectively for the arithmetic mean and standard deviation values over the 10 models generated by each method. The best results are shown in boldface.

Table 1. Results obtained in the rice taste evaluation problem

	#R		**MSE_{tra}**		**MSE_{tst}**		**EBS**	
Method	$\bar{x}$	σ	$\bar{x}$	σ	$\bar{x}$	σ	$\bar{x}$	σ
WM	**15**	0.632456	0.013284	0.005987	0.013119	0.004239	–	–
NIT	64	**0.000000**	0.008626	0.000345	0.009851	0.001931	–	–
COR-SA	32	**0.000000**	0.007076	**0.000571**	0.008012	0.001766	3,963	**110**
COR-TS	32	**0.000000**	0.007213	0.000553	0.008398	0.001638	**433**	118
COR-GA	32	**0.000000**	**0.006845**	0.000574	0.007830	**0.001457**	5,123	1,632
COR-AS	32	**0.000000**	0.006943	0.000602	**0.007702**	0.001594	1,108	307

In view of the obtained results, the methods based on the COR methodology perform a good learning process generating accurate models in both approximation – MSE_{tra} – and generalization – MSE_{tst} –, overcoming the WM and NIT methods.

Within the COR-based methods, the global search techniques (GAs and ACO) obtain better results than the neighborhood-based ones (SA and TS). Between the COR-GA and COR-AS methods, though they both generate models with similar accuracy, the latter only needs a fifth of the evaluations to find the solution, which is an interesting aspect to take into account. This fact seems to be related to the consideration of heuristic information made by ACO algorithms.

Figure 6 illustrates the behavior of the four analyzed techniques showing their evolution charts in the first data set partition. While the COR-TS method performs a gradual descent, the other three methods show a strong decrease at the beginning, although the COR-SA method becomes stabilized after several initial evaluations. As may be observed, the COR-AS method presents the best behavior quickly obtaining good solutions.

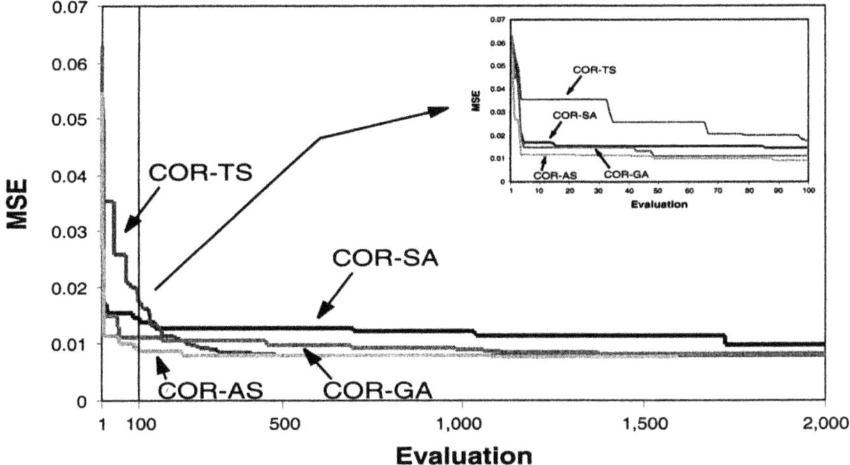

Fig. 6. Evolution chart of the four COR-based methods in the first data set partition

5 Concluding Remarks

A learning methodology to quickly generate accurate and simple linguistic models has been presented in this contribution: the COR methodology. It is based on considering the cooperation among the fuzzy rules in the generation process making good use of the interpolative reasoning developed by the finally designed FRBS. One of its interesting advantages is its flexibility allowing it to be used with different combinatorial search techniques.

Thus, four specific metaheuristics (SA, TS, GAs, and ACO) have been considered. Their good performance has been shown when solving a real-world problem. From this experimental study, the best results have been obtained by the ACO learning method thanks to it considers heuristic information to guide the search.

The obtained results lead us to conclude that the consideration of cooperative rules improves the performance of the linguistic models and the derivation of linguistic rules by firstly generating a candidate rule set and then searching the best combination of rules is a good way to accomplish this aspect.

References

1. Baker J.E. (1987) Reducing bias and inefficiency in the selection algorithm, Proceedings of the 2nd International Conference on Genetic Algorithms, Lawrence Erlbaum, Hillsdale, NJ, USA, 14–21.
2. Bárdossy A., Duckstein L. (1995) Fuzzy rule-based modeling with application to geophysical, biological and engineering systems. CRC Press, Boca Raton, FL, USA.

3. Casillas J., Cordón O., Herrera F. (2000) A methodology to improve ad hoc data-driven linguistic rule learning methods by inducing cooperation among rules. Technical Report #DECSAI-00-01-01, Dept. Computer Science and A.I., University of Granada, Spain.
4. Casillas J., Cordón O., Herrera F. (2000) Improving the Wang and Mendel's fuzzy rule learning method by inducing cooperation among rules. Proceedings of the 8th Information Processing and Management of Uncertainty in Knowledge-Based Systems Conference, Madrid, Spain, 1682–1688.
5. Cordón O., Herrera F., Hoffmann F., Magdalena L. (2001) Genetic fuzzy systems: evolutionary tuning and learning of fuzzy knowledge bases. World Scientific, Singapore. In press.
6. Cordón O., Herrera F., Peregrín A. (1997) Applicability of the fuzzy operators in the design of fuzzy logic controllers. Fuzzy Sets and Systems 86:15–41.
7. Dorigo M., Di Caro G. (1999) The ant colony optimization meta-heuristic. In: Corne D., Dorigo M., Glover F. (Eds.) New Ideas in Optimization. McGraw-Hill, 11–32.
8. Dorigo M., Maniezzo V., Colorni A. (1996) The ant system: optimization by a colony of cooperating agents. IEEE Transactions on Systems, Man, and Cybernetics. Part B: Cybernetics 26(1):29–41.
9. Fullér R. (2000) Introduction to neuro-fuzzy systems. Springer-Verlag, Berlin/New York, Germany/USA.
10. Glover F., Laguna M. (1997) Tabu search. Kluwer Academic, Dordrecht/Norwell, MA, USA.
11. Herrera F., Verdegay J.L. (Eds.) (1996) Genetic algorithms and soft computing. Physica-Verlag, Heidelberg, Germany.
12. Holland J.H. (1975) Adaptation in natural and artificial systems. Ann arbor: The University of Michigan Press.
13. Kirkpatrick S. (1984) Optimization by simulated annealing: quantitative studies. Journal of Statistical Physics 34:975–986.
14. Michalewicz Z. (1996) Genetic algorithms + data structures = evolution programs. Springer-Verlag, Berlin/New York, Germany/USA.
15. Nauck D., Klawonn F., Kruse R. (1997) Fundations of neuro-fuzzy systems. John Wiley & Sons, New York, USA.
16. Nozaki K., Ishibuchi H., Tanaka H. (1997) A simple but powerful heuristic method for generating fuzzy rules from numerical data. Fuzzy Sets and Systems 86:251–270.
17. Pedrycz W. (Ed.) (1996) Fuzzy modelling: paradigms and practice. Kluwer Academic, Dordrecht/Norwell, MA, USA.
18. Pedrycz W. (Ed.) (1997) Fuzzy evolutionary computation. Kluwer Academic, Dordrecht/Norwell, MA, USA.
19. Sugeno M., Yasukawa T. (1993) A fuzzy-logic-based approach to qualitative modeling. IEEE Transactions on Fuzzy Systems 1(1):7–31.
20. van Laarhoven P.J.M., Aarts E.H.L. (1987) Simulated annealing: theory and applications. Kluwer Academic, Dordrecht/Norwell, MA, USA.
21. Wang L.X., Mendel J.M. (1992) Generating fuzzy rules by learning from examples. IEEE Transactions on Systems, Man, and Cybernetics 22(6):1414–1427.
22. Zadeh L.A. (1975) The concept of a linguistic variable and its application to approximate reasoning. Information Science 8:199–249, 8:301–357, 9:43–80.

Retrieval of Information

Evaluation of Flexible Queries: The Quantified Statement Case

Patrick Bosc **Ludovic Liétard*** **Olivier Pivert**

IRISA/ENSSAT
Technopole ANTICIPA BP 447
22305 Lannion FRANCE
e-mail: bosc|pivert@enssat.fr

IRISA/IUT*
Rue Édouard Branly BP 150
22305 Lannion FRANCE
e-mail: lietard@iut-lannion.fr

Abstract

Many propositions to extend database management systems have been made in the last decade. Some of them aim to support a wider range of queries involving fuzzy predicates expressing preferences and this paper focuses on the evaluation of a particular subset of queries, namely those using fuzzy quantified statements. More precisely, we consider the queries calling on a partitioning where a linguistic quantifier appears in the set-oriented condition. This condition is expressed by a quantified statement of type "Q X are A" and its degree of truth is assumed to be computed via the Sugeno fuzzy integral. This paper proposes algorithms to evaluate such queries and the main objective is to reduce processing time by saving data access. Heuristics are integrated into the algorithms in order to conclude on the result without accessing all elements of the referential.

1 Introduction

When querying a database by usual means, it may happen that no data fulfill the requirements expressed by the query. In this case, the answer is said to be empty and this situation generally does not cope with users' expectations. Moreover, the user does not dispose of information about the content of the database which could help him reformulate his query in a more appropriate manner. A solution to avoid empty answers resides on flexible querying which mainly relies on the expression of conditions allowing for preferences. It is then possible to express that among acceptable answers, some are preferred. An advantage of flexible queries is to rank-order the best replies rather than to provide the user with a set of undifferentiated answers.

Let us consider the example of a user who is looking for "*economical* restaurants *not too far* from downtown". The Boolean query: "retrieve the restaurants having a menu less than $20 and situated less than 2 miles far from town hall" delivers an empty answer if no restaurant of the database satisfies both conditions. If the most interesting restaurant of the database has a menu of $22 and is located at 1.5 mile from town hall, this restaurant cannot be an answer, whereas it could be a *somewhat acceptable* response in the context of a flexible query including a condition stating that $22 is not ideal, but still *somewhat acceptable*.

This paper is set in the field of relational databases where it has been shown [1] that fuzzy set theory defines a more general framework for expressing flexible queries. In this context, flexible queries are based on predicates expressing preferences (also called vague or fuzzy predicates) modeled by fuzzy sets [2].

Vague predicates correspond to adjectives alone or with an adverb acting as a modifier [3, 4] (*young, very young*) and it is also possible to consider flexible connectors expressing preferences or compensation between the different levels of satisfactions.

This paper deals with particular flexible connectors, namely linguistic quantifiers [5] which model linguistic expressions (*about the half, most of, around 3*, ...) and allow for preferences. Such quantifiers express intermediate attitudes between the negation (*none*) and the generalized conjunction (*all*). In the following, a sentence involving a linguistic quantifier (as "*most of* the employees are *young*") is called a quantified statement. To compute or evaluate a quantified statement consists in determining its degree of truth (the extent to which "*most of* employees are *young*" can be considered true).

An extension of the SQL language to flexible querying using fuzzy sets (namely SQLf language [6, 7]) is considered in this paper. Our objective is to propose efficient algorithms to evaluate SQLf queries involving linguistic quantifiers. These algorithms are adapted to save processing time and they involve heuristics in order to conclude on the result before each data is accessed (the processing is then stopped earlier). When referring to the previous example ("*most of* the employees are *young*"), the heuristics aim at stopping the processing of the computation before each employee is accessed. Due to the lack of room, we limit this paper to a single use of linguistic quantifiers (the partitioning of relations) and to the interpretation of quantified statements based on the Sugeno fuzzy integral.

Section 2 is devoted to the interpretation of quantified statements by Sugeno fuzzy integral and their use in flexible queries involving a partitioning. Algorithms are proposed in Section 3. In the following, X denotes a finite and discrete set and P(X) its power set.

2 Linguistic quantifiers and flexible querying

Linguistic quantifiers are represented by fuzzy sets and are involved in statements of type "Q X are A" where Q is a linguistic quantifier, X a set of elements taken as a referential and A a vague predicate. Such an expression expresses that "in set X, Q elements satisfy the vague condition A" (e.g., "*almost all* employees are *young*"). Another type of quantified statements can also be considered such as "*almost all well-paid* employees are *young*" but their interpretation is much more tricky because of a fuzzy referential (see for instance [8]). Moreover they are probably less useful in flexible querying from a practical point of view and this paper deals with expressions of type "Q X are A".

It is possible to distinguish between absolute quantifiers (which refer to an absolute number such as *about 3, at least 2*, ...) and relative quantifiers (which refer to a proportion such as *about the half, at least a quarter*, ...). An absolute (resp. relative) quantifier Q in the statement "Q X are A" means that the number (resp. proportion) of elements satisfying condition A is compatible with Q.

A linguistic quantifier can also be increasing (resp. decreasing) [9] which means that an increase in the satisfaction to condition A cannot decrease (resp. increase) the degree of truth of the statement "Q X are A". *At least 3*, *almost all* (resp. *at most 2*, *at most the half*) are examples of increasing (resp. decreasing) quantifiers.

Subsection 2.1 is devoted to the representation of linguistic quantifiers; subsection 2.2 to the interpretation of quantified statements by Sugeno fuzzy integral. The integration of quantified statements into flexible queries calling on a partitioning is described in subsection 2.3.

2.1 Representation of linguistic quantifiers

The representation of an absolute quantifier is a fuzzy subset Q with membership function μ_Q defined on the natural numbers. A relative quantifier is a fuzzy subset Q with membership function μ_Q defined on the unit interval [0,1]. In both cases, the membership degree $\mu_Q(j)$ represents the degree of truth of the statement "Q X are A" when j elements in X completely satisfy A, whereas A is fully unsatisfied by the others (j being a number or a proportion). Consequently, the definition of a linguistic quantifier gives the degree of truth in case of Boolean predicates.

The representation of an increasing linguistic quantifier satisfies: i) $\mu_Q(0) = 0$, ii) $\exists$ m such as $\mu_Q(m) = 1$, iii) $\forall$ a, b if a > b then $\mu_Q(a) \geq \mu_Q(b)$.. The representation of a decreasing quantifier satisfies: i) $\mu_Q(0) = 1$, ii) $\exists$ m such as $\mu_Q(m) = 0$, iii) $\forall$ a, b if a > b then $\mu_Q(a) \leq \mu_Q(b)$.

Example 1. The linguistic quantifier (absolute and increasing) *at least 5* is given by Figure 1.

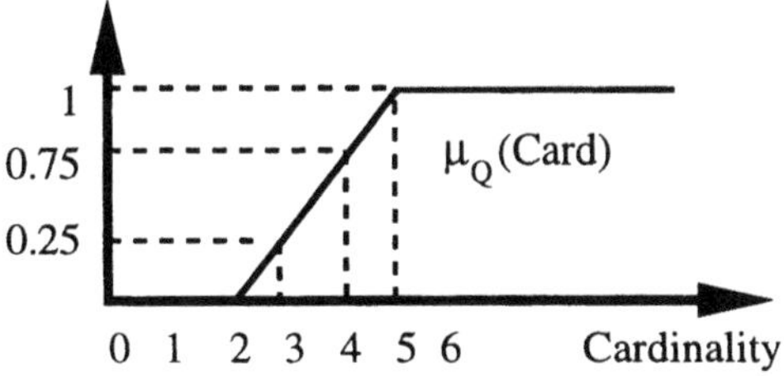

Figure 1: The quantifier *at least 5*

Let us consider X a set of individuals and the quantified statement "*at least 5* individuals are over 25 years old". As a Boolean predicate is involved, this statement is true at a degree $\mu_Q(s)$ with s the number of individuals being over 25 years old ♦

2.2 Interpretation of quantified statements by Sugeno fuzzy integral

In the general case, the predicate A appearing in "Q X are A" is fuzzy. The Sugeno fuzzy integral $S_m(A)$ has been proposed [10, 11] to determine the degree of truth of the quantified statement "Q X are A" when Q is increasing and absolute (resp. relative):

$$S_m(A) = \max_{1 \le i \le n} \min(\mu_A(x_i), \mu_Q(i)) \quad (1)$$

$$(\text{resp. } S_m(A) = \max_{1 \le i \le n} \min(\mu_A(x_i), \mu_Q(i/n)))$$

where $X = \{x_1, x_2, ..., x_n\}$ such that $\mu_A(x_1) \ge \mu_A(x_2) \ge ... \ge \mu_A(x_n)$. It is possible to show [11, 12] that this interpretation of quantified statements reverts to Yager's competitive type aggregation [13] and can be extended to decreasing quantifier.

Example 2. Set X is made of 6 individuals $\{e_1, e_2, e_3, e_4, e_5, e_6\}$ such that : $\mu_{young}(e_1) = \mu_{young}(e_2) = \mu_{young}(e_3) = 1$; $\mu_{young}(e_4) = 0.8$; $\mu_{young}(e_5) = 0.2$; $\mu_{young}(e_6) = 0.1$. The linguistic quantifier is given by Figure 1. The degree of truth of the statement "*at least 5* X are *young*" is given by:

$$S_m(A) = \max(\min(\mu_{young}(e_1),\mu_Q(1)),$$

$$= \max \min(\mu_{young}(e_2),\mu_Q(2)), \min(\mu_{young}(e_3),\mu_Q(3)),$$

$$\min(\mu_{young}(e_4),\mu_Q(4)), \min(\mu_{young}(e_5),\mu_Q(5)),$$

$$\min(\mu_{young}(e_6),\mu_Q(6))).$$

The computations return:

$S_m(A) =$
$\max(\min(1,0), \min(1,0), \min(1,0.25), \min(0.8,0.75), \min(0.2,1), \min(0.1,1)) =$ 0.75.

It can be checked that the result (0.75) is closed to 1 since, it appears that around 4 people (e_1, e_2, e_3, e_4) can be considered *young*♦

2.3 Partioning with linguistic quantifiers

In SQL, a relation may be partitioned into subsets according to the value of one or several attributes mentioned in a **group by** clause. In so doing, each subset gathers tuples which have the same value on the considered attribute(s) and further operations apply no longer to individual tuples but to subsets. This functionality is retained in SQLf, and in this context, the **having** clause can be used along with a set-oriented vague condition aiming at the selection of subsets. When the set-oriented vague condition involves a linguistic quantifier, the query is written:

select <calibration> <retained_attribute(s)>
from <regular relations> **where** <Boolean condition>
group by <attribute(s)> **having** (<quantifier> **are** <vague condition>)

As in SQL, for the query to be meaningful, the set of retained attributes (<retained_attribute(s)>) must be included in that of attributes appearing in the **group by** clause. The <calibration> indicates a threshold to be reached by an answer to be retained (qualitative calibration). Each subset p is assigned the degree $\mu_{svc}(p)$ expressing its satisfaction to the set-oriented vague condition (<quantifier> **are** <vague condition>). This degree is the degree of truth of the statement "*Q* X are *A*" where X is the considered subset, *Q* the linguistic quantifier <quantifier> and *A* the fuzzy predicate <vague condition>.

In the following we consider that <attribute(s)> and <attribute(s)_retained> are a same single attribute without loss of generality.

Example 3. Relation R(#emp, age, #dpt) describes the ages of employees (#emp, age) working in different department stores (#dpt). The SQLf query "retrieve the departments satisfying *at least 5* employees are *young* with a minimum level of satisfaction of 0.7" is expressed by:

select 0.7 #dpt **from** R **group by** #dpt **having** "*at least 5* **are** *young*".

The linguistic quantifier *at least 5* is given by Figure 1. According to this query, relation R is split into different subsets of employees, each of them being associated with a given department. We consider the following subset associated with department #1:

#emp	age	#dpt
e_1	22	#1
e_2	23	#1
e_3	22	#1
e_4	30	#1
e_5	45	#1
e_6	55	#1

such that: $\mu_{young}(e_1) = \mu_{young}(e_2) = \mu_{young}(e_3) = 1$; $\mu_{young}(e_4) = 0.8$; $\mu_{young}(e_5) = 0.2$; $\mu_{young}(e_6) = 0.1$. Department #1 satisfies the query at a degree $\mu_{svc}(\#1)$ given by the degree of truth of "*at least 5* X are *young*" with $X = \{e_1, e_2, e_3, e_4, e_5, e_6\}$. Computations returns the value 0.75 (cf. example 2). This degree of truth is over the threshold (0.7) and consequently department #1 is retained by the query ♦

3 On the evaluation of SQLf queries involving quantified statements and partitioning

3.1 Introduction

This Section deals with the design of algorithms for the evaluation of SQLf queries calling on a partitioning with linguistic quantifier. It is assumed that a qualitative calibration (i.e. a threshold to be reached) is specified in the query. This kind of query applies to subsets of tuples. For each subset X, the quantified statement "*Q* X are *A*" is evaluated to check if its degree of truth is over the threshold (cf. example 3).

Basically, such algorithms aim at computing, by means of a Sugeno fuzzy integral, the degree of truth of the quantified statement "*Q* X are *A*" involved in the query (*Q* being increasing). When "*Q* X are *A*" does not reach the threshold, the set X is not retained by the query. These algorithms have to be performed for each subset resulting from the partitioning.

We assume that membership degrees $\mu_A(x)$ and $\mu_Q(i)$ are provided by two functions Q and A and that functions Max and Min are available.

Our objective is to save data access by proposing conditions and heuristics to conclude on the result (and thus to stop the algorithm) before set X is entirely accessed. Subsection 3.1 introduces a naive algorithm (i.e. without heuristics). Subsection 3.3 defines principles for the design of heuristics. These heuristics are detailed in subsection 3.4 whereas subsection 3.5 proposes the final algorithm.

3.2 A naïve algorithm

The algorithm proposed here is based on a two stage process: i) an access to each element of X (each A(x) value and the cardinality of set X are computed); ii) the Sugeno fuzzy integral is computed and compared with the threshold α. The algorithm delivers the degree of truth of "*Q* X are *A*" when it is over the threshold and a zero if it is not the case. The introduced algorithm considers an absolute quantifier. It can be adapted to a relative quantifier (the modifications are in italics).

```
Procedure Naive_Algo(out res) is
    Deg : array of real;            % contains the μA(x)'s %
    Card : integer;                 %the cardinality of set X %
    Sug : real ;                    % the Sugeno fuzzy integral%
    i : integer                     % an index %

begin
    Card:=0;
    for each x in X do:             % step 1: access to elements %
      sorted insertion (decreasing order) of
      A(x) in Deg;
      Card := Card + 1;
    done;
                                    % step 2: computation of the integral %
    Sug:=min(Deg[1],Q(1));           % absolute%
    Sug:=min(Deg[1],Q(1/Card));     %relative%
    for i:= 2 until Card do
      Sug:= Max(Sug,min(Deg[i],Q(i));
      Sug:=Max(Sug,min(Deg[i],Q(i/Card));
    done
    if Sug ≥ α then
      res := Sug;                   % success: interpretation is Sug%
    else
      res := 0;                     % failure : under the threshold %
    endif;
end.
```

3.3 Principle of heuristics

This subsection proposes bases for improved algorithms to compute the degree of truth of quantified statements. Our objective is to reduce processing time by saving data access. Heuristics are integrated into the previous algorithm to determine if the evaluation is over (or under) the specified threshold before X is entirely accessed (i.e. before the end of step 1). Two kinds of heuristics can be considered : i) failure heuristics which conclude that the threshold cannot be reached; ii) success heuristics which conclude that the threshold will certainly be reached. It is important to notice that, when used, none of these heuristics delivers the actual value of the degree of truth (since the accesses are not completed). Consequently, they can be used only if that actual value is not needed which is always the case for a failure (the degree of truth being under the threshold, its actual value is not needed) but not for a success. In consequence, this paper mainly deals with failure heuristics.

3.4 Quantifier guided heuristics

This subsection proposes failure heuristics whose objective is to save data accesses. For the sake of simplicity the quantifier is considered to be absolute. In the following, n denotes the cardinality of set X.

A first failure heuristic appears when n is such that $\mu_Q(n) < \alpha$. In that case we have:

$\mu_Q(n) < \alpha \Rightarrow \mu_Q(1) \leq ... \leq \mu_Q(n) < \alpha$ (Q being increasing) $\Rightarrow S_m(A) < \alpha$.

This heuristics does not need to access any element in X. Consequently it can be checked first and the other failure heuristics assumes that $\mu_Q(n) \geq \alpha$.

A second failure heuristic relies on the smallest cardinality c such that $\mu_Q(c) \geq \alpha$. At first, we consider an example to illustrate the nature of that cardinality. Heuristics are then introduced.

Example 4. The linguistic quantifier (absolute and increasing) *at least 5* is given by Figure 1. We consider a threshold equal to 0.7 and the statement "*at least 5* X are *A*". According to the quantifier, the threshold is reached when at least 4 elements x in X satisfy $\mu_A(x) = 1$ (since $\mu_Q(4) \geq 0.7$ while $\mu_Q(3) < 0.7$). This cardinality of 4 defines the smallest quantity of *entirely A* elements that allows to reach the threshold. In other words when the condition "at least 4 are entirely *A*" holds it is certain that the threshold is reached (however, the threshold can be reached while "at least 4 are entirely *A*" does not hold). This condition involves a crisp quantifier and a crisp condition. It defines the requirement related to the degree of truth no longer in terms of a threshold but in terms of a quantity of entirely *A* elements. This quantity can be defined as the smallest cardinality c such that $\mu_Q(c) \geq 0.7$ ♦

The corresponding heuristics is based on the following property:

$$\mu_A(x_c) < \alpha \Rightarrow S_m(A) < \alpha \qquad (2)$$

where $X = \{x_1, x_2, ..., x_n\}$, $\mu_A(x_1) \geq \mu_A(x_2) \geq ... \geq \mu_A(x_n)$. If cardinality c is greater than n we consider dummy values $\mu_A(x_{n+1}) \geq .... \geq \mu_A(x_c)$ (each of them being 0) and $\mu_A(x_c) = 0$. The proof of that property is in annex 1. Let UB be an upper bound of $\mu_A(x_c)$. The heuristics is then:

when UB $< \alpha$,
it is possible to conclude that $S_m(A) < \alpha$.

We propose to dynamically compute UB at each step of the algorithm (i.e. after each access). In consequence, it is necessary that UB decreases for the heuristic to be useful. UB is defined according to the process defined hereafter.

At step j of the algorithm, j values $\mu_A(x)$s are known and we assume the (n-j) missing values $\mu_A(x)$s to be 1s. We consider a sort of these n values:

$$a_1 \geq \ldots \geq a_n.$$

Thus value a_c can be chosen for UB. Remark that c is between 1 and n (since $\mu_Q(n) \geq \alpha$ we have $c \leq n$). In annex 2, we demonstrate the validity of this choice (a_c) for UB.

A last point is devoted to the measure of the effective benefit provided by the heuristics. Let us illustrate this point by reconsidering example 4. As a threshold of 0.7 is specified in the query, the threshold is reached as soon as there are 4 degrees $\mu_A(x)$ set to 1 (since $\mu_Q(4) \geq 0.7$ while $\mu_Q(3) < 0.7$). In consequence, as long as there are 4 unaccessed elements x it is impossible to conclude on a failure (as no particular assumption is made on these unaccessed elements, they could satisfy *A* with full satisfaction which would give a result over the threshold).

This can be generalized to any quantifier *Q* and any threshold α by considering the smallest cardinality c such that $\mu_Q(c) \geq \alpha$. Consequently, as long as there are still c unaccessed elements, failure heuristics cannot allow to conclude (since the c unaccessed elements may be set to 1, thus giving a result over α). It means that there is no interest in checking a failure heuristic before the $(n+1-c)^{th}$ accesses. The smaller (n+1-c), the sooner heuristics can be checked. In other words, the more c is near to n, the more useful the failure heuristics are. As an example, if c = 90 and n = 100, we could expect an improvement from failure heuristics as soon as the 11th element is accessed. Since the total number of accesses is 100, the use of heuristics is of interest. However, when c = 3 and n = 100, we could not expect an improvement from heuristics before the 98th element is accessed. In this last situation, it appears that the heuristics provides (almost) no benefit.

3.5 Final algorithm

As we deal with queries involving a partitioning, set X contains tuples of a same relation sharing a same value for a given attribute <attribute>. The relation is stored on an external support (in a file for example) whose access is supposed to be time consuming. Consequently, it is assumed that the elements in X are accessed from the external support via an index on <attribute> (if it is not the case, subset X must be built first which implies that accesses have been already made).

Moreover, previous heuristics assume the knowledge of the cardinality of set X. In the context of this paper, the cardinality of X can be known in advance if the index incorporates a counter of the elements sharing a same entry (i.e. belonging to a same subset). However this assumption does not always hold in practise (if the index does not incorporate a counter) but an upper bound of that cardinality is assumed to be known from a global variable (it is realistic in some cases, for example when subsets describe employees of a same department, and it is known that a department has at most 30 employees).

It can be shown (cf annex 3) that the heuristics still apply when an upper bound is known (the actual cardinality is replaced by its upper bound in data structures and computations).

At least, success heuristics appear when it is certain that the degree of truth will be 1. In that case the threshold is obviously reached and the degree of truth is known. These success heuristics rely on value M defined as the smallest cardinality m such that $\mu_Q(m) = 1$. In that case, when M degrees set to 1 are accessed, we are sure that the final degree will equal 1. Consequently, a success heuristic allows to conclude when a number M of already accessed elements are such that $\mu_A(x) = 1$.

The algorithm introduced in 3.2 is modified to integrate the previous heuristics (where n' denotes our knowledge on the cardinality of set X, i.e., either the actual cardinality or an upper bound):

```
Procedure Improved_Algorithm(out res) is
   M, c, UB: integer;
   A: array 1..n' of real;         %store 1s and values A(x)s%
   Cpt : integer;                  % To count A(x) with A(x) = 1 %
begin
   if Q(n') < α then res:=0;exit; endif;  % failure heuristic : Sm(A) < α %
   procedure_initialize;           % computation of c and M from α and Q%
   Card := 0;                      % Array A is initialized ∀i, A[i] = 1%
   Cpt := 0;
   for each x in X do:             % via the index%
     Card := Card + 1;
     if (A(x) = 1) then Cpt := Cpt +1; endif;
     if (Cpt = M) then res := 1; exit; endif;     % success heuristic %
     sorted insertion of A(x) in A;               % it replaces a 1%
     UB:=A[c];
     if UB < α then res:=0; exit endif;           % failure heuristic %
   done;
% No heuristics are used: and computations are performed %
   Sug:=min(A[1],Q(1));
   for i:= 2 until Card do
     Sug:= Max(Sug,min(Deg[i],Q(i));
   done
    if Sug ≥ α then res := Sug;          % success: degree of truth is Sug%
    else res := 0;                       % failure: under the threshold %
   endif;
end.
```

Example 5. We apply the previous algorithm to the query:

select 0.7 #dpt **from** R
group by #dpt **having** "*at least 5* **are** *young*".

The linguistic quantifier *at least 5* is given by Figure 1.

Department #2 contains 6 employees (X = $\{e_1, e_2, e_3, e_4, e_5, e_6\}$) such that $\mu_{young}(e_1) = 0.9$; $\mu_{young}(e_2) = 0.8$; $\mu_{young}(e_3) = 0.6$; $\mu_{young}(e_4) = 0.5$; $\mu_{young}(e_5) = 0.4$; $\mu_{young}(e_6) = 0.1$. Department #2 is not retained by the query since the degree of truth of "*at least 5* X are *young*" does not reach the threshold (0.7):

$S_m(A) = \max \min(\mu_{young}(e_1),\mu_Q(1)), \min(\mu_{young}(e_2),\mu_Q(2)), \min(\mu_{young}(e_3),\mu_Q(3)), \min(\mu_{young}(e_4),\mu_Q(4)), \min(\mu_{young}(e_5),\mu_Q(5)), \min(\mu_{young}(e_6),\mu_Q(6))$.

The computations return:

$S_m(A) =$
$\max \min(0.9,0), \min(0.8,0), \min(0.6,0.25), \min(0.5,0.75), \min(0.4,1), \min(0.1,1) = 0.5$

which is under 0.7.

The previous algorithm assumes that the employees are accessed from external memory via an index. The access is not ordered (random access) and, in that example, the first element to be accessed is e_6 then e_4, then e_3, then e_5, then e_1, then e_2. The upper bound of the cardinality is assumed to be n' = 7. As the threshold is 0.7, we compute from the quantifier *at least 5* (cf. Figure 1) the value of c: here, c equals 4 (it is computed as the smallest cardinality c such that $\mu_Q(c) \geq 0.7$). Value M equals 5 (M being the smallest value i with $\mu_Q(i) = 1$). However, as the department does not satisfy the requirement, we ilustrate the use of failure heuristics and value M is not used hereafter. Array A is of size n' (n' = 7) and before the first access it contains 1s:

A = | 1 | 1 | 1 | 1 | 1 | 1 | 1 |

After each access, the content of A is modified and A[c] (i.e. A[4]) is checked. When it is under 0.7, the processing is stopped since it is certain that $S_m(A) < 0.7$.

access to e_6: $\mu_{young}(e_6)$ is computed ($\mu_{young}(e_6) = 0.1$) and inserted into A which becomes:

A = | 1 | 1 | 1 | 1 | 1 | 1 | 0.1 |

As A[4] > 0.7, the processing is continued.

access to e_4: $\mu_{young}(e_4)$ is computed ($\mu_{young}(e_4) = 0.5$) and inserted into A which becomes:

A = | 1 | 1 | 1 | 1 | 1 | 0.5 | 0.1 |

As A[4] > 0.7, the processing is continued.

access to e_3: $\mu_{young}(e_3)$ is computed ($\mu_{young}(e_3) = 0.6$) and inserted into A which becomes:

A = | 1 | 1 | 1 | 1 | 0.6 | 0.5 | 0.1 |
|---|---|---|---|---|---|---|

As A[4] > 0.7, the processing is continued.

access to e_5: $\mu_{young}(e_5)$ is computed ($\mu_{young}(e_5) = 0.4$) and inserted into A which becomes:

A = | 1 | 1 | 1 | 0.6 | 0.5 | 0.4 | 0.1 |
|---|---|---|---|---|---|---|

As A[4] < 0.7 (A[4] = 0.6), the processing is stopped and it is certain that $S_m(A) < 0.7$. Two accesses have been saved and it represents 33% of set X♦

4 Conclusion

In this paper we have considered flexible querying based on fuzzy sets and SQLf language (an extension of SQL to flexible querying). In this context, conditions express preferences instead of strict requirements. Each answer is associated with a degree of satisfaction which represents its adequation with the query (i.e. with the preferences). To ensure a calibration of answers, a query involves a threshold to be reached by each answer to be retained. Various patterns of query are available and some queries may involve linguistic quantifiers such as *most of*, *at least 4* to allow for an intermediate attitude between the negation (*none*) and the conjunction. A quantifier is relative (*most of*) when it refers to a proportion, it is absolute when it refers to a number (*at least 4*).

This paper was devoted to queries calling on a partitioning where a linguistic quantifier appears in the set-oriented condition. This condition is expressed by a quantified statement of type "*Q* X are *A*" and its degree of truth is assumed to be computed by means of the Sugeno fuzzy integral.

We have proposed algorithms to evaluate such queries and our objective was to reduce processing time by saving data access. Heuristics are integrated into the algorithm in order to conclude on the result before the accesses are completed. Two kinds of heuristics can be considered: i) failure heuristics which allow to conclude that the threshold will not be reached; ii) success heuristics which conclude that the threshold will certainly be reached. These heuristics are suitable for absolute quantifiers and rely on both a property of the Sugeno fuzzy integral and on the quantifiers' definition. In [14] another kind of heuristics, based on the properties of median operators, is proposed (since a Sugeno fuzzy integral is a median). In this previous work, it is assumed that the cardinality of the universe is known. This assumption related to cardinality is generally too demanding and this present paper has considered the situation where the cardinality is not known in advance (*Q* being absolute). In addition, we have shown how the potential benefit provided by heuristics can be estimated.

In the near future we intend to extend this work to relative quantifiers. A comparison of the heuristics introduced here with the ones proposed in [14] could also be a matter of future research.

References

[1] P. Bosc, O. Pivert (1992), Some Approaches for Relational Databases Flexible Querying, *Journal of Intelligent Information Systems,* 1, pages 323-354.

[2] L.A. Zadeh (1965), Fuzzy sets, *Information and Control*, 8, pages 338-353.

[3] L.A. Zadeh (1972), A fuzzy-set-theoric interpretation of linguistic hedges, *Journal of Cybernetics,* 2, pages 4-34.

[4] B. Bouchon-Meunier (1992), Fuzzy logic and knowledge representation using linguistic modifiers, in *Fuzzy Logic for the Management of Uncertainty*, (L.A. Zadeh, J. Kacprzyk eds), John Wiley and Sons, pages 399-414.

[5] L.A. Zadeh (1983), A computational approach to fuzzy quantifiers in natural languages, *Computer Mathematics with Applications* , 9, pages 149-183.

[6] P. Bosc, M. Galibourg and G. Hamon (1988), Fuzzy querying with SQL: extensions and implementation aspects, *Fuzzy Sets and Systems*, 28, pages 333-349.

[7] P. Bosc, O. Pivert (1995), SQLf: A relational database language for fuzzy querying, *IEEE Transactions on Fuzzy Systems,* 3, pages 1-17.

[8] P. Bosc, L. Liétard, H. Prade (1996), On fuzzy queries involving fuzzy quantifiers, *Proceedings of the 12th European Conference on Artificial Intelligence (ECAI'96),* pages 6-10, Budapest (Hungary).

[9] R.R. Yager (1988), On ordered weighted averaging aggregation operators in multicriteria decisionmaking, *Transactions on Systems, Man, and Cybernetics,* 18, pages 183-190.

[10] P. Bosc, L. Liétard (1996), Fuzzy integrals and database flexible querying, *Proceedings of the FUZZ-IEEE 1996 Conference (FUZZ-IEEE'96),* pages 100-106, New-Orleans (Louisiana).

[11] P. Bosc, L. Liétard (1994), Monotonous quantifications and Sugeno fuzzy integrals, *Proceedings of the 5th IPMU Conference,* pages 1281-1286, Paris (France).

[12] H. Prade (1990), A two-layer fuzzy pattern matching procedure for the evaluation of conditions involving vague quantifiers, *Journal of Intelligent and Robotic Systems*, 3, pages 93-101.

[13] R.R. Yager (1984), General multiple-objective decision functions and linguistically quantified statements, *International Journal of Man-Machine Studies,* 21, pages 389-400.

[14] P. Bosc, L. Liétard and O. Pivert (1995), Quantified statements and database fuzzy querying, in *Fuzziness in Database Management Systems,* (P. Bosc, J. Kacprzyk eds), Physica-Verlag, pages 275-308.

Appendix

Annex 1. When $c > n$ it means $\mu_A(x_c) = 0$. As $c > n$ and c being the smallest value such that $\mu_Q(c) \geq \alpha$ we have $\mu_Q(n) < \alpha$. In that case $S_m(A) < \alpha$ holds (since $\mu_Q(1) \leq \mu_Q(2) \leq \ldots \leq \mu_Q(n) < \alpha$) and $\mu_A(x_c) < \alpha \Rightarrow S_m(A) < \alpha$ holds.

When $c \leq n$ it means $\mu_A(x_c) \neq 0$ and we establish that $S_m(A) \geq \alpha \Rightarrow \mu_A(x_c) \geq \alpha$.
Let us consider that $S_m(A) \geq \alpha$. From the definition of Sugeno fuzzy integral, we get:

$S_m(A) = \max_i \min (\mu_A(x_i), \mu_Q(i)) \geq \alpha$.

If indix j is such that $S_m(A) = \min (\mu_A(x_j), \mu_Q(j))$, it implies that:

$\exists$ j such that: $\min (\mu_A(x_j), \mu_Q(j)) \geq \alpha$

which leads to :

$\exists$ j such that: $\mu_A(x_j) \geq \alpha$ and $\mu_Q(j) \geq \alpha$.

Since the values $\mu_A(x)$ and $\mu_Q(i)$ are sorted we get:

$$\mu_A(x_1) \geq .... \geq \mu_A(x_j) \geq \alpha \qquad \text{(E1)}$$

$$\mu_Q(n) \geq ... \geq \mu_Q(j) \geq \alpha \qquad \text{(E2).}$$

If $c = 1$, (E1) gives $\mu_A(x_1) \geq \alpha$ which ends the proof (since $\mu_A(x_c) \geq \alpha$). If c differs from 1 its definition gives: $\mu_Q(c\text{-}1) < \alpha$. From (E2) and $\mu_Q(c\text{-}1) < \alpha$ we conclude that $c \leq j$ (if $c > j$ then $c\text{-}1 \geq j$ and from (E2) we get $\mu_Q(c\text{-}1) \geq \alpha$ which is impossible). From $c \leq j$ and (E1) we get $\mu_A(x_c) \geq \alpha$♦

Annex 2. First, we demonstrate that the value of a_c decreases after the computation of a new $\mu_A(x)$ (when moving from step j to step j+1). Then we demonstrate that a_c (at any step j) is an upper bound of value $\mu_A(x_c)$ given in property (2).
Decrease. When moving from step j to step (j+1) a value 1 in $a_1 \geq .... \geq a_n$ is replaced by a grade a fullfilment thus a_c cannot increase.
Upper bound. Since the value of a_c cannot increase after each acess, it is just necessary to show that a_c is an upper bound *once all elements are accessed* (is the last computed value a_c is an upper bound, the previous ones are also upper bounds since they are larger or equal to that last value). Once the n elements are accessed, we dispose of each degrees (n degrees) and we get:

$a_1 \geq .... \geq a_n$

which are respectively:

$\mu_A(x_1) \geq .... \geq \mu_A(x_n)$,

where a_c is coming from. This value a_c has to be compared with value $\mu_A(x_c)$ given by property (2). If $(c > n)$ we have $\mu_A(x_c) = 0$ thus $a_c \geq \mu_A(x_c)$. If $(c \leq n)$ the value $\mu_A(x_c)$ is given by the following sort:

$\mu_A(x_1) \geq \mu_A(x_2) \geq ... \geq \mu_A(x_c) \geq ... \geq \mu_A(x_n)$.

When comparing the two previous sorts, we obviously get $a_c \geq \mu_A(x_c)$♦

Annex 3. In the following, n denotes the actual cardinality of set X whereas n' denotes our knowledge on that cardinality (either n itself of an upper bound). Thus we have $n \leq n'$. This proof is very similar to the one introduced in annex 2.

First, we demonstrate that the value of a_c decreases after the computation of a new $\mu_A(x)$ (when moving from step j to step j+1). Then we demonstrate that a_c (at any step j) is an upper bound of value $\mu_A(x_c)$ given in property (2).

Decrease. When moving from step j to step (j+1) a value 1 in $a_1 \geq .... \geq a_{n'}$ is replaced by a grade a fullfilment thus a_c cannot increase.

Upper bound. Since the value of a_c cannot increase after each acess, it is just necessary to show that a_c is an upper bound *once all elements are accessed* (is the last computed value a_c is an upper bound, the previous ones are also upper bounds since they are larger or equal to that last value). Once the n elements are accessed, we dispose of each degrees (n degrees) added to (n'-n) values to 1 and we get:

$$a_1 \geq .... \geq a_n \geq ... \geq a_{n'}$$

which are respectively:

$$1 \geq 1 \geq .... \geq 1 \geq \mu_A(x_1) \geq .... \geq \mu_A(x_n),$$

where a_c is coming from. This value a_c has to be compared with value $\mu_A(x_c)$ given by property (2). If $(c > n)$ we have $\mu_A(x_c) = 0$ thus $a_c \geq \mu_A(x_c)$. If $(c \leq n)$ the value $\mu_A(x_c)$ is given by the following sort:

$$\mu_A(x_1) \geq \mu_A(x_2) \geq ... \geq \mu_A(x_c) \geq ... \geq \mu_A(x_n).$$

When comparing the two previous sorts, we obviously get $a_c \geq \mu_A(x_c)$♦

Intelligent Filtering with Genetic Algorithms and Fuzzy Logic

María J. Martín-Bautista[1†], María-Amparo Vila[1], Daniel Sánchez[1], and Henrik L. Larsen[2‡]

[1] Dept. of Computer Science and Artificial Intelligence, Granada University, Avda. Andalucía 37, 18071 Granada, Spain
[2] Dept. of Computer Science, Roskilde University, P.O. Box 260, DK-4000 Roskilde, Denmark

Abstract. We present two different approaches combining fuzzy information retrieval of documents with genetic algorithms, and the pre-processing stage of classification called feature selection. The differences between these approaches lie basically in the target of the fitness function selected. In the first approach, the Term-Oriented Model, the fitness function is based on a measure to find the most discriminatory terms, by rewarding not only the terms from the good documents, but also those from the bad ones, if they are considered as good partial classifiers. However, the aim of the Document-Oriented Model, as traditionally, is to rank the documents by relevance. So, the best chromosome represents the optimal query. The fuzzy weighting scheme used in this model considers also the discriminatory terms by introducing the knowledge about the user preferences in the genes, but rewarding the genes belonging to the good documents.

1 Introduction

Research in Information Retrieval has been increased and wide-opened to new technologies in the recent years. Text and Web Retrieval have become essential researching areas due to the explosion of the communications and the information highway. Some other tasks associated to the retrieval of information in the Web, in particular classification management of information overload and the building of user profiles have lead Information System researchers to import some techniques from other disciplines such as Machine Learning and Soft Computing, and get into a new research field called Data Mining.

The efficiency of the different methods utilized in query and matching processes is usually diminished by a poor categorization of the documents.

As most of the techniques used in text classification are determined by the occurrences of the words (terms) appearing in the documents, the fixing of the set of most relevant terms seems to be an important stage in this process.

† Correspondence author: mbautis@decsai.ugr.es

‡ Henrik L. Larsen was partly supported by the Danish Natural Science Research Council (project No.51-00-0376), and the IT-University of Copenhagen

One of the first stages of the classification process is the Feature Selection (FS), by means of which the complexity of the problem is reduced by the elimination of irrelevant features to be considered later in the classification stage. This paper concerns the following problem: the selection of the most relevant features in classification processes by utilizing a Genetic Algorithm (GA). The initial results in the experimentation with our model reveal GAs as a powerful tool to reduce the dimensionality of classification problems.

2 Genetic Algorithms and Fuzzy Information Retrieval

Artificial Intelligence (AI) and Machine Learning (ML) have been used as support to Information Retrieval in order to speed and improve retrieval processes such as indexing, matching, querying and classification. While in AI the rules are applied upon the patterns, in Machine Learning the patterns are learned. This learning process may be aided by other techniques coming from Soft Computing such as Fuzzy Logic [29] and Genetic Algorithms (GAs) [8]. Some combinations of these techniques are presented by Chen [5].

GAs help in the retrieving process by searching the query space and build user profiles. While in the classical static profiles there is no learning and the profile is typically a query selected by the user, GAs allow us to build adaptive profiles, by using inductive techniques to refine and maintain a representation of the user needs in the area of interest [14].

In [28], GAs are used to optimize queries, using as fitness function a parametric combination of precision and recall. The authors make a comparative study of the influence of the crossover and mutation in the population through the generations. The main disadvantage of this approach is the lack of ability to handle imprecision. The classical Boolean models [23] are easy to implement and execute, but also are very unfriendly to the user and have a lack of flexibility in the representation of the user information needs. Fuzzy information systems attempt to solve this problem [11].

Fuzzy Logic has been introduced in several tasks of the Information Retrieval process [4], [10].

In the matching task, the criteria are allowed to be soft and the grades of importance both in the side of the system and the user can be fuzzy [1], [2]. However, these systems present a major drawback on the side of the user, in the case of non-expert users, for which handling the fuzzy grades may be hard. This problem may be solved by linguistic labels, as is proposed in [3].

In the representation task, the presence of the terms in documents is represented by fuzzy sets, encoded into the genes of a GA [16], [17].

Fuzzy Logic has been also introduced in the information retrieval measures, as is presented in [7], [22].

In this paper, the role of the GAs in the information retrieval systems is established. In the next section, we will explain the classical case where the function to optimize depends on the document classification. In section

4, we present a new tested model where the GA has a fitness function to optimize the selection of the terms. A hybrid approach with a fitness based on documents, but with a selection scheme calculated from the goodness of the terms is proposed in section 5. Finally, in the last section, we will present some discussion and future trends.

3 The Classical Case: The Document–Oriented Model

The combination of Genetic Algorithms and Fuzzy Logic has been widely used in Information Retrieval Systems to optimize new measures related to the documents such as fuzzy precision and fuzzy recall, as an alternative to the classical measures. Several approaches can be found in the literature in this field. In [22], the authors test the performance of the system by certain combinations of these fuzzy measures. The coding of the genes is a fuzzy set representing the weights of the terms in the query.

In [20], genetic programming (non-standards GAs) is applied to a fuzzy information retrieval system that is optimized via relevance feedback. For this purpose, the fitness function is not a combination of recall-precision as in the former approach, but a combination of a similarity measure between the document and the query, weighted by the relevance feedback.

The reasons to use this fitness function instead of the recall-precision measures are given by the authors: if no relevant documents are retrieved by a chromosome, its fitness will be zero, and a lack of selection pressure will lead the chromosome to be push out of the population.

A comparison of three possible fitness functions: recall, recall-precision and similarity-relevance feedback can be found in [12].

In all the mentioned approaches, the fitness function is oriented towards the relevance of the documents, and the genes are represented by a fuzzy value calculated from the frequency of the term in the document.

4 The Term–Oriented Model

When a user retrieves documents from an information system (for instance, from the Internet), systems typically have a lack of building a user profile. Hence, the user cannot use the previous queries to the system for future requests. These needs may be represented by terms extracted from those documents evaluated by the user as interesting and be learned.

One of the main problems studied in this field is the construction of user profiles by means of the discovering of the most relevant and representative terms (features) which information filtering systems can use to determine the most useful information to a given user. We must distinguish between those terms that best represent the information user needs, and those that allow us to discern between relevant and non-relevant, that is, the discriminatory terms for a certain classification.

This problem can be tackled in the classification task by the Feature Selection (FS), one of the first stages of the classification process by means of which the complexity of the problem is reduced by the elimination of irrelevant features to be considered later in the classification stage.

By this preprocessing, the complexity of the problem is reduced by the elimination of irrelevant features in the classification. Several approaches with Genetic Algorithms (GAs) to solve the feature selection problem have been proposed in the literature [9], [21], [24], [25], and [26]. The relative insensitivity of GAs to noise, and the requirement of no domain knowledge make GAs a powerful tool to identify and select the best subset of features to be used by the rule induction module in a classification system.

Several approaches using GAs related to user profiles construction can be found in the literature, for instance, [6], [13] and [19]. Another approach using GAs is presented in [18], where a user profile is built from the user preferences, represented by a population of chromosomes. Each chromosome is a vector of fuzzy genes, where every gene represents by a fuzzy set the number of occurrences that a term should have in the document required by the user.

5 Fuzzy Genes

Most of the techniques used in text classification are determined by the occurrences of the words (terms) appearing in the documents, combined with the user feedback over the documents retrieved. However, in this approach, the most relevant terms will be selected from a previous fuzzy classification given by the genetic algorithm guided by the user feedback, but using techniques from Machine Learning.

In our model, a gene in a chromosome is defined by a term and a fuzzy number $\tilde{\eta}$ of occurrences of the term in documents belonging to the class of documents that satisfy the user's information need.

Let $\Theta=\{D_1, \dots, D_m\}$ be the set of documents evaluated by the user, and let $u_i \in [0, 1]$ be the user's evaluation of the document D_i, $i=1, \dots, m$, that is, u_i is the degree to which the user finds that the document D_i satisfies his needs. We shall assume that an evaluation $u>0.5$ indicates a good document, with $u=1$ representing a highly relevant document, while $u \leq 0.5$ indicates a bad document, $u=0$ representing a document that is not relevant at all.

We will, without loss of generalization, assume that Ω is ordered decreasingly by u_i: $\Omega = \{D_1, \dots, D_k, D_{k+1}, \dots, D_m\}$, such that the subsets $R = \{D_1, \dots, D_k\}$ and $NR = \{D_{k+1}, \dots, D_m\}$ contains, respectively, the good (relevant, R) and the bad documents (non-relevant NR).

Let $T = \{t_1, \dots t_n\}$ be the set of symbols extracted from Ω, and x_{ij} the relative frequency of symbol t_j in document D_i.

Therefore, a gene G is a pair $G(t, \tilde{\eta})$, where t is a term, and $\tilde{\eta}$ is a fuzzy number characterized by the membership function $\mu_{\cong\eta}$ as follows:

$$\mu_{\simeq\eta}(x) = \begin{cases} 0 & x = 0 \\ e^{-1/2\left(\frac{x-\eta}{\sigma}\right)^2} & x > 0 \end{cases} \quad (1)$$

The membership function is a Gaussian one, assuming that the relative symbol occurrence frequency is normal distributed $N(\eta,\sigma^2)$, where the parameters η, $\sigma \in R^+$.

The parameter η is represented by the weighed average $\bar{x}_j$ of the relative frequency of the term t_j based on the relevance of the document.

$$\bar{x}_j = \frac{\sum_{i=1}^{m}(u_i \cdot x_{ij})}{\sum_{i=1}^{m} u_i} \quad (2)$$

As for the value of parameter σ^2, is given by the standard deviation of the value η:

$$\sigma_j^2 = \frac{\sum_{i=1}^{m}(u_i x_{ij} - \bar{x}_j)^2}{\sum_{i=1}^{m} u_i} \quad (3)$$

This fuzzy representation is referred as the *relevant scheme*, since it rewards the genes based on the estimated relevance of the documents. It provides a more accurate characterization of the documents that satisfy the user's information need.

A comparison with the others approaches is carried out in other author work (see [15]), in order to reveal the importance of a fuzzy weighting considering the user preferences.

6 TO–GENFES: A Term–Oriented Model with Genetic Feature Selection

The main idea of this approach is to build user profiles from a group of terms coming from the fittest chromosome of a population in the GA [17]. However, the selection of the terms to survive are not based on how good those terms describe the documents, but on how good they are to distinguish the documents that are relevant from those that are not relevant, according to the user preferences.

6.1 The Fitness Function

The fitness function (4) to maximize is term-oriented, and is based on classical similarity measures in Information Retrieval, such as the coefficients of Jaccard (5) and Dice (6). These measures are weighted by the discriminatory power of the terms in the chromosomes (7).

$$P(y) = S^*(C_y, V_h) + q_y \quad (4)$$

where $S^*(C_y, V_h)$ represents a similarity measure between a chromosome and the discriminatory vector by:

$$S^J(C_y, V_h) = \frac{\sum_{j=1}^{|T|} C_y(t_j) \cdot V_h(t_j) \cdot G(t_j)}{\sum_{j=1}^{|T|} C_y(t_j) + \sum_{j=1}^{|T|} V_h(t_j) \cdot G(t_j) - \sum_{j=1}^{|T|} C_y(t_j) \cdot V_h(t_j) \cdot G(t_j)} \quad (5)$$

or by:

$$S^D(C_y, V_h) = \frac{2 \cdot \left[\sum_{j=1}^{|T|} C_y(t_j) \cdot V_h(t_j) \cdot G(t_j)\right]}{\sum_{j=1}^{|T|} C_y(t_j) + \sum_{j=1}^{|T|} V_h(t_j) \cdot G(t_j)} \quad (6)$$

where:

- $C_y(t_j) = \mu_{\cong}(t_j)$, as defined in (1), and represents the relative frequency of every term t_j appearing in the gene of the chromosome C_y.
- $V_h(t_j) = \mu_{\cong}(D_i(t_j)) \cdot \mu_{\cong}(D_k(t_j))$ is the discriminatory vector based on the comparison of the term t_i appearing in documents D_i and D_k, where $i, k \in \{1, ..., |\Omega|\}$.
- $G(t_j) = \frac{g(t_j)}{\sum_{i=1}^{|T|} g(t_i)}$, with $g(t_j)$ being the accumulated value of t_j for all the discriminatory vectors, and, q_y represents the capability of the chromosome itself, calculated by adding the accumulated discriminatory values of every term presented into the chromosome, as it is shown below.

$$q_y = \frac{\sum_{j=1}^{|T|} C_y(t_j).g(t_j)}{\sum_{j=1}^{|T|} g(t_j)} \quad (7)$$

The fuzzy recall-precision measure is applied in experimental situations where user has evaluated all documents in the collection queried.
Let $\Omega = \{\omega_1, \ldots, \omega_m\}$ be the collection queried, and let u_i and s_i be the (expert) user's and the system's evaluation of the document ω_i, respectively. We define the fuzzy recall-precision τ by:

$$\tau = \rho^{v_1} \psi^{v_2} \quad (8)$$

where ρ is the fuzzy recall, and ψ is the fuzzy precision defined by:

$$\rho = \frac{\sum_{i=1}^{m} min(u_i, s_i)}{\sum_{i=1}^{m} u_i} \qquad \psi = \frac{\sum_{i=1}^{m} min(u_i, s_i)}{\sum_{i=1}^{m} s_i} \quad (9)$$

and v_1, v_2 are the importance of high recall and high precision, respectively.

For an internet information retrieval system, we expect that precision is more important than recall, and therefore $v_1 < v_2$.

Notice, that applied to the subset of Ω comprising the documents evaluated by the user in the answer retrieved by the system, the fuzzy recall-precision τ measures how close the system's evaluation is to the user's evaluation.

6.2 DO–GENFES: A Document–Oriented Model with Feature Selection

In the previous sections, the role of the GAs in the information retrieval systems has been established. On the one hand, in Sect. 3 we explain the classical case, in which the fitness function is document-oriented. The classical Information Retrieval uses measures such as precision and recall, and those based on similarity measure combined with relevance feedback. The classification obtained from this process is a ranked list of documents ordered by relevance.

On the other hand, in Sect. 4 we have presented the term-oriented model, where the GA has a fitness function to optimize the selection of the terms. A classification of the terms based on their discriminatory power is carried out. From the best chromosome, a fuzzy recall-precision measure can be calculated in order to obtain a ranked list of documents as well as a user profile. However, we must point out that there is no optimization in the information retrieving process operating directly over the documents.

DO-GENFES is a document-oriented approach. It is document-oriented due to the use of document relevance measures in the fitness function. The most discriminatory terms are selected by means of the information about the user preferences maintained in the fuzzy genes.

In this model, the representation of the terms in the genes follows the same fuzzy function (1) as in the term-oriented model. However, the estimation of parameters η and σ will be calculated by new expressions (10) and (11), that helps the terms more discriminatory.

The feature selection is embedded in the fuzzy weighting scheme in the genes. The fuzzy weighting scheme used in this model considers the discriminatory terms by introducing the knowledge about the user preferences in the genes, but distinguishing the genes belonging to good and bad documents. This representation in the genes is called the *discriminatory scheme.*

$$\bar{x}_j = \frac{\sum_{i=1}^{k} (u_i \cdot x_{ij})}{\sum_{i=1}^{k} u_i} \quad \bar{x}'_j = \frac{\sum_{i=k+1}^{m} ((1 - u_i) \cdot x_{ij})}{\sum_{i=k+1}^{m} (1 - u_i)} \tag{10}$$

$$\sigma_j^2 = \frac{\sum_{i=1}^{k} (u_i x_{ij} - \bar{x}_j)^2}{\sum_{i=1}^{k} u_i} \quad \sigma_j'^2 = \frac{\sum_{i=k+1}^{m} \left((1 - u_i)\, x_{ij} - \bar{x}'_j\right)^2}{\sum_{i=k+1}^{m} (1 - u_i)} \tag{11}$$

Both fuzzy schemes, the one in the term-oriented model and the presented above will be compared in the experimental stage (Sect. 7).

6.3 Fitness Function

The fitness function to maximize is document-oriented, and is based on the classical effectiveness measures in Fuzzy Information Retrieval, presented in (8) and (9).

7 Experiments

The aim of these experiments is to test the differences between the fuzzy weighting schemes proposed for the Term and the Document-Oriented models, and their fitting to a certain model based on the objective of the approach. The length of the chromosome is fixed to 10. With the purpose of keep the diversity of the population, the mutation population should be incremented to 0.2 (that is, large as compared to the standard mutation probability [8]), as it is the only way to introduce new terms into the population.

Therefore, for the experimental stage, the parameters of the GA have been fixed as follows:

- Number of Generations: 1000
- Size of the population: 80
- Chromosome Length: 10
- Probability of Crossover: 0.6
- Probability of Mutation: 0.2

The collection of documents is corresponding to the follow query in the INSPEC database of Jul-Sep 1998: *"Information Retrieval and Classification"*.

The number of documents retrieved was 22, and the number of terms extracted (after removing stop-list words and stemming) is 616.

Let suppose that the user needs are oriented towards the query topic in the contexts of *Web* and *Internet*, to which the user will give the higher evaluation. Since the previous query must be refined specially in terms of precision, the values for the weights of the fuzzy recall (v_1) and fuzzy precision (v_2) will be $v_1 = 0.67$ and $v_2 = 1$. The performance of the system is shown in Table 1 and Table 2.

8 Conclusions and Future Work

We presented two different retrieval models combined with genetic algorithms and fuzzy logic. The classical model has been considered as document-oriented. The optimization of measures such as precision and recall are the target in this kind of models. A ranked list of documents ordered by relevance is obtained when the system is queried.

Table 1. Table 1. Fuzzy Recall–Precision in the Term–Oriented Model (Relevant Scheme)

Fitness Function	Fuzzy Recall–Precision	Fuzzy Recall	Fuzzy Precision
Jaccard Score	0.409098	0.650997	0.545455
Dice Coefficient	0.407604	0.659943	0.538562
Without Feature Selection	0.395036	0.632279	0.536783

Table 2. Table 2. Relevant Scheme *vs.* Discriminant Scheme

Term–Weighting Scheme	Fuzzy Recall–Precision	Fuzzy Recall	Fuzzy Precision
Relevant Scheme (Term–Oriented M.)	0.409098	0.650997	0.545455
Discriminatory Scheme (Document–Oriented M.)	0.336786	0.581604	0.484764

TO-GENFES (Term-Oriented model with Genetic Feature Selection) has been revealed as a valid tool for the construction of user profiles and classification of documents ranked by relevance. The good performance of the implemented system demonstrates the necessity of a preprocessing stage in the classification process. This approach considers the selection of the most discriminatory terms as fitness function, that is, those with the facility to separate the documents in relevant and non-relevant. The evaluation of the documents is carried out by the evaluation of a fuzzy recall-precision measure, and a user profile is obtained from the final population. Although a ranked list of documents is also obtained in this approach, it must be pointed out that the target of the GA is not the optimization of the classification of the documents but to discern between the relevant and non-relevant terms for the document classification.

DO-GENFES (Document-Oriented model with Genetic Feature Selection) is proposed as a variation of the classical model, modifying it by introducing pre-selection of the most discriminatory terms. The fuzzy weighting scheme utilized in this model rewards the more discriminatory terms appearing in good and bad documents.

In both models, the most representative and discriminatory terms have been identified without a diminution of the performance of the system. The reduction of the number of terms to be in the user profile is an important aspect of the system both from the computational and storage space point of view, since these terms can be used to optimize the retrieving process for the same user instead of all the indexing terms.

The grouping of the profiles by interest areas may help us to extract common preferences for the users. The mining of these profiles in a following stage in order to get general profiles may be our main objective for a future work.

References

1. Bookstein A. (1980). "Fuzzy Requests: An Approach to Weighted Boolean Searches". *Journal of the American Society for Information Science,* **31**, number 4, 240–247.
2. Bordogna, G., Carrara, P., and Pasi, G. (1995). "Fuzzy Approaches to Extend Boolean Information Retrieval". In Bosc, P. and Kacprzyck, J. (Eds.) *Fuzziness in Database Management Systems*, 231–274. Physica-Verlag.
3. Bordogna, G. and Pasi, G. (1993). "A Fuzzy Linguistic Approach Generalizing Boolean Information Retrieval: A Model and its Evaluation". *Journal of the American Society for Information Science,* **44**, number 2, 70–82.
4. Buell, D.A. (1982). An Analysis of some Fuzzy Subset Applications to Information Retrieval Systems. *Fuzzy Sets and Systems,* 35–42. North-Holland.
5. Chen, H. (1995). "Machine Learning for Information Retrieval: Neural Networks, Symbolic Learning, and Genetic Algorithms". *Journal of the American Society for Information Science,* **46**, number 3, 194–216.
6. Ferguson, S. (1995). "BEAGLE: A genetic algorithm for Information Filter Profile Creation". *Technical Report CS-692.*University of Alabama.
7. Gedeon, T.D. and Kczy, L.T. (1995) "Learning Fuzzy Measure Functions for Information Retrieval". In *Proc. of the FUZZ-IEEE/IFES'95 Workshop on Fuzzy Database Systems and Information Retrieval,* Yokohama, Japan.
8. Holland, J.H. (1992) *Adaptation in Natural and Artificial Systems.* Massachusetts: MIT Press.
9. Kelly, J.D. and Davis, L. (1991) "Hybridizing the Genetic Algorithm and the K Nearest Neighbors Classification Algorithm". In *Proc. of the Fourth International Conference on Genetic Algorithms and their Applications (ICGA),* 377–383.
10. Kraft, D.H. and Buell, D.A. (1993). "Fuzzy Sets and Generalized Boolean Retrieval Systems". In D. Dubois and H. Prade (Eds.), *Readings in Fuzzy Sets for Intelligent Systems,* 648–659. San Mateo, CA: Morgan Kaufmann Publishers.
11. Kraft, D.H. and Petry, F.E. (1997). "Fuzzy Information Systems: Managing Uncertainty in Databases and Information Retrieval Systems". *Fuzzy Sets and Systems,* 183–191. Elsevier Science.
12. Kraft, D.H., Petry, F.E., Buckles, B.P., and Sadasivan, T. (1995). "Applying Genetic Algorithms to Information Retrieval Systems via Relevance Feedback". In P. Bosc and J. Kacprzyk (Eds.), *Fuzziness in Database Management Systems,* 330–344. Germany: Physica-Verlag.

13. Lam, W. (1999). "Intelligent Content-Based Document Delivery via Automatic Filtering Profile Generation". *Intelligent Journal of Intelligent Systems,* **14**, number 10, 963–979. John Wiley & Sons.
14. Larsen, H.L., Andreasen, T. and Christiansen, H. (1998) "Knowledge Discovery for Flexible Querying". In Christiansen, H., Andreasen, T. and Larsen, H.L. (Eds.) *Flexible Query Answering System.* Lecture Notes in Artificial Intelligence, **1495**, 227–235. Berlin: Springer-Verlag.
15. Martín-Bautista, M.J., Larsen, H.L. and Vila, M.A. (2000). "Fuzzy Genes: Improving the Effectiveness of Information Retrieval". In *Proc. of the Congress on Evolutionary Computation (CEC 2000),* **1**, pp. 471–478 .San Diego, CA. July 2000.
16. Martín-Bautista, M.J., Larsen, H.L. and Vila, M.A. (1999a). "A Fuzzy Genetic Algorithm Approach to an Adaptive Information Retrieval Agent". *Journal of the American Society for Information Science,* **50**, number 9, 760–771.
17. Martín-Bautista, M.J., Larsen, H.L. and Vila, M.A. (1999b). "A Genetic Fuzzy Classifier to Adaptive User Interest Profiles with Feature Selection". *Proc. of the European Society for Fuzzy Logic and Technology (Eusflat-Estylf) Joint Conference* 327–330. Palma, Spain.
18. Martín-Bautista, M.J. and Vila, M.A. (1998) "Applying Genetic Algorithms to the Feature Selection Problem in Information Retrieval". In Christiansen, H., Andreasen, T. and Larsen, H.L. (Eds.), *Flexible Query Answering System.* Lecture Notes in Artificial Intelligence, **1495**. Berlin: Springer-Verlag.
19. Pazzani, M. and Billsus, D. (1997) "Learning and Revising User Profiles: The identification of interesting web sites". *Machine Learning* **27**, 313–331. Kluwer Academic Publishers.
20. Petry, F.E., Buckles, B.P. and Prabhu, D. (1993) "Fuzzy Information Retrieval Using Genetic Algorithms and Relevance Feedback". In *Proc. of the 56th ASIS Annual Meeting,* **30**, 122–125, Columbus, Ohio.
21. Punch, W.F., Goodman, E.D., Pei, M., Chia-Sun, L., Hovland, P. and Enbody, R. (1993) "Further Research on Feature Selection and Classification Using Genetic Algorithms". In *Proc. of the Fifth International Conference on Genetic Algorithms and their Applications (ICGA),* 557–564. San Mateo, CA: Morgan Kauffmann Publishers.
22. Rochet, S., Sanchez, E., and Tassier, C. (1996) "Fitness Landscape and Performance Algorithms in Fuzzy Information Retrieval". In *Proc. of Fourth European Congress on Intelligence Techniques and Soft Computing,* vol.2, pp.831-835, Aachen, Germany.
23. Salton, G and McGill, M.J. (1983) *Introduction to Modern Information Retrieval.* New York: McGraw-Hill.
24. Siedlecki, W. and Sklansky, J. (1989) "A Note on Genetic Algorithms for Large-Scale Feature Selection". *Pattern Recognition Letters* **10**, 335–347, North Holland: Elsevier Science Publishers.
25. Smith, J.E., Fogarty, T.C. and Johnson, I.R. (1994) "Genetic Selection of Features for Clustering and Classification". In *IEE Colloquium on Genetic Algorithms in Image Processing & Vision,* IEE Digest 1994/193, London.
26. Vafaie, H. and De Jong, K., (1992) "Genetic Algorithms as a Tool for Feature Selection in Machine Learning". In *Proceeding of the 4th International Conference on Tools with Artificial Intelligence,* Arlington, VA.
27. Van Rijsbergen, C.J. (1979). *Information Retrieval.* London: Butterworths.

28. Yang, J. and Korfhage, R.R. (1993) "Query Optimization in Information Retrieval Using Genetic Algorithms". In *Proc. of the Fifth International Conference of Genetic Algorithms (ICGA'93)*, 603–611. University of Illinois at Urbana-Champaign, Illinois.
29. Zadeh, L.A. (1965). Fuzzy Sets. *Information and Control*, **83**, 338–353.

Using Semantic and Phonetic Term Similarity for Spoken Document Retrieval and Spoken Query Processing

Fabio Crestani

Department of Computer Science, University of Strathclyde, 26 Richmond Street, Glasgow G1 1XH, Scotland, UK. Email: F.Crestani@cs.strath.ac.uk

Abstract In classical Information Retrieval systems a relevant document will not be retrieved in response to a query if the document and query representations do not share at least one term. This problem is known as "term mismatch". A similar problem can be found in spoken document retrieval and spoken query processing, where terms misrecognized by the speech recognition process can hinder the retrieval of potentially relevant documents. I will call this problem "term misrecognition", by analogy to the term mismatch problem.

This paper presents two classes of retrieval models that attempt to tackle both the term mismatch and the term misrecognition problems at retrieval time using term similarity information. The models make effective use of complete or partial knowledge of semantic and phonetic term similarity evaluated using statistical methods for the corpus.

1 Introduction

In Information Retrieval (IR), document and query are commonly represented by sets of weighted terms (index terms) extracted from their text. Documents are ranked and presented to the user according to how well their representation matches the query representation [14].

A fundamental problem of IR is *term mismatch*. A query is usually a short and incomplete description of the user information need. Users and authors of documents often use different terms to refer to the same concepts. This produces an incorrect relevance ranking of documents with regards to the information need expressed in the query.

A similar problem can be found in spoken document retrieval and spoken query processing, where terms misrecognized by the speech recognition process or out of the vocabulary of the speech recognition system are found not matching in query and document representations. Naturally, this hinder the effectiveness of the IR system in a way similar to the term mismatch problem. I will call this problem *term misrecognition*, by analogy to the term mismatch problem.

This paper addresses the term mismatch and the term misrecognition problems proposing a set of retrieval models that exploits the knowledge of semantic and phonetic term similarity in the term space. The term similarity is used at retrieval time to estimate the relevance of a document in response to a query by looking not only at matching terms, but also at non-matching terms whose semantic and/or phonetic similarity are above a predefined threshold.

The paper is structured as follows. In section 2 and 3 I briefly present the term mismatch and misrecognition problems. Section 4 gives a definition of term similarity and a description of it properties that are useful in section 5, the core of this paper, where a set of models for exploiting term similarity at retrieval time are presented. Section 6 describe two measures of similarity that the proposed models enable to combine to address both the semantic and term mismatch and misrecognition problems: semantic and phonetic similarity. The combination of these measures of similarity is presented in section 7 and current work on the evaluation of this proposal is presented in section 8. Section 9 concludes the paper outlining future work. This paper is revised and extended version of [3].

2 The Term Mismatch Problem

Representing the user information need and the document informative content is a very difficult. Attempts to using advanced Natural Language Processing techniques or complex logical models have failed to solve the problem and IR is still using the classical technique of the "bag of terms" [12]. Terms are automatically extracted from or manually assigned to documents or queries. This method of representing documents and queries is common to both the Vector Space model [11] and the Probabilistic model [14], the two most important models of IR. However, representing documents and queries using a set of terms has a very serious side effect: the term mismatch problem.

Users of IR systems often use different terms to describe concepts in their queries than the authors use to describe the same concepts in their documents. It has been observed that two people use the same term to describe the same concept in less than 20% of the cases [6]. It has also been observed that this problem is more severe for short casual queries than for long elaborate ones because, as queries get longer, there is a higher chance of some important term co-occurring in the query and the relevant documents [17]. The term mismatch problem does not have only the effect of hindering the retrieval of relevant documents, it also naturally produces bad rankings of relevant documents.

A number of approaches have been attempted to solve the term mismatch problem:

- dimensionality reduction (e.g., stemming and conflation, manual thesauri, clustering or automatic thesauri, or Latent Semantic Indexing);
- query expansion (e.g., automatic query expansion, or relevance feedback);
- imaging (e.g., retrieval by general logical imaging).

In [5] I argued that none of these approaches can completely solve the problem, since each approach has its drawbacks, and I proposed a new set of models that tackles this approach in a more natural and effective way.

3 The Term Misrecognition Problem

The term misrecognition problem is analogous to the term mismatch problem. The problem is caused by the incorrect recognition of a term in a document or in a query. If a term t_j was actually present in both query and document, but was incorrectly recognized for t_k, then a number of potentially relevant documents containing t_j are not going to be retrieved, while a number of documents likely to be non-relevant and containing t_k are going to be retrieved. The incorrect ranking of these retrieved document is in direct relation to how many of these incorrect term recognitions are made.

This problem can be found when documents (or queries) are not in a textual form directly comparable to queries (or document), like for example in spoken document retrieval and spoken query processing, or with OCRed documents of queries. It is plausible to assume that mistakes in speech recognition are related to how close words sound like [8], while in OCR it is related to how similar their shapes are [7]. In this paper I will be mainly concerned with the term misrecognition problem found in spoken document retrieval and spoken query processing, since this work is important in the context of the SIRE Project. The main objective of SIRE project is to enable a user to interact via voice (i.e. submit queries, commands, relevance assessments, and receive summaries of retrieved documents) with a probabilistic IR system over a low bandwidth communication line, like for example a telephone line [2].

4 Term Similarity

All the approaches to the term mismatch problem proposed so far assume the availability of a measure of the similarity between terms. In fact, a similarity measure between pairs of terms in necessary in order to build an automatic thesaurus, expand the query, or perform indexing weights transfer. The approach proposed in this paper requires it too.

Let us suppose we have a measure of similarity that enables us to evaluate for each pair of terms a real value which estimates how close the terms are according to a metrics based on some property of the space that we want to observe. Let us also assume that such a measure of similarity has been normalised:

$$\forall(t_i, t_j), 0 \leq Sim(t_i, t_j) \leq 1$$

Such function Sim, should have the following properties:

1. $Sim(t_i, t_j) = 1$ iff $t_i = t_j$;
2. $Sim(t_i, t_j) \rightsquigarrow 1$ if t_i and t_j are semantically close, that is if t_i and t_j can be (and have been) used to express the same concepts;
3. $Sim(t_i, t_j) \rightsquigarrow 0$ if t_i and t_j are not semantically close, that is if t_i and t_j cannot be (and have not been) used to express the same concepts.

Symmetry, although often found in many similarity measures used experimentally is not a desired property, since it does take into consideration the generalisation and specialisation characteristics of the terms.

In the following sections, I will present two classes of retrieval models that exploit this measure of similarity to approach the term mismatch and the term misrecognition problem.

5 Exploiting Term Similarity

Classical IR models evaluate the RSV of a document with regard to a query using some variant of the following formula:

$$RSV(d,q)_c = \sum_{t \in (d \cap q)} w_d(t) \cdot w_q(t) \tag{1}$$

where $w_d(t)$ is the indexing weight assigned to term t in the context of document d, and $w_q(t)$ is the indexing weight assigned to term t in the context of query q. The sum of the product of the indexing weights is performed over all terms occurring in both the document and the query. Classical IR models fall into the term mismatch problem since they do not take into account that the same concept could be expressed using different terms in documents and query. However, supposing we had semantic similarity information on the term space, we could use it in the evaluation of the RSV to account for the term mismatch problem.

In the following two sections I will present some models that exploit term similarity information at retrieval time in this fashion.

5.1 The q ⊳ d Models

If we consider the point of view of a query, then we could take a query term for which we cannot find a matching document term and look for semantically close document terms. We could then evaluate the RSV using the following general formula:

$$RSV_{f(q \triangleright d)}(d,q) = \phi_{t_k \in q}(w_d(t_j), w_q(t_k), f(Sim(t_j, t_k), t_k)) \tag{2}$$

where t_j and t_k are respectively a document and a query term, and f indicates the use we can make of the known similarity between the two terms.

Let us take, for example, the following f, indicated by max:

$$f(Sim(t_j, t_k), t_k) = max_{t_j} Sim(t_j, t_k) \cdot w_d(t_j)$$

The rationale behind this formula is that in the presence of complete similarity information on the term space, we can easily determine the closest document term to t_k, that is the document term for which we have the maximum value of similarity with the query term t_k. Supposing the similarity measure has been normalised in the range $[0, 1]$, we could introduce the similarity value in the computation of the RSV as follows:

$$RSV_{max(q \triangleright d)}(d, q) = \sum_{t \in q} Sim(t, t^*) \cdot w_d(t^*) \cdot w_q(t) \quad (3)$$

where t^* is a document term for which the value of $Sim(t, t^*)$ is maximum given the query term t, $w_d(t^*)$ is the indexing weight assigned to term t^* in the context of document d, $w_q(t)$ is the indexing weight assigned to term t in the context of query q, and $Sim(t, t^*)$ is the similarity value between t and t^*.

Formula 3 enables to consider non-matching terms in the evaluation of the RSV. Two non-matching terms for which the similarity measure is maximum, will contribute to the RSV in a way that is proportional to their similarity value. Formula 3 is a generalisation of formula 1, as it can be easily proved if we assume $Sim(t_j, t_k) = 1$ if $t_k = t_j$ and $Sim(t_k, t_j) = 0$ otherwise.

Another example of function f enables us to consider the total value of the contribution of all non-matching terms in the evaluation of the RSV. We can the use the following f, indicated hereby with *tot*:

$$f(Sim(t_j, t_k), t_k) = \sum_{t_j} Sim(t_j, t_k) \cdot w_d(t_j)$$

In this case we could evaluate the RSV using the following formula:

$$RSV_{tot(q \triangleright d)}(d, q) = \sum_{t_k \in q} (\sum_{t_j \in d} Sim(t_k, t_j) \cdot w_d(t_j)) \cdot w_q(t_k) \quad (4)$$

where symbols are defined as in formula 3. Again, formula 4 is a generalisation of formula 1.

Notice that formula 3 and formula 4 are just some of the possible ways of considering the contribution of non-matching terms in the evaluation of the RSV using term similarity. Other, more complex strategies can be considered, like for example the use of a term representative of the document content (e.g. the centroid), or using terms representative of topical concepts or structural sections of a document. I will not address these more complex formulas in this paper.

5.2 The d ⊳ q Models

If we consider the point of view of a document, then we have the $d \rhd q$ models defined in general terms as follows:

$$RSV_{f(d \rhd q)}(d, q) = \phi_{t_j \in d}(w_d(t_j), w_q(t_k), f(Sim(t_j, t_k), t_j)) \tag{5}$$

The evaluation of the RSV could then be obtained, for example and mutatis mutandis with respect to the models presented in the previous section, using the following formula for the evaluation of $RSV_{max(d \rhd q)}(d, q)$:

$$RSV_{max(d \rhd q)}(d, q) = \sum_{t \in d} Sim(t, t^*)\ w_d(t)\ w_q(t^*) \tag{6}$$

where t^* is a query term for which the value of $Sim(t, t^*)$ is maximum given the document term t, $w_d(t)$ is the indexing weight assigned to term t in the context of document d, $w_q(t^*)$ is the indexing weight assigned to term t^* in the context of query q, and $Sim(t, t^*)$ is the similarity value between t and t^*.

Alternatively, we could evaluate $RSV_{tot(d \rhd q)}(d, q)$ in a way similar to the one reported in formula 4:

$$RSV_{tot(d \rhd q)}(d, q) = \sum_{t_j \in d} (\sum_{t_k \in q} Sim(t_k, t_j) \cdot w_q(t_k)) \cdot w_d(t_j) \tag{7}$$

As can be noticed, the only difference between the $q \rhd d$ and the $d \rhd q$ models is the point of view taken. Again, more complex ways of considering the contribution of non-matching terms in the evaluation of the RSV can also be devised, in ways similar to those already discussed for the $q \rhd d$ class of models.

5.3 Consideration on the q ⊳ d and d ⊳ q Models

In a related area of research, aimed at modelling the IR process as logical model, Wong and Yao demonstrated that most current IR models can be explained in terms of the formula $P(E \rightarrow H)$ that is evaluated as $P(H \mid E)$ [15]. The latter formula evaluates the degree of confirmation (or belief, according to the view taken) of the sentence H given evidence E. Conventional IR models can be obtained by associating either d or q to H or E, and by defining different ways of evaluating the probabilities by means of probabilistic inference on a concept space. Earlier, Nie showed that the two conditionals $d \rightarrow q$ and $q \rightarrow d$ have a very interesting interpretation in the context of IR [10]. The conditional $d \rightarrow q$ expresses the *exhaustivity* of the document to the query, i.e. how much of the document content is specified by the query content. In fact $d \rightarrow q$ is intuitively equivalent to $d \subseteq q$. The conditional $q \rightarrow d$, instead, expresses the *specificity* of the document to the query, i.e. how much of the query content is specified in the document content. In fact,

$q \rightarrow d$ is intuitively equivalent to $q \subseteq d$. The models proposed in this paper can be interpreted in this way too.

In fact, the $q \triangleright d$ models, by taking the query point of view, measure how much of the query content is specified in the document. This is done in a complete way by $tot(q \triangleright d)$, or in a partial way by $max(q \triangleright d)$, considering only the most important contributions. So, $q \triangleright d$ enables to measure the specificity of the document to the query. On the other hand, the $d \triangleright q$ models, by taking the document point of view, measure how much of the document content is required by the query. Again, this is done in a complete way by $tot(d \triangleright q)$, or in a partial way by $max(d \triangleright q)$. So, $d \triangleright q$ enables to measure the exhaustivity of the document to the query.

Different applications require different levels of specificity and exhaustivity. In fact, specificity is precision oriented, while exhaustivity is recall oriented. Precision and recall are the two most commonly used measures of performance evaluation of IR systems. They are defined, respectively, as the fraction of retrieved documents that are relevant, and the fraction of relevant documents that are retrieved.

5.4 The q ▷ d and d ▷ q Models with Partial Similarity Information

In the above discussion I have supposed the availability of full similarity information. This case is often unrealistic, especially for large term spaces, given the computational burden of the evaluation of $Sim(t_i, t_j)$ for every pairs of terms in the term space. The evaluation and the storing of complete similarity information is in fact a very expensive process. In most practical cases it makes more sense to evaluate and store similarity information only for pairs of terms that are most similar. These often are a very small subset of all terms in the term space. Moreover, this case makes it possible to use a thesaurus for the evaluation of $Sim(t_i, t_j)$, since a thesaurus contains information regarding only the most similar pairs of terms. The formulas presented in the two previous sections do not need to be modified in case of availability of only partial similarity information. They can be used as their are. Moreover, it can be easily proved that, for most f:

$$RSV_{f(q \triangleright d)} \rightarrow RSV_c \quad \text{for} \quad \mathbf{SS} \rightarrow \mathbf{n.a.}$$

and

$$RSV_{f(d \triangleright q)} \rightarrow RSV_c \quad \text{for} \quad \mathbf{SS} \rightarrow \mathbf{n.a.}$$

where **SS** is the similarity matrix, and **n.a.** is the matrix on all $n.a.$ values, where with $n.a.$ we indicate the non-availability of similarity information for a pair of terms.

Notice that if we have complete similarity information and the similarity measure is symmetric, than $RSV_{tot(q \triangleright d)}(d, q) = RSV_{tot(d \triangleright q)}(d, q)$.

Incidentally, in this case, given an appropriate term weighting function, $RSV_{tot(q \triangleright d)}(d,q)$ and $RSV_{tot(d \triangleright q)}(d,q)$ yield the same ranking of the Generalised Vector Space Model [16].

6 Different Forms of Similarity

So far, in the presentation of the $d \triangleright q$ and $q \triangleright d$ models, I have always talked about similarity from a generic point to view, meaning any possible way of establishing a metric in the term space that has the properties discussed in section 4. However, there are two forms of similarity that it would be very important to combine for spoken document retrieval and spoken queries processing:

- *semantic similarity*;
- *phonetic similarity*.

These two types of similarity are related to the two main types of uncertainty present in spoken document retrieval and spoken query processing and that are the causes of the term mismatch problem and the term misrecognition problem.

The next sections will examine how we can evaluate semantic and phonetic term similarity. Later I will explain how they can be combined together in a retrieval model.

6.1 Semantic Term Similarity

There are many different techniques for estimating semantic similarity between terms. Semantic similarity may be estimated from external knowledge, like for example a thesaurus or a dictionary. It can also be estimated from the document collection itself, given a large enough corpus. Most of these techniques are based on statistical analysis of the patterns of occurrence of terms in the documents.

One of the most often used measure of semantic similarity is the Expected Mutual Information Measure (EMIM), a well accepted measure in Lexicography [1]. EMIM is defined as follows:

$$\begin{aligned}
&SSim(t_i,t_j) = \\
&\quad = EMIM(t_i,t_j) = \\
&\quad = \textstyle\sum_{t_i,t_j} P(t_i \in d, t_j \in d) \cdot \log \frac{P(t_i \in d, t_j \in d)}{P(t_i \in d) P(t_j \in d)} \\
&\quad = \textstyle\sum_{t_i,t_j} P(t_i,t_j) \cdot \log \frac{P(t_i,t_j)}{P(t_i)P(t_j)}
\end{aligned}$$

where t_i and t_j are any two terms of the term space T. The EMIM between two index terms is often interpreted as a measure of the statistical information contained in one term about the other (and vice versa, it being a symmetric measure). For our purposes we can estimate EMIM using the technique proposed by Van Rijsbergen in [14, p.130], which rely on the availability of occurrence and co-occurrence data that can be derived by a statistical analysis of the term distribution in the collection.

$SSim(t_i, t_j)$ can easily be normalised in $[0, 1]$ once its maximum and minimum values for the available data have been found. The important point is that any measure of semantic similarity, can be used with the models proposed in this paper. The better the measure, the better the performance of the models. We will indicate semantic similarity with $SSim$ in the rest of this paper.

6.2 Phonetic Term Similarity

Phonetic similarity (henceforth indicated with $PSim$) is often estimated using a Phone Confusion Matrix (PCM). A PCM is a matrix that reports for each phone in row the number of times that phone has been mistaken with the phone in column. In other words, if we call reference (r) the real value of the phone being observed and hypothesis (h) the phone actually observed, $PCM(r, h)$ gives as the number of times phone r is confused with phone h.

In most cases, the PCM is derived with parameters that model the performance of the speech recogniser for "good speech" (e.g., produced by a native-speaker in a non-spontaneous manner). The numbers are synthetic, which means that they are not generated based on measurements of phone confusions, but rather on a model of how the speech recognition system works.

In order to use a PCM with the models proposed here, we have to derive similarity values at term level, rather than phone level. However, building an error recognition confusion matrix at term level would be too expensive, since the number of terms in the term space is too large. Moreover, such a matrix would be very sparse. On the other hand, there exist a limited number of phones (the exact number depends on the phonetic system used, the US English system having 54 phones), making it easier to build such a matrix. With and PCM built at phones level, and assuming that phones comprising each term are independent, we can evaluate $PSim(t_i, t_j)$ using the dynamic programming procedure proposed in [9]:

$$PSim(t_i, t_j) = A(l_i, l_j)$$

where l_i and l_j are respectively the length of t_i and t_j, and A is the $l_i \times l_j$ dynamic programming matrix evaluated recursively as reported in formula:

$$A(m,n) = \begin{cases} 1 & m = 0, n = 0 \\ A(0, n-1) \cdot C_n(0, j[n-1]) & m = 0, n > 0 \\ A(m-1, 0) \cdot C_n(i[m-1], 0) & m > 0, n = 0 \\ max \begin{cases} A(m-1, n) \cdot C_n(i[m-1], 0) \\ A(m-1, n-1) \cdot C_n(i[m-1], j[n-1]) \\ A(m, n-1) \cdot C_n(0, j[n-1]) \end{cases} & m > 0, n > 0 \end{cases} \tag{8}$$

In formula 8 $C_n(r,h)$ is the probability (actually the normalised frequency) of observing h given that it really was r. This is obtained as:

$$C_n(r,h) = \frac{PCM(r,h)}{\sum_{k\in\{h\}} PCM(r,k)}$$

where $PCM(r,h)$ is a value of the PCM matrix with row 0 for insertion and column 0 for deletion errors. Notice that with this estimation procedure we can interpret $PSim(t_i,t_j) \approx P(t_i \mid t_j)$. An example of such matrix is depicted in figure 1[1].

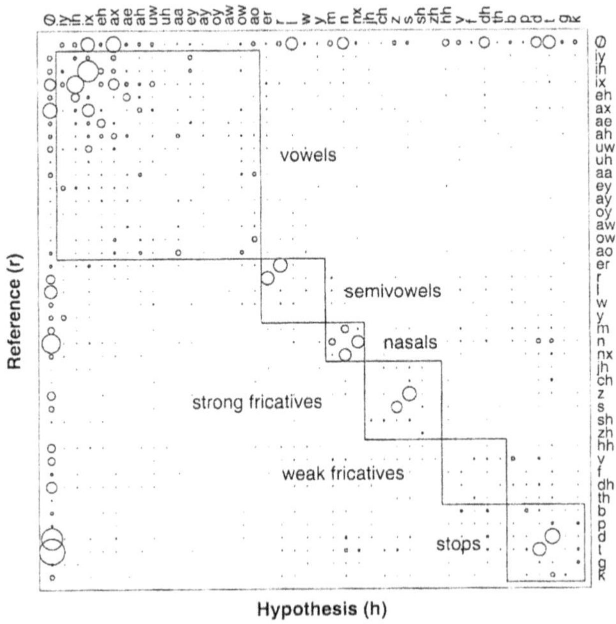

Figure1. Example of a Phone Confusion Matrix.

Other techniques based, for example, on Hidden Markov Models can also be used to estimate $PSim$ [8].

7 Combination of Semantic and Phonetic Similarity for Spoken Document Retrieval and Spoken Query Processing

We can easily adapt the models presented in section 5 to dealing with the misrecognition problem. This can be done by using phonetic similarity, in-

[1] Reproduced from [9], with permission.

stead of, or in conjunction with, semantic similarity. So for example if we are only considering phonetic similarity, formula 3 can be rewritten as:

$$RSV_{max_p(q \triangleright d)}(d,q) = \sum_{t \in q} PSim(t, t^{p*}) \cdot w_d(t^{p*}) \cdot w_q(t) \tag{9}$$

where t^{p*} is a document term for which the value of $PSim(t, t^{p*})$ is maximum given the query term t, $w_d(t^{p*})$ is the indexing weight assigned to term t^{p*} in the context of document d, $w_q(t)$ is the indexing weight assigned to term t in the context of query q, and $PSim(t, t^{p*})$ is the phonetic similarity value between t and t^{p*}.

While if we consider only the semantic similarity, the formula for $RSV_{max_s(q \triangleright d)}$ can be written using $SSim$ instead of $PSim$. On the other hand, if both measures of similarity were normalised, we could consider the combination of both the semantic and phonetic similarity. So, for example, we could write:

$$\begin{aligned} & RSV_{max_{ps}(q \triangleright d)}(d,q) = \\ & \quad = \alpha \cdot RSV_{max_p(q \triangleright d)}(d,q) + \beta \cdot RSV_{max_s(q \triangleright d)}(d,q)) = \\ & \quad = \textstyle\sum_{t \in q} \left(\alpha \cdot PSim(t, t^{p*}) \cdot w_d(t^{p*}) + \beta \cdot SSim(t, t^{s*}) \cdot w_d(t^{s*})\right) w_q(t) \end{aligned} \tag{10}$$

where α and β are tow parameters (with $\alpha + \beta = 1$) allowing to give weighted preference to $PSim$ or $SSim$. Notice that the properties described in section 5.4 are preserved.

Analogously, $RSV_{tot_{ps}(q \triangleright d)}(d,q)$ can be easily evaluated as:

$$RSV_{tot_{ps}(q \triangleright d)}(d,q) = \sum_{t_k} (\sum_{t_j} (\alpha \cdot PSim(t_k, t_j) + \beta \cdot SSim(t_k, t_j)) \cdot w_d(t_j)) \cdot w_q(t_k) \tag{11}$$

Formulas 10 and 11 are very simplistic linear combinations of semantic and phonetic similarities, and other more complex combinations can be devised. We also leave to the reader the task of deriving $RSV_{max_{ps}(d \triangleright q)}$ and $RSV_{tot_{ps}(q \triangleright d)}$ where semantic and phonetic similarity are combined.

8 Evaluation

In [5] an extensive evaluation of the how the models reported in this paper enable to tackle the term mismatch problem has been reported. The use of semantic similarity enabled to achieve significant improvements in the performance over standard IR models. Recently, these results have been proved also for a much larger test collection than the ones used in [5].

I am currently experimenting with the combination of semantic and phonetic similarity for spoken query processing using a collection of spoken queries with a range of word error recognition rates. The baseline performance of standard IR for the spoken query processing task using this set of queries has already been established [4]. The first results of the use of a combination of semantic and phonetic similarity with the $d \rhd q$ and $q \rhd d$ models seems promising.

The use of phonetic similarity derived form PCM has been recently addressed in a similar way in [13]. In that paper, a phonetic approach, rather that a term-based approach was used. The performance results obtained in video-based distributed learning setting were very encouraging. I expect to obtain similar or better levels of performance, since in [13] only single-term queries were used and there was no attempt was made to combine term-based retrieval and phonetic retrieval.

9 Conclusions and Future Work

In this paper I presented a set of models for dealing with the term mismatch and the term misrecognition problems in spoken document retrieval and spoken query processing. An experimental evaluation is currently being carried out. These experimental results will provide useful feedback on the effectiveness of the models proposed and on how to effectively combine semantic and phonetic similarity.

References

1. K.W. Church and P. Hanks. Word association norms, mutual information and lexicography. In *Proccedings of ACL 27*, pages 76–83, Vancouver, Canada, 1989.
2. F. Crestani. Vocal access to a newspaper archive: design issues and preliminary investigation. In *Proceedings of ACM Digital Libraries*, pages 59–68, Berkeley, CA, USA, August 1999.
3. F. Crestani. Combination of semantic and phonetic term similarity for spoken document retrieval and spoken query processing. In *Proceedings of the 8th Conference on Information Processing and Management of Uncertainty in Knowledge-Based Systems (IPMU)*, pages 960–967, Madrid, Spain, July 2000.
4. F. Crestani. Effects of word recogntion errors in spoken query processing. In *Proceedings of the IEEE ADL 2000 Conference*, pages 39–47, Washington DC, USA, May 2000.
5. F. Crestani. Exploiting the similarity of non-matching terms at retrieval time. *Journal of Information Retrieval*, 2(1):23–43, 2000.
6. S. Deerwester, S.T. Dumais, G.W. Furnas, T. Landauer, and Harshman. Indexing by latent semantic analysis. *Journal of the American Society for Information Science*, 41(6):391–407, 1990.
7. J. Heid. Getting started with optical character recognition. *MacWorld*, pages 77–83, October 1990.
8. J.A. Markowitz. *Using speech recognition.* Prentice Hall, Upper Saddle River, NJ, USA, 1996.

9. K. Ng. Towards robust methods for spoken document retrieval. In *Proceedings of Int. Conf. on Spoken Language Processing*, volume 3, pages 939–942, Sydney, Australia, November 1998.
10. J.Y. Nie. An outline of a general model for Information Retrieval. In *Proceedings of ACM SIGIR*, pages 495–506, Grenoble, France, June 1988.
11. G. Salton. *Automatic information organization and retrieval.* McGraw Hill, New York, 1968.
12. A.F. Smeaton. Progress in the application of Natural Language Processing to Information Retrieval tasks. *The Computer Journal*, 35(3):268–278, 1992.
13. S. Srinivasan and D. Petkovic. Phonetic confusion matrix based spoken document retrieval. In *Proceedings of ACM SIGIR*, pages 81–87, Athens, Greece, July 2000.
14. C.J. van Rijsbergen. *Information Retrieval.* Butterworths, London, UK, second edition, 1979.
15. S.K.M. Wong and Y.Y. Yao. On modelling Information Retrieval with probabilistic inference. *ACM Transactions on Information Systems*, 13(1):38–68, 1995.
16. S.K.M. Wong, W. Ziarko, V.V. Raghavan, and P.C.N. Wong. On modelling of information retrieval concepts in vector spaces. *ACM Transactions on Information Systems*, 12(2):299–321, 1987.
17. J. Xu. *Solving the word mismatch problem through automatic text analysis.* Ph.D. Thesis, Department of Computer Science, University of Massachusetts, Amherst, MA, USA, May 1997.

Knowledge-Based Extrapolation of Cases: A Possibilistic Approach*

Eyke Hüllermeier[1], Didier Dubois[2], and Henri Prade[2]

[1] Statistics and Decision Theory
University of Paderborn, Germany
eyke@upb.de
[2] IRIT, Université Paul Sabatier
Toulouse, France
{dubois,prade}@irit.fr

Abstract. The paper presents a formal framework of instance-based prediction in which the generalization beyond experience is founded on the concepts of similarity and possibility. The underlying extrapolation principle is formalized by means of possibility rules, a special type of fuzzy rules. Thus, instance-based prediction can be realized as fuzzy set-based approximate reasoning. The basic model is extended by means of fuzzy set-based (linguistic) modeling techniques, including the discounting of untypical cases and the flexible handling and adequate adaptation of different similarity relations. This extension provides a convenient way of incorporating domain-specific (expert) knowledge. Our approach thus allows for combining knowledge and data in a flexible way and favors a view of instance-based reasoning according to which the user interacts closely with the system.

1 Introduction

In instance-based reasoning methods, such as nearest neighbor classification [3], instance-based learning [2], and case-based reasoning [1], observed cases are extrapolated based on some kind of *closeness* or *representativeness* assumption. Typically, the concept of *similarity* (or distance) plays a crucial role in the inference process. In case-based reasoning (CBR), for example, problem solving proceeds from the assumption that "similar problems have similar solutions." This type of assumption will subsequently be referred to as the SBR hypothesis, where the latter acronym stands for *similarity-based reasoning.*

In this paper, we propose to formalize the SBR hypothesis and the related inference principle in the framework of fuzzy rules and fuzzy set-based approximate reasoning, with a special emphasis on the performance task of *prediction* [5,11]. There are several aspects which motivate the combination of SBR and fuzzy set-based modeling and reasoning techniques [15], and especially the use of fuzzy rules in the context of SBR [5]. Firstly, the SBR

---

* Expanded and updated version of a paper with the same title presented at the 8th International Conference on Information Processing and Management of Uncertainty in Knowledge-Based Systems, pages 1575–1582, Madrid, Spain, 2000.

hypothesis itself can be considered as an *if-then* rule. Secondly, the notion of *similarity*, which lies at the heart of SBR, is also strongly related to the theory of fuzzy sets. Indeed, one of the main interpretations of the membership function of a fuzzy set is that of a similarity relation, i.e. membership values can be thought of as degrees of similarity [10]. Thirdly, linked with the framework of possibility theory, fuzzy sets provide a tool for modeling and processing *uncertainty*. In connection with SBR, this aspect seems to be of special importance if one realizes the *heuristic* character of this type of reasoning method [12].

The basic SBR framework we proceed from is stated in Section 2. In Section 3, we present a possibilistic model of *similarity-based inference* (SBI). This model makes use of possibility rules, a special type of fuzzy rules, in order to formalize the SBR hypothesis.[1] In Section 4, we outline some extensions of the basic model. These extensions, which make use of fuzzy set-based modeling techniques, enable domain-specific knowledge to be translated into a particular SBR model.

2 The Basic Framework

A *case* is a tuple $\langle s, r\rangle \in \mathcal{C} = \mathcal{S} \times \mathcal{R}$ consisting of a *situation* $s \in \mathcal{S}$ and an associated *result* or *outcome* $r \in \mathcal{R}$.[2] We do not assume that a situation determines a unique outcome, which would be too restrictive for certain applications. That is, cases $\langle s, r\rangle$ and $\langle s, r'\rangle$ might be encountered such that $r \neq r'$. Let $\varphi \subset \mathcal{S} \times \mathcal{R}$ denote the class of potential observations. Thus, a case is always an element of the relation φ.

Data is assumed to be given in the form of a memory

$$\mathcal{M} = \{\langle s_1, r_1\rangle, \langle s_2, r_2\rangle, \ldots, \langle s_n, r_n\rangle\} \tag{1}$$

of precedent cases. The similarity of situations resp. results is specified by means of similarity relations

$$\sigma_{\mathcal{S}} : \mathcal{S} \times \mathcal{S} \to \mathcal{L}, \quad \sigma_{\mathcal{R}} : \mathcal{R} \times \mathcal{R} \to \mathcal{L},$$

where $\mathcal{L}$ is an *ordinal* scale. Usually, $\mathcal{L}$ will be taken as $\{0, 1/N, 2/N, \ldots, 1\}$ without loss of generality, where 1 (0) stands for complete (dis)similarity.

As already mentioned above, our focus is on similarity-based prediction: We consider the task of exploiting past experience (in the form of the memory $\mathcal{M}$) against the background of the SBR hypothesis in order to predict the *result* or *outcome* $r_0 \in \mathcal{R}$ associated with a new situation $s_0 \in \mathcal{S}$. To this

[1] Let us mention that other types of fuzzy rules might be used, and that corresponding models can also be formalized within a more logic-oriented framework [5,14].

[2] We prefer these expressions for reasons of generality to the terms "problem" and "solution" which are commonly used in CBR.

end, we shall quantify the possibility that $r_0 = r$, i.e. that $\langle s_0, r\rangle \in \varphi$, for all outcomes $r \in \mathcal{R}$. As will be seen in Section 3, this kind of prediction makes the formulation of rather general types of queries possible, especially if s_0 is allowed to be incompletely specified. Moreover, a prediction of this kind can be used in various ways, e.g. for helping a user in making decisions. In CBR, it can also support the overall process of problem solving in the sense that it allows subsequent stages of this process to focus on the most likely outcomes. For instance, if r_0 corresponds to the solution of a new problem, s_0, a possibilistic valuation allows one to consider the most promising candidates first, before taking other solutions into account.

Example 1 *For illustration purposes we will use the (real-world)* AUTOMOBILE DATABASE[3] *throughout the paper. This database contains 205 cars, each of which is characterized by 26 attributes. Thus, a case corresponds to a car which is characterized by means of an attribute–value representation including properties such as, e.g., its horsepower and fuel-type. For the sake of simplicity, we shall consider only some of the attributes available, i.e. our memory* $\mathcal{M}$ *is actually a projection of the complete database. One of the attributes, namely the price of a car, has been chosen as the outcome associated with a case. The latter is hence a tuple* $\langle s, r\rangle$*, where the situation* $s = (a_1, \ldots, a_L)$ *is a vector of attribute values describing a car, and* r *is the associated price. The similarity between two cars* s *and* s' *will be defined as a combination of the similarities between the respective attribute values* a_j *and* a'_j $(1 \leq j \leq L)$.

3 Possibility Rules and Similarity-Based Inference

3.1 Possibility rules

Fuzzy rules provide a local, rough and soft specification of the relation between variables X and Y ranging on domains D_X and D_Y, respectively [9]. They are generally expressed in the form "if X is A then Y is B," where A and B are fuzzy sets associated with symbolic labels and modeled by means of membership functions on D_X resp. D_Y.[4] Fuzzy rules can be formalized as possibility distributions constrained by some combination of the membership functions which define, respectively, their condition and conclusion part [7].

A *possibility rule* involving fuzzy sets A and B, subsequently symbolized by $A \rightsquigarrow B$, is a special type of fuzzy rule which corresponds to the statement that "the more X is A, the more *possible* B is a range for Y." More precisely, it can be interpreted as a collection of rules "if $X = x$, it is possible at least to the degree $A(x)$ that B is a range for Y." The intended meaning of this kind of *possibility-qualifying* rule is modeled by the following constraint which

[3] Available at `http://www.ics.uci.edu/~mlearn`.

[4] We use the same notation for a label, the name of an associated fuzzy set, and the membership function of this set.

guarantees a certain lower bound to the possibility, $\pi(x,y)$, that (x,y) is an admissible instantiation of (X,Y):

$$\pi(x,y) \geq \min\{A(x), B(y)\}. \tag{2}$$

As suggested by the rule-based modeling of the relation between X and Y, these variables often play the role of an input and an output, respectively, and one is interested in possible values of Y while X is assumed to be given. By letting $\pi(y \,|\, x) = \pi(x,y)$, the constraint (2) can also be considered as a lower bound to a *conditional* possibility distribution. That is, given the value $X = x$, the possibility that $Y = y$ is lower-bounded by $\pi(x,y)$ according to (2). Observe that *nothing* is said about Y in the case where $A(x) = 0$ since we then obtain the trivial constraint $\pi(y \,|\, x) \geq 0$. Besides, it should be noticed that the lower bound-interpretation is also consistent with conditional distributions $\pi(\cdot \,|\, x)$ which are not normalized, i.e. for which $\sup_y \pi(y \,|\, x) < 1$.

3.2 Formalizing the SBR hypothesis

A basic idea of the approach discussed in this paper is to use a possibility rule as defined above in order to formalize the SBR hypothesis. In fact, interpreting X and Y as degrees of similarity between two situations and two results, respectively, and A and B as fuzzy sets of "large similarity degrees" (with strictly increasing membership functions) amounts to expressing the following version of the SBR hypothesis: "The more similar two situations are, the more *possible* it is that the corresponding outcomes are similar" [5]. Note that this formalization takes the heuristic nature of the SBR hypothesis into account. In fact, it does not impose a deterministic constraint, but only concludes on the *possibility* of the outcomes to be similar.

In the sense of the above principle, an observed case $\langle s_1, r_1 \rangle \in \mathcal{M}$ is taken as a piece of evidence [4] which qualifies similar (hypothetical) cases $\langle s, r \rangle$ as being possible. According to (2) it induces lower bounds[5]

$$\pi(s,r) \geq \min\left\{\sigma_{\mathcal{S}}(s,s_1), \sigma_{\mathcal{R}}(r,r_1)\right\} \tag{3}$$

to the possibility that $\langle s, r \rangle \in \varphi$. This can be interpreted as a similarity-based *extrapolation* of case-based information: The observation $\langle s_1, r_1 \rangle$ is considered as a typical case or, say, prototype, which is extrapolated in accordance with the SBR hypothesis. The more similar $\langle s, r \rangle$ and $\langle s_1, r_1 \rangle$ are in the sense of the (joint) similarity measure

$$\sigma_{\mathcal{C}} : (\langle s,r \rangle, \langle s',r' \rangle) \mapsto \min\left\{\sigma_{\mathcal{S}}(s,s'), \sigma_{\mathcal{R}}(r,r')\right\},$$

the more plausible the (hypothetical) case $\langle s, r \rangle$ becomes and, hence, the larger is the (lower) possibility bound (3). In other words, a high degree of

[5] Without loss of generality, we assume the membership functions of the fuzzy sets of "large similarity degrees" to be given by the identical function $\mathrm{id} : x \mapsto x$.

possibility is assigned to a hypothetical case as soon as the *existence* of a very similar case is guaranteed (by observation).

Applying (3) to all cases in the memory $\mathcal{M}$ we obtain the possibility distribution $\pi_{\mathcal{C}}$ defined by

$$\pi_{\mathcal{C}}(s,r) = \max_{1 \leq i \leq n} \min \left\{ \sigma_{\mathcal{S}}(s, s_i), \sigma_{\mathcal{R}}(r, r_i) \right\} \tag{4}$$

for all $c = \langle s, r \rangle \in \mathcal{S} \times \mathcal{R}$. This distribution can be interpreted as a possibilistic approximation of the relation φ of existing cases. It is of provisional nature and actually represents lower bounds to possibility degrees (the equality in (4) is justified by a principle of *maximal informativeness*). In fact, the degree of possibility assigned to a case c may increase when gathering further evidence by observing new sample cases, as reflected by the application of the maximum operator in (4).

3.3 Similarity-based inference

The distribution (4) can be taken as a point of departure for various inference tasks. For example, given a new situation s_0, a prediction of the associated outcome r_0 is obtained in the form of the conditional distribution $\pi_{\mathcal{R}}$ defined by

$$\pi_{\mathcal{R}}(r) = \pi_{\mathcal{R}}(r \mid s_0) = \pi_{\mathcal{C}}(s_0, r) \tag{5}$$

for all $r \in \mathcal{R}$.

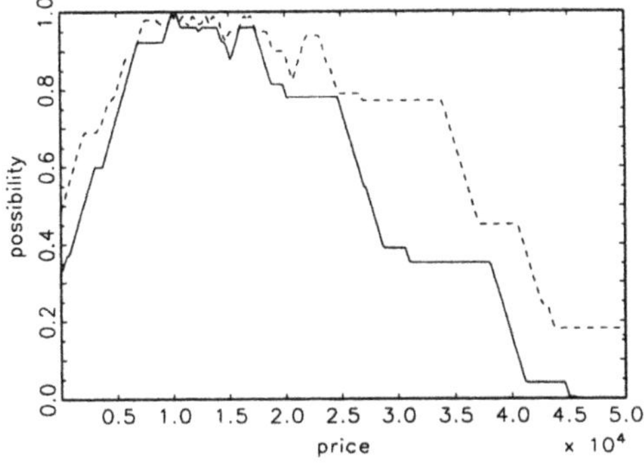

Fig. 1. Prediction (5) of the price of a car based on the original hypothesis (dashed line) and its modified version (10) (solid line).

Example 2 *Reconsider Example 1 and suppose a car to be characterized by only one attribute, namely its horsepower. Thus, the* SBR *hypothesis should* *simply be understood in the sense that "cars with similar horsepower have similar prices." Let* $\sigma_{\mathcal{S}} = \sigma_{hp} = f_{100}$ *with*

$$f_M : (x, x') \mapsto [\max\{1 - |x - x'|/M, 0\}]_{\mathcal{L}}, \tag{6}$$

where $\mathcal{L} = \{0, 1/100, \ldots, 1\}$ *and* $[x]_{\mathcal{L}} = \max\{\lambda \in \mathcal{L} \mid \lambda \leq x\}$. *Moreover, let the similarity between two outcomes (= prices) be given by* $\sigma_{\mathcal{R}} = f_{10000}$. *Figure 1 shows the prediction (5) for* $s_0 = 100$. *This prediction corresponds to the "more or less" possible range of prices for the class of cars whose horsepower is 100. As can be seen, the evidence contained in the memory* $\mathcal{M}$ *of cases strongly supports prices between* \$10,000 *and* \$17,000. *At the same time, however, it does not completely rule out prices which are slightly lower or higher.*

Suppose that we are interested in, say, the price of a car whose horsepower is between 90 and 110. This amounts to predicting the outcome of a situation s_0 with incompletely specified attributes. The following generalization of (5) is in accordance with the semantics underlying our approach:

$$\pi_{\mathcal{R}}(r) = \pi_{\mathcal{R}}(r \mid \mathcal{S}_0) = \inf_{s \in \mathcal{S}_0} \pi_{\mathcal{C}}(s, r), \tag{7}$$

where $\mathcal{S}_0$ denotes the set of situations $s \in \mathcal{S}$ which are compatible with the characterization of s_0 (i.e. the interval [90, 110] in our example). Indeed, each potential situation $s \in \mathcal{S}_0$ gives rise to a lower bound $\pi_{\mathcal{C}}(s, r)$ according to (4). Without additional knowledge, however, we can guarantee but the smallest of these bounds to be valid. This is in agreement with the idea of *guaranteed possibility* (of an event $X \subset \mathcal{X}$), which is formally derived from a possibility distribution π on $\mathcal{X}$ according to $\Delta(X) = \inf_{x \in X} \pi(x)$.

The prediction (7) can be generalized further by modeling imprecise knowledge about s_0 in the form of a possibility distribution π_0 on $\mathcal{S}$, where $\pi_0(s)$ corresponds to the degree of possibility that $s_0 = s$. A horsepower of 100, for instance, might appear somewhat more plausible than a horsepower of 90, even though the latter is not completely excluded. A graded modeling of $\mathcal{S}_0$ is useful, e.g. if some attributes are specified linguistically.

Observe that (7) can be interpreted as the possibility of the tuple $\langle s, r \rangle$ which is *guaranteed* by each *possible* situation $s \in \mathcal{S}_0$. Therefore – taking into account the possibility distribution π_0 which represents the imprecisely known situation s_0 – (7) can be generalized as follows:

$$\pi_{\mathcal{R}}(r) = \inf_{s \in \mathcal{S}} \max\{\pi_{\mathcal{C}}(s, r), 1 - \pi_0(s)\}. \tag{8}$$

One obviously recovers (7) from (8) by associating the set $\mathcal{S}_0$ in (7) with a related $\{0, 1\}$-valued possibility distribution, i.e. $\pi_0(s) = 1$ if $s \in \mathcal{S}_0$ and 0 otherwise. (8) estimates the inclusion of the fuzzy set of situations compatible with $\mathcal{S}_0$ in the fuzzy set of situations which are possibly associated with the result r; it represents the *certainty* that a situation, fuzzily restricted by

$\mathcal{S}_0$, is possibly associated with r. In the extreme case where $\mathcal{S}_0$ is completely unspecified ($\pi_0 \equiv 1$), (8) yields $\pi_{\mathcal{R}}(r) = \inf_{s \in \mathcal{S}} \pi_{\mathcal{C}}(s,r)$, that is a fully uninformative result usually equal to 0. This is clearly in agreement with the idea that $\pi_{\mathcal{R}}$ is a lower bound.

A further generalization becomes necessary when allowing for incompletely specified sample cases. Let the ith case in the memory be characterized by the (crisp) set $\mathcal{C}_i = \mathcal{S}_i \times \mathcal{R}_i \subset \mathcal{C}$. Then, (4) becomes

$$\pi_{\mathcal{C}}(s,r) = \max_{1 \leq i \leq n} \inf_{c_i \in \mathcal{C}_i} \sigma_{\mathcal{C}}(\langle s,r \rangle, c_i),$$

which is in accordance with (4) and (7). Moreover, we obtain

$$\pi_{\mathcal{C}}(s,r) = \max_{1 \leq i \leq n} \inf_{c_i \in \mathcal{C}_i} \max\{\sigma_{\mathcal{C}}(\langle s,r \rangle, c_i), 1 - \pi_i(c_i)\}$$

if the ith case is characterized by means of a possibility distribution π_i rather than by a crisp set $\mathcal{C}_i$. Observe that this expression of $\pi_{\mathcal{C}}(s,r)$ can be inserted into (8) in order to handle incomplete specifications of both, the sample cases and the new situation.

4 Controlling the Generalization Beyond Data

The possibilistic extrapolation of case-based information in the sense of (3) relies on the heuristic assumption underlying SBR. It should, therefore, take into account whether the related reasoning principle is actually valid. That is, the less the current application seems to meet the SBR hypothesis, the more cautious one should be when considering an observed case as evidence for the existence of similar cases. In this section, several extensions of the basic model of Section 3 are proposed in order to modulate the extent of case-based extrapolation. The methodological framework outlined below includes the adaptation of similarity relations and inference rules, the modeling of the SBR hypothesis by combining several rules, the discounting of untypical cases, and the local restriction of inference rules.

4.1 Modified possibility rules

The basic model can be rendered more flexible by making use of (linguistic) modifiers [16] in (4), i.e. non-decreasing functions $m_1, m_2 : \mathcal{L} \to \mathcal{L}$. This leads to possibility rules $m_1 \circ A \overset{m_2}{\rightsquigarrow} B$ with associated distributions

$$\pi_{\mathcal{C}} : (s,r) \mapsto \max_{1 \leq i \leq n} m_2 \left(\min \left\{ m_1(\sigma_{\mathcal{S}}(s,s_i)), \sigma_{\mathcal{R}}(r,r_i) \right\} \right). \tag{9}$$

Both modifiers in (9) control the extent to which a sample case is extrapolated, i.e. the extent to which other (hypothetical) cases are supported by an observation. The larger (in the sense of the partial order of functions on $\mathcal{L}$)

m_1 and m_2 are, the stronger (in the sense of asserted possibility degrees) a case $\langle s_i, r_i \rangle$ is extrapolated.

In connection with the linguistic modeling of fuzzy concepts, modifiers such as $x \mapsto x^2$ or $x \mapsto \sqrt{x}$ are utilized for depicting the effect of linguistic hedges such as "very" or "almost" [16]. Applying the modifier $m_1 : x \mapsto x^2$ might thus be seen as replacing the original hypothesis that "similar situations induce similar outcomes" by the weaker assumption that only "*very* similar situations induce similar outcomes." The modifier m_2 acts on the possibility-qualifying part of a rule. It can be thought of as modifying the possibility distribution associated with the rule $m_1 \circ A \rightsquigarrow B$. In fact, it allows for modeling rules of the form "for m_1-similar situations it is m_2-possible that the respective results are similar," where "m_2-possible" stands for expressions such as, e.g., "more or less possible." Linguistic hedges such as "more or less" basically bring a discounting of the rule $m_1 \circ A \rightsquigarrow B$ about. Discounting a possibility distribution π within the framework of (qualitative) possibility theory can be realized, e.g., by modifying π into $\min\{1-\lambda, \pi\}$ [8]. The constant λ plays the role of a discounting factor and defines an upper bound to the support that can be provided by an underlying (possibility) rule. Indeed, π remains unchanged if $\lambda = 0$. As opposed to this, the original support expressed by π is completely annulled if the discounting is maximal ($\lambda = 1$). By taking m_2 as the mapping $x \mapsto \min\{x, 1-\lambda\}$, the distribution (9) becomes

$$\pi_C : (s,r) \mapsto \max_{1 \leq i \leq n} \min \{1 - \lambda, \min \{m_1(\sigma_S(s, s_i)), \sigma_{\mathcal{R}}(r, r_i)\}\} . \tag{10}$$

Example 3 *Consider as an example the hypothesis that "it is completely possible that cars with* very *similar horsepower have similar prices." Applying the modifier $m_1 : x \mapsto x^2$ to the relation σ_{hp} and modeling the (non-)effect of "completely" by $\lambda = 0$, the prediction $\pi_{\mathcal{R}}$ based on (10) yields the possibility distribution shown in Figure 1. Compared to the prediction (5), the degree of possibility is smaller for most of the prices $r \in \mathcal{R}$. This is caused by the fact that the* SBR *hypothesis is now modeled in a more cautious way.*

It deserves mentioning that the modifier functions m_1 and m_2 in (9) are not necessarily predefined. Rather, they are intended to adapt the SBR model to the given data. In general, this comes down to choosing optimal modifiers from (parametrized) classes of functions associated with respective linguistic hedges. Details of this procedure, such as e.g. the specification of a consistency criterion to be optimized with respect to some set of (typical) cases, are discussed in [6].

4.2 Combination of several rules

Rather than making use of a single possibility rule, the SBR hypothesis can be expressed by means of a combination (conjunction) of several rules. Suppose m such rules to be specified. Denoting by π_C^k the possibility distribution (10) induced by the kth rule ($1 \leq k \leq m$), the overall extrapolation is then given by

$$\pi_C = \pi_C^1 \vee \pi_C^2 \vee \ldots \vee \pi_C^m. \tag{11}$$

The *disjunctive* combination of possibility distributions in (11) shows that a hypothetical case can be supported by any observed case in connection with any rule. Note that each rule might involve different similarity relations, or different modifications of basic relations. Within our framework, it seems particularly interesting to combine similarity measures from a set of elementary relations (associated with individual attributes) by means of fuzzy set-based modeling techniques.

Suppose, as in our running example, that an attribute–value representation is used in order to characterize cases. That is, let situations correspond to vectors $s = (a_1, \ldots, a_L) \in \mathcal{S} = \mathcal{A}_1 \times \ldots \times \mathcal{A}_L$, where $\mathcal{A}_j$ denotes the set of values of the jth attribute. Moreover, let σ_j be an elementary similarity relation defined over $\mathcal{A}_j$. By making use of logical connectives, the if-part of a possibility rule can then be composed of these elementary measures or modified versions thereof. Restricting ourselves to the logical connective $\wedge$, we obtain rules of the form

$$m_{11}(\sigma_1(a_1, a_1')) \wedge \ldots \wedge m_{1L}(\sigma_L(a_L, a_L')) \overset{m_2}{\rightsquigarrow} \sigma_{\mathcal{R}}(r, r'). \tag{12}$$

A rule of the form (12) can also be expressed as $\sigma_{\mathcal{S}}' \overset{m_2}{\rightsquigarrow} \sigma_{\mathcal{R}}$, where

$$\sigma_{\mathcal{S}}'(s, s') = \min_{1 \leq j \leq L} m_{1j}(\sigma_j(a_j, a_j')). \tag{13}$$

Let us remark that an aggregation (13) requires the elementary similarity relations to be commensurate.

Of course, one might think of replacing the min-operator in (13) by other t-norms in order to model the logical $\wedge$-connective. Moreover, the condition part in (12) can be generalized such that only some of the attributes are used, i.e., each rule can concern different attributes. Leaving the jth attribute out of account can be interpreted in two ways. Firstly, this attribute might be irrelevant for the similarity of situations, which is adequately reflected by $m_{1j} \equiv 1$. Secondly, the rule might be interpreted as expressing a ceteris paribus condition, i.e. it might be assumed implicitly that $a_j = a_j'$. In this case, m_{1j} should be defined by $m_{1j}(1) = 1$ and $m_{1j}(x) = 0$ for $0 \leq x < 1$.[6] For example, when saying that two cars with similar horsepower have similar prices, it might be taken for granted that both cars have the same type of aspiration (standard or turbo).

Suppose that m possibility rules have been defined by using the same modifier m_2. Moreover, let $\sigma_{\mathcal{S}}^k$ ($1 \leq k \leq m$) denote the (aggregated) measure

[6] Besides, σ_j should be separating: $\sigma_j(a_j, a_j') = 1 \Leftrightarrow a_j = a_j'$.

(13) associated with the condition part of the kth rule. Thus, the rules specify different conditions (in the form of conjunctions of elementary similarity relations between attributes) which all allow to draw the same conclusion. The m individual rules are then equivalent to one (aggregated) rule of the form $\sigma_S \overset{m_2}{\rightsquigarrow} \sigma_{\mathcal{R}}$, where

$$\sigma_S(s, s') = \max_{1 \leq k \leq m} \sigma_S^k(s, s').$$

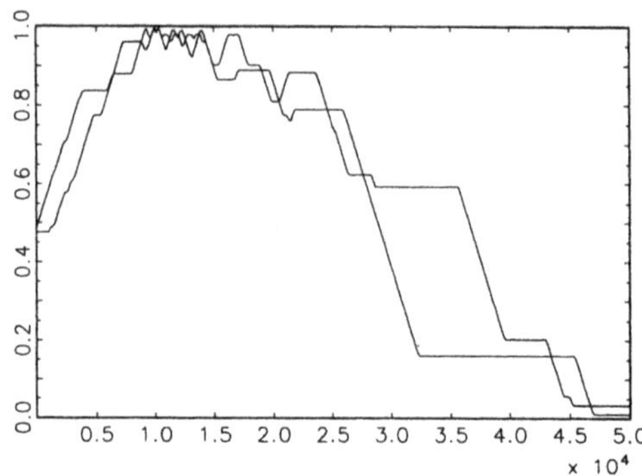

Fig. 2. Prediction (9) of the price of a car with horsepower 100, engine-size 110 and peak-rpm 5500, induced by two different rules.

Example 4 *Consider the following rules as an example: (1) Cars with* very similar *horsepower possibly have similar prices. (2) Cars with* similar *engine-size and* approximately similar *peak-rpm possibly have similar prices. Making use of the similarity measures* σ_{eng} *and* σ_{rpm} *defined by (6) with* $M = 100$ *and* $M = 1000$*, respectively, and modeling the effect of the linguistic hedge "approximately" by means of* $x \mapsto [\sqrt{x}]_{\mathcal{L}}$*, the two rules yield the two predictions shown in Figure 2. The overall prediction associated with the conjunction of the rules (i.e. the disjunction of the two premises) corresponds to the pointwise maximum of these distributions.*

Of course, different rules (12) will generally use different modifiers m_2. They should then be consistent in the sense that a strengthening of the premise of a rule does not entail a reduction of extrapolation. Thus, consider two rules (12) modeled by means of modifiers m_{1j}^1, m_2^1 and m_{1j}^2, m_2^2 $(1 \leq j \leq L)$, respectively. The first rule is obviously redundant with respect to the second one if

$$\forall 1 \leq j \leq L : m_{1j}^1 \leq m_{1j}^2 \quad \text{and} \quad m_2^1 \leq m_2^2.$$

In fact, we then have $\pi_C^1 \leq \pi_C^2$ for the possibility distributions induced by these two rules in connection with any observed case.

Consider the following rules as an example: (1) For cars with *similar* horsepower it is *completely* possible that the associated prices are similar. (2) For cars with *very similar* horsepower it is *more or less* possible that the associated prices are similar. This example reveals that redundancy always emerges in connection with somewhat conflicting rules (a stronger condition entails a weaker conclusion). Therefore, redundant rules should generally be avoided.

4.3 Discounting of cases

Given a possibility rule (or a set of such rules as in Section 4.2) expressing the SBR hypothesis, each observed case $\langle s, r \rangle$ leads to an *instantiation* of that rule. The meta-rule "similar situations possibly have similar outcomes" thus becomes a specific rule related to $\langle s, r \rangle$: "If a situation is similar to s, the corresponding outcome is possibly similar to r." Of course, this rule and, hence, the induced extrapolation of $\langle s, r \rangle$ might be misleading if the case $\langle s, r \rangle$ is a rather "untypical" or "exceptional" one. In our database, for instance, the 106th car has a rather low price ($19,699), at least in comparison with its horsepower (200). Thus, applying the similar horsepower–similar price assumption in connection with this case might provide unjustified support of low prices (for cars with similar horsepower) in further predictions.

Methods for discounting a prediction can be used in order to prevent untypical cases from providing unjustified support of other (hypothetical) cases. The discounting of possibility degrees x according to $x \mapsto \min\{x, 1-\lambda\}$ has already been discussed in Section 4.1 where it served for upper-bounding the potential support provided by a rule. In connection with the discounting of cases one might think of more general approaches since *restricting* does not necessarily mean *bounding* the extrapolation. Principally, any (non-increasing) mapping $\mathcal{L} \to \mathcal{L}$ can be used for modifying possibility degrees. The function

$$x \mapsto \begin{cases} x & \text{if } \; x \geq x_0 \\ \min\{x, 1-\lambda\} & \text{if } \; x < x_0 \end{cases}, \tag{14}$$

for instance, defines an obvious generalization of $\min\{x, 1-\lambda\}$ (and does also make sense within an ordinal setting). By letting $x_0 \leq 1$, (14) allows to restrict the scope of the extrapolation to highly similar situations without discounting the observed case itself, as $\min\{x, 1-\lambda\}$ would do. When choosing $x_0 = \lambda = 1$, for instance, a sample case $\langle s, r \rangle$ is not extrapolated at all (at least if σ_C is separating). However, the possibility $\pi_C(s, r) = 1$ is assigned to the case itself, which reflects the fact that it indeed belongs to φ.

Suppose that a "level of typicality" is assigned to each observed case by some expert. Thus, a case can be thought of as a triple $\langle s, r, t \rangle$ with $t \in \mathcal{L}$. (Numerical levels can be associated with linguistic labels, such as e.g. "very typical" or "completely exceptional.") Let $\delta_t : \mathcal{L} \to \mathcal{L}$ denote a discounting function which depends on the level t of typicality, i.e. $\delta_t \leq \delta_{t'}$ for $t \leq t'$. The prediction (9) can then be generalized as follows:

$$\pi_C : (s, r) \mapsto \max_{1 \leq i \leq n} m_2 \left(\delta_{t_i} \left(\min \left\{ m_1(\sigma_S(s, s_i)), \sigma_{\mathcal{R}}(r, r_i) \right\} \right) \right) . \qquad (15)$$

This mapping reveals the combination of two types of discounting, namely that of the complete rule (via m_2) and that of individual observations (via δ_{t_i}).

4.4 Local extrapolation

So far, the possibility rules which define a model of the SBR hypothesis have been used *globally* in the sense that they apply to all cases of the instance space $\mathcal{S} \times \mathcal{R}$. Needless to say, the SBR hypothesis does not necessarily apply equally well to all parts of this space. That is to say, the degree of extrapolation of a case $\langle s, r \rangle$ that can be justified by the SBR hypothesis might depend on the region to which it belongs.

In our database, for instance, the variance of the price is smaller for cars with aspiration "turbo" than for cars with aspiration "standard" (even though the average price is higher for the former). Thus, the hypothesis that similar cars possibly have similar prices seems to apply better to turbo than to standard cars. Likewise, a statistical analysis suggests that the variation of the price is an increasing function of the size of cars. Again, the smaller a car is, the better the SBR hypothesis seems to apply (at least if the similarity of two lengths x, x' is a function of $|x - x'|$). Consequently, the extrapolation of case-based information should be larger for small cars than for large cars.

In order to adapt the formalization of the SBR hypothesis one might think of defining different rules for different regions of the input space. Restricting the application of a rule to a certain (fuzzy) range of this space can be accomplished by means of a fuzzy partition $\mathcal{F}$ of $\mathcal{S}$. The condition part of a rule then appears in the form

$$F(s) \wedge F(s') \wedge m_1(\sigma_S(s, s')), \qquad (16)$$

where the fuzzy set $F \in \mathcal{F}$ is identified by its membership function $F : \mathcal{S} \to [0, 1]$. The condition (16) can be associated with an extended possibility rule "the more both situations are in F *and* the more similar they are, the more possible it is that the related outcomes are similar." This way, one might express, for instance, that "it is *completely* possible that small cars of similar size have similar prices" and "it is *more or less* possible that large cars of similar size have similar prices." The fuzzy set F in (16) is then given by the set of small cars and large cars, respectively. Note that the attribute "aspiration" defines a crisp rather than a fuzzy partition.

On the basis of (16), the inference scheme (9) becomes

$$\pi_{\mathcal{C}} : (s,r) \mapsto \max_{1 \le i \le n} \min \{F(s), F(s_i), \\ m_2 (\min \{m_1(\sigma_{\mathcal{S}}(s,s_i)), \sigma_{\mathcal{R}}(r,r_i)\})\} . \tag{17}$$

Observe that $\pi_{\mathcal{C}} \equiv 0$ as soon as $F(s) = 0$, thus expressing that a rule has no effect outside its region of applicability. Besides, it is worth mentioning that (17) is closely related to ideas of discounting as discussed in previous sections. This becomes especially apparent when writing (17) in the form

$$\pi_{\mathcal{C}} : (s,r) \mapsto \max_{1 \le i \le n} m_{2i}(x_i), \tag{18}$$

with $x_i = \min\{m_1(\sigma_{\mathcal{S}}(s,s_i)), \sigma_{\mathcal{R}}(r,r_i)\}$, $m_{2i} : x \mapsto \min\{F(s), F(s_i), m_2(x)\}$. In fact, (18) shows that the original support provided by the cases is discounted by means of the modifiers m_{2i}. As opposed to (10), however, this is not realized by using a constant factor λ. Rather, the discounting of a rule now depends on the situations s and s_i to which it is applied.

5 Concluding Remarks

The method proposed in this paper provides a formalization of the inference principle underlying similarity-based reasoning methods. Taking the SBR hypothesis for granted, an already encountered case is considered as evidence for the existence of *similar* cases. This evidence is expressed in terms of degrees of possibility assigned to hypothetical cases. In accordance with the heuristic nature of the SBR hypothesis, the extrapolation of observed cases is hence *possibilistic* in the sense that predictions take the form of possibility distributions on the set of outcomes, rather than precise (point-)estimations.

As an important aspect of our method let us again mention that it provides an interesting approach to combining *knowledge*, expressed in the form of (fuzzy) extrapolation rules, and *data* which is represented by cases. Loosely speaking, a rule-based model provides an "instruction" of how to generalize beyond observed data, thereby making the "inductive bias" underlying this generalization very explicit. A prediction in the form of a possibility distribution thus results from the combination of two ingredients, namely the observed cases and the (heuristic) "SBR knowledge" which dictates how to extrapolate the data.

Apart from possibility rules, other types of fuzzy rules can be used in order to formalize the SBR hypothesis, which leads to different principles of similarity-based inference. Investigating the relationship between these approaches and combining their merits is an important aspect of future work. In fact, a combination of (example-based) possibility rules and (implication-based) certainty rules seems to be particularly interesting in connection with the determination (learning) of optimal modifiers [13]. Besides, our approach is closely related to instance-based learning [2] and non-parametric statistical methods. These relations are explored in an extended (forthcoming) version of this paper [6].

References

1. A. Aamodt and E. Plaza. Case-based reasoning: Foundational issues, methodological variations, and system approaches. *AI Communications*, 7(1), 1994.
2. D.W. Aha, D. Kibler, and M.K. Albert. Instance-based learning algorithms. *Machine Learning*, 6(1):37–66, 1991.
3. B.V. Dasarathy, editor. *Nearest Neighbor (NN) Norms: NN Pattern Classification Techniques*. IEEE Computer Society Press, Los Alamitos, 1991.
4. T. Denoeux. A k-nearest neighbor classification rule based on Dempster-Shafer Theory. IEEE *Trans. on Systems, Man, and Cybernetics*, 25(5):804–813, 1995.
5. D. Dubois, F. Esteva, P. Garcia, L. Godo, R. Lopez de Mantaras, and H. Prade. Fuzzy set modelling in case-based reasoning. *International Journal of Intelligent Systems*, 13:345–373, 1998.
6. D. Dubois, E. Hüllermeier, and H. Prade. Instance-based prediction in the framework of possibility theory. Submitted for publication.
7. D. Dubois and H. Prade. A typology of fuzzy "if ... then ..." rules. In *Proc. 3rd Int. Fuzzy Systems Association (IFSA) Congress*, pages 782–785, 1989.
8. D. Dubois and H. Prade. On the combination of evidence in various mathematical frameworks. In J. Flamm and T. Luisi, editors, *Reliability Data Collection and Analysis*, pages 213–241. Kluwer Academic Publishers, 1992.
9. D. Dubois and H. Prade. What are fuzzy rules and how to use them. *Fuzzy Sets and Systems*, 84:169–185, 1996.
10. D. Dubois and H. Prade. The three semantics of fuzzy sets. *Fuzzy Sets and Systems*, 90(2):141–150, 1997.
11. B. Faltings. Probabilistic indexing for case-based prediction. *Proceedings* ICCBR-97, pages 611–622. Springer-Verlag, 1997.
12. E. Hüllermeier. Toward a probabilistic formalization of case-based inference. *Proceedings* IJCAI-99, pages 248–253, Stockholm, 1999.
13. E. Hüllermeier, D. Dubois, and H. Prade. Fuzzy rules in case-based reasoning. In *Conférences* AFIA-99, *Proc.* RÀPC—99, pages 45–54, Paris, 1999.
14. E. Plaza, F. Esteva, P. Garcia, L. Godo, and R. Lopez de Mantaras. A logical approach to case-based reasoning using fuzzy similarity relations. *Information Sciences*, 106:105–122, 1998.
15. R.R. Yager. Case-based reasoning, fuzzy systems modelling and solution composition. *Proceedings* ICCBR-97, pages 633–643, Providence, RI, USA, 1997.
16. L.A. Zadeh. A fuzzy-set theoretic interpretation of linguistic hedges. *J. Cybernetics*, 2(3):4–32, 1972.

A Methodology to Improve Object Oriented Database Systems with Fuzzy Types

Nicolás Marín, Olga Pons, Ignacio J. Blanco, and María Amparo Vila

Department of Computer Science and Artificial Intelligence
E.T.S.I.I., University of Granada
Avenida de Andalucía, 38, 18071, Granada, Andalusia, Spain
{nicm,opc,iblanco,vila}@decsai.ugr.es

Abstract. Fuzzy Types are a desirable feature that an Object Oriented Database System (OODB) must have in order to deal with vague structures. This kind of types are defined by means of different levels of precision or amplitude where properties are ordered according to their relationship with the concept represented by the type. The implementation of this new tool can be made building a new layer on an existing OODB, avoiding the development of a whole system which incorporates fuzzy types as an intrinsic characteristic. In this paper, we explain how the typical classes of an OODB can be used in order to represent a fuzzy type. New mechanisms of instantiation and inheritance are also modeled using this approach.

1 Introduction

In the last few years, Fuzzy Object Oriented Database Models (FOODM) have appeared, making possible the management of vagueness in the Object-Oriented Database Model. The study of vagueness has been focused on different levels, tackling topics such as fuzzy attribute domains in the database, fuzzy membership of an object to a class, more relaxed superclass–subclass relationships, and, even, fuzzy behavior of the objects.

We can find in the literature important papers by authors such as A. Yazici et al. [7,19–21], G. Bordogna et al. [1–4] and D. Dubois et al. [16]. They have been working directly on the object-oriented model, proposing different approaches to deal with imperfect information in this model. Other authors, such as M.A. Vila et al. [17,18], have preferred to introduce a previous step through a semantic data model. N.V. Gyseghem and R. De Caluwe [8] have investigated some proposals to incorporate vagueness into the behavior of the objects. These two last authors propose in [9] a complete model to deal with imperfect information (i.e. fuzzy, uncertain, imprecise) at all the layers of the OODB Model (data level as well as the metalevel). Moreover, this model allows the modeling of hypothetical information.

When an object is created, it must be represented by means of a crisp set of properties, independently from the applicability degree of each one of these properties to the object. We can manage vague information about the structure of the object, and it is possible that this information might be stored in a certain way, but we have to represent the object by a crisp structure. Recently [10], we have proposed the possibility of defining the structure and the behavior of a class (i.e., its type) in a soft or fuzzy way, in order to improve the modeling of an important group of real world problems [5,6,14,15]. We introduced Fuzzy Types as a new way to handle vague structures. With this new concept of type, we have modified the idea of instantiation and inheritance mechanisms in order to take advantage of the new capabilities that the object-oriented model acquires with the use of fuzzy types.

The development of a system that incorporates vagueness into its types can be established by means of two different strategies. The first one consists of developing a full object-oriented database system which incorporates Fuzzy Types as an intrinsic characteristic. From a general point of view, it could be the best choice, but it requires a large amount of effort which may not be interesting in particular situations.

A second strategy can be the addition of a new layer which implements Fuzzy Types on an existing Object-Oriented Database System, minimizing the effort needed to get the new capabilities. In this paper we explain a methodology that can be followed to implement this extra layer. We will describe how the typical classes of an OODB can be used in order to represent a fuzzy type, and how the mechanisms of instantiation and inheritance must be implemented to work accurately with our new kind of types.

The paper is organized as follows: Section 2 is devoted to explain the main characteristics of the Fuzzy Type concept, presenting at the same time the methodology that has to be used in order to develop Fuzzy Types in a classical OODB. We focus on the structure and the behavior of the type, as well as instantiation and inheritance topics. Section 3 presents Fuzzy Types as part of a general fuzzy object oriented database model, pointing out the architecture of FOODB built on the basis of an existing OODB. Some concluding remarks are outlined in Sect. 4.

2 Fuzzy Types: Concept, Instantiation, and Inheritance

2.1 A New Concept of Type

As we have mentioned in the introduction, Fuzzy Types have been introduced in a previous paper as a new way of managing vague structures. Let us now have a look at a brief summary of this concept and its most important characteristics. In order to discover more about the problems where fuzzy types can be useful, and a detailed presentation of the concept, see [10].

A fuzzy structure is a fuzzy set defined over the set of all the attributes possible in our model. Taking this definition into account, a fuzzy type is a type whose structural part S is a fuzzy structure. Let T be a type associated to a given class C. The membership function that characterizes the structural component of the type has the following form:

$$\mu_S : A \rightarrow [0, 1]. \tag{1}$$

In (1) A is the set of all attributes which can be used in our model. The set of attributes that can be used to characterize the type at any moment is the support set of the fuzzy set associated to the type. The kernel set contains the basic attributes characterizing the type. Finally, each one of the α-cuts defines a precision degree with which the type can be considered.

For example, imagine that we are dealing with the concept of *book* in the library of a certain university department. We can characterize this concept by means of the following three precision levels:

- *Basic properties*: title, author, editorial, numberOfPages, ISBN, date
- *First level of precision*: review, chapterSummaries, appropriateUse
- *Second level of precision*: costPrize, publisherInfo, sourceText, contributors

In this way we can typify a certain book (or class of books) choosing among three different levels of amplitude according to the knowledge that we have about the book or the use that we are going to do with it. In our library, we may have books we only need to register in our database. The first level of properties will be enough to characterize these objects. However, books of special interest which had been analyzed by an expert of the department will need additional information in order to express a review of the book, a description of its chapters, and a list of subjects for which it may result an interesting reading. These books will need the two first levels of the type. Finally, it may happens that the department had edited some of the books existing in the database. In this case, the books will need extra properties to store information about the publisher, cost of edition, source files with the text, and, when required, information about the contributors.

This structure can be expressed using the following fuzzy set:

S=1/title + 1/author + 1/editorial + 1/numberOfPages + 1/ISBN + 1/date + 0.9/review + 0.9/chapterSummaries + 0.9/appropriateUse + 0.8/costPrize + 0.8/publisherInfo + 0.8/sourceText + 0.8/contributors.

Therefore, we have the following relevant α-cuts:

- S_1 ={title, author, editorial, numberOfPages, ISBN, date}
- $S_{0.9} = S_1 \cup$ {review, chapterSummaries, appropriateUse}
- $S_{0.8} = S_{0.9} \cup$ {costPrize, publisherInfo, sourceText, contributors}

When the user of our type wants to create an instance of the class Book, he will be able to make it incorporate the attributes of either S_1, or $S_{0.9}$, or $S_{0.8}$, according to the precision degree required by this object to be represented.

It must be underlined that the concrete values used for α may not be very important when the only purpose is to organize a structure in a certain number of precision levels. In this situation, the important aim is the number of relevant α-cuts that can be used. Nevertheless, in other situations, giving some semantic to these values may be interesting. Let see an example.

In [11] we presents a set of techniques for exploring data sets and for extracting the definition of the underlying fuzzy type. Data sets have a plain structure, characterized by a crisp set of attributes. The objects of the data set are represented by tuples formed by the values of these attributes in relation with this object. However, it may happen that there is a high number of null values in the data set. This may be due to the limitations imposed by the plain representation in the structure of the data set: an object has to incorporate all the properties, independently from it needs them or not.

For instance, we may have to face a situation of this kind when merging several databases. In this case, each database treats the objects of a given class with a particular level of precision in its descriptions, considering different sets of attributes to describe them. After merging, we have to represent each class with a set of attributes that contains any attribute used in any of the databases to characterize the type of this class. Many null values, of several kinds, will appear. In general, dealing with objects that come from different sources would lead us to a problem of this type.

The use of a fuzzy type for representing the structure in the data set can improve the representation of the objects, contributing both a better definition of the underlying type and an important reduction of the amount of null values. In these situations, when the structure is being inferred from a set of instances, the value of α can be calculated to indicate the relevance of each attribute within the type that is being defined.

After this discussion about the semantic of membership degrees, let us now look at the effect of structural vagueness on the methods that define the behavior of the class.

A method of a given class has in its code a set of references to attributes of the instance on which it is applied. It can also have messages sent to the receptor object itself which reference other methods of the same class. These methods will in turn reference other sets of attributes and methods.

So far, in the object-oriented model, every instance of a class could reference any of the attributes of the class (instance variables). However, with our new kind of types, an instance of a given class may or may not incorporate certain attributes according to the α-cut of the class structure with which it has been created.

Each one of the methods defined in a class must have an associated precision level (as is the case with the attributes or instance variables). The minimum precision that an instance must have in order to incorporate a method in its behavior must be determined. This level of precision, which depends on the attributes and other methods referenced in the code of the methods, will be called N_m. If we consider a class C and a method m defined for that class, the precision level N_m of this method can be obtained by the formulation shown in table 2.1.

Table 1. Calculation of the precision level

$Attr(m)$[a]	$Ref(m)$[b]	Precision Level N_m
$\neq \emptyset$	$\neq \emptyset$	$\min(\min_{x \in Ref(m)}\{N_x\}, \min_{x \in Attr(m)}\{\mu_S(x)\})$
$\neq \emptyset$	$= \emptyset$	$\min_{x \in Attr(m)}\{\mu_S(x)\}$
$= \emptyset$	$\neq \emptyset$	$\min_{x \in Ref(m)}\{N_x\}$
$= \emptyset$	$= \emptyset$	1

[a] set of attributes referenced in the code of the method m

[b] set of methods referenced in this code (excluding recursive references)

At this point we are ready to define the behavior component B of a fuzzy type or class. This component consists of a fuzzy set defined over the set M of all the methods which can be defined in our model. It has the following membership function:
$\mu_B : M \rightarrow [0,1]$

$$\mu_B(m) = \begin{cases} 0 & \text{if the method } m \text{ has not been defined for the class} \\ N_m & \text{if } m \text{ has been defined for the class.} \end{cases} \tag{2}$$

It is important to emphasize that this behavior component does not add any new level of precision. It simply completes the precision levels already fixed by the structural component, with the appropriate conduct. Of course, we could also let the programmer of the type put a method in a precision level lower than the one corresponding to this method according to its code. This variation may be useful if the programmer intends to make this method inaccessible to some instances of the type. In this situation, if U_m stands for the precision value of a method m given by the programmer, the membership function written above changes as follows:
$\mu_B : M \rightarrow [0,1]$

$$\mu_B(m) = \begin{cases} 0 & \text{if the } m \text{ has not been defined for the class} \\ \min(U_m, N_m) & \text{if } m \text{ has been defined for the class.} \end{cases} \tag{3}$$

For example, in relation to the type Book, it is possible to find methods with a precision level 1 (e.g. getAuthor(...)), with a precision level 0.9 (e.g. addNewChapterSummary(...)) or even with a level 0.8 (e.g. calculateCost-Prize(...)).

2.2 Building Fuzzy Types in the Crisp Object Oriented Model

This new way of considering the type definition can be easily modeled over a traditional object oriented model, using the concept of 1–ramified hierarchy of classes [12]. The classes which appear in the hierarchy correspond to the different levels of precision with which the concept represented by the fuzzy type can be considered. This idea is explained in Fig. 1.

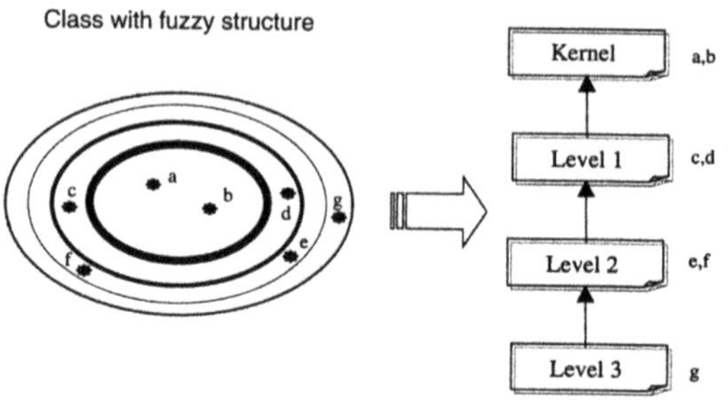

Fig. 1. Representation of a Fuzzy Type

A *1–ramified hierarchy of classes* is defined as a series of classes C_1, ..., C_{i-1}, C_i, C_{i+1}, ..., C_n verifying the following properties:

- $Sub_{Ci} = \{C_{i+1}\}, i = 1..n-1$ (Sub_{Ci} stands for the set of subclasses of C_i).
- $Sup_{Ci} = \{C_{i-1}\}, i = 2..n$ (Sup_{Ci} stands for the set of superclasses of C_i).
- A finite sequence of values $\{\alpha_i\}$ exists, associated to the hierarchy, such that $\alpha_1 = 1$, $\alpha_n > 0$ and $\alpha_i > \alpha_{i+1}$.

We are dealing with support sets of a finite nature. Therefore, the number of relevant α-cuts which can be considered is also finite. As can be seen in the last figure, for each of those relevant α-cuts a crisp class is introduced into the hierarchy which represents the type. This class will have the structure and behavior appropriate to the distance or precision with which the concept represented by the fuzzy type is considered at that level. The root of the hierarchy will have the properties (attributes and methods) of the kernel set, the next subclass will incorporate these properties, thanks to the crisp inheritance mechanism, and will add the appropriate ones of that precision level, and so on.

For instance, our type Book would be represented by means of a hierarchy of three classes. A class (C_1 with $\alpha_1 = 1$) at the top of the hierarchy containing basic attributes and the appropriate behaviour, a subclass (C_2 with $\alpha_2 = 0.9$) embodying the first level of precision (i.e. reviews and chapter summaries), and, finally, another subclass (C_3 with $\alpha_3 = 0.8$) implementing the last level of amplitude, for those books edited by the department.

2.3 Calling Objects into Being

The change proposed in the concept of type involves modifications being made to the idea of instantiation and inheritance. The instantiation mechanism must allow us to choose the α-cut of properties of the type that will be used to represent every new object.

Let us suppose the existence of a generic method new(α) (with $\alpha \in (0,1]$). The receptor of this method can be any class C, while the argument is the level α of the structure that is needed to represent the new object. The effect of sending the message new(α) to a class C with structural component S and behavior component B, consists of creating an object incorporating the set S_α of attributes. The set B_α of methods defines the behavior of this object.

Using this kind of hierarchies we can model easily the instatiation mechanism (we only have to chose the right class of the hierarchy and apply the classical *new* method). Figure 2 presents this idea adapted to our type Book.

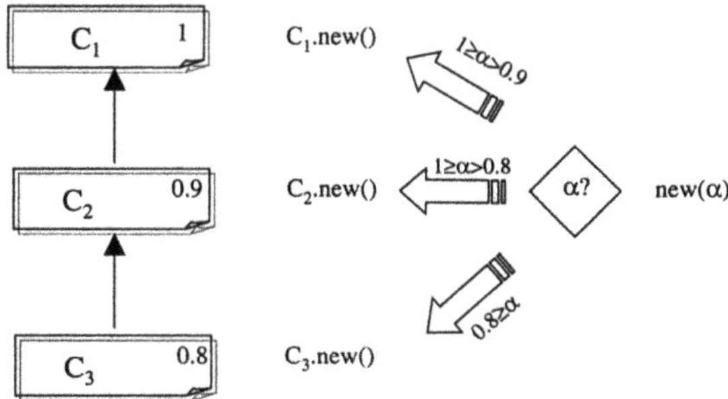

Fig. 2. Instantiation of a Fuzzy Type

2.4 Inheriting Fuzzy Types

The inheritance mechanism H must enable part of the class structure and behavior to be inherited by its subclasses. As we have done with the instantiation mechanism, we add a threshold to indicate which subset of properties we want to be inherited. Two different forms of inheritance can be considered:

- Incorporating inherited attributes and methods to the kernel set of the structural and behavior components of the subclass, respectively. In this way, the vagueness of the inherited properties will be eliminated. This type of inheritance will be called *inheritance without vagueness propagation* H_{crisp}.
- Keeping the vagueness, by inheriting both properties and methods affected by the corresponding membership degree. This type of inheritance will be called *inheritance with vagueness propagation* H_{fuzzy}.

Let us suppose we are creating a new class C. We would like it to inherit from another class C' without vagueness propagation and with a threshold α. S_{Sub} and B_{Sub} stand for the structural and behavior components defined for the new class. S_{Sup} and B_{Sup} stand for the respective components of the superclass. The resulting type for the class C will have the following components:

$$S_C = S_{Sup-\alpha} \cup S_{Sub}, \tag{4}$$

$$B_C = B_{Sup-\alpha} \cup B_{Sub}. \tag{5}$$

However, in order to inherit with vagueness propagation, the new components would be:

$$S_C = S_{Sup-fuzzy-\alpha} \cup S_{Sub}, \tag{6}$$

$$B_C = B_{Sup-fuzzy-\alpha} \cup B_{Sub}. \tag{7}$$

In these last formulations, for any fuzzy set Y, $Y_{fuzzy-\alpha}$ stands for the fuzzy cut at level α of Y, defined by the following membership function:

$$\mu_{Y-fuzzy-\alpha}(m) = \begin{cases} 0 & \text{if } \mu_Y(x) < \alpha \\ \mu_Y(x) & \text{otherwise.} \end{cases} \tag{8}$$

In the two kinds of inheritance, $B_{Sup-\alpha}$, $B_{Sup-fuzzy-\alpha}$ and B_{Sub} are recalculated once the definitive structural component S_C is known.

2.5 Overriding Policy

One of the main advantages contributed by OODBS is the capability of redefining inherited properties when a subclass is created. The addition of fuzzy types to the object oriented paradigm of databases requires the definition of a new policy to manage overriding. We extend the concept of redefinition for our fuzzy types by using the following rule in order to decide which method will be applied when a message is received by an instance created with a precision level α:

- Start at the fuzzy class the instance belongs to.
- Look for a method of that class that matches the signature of the message and with a level of precision higher than α.
- If only one is found, apply it.
- If there are several ones, use the most specific one (the one with the lowest $\mu_B(m)$).
- Otherwise, go up a level in the inheritance hierarchy of fuzzy classes, and go to the second step of this process (if it is possible).
- Finally, when no method is found, the appropriate error message will appear.

Taking the rule explained in this section into account, let now see how can be performed the implementation of both kinds of inheritance mechanisms (with and without vagueness propagation) preserving this policy.

2.6 Dealing with Inheritance in Existing OODBS

First, let us have a look to the case in which there is no vagueness propagation. Let C_1, ..., C_{i-1}, C_i, C_{i+1}, ..., C_n be the hierarchy representing the fuzzy type of the superclass, D_1, ..., D_{j-1}, D_j, D_{j+1}, ..., D_n be the hierarchy representing the structural component of the fuzzy type defined for the subclass, and α be the threshold used in order to inherit. Let also C_i be such that $\alpha_i \geq \alpha > \alpha_{i+1}$. In such a situation, C_i represents the α-cut of superclass properties that we want to be inherited ($S_{Sup-\alpha}$ and $B_{Sup-\alpha}$). In order to get a representation of the new obtained type, we only have to make the hierarchy D_1, ..., D_{j-1}, D_j, D_{j+1}, ..., D_n incorporate this α-cut in all its classes. There is a simple way of doing this: making D_1 inherit from C_i. Finally, it only remains to complete the obtained hierarchy, adding the methods defined for the subclass on the appropriate level, because now the level of the hierarchy where they have to be placed can be calculated.

Again in relation with our library example, think in the creation of a class Dictionary. This new class inherits without vagueness propagation from Book. The first level is enough, because in the library they do not expect to review nor edit any dictionary. They add some characteristic properties to the inherited type, in order to store the number of cited words, the involved languages, and the category of the dictionary (e.g. pocket, normal, advanced). Figure 3 explains this idea.

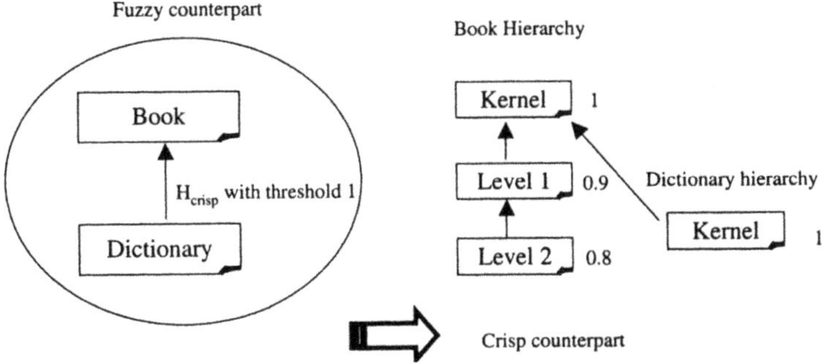

Fig. 3. Creating the class Dictionary

The case in which we want vagueness to be propagated is a bit more complex. Since it is possible for users to redefine the precision level of a variable, and those methods which they consider appropriate, the fuzzy inherited conduct may differ from that of the superclass (for example, some methods may change their N_m when the precision level of some of their referenced instance variables is redefined).

First, we must obtain both the structural and the behavior component of the new type by means of the union operator, in the form of fuzzy sets of properties (as indicated in previous sections). After that, the appropriate 1–ramified hierarchy must be built to represent our type by means of precision levels.

In order to keep the right overriding policy, this must be done following the next schedule:

- The first step is to create a hierarchy of classes representing the relevant α-cuts of the obtained structural component.
- The second step consists of adding the different methods to each level, according to the N_m calculated for them. However, this cannot be done just as it is. Remember that there may be some redefined methods, and the system must choose the right method to apply for each level of precision, according to the rule set out at Sect. 2.4. Therefore, instead of incorporating all the methods in their corresponding level, we keep only those methods that have some possibility of being applied.

Normally, a number of precision levels that are equal to or higher than the one inherited from the subclass is obtained (unless the precision levels of the attributes are redefined). Unlike the inheritance without vagueness propagation, this implementation does not imply any relationship of crisp inheritance between the superclass hierarchy and the new hierarchy obtained for the subclass. Care must be taken with the corresponding problems of redundancy.

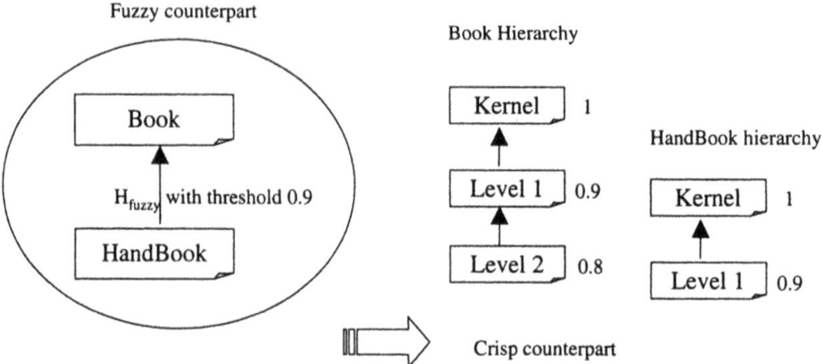

Fig. 4. Creating the class HandBook

For instance, consider the creation of a class HandBook in our library example. The department does not publish any one, but they want to preserve the two first levels of precision of the type Book, in order to deal with the handbooks that had been analyzed by a member of the department. At the same time, specific properties related to handbooks are added to this levels. For instance, an attribute to store the kind of system which the handbook refers to (e.g. database, program environment, program language) and another attribute indicating the name of such system can be added to the basic properties (i.e. the inherited kernel). In order to store the level of the handbook (e.g. novice, normal, advanced, expertise), the presence of examples and a measure of the quality, three attributes – goalLevel, examples, and quality – can be added to the second inherited level. Figure 4 shows the necessary classes hierarchies that have to be implemented to accomplish the creation of the class HandBook.

2.7 Two Different Levels of Abstraction, one Hidden to the User

According to that put forward in the last paragraphs, it should be noted that any problem that we wish to represent following this schema generates a graph with two layers. The first layer, called the fuzzy layer, shows the classes with a fuzzy structure that make up the conceptual hierarchy of the problem that is being modeled. Arcs of this layer are labeled so that each is associated with a kind of inheritance (with or without vagueness propagation) and a threshold. Below, there is another layer, called the crisp layer, made up of classes with a crisp structure, containing the different hierarchies used to represent the fuzzy classes of the other layer. Figure 5 illustrates both levels. Of course, from the user point of view, the crisp level must be transparent.

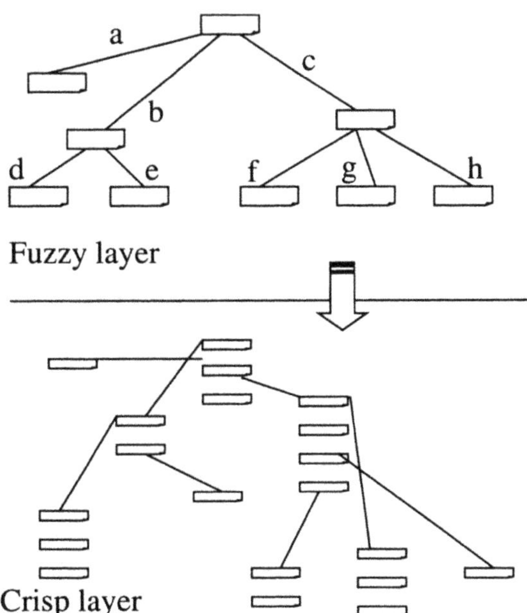

Fig. 5. Bilayered graph

3 Fuzzy Types as Part of a General Model

We have explained in Sect. 2 the characteristics of Fuzzy Types and how they can be implemented over a classical object oriented database system. Nevertheless, as we mentioned in the introduction, a Fuzzy Object Oriented Database System must be able to handle vagueness at several levels (imprecise and uncertain attribute domains, fuzzy extents in classes, fuzzy superclass–subclass relationships, ...). In this context, Fuzzy Types allows us to manage vague structures in types, dealing with objects characterized by different levels of precision within the same type.

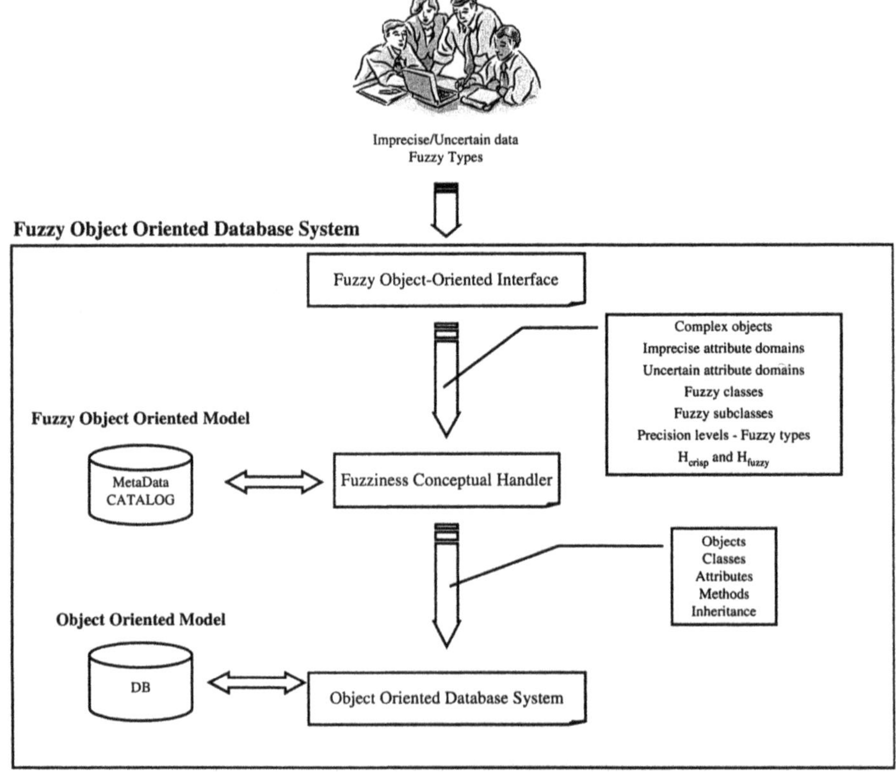

Fig. 6. Fuzzy Object Oriented DB Arquitecture

In [13] we summarize a full proposal in this area in which the different sources of vagueness in data can be managed over a traditional object-oriented database system (OODBMS). We explain the new object-oriented structures to be considered in order to describe vagueness. The basis of our proposal is to consider that the classical object-oriented database model is wide and general enough to be the base for developing a Fuzzy Object Oriented Database Model. With the methodology described in Sect. 2 we can add Fuzzy Types to this model keeping this policy.

Figure 6 explains how a fuzzy object oriented database system can be built taking as basis a classical one.

The user of a Fuzzy Object Oriented Database System works with imprecise or uncertain data, possibly organized by means of fuzzy types. A fuzzy object oriented interface allows this user to manage its real world problem via a fuzzy object oriented model of database. The central tasks in the system are performed by a Conceptual Fuzzy Handler. Among its responsibilities:

- Storing the fuzzy object oriented schema. A metadata catalog helps to achieve this aim.
- Translating the fuzzy object oriented model into a crisp object oriented model, according to the structures mentioned in [13].
- Storing the crisp object oriented model in a classical object oriented database system, basis of the full architecture.

4 Conclusions and Further Work

The addition of vagueness to the concept of type can be considered as a new step towards the achievement of a better fuzzy object-oriented model. Incorporating the possibility of handling fuzzy types as a new layer in a traditional Object-Oriented Database System, allows us to easily obtain our new capabilities, avoiding the development of a full system, with all the effort that this task would require.

Described using the methodology explained in this paper, Fuzzy Types can be included as part of a general Fuzzy Object Oriented Database System built on the basis of an existing object oriented database system, and capable of managing vagueness in data from different sources. At this moment, our research effort is aimed to the study of the development of such a System. To accomplish this goal, a prototype is being implemented.

References

1. Bordogna G., Lucarella D., Pasi G. (1994) A fuzzy object oriented data model. In: Proceedings of FUZZ-IEEE, 313–317.
2. Bordogna G., Pasi G. (1998) Management of linguistic qualification of uncertainty in fuzzy databases. In: Proceedings of Information Processing and Management of Uncertainty in Knowledge Based Systems.
3. Bordogna G., Pasi G. (1999) Typicality based on soft aggregations in fuzzy object oriented databases. In: Proceedings of EUSFLAT, 489–492.
4. Bordogna G., Pasi G., Lucarella D. (1999) A fuzzy object oriented data model for managing vague and uncertain information. International Journal of Intelligent Systems 14:623–651.

5. Buneman P., Davidson S., Suciu D. (1995) Programming constructs for unstructured data. In: Proceedings of DBPL.
6. Buneman P., Davidson S., Fernandez M., Suciu D. (1997) Adding structure to unstructured data. In: Proceedings of ICDT, 336–350.
7. George R., Buckles B., Petry F. (1993) Modelling class hierarchies in the fuzzy object-oriented data model. Fuzzy Sets and Systems 60:259–272.
8. Gyseghem N. V., Caluwe R. D. (1994) Fuzzy object-oriented databases: Some behavioral issues. In: Proceedings of EUFIT, 361–364.
9. Gyseghem N. V., Caluwe R. D. (1998) Imprecision and uncertainty in the UFO database model. Journal of the American Society for Information Science 49:236–252.
10. Marín N., Vila M.A., Pons O. (2000) Fuzzy types: A new concept of type for managing vague structures. International Journal of Intelligent Systems 15:1061–1085.
11. Marín N., Blanco I.J., Pons O., Vila M.A. (2000) Extracting fuzzy types from datasets analyzing null values in attributes. Tech. Rep. DECSAI-00-01-21. Department of Computer Science and Artificial Intelligence, Universitiy of Granada.
12. Marín N., Blanco I.J., Pons O., Vila M.A. (2000) Fuzzy types as a new layer on an object oriented database system. In: Proceedings of IPMU, 1099.
13. Marín N., Pons O., Vila M.A. (2000) Softening the object-oriented database model: imprecision, uncertainty, and fuzzy types. Tech. Rep. DECSAI-00-01-22. Department of Computer Science and Artificial Intelligence, Universitiy of Granada.
14. Nestorov S., Abiteboul S., Motwani R. (1997) Inferring structure in semistructured data. In: Proceedings of Workshop on Management of Semistructured Data held in conjunction with SIGMOD.
15. Papakonstantinou Y., Garca-Molina H., Widom J. (1995) Object exchange across heterogeneous information sources. In: Proceedings of IEEE International Conference on Data Engineering.
16. Rossazza J.-P., Dubois D., Prade H. (1998) Fuzzy and Uncertain Object-Oriented Databases. Concepts and Models. A hierarchical model of fuzzy classes. 13:21–61. Advances in Fuzzy Systems- Applications and Theory.
17. Vila M.A., Cubero J.C., Medina J.M., Pons O. (1996) A conceptual approach for dealing with imprecision and uncertainty in object-based data models. International Journal of Intelligent Systems 11:791–806.
18. Vila M.A., Cubero J.C., Medina J.M., Pons O. (1998) A fuzzy object-oriented data model represented by means of a semantic data model. Tech. Rep. DECSAI-98-00-00. Department of Computer Science and Artificial Intelligence - University of Granada.
19. Yazici A., Aksoy D., George R. (1996) The similarity-based fuzzy object-oriented data model. In: Proceedings of IPMU, vol. 3, 1177–1182.
20. Yazici A., Koyuncu M. (1997) Fuzzy object-oriented database modeling coupled with fuzzy logic. Fuzzy Sets and Systems 89:1–26.
21. Yazici A., George R., Aksoy D. (1998) Design and implementation issues in the fuzzy object-oriented data model. Journal of Information Sciences 108:241–260.

GPSR Compliance
The European Union's (EU) General Product Safety Regulation (GPSR) is a set of rules that requires consumer products to be safe and our obligations to ensure this.

If you have any concerns about our products, you can contact us on

ProductSafety@springernature.com

In case Publisher is established outside the EU, the EU authorized representative is:

Springer Nature Customer Service Center GmbH
Europaplatz 3
69115 Heidelberg, Germany

www.ingramcontent.com/pod-product-compliance
Ingram Content Group UK Ltd.
Pitfield, Milton Keynes, MK11 3LW, UK
UKHW021858190726
13853UKWH00003B/1329